THE CREATIVE IMPULSE

FOURTH EDITION

THE
CREATIVE
IMPULSE

An Introduction to the Arts

FOURTH EDITION

DENNIS J. SPORRE

Prentice Hall, Upper Saddle River, NJ 07458

This book was designed and produced by
CALMANN & KING LTD
71 Great Russell Street, London WC1B 3BN

Designed by Richard Foenander
Typeset by Bookworm Typesetting, Manchester, England
Printed and bound in Hong Kong

Front cover: Jan Vermeer, *The Lacemaker*, c. 1669–70. Oil
on canvas (attached to panel), c.9 x 8 ins (24.5 x 21 cm).
The Louvre, Paris.

Back cover: Junaid, *Bihzad in the Garden*, from the poems
of Khwahju Kirmani. Manuscript illumination, 1396.
British Museum, London.

Frontispiece: Alberto Giacometti, *Man Pointing*, 1947.
Bronze, c.70 ins (179 cm) high, at base 12 x c.13 ins (30.5 x
33.7 cm). Museum of Modern Art, New York. Gift of Mrs
John D. Rockefeller 3rd.

Picture Credits

The author, the publishers, and Calmann & King Ltd wish to thank the
museums, galleries, collectors, and other owners who have kindly
allowed their works to be reproduced in this book. In general, museums
have supplied their own photographs; other sources are listed below.

Actors' Theatre of Louisville/David S. Talbott: 18.40, 18.41; AKG,
London: front cover, 1.6, 5.12, 5.15, 7.3, 8.5, 9.3, 9.16, 10.13, 10.14,
10.15, 10.20, 10.22, 10.27, 10.29, 10.30, 10.31, 10.32, 11.2, 11.7, 11.11,
11.19, 11.20, 11.29, 12.2, 12.3, 12.8, 12.10, 12.11, 12.12, 12.13, 12.14,
12.16, 12.18, 12.20, 12.21, 12.24, 12.25, 13.2, 13.4, 14.4, 15.22, 17.21,
17.23, 17.25; Arcaid: 16.30; Archivi Alinari, Florence: 10.3, 11.26;
Ancient Art & Architecture Collection, London: 5.2, 8.30, 13.26; Wayne
Andrews, Chicago: 14.21; The Architectural Association, London: 17.24,
18.30, 18.35; James Austin, Cambridge: 10.5; Bildarchiv Preussischer
Kulturbesitz, Berlin: 14.31; Bilderberg/Wolfgang Volz, Hamburg: 0.3,
18.25; Bridgeman Art Library: 7.9, 9.15, 11.4, 11.8, 11.10, 12.1, 12.17,
12.26, 14.7, 14.18, 14.28, 15.4, 16.6, 16.17; Bulloz, Paris: 7.19;
CNMHS/SPADEM, Paris: 7.17, 7.24; The Carnegie Museum of Art
(Museum purchase: gift of Kaufmann's, the Women's Committee and the
Fellows of the Museum of Art 85.62): 18.15; Cement & Concrete
Association, Slough: 18.36; Trudy Lee Cohen © 1986, Philadelphia:
16.27; Courtauld Institute of Art, London: 13.12; Deutsches
Archäologisches Institut, Athens: 2.9; Deutsches Archäologisches
Institut, Rome: 4.29; Jean Dieuzaide, Toulouse: 7.12; John Donat,
London: 17.23; Dumbarton Oaks (Byzantine Photograph Collection),
Trustees of Harvard University, Washington D.C.: 6.16; Esto
Photographics, Inc., Mamaroneck, New York: 18.31; ET Archive: 9.6;
Mary Evans Picture Library: 12.4, 12.5, 13.5; Fisk University (Vechten
Gallery of Fine Arts) Nashville, Tennessee: 17.16; Fotografica Foglia,
Naples: 4.12; Werner Forman Archive, London: 5.27, 9.19; Fotomas
Index: 15.3; Alison Frantz, Princeton, New Jersey: 3.23, 3.26, 6.19;
Solomon R. Guggenheim Museum, New York: 18.32; Hal Tiné, South
Salem, New York: 18.42; Sonia Halliday, Weston Turville, U.K.: 3.1
6.30, 6.34, 8.12, 8.14; Robert Harding Pictures Library, London: 11.30,
13.22, 13.23; Clive Hicks, London: 7.13, 8.9, 8.11, 8.13; Colorphoto Hans
Hinz, Allschwil, Switzerland: 1.1, 1.5; Hirmer Fotoarchiv, Munich: 1.16,
1.18, 1.24, 2.18, 2.21, 3.8, 3.20, 3.22, 3.30, 6.3, 6.4, 6.6, 6.10, 6.36, 8.8;
Hirshhorn Museum and Sculpture Garden, Smithsonian Institution, Gift
of Joseph H. Hirshhorn, 1972 (photo Lee Stalsworth): 18.11; Holly
Solomon Gallery, New York: 18.26; Angelo Hornak, London: 9.29,
16.29; Hulton Deutsch Collection: 6.14, 12.23, 14.30; By courtesy of the
Trustees of Sir John Soane's Museum, London: 14.12; Hubert Josse:
A.F. Kersting: 1.14, 3.19, 3.33, 7.18, 8.7, 8.15, 8.17, 9.1, 9.7, 9.8, 9.10,
9.13, 9.26, 9.27, 9.28, 9.30, 9.31, 11.23, 13.1, 13.33, 13.35, 14.10, 15.14;
G.E. Kidder Smith, New York: 15.6; Lauros-Giraudon/Bridgeman,
London: 8.10, 8.18, 8.19, 8.20, 13.14; Ralph Liebermann, North Adams,
MA: 16.21, 17.25, 18.33; Louisiana Office of Tourism/Al Godoy: 18.39;
Mansell Collection: 3.4, 3.9, 3.10, 3.17, 4.16, 4.17, 4.19, 4.20, 4.24, 9.17,
10.6, 10.9, 10.10, 10.11, 10.19, 10.28, 11.24, 11.27, 13.9, 13.10, 13.11;
Bildarchiv Foto Marburg, Germany: 3.35, 5.23, 5.26, 8.29, 14.34, 14.35;
Jean Mazenod, L'Art de L'Ancienne Rome, Editions Mazenod, Paris:
4.13; Menil Collection: 18.12; Lucia Moholy, Zürich: 17.27; Peter Moore,
New York: 18.29; Ann Münchow, Aachen: 7.27, 7.28; Musée d'Art et
d'Histoire, Auxerre: 7.23; Musei Capitolini, Rome/Barbara Malter: 4.26;
National Film Archive, London: 16.28, 17.26; Courtesy of the Oriental
Institute, University of Chicago: 1.8, 1.10, 1.11; Österreichische
Akademie der Wissenschaften-Mosaikenkommission, Vienna: 6.5;
Pentogram Design/Theo Crosby: 12.27; Photoresources, Canterbury: 2.3;
Josephine Powell, Rome: 6.2; Prestel Verlag Munich: 18.24; Quattrone
Mario Fotostudio, Florence: 10.18; Range/Bettmann: 17.6; Réunion des
Musées Nationaux, Paris: 2.11, 6.12, 6.13, 7.25, 13.7, 13.16, 13.21, 14.14;
Scala, Florence: 2.1, 6.1, 6.9, 6.31, 6.38, 7.1, 9.18, 9.21, 10.1, 10.16,
11.14, 11.18, 11.33, 11.38, 13.6, 13.13, 13.19, 13.20, 13.27; Peter Sanders
Collection: 6.20; Scala: 5.1, 5.6, 8.1, 10.21, 11.1; Bob Schalkwijk, Mexico
City: 17.18; Schomburg Center for Research in Black Culture (Art &
Artifacts Division); The New York Public Library; Astor Lenox and
Tilden Foundations: 17.17; Science Photo Library/Hank Morgan: 18.2;
Edwin Smith, Saffron Walden: 14.32, 14.33; Sperone Westwater: 18.14;
Wim Swaan: 9.9; Telegraph Colour Library/T. Yamada: 12.27; Vatican
Museums: 11.31, 11.34; Roger-Viollet: 9.12; Weidenfeld & Nicolson,
London: 14.19; Peter Wexler, Inc., New York: 18.44; Whitney Museum
of American Art, New York/photo Geoffrey Clements: 18.9; Whitney
Museum of American Art, New York/photo Sandak, Inc./G.K. Hall,
Boston, Massachusetts): 18.22.

CONTENTS

PICTURE CREDITS 4
PREFACE 9

Introduction: What Are the Arts and How Do We Respond to and Evaluate Them? 10

THE HUMANITIES AND THE ARTS 12
WHAT IS ART? 13
   Nonrestrictiveness 13 Human Enterprise 14 Medium of Expression 14 Communication 14
THE FUNCTIONS OF ART 15
   Entertainment 15 Political and Social Commentary 15 Therapy 15 Artifact 16
LOOKING, LISTENING, AND RESPONDING 16
   Two-dimensional Art 17 Media 17 Composition 17 Sculpture 19 Dimensionality 19 Texture 19 Architecture 21 Structure 21 Music 22 Genres 22 Melody and Structure 22 Theatre 22 Genres 22 Plot, Character, Thought, and Visual Elements 22 Literature 23 Genres 23 Point of View, Character, and Plot 23 Theme and Language 23 Film 23
EVALUATING WORKS OF ART 24
   Types of Criticism 26 Formal Criticism 26 Contextual Criticism 26 Making Judgments 27 Craftsmanship 27 Communication 27

1 The Ancient World 28

THE HUMAN JOURNEY 30
ICE AGE BEGINNINGS 30
   Time and Ice 30 TECHNOLOGY: *OUR EARLIEST TOOLS* 32 Ice Age Culture 32 Our Earliest Art 32
   MASTERWORK: *THE WOMAN FROM WILLENDORF* 33 Venus Figures 34 The Cave of Lascaux 34
MESOPOTAMIA 36
   From Prehistory to History 36 Sumer 36 Religion 36 Writing 38 TECHNOLOGY: *THE INVENTION OF THE WHEEL* 38
   MASTERWORK: *THE TELL ASMAR STATUES* 39 Art 40 Music 40 Hammurabi and the Law 40 The Assyrians 41
ANCIENT EGYPT 43
   Religion 43 OUR DYNAMIC WORLD: *ANCIENT CHINA* 44 Art 44 Materials and Conventions 45 Old Kingdom 45 Pyramids 45 Sculpture 46 MASTERWORK: *THE TOMB OF NEFERTARI* 48 Middle Kingdom 50 The Scribes 50 New Kingdom 50 Tutankhamun 50 Theban Rock Tombs 50
MUSIC 51
SYNTHESIS: AKHENATON AND MONOTHEISM: THE TELL EL AMARNA PERIOD 52
   PROFILE: *AKHENATON* 53

2 Archaic Greece and the Aegean 54

THE MINOANS 57
THE MYCENAEANS 58
BETWEEN MYTH AND HISTORY 60

THE ARCHAIC GREEK WORLD 61
   The Polis 61 The Hellenes 62 TECHNOLOGY: *THE OLIVE PRESS* 63 The Persian War 63 Religion 63 Philosophy 64 Art 66 Vase Painting 66 MASTERWORK: *THE DIPYLON VASE* 67 Sculpture 68 OUR DYNAMIC WORLD: *NATIVE AMERICAN CULTURE* 69 Archaic Style 69 Architecture— The Doric Order 72 Music 73 Literature 74 Sappho 74 Hesiod 75
SYNTHESIS: THE ILIAD OF HOMER 76

3 Greek Classicism and Hellenism 78

THE CLASSICAL WORLD 80
   The Persian War 80 The Age of Pericles 82 The Peloponnesian War 83 Philosophy 84 Humanism and Intellectualism 84 Sophistry: The Distrust of Reason 84 Socrates, Plato, and Aristotle 85 Literature: The Platonic Dialogues 86 OUR DYNAMIC WORLD: *PHILOSOPHY AND RELIGION IN EAST ASIA* 89 History and Science 91 The Classical Style 92 Vase Painting 92 Sculpture 94 MASTERWORK: *MYRON—DISCUS THROWER* 95 Late Classical Style 98 Architecture 99 MASTERWORK: *THE PARTHENON* 100 Theatre 103 Aeschylus 105 PROFILE: *AESCHYLUS* 105 Sophocles 106 MASTERWORK: *SOPHOCLES—OEDIPUS THE KING* 106 Euripides 106 Aristotle's Theory of Tragedy 107 Aristophanes 107 Costume 107 Theatre Design 107 OUR DYNAMIC WORLD: *THE NOK STYLE OF AFRICA* 108 Music 109
THE HELLENISTIC AGE 111
   Alexander and Hellenistic Culture 111 Theatre and Literature 112 Philosophy and Religion 113 TECHNOLOGY: *HERO'S STEAM TURBINE* 113 Hellenistic Style 115 Sculpture 115 OUR DYNAMIC WORLD: *QIN DYNASTY REALISM—TERRACOTTA WARRIORS* 116 Architecture 117
SYNTHESIS: FROM IDEALISM TO REALISM— PROMETHEUS AND HECUBA 120

4 The Roman Period 122

ROMAN CIVILIZATION 124
THE ETRUSCANS 124
THE ROMAN REPUBLIC 124
   Military Expansion 126 The Roman Civil War 127 The Visual Arts and Architecture 127 Wall Painting 127 Sculpture 129 Architecture 130 Theatre 130 Philosophy and Religion 131
THE ROMAN EMPIRE 132
   Augustus 132 Pax Romana 134 Roman Law 135 Philosophy 136 Seneca 136 Marcus Aurelius and Epictetus 136 Plotinus: Beauty and Symbol 136 Religion 136 Two-dimensional Art 137 Sculpture 139 OUR DYNAMIC WORLD: *HAN DYNASTY PAINTING* 140 Architecture 143 MASTERWORK: *THE PANTHEON* 144 TECHNOLOGY: *CEMENT* 146 Music 148 PROFILE: *VERGIL* 148 Literature 149
SYNTHESIS: AUGUSTUS—CLASSICAL VISIONS 150

5 Judaism and Early Christianity 152

THE PEOPLE OF ISRAEL 155
The Patriarchs 155 Abraham 155 Moses 155 The
Selection of Israel 156 **The Ten Commandments 157**
Conquest and the Judges 157 The United Monarchy
158 **The Divided Kingdom and Exile 158 The Post-**
exilic Period and Beyond 158 PROFILE: *SOLOMON* 159
The Hebrew Bible 159 The Torah 160 The Prophets
160 The Writings 161 **Jewish Art and Architecture**
161 Visual Art 161 MASTERWORK: *THE TEMPLE OF*
JERUSALEM 162 Music 164
CHRISTIANITY 164
OUR DYNAMIC WORLD: *SHINTO SCULPTURE IN JAPAN* 165
Jesus Christ and His Teachings 165 The Apostolic
Mission 167 The Early Christian Church 168 The
Popes 169 Early Christian Thought 170
CHRISTIANITY AND THE LATE ROMAN EMPIRE 171
Diocletian and Constantine 171 The Barbarians 173
LATE ROMAN AND EARLY CHRISTIAN ART 174
The Visual Arts and Architecture 174 Visual Art 174
Architecture 179 **Literature 181 Music 181**
TECHNOLOGY: *MATCHES* 182
SYNTHESIS: **ST PAUL AND THE WESTERNIZATION OF**
CHRISTIANITY 184

6 Byzantium and the Rise of Islam 186

BYZANTIUM 188
Justinian 188 Reorganization of the Eastern Empire
189 **The Isaurian Emperors and Iconoclasm 190 From**
Rise to Fall (867–1453) 190 Byzantine Intellectualism
192 **The Arts of Byzantium 193** Two-dimensional Art
193 Sculpture 198 MASTERWORK: *THE HARBAVILLE*
TRIPTYCH 199 Literature 200 Theatre and Music 201
OUR DYNAMIC WORLD: *CHINESE THEATRE* 202 Architecture
203
THE RISE OF ISLAM 205
The Religion of Islam 205 PROFILE: *MUHAMMAD* 207 **The**
Spread of Islam 208 Islamic Style in the Arts 208
Visual Art 208 Literature 209 Architecture 209
SYNTHESIS: **IN PRAISE OF THE EMPEROR—THE MARK OF**
JUSTINIAN 213
PROFILE: *ANTHEMIUS OF TRALLES* 213 TECHNOLOGY: *SPANNING*
SPACE WITH TRIANGLES AND POTS 216

7 The Early Middle Ages 218

THE MIDDLE AGES 220
THE MEDIEVAL CHURCH 221
Devils and Division 221 The Roman Papacy 221
Monasticism 222 PROFILE: *POPE GREGORY I* 223
CHARLEMAGNE'S EMPIRE 224
FEUDALISM 226
Feudal Lords 226 Serfs and Women 226
TECHNOLOGY: *THE VIKING SHIPS* 227
THE OTTONIANS 229
THE VISUAL ARTS 229
Manuscript Illumination and Sculpture 229
Romanesque Style in Architecture and Sculpture 231
MASTERWORK: *THE BRONZE DOORS OF HILDESHEIM CATHEDRAL*
232 OUR DYNAMIC WORLD: *IGBO-UKWU* 234
MUSIC 237
Sacred Music 237 Gregorian Chant 237 Sequences and
Tropes 237 **Secular Music 238**
LITERATURE 238
THEATRE 238
SYNTHESIS: **THE CAROLINGIAN RENAISSANCE 240**
Manuscript Illumination and Wall Painting 241
Sculpture 244 Carolingian Design 244 Song of Roland
245

8 The High Middle Ages 246

THE SOCIAL ORDER OF THE HIGH MIDDLE AGES 248
The Rise of Cities 248 The Middle Class 249
TECHNOLOGY: *A BETTER HORSE COLLAR* 249 **Feudal**
Monarchs and Monarchies 250 Chivalry 250
THE CHRISTIAN CHURCH 251
Reform in the Christian Church 251 St Bernard of
Clairvaux and Mysticism 252 The Crusades 252
PHILOSOPHY AND THEOLOGY 255
The Rise of Universities 255 Abelard and Realism 256
St Thomas Aquinas and Aristotelianism 256 PROFILE:
ST FRANCIS OF ASSISI 257
LITERATURE 258
Courtly Romances 258 Dante and the Divine Comedy
258
GOTHIC STYLE 260
Architecture 260 MASTERWORK: *SALISBURY CATHEDRAL* 265
Sculpture 267 Painting 268
MUSIC 271
Ars Antiqua 271
THEATRE 271
OUR DYNAMIC WORLD: *BUDDHISM IN JAPANESE ART* 272
SYNTHESIS: **SUGER AND THE ABBEY CHURCH OF SAINT-**
DENIS 275

9 The Late Middle Ages 278

THE END OF THE MIDDLE AGES 280
Secularism and Transition 280 The Hundred Years'
War 281 PROFILE: *JOAN OF ARC* 282 **The Secular**
Monarchies 283 The Plague 283 Economics and
Industrialization 283 Religion and the Great Schism
284 TECHNOLOGY: *KEEPING TIME* 285
LITERATURE 286
Petrarch and Boccaccio 286 Petrarch 286 PROFILE:
GEOFFREY CHAUCER 287 Boccaccio 287 **Froissart's**
Chronicles 288
ART AND ARCHITECTURE 288
Late Gothic Architecture 288 Late Gothic Sculpture
290 **Painting 292** Italy 292 Flanders and the North
296 MASTERWORK: *JAN VAN EYCK—THE ARNOLFINI MARRIAGE*
297
MUSIC 299
Ars Nova 299 Guillaume de Machaut 299 OUR DYNAMIC
WORLD: *NOH THEATRE OF JAPAN* 300
THEATRE 300
SYNTHESIS: **THE LATE GOTHIC TEMPERAMENT IN**
ENGLAND 301

10 The Early Renaissance 306

THE RENAISSANCE 308
THE RENAISSANCE VIEWPOINT 309
    Antiquity Revisited and Measured 309 Humanism 310
    Neo-Platonism 310 PROFILE: *NICCOLÒ MACHIAVELLI* 311
    Capitalism 313 Discovery 313 The Papal States 314
    Italian City-states 314 TECHNOLOGY: *FLYWHEELS AND CONNECTING RODS* 315
THE BEGINNINGS OF RENAISSANCE ARCHITECTURE 316
    Brunelleschi 318
SCULPTURE 320
    Donatello 320 Ghiberti 321
PAINTING 324
    Masaccio 324 MASTERWORK: *MASACCIO—THE TRIBUTE MONEY* 324 The Heritage of Masaccio 326 Lyrical
    Poetry in Painting 329 OUR DYNAMIC WORLD: *THE MING DYNASTY IN CHINA* 330
MUSIC 333
    Music in Renaissance Florence 333 The Spread of the Renaissance Style 334
THEATRE 335
SYNTHESIS: FLORENCE IN THE QUATTROCENTO 336
    Cosimo de Medici 337 Piero de Medici 338 Lorenzo de Medici 339

11 The High Renaissance and Mannerism 340

THE HIGH RENAISSANCE 342
SOUTHERN EUROPE IN THE SIXTEENTH CENTURY 343
    The Expanding World 343 OUR DYNAMIC WORLD: *INDIA FROM ALEXANDER TO AKBAR* 345 The Ottoman Turks 346
    The Italian Wars 346 The Papal States 347
    TECHNOLOGY: *LEONARDO: TURNING THE SCREW* 348 Spain's
    Golden Century 349
THE VISUAL ARTS 351
    The High Renaissance 351 Leonardo da Vinci 351
    PROFILE: *MICHELANGELO* 353 Michelangelo 354
    MASTERWORK: *MICHELANGELO—DAVID* 356 Raphael 357
    Titian and Tintoretto: The High Renaissance in Venice 358 Mannerism 359
ARCHITECTURE 361
THE PERFORMING ARTS 363
    Music 363 Drama 364 Commedia dell' Arte 364
LITERATURE 366
    Baldassare Castiglione 366 Ludovico Ariosto 366
SYNTHESIS: PAPAL SPLENDOR—THE VATICAN 368

12 Renaissance and Reformation in Northern Europe 372

THE REFORMATION 374
    The Background 374 Erasmus and Christian
    Humanism 376 Martin Luther 377 Ulrich Zwingli and
    Zurich 380 John Calvin and the New Jerusalem 381
SCIENCE AND THE INTELLECT 382
    The Scientific Revival 382 TECHNOLOGY: *NAVAL ARTILLERY* 383 Michel de Montaigne 384
THE VISUAL ARTS AND ARCHITECTURE 384
    Germany 384 Albrecht Dürer 385 Matthias Grünewald 387 Albrecht Altdorfer 389 The Netherlands 389
    Hieronymus Bosch 389 Pieter Bruegel the Elder 390

France 392 OUR DYNAMIC WORLD: *MING DYNASTY PORCELAIN* 393
MUSIC 394
    Germany 394 France 395
SYNTHESIS: THE GREAT AGE OF THE TUDORS 396
    Visual Art and Architecture 397 Literature and Drama
    397 PROFILE: *CHRISTOPHER MARLOWE* 399 MASTERWORK:
    MARLOWE—DOCTOR FAUSTUS 400 Music 402

13 The Baroque Age 404

SCIENTIFIC REVOLUTION AND SYSTEMATIC RATIONALISM 406
    Francis Bacon 406 Galileo Galilei 407 Johannes
    Kepler 407 René Descartes 407 Isaac Newton 408
    TECHNOLOGY: *STANDARDIZED MEASUREMENT* 409
SOCIAL THEORY 409
    Thomas Hobbes 410 John Locke 410
THE COUNTER-REFORMATION 410
    The Council of Trent 410 The Wars of Religion 413
ABSOLUTISM AND THE RISE OF THE BOURGEOISIE 414
THE VISUAL ARTS AND ARCHITECTURE 414
    Baroque Style 414 Counter-Reformation Baroque 416
    Caravaggio 416 El Greco 417 Sculpture 418
    Architecture 419 Aristocratic Baroque 420 Rubens 420
    Poussin 421 Sculpture 422 Architecture 422 OUR
    DYNAMIC WORLD: *MUSLIM VERSUS HINDU ARCHITECTURE* 426
    Bourgeois Baroque 428 Rembrandt 428 MASTERWORK:
    REMBRANDT—THE NIGHT WATCH 429 Van Ruisdael 430
LITERATURE 432
    Poetry and Satire 432 The Rise of the Novel 432
MUSIC 433
    The Counter-Reformation 433 Baroque Style 433
    Secular Music 433 Opera 433 Cantata 434
    PROFILE: *JOHANN SEBASTIAN BACH* 435 MASTERWORK: *BACH—
    FUGUE IN G MINOR* 436 Instrumental Music 436
FRENCH NEOCLASSICAL THEATRE 437
SYNTHESIS: ENGLISH BAROQUE—SEVENTEENTH-CENTURY LONDON 439
    MASTERWORK: *WREN—ST PAUL'S CATHEDRAL* 440 English
    Baroque Architecture 441 PROFILE: *SIR CHRISTOPHER WREN*
    442 English Baroque Oratorio: George Frederick Handel
    442 English Baroque Theatre 443

14 The Enlightenment 444

THE ENLIGHTENMENT 446
    Technology 447 TECHNOLOGY: *JAMES WATT AND THE STEAM
    ENGINE* 448 Philosophy 449 The Philosophes 449
    PROFILE: *VOLTAIRE* 450 Economics and Politics 451
    Aesthetics and Classicism 453
THE VISUAL ARTS AND ARCHITECTURE 454
    Rococo Style 454 Humanitarianism and Hogarth 458
    Landscape and Portraiture 458 Genre 459 Neoclassicism
    460 MASTERWORK: *DAVID—THE OATH OF THE HORATII* 462
LITERATURE 464
    Goldsmith 464 Johnson 464 The Preromantics 465
MUSIC 466
    Pre-classical 466 Expressive Style 466 Classical Style
    466 Haydn 467 Mozart 468 Beethoven 469
THEATRE 470
    Britain 470 America 470 OUR DYNAMIC WORLD: *JAPANESE
    KABUKI THEATRE* 471 France 472 Germany 472
SYNTHESIS: THE ENLIGHTENED DESPOT—FREDERICK THE GREAT 474

15 The Romantic Age 478

THE AGE OF INDUSTRY 480
Technology 480 TECHNOLOGY: *EXACT TOLERANCE* 482
Social Changes 482 Philosophy 484 Idealism 484
Hegel's Aesthetic Theory 484 Positivism and
Materialism 485 Internationalism 485 Patronage 486
THE VISUAL ARTS AND ARCHITECTURE 487
Classicism 487 The United States 487 Romanticism
489 MASTERWORK: *GÉRICAULT—THE RAFT OF THE "MEDUSA"*
492 PROFILE: *ROSA BONHEUR* 496
LITERATURE 498
Wordsworth 499 Jane Austen 499 Other Nineteenth-
century Romantics 499
MUSIC 500
Lieder 500 Piano Works 501 Program Music 501
Symphonies 502 Nationalism 503 Choral Music 503
Opera 503 PROFILE: *JOHANNES BRAHMS* 503
THEATRE 505
Romanticism 505 Melodrama 507
SYNTHESIS: THE VICTORIANS—THE NINETEENTH
CENTURY IN BRITAIN 508

16 The Beginnings of Modernism 512

THE WORLD IN TURMOIL 514
European Migration 514 Business and Industry 514
Workers and Socialism 515 The German Reich 517 A
Scientific Explosion 518 Physics 518 TECHNOLOGY:
COCA-COLA 518 Biology 519
PHILOSOPHY AND PSYCHOLOGY 519
Friedrich Nietzsche 519 Sigmund Freud 519 Carl
Jung 521
THE VISUAL ARTS AND ARCHITECTURE 521
Realism 521 MASTERWORK: *RENOIR—LE MOULIN DE LA
GALETTE* 524 Impressionism 525 Post-impressionism
528 Experimentation and Art Nouveau 531 PROFILE:
LOUIS SULLIVAN 532 Cubism 534 MASTERWORK: *PICASSO—
LES DEMOISELLES D'AVIGNON* 535 Mechanism and
Futurism 536 Expressionism 536 Fauvism 537
LITERATURE 538
Realism 538 OUR DYNAMIC WORLD: *NATIVE AMERICAN
WOMEN IN LITERATURE* 539 Symbolism 540
MUSIC 540
Impressionism 540 Naturalism in Opera 541
Nontraditional Transitions 542 Stravinsky 543
PROFILE: *IGOR STRAVINSKY* 543 Schoenberg 544 Jazz 544
THEATRE 544
Realism and Naturalism 544 Symbolism 545
FILM: ART AND MECHANIZATION 545
SYNTHESIS: AMERICA'S GILDED AGE 548
The Breakers 548 Whitehall 550 Biltmore House 551

17 Modernism 552

THE MODERN WORLD IN CONFLICT 554
The Economy Before World War I 554 Toward World
War I 554 The Great War 556 Revolution and Civil
War in Russia 558 The Aftermath 559
BETWEEN THE WARS 560
The Great Depression 560 Hitler's Conquests 561
WORLD WAR II 562
Europe and Africa 562 The Pacific 563
SCIENCE AND WAR 564

TECHNOLOGY: *COMPUTERS* 564
PHILOSOPHY 565
Pragmatism 565 Existentialism 565
LITERATURE 566
The Novel 566 PROFILE: *LANGSTON HUGHES* 567 Poetry
567 OUR DYNAMIC WORLD: *NATIVE AMERICAN FICTION* 568
THE VISUAL ARTS AND ARCHITECTURE 569
Abstraction 569 Dada 570 Surrealism 571 American
Painting 571 PROFILE: *GEORGIA O'KEEFFE* 573 The Harlem
Renaissance 574 Central American Painting 575
African and Primitive Influences 575 MASTERWORK:
MOORE—RECUMBENT FIGURE 577 Architectural
Modernism 578 MASTERWORK: *WRIGHT—KAUFMANN HOUSE*
579
MUSIC 581
Modern Traditionalism 581 Departures 581
Hindemith 581 Bartók 581 Berg 582 Ives and Copland
582
THEATRE 582
Expressionism 582 Epic Theatre 583 Absurdism 583
FILM 584
European Film 584 The Glorious Twenties 584 The
Thirties 585
SYNTHESIS: THE BAUHAUS—INTEGRATION OF THE
ARTS 586

18 An Age of Pluralism 588

A PLURALISTIC WORLD ORDER 590
Decolonization 591 The Cold War 592 A Unified
Europe 592 TECHNOLOGY: *ROBOTS* 593 Science and
Liberty 593 Toward Another Millennium 594
THE VISUAL ARTS AND ARCHITECTURE 594
Abstract Expressionism 594 Pop Art 597 Op Art 599
Hard Edge 599 Photorealism and Conceptualism 600
Neo-expressionism 600 Primary Structures 602
Abstraction 603 Found Sculpture and Junk Culture
605 Minimalism 605 Light Art 605 Ephemeral and
Environmental Art 607 PROFILE: *ROBERT SMITHSON* 608
Installations 608 Postmodernism 608 Neo-abstraction
610 Video Art 610 Architectural Modernism 611
Architectural Postmodernism 614
PLURALISM IN LITERATURE 617
MUSIC 618
Serialism 618 Aleatory Music 619 Improvisation 619
Electronic Music 619 Pluralism 619 Penderecki 620
PROFILE: *KRZYSZTOF PENDERECKI* 621 Pop Music 621
THEATRE 623
Realism 623 Absurdism 623 Pluralism 623
Spectacularism 624
FILM 624
Neo-realism 624 The Demise of the Studio 625
Pluralism 626
SYNTHESIS: NATIVE AMERICAN AND AFRICAN-
AMERICAN ARTS 627
Native American Poetry 627 Native American
Ceramics and Painting 627 Native American Music 628
African-American Popular Music—Jazz 628 African-
American Theatre 628 African-American Writers 630

GLOSSARY 631
NOTES 636
FURTHER READING 637
INDEX 641

PREFACE

This is the fourth edition of a work that has been used by hundreds of programs in the United States and has enjoyed separate editions in Britain and Australia. Such wide usage has produced many suggestions for improvement from those who have used the book on a daily basis, year in and year out. Consequently, the fourth edition of *The Creative Impulse* makes some basic changes in both format and content. However, it maintains its overall focus and intent—that is, to present an overview of the arts in the Western tradition in the contexts of the philosophy, religion, aesthetic theory, economics, and politics surrounding them. The text remains an historical introduction to the humanities from which the reader will gain a basic familiarity with major styles, some understanding of the ideological, chronological, and technical implications of those styles, and also a feeling for the historical development of individual arts disciplines.

The changes in this edition accomplish three ends. First, they strengthen the depth and scope of coverage. For example, each chapter contains major additions dealing with general history. There are also completely new chapters providing new material—for example, Chapter 5: Judaism and Early Christianity and Chapter 6: Byzantium and the Rise of Islam. Other material has been expanded into several chapters—for example, the Middle Ages are now covered in three chapters rather than two, and the Renaissance is now discussed in three chapters rather than one. In addition, each chapter contains feature boxes on non-Western art and culture: Chinese, Japanese, Indian, African, and Native American. Feature boxes on technology strengthen the contextual materials, and "Profile" sections give biographies of key figures to enhance the human side of arts history. A completely new Introduction gives the student a thorough grounding in what the arts are and how we evaluate them.

The second major change consists of the reorganization of some material. Given the limits of space and the reactions of those who have used the text, this edition reduces the material on the Ice Age, Mesopotamia, and Ancient Egypt into one chapter rather than three. In those chapters in which more than one historical period is covered, general history and the arts have been juxtaposed, rather than presenting all the history and then all the arts material. This change gives students a better and easier sense of the relationship between art and its times. The order of presentation of the arts has also been changed so that architecture is brought closer to the visual arts because of their similarities in styles. As in the previous editions, each chapter ends with a "Synthesis" section, in which we concentrate on one specific location whose arts provide in some way a microcosm of the period.

The third major change in this edition is the insertion of devices to help students focus on the material covered. Each chapter begins with an "At a Glance" section that outlines the entire chapter. Appropriate sections of each chapter begin (and end) with a series of Critical Look and Critical Review sections that highlight the material following and summarize foregoing text. The aim here is to direct students in their work, stimulate critical thinking, and make the art and history relevant to today. Unlike some texts, we have not included chapter summaries. I have used summaries in other texts, and feedback suggests that students—ever seeking the path of least resistance—often substitute the summary for the main body of the text.

From the old editions we have kept the numerous, high-quality illustrations—more than in any other text currently on the market. Also remaining is the formal analysis of artworks in addition to discussion about them. This is critical if students are to carry an interest in the arts beyond the confines of the classroom and into the rest of their lives: that, I would hope, is the ultimate purpose for humanities courses. When encountering an artwork for the first time—whether in a museum, a theatre, a concert hall, or on the street—we usually do not have access to biographical or other contextual materials. We have only the artwork and the ability to confront it. Thus, by doing analyses—that is, by approaching artworks on the basis of how they work in terms of line, form, color, melody, plot, and so on—we are presenting to students a means by which artworks can be confronted and responded to in an on-the-spot manner: the way we actually meet them in real life.

Finally, it should be clear that a work such as this depends upon a multitude of sources other than the general knowledge of its author. In the interest of readability and in recognition of the generalized purpose of this text, copious footnoting has been avoided. I hope the method chosen for presentation and documentation of the works of other authors meets the needs of both responsibility and practicality. The Further Reading section at the end of the text is a compilation of the works used in the preparation of this text. I am indebted to these authors, to my colleagues around the country, and specifically to John Myers, Sherrill Martin, and David Kechley.

D. J. S.

INTRODUCTION

WHAT ARE THE ARTS AND HOW DO WE RESPOND TO AND EVALUATE THEM?

AT A GLANCE

The Humanities and the Arts

What is Art?
Nonrestrictiveness
Human Enterprise
Medium of Expression
Communication

The Functions of Art
Entertainment
Political and Social Commentary
Therapy
Artifact

Looking, Listening, and Responding
Two-dimensional Art
Sculpture

Architecture
Music
Theatre
Literature
Film

Evaluating Works of Art
Types of Criticism
Making Judgments

0.1 Antonio Canova, *Perseus Holding the Head of Medusa,* 1804-08. Marble, 7 ft 2⅝ ins (2.20 m) high. The Metropolitan Museum of Art, New York, Fletcher Fund, 1967.

A CRITICAL LOOK

We are about to begin a journey through the history of human life, mostly in the Western tradition, especially with its relationship to the arts. Before we begin that journey, however, we will briefly examine some basic concepts and learn some fundamental vocabulary that will make the journey more rewarding. The arts are ways of knowing about life, and their study can enhance our ability to think, to feel, and to cope. In the first two sections of this Introduction we will learn to see the arts as one of the general ways in which humans deal with the universe. Then we will examine in a more precise way what we mean when we try to define "art" or "works of art." In these first two sections, several important terms and questions confront us.

What do we mean by the term "humanities" and how do the humanities differ from other ways of knowing?

What do we mean when we contend that the arts are processes, products, and experiences?

Why does a definition of a "work of art" imply nonrestrictiveness, human enterprise, a medium of expression, and communication?

Humans are a creative species. Whether in science, politics, business, technology, or the arts, we depend on our creativity almost as much as anything else to meet the demands of daily life. That is why this book, which traces all aspects of human history, is called *The Creative Impulse*. It is a story about us: our perceptions of the world as we have come to see it, respond to it, and communicate our understandings to each other since the Ice Age, more than 35,000 years ago (Fig. **0.2**). At that time, we were already fully human. Although we have learned a great deal about our world and how it functions, and we have changed our patterns of existence, the fundamental characteristics that make us human—that is, our ability to

intuit and to symbolize—have been with us from the beginning. Our art—the major remaining evidence of our earliest times—tells us this in terms that are inescapable.

Thus, as we begin our study, which will focus to a large extent on artistic creativity, we need some touchstones to help us to understand, perceive, respond to, and evaluate works of art. This chapter gives us that necessary foundation.

THE HUMANITIES AND THE ARTS

The humanities can broadly be defined as those aspects of culture that look into the human spirit. But despite our desire to categorize, there really is no clear boundary between the humanities and the sciences. The basic difference lies in the approach that distinguishes investigation of the natural universe, technology, and social science from the sweeping search of the arts for human reality and truth.

Within the educational system, the humanities have traditionally included the fine arts, literature, philosophy, and, sometimes, history. All these subjects are concerned with exploring what it is to be human, what human beings think and feel, what motivates their actions and shapes their thoughts. Many of the "answers" lie in the millions of artworks all around the globe, from the earliest sculpted fertility figures to the video art of the 1990s. These ARTIFACTS and images are themselves expressions of the humanities, not merely illustrations of past or present ways of life.

Artistic styles, schools, and conventions are the stuff of art history, but change in the arts differs from change

0.2 Bison, after 15,000 B.C. Modeled clay, 25 and 24 ins (63.5 and 61 cm) long. Tuc d'Audoubert, Ariège, France

in the sciences in one significant way. Whereas new technology usually displaces the old, and new scientific theory explodes the old, new art does not invalidate earlier human expression. Obviously, not all artistic styles survive, but Picasso cannot do to Rembrandt what the theories of Einstein did to those of Newton.

Works of art also remain, in a curious way, always in the present. We react at the time we hear or see it to the sound of a symphony or to the color and composition of a painting. There can be no doubt that an historical perspective on the composer or painter and a knowledge of the circumstances in which the art was created enhance our understanding and appreciation, but for most of us, it is today's reaction that is most important.

WHAT IS ART?

In a broad sense, the arts are *processes*, *products*, and *experiences* that communicate aspects of the human condition in a variety of means, many of which are nonverbal. *Processes* are the creative thoughts, materials, and techniques artists combine to create *products*—the artworks. *Experiences* are the human interactions and responses that occur when people encounter the vision of the artist in the artwork.

But what is art? Attempts to answer this question have been made by scholars, philosophers, and aestheticians for centuries without yielding many adequate answers. The late Pop artist Andy Warhol reportedly said that "Art is anything you can get away with." Perhaps we should be a little less cynical—and a little more specific. Instead of asking "What is art?", let us ask "What is a work of art?" A work of art is one person's vision of human reality, our hopes, desires, fears, and experiences which is expressed in a particular artistic medium, and shared with other people. Now we can explore the terms of this definition.

NONRESTRICTIVENESS

First, our definition is fairly nonrestrictive: an artwork is anything that attempts to communicate a vision of human reality through a means traditionally associated with the arts—drawing, painting, printmaking, sculpture, as well as works of music, dance, literature, film, architecture,

0.3 Christo, *Running Fence*, Sonoma and Marin Counties, California, 1972–6. Woven nylon fabric and steel cables, 18 ft (5.49 m) high, 24½ miles (39.2 km) long. Erected September 1976, two weeks.

and theatre. If the originator intends it as a work of art, it is one. Whether it is good or bad, sophisticated or naive, profound or inconsequential matters little. A child's drawing that expresses some feeling about mother, father, and home is as much an artwork as Michelangelo's Sistine Chapel frescoes. The music of the Grateful Dead and that by Mozart both qualify as artworks under our definition, even though the qualities we might give to these artworks probably would be different. (We will discuss value judgments later in this chapter.)

HUMAN ENTERPRISE

The second implication of our definition is that art is a human enterprise: whenever we experience a work of art we come into contact with another human being. Artworks are intended to engage us and to animate a desire to respond. In the theatre, for example, we are exposed to a variety of visual and aural stimuli that attempts to make us feel, think, or react as the artists wish us to react.

MEDIUM OF EXPRESSION

Although we can readily accept the traditional media—painting, traditional sculpture, music using traditional instruments, theatre using a script and performed in an auditorium, and so on—sometimes, when a medium of expression does not conform to our expectations or experiences, we may reject the artwork. For example, Figure **0.3** shows a gigantic environmental installation, consisting of a 24½-mile-long steel and nylon fence, created (and financed) by the artist Christo. For Christo, this work—which existed for only a short time—was an artwork. For other people, it most definitely was not. Even though the medium was unconventional, and the work transitory, our working definition would allow it because the intent of the work was artistic.

COMMUNICATION

Artworks involve communication and sharing. The common factor in all artwork is the humanizing experience, which needs other human beings with whom artists can share their ideas. When artworks and humans interact, a wide range of possibilities can occur. Interaction may be casual and fleeting, as in the first meeting of two people, when one or both are not at all interested in interaction. Similarly, the artist may not have much to say, or may not say it very well. For example, a play may have little skill in its writing or fail to engage the audience. Or we may be ignorant, self-absorbed, preconditioned, or distracted; our preconceptions may be rigid or not met by the production, or we may be so preoccupied by what occurred outside the theatre that we find it impossible to perceive what the production offers. In such circumstances, the artistic experience fails. On the other hand, all conditions may be optimum, resulting in a profoundly exciting and meaningful experience. The play may treat a significant subject in a unique manner, the acting, directing, and design may be excellent, and the audience may be receptive. Or, the interaction may fall somewhere between these two extremes. In any case, a human interchange occurs, and that is fundamental to art.

In discussing art as communication, we need to note one important term, and that is SYMBOL. Symbols suggest something less tangible or less obvious. Symbols differ from signs, which suggest facts or conditions. Signs are what they denote. Symbols carry deeper, wider, and richer meanings. Look at Figure **0.4**. What do you see? You might identify this figure as a sign, which looks like a plus sign in arithmetic—it is what it seems to be. On the other hand, it might be a Greek cross, in which case it is a symbol

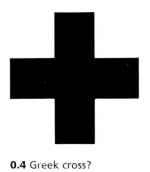

0.4 Greek cross?

| **A CRITICAL LOOK** |

Art, like anything else, can have a number of functions. In the next section, we will examine some of them. As you read, remember that functions can be determined as much by those who experience works of art as by those who make them, in the same sense that "meaning"—in any communicative medium—is determined as much by the person who hears or reads as it is by the person who speaks or writes. This section is fairly short and straightforward, and we will master its content by focusing on three things:

What are the major functions of art?

How is it possible for a work of art to fulfill more than one function?

In the context of cultural artifact, how may religious ritual qualify as "art"?

ITICAL EVIEW p. 14

because it suggests a wide variety of images, meanings, and implications. Artworks use symbols to convey meaning that goes well beyond the surface of the work, offering glimpses of human reality that cannot be sufficiently described in any other manner. Symbols make artworks into doorways, through which we pass in order to experience, in limited time and space, more of life.

THE FUNCTIONS OF ART

ITICAL LOOK abovo

Art can function in many ways: as entertainment, as political or social weapon, as therapy, and as artifact. One function is no more important than the others. Nor are they mutually exclusive: a single artwork can pursue any or all of them. Nor are these the only functions of art. Rather, they serve as indicators of how art has functioned in the past, and can function in the present. Like the types and styles of art we will examine later in the book, these four functions are options for artists and depend on what artists wish to do with their artworks.

ENTERTAINMENT

Plays, paintings, concerts, and so on can provide escape from everyday cares, treat us to a pleasant time, and engage us in social occasions; they entertain us. They also give us insights into our hopes and dreams, likes and dislikes, as well as other cultures; and we can find healing therapy in entertainment.

The role of any one function depends on us. An artwork in which one person finds only entertainment may function as a social and personal comment for someone else. A Mozart symphony, for example, can relax us, but it may also comment on the life of the composer and/or the conditions of eighteenth-century Austria.

POLITICAL AND SOCIAL COMMENTARY

When art seeks to bring about political change, or to modify the behavior of large groups of people, it has political or social functions. In Ancient Rome, for example, the authorities used music and theatre to keep masses of people occupied in order to quell urban unrest. On the other hand, Roman playwrights used their plays to attack incompetent or corrupt officials. The Greek playwright Aristophanes used comedy in such plays as *The Birds* to attack the political ideas of the leaders of Athenian society. In *Lysistrata* he attacked war by creating a story in which all the women of Athens go on a sex strike until Athens is rid of war and warmongers.

In late nineteenth-century Norway, Henrik Ibsen used his play *An Enemy of the People* (1882) as a platform for airing the issue of whether a government should ignore pollution. In the United States in the 1990s, many artworks advance social and political causes and sensitize viewers, listeners, or readers to particular cultural situations.

THERAPY

As therapy, art can help treat a variety of illnesses, both physical and mental. Role-playing, for example, frequently acts as a counseling tool in treating dysfunctional family situations. In this context, often called psychodrama, mentally ill patients act out their personal circumstances in order to find and cure the cause of their illness. The focus of this use of art as therapy is the individual. However, art in a much broader context acts as a healing agent for society's general illnesses as well. Artworks can illustrate society's failings and excesses in hopes of saving us from disaster. The laughter caused by comedy releases endorphins, chemicals produced by the brain, which strengthen the immune system.

ARTIFACT

Art also functions as an artifact: a product that represents the ideas and technology of time and place. Artifacts, like plays, paintings, poems, and buildings, connect us to our past. In this text, the function of art as artifact—as an example of a particular culture—takes on a central role.

When we examine art in the context of cultural artifact, one of the issues we face is the use of artworks in religious ritual. We could consider ritual as a separate function of art. Although we may not think of religious ritual as "art," in the broad context that we have adopted for this text, ritual often meets our definition of human communication using an artistic medium. Music, for example, when part of a religious ceremony, meets the definition, and theatre—if seen as an occasion planned and intended for presentation—would include religious rituals as well as events that take place in theatres. Often, it is difficult to discern when ritual stops and secular production starts—for example, Ancient Greek tragedy seems clearly to have evolved from ritual. When ritual, planned and intended for presentation, uses traditionally artistic media like music, dance, and theatre, we can study it as "art" and artifact of its particular culture.

CRITICAL REVIEW below

A CRITICAL REVIEW

In what ways do the films, television, and music we watch and listen to affect our health and actions? Why do we listen to music? To relax? Get energized? Interact with other people?

How many times a day do we come into contact with artistic devices, and what function have these artistic devices played in our lives to make us feel good (about a product, perhaps), and so on. Also will the functions of these artworks change through time? As an experiment, pick two or three examples of art that have been made during the last five years and project yourself one hundred years into the future. How will that art makes us appear to our great-grandchildren?

We discussed four functions of art. What are some others?

In your own experience, what items from the past have been most revealing about the people who lived then? In what ways is understanding the past important for us, as we live in the present?

A CRITICAL LOOK

When we begin to study any discipline, perhaps one of the most challenging tasks we face is an onslaught of new vocabulary. For example, if we study biology, we need to know what phyla, species, and so on are. We also need to know what constitutes the various sub-areas of biology—for example, vertebrate, invertebrate, genetics, and so on. It seems that before we can begin to deal with concepts and applications to life, we must memorize. In the next section, therefore, we study the various media that comprise the arts and some of the things within each of those art forms that we can look for and listen for to help us enjoy art more. Identifying the media of the arts and their basic characteristics will be fairly simple, but some of the more technical elements will present challenges, because this section extends through seven different art forms.

In two-dimensional art and sculpture, we speak of the "elements" and "principles" of composition. What are they?

Throughout the text, when we study examples of sculpture, we will refer to its dimensionality. What does this term mean and how does it affect works of sculpture?

What are the different types of architectural structure? Explain them.

LOOKING, LISTENING, AND RESPONDING

CRITICAL LOOK above

Learning what to see and listen for helps us to focus our attention on important characteristics in works of art and to discount what is insignificant. In the section that follows, we explain a few of the formal and technical aspects of two-dimensional art, sculpture, architecture, music, theatre, literature, and film. Our examination will be limited to terms and concepts appropriate to the creative accomplishments of humanity discussed in the remainder of the text.

TWO-DIMENSIONAL ART

Two-dimensional art consists of paintings, drawings, prints, and photographs, which differ from each other primarily in the technique of their execution. Probably, our initial response to all four is a response to subject matter—that is, we first notice what the painting, drawing print, or photograph is about. Such recognition leads us into the work's meaning and begins to shape our response to it. Beyond the recognition of subject, however, lie the technical elements chosen by artists to make their vision appear the way they wish it to appear, and these include MEDIA and COMPOSITION.

MEDIA

The media of the two-dimensional arts are paintings, drawings, prints, and photography. Paintings and drawings can be executed with oils, watercolors, tempera, acrylics, ink, and pencils, to name a few of the more obvious. Each physical medium has its own characteristics. As an example, let us look at the differences between oil and ink.

Oils are one of the most popular of the painting media and have been since their development around the beginning of the fifteenth century. They offer artists a broad range of color possibilities; they do not dry quickly and can, therefore, be reworked; they present many options for textural manipulation; and they are durable. Look at the texture in the obvious brushwork of Van Gogh's *The Starry Night* (Fig. **0.6**). This kind of manipulation is a characteristic of oil. Now, examine the fluidity of Chu Ta's *Lotus* (Fig. **0.5**). Very similar to another physical medium, watercolor, ink has a translucence and delicacy that gives it a unique spontaneity and appeal that oil, for example, cannot achieve. Whatever the physical medium—that is, painting, drawing, print, or photograph—we can find identifiable characteristics that make the final work of art what it is. Had the artist chosen a different physical medium, the consequent work—all other things being equal—would not look the same.

COMPOSITION

The second technical area we can isolate and respond to involves artists' use of the *elements* and *principles of composition*. These are the building blocks of two-dimensional works of art. Among others, these elements and principles include line, FORM, color, repetition, and BALANCE.

ELEMENTS The primary element of composition is *line*. In Joan Miró's *Composition* (Fig. **0.7**) we see amorphous shapes. Some of these are like cartoon figures—they are identifiable from the background because of their outline—but the other shapes also exemplify line, and they

0.5 Chu Ta (Pata-shan-jen), *Lotus*, 1705. Brush and ink, 6½ × 28 ins (17 × 71 cm). Palmer Museum of Art, Pennsylvania State University.

do so because they form boundaries between areas of color and between shapes or forms. Essentially, line is either curved or straight, and it is used by artists to control our vision and to create unity, emotional value, and, ultimately, meaning.

0.6 Vincent van Gogh, *The Starry Night*, 1889. Oil on canvas, 29 × 36¼ ins (74 × 92 cm). Collection, Museum of Modern Art, New York (acquired through the Lillie P. Bliss Bequest).

0.7 Joan Miró, *Composition*, 1933. Oil on canvas, 51⅜ × 64 ins (130.5 × 165 cm). Wadsworth Atheneum, Hartford, Connecticut.

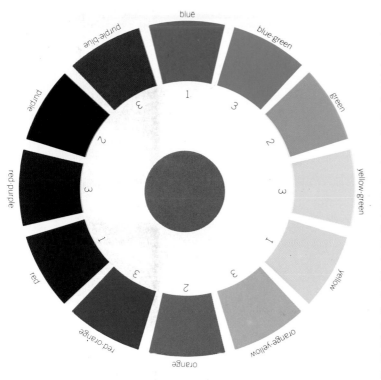

0.8 Color wheel.

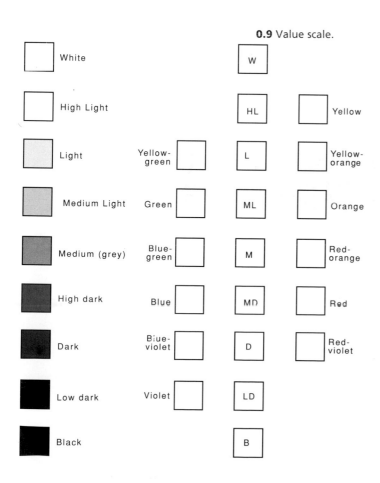

0.9 Value scale.

Form and line are closely related. Form as a compositional element is the SHAPE of an object. It is the space described by line. A building is a form. So is a tree. We perceive them as buildings or trees, and we perceive their individual details. because of the line by which they are composed. *Color* is a somewhat complex compositional element. The word HUES is used to describe the basic, perceivable wavelength differences of the color spectrum (see Fig. **0.8**). Color also includes VALUE, the apparent whiteness or grayness of a color (see Fig. **0.9**). When we observe a work of art, we can, among other aspects of color, identify and respond to the breadth of the *palette*— how many different hues and values the artist has used— and the way the artist has used those hues and values to create images and moods.

PRINCIPLES The principles of composition include *repetition* (how the elements of the picture are repeated or alternated) and *balance* (how the picture stands on its axes). In Picasso's nearly symmetrical *Girl Before a Mirror* (Fig. **0.10**), the artist has ordered the recurrence of elements in a regular manner. He has placed hard angles and soft curves side by side, and, in addition, has used two geometric forms, the oval and the diamond, over and over again to build up the forms of the work.

SCULPTURE

Sculpture is a medium of three dimensions. Thus, in addition to those qualities of composition just noted, we can approach sculpture by another element of composition called MASS: the size, shape, and volume of the forms. Sculpture appeals to us by how large or small it is and by the appearance of weight and density in its materials.

DIMENSIONALITY

As we have seen, sculpture defines actual space. Sculpture may be FULL ROUND, relief, or linear. Full round works are freestanding and fully three-dimensional. Relief sculpture projects from a background and cannot be seen from all sides. Linear sculpture emphasizes construction with thin, tubular items such as wire or neon tubing.

TEXTURE

The surface texture of a work of sculpture is as important as its dimensionality. A work such as Michelangelo's *David* (Fig. **11.16**) is created from marble, but the artist's treatment of texture makes the stone seem alive and warm like living flesh. Throughout this book, we will see a variety of surface textures that give the sculptures part of their communicative value.

0.10 Pablo Picasso, *Girl Before a Mirror*, Boisgeloup, March 1932. Oil on canvas, 64 × 51¼ ins (162.3 × 130.2 cm). Collection, Museum of Modern Art, New York (gift of Mrs. Simon Guggenheim).

ARCHITECTURE

Architecture is often described as the art of sheltering, and it is the one art form that combines aesthetic considerations with intensely practical ones. Our formal responses to architecture often involve the purpose of the building: a church, an office building, a residence, and so on. The way architects merge interior function with exterior form provide much of our encounter with works of architecture.

Although a variety of fundamental technical elements exist in architecture, we will only discuss one: *structure*.

STRUCTURE

There are many systems of structure in architecture. As we travel through the centuries in our examination of human creativity, we will see examples of POST-AND-LINTEL, CANTILEVER, ARCH, bearing wall, and skeleton frame. Laying horizontal members (LINTELS) across vertical supports (posts) gives us one of our oldest structural systems—that is, post-and-lintel (see Fig. **4.25**). When unimpeded interior space became an architectural necessity, the arch gave architects a means of solving the practical

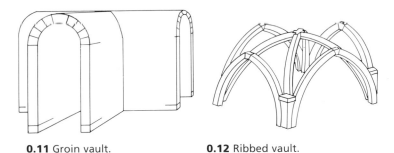

0.11 Groin vault.   **0.12** Ribbed vault.

problems involved. Whether it was used in VAULTS (arches joined end to end) or in domes (concentric arches), as we shall see in the great Gothic cathedrals of the Middle Ages or the dome of the Pantheon (see Fig. **4.22**), the arch opened interior space to usable proportions. When vaults cross at right angles, they create a GROIN VAULT (see Fig. **0.11**). The protruding masonry that indicates a diagonal juncture of arches in a tunnel vault is RIB VAULTING (see Fig. **0.12**). Cantilever, as exemplified in the Zarzuela Race Track (see Fig. **0.13**), provided architects with dramatic

0.13 Eduardo Torroja, Grandstand, Zarzuela Race Track, Madrid, 1935.

means for expression, for here, unsupported, overhanging precipices define space.

The system of bearing wall has had ancient and modern applications. In it, the wall supports itself, the floors, and the roof, and both log cabins and solid masonry buildings are examples in which the wall is the structure. When the wall material is continuous (not joined or pieced together) it is called MONOLITHIC.

Finally, skeleton frame structure uses a framework to support the building. The walls are attached to the frame, thus forming an exterior skin. When skeleton framing makes use of wood, as in house construction, the technique is called balloon construction. When metal forms the frame, as in skyscrapers, the technique is known as steel-cage construction.

MUSIC

GENRES

Listening to music often begins with generic identification, simply because it is helpful to know exactly what kind of composition we are hearing. Being aware that we are listening to a SYMPHONY—a large musical composition for orchestra, typically consisting of four separate sections called "movements"—provides us with clues that are different from a MASS—a choral setting of the Roman Catholic service, the Mass. A CONCERTO, a composition for solo instrument with accompaniment, gives us different experiences from an opera or ORATORIO, a large-scale choral work like Handel's *Messiah* performed in concert form.

MELODY AND STRUCTURE

Whatever the generic identification of the piece, all music employs the same technical elements—melody and STRUCTURE are perhaps the two most obvious. We will introduce others at appropriate points in the text.

Melody is a succession of sounds with rhythmic and tonal organization. Any organization of musical tones constitutes a melody. Melody can have particular qualities beyond being a mere succession of sounds. Musical ideas, for example, come to us in melodies called THEMES; shorter versions, brief melodic or rhythmic ideas, are called MOTIVES or MOTIFS.

Structure, like the principles of communication in visual art, gives musical compositions shape and organization. Structure is the means by which composers arrange musical elements and relationships into successive events or sections. Essentially, we can listen for two types of structure: closed and open. Closed forms direct our attention back into the composition by restating at the end of a thematic section the element that formed the

beginning. The typical organization of the opening movement of a symphony exemplifies closed form. In this form, which is often called sonata-allegro form, the pattern of development gives us an ABA or AABA type of arrangement of thematic material. Open form, on the other hand, allows us to escape from the structure. Repetition of thematic material serves only as a departure point for further development, and the composition ends without repetition of the opening section.

THEATRE

The word "theatre" comes from the Greek *theatron*: the area of the Greek theatre building where the audience sat. Its literal meaning is "a place for seeing." Like the other performing arts, theatre is an interpretive discipline, because between the playwright and the audience stand the director, the designers, and the actors.

GENRES

At the formal level, we begin our response by understanding the genre—that is, the type of play—from which the performance evolves. We are probably most familiar with the genres of TRAGEDY and comedy, but there are others—for example, melodrama.

We commonly describe a tragedy as a play with an unhappy ending, and typically, tragic heroes make free choices that cause suffering and defeat or sometimes triumph out of defeat. Often, the hero—the protagonist—undergoes a struggle that ends disastrously. In many respects, comedy is much more complex than tragedy and even harder to define. Comedy embraces a wide range of theatrical approaches, and when it is defined in its broadest terms, comedy may not even involve laughter. Although we can say, probably with some accuracy, that humor forms the root of all comedy, many comedies employ satire, and comedies often treat serious themes while remaining basically lighthearted in spirit.

These and the other genres of theatre guide our expectations as we witness a production. If we know the genre in advance, our responses move according to those expectations. If we do not know the genre, we have to work it out as the production unfolds.

PLOT, CHARACTER, THOUGHT, AND VISUAL ELEMENTS

At the technical level, theatrical productions are shaped to a large degree by the elements of *plot*—that is, the structure of the play—the skeleton that gives the play shape, and on which the other elements hang. The nature of the plot determines how a play works—the ways in which it moves from one moment to another, the means by which conflicts are structured, and, ultimately, the way in which the experience comes to an end.

Plays also turn on *character*: the motivating psychological makeup of the people in the play. Although many plays focus on visual elements such as settings, lighting, and costumes, we find theatre engrossing because of the way human behavior and conflict are reflected in the decisions and actions of the people in the play. Thus, when we attend a performance of a play, we give primary attention to the way in which character is revealed through the dialogue provided by the playwright and through the actions of the actors. Most plays develop from beginning to end on the actions and decisions of one major character, the protagonist, and when we follow his or her development and the consequences of his or her actions, we are led to an understanding of what the play means.

The meaning of the play—sometimes called its *thought*—like the meaning of any work of art, reveals what artists are trying to communicate to us about our universe.

LITERATURE

Literature operates through a system of language in which the words themselves are the triggers for our understanding.

GENRES

Like many of the other arts, we approach literature first through the formal door of its genres. These are fiction, poetry, biography, and essay.

Fiction is a work created from the author's imagination rather than from fact. Normally, it takes one of two approaches to its subject matter: realistic—the appearance of observable, true-to-life details—or nonrealistic—fantasy. Other literary forms, like narrative poetry, can also be fiction, and fictional elements can be introduced into forms such as biography and epic poetry. Traditionally, fiction is divided into novels and short stories. *Poetry* is a type of work designed to convey a vivid and imaginative sense of experience. It uses condensed language, selected for its sound, suggestive power, and meaning, and employs specific technical devices such as meter, rhyme, and metaphor. Poetry can be divided into three major types: *narrative*, which tells a story, *dramatic*, which utilizes dramatic form or technique, and LYRIC, which consists of brief, subjective treatments employing strong imagination, melody, and feeling to create a single, unified, and intense impression of the personal emotion of the poet.

Over the centuries, *biography*, a written account of a person's life, has taken many forms, including literary narratives, simple catalogues of achievement, and psychological portraits. Accounts of the lives of the saints and other religious figures are called hagiographies.

Traditionally, the *essay* is a short literary composition on a single subject, usually presenting the personal views of the author. Essays include many subforms and a variety of styles, but they uniformly present a personal point of view with a conscious attempt to achieve grace of expression. Characteristically, essays are marked by clarity, good humor, wit, urbanity, and tolerance.

POINT OF VIEW, CHARACTER, AND PLOT

In fiction, we note the author's *point of view*: first person; epistolary form through the use of letters written by the characters; third person; or stream of consciousness (wherein a flow of thoughts and feelings come from a specific character's psyche). As in theatre, *character* also represents an important focus for our attention. The people in the work and their struggles with some important human problem give literature much of its appeal. *Plot* in a work of literature may be the major or subordinate focus. Like the theatrical plot, literary plots unfold the structure of the work and may come to a climax and resolution or they may leave the characters in a convenient place, allowing us to imagine their future lives continuing as their characters will dictate.

THEME AND LANGUAGE

Most good stories have an overriding idea or theme by which the other elements are shaped. Although some critics argue that the quality of a theme is less important than what the author does with it, the best artworks are often those in which the author has taken a meaningful theme and developed it exceptionally.

In poetry, *language* that includes imagery—figures, which take words beyond their literal meaning, and METAPHORS, which give new implication to words—also provides an important focus.

FILM

A product of modern technology, film brings us into a world that, apart from a want of three-dimensionality, is often mistaken for reality. We are most familiar with the *narrative* film—that is, one that tells a story, such as the films directed by Alfred Hitchcock (Fig. **0.14**). Two other types of film also exist—documentary film and absolute film. *Documentary* film is an attempt to record actuality, using either a sociological or a journalistic approach, and it is normally not reenacted by professional actors but

A CRITICAL REVIEW

One way to see all the terminology we have just encountered is as a can opener that allows us to get into a work of art and to feel confident that we know what to look at and listen for. When we hear a new piece of music or see a painting for the first time, we now have adequate tools to begin to experience the work in a new way. Rather than depending totally on our visceral reactions—that is, how the song or painting, or any other work of art, makes us "feel" or whether we immediately "like" it or not—we can call to mind aspects such as line and form, melody and structure and ask ourselves how the artist has chosen to use those elements in the work. Knowing this terminology gives us the confidence not only to approach works of art in a new and meaningful way, but also boosts our confidence in sharing our discoveries with others.

Examine one of the buildings on your campus and write an extended description of it, using each of the appropriate terms in the architecture division as a general topic.

Listen to any piece of music—popular or classical—and write an analysis of the piece using the terms from the music division of this section.

0.14 Alfred Hitchcock (director), *North by Northwest*, 1959. 136 minutes, MGM Studios, USA.

shot as the event occurs. *Absolute* film is film that exists for its own sake, for its record of movement or form. It does not use narrative techniques—although documentary techniques can be used in some instances. Created neither in the camera nor on location, absolute film is built carefully, piece by piece, on the editing table or through special effects and multiple-printing techniques.

CRITICA REVIEW above

EVALUATING WORKS OF ART

One of the questions everyone seems to ask about an artwork is, "Is it any good?" Whether it is rock music, a film, a play, a painting, or a classical symphony, judgments about the quality of a work often vary from one extreme to the other, ranging from "I liked it" and "interesting," to specific reasons why the artwork is thought to be effective or ineffective.

CRITICA LOOK p. 25

Because the word "criticism" implies many things to many people, we must first agree on what it means. Criticism is a detailed process of analysis undertaken to gain understanding and appreciation. First we examine an artwork's many facets and trying to understand how they work together to create meaning or experience. We then try to state what that meaning or experience is. Only when the process is complete do we attempt judgment.

We also apply a set of standards developed essentially from personal experience. The application of such standards is what makes value judgment a tricky task. Our knowledge of an art form can be shallow, our perceptual skills may be faulty, and the range of our experiences may be limited. The application of standards may be especially difficult if we try to judge an artwork as "good" or "bad" based on pre-established criteria: if we

A CRITICAL LOOK

Whether we like it or not, we are bombarded with art and art experiences all our lives, and how other people view us may depend on our ability to approach art critically. That process is what we call criticism, and in that process, the process itself is often more important than the results it yields, as the following section will illustrate. Sometimes, the process is frustrating, because there may not be any "right" or "wrong" answers.

Define criticism and explain what the process entails.

Describe two types of criticism.

Explain criteria for making judgments.

believe that a plot is the most important element in a film or play, any film or play that does not depend heavily on a plot may be judged as being faulty, despite the other qualities it may possess. Such pre-established criteria account for some of the difficulty new or experimental approaches in the arts often have in achieving critical acclaim. History is full of examples of new attempts that received terrible receptions from so-called experts, whose ideas of what an artwork ought to be could not allow for experimentation or departures from accepted practice. In 1912, when Vaslav Nijinsky choreographed the ballet *Rite of Spring* to music by Igor Stravinsky, the departures from conventional music and choreography caused a riot.

Audiences and critics could not accept the fact that the ballet did not conform to traditional standards. Today, both the music and the choreography are considered masterpieces. Similarly, Samuel Beckett's *Waiting for Godot* (1953) (Fig. **0.15**) does not have a plot, characters, or thoughts that are expressed in the conventional manner of the late nineteenth century. In the play, two tramps wait beside the road by a withered tree for the arrival of someone named Godot. They tell each other stories, argue, eat some food, and are interrupted by a character named Pozzo leading a slave, Lucky, by a rope. After a brief conversation, Lucky and Pozzo leave. At the end of Act One a boy enters the stage to announce that Godot

0.15 Samuel Beckett, *Waiting for Godot*, Utah Shakespearean Festival, 1990. Director: Tom Marlens.

will not come today. In Act Two much the same sequence of events occurs. Now Pozzo is blind and led by Lucky. The tree has sprouted a few leaves. The play ends as the young boy returns to indicate that Godot will not arrive that day either. If our standards indicate that a successful play must have a carefully fashioned plot, wrapped around fully developed characters, and a clear message, then *Waiting for Godot* cannot possibly be a good play. Some people agree with such an assertion, others disagree vehemently. What, then, are we to conclude? What if my criteria do not match yours? What if two experts disagree on the quality of a movie? Does that make any difference to our experience of it?

The easiest answer to such questions is that value judgments are intensely personal—but such an answer is not a satisfying one. Some opinions are more informed than others and represent more authoritative judgment. However, sometimes even knowledgeable people disagree. The best we can conclude is that value judgments simply may not be important or essential. Disagreements about quality, however, can enhance the experience of a work of art when they lead to thought about why the differences exist, resulting in a deeper understanding of the artwork. None the less, criticism can be exercised without involving any judgment. We can thoroughly dissect any work of art, describe what it consists of—recount and analyze, for example, plot, character, language, aural and visual elements, and thought—and how all of these factors affect an audience and its response. We can spend a significant amount of time doing this and never pass a value judgment at all.

Does this mean that all artworks are equal in value? Not at all. It means that in order to understand what criticism involves, we must separate descriptive analysis, which can be satisfying in and of itself, from the act of passing value judgments. Analysis necessarily leads to enhanced understanding. We may not like the work we have analyzed, but we have understood something that we did not understand before. One important value of criticism is the sharing process: our mutual agreement is less important than the enhanced perception that results from going through the process of understanding and sharing it with someone else.

Now that we have examined briefly what criticism is and why we might do it, what criteria or approaches can we use?

TYPES OF CRITICISM

There are two basic types of criticism. Examination of a single artwork is called *formal criticism*. Examination of the same work in the context of the events surrounding it, and perhaps the circumstances of its creation, is called *contextual criticism*.

FORMAL CRITICISM

Here, we are interested primarily in the artwork itself. We can allow the work to stand by itself, applying no external conditions or information. We analyze the artwork just as we find it: if it is a painting, we look only within the frame; if it is a play, we analyze only what we see and hear. Formal criticism approaches the artwork as an entity within itself. As an example, we will do a brief analysis of Molière's comedy *Tartuffe* (1664):

Orgon, a rich bourgeois, has allowed a religious conman, Tartuffe, to gain complete hold over him. Tartuffe has moved into Orgon's house and tries to seduce Orgon's wife at the same time that he is planning to marry Orgon's daughter. Tartuffe is unmasked, and Orgon orders him out. Tartuffe seeks his revenge by claiming title to Orgon's house and blackmailing him with some secret papers. At the very last instant, Tartuffe's plans are foiled by the intervention of the king, and the play ends happily.

We have just described a story. Were we to go one step further and analyze the plot, we would look, among other things, for points at which crises occur and cause the characters to make important decisions; we would also want to know how those decisions moved the play from one point to the next. In addition, we would try to locate the extreme crisis—the climax. Meanwhile, we would discover auxiliary parts of the plot such as reversals: for example, when Tartuffe is discovered and the characters become aware of the true situation. Depending on how detailed our criticism were to become, we could work our way through each and every aspect of the plot. We might then devote some time to describing and analyzing the driving force—the character—of each person in the play and how the characters relate to each other. Has Molière created fully developed characters? Are they types, or do they seem to behave more or less like real individuals? In examining thought, we would no doubt conclude that the play deals with religious hypocrisy, and that Molière had a particular point of view on that subject. In this approach, information about the playwright, previous performances, historic relationships, and so on is irrelevant.

CONTEXTUAL CRITICISM

The other general approach to criticism seeks meaning by examining related information "outside" the artwork, such as the artist's life, his or her culture, social, and political conditions and philosophies, public and critical reactions to the work, and so on. These can all be researched and applied to the work in order to enhance perception and understanding. This approach tends to view the artwork as an artifact generated from particular contextual needs, conditions, and/or attitudes. If we carry our criticism of *Tartuffe* in this direction, we would note that certain historical events help to clarify the play. For example, the object of Molière's attention probably was the Company of the Holy Sacrament, a secret, conspiratorial, and influential society in France at the time. Like many fanatical religious sects—including those of our own time—the society sought to enforce its own view of morality by spying on the lives of others and seeking out heresies, in this case, in the Roman Catholic Church. Its followers were religious fanatics, and they had a considerable effect on the lives of the citizenry at large. If we were to follow this path of criticism, any and all such contextual matters that might illuminate or clarify what happens in the play would be pursued.

MAKING JUDGMENTS

Now that we have defined criticism and noted two approaches we might take in pursuing it, we can move on to the final step—making value judgments.

There are several approaches to the act of judgment. Two characteristics, however, apply to all artworks: they are crafted, and they communicate something to us about our experiences as humans. Making a judgment about the quality of an artwork should address each of these.

CRAFTSMANSHIP

Is the work well made? To make this judgment, we first need some understanding of the medium in which the artist works. For example, if the artist proposes to give us a realistic vision of a tree, does the artist's handling of the paint yield a tree that looks like a tree? If craftsmanship depended only on the ability to portray objects realistically, judgment would be quite simple. However, we must remember that judgments about the craftsmanship of the artwork require some knowledge about the techniques of its medium. Although we may not yet be ready to make judgments about all of the aspects of craftsmanship in any art form, we can apply what we do know.

COMMUNICATION

Evaluating what an artwork is trying to say offers more immediate opportunity for judgment and less need for expertise. Johann Wolfgang von Goethe, the nineteenth-century poet, novelist, and playwright, set out a basic, commonsense approach to communication. Because it provides an organized means for discovering an artwork's communication by progressing from analytical to judgmental functions, Goethe's approach is a helpful way in which to end our discussion on criticism and this introductory chapter. Goethe posed three questions: What is the artist trying to say? Does he or she succeed? Was the artwork worth the effort? These questions focus on the artist's communication by making us identify, first, what was being attempted and, second, the artist's success in that attempt. Whether or not the project was worth the effort asks us to decide if the communication was important. Was it worthwhile?

A CRITICAL REVIEW

Making a judgment about the quality of a work of art may be the least important relationship we can have with it. Of course, some people are naturally more critical than others, which means that whenever we meet new people or experience new things, the first thing many of us do is to express what we find wrong with them or it. The bases for such predispositions are in the realm of psychology, not of art, and so we will not go into them here. However, you may find it revealing to study your own tendencies in this regard. Do you find the act of judgment more rewarding than the process of investigation and description? Why? Certainly it is easier and quicker. But is it the most rewarding?

Go to a play, a museum, or a concert. Write a page or two on your tendencies with regard to process of judgment as it relates to your encounter with the play or one of the works in the museum or on the concert program. What did you find in the work and, more importantly, what did those reactions reveal to you about yourself?

CHAPTER ONE

THE ANCIENT WORLD

AT A GLANCE

The Human Journey

Ice Age Beginnings
Time and Ice
  TECHNOLOGY: Our Earliest Tools
Ice Age Culture
Our Earliest Art
  MASTERWORK: The Woman from
    Willendorf

Mesopotamia
From Prehistory to History
Sumer
  TECHNOLOGY: The Invention of the
    Wheel
  MASTERWORK: The Tell Asmar Statues
The Assyrians

Ancient Egypt
Religion
  OUR DYNAMIC WORLD: Ancient China
Art

Old Kingdom
  MASTERWORK: The Tomb of Nefertari
Middle Kingdom
New Kingdom

Music

**Synthesis: Akhenaton and
  Monotheism—The Tell el Amarna
  Period**
  PROFILE: Akhenaton

1.1 Black bull, detail, c. 16,000–14,000 B.C. Paint on limestone, total length of bull 13 ft (3.96 m). Lascaux, France.

A CRITICAL LOOK

Humankind is a continually evolving species, like all other species. Over millions of years our physical characteristics have changed, but more dramatic have been the changes in the way in which we go about life. We might even conclude that we are less human today than we were 15,000 years ago, the time period we examine in the first section of this chapter. We are going back to our earliest documented existence—the period in which at least a modicum of record exists. In so doing we will find that the creative impulse, from which this book draws its title, lies at the heart of our humanity. Thus, as we start our story of humankind's creative impulse, let's look for answers to three questions.

What were the three original periods of human cultural development and how do we distinguish among them?

Why might Ice Age artists have chosen to represent figures nonrealistically rather than realistically?

What does the Cave of Lascaux reveal of our early human predecessors?

THE HUMAN JOURNEY

The human journey began long before the chronicles of history. Several million years may have passed as humankind journeyed from prehistory to city life, civilization, and history. As humankind evolved culturally, they adapted to a changing environment with creative discoveries and ingenious applications of those discoveries in technology and social inventions. They migrated across the globe.

The first stage of human culture was the Paleolithic or Old Stone Age, reaching back beyond one million years B.C. Here, humans were hunters and gatherers. But in the Paleolithic period, humans discovered fire, clothing, basic techniques for hunting and gathering food, and simple social organization. Toward the end of the period, our ancestors probably began to think in artistic and religious terms (Map **1.1**).

The second stage of human culture was the Neolithic period or New Stone Age. Between approximately 8000 B.C. to 3000 B.C. people began to settle down and to raise crops rather than to hunt and gather. This was our agricultural phase. Stone tools improved dramatically, and we learned to make pottery and textiles. Social structure changed as well, as humans learned how to live together in small villages.

When villages evolved into cities, a third stage of cultural development occurred called civilization. From that time on, humans have engaged in complex cultures evolving around urban centers and empire building. They learned how to work with metals, to build monumental architecture, to write, to organize centralized bureaucracies, and to stratify social classes.

We begin our study of humankind's creative impulse in the Old Stone Age, where our earliest records reveal not only our humanity but also our creativity.

ICE AGE BEGINNINGS

In the last part of the Old Stone Age, some 50,000 years ago, humankind began to grasp the notions of selfhood and individuality. They began to make symbols as part of a strategy for comprehending reality and for telling each other what they discovered. They learned to make art in order to express more fully what they believed was their unique essence. They thought. They became aware of death and buried their dead with care and reverence. They realized that they had a complex relationship with the world into which they were born in mystery, in which they lived in mystery, and from which they departed in mystery. Progress since that early time in technological and socioeconomic sophistication has been immense, but we are no more human now than they were at first.

If we have any tendency to think of our prehistoric predecessors as somehow less human than ourselves, we have only to consider the profundity of their art to set our thinking straight. However, because we are dealing with prehistory—that is, before recorded history—we can make only the broadest of conjectures, based on the slimmest of evidence. Studies of prehistoric societies and art leave us without a unified consensus on which to build, but even if we cannot accurately grasp all the whys or wherefores of the artifacts (see Introduction) that remain for us to study, we cannot escape the power of the human spirit that they express.

TIME AND ICE

Between 500,000 and one million years ago great shifts of climate, ranging from temperate to arctic, occurred when four glacial periods, separated by three interglacial periods, wrought tremendous changes on geography and ani-

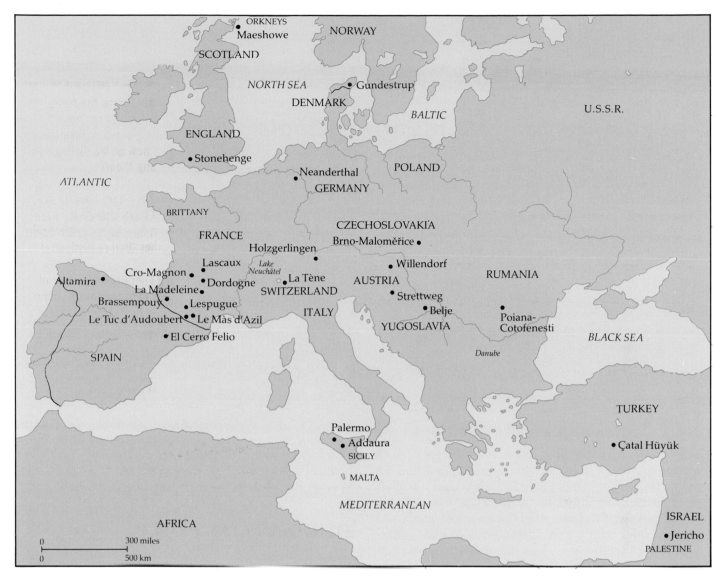

Map 1.1 Sites of prehistoric importance in Europe.

B.C.	GENERAL EVENTS	LITERATURE & PHILOSOPHY	VISUAL ART & ARCHITECTURE	THEATRE & MUSIC
1,000,000	Stone weapons			
500,000	Flint axes	Human symbols		
50,000	*Homo neanderthalensis* Tool making			
30,000	*Homo sapiens*	Cuneiform writing	Woman from Willendorf (**1.4**) Man from Bruno Animals from Vogelherd	
20,000			Woman from Dolní Venus of Lespugue Horse from Gargas (**1.3**) Bison from La Grèze Cave of Lascaux (**1.1, 1.5**)	
15,000	Last glaciers in Europe Agricultural settlements Pottery		Cave of Altamira	Dancing figures
10,000				

Timeline 1.1 The prehistoric world.

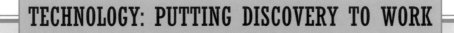

TECHNOLOGY: PUTTING DISCOVERY TO WORK

Our Earliest Tools

The technology that accompanied the transition of early humans into social organizations helped them to survive. Perhaps as early as two million years ago, our forebears began to use crudely split stones for cutting and scraping. In the millennia that followed, throughout Africa, Europe, and Asia, scrapers, spears, axes, and knives emerged, followed by bows and arrows with chipped flint heads. As early as 250,000 years ago, hand axes were made either from flint or from a fine-grained rock that would provide a sharp edge (Fig. **1.2**). Beginning with a suitable piece of stone, flakes were hammered off in a series around the edge, so that eventually both sides of the tool were covered with scars from which the flakes had been detached. At first, the flakes seem to have been discarded, but in time they were used unaltered as small tools, while, later still, they were often trimmed to provide knives and scrapers.

1.2 Hand-axe from Swanscombe, Kent, U.K., c. 25,000 B.C. Flint, 6³⁄₈ ins (15.8 cm) high.

mal life. During the glacial periods in northern Europe glaciers at the pole and those in mountain ranges such as the Alps expanded to occupy huge areas. When the ice sheets were at their maximum extent, they were, on average, approximately 3,000 feet (910 meters) thick. This resulted in a drop in the levels of the oceans of nearly 270 feet (80 meters), with the result that during the last glaciation, the sea level dropped so far that the British Isles and the Scandinavian peninsula were joined to the European continent. During the interglacial periods, the glaciers contracted and the sea rose to 60 or 90 feet (18–27 meters) above its present level. Stretches of Ice Age beaches containing shells from tropical seas can still be found in the cliffs high above the Mediterranean shores. Between 10,000 and 8,000 years ago, the climate again changed drastically and the Ice Age ended. The ice receded and the seas rose. Forests sprang up where only tundra had existed.

ICE AGE CULTURE

Our earliest ancestors moved slowly to the acquisition of artistic capacity. Stereoscopic vision, manual dexterity, communicative ability, conceptual thought, symbol-making, and artistic intuition all contributed to this development, and by the time of the last Ice Age a human ancestor of far greater complexity, self-awareness, and clearer artistic gifts emerged. Perhaps as early as 30,000 B.C. the Ice Age hunter of western Europe was using a complex system of notation, for examples of human notation, scratched and engraved in bone and stone, appear across Europe, from Spain to Russia.

Thus, what we find remaining of Ice Age culture—its art—may be the product of a technologically and economically unsophisticated people, but they used art, symbol, rite, and story just as "modern" humans do.

OUR EARLIEST ART

The first known drawings date from approximately 30,000 to 15,000 B.C. Figures were scratched on stones that have been found in deposits on cave floors, among tools and weapons that scholars have used to date them. Among these early works is a horse engraved on a cave wall at Gargas, France, dating from approximately 17,000 to 13,000 B.C. (Fig. **1.3**). The strong, curving outline captures the grace and strength of the horse, and in this smooth and sophisticated depiction, the artist uses realistic proportions and captures details like the hair under the muzzle. Although the use of line is economical, the essentials of the subject are nevertheless there. The caves at Gargas were also occupied by much later peoples, which raises some questions about the date of the drawings there, but they still provide us with a remarkable illustration of the perceptions and style of our prehistoric ancestors.

1.3 Horse's head, c. 17,000–13,000 B.C. Engraving on rock, about 8 ins (20 cm) high. Gargas, France.

The Woman from Willendorf

The Woman from Willendorf is the best-known example of the Venus figures. Like the others, she is a recognizable or realistic, portrayal within a stylized framework. The emphasis on swollen thighs and breasts and prominent genitals leaves no doubt that the image is a fertility symbol. Some have suggested that such works reveal this as an obsession of their makers. Carved from limestone, the figure was originally colored red, the color of blood, perhaps symbolizing life itself. Corpses were painted red by many primitive peoples.

The Willendorf Woman is remarkable in several respects. The figure is complete, with the legs finished off, intentionally, at the calves. The hands and arms are laid casually across the breasts. The head is tilted forward, in a similar fashion to other Venus figures. Obesity lends the figure a certain vitality: the REALISM of the folds and contours of flesh strikes a sophisticated balance with symbolic overstatement. The bulging fat of breasts, sides, belly, and thighs creates a subtle repetition of line and form that moves the eye inevitably toward the reproductive organs. She may be pregnant. She may very well be an Earth Mother, or goddess of fertility.

She is generalized in her facelessness, yet her form strongly suggests an individual woman rather than an abstraction, however grossly exaggerated her torso. Why, then, does the woman have no face? We know that artists at this time were able to render facial features; so it is clear that the sculptor deliberately decided to leave them out. Perhaps the conventions of the form itself predate the carving, coming from a time when artists lacked the skill to depict faces. Alternatively, the facelessness may reflect an idealized quality of the goddess handed down from the past.

Although faceless, these Venus figures usually have hair, often wear bracelets, beads, aprons, or waistbands, and often show markings that may represent tattoos. These details are interesting for what they reveal about female ornamentation. In addition, although the culture would have been dominated by the male hunting ethos, the statues we have largely represent females and emphasize their sexuality. The mystery and apparent miracle of birth, along with the seemingly exclusive female role therein, must have held great importance for these people. Thus, the Venus figurines, which seem to blend women's practical and symbolic roles, undoubtedly had a powerful, if unnameable, mystical significance.

1.4 Woman from Willendorf, Lower Austria, c. 30,000-25,000 B.C. Limestone, 4⅓ ins (11 cm) high. Naturhistorisches Museum, Vienna.

1.5 Main Hall, or Hall of the Bulls, Lascaux, France.

VENUS FIGURES

Venus figures have been found in burial sites in a band stretching approximately 1,100 miles (1,770 kilometers) from western France to the central Russian plain. Many scholars believe that these figures are the first works in a REPRESENTATIONAL style—that is, they are works that attempt to portray their subjects realistically. The figures, which share certain stylistic features and are remarkably similar in overall design, may be fertility figures or they may have been no more than objects for exchange. Whatever their purpose, all the figures have the same tapering legs, wide hips, and sloping shoulders (Fig. **1.4**).

THE CAVE OF LASCAUX

The Cave of Lascaux in France lies slightly over a mile (about 2 kilometers) from the little town of Montignac, in the valley of the Vézère River. The cave itself was discovered in 1940 by a group of children who, while investigating a tree uprooted by a storm, scrambled down a fissure into a world undisturbed for thousands of years. The cave was sealed in 1963 to protect it from atmospheric damage, and visitors now see Lascaux II, an exact replica, which is sited in a quarry 600 feet (180 meters) away.

An overwhelming sense of power and grandeur emerges from the Main Hall, or Hall of the Bulls (Fig. **1.5**).

The thundering herd moves below a sky formed by the rolling contours of the stone ceiling of the cave, sweeping our eyes forward as we travel into the cave itself. At the entrance of the hall, the 8-foot (2.4-meter) "unicorn" begins a larger-than-life-size montage of bulls, horses, and deer, which are up to 12 feet (3.7 meters) tall. Their shapes intermingle one with another, and their colors radiate warmth and power. These magnificent creatures remind us that their creators were capable technicians who, with artistic skills at least equal to our own, were able to capture the essence beneath the visible surface of their world. The paintings in the Main Hall were created over a long period of time and by a succession of artists, yet their cumulative effect in this 30- by 100-foot (9 by 30 meters) domed gallery is that of a single work, carefully composed for maximum dramatic and communicative impact. We must remember, however, that we see the work illuminated by electric floodlighting, very differently from the people by and for whom it was created, who could only ever see small areas at a time, lit by flickering stone lamps of oil or animal fat.

We cannot reconstruct what life was like during the latter half of the Old Stone Age, when the artistic achievements we have just examined occurred. There is some evidence that perhaps as early as 100,000 B.C. these people had some sort of religion. Some historians have suggested that they put up the skulls of cave bears as though to worship these rivals for the spaces in which they lived. By 50,000 B.C., Neanderthal people are known to have buried their dead with ceremony and care, behavior suggesting a belief in the hereafter, for ancient corpses were painted with red ochre, positioned with their knees raised, and provided with weapons. There is no proof for such conjecture, but the evidence does suggest that religion was among the earliest examples of human capacity to think in the abstract. As we have seen, there can be little doubt that art was another example.

In the New Stone Age—that is, the period from 8000 B.C. to perhaps 3500 B.C.—the final link was forged from our earliest, unknown ancestors to our earliest known ancestors, who emerged from the darkness of prehistory into the light of history and civilization. That link leads us from Europe to a place in the Middle East called Mesopotamia.

CRITICAL REVIEW below

A CRITICAL REVIEW

In the Introduction, we discussed how works of art can function as artifacts, and in the previous section, we have examined some artifacts from the earliest documentable periods of human culture. Nevertheless, striking as these cultural artifacts may be, they can give us only a rudimentary picture of our ancestors. While the artifacts offer us a remarkable record of what our predecessors did artistically, they give us no insight into knowing why they did it. When we begin to apply our definition of artworks as human enterprises, however, we come closer to these people as humans. More importantly, perhaps, the artworks of the Ice Age help us to focus on such questions as what it really means to be human and where we stand today in our "civilized" culture in that regard. In one sense, it could be asserted that our Ice Age predecessors were not as fully human as we are today—what does it mean to be "human"?

It seems fairly clear that the way in which Ice Age people portrayed human and animal figures was a choice rather than a matter of basic artistic ability. What qualities can a work of art gain if it does not represent an object realistically?

Using the vocabulary from the visual art section of the Introduction, write a page or two in which you analyze and speculate on possible interpretations of the Venus figures.

A CRITICAL LOOK

Just as it is important for us to understand what it means to be "human," so we must understand what it means to be "civilized." In the next section, we will investigate some of the characteristics that scholars have used to distinguish between human cultures that are "primitive" as opposed to those that are regarded as "civilized." Using those criteria, we will move ahead chronologically to examine what are acknowledged to be the earliest "civilizations" we know about. Our journey takes us to what today we call the Middle East, to the areas around the Rivers Tigris and Euphrates in Mesopotamia.

There are several important issues to consider. The first of these is the criteria we use to define civilized cultures, another is the role of language, specifically written language, in the emergence of a civilized culture, and a third area of exploration lies in the relationship of government, art, and religion and how each affects the other.

What form or forms may the Sumerian gods have taken?

How did artists achieve a sense of dignity in the Tell Asmar statues?

MESOPOTAMIA

CRITICAL LOOK p. 35

In myth the Tower of Babel rose to connect heaven and earth. In much the same way, the arts of the Mesopotamians symbolized the people's relationship to their kings and, through them, to their gods. Bridging prehistory and history, the cities and empires of the Fertile Crescent, the land "between the rivers"—the Tigris and the Euphrates—were our prototype civilizations. Here, for the first time, agriculture, metal technology, literacy, the specialization of labor, and a hierarchically organized urban community were combined. Kingdoms rose and fell as one power plundered its enemies and obliterated their cities, only in turn to be itself plundered and obliterated. Finally, spilling out of the crescent north into Asia Minor and south as far as Egypt, the vast empires of Mesopotamia reached outward in space and forward in time to clash with and influence the Greeks.

FROM PREHISTORY TO HISTORY

Before civilization could begin, human beings had to produce an economic surplus beyond their daily needs so that some people could take up "non-productive" activi-

ties such as trading. To reach such a stage, they had to progress from hunting and gathering to planting and farming. As our ancestors moved out of the New Stone Age and into the Age of Metals, they also moved from hunting to agriculture. Societal complexity, which may be the basic quality of civilization, could then emerge. At some time around 6000 B.C. the first recognizable civilization appeared in that part of the Near East that we call Mesopotamia (see Maps **1.2** and **1.3**), and the earliest recognizable culture to emerge in this area was that of Sumer.

SUMER

The Sumerians had a way of life similar to that of the other peoples in the region. They lived in villages and organized themselves around several important religious centers, which grew rapidly into cities.

RELIGION

Religion and government shared a close relationship in Sumer. Religion permeated the social, political, and economic, as well as the spiritual and ethical life of society. A long EPIC poem, the *Gilgamesh Epic*, gives us an insight into this religion around which Sumerian society was

Map 1.2 Mesopotamia.

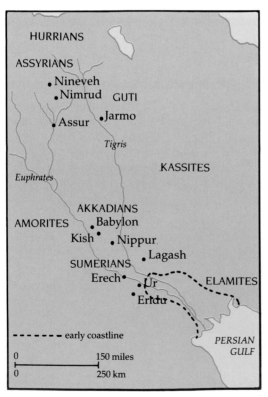

Map 1.3 Ancient Egypt and the Middle East.

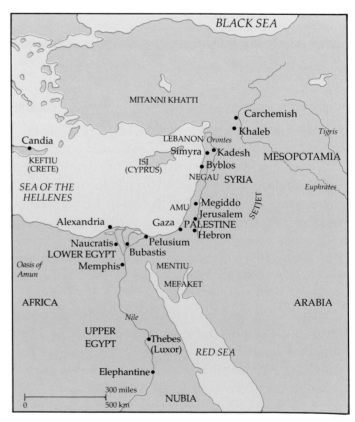

B.C.	GENERAL EVENTS	LITERATURE & PHILOSOPHY	VISUAL ART & ARCHITECTURE	THEATRE & MUSIC
8000	Mesopotamian farming villages Sumerian civilization		Ritual painted vases Stamp seals	Religious dances
3000	Invention of the wheel Bronze casting Sargon I Haram Sin Dynasties I and II in Egypt	*The Book of the Dead* Sumerian pantheon	Head of goddess Lambs sacred to E-Anna Cylinder seals Tell Asmar temple and statues (**1.8**) Royal harp He-goat from Ur (**1.9**) Ground-level temples Sin Temple, Khafaje Temple of Khentiamentiu Saqqara tombs Abydos tombs	
2000	Ur Old Kingdom of Egypt Middle Kingdom of Egypt	Epics, love songs Babylonian literature Rage of the God Ezra Love songs	Ziggurat at Ur Rhomboidal Pyramid Pyramid of Cheops (**1.14, 1.15**) Sphinx Rahotep and Nofret (**1.16**)	
1000	New Kingdom of Egypt Amenhotep IV Tutankhamun Hittite Empire Hammurabi		Temple at Luxor Valley of the Queen (**1.17**) Thebes (**1.18**) Tell el Amarna (**1.22, 1.23**)	Abydos passion play Funeral dances
900	Assyrian Empire			
700	Sargon II		Citadel at Dur Sharrukin (**1.10, 1.11**) Winged bull Basalt reliefs	
500	Nebuchadnezzar II Darius I Xerex I	Gilgamesh Epic		
300	Ptolemy II			

Timeline 1.2 The Ancient Near East and Ancient Egypt.

organized. The list of gods is a long one. By about 2250 B.C., the Sumerians worshipped a well-developed and generally accepted PANTHEON of gods. Temples were erected throughout Sumer for the sacrifices that were thought necessary to ensure good harvests. It appears that each individual city had its own god, and these local gods had their places in a larger HIERARCHY. Like the Greeks later (see Chapter 2), the Sumerians gave human forms and attributes to their gods. The gods also had individual responsibilities. Ishtar was the goddess of love and procreation, for example. There was a god of the air, one of the water, one of the plow, and so on. Three male gods at the top of the hierarchy demanded sacrifice and obedience. To those who obeyed the gods came the promise of prosperity and longevity. The elaborate and intricate rituals focused on cycles involving marriage and rebirth: a drama of creation witnessed in the changing seasons.

Sumerian religion was concerned with life, and it seems to have perceived the afterworld as a rather dismal place. Nonetheless, there is evidence to suggest not only the practice of ritual suicide but also the belief that kings and queens would need a full complement of earthly possessions when they entered the next world.

Sumerian religion had important political ramifications as well. It ascribed ownership of all lands to the gods. The king was a king-priest, responsible to the gods alone. Below him, an elaborate class of priests enjoyed worldly power, privilege, and comfort, and to this class fell the responsibility for education and the writing of texts. And it is writing that undoubtedly represents the Sumerians' greatest contribution to the advancement of general civilization.

WRITING

Various primitive peoples had used picture writing to convey messages. Sumerian writing, however, initiated the use of pictorial symbols that were qualitatively different: the Sumerians (and later the Egyptians) used pictures to indicate the syllabic sounds that occurred in different words rather than simply to represent the objects themselves. Sumerian language consisted of monosyllables used in combination, and so Sumerian writing came to consist of two types of sign, one for syllables and one for words. Writing materials were an unbaked clay tablet and a reed stylus, which, when pressed into the soft clay, produced a wedge-shaped mark. The wedges and combinations of wedges that made up Sumerian writing are called "cuneiform," from the Latin *cuneus*, meaning "wedge" (Fig. **1.6**).

Written language can cause many things to happen in a society, and it also reveals many things about that society. As well as opening up new possibilities for communication, it has a stabilizing effect on society, because it fixes the past by turning it into a documentable chronicle. In Sumer, records of irrigation patterns and practices, tax collections, and harvest and storage details were among

1.6 Clay tablet with cuneiform writing from Palace G, Elba, c. 2,400 B.C. National Museum of Aleppo, Syria.

TECHNOLOGY: PUTTING DISCOVERY TO WORK

The Invention of the Wheel

Insofar as Sumerians were capable of discerning scientific knowledge, they were also capable of applying that knowledge as technology. Sumerian mathematics employed a system of counting based on 60, and that system was used to measure time (we still have 60 minutes in 1 hour) and circles, divided into 360 degrees. The invention of number positioning—for example, 6 as a component of 6 or 60—made Sumerian mathematics unusually sophisticated. Mathematical calculation formed the basis for architectural endeavor, which, in turn, gave rise to higher levels of brick-making technology. Pottery was mass-produced and made the first known use of the potter's wheel. The wheel itself appeared as a transportation device in Sumer as early as 3000 B.C. By the same time. Sumerian technology had accomplished the casting of bronze and the invention of glass.

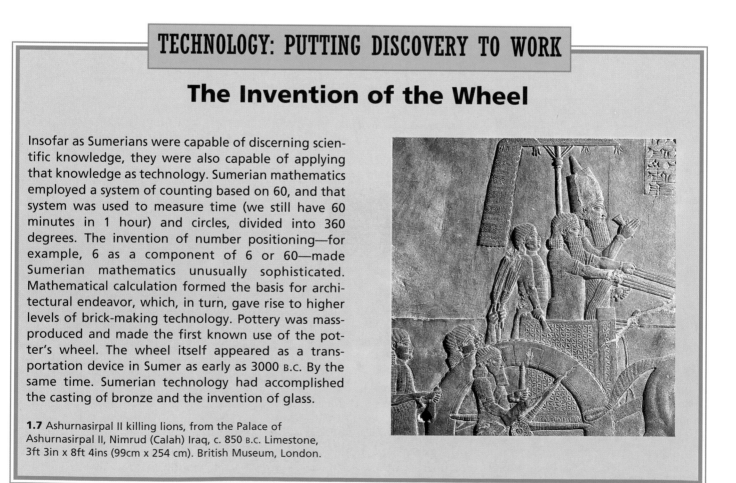

1.7 Ashurnasirpal II killing lions, from the Palace of Ashurnasirpal II, Nimrud (Calah) Iraq, c. 850 B.C. Limestone, 3ft 3in x 8ft 4ins (99cm x 254 cm). British Museum, London.

The Tell Asmar Statues

Undoubtedly the most striking features of these figures are their enormous, staring eyes, with their dramatic exaggeration. Representing Abu, the god of vegetation (the large figure), a goddess assumed to be his spouse, and a crowd of worshippers, the statues occupied places around the inner walls of an early temple, as though they were at prayer, awaiting the divine presence. The figures have great dignity, despite the stylization and somewhat crude execution. In addition to the staring eyes, our attention is drawn to the distinctive carving of the arms, which are separate from the body. The lines of each statue focus the eye of the viewer on the heart, adding to the emotion suggested by the posture. The composition is closed and self-contained, reflecting the characteristics of prayer.

Certain geometric and expressive qualities characterize these statues. In typical Sumerian style, each form is based on a cone or cylinder, and the arms and legs are stylized and pipe-like, rather than being realistic depictions of the subtle curves of human limbs.

The god Abu and the mother goddess may be distinguished from the rest by their size and by the large diameter of their eyes. The meaning in these statues clearly bears out what we know of Mesopotamian religious thought. The gods were believed to be present in their images. The statues of the worshippers were substitutes for the real worshippers, even though no attempt appears to have been made to make the statues look like any particular individual: every detail is simplified, focusing attention on the remarkable eyes, which are constructed from shell, lapis lazuli, and black limestone.

Large and expressive eyes appear to be a basic convention of Sumerian art—although it is a convention found in other ancient art as well. Its basis is unknown, but the idea of the eye as a source of power permeates ancient folk-wisdom. The eye could act as a hypnotizing, controlling force, for good or for evil, hence the term "evil eye," which is still used today. Symbolic references to the eye range from "windows of the soul" to the "all-seeing" vigilance of the gods.

The Sumerians used art, like language, to communicate through conventions. Just as cuneiform script condensed wider experiences and simplified pictures into signs, so Sumerian art took reality, as it was perceived by the artist, and reduced it to a few conventional forms, which, to those who understood the conventions, communicated larger truths about the world.

1.8 Statues of worshipers and deities from the Square Temple at Tell Asmar, Iraq, c. 2750 B.C. Gypsum, tallest figure 30 ins (76 cm) high. Iraq Museum, Baghdad, and Oriental Institute, University of Chicago.

the first things written down. Writing was also a tool of control and power. In the earliest times, the government and the priestly class of Sumer held a monopoly on literacy, and literacy served to strengthen their government.

But literacy also led to literature, and the oldest-known story in the world comes to us from earliest Sumer. The *Gilgamesh Epic*, an episodic tale of a hero's adventures, is from this era, although its most complete version dates from as late as the seventh century B.C. Gilgamesh was a real person, a ruler at Erech (or Uruk), and one fascinating part of this epic describes a flood, which parallels that in the story of Noah's ark in the Bible. Other epics too, and even love songs, have survived from the literature of ancient Sumer.

ART

Sumerian art progressed from stereotypical and anonymous portrayals to depictions of actual individuals, usually kings, who were portrayed in devotional acts rather than as warlords. The famous statues from Tell Asmar and the Temple of Abu illustrate this well (see Fig. **1.8**).

But if crudity marks the depiction of the human figure in these votive statues, grace and delicacy are evident in works from the golden splendor of the Sumerian court.

1.9 He-goat from Ur, c. 2600 B.C. Wood with gold and lapis lazuli overlay. 20 ins (50.8 cm) high. University Museum, University of Pennsylvania.

Inlaid in gold, the bearded bull symbolizes the royal leadership of ancient Sumer and masculine fertility (Fig. **1.9**). Here, we glimpse an idea basic to Sumerian culture: the wisdom and perfection of divinity embodied in animal power. In this case, the goat is the earthly manifestation of the god Tammuz, and his superhuman character is crisply and elegantly conveyed.

MUSIC

The early Sumerians made music as an essential and lively part of their culture, and they had many musical instruments. Music fulfilled a variety of functions in Sumerian life. It seems to have been most popular as secular entertainment, but religious ceremonies also employed music. Solo performances, instrumental ensembles of single and mixed instruments, and solo and choral vocal music with instrumental accompaniment are all documented in surviving artifacts.

We can only speculate on what Sumerian music would have sounded like. Clearly, stringed instruments were predominant, while percussion and rhythm instruments seem to have been less popular, and the trumpet was mainly military in application. Thus, we may assume that Sumerian music favored lyrical, soft, restrained tones, rather than loud, brash ones.

HAMMURABI AND THE LAW

As Sumerian civilization coalesced, corresponding developments took place among the surrounding peoples. But the region, which by this time had begun to feel the influence of the Egyptian civilization, remained in flux until the next great ruler emerged in the early 1700s B.C. This ruler was Hammurabi. His capital was Babylon, and Babylon became the hub of the world—at least for a while. The first Babylonian empire encompassed the lands from Sumer and the Persian Gulf to Assyria. It included the cities of Nineveh and Nimrud on the Tigris and Mari on the Euphrates, and extended up the Euphrates to present-day Aleppo (see Map **1.3**). This empire, of approximately 70,000 square miles (181,300 square kilometers), rested on an elaborate, centralized, administrative system. It maintained its order through a wide-ranging judicial code, which we have come to call the Code of Hammurabi. These laws consist of 282 articles, which address the legal questions of the time.

Foremost in importance among the articles was the precept of "an eye for an eye." Before Hammurabi's time, damages for bodily injury were assessed on a monetary basis—for example, a lost eye would be assessed at 60 shekels. Under Hammurabi, the monetary system was retained only for an injury inflicted by a free man on one of lower status. If, however, the parties were of equal status, exact retribution was called for: "An eye for an eye, a tooth for a tooth," and so forth. We do not know what retribution was exacted for injury inflicted on a person of higher degree, but the penalty in such a case was undoubtedly even more severe. Hammurabi's code was pragmatic and clearly based on a rigid class system. Only the rich were allowed to escape retributive mutilation by monetary payment. A sliding scale, based on ability to pay, determined compensation for medical expenses and legal fees.

The rights and place of women, likewise, were specifically spelled out. The purpose of a wife was to provide her husband with legitimate sons and heirs. The penalty for adultery (by a wife) was drowning for both wife and paramour. Men were allowed "secondary" or "temporary" wives as well as slave concubines. On the other hand, beyond the area of procreation, women were largely independent. They could own property, run businesses, and lend and borrow money. A widow could remarry, which allowed greater population growth than was possible in cultures where the wife had to throw herself on her husband's funeral pyre.

In essence, the Code of Hammurabi dealt with wages, divorce, fees for medical services, family matters, commerce, and land and property, which included slaves. Hammurabi, like the rulers who preceded him, took his authority and also his law from the gods. Thus the concept of law as derived from extraordinary and supernatural powers continued unchallenged.

THE ASSYRIANS

Hammurabi reigned for forty-two years, and in that time he achieved much. Cuneiform writing saw further development and spread widely throughout the Near East. Astrology stimulated the observation of nature. The patron god of the Babylonians, Marduk, surpassed his rivals to assume supremacy in the pantheon. Some 125 years after Hammurabi's death, his dynasty ended as yet another power from Asia Minor and northern Syria, the Hittites, plundered Babylon. The conquerors apparently maintained control until nearly 1100 B.C., but no notable figures emerged.

By the year 1000 B.C. a new power had arisen in Mesopotamia—the Assyrians. These were northern peoples from Ashur on the River Tigris. Their military power and skill enabled them to maintain supremacy over the region, including Syria, the Sinai peninsula, and as far as lower Egypt, where they destroyed Memphis. For nearly 400 years they appear to have engaged in almost continuous warfare, ruthlessly destroying their enemies and leveling the conquered cities. Finally, they, too, felt the conqueror's sword, and all their cities were utterly destroyed.

1.10 Reconstruction of Sargon II's citadel at Dur Sharrukin (Khorsabad, Iraq).

1.11 Gate of Sargon II's citadel at Dur Sharrukin (during excavation) with pair of winged and human-headed bulls. Limestone.

Under Sargon II, who came to power in 722 B.C., the high priests of the country regained many of the privileges they had lost under previous kings, and the Assyrian Empire reached the peak of its power. Early in his reign, Sargon II founded the new city of Dur Sharrukin (Khorsabad, Iraq). His vast royal CITADEL, which occupied some 250,000 square feet (23,225 square meters), was built as an image not only of his empire, but also of the cosmos itself. This citadel, a reconstruction of which appears in Figure **1.10**, synthesizes the developments in Assyrian architecture and demonstrates the pri-orities of Assyrian civilization. In Sargon's new city, secular architecture clearly takes precedence over religious architecture, and the rulers of Assyria seem to have been far more concerned with building fortifications and imposing palaces than with erecting religious shrines. The citadel rises like the hierarchy of Assyrian gods, from the lowest levels of the city, through a transitional level, to the king's palace, which stands on its own elevated terrace. Two gates connect the walled citadel to the outside world. The first was undecorated; the second was adorned with, and guarded by, winged bulls (Fig. **1.11**).

CRITI REVIE below

A CRITICAL REVIEW

One of the critical challenges facing any culture is the manner in which it accommodates the viewpoints of those who dwell in it. By today's standards, the earliest "civilizations" were hardly more than counties on our political maps, but what distinguished them from other "civilizations" were what we might call their cultural ethos: that spirit or commonality that held them together as a people. Military conquest seems always to have been a major means of expanding that ethos beyond the immediate confines of the civilization, but once one people had conquered another, the question arose of how those who had been conquered were to be incorporated into the ethos of the ruling civilization. The question this raises, as we look back at the history of humankind's earliest civilization, is why do we find it so difficult to get along with people who are different from ourselves?

What is the difference between "primitive" and "civilized" culture? Do those differentiations have any "quality" connotations? That is, is life better in one circumstance than in another? In what ways?

Sumerian society had a definite link between government, religion, and art. In an extended paragraph, describe this relationship and how it contributed to a unified cultural ethos.

A CRITICAL LOOK

We interrupt this next section of our journey through the ancient world with a feature that will recur in every chapter (Our Dynamic World), by which we can glimpse cultures outside the Western tradition. Somewhere around a thousand years later than in Sumer, recorded Chinese history began, and another of the world's great civilizations rose. Look closely at the concept called the *pao-chia* system. It is a system that defines how the Chinese relate to each other and how they see themselves as individuals.

After this short detour to China, we move back to the main focus of the text to study the great civilization of Ancient Egypt. We look to Ancient Greece as the cauldron from which emerged the Western cultural tradition, but the Greeks acknowledged the role of the Egyptians in their development. We will see in a later chapter that the Egyptians also played an important role in the Judeo-Christian aspects of Western civilization.

Describe Egyptian religion and the role it played in social life.

Describe the development of hieroglyphic writing.

Explain how the works of art of Egypt exemplified or supported its religious beliefs.

Describe how Akhenaton and the Tell el Amarna period stood in contrast to the art and religion of its Egyptian predecessors.

ANCIENT EGYPT

Protected by deserts and confined to a narrow river valley (see Map **1.3**, p. 36), Ancient Egypt experienced a relatively isolated cultural history, virtually unbroken for thousands of years. It was a civilization unique in its dependence upon the regular annual flooding of a single river, for each year, as the Nile overflowed its banks to deposit a rich and fertile silt on the surrounding fields, it bore witness to the rhythm of a beneficent natural order that would continue beyond the grave. Death—or, rather, everlasting life in the hereafter—was the focus of the life and the arts of the Egyptians. Created mostly in the service of the cult of a god, or to glorify the power and wealth of a pharaoh, art and architecture centered on the provision of an eternal dwelling place for the dead. Life was celebrated and recreated in images intended to provide an eternal substitute for the mortal body.

RELIGION

From the beginning of Egyptian civilization, the king was always identified with a god. At the time when Upper and Lower Egypt were united, in Dynasty I, the king was considered to be the earthly manifestation of the god Horus, deity of the sky. The king was also considered to be the "Son of Ra," and thus represented a direct link between the royal line and the creator sun god.

Egyptian religion was a complex combination of local and national gods, and in a cumulative process new beliefs and gods were added over the thousands of years of Egyptian dynastic history. Two gods could be amalgamated and yet retain their separate entities. The same god could appear in various manifestations. For example, Horus may be the avenger of his father, Osiris, or the infant son of Isis, or the sky god, whose wings span the heavens and whose eyes are the sun and the moon.

Religion played a central role in an Egyptian's personal and social life, as well as in civil organization. Death was believed to be a doorway to an afterlife, in which the departed could cultivate his or her own portion of the elysian fields with water apportioned by the gods. Life continued for the dead as long as the corpse, or some material image of it, continued to exist. Careful burial in dry sand, which preserved the corpse, was therefore essential, as was skillful mummification. The art of embalming had reached a proficient level as early as 3000 B.C. Great pains were taken to ensure a long existence for the corpse, and mortuary buildings became the most important architectural features of the culture, reflecting their role as eternal homes. These tombs and burial places, rich in funereal imagery and narrative, have provided most of what we know of Egyptian history. Religious practice dictated that only good things be said of the departed, however. Thus the picture of a country populated by young, handsome, well-fed men and women, and ruled by beneficent pharaohs who inspired reverence, optimism, and productivity, even among the lowest slaves, may need careful adjustment.

The pharaoh acted as a link between mortals and the eternal. Priests, or servants of the god, were delegates of the pharaoh. The common people relied on their ruler for their access to the afterlife: the offerings that would secure the pharaoh's existence in the afterlife were the people's only key to the eternal. It was, therefore, in every Egyptian's interest to be sure that the pharaoh's tomb could sustain and maintain him. Images and inscriptions in the tombs included the lowliest servants, ensuring that

OUR DYNAMIC WORLD

Ancient China

From the earliest times China witnessed the crowding of populations into tight-walled villages, and this packing together of people governed both social and family relationships. The family, rather than the individual, the state, or the church, formed the most significant social unit, and this was reinforced by the religious practice of ancestor worship. The family also formed the basic political unit. A system of mutual responsibility, called the *pao-chia* system, made individuals in the same household responsible for each other's actions. In this way, the individual became subordinate to the family, and norms for social conduct, such as loyalty, sincerity, and benevolence, were inculcated in the family system.

At a time slightly before the Hebrews' enslavement in Egypt (see page 154), verifiable Chinese history was beginning. The earliest Chinese books date to the early centuries of the first millennium B.C. Mostly mythological, these early histories wove a pattern of ethics, philosophy, and mythology.

From the Shang dynasty, which began c. 1400 B.C., come elaborately designed bronze ceremonial vessels. The craftsmanship of the design is exquisite and surpasses the quality of virtually every era, including the Western Renaissance. Each line has perfectly perpendicular sides and a flat bottom, meeting at a precise 90-degree angle, in contrast, for example, with incising, which forms a groove. The approach to design seen in animal representation reveals a vision unlike that of Western culture but similar to that of Pacific Northwest Native American design, in which the animal appears as if it had been skinned and laid out with the pelt divided on either side of the nose. A rigid bilateral balance occurs. The grace and symmetry of the bronze ritual vessel of the shape known as *hu*

1.12 Ritual wine vessel or *hu*, c. 1300–1100 B.C. Bronze, 16 ins (40.6 cm) high, 11 ins (27.9 cm) wide. Nelson Gallery, Atkins Museum, Kansas City.

(Fig. **1.12**) exhibits subtle patterns carefully balanced and delicately crafted. The graceful curves of the vessel are broken by deftly placed ridges and gaps, and while the designs are delicate, the overall impression exhibits solidity and stability.

they, too, would participate forever in the pharaoh's immortality. Magic charms for the revivification of the deceased king, which were at one time spoken by priests, came to be inscribed on the walls of the tomb so that, if necessary, the deceased could read them. Eventually the nobility began to usurp these magic formulas, and by the end of the twenty-first century B.C., they were copied regularly, and almost everyone could share the once-unique privilege of the pharaoh.

The pharaoh joined the gods in the nether world after death. As befitting a ruler whose entourage also existed in the afterlife, he came to be associated with Osiris, king of the dead.

ART

The most productive artistic periods in Ancient Egypt were those when prosperity was high and the nation was at peace. There also appears to be a correlation between artistic vitality and strong rulers. To a certain degree, religious forces also affected the focus and tenor of art. For example, when Mena, the first historic king, made Memphis his capital, art flourished and reached high levels of prominence because the major god of Memphis happened to be Ptah, the god of art and all handicrafts. One of the functions of the high priest of Ptah was that of

"Chief of the Stone Cutters and Artist to the King." As long as Memphis retained a central position in Egyptian life—as it did until the fall of the Middle Kingdom—art maintained its importance. During Dynasty XXVI, Memphis reemerged as a political center, and art was once again cultivated.

Egyptian painting was subordinate to sculpture. According to some sources, the Egyptians may not even have regarded it as an art form. Painting was, for the most part, a decorative medium which provided a surface finish to a work of sculpture. Sculptures in relief and in the round were painted. Flat surfaces were also painted, although such paintings often appear to be substitutes for relief sculpture.

In the Middle Kingdom this substitution became general, and painting largely replaced relief sculpture. The scenes vividly portrayed subjects of genuine human interest with original insight. The same may be said of painting in the New Kingdom. Here we often find humor in portrayals of daily life, put across with a high level of technical craftsmanship. Nonetheless, the only time when painting was regarded as a true art was during the reign of Akhenaton in the New Kingdom. Painting appears to have died out, as even a subsidiary art, after the New Kingdom.

MATERIALS AND CONVENTIONS

We know a little about the materials used by Egyptian painters, thanks to analysis by the famous Egyptologist Sir Flinders Petrie, of the mastaba, or tomb, decorations of Rahotep and Nofret at Maidum. Rahotep's tomb walls date from the Old Kingdom. They show careful preparation: the sun-dried mud brick was covered with a layer, 1½ ins (4 cm) thick, of mud plaster mixed with chopped straw. This, in turn, was covered by a very thin layer of fine GESSO. Paint was then applied with a brush. Petrie's analysis did not determine the actual pigments used, but the colors were black, blue, brown (of several values), green, gray, orange, red, white, and yellow. White gypsum was used to raise the value of any hue. It is clear that Egyptian artists had a formulaic approach to the human figure, although proportions varied from one period to another. The basic figure was the standing male, and his proportions dictated those of other figures. To maintain proper proportions, the painting surface was first ruled into squares. The CANON of proportion prescribed during the Middle Kingdom is as follows.

Head (hair to shoulder) 1 unit
Shoulder to hem of kilt 5 units
Hem to ground 3 units
Ground to nipple 7 units
Ground to belt (front) 5 units
Ground to base of hip 4½ units
Ground to base of knee 2½ units
Across shoulders 2½ units
Across waist 1⅛ units
Across feet 3¾ units[1]

As we examine painting from the Old, Middle, and New Kingdoms, we notice some prevailing conventions and some changes. In Old Kingdom painting, VERISIMILITUDE and intricacy are combined with flat, or two-dimensional, figure portrayal in which no attempt is made to give an impression of solidity by shading, modeling, or foreshortening. During the Middle Kingdom, technical refinement is replaced by a decorative approach to color as realism loses its importance: fabrics are clearly stylized. Now focus shifts to lesser nobles and paintings display a new humor and liveliness. New Kingdom painting continues the convention of two-dimensional figure depiction, with a few exceptions, and color remains vibrant.

OLD KINGDOM

Egypt's political organization centered around its all-powerful rulers, the pharaohs. The Egyptians themselves used no other dating system than that of their pharaonic dynasties, and the traditional chronology of Egyptian development also follows the dynasties of its rulers.

The first significant achievement we can mark is the establishment of the Old Kingdom (c. 2778–2263 B.C.). The Old Kingdom, whose capital was Memphis, had a planned economy and strict social order, while relying on the agricultural system based on the annual Nile floods. We know little of the earliest dynasties, but during the reign of Snofru and other rulers of Dynasty IV, there emerged the structure that has come to symbolize Egyptian accomplishment—the pyramid. According to one ancient source, Snofru "arose as a beneficent king over all the earth." He was a great builder, and his mortuary temple contains a list of the strongholds and cities he founded. The Egyptians attributed a standard list of accomplishments to beneficent rulers, and we can infer that Snofru built many temples and more than satisfied the appetites of the gods for offerings. The propensity for building reflected the fact that no ruler wished to dwell in his father's palace. Usually he built his own, as close as possible to his mausoleum.

PYRAMIDS

Pyramid-building proliferated in the Old Kingdom. Dynasty IV produced the most remarkable edifices of Egyptian civilization, the images that come to mind whenever we think of Egypt—the pyramids at Giza (Fig. **1.13**). In addition to the three most obvious pyramids, the area contains burial places for almost all the important people of Dynasties IV and V. The largest pyramid, that of Cheops (Fig. **1.15**), measures approximately 750 feet square (70 meters square) and rises at an angle of approximately 51 degrees to a height of 481 feet (147 meters). The burial chamber of the king lay hidden in the middle of the pyramid (Fig. **1.14**). Construction consisted of irregularly placed, rough-hewn stone blocks covered by a carefully dressed limestone facing, approximately 17 feet (5 meters) thick.

The famous Sphinx is a colossal figure carved from an outcrop of rock, lying at the head of the causeway leading from the funerary temple that adjoins the pyramid of Cheops' son Chephren (see Fig. **1.13**). His pyramid originally measured 707 feet square (65 meters square), and rose, at an angle of 52 degrees, to a height of 471 feet (144

meters). The Egyptian sphinx is a mythological creature, having the body of a lion and the head of a man, ram, or hawk. At Giza the giant Sphinx acts as a guardian, to protect the tombs.

SCULPTURE

Sculpture was the major art form of the Egyptians. By the time of the Old Kingdom, sculptors of the first two dynasties had overcome many of the difficulties that plagued their predecessors of the pre-dynastic period. During those archaic times, religious tenets may have confounded sculptors, for many primitive peoples throughout history have regarded the realistic portrayal of the human figure as dangerous. A close likeness of a person might have been thought capable of capturing the soul. There were also technical problems to be overcome. Pre-dynastic sculpture left detailing rough and simple, and convention rather than naturalism prevailed. Sculptors seem to have relied on memory to portray the human form, rather than working from live models.

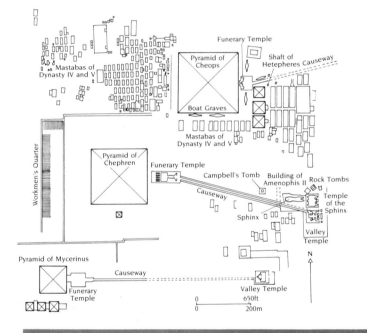

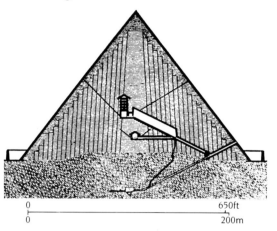

1.13 (*above left*) Plan of the Giza pyramid complex.

1.14 (*above*) Longitudinal section, direction south-north, of the Great Pyramid of Cheops, Giza, Egypt, Dynasty IV (2680–2565 B.C.).

1.15 (*left*) Great Pyramid of Cheops, Giza, Egypt, Dynasty IV (2680–2565 B.C.).

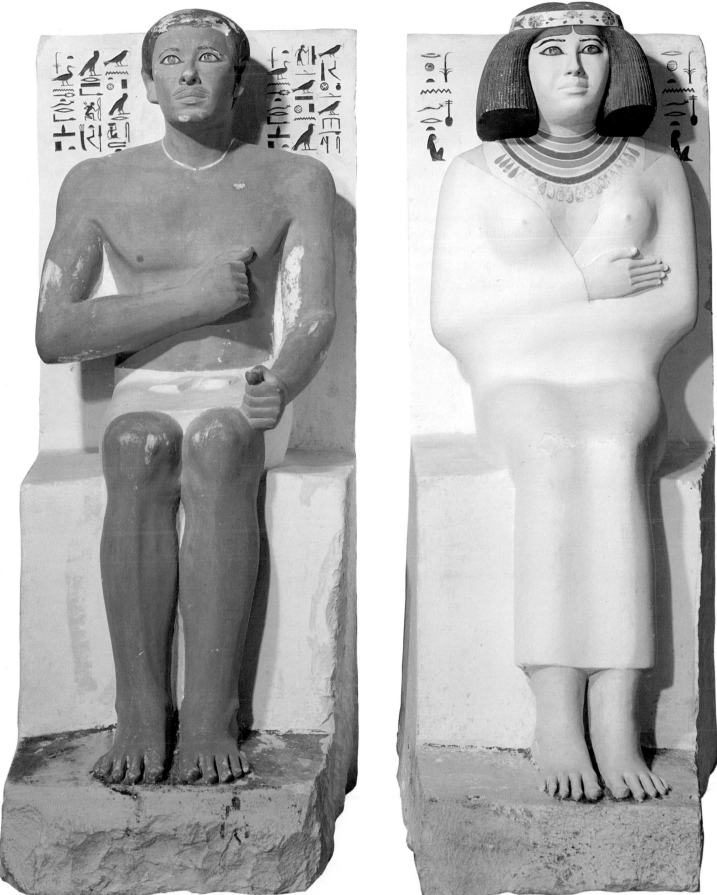

1.16 Prince Rahotep and his wife Nofret from Maidum, c. 2580 B.C. Painted limestone, 3 ft 11½ ins (1.2 m) high. Egyptian Museum, Cairo.

The Tomb of Nefertari

Queen Nefertari-mi-en-Mat, of Dynasty XIX, was the favorite among the four principal wives of King Ramesses II. Her tomb, which lies in the Valley of the Queens in western Thebes, rests under the precipitous cliff walls at the end of the gloomy valley of Biban el Harin. We enter through the First Room, to the east of which lies the Main Room, or offering chamber. The major part of the tomb is connected to these chambers by a flight of stairs. The Hall of Pillars, or Sarcophagus Chamber, provides the central focus of the tomb. Three side rooms open off the Hall of Pillars (Fig. **1.17**).

The paintings adorning the walls of Nefertari's tomb are elegant, charming, and alive with color. The northeast wall of the First Room carries a vibrant painting (Fig. **1.18**) showing, on the extreme left, the goddess Selkis with a scorpion on her head. On the extreme right appears the goddess Maat. On her head rests her hieroglyph, the feather. The rear wall of the recess depicts Queen Nefertari led by Isis toward the

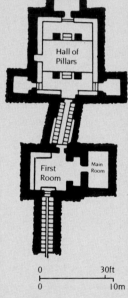

0   30ft
0   10m

1.17 Ground plan of Tomb of Queen Nefertari-mi-en-Mat in the Valley of the Queens, western Thebes, Egypt. 1290–1224 B.C.

1.18 Queen Nefertari guided by Isis, from the northeast wall of the tomb of Queen Nefertari at Thebes, Egypt. 1290–1224 B.C.

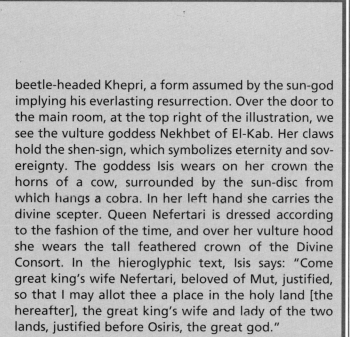

beetle-headed Khepri, a form assumed by the sun-god implying his everlasting resurrection. Over the door to the main room, at the top right of the illustration, we see the vulture goddess Nekhbet of El-Kab. Her claws hold the shen-sign, which symbolizes eternity and sovereignty. The goddess Isis wears on her crown the horns of a cow, surrounded by the sun-disc from which hangs a cobra. In her left hand she carries the divine scepter. Queen Nefertari is dressed according to the fashion of the time, and over her vulture hood she wears the tall feathered crown of the Divine Consort. In the hieroglyphic text, Isis says: "Come great king's wife Nefertari, beloved of Mut, justified, so that I may allot thee a place in the holy land [the hereafter], the great king's wife and lady of the two lands, justified before Osiris, the great god."

The painting itself is rich, warm, and highly stylized. A black base with colored bands borders the composition, providing it with a solid anchor and raising the body of the painting above the chamber floor. A black band forms the upper terminal accent of the recessed panel and continues on to the right. The black ceiling, with its conventional ocher stars, provides a color link which unifies the entire composition. A small black band decorated with stars runs just below the upper motif on the left panel. A similar black band without the stars reappears above the extreme right panel. The limited palette consists of only four hues, and these never change in value. Yet the overall effect of this wall decoration is one of great variety.

In the conventional style established since Dynasty I, the human forms appear only in flat profile. The pictures lie strictly on the surface. Naturalistic proportions are adhered to only minimally. Eyes, hands, head, and feet show no attempt at verisimilitude. On the contrary, the fingers become extenuated designs, elongating the arms to balance the elegant and sweeping lines of legs and feet. The matching figures of Selkis and Maat (extreme left and right) have arms of unequal length and proportion. Although the basic style remains consistent, we can observe a significant change in body proportions from those of the Old and Middle Kingdoms.

Because pre-dynastic sculpture predates written history, we can do no more than speculate on how much conventionalization reflected lack of technical proficiency, or philosophy, or both. When we examine CLASSICAL Greek sculpture, for example, we are certain that the IDEALIZATION of FORM was philosophical because the technical command necessary to produce naturalistic or any other type of representation was obviously there. But in pre-dynastic Egypt, the reverse appears more likely.

Old Kingdom sculpture shows full technical mastery of the craft. Life-size sculpture, capturing the human form in exquisite natural detail, became very popular. At the same time, the conventional representation of certain ideals of the pharaoh's demeanor persisted. His divine nature dictated a dignified and majestic portrayal. Although this treatment became less rigid as time went on, the more human qualities that this softening connotes never compromised the divine repose of the pharaonic statue.

The sculpture of Prince Rahotep and his wife Nofret (Fig. **1.16**) comes from the tomb of the Prince, who was one of Snofru's sons. The lifelike colors of the statues exemplify the Egyptian tendency to use paint as a decorative surface for sculpture, but the work is in no way commonplace. The eyes of both figures are made of dull- and light-colored quartz. The eyelids are painted black. Both figures wear the costume of the time. As was conventional, the skin tones of the woman are several shades lighter than those of the man: a woman's skin was traditionally painted a creamy yellow hue, whereas a man's skin ranged from light to dark brown. The kings of Dynasty IV rose from peasant stock, an ancestry that is apparent in the sturdy, broad-shouldered, well-muscled physique of the prince. At the same time, his facial characteristics, particularly the eyes and expression, exhibit alertness, wisdom, strength, and capacity. The portrayal of Nofret expresses similar individuality. This may be the earliest example of Egyptian art with the full development of the NATURALISTIC, three-dimensional female figure. Nofret wears a gown typical of the period, cut to reveal voluptuous breasts. The artist has been meticulous in his observation and depiction in the upper portions of the statues.

The Egyptian admiration for the human body is clearly revealed in both statues. Precise modeling and attention to detail are evident in even the smallest items. Nofret's gown both covers and reveals the graceful contours of her body. Her facial features reveal an individual of less distinct character than her husband: she has a sensual and pampered face. She wears a wig shaped in the style of the day, but beneath the constricting headband we can see Nofret's much finer hair, parted in the center and swept back beneath the wig. The treatment of the hand held open against the body reveals not only the artist's skill and perceptiveness, but also the care and attention Nofret has bestowed on it. The hand is, indeed, delicate: small dimples decorate the fingers, and the nails exhibit extraordinary detail. The unpainted nails are correctly observed as being lighter than skin tone.

The artist's attention and precision, so carefully expressed in the upper body, deteriorate almost to the point of crudity in the lower body, as is typical of sculpture of this era. The legs of both figures are lumpy, ill-defined, and coarse. The feet are nearly unrecognizable as parts of the human anatomy, except in that they have five toes. Parts of the thrones on which the figures sit show even less attention to detail—they remain rough blocks of limestone, still bearing the marks of the quarry.

MIDDLE KINGDOM

In about 2130 B.C. the governor of Thebes successfully subdued his rivals and founded a new dynasty (XI) that unified Egypt. Dynasties XI, XII, and XIII succeeded in maintaining an effective central government for the next 400 years, a period known as the Middle Kingdom. This was an age of recovery, expansion, and material replenishment. Egypt conquered Nubia to the south, and expanded its trade to regions previously unreached. Theological changes also occurred, consolidating the diverse religious cults under the sun-god Ra.

Life, however, remained precarious, even for a pharaoh. Like many of his predecessors, Amenemhet I, the founder of Dynasty XII, was assassinated in a palace conspiracy. He had assumed the throne twenty-nine years earlier in the same way by overthrowing the last ruler of Dynasty XI.

By the mid-nineteenth century B.C. the entire Egyptian domain was administered directly from the pharaoh's palace. Its sphere of influence included the conquered Nubia and extended to southern Syria. By the early 1900s B.C., the rulers of Byblos, in the Negev, were using the Egyptian form of writing— HIEROGLYPHS, or symbols that are conventionalized pictures of the things they represent—and Egyptian titles. A carefully designed system of fortresses guarded the southern approach to Egypt and the isthmus of Suez. Entry into Egypt proper was tightly controlled, even for commercial purposes, although, according to the biblical story, Abraham led his people down to sojourn in Egypt when there was famine in his own land.

THE SCRIBES

During the Middle Kingdom, the importance of scribes to the economy increased, as did their numbers. The profession of scribe was open to anyone with talent, and the common people could send their children to the scribal school, along with the children of the high born. Scribes were essential, and they were everywhere. All governmental functions needed to be recorded—the activities of armies, the counting of crops, the monthly inspections of utensils in the temples, and even the wicks, made of old rags, to light the work in royal tombs. In a carefully organized hierarchy, lower scribes labored diligently to become higher scribes, and even the most highly born youth started at the bottom of the bureaucratic ladder. As early as the twenty-first century B.C. we encounter the aphorism, "the pen is mightier than the sword."

NEW KINGDOM

Dynasty XVIII witnessed a flood of activity encompassing both a renaissance in the arts and significant military accomplishments. Royal authority was consolidated and centralized, becoming more powerful than ever before. Around 1486 B.C. a woman, Hatshepsut, came to the throne as the first queen. Commerce expanded during her reign, and it was reinforced in successive reigns by further military and imperial expansion. Thutmose III took Egyptian boundaries to the Euphrates. Monuments document marriages to Asiatic princesses. Temple decoration grew lusterous, and sculpture in the round came into favor.

TUTANKHAMUN

Akhenaton was succeeded by the pharaoh perhaps best known to us, Tutankhamun. Amenhotep IV had changed his name to Akhenaton to erase the relationship of the pharaohs with the cult god Amun-Ra and to establish his identity with Aton. Tutankhamun changed his name, from Tutankhaton, to make the opposite point. The splendor of his burial may, in fact, be attributable to the gratitude of the people for this reversal of policy.

Tutankhamun reigned only briefly. After his death, Egypt began a 200-year slide toward the end of the New Kingdom. After 1150 B.C. strikes and serious economic troubles proliferated. The power of the pharaoh gradually declined and internal disorganization increased.

THEBAN ROCK TOMBS

The painted tombs of Thebes provide most of our knowledge of Egyptian painting in the New Kingdom. Representations of gods are found for the first time in these tombs. Elaborate ceiling decorations are common, and the paintings portray the vivacity and humor of daily life. Depictions of workers and peasants differ from those of the Old Kingdom, particularly in the shape of the heads and in the types of garments.

These tombs generally have a square forecourt, which leads into a transverse hall. From there a long, narrow

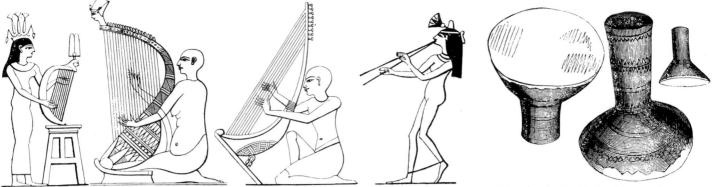

1.19 Egyptian harps.

1.20 The double pipe.

1.21 The darabukkah of the modern Egyptians.

hall leads to the ritual chapel. This contained seated statues of the deceased and of his or her family. Beneath the chapel lay the burial chamber, access to which was gained by way of a sloping corridor, steep stairs, or a vertical shaft. The walls of the transverse and long halls were often painted with hunting or farming scenes, which were intended to ensure supplies of food for the dead in the hereafter.

MUSIC

The Egyptians had many contacts with other peoples of the Mediterranean world and cross-cultural influence appears to have been strong in the area of music. We know, for example, that the Egyptians were fond of Assyrian music, and vice versa, but we cannot know how their musical systems sounded. We do not have musical scores, and even if we did, we would not know how to play them. Scales, HARMONIES, textures, pitches, intervals, dynamics, and so on, remain a mystery. We can nonetheless examine some of the instruments and perhaps speculate on their musical timbre, the basic quality of sound.

The modern world is fairly well acquainted with Egyptian muscial instruments: sculptures and paintings depict them, and fragments and even nearly complete instruments have been found. Harps, lyres, and numerous other stringed instruments, along with pipes, flutes, cymbals, and bells were all in the storechest of the Egyptian musician. As in Mesopotamia, the basic instrument in the Egyptian scheme was probably the harp. Harps varied tremendously in size, complexity, shape, and ornamentation (Fig. **1.19**). Harps are depicted with four, seven, and ten strings. Some are very plain, others ornate and brightly colored. How much of this variety is real and how much lies in the imagination of the painter, we do not know, but the frequent depiction of the harp does assure us of its popularity. Wall paintings also indicate that the larger harps, some of which appear to stand nearly six feet tall, were played essentially as modern harps are.

The tamboura of ancient Egypt had two basic shapes, one oval and the other with sides slightly incurved, like a modern violin or guitar. The overall design of this long, narrow instrument is reminiscent of a simple, home-made guitar. Illustrations show from two to four tuning pegs, and also indicate that the tamboura could be either with or without frets. The number of frets in some illustrations, if they are accurate, suggests that the instrument could produce a large number of pitches on each string. Analysis of tambouras found with strings intact shows that the Egyptians used cat gut for stringing. Additional stringed instruments of innumerable shapes and sizes defy classification, but this variety certainly indicates that music, whatever its texture and tonal nature, held an important place among the arts of ancient Egypt.

Wind instruments were very varied in shape, size, and ornamentation. Small pipes made of reed with three, four, five, and more finger holes have been found in great quantity. Some of these appear to have been played by blowing directly across the opening at the end, and others seem to have required a reed, like the modern clarinet or oboe. The long double pipe illustrated in Figure **1.20** was made of wood or reed-stem.

The Egyptians also enjoyed rhythmic emphasis, as we can deduce from a variety of percussion instruments. Three kinds of drum appear. One is a small and longish hand drum. A second appears more like an American Indian tom tom, with cords stretching between the drum heads. A third type is still found in Egypt and is called a darabukkah (Fig. **1.21**). Tambourines, bells, cymbals, and other rhythm instruments are also depicted.

Extrapolating from the shape of the stringed instruments and the number of strings, as well as from the number of finger holes in flute-type instruments, some musicologists have suggested that Egyptian music was based on pentatonic scales. But none of the extant instruments is in good enough condition to produce sufficient tones to prove them right or wrong. Scholars have also argued that Egyptian musical theory exerted a profound influence on Greek music.

SYNTHESIS

Akhenaton and Monotheism: The Tell el Amarna Period

The reign of Akhenaton marked a break in the continuity of artistic style. The stiff poses disappeared to be replaced by a more natural form of representation (Fig. **1.22**). The pharaoh, moreover, was depicted in intimate scenes of domestic life, rather than in the ritual or military acts that were traditional. He is no longer seen associating with the traditional gods of Egypt. Rather, he and his queen are depicted worshipping the disc of the sun, whose rays end in hands that bless the royal pair or hold to their nostrils the *ankh*, the symbol of life.

The cause of this revolution is not certain, but some evidence suggests that the priesthood of Heliopolis, the ancient seat of the sun cult, were seeking to reestablish the primacy of their god.

1.22 *King Smenkhkare and Meritaten*, Tell el Amarna, Egypt, c. 1360 B.C. Painted limestone relief, c. 5 ft (1.53 m) high. Staatliche Museen, Berlin.

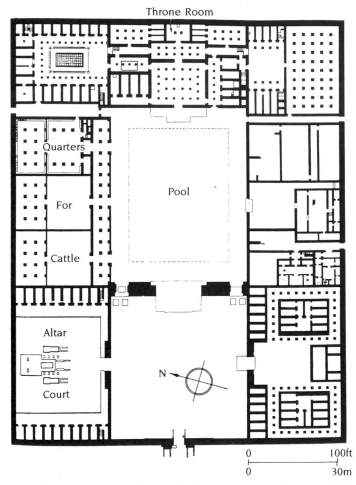

Throne Room

Quarters

Pool

For

Cattle

Altar

Court

N

0   100ft
0   30m

1.23 Plan of the North Palace, Tell el Amarna, Egypt, Dynasty XVIII (1570–1314 B.C.).

In the fifth or sixth year of his reign, Akhenaton moved his court to the city of Tell el Amarna, newly constructed in the sandy desert on the east bank of the Nile. It was a new city for a new king intent on establishing a new order based on a new religion. Akhenaton failed, and Tell el Amarna, abandoned at his death, was never built over again because it lay away from cultivated land. It thus provides us with an unspoiled record of Akhenaton's social and cultural vision.

The town is dominated by the large estates of the wealthy. They chose the best sites and laid them out in the style of the Egyptian country house, with large gar-

Akhenaton

Amenhotep IV, as Akhenaton was called before changing his name to reflect his god, was himself unusual. He possessed a "strange genius" for religious experience and its expression. The realistic trends of the period and Akhenaton's desire for truth seem to have resulted in the graphic depiction of his physical deformities. He is shown as having a misshapen body, an elongated head, and a drooping jaw. Yet the eyes are deep and penetrating. The effect is one of brooding intensity.

In a hymn of praise to Aton, the sun god, thought to have been written by the king, Akhenaton exhibits a spirit of deep joy and devotion to the deity. In his lyrical description of the way the earth and humankind react to the rising and setting of the sun, we glimpse a man of sensitive character. His vision is universal: Aton is not merely a god of Egypt, but of all people, and Akhenaton himself is the sole mediator between the two.

dens, numerous out-buildings, and a wall enclosing the entire establishment. Between these large estates lay the smaller dwellings of the less wealthy. The new city was complete, it seems, with a slum area outside the northern suburb. Near this area stood the grand North Palace (Fig. **1.23**).

In many ways the architecture of Tell el Amarna reflects the common features of New Kingdom domestic architecture although it is less sumptuous. Its lines and style seem relatively simple. Structures are open. At Amarna numerous unroofed areas lead to the altar of the sun god, Aton, left open to provide access to his rays.

Sculpture at Tell el Amarna departs from tradition. It is more secular, with less apparent emphasis on statues and reliefs for tombs and temples. The Amarna sculptors seem to have sought to represent the uniqueness of human beings through their faces. Amarna sculpture is highly naturalistic, but it transcends the merely natural and enters the spiritual realm. The statue of Akhenaton shown in Figure **1.24** depicts the curious physical features of the king that we noted earlier, and yet the stylization of the approach is also clear.

In the relief sculptures and wall paintings, the conventions of body proportions differ significantly from those of the other periods. In the Old, Middle, and early New Kingdoms, head and body proportions seem to be close to a ratio of 1:8. The total figure is thus nine head lengths from top to bottom. At Tell el Amarna, the total figure is seven to eight head lengths: in other words, the head is larger. Body proportions are also different. Arms are thinner and hands are larger. Abdominal and pelvic areas are emphasized in contrast to the focus on the shoulders and upper torso of earlier periods.

Many of the structural details of Armarna architecture are strikingly original. Plant motifs seem to have been favored, and palm-shaped columns are found in abundance. The stone version has a certain stoutness or heaviness, which is typical of Egyptian architecture. Also popular at Amarna were papyrus-bundle columns with CAPITALS of clustered, open flowers, sometimes made of alabaster inlaid with blue paste. Most original are kiosklike structures carved with convolvulus vines. The palace

1.24 King Amenhotep IV, later Akhenaton, from a pillar statue in the temple of Aton near the temple of Amun at Karnak, 1364–1347 B.C. Sandstone, 13 ft (3.96 m) high. Egyptian Museum, Cairo.

walls dazzled the eye with colored glazed tiles and painted stone reliefs. Indeed, the entire city must have shimmered in the sunlight of Akhenaton's single god.

Isolated from other periods by geographical and religious circumstance, the Tell el Amarna period encapsulates the artistic expressions of a single religious and philosophical concept. The religious reforms of Akhenaton were doomed to fail. Yet this Egyptian experiment in MONOTHEISM has left us with a vivid portrait of an integrated life-scheme.

CHAPTER TWO

ARCHAIC GREECE AND THE AEGEAN

AT A GLANCE

The Minoans

The Mycenaeans

Between Myth and History

The Archaic Greek World
The Polis

The Hellenes
    TECHNOLOGY: The Olive Press
The Persian War
Religion
Philosophy
Art
    MASTERWORK: The Dipylon Vase
Sculpture

OUR DYNAMIC WORLD: Native American
    Culture
Architecture—The Doric Order
Music
Literature

Synthesis: The Iliad of Homer

2.1 Geometric amphora, c. 760 B.C. National Archeological Museum, Athens.

A CRITICAL LOOK

The Western tradition traces its roots to a very specific time and place—classical Greece or the golden age of Athens—which we will examine in the next chapter. However, the Western tradition did not simply blossom from nothing. It occurred because of an amalgamation of forces, ideas, and events that coalesced fortuitously. We have already suggested that the influences that led to the beginnings of Western culture reached as far as Ancient Egypt and Mesopotamia. But these influences also came from areas closer to Athens—that is, the entire eastern Mediterranean Sea and specifically the Aegean Sea. Much of what we think we know of the local roots of the golden age of Greece has been pieced together from fragmentary, recently discovered remains, but as we shall see, much is still a mystery, and much is still conjecture.

What do archeology and art tell us about daily life among the Minoans and Mycenaeans?

When, in historical terms, did the civilizations of Minoa and Mycenaea occur?

What approaches to political life and commerce did each of these civilizations take?

What were the religious beliefs of these civilizations?

We leave the cradle of civilization in the Middle East and turn northeastward to the Aegean Sea and the area we know as Greece (Map **2.1**). It was here that the roots of Western civilization—the major focus of this book—took hold. There is little doubt that Egypt and Mesopotamia had an effect on the emerging culture of Greece—the Greeks of the classical period noted this, and the latest holders of Mesopotamian power, the Persians, conquered parts of the Grecian world, including Athens—but before there were "Greeks," there were others in the region.

As early as the first centuries of the Bronze Age, a collection of civilizations made up of farmers, shepherds, and seafaring traders had begun a succession of settlements of the Aegean world. From continental Greece and the Peloponnese, they spread around the Aegean Sea, and although they are now identifiable to us mainly by their art, we know that they moved outward from Minoa and Mycenae to colonize Cyprus, Phoenicia, Egypt, and Italy. But by 1200 B.C. they had disappeared, and a "dark age" lasting 400 years ensued. Then the cloud of history recedes to reveal established CITY-STATES. The artists of these city-states laid the foundations of the archaic style

B.C.	GENERAL EVENTS	LITERATURE & PHILOSOPHY	VISUAL ART & ARCHITECTURE	THEATRE & MUSIC
3000	Mycenean traders in the Aegean Early Minoan Age	Pictorial writing	Palace of Minos, Knossos (**2.2**)	
1200	Late Minoan Age Destruction of Troy		Lion Gate, Mycenae (**2.4**) *Boar hunt* (**2.3**)	
800	"Dark Ages" Carthage founded (traditional)		Protogeometric vases (**2.8**)	
700	First Olympic games First Greek inscription	Homer, *Iliad*, *Odyssey* Hesiod, *Works and Days*	Geometric vases (**2.1**) Diplyon Vase (**2.9**)	
600		Draco's laws Ionian poets Sappho of Lesbos	Doric order	
500	Babylon taken by Persians	Pythagoras	Perseus bowl (**2.10**) Kouroi and korai (**2.14**, **2.15**, **2.16**, **2.17**) "Basilica," Paestum (**2.21**) Lydos, krater Makron, skyphos (**2.11**)	Choric dance festivals First tragic competitions
400			Red figure krater (**2.7**) *Kritios Boy* (**2.18**)	

Timeline 2.1 Archaic Greece and the Aegean.

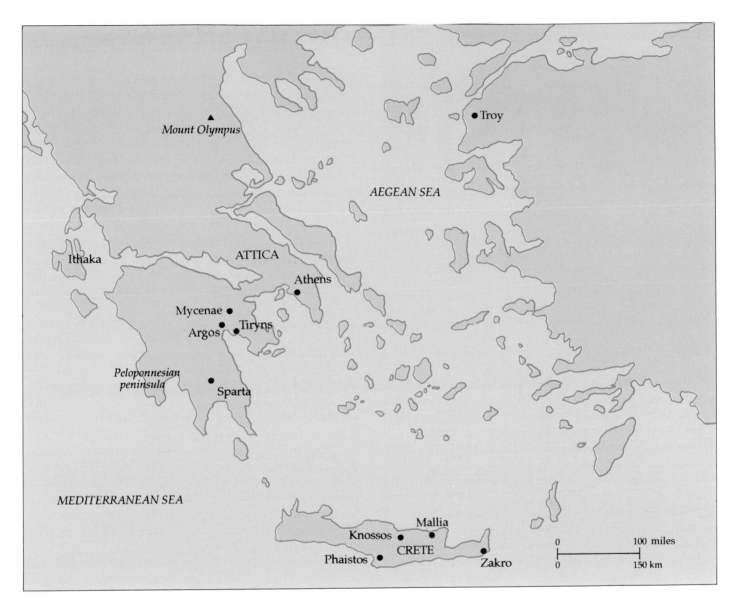

Map 2.1 The Aegean.

and created the philosophical and cultural conditions necessary for the spark that was to ignite the crucible of Western civilization.

THE MINOANS

Around 3000 B.C., while pyramids were rising in Egypt and sizable cities were being built in Mesopotamia, small towns on the island of Crete began to expand into large urban centers. The Minoan civilization, named after the legendary King Minos, emerged at this time, and by 1800 B.C. a great palace had arisen in the city of Knossos on Crete. Not much is known about the Minoans, but we can tell from the ruins of their palaces and their wall paintings that they were rich and adventurous. They depended on their naval power for defense, and their palaces,

which were not fortified, were elaborate complexes, with the private homes of the aristocracy and religious leaders clustered around them. These palaces had running water and elaborate drainage systems, and, below ground, storage areas contained large earthenware pots of grains, oil, and wine. They also had systems for cooling during the summer and heating in winter. Through trading posts around the Aegean, Minoan Crete carried on a lively and rewarding commerce as far away as Egypt, exporting pottery, bronze, olive oil, and timber.

Many well-preserved archeological sites allow us to deduce a certain amount of information about the Minoan lifestyle and culture, even though their writing has yet to be fully deciphered. Wall paintings, executed in brilliant colors and displaying spontaneity and a deep love of nature, reveal accurately depicted portraits of royalty and scenes of nature. They reflect a flighty court life with

2.2 Queen's chamber, Palace of Minos at Knossos, Crete, c. 1500 B.C.

THE MYCENAEANS

The Mycenaeans were early, barbaric, Indo-European conquerors who settled the rugged southeastern coastline of mainland Greece and who, by the fourteenth century B.C., had supplanted the Minoans as rulers of Crete. Homer called them "tamers of horses," because they fought from chariots, and they left the lands they conquered in ruins. Unlike the Minoans, of whom the later Greeks were unaware, the Mycenaeans, through Homer, provided Greece with myths, legends, and heroes like the mighty Achilles in the *Iliad* and the wandering Odysseus in the *Odyssey*. The Greeks also found in this people a source of ethics and moral order, and Homer's epics give a glimpse of a social organization in which the *oikos* (household domain) was the center of economic and social power.

Although conquest seems to have been their main occupation, the Mycenaeans did engage in some trade, their traders traveling throughout the Mediterranean between 1400 and 1200 B.C. Above all, however, they were warriors, and their rule was maintained by the strength of their military. It was their soldiers and armada of ships that reportedly conquered the legendary Troy and gave Homer the basis for his epic, the *Iliad*.

Their political structure appears to have been similar to the feudal system of medieval Europe. Petty kings controlled small, fortified city-states and the surrounding countryside, while a rigid class system gave preeminence to warriors. Just below the ruling class came a large body of bureaucrats and retainers, essential for collecting taxes and supplying the military.

A variety of local deities and household gods and goddesses, some of which appear also to have been predecessors of Greek deities, were worshipped in caves and at natural shrines. Religious practice included burying the dead with honor, and, like the Egyptians, the Mycenaeans mummified corpses and buried them with precious objects.

Most of what we know of the world of the ancient Mycenaeans comes from fragmentary remains of their art. The walls of their palaces bear decorative paintings, which also represent the activities of the time. The *Boar Hunt* (Fig. **2.3**) shows a group of dogs, hunting as a pack and attacking their prey. That the hounds are domesticated is evident from their collars, which appear to be tied around the neck. The hand and what looks like the lance of the hunter at the extreme right of the fragment indicate that the dogs have chased the boar into the vicinity of the hunters. This painting is clearly a testament not only to a successful hunt, but also to the dog breeder, whose well-trained dogs carry out their owner's commands.

The central city of Mycenae boasted a great palace complex and great wealth. The palaces of the Mycenaeans

high-born, bare-breasted ladies, bedecked in jewels, strolling in lovely gardens. Sportive youths frolic and raise golden goblets of wine. Life was lavish in the labyrinthine palaces of Knossos, with their complex rooms and passageways. There were bureaucrats and scribes in abundance, but few soldiers, and Minoan civilization clearly had trade, not militarism or politics, at its center.

The Minoans were a wealthy and secure people. If the so-called Palace of Minos (Fig. **2.2**) is representative, they not only enjoyed comfort, but were also capable of sophisticated elegance in decor and design. The palace had so many rooms that it was remembered in Greek myth as the "labyrinth of the Minotaur." The walls were built of masonry and decorated with murals and geometric motifs. Rectangular and circular COLUMNS, employed as supports, took the form of tapering wooden SHAFTS, perhaps reflecting their origin as unworked tree-trunks, with heavy, geometric capitals. The total impression is one of openness and lightness, combined with luxury and attention to detail.

The religion had a variety of gods, goddesses, and myths. Early versions of Athena—who later emerged as the patron goddess of Athens—first appeared here. The Minoans also had a cult of the sacred bull, which was celebrated by terrifying "bull dancing" or "bull leaping," a rite performed by naked young men and women on the backs and over the horns of the bulls. This was probably the origin of the Minotaur of Greek legend.

It was, however, a comparatively short-lived glory. By 1500 B.C. the Minoans had been swept into darkness, perhaps by a series of earthquakes and volcanic eruptions or perhaps merely through conquest by their neighbors. However, their influence was felt on a later civilization that also emerged in the Aegean, that of the Mycenaeans.

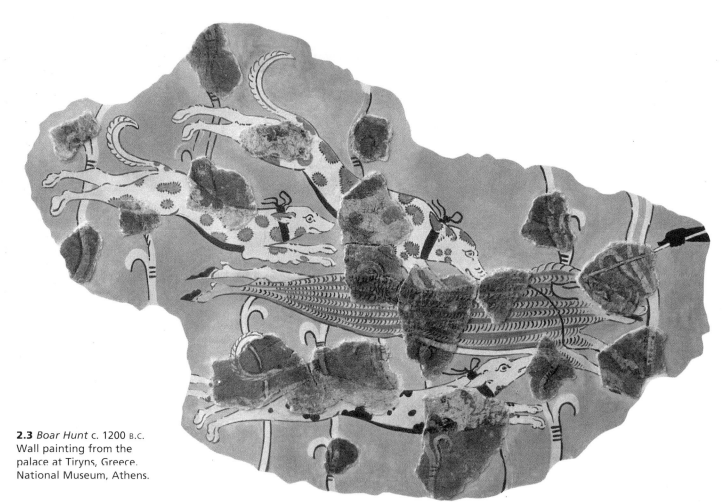

2.3 *Boar Hunt* c. 1200 B.C.
Wall painting from the
palace at Tiryns, Greece.
National Museum, Athens.

2.4 The Lion Gate, Mycenae, Greece, c. 1250 B.C.

were very different from those of the Minoans, for they
were fortresses constructed of large, rough stone blocks
placed at the center of a settlement on top of the highest
hill. The individual boulders were so huge that the
Greeks who viewed them centuries later called them
"Cyclopean," believing that only cyclopses—mythological giants with one eye in the center of their foreheads—
could have moved them.

The Lion Gate at the Palace of Mycenae (Fig. **2.4**)
demonstrates the powerful effect of juxtaposing smoothly
carved elements with the massive blocks of stone. In an
alcove on top of the lintel, two lions, obviously intended
as guardians, flank a tapering column similar to those
found in Minoan palaces. The careful carving of the animals' musculature expresses strength, and it contrasts
with the rough stone masonry, creating a slightly uncom-
fortable effect, which is reinforced by the cramped nature
of the composition within the alcove. Yet, despite any
crudity in the design, the execution is remarkably skillful,
and the jointure of the stone is tight.

In spite of its great defenses and massively fortified
palaces, the Mycenaean civilization collapsed shortly
after 1200 B.C.

TICAL
EVIEW
p. 60

A CRITICAL REVIEW

Piecing together a picture of a civilization from archeological and artistic artifacts and supplementing it by mythological illuminations of later cultures does not yield a complete depiction. Just as viewing the paintings and deposits of the Cave of Lascaux allows us to see only a part—the whats but not the whys—in the cases of Minoa and Mycenaea, we see a picture of muted colors and blurred edges. The image is there, but it remains slightly out of focus. We would like to know why the Minoans, seemingly a peaceful, non-military culture, rose to prominence, and then disappeared. We would like to know the same about the Mycenaeans, replacing the mythology of the later Greeks with facts. But again, it is the art of the time that gives us our best information. We sense in the art of both civilizations something of the character of these peoples. We come closer to them as humans—rather than historical curiosities—in the intimacy of their worship and daily life, as portrayed in their art.

In an extended paragraph, compare the religions of Minoa, Mycenaea, ancient Egypt, and Mesopotamia.

Compare the basic approach to life, government, and commerce of the Minoans and Mycenaeans, and extend that comparison to the civilizations we studied in Chapter 1.

A CRITICAL LOOK

At some time and in some way a cultural ethos developed in the disparate settlements around the Aegean Sea. These people began to see themselves as alike in critical ways, and their backgrounds began to blur into a single identity from which a common culture, philosophy, art, politics, and religion emerged. A number of critical concepts and topics will be explored in the next section, including government, religion, philosophy, and the historical context in which it all took place. As you study the material, keep in mind that the specifics lie beneath a broader concept of that overall cultural ethos. This ethos, called Hellenism, is the foundation of Western culture.

Explain how a "Greek" cultural ethos developed in the Aegean and Mediterranean in the period from 800 to 480 B.C.

Discuss the three pre-Socratic philosophical systems of the period.

Describe the Greek pantheon and the way the Greeks viewed their deities.

BETWEEN MYTH AND HISTORY

CRITICAL LOOK above

Between the time of the Mycenaean civilization, with its art and palaces, and that of the Greek city-states of the eighth century B.C. lies a historical vacuum of four centuries. Historians call this time the "Greek Middle Ages" or the "dark centuries," and it was during this period that wave upon wave of Indo-European peoples filtered into the area and spread throughout Asia Minor. The building of palaces ceased and what little artistic activity existed— for example, pottery—was crude. Although the Mycenaeans had writing, the skill seems to have vanished during this time, leaving only archeology to testify to the existence of these peoples. Life switched from fortified cities to isolated farming communities, and trade and

commerce among communities isolated by the mountainous terrain was minimal if it had not ceased altogether.

Nonetheless, life was not static nor all dark. During this time, iron replaced bronze for tools and weapons, significant changes occurred in burial practices, the political hierarchy shifted from kings to powerful families, and new peoples drifted into the valleys, to neighboring islands, and to the shores of Asia Minor. The Dorians settled in the Peloponnese and became the ancestors of the militaristic Spartans. The Ionians moved to islands and the Asian coast of the Aegean, where they came into contact with the older civilizations of the Near East and started the flame that would later ignite in the intellectual and cultural fire of the Greek Golden Age. Toward the end of the eighth century B.C., gatherings of Greeks listened rapturously to the epic poems of Homer and Hesiod, looking back on the heroes of Mycenae. And indeed, they did look backward, because it seemed that all glory lay in the past, with little to look forward to.

It seems clear that at the end of the thirteenth century B.C. a wave of destruction swept across the area. Existing cities were abandoned, and their populations moved to new sites. Some centers, such as Athens, appear to have remained intact, but the period seems to have been typified by waves of migrants passing from one place to another, not as warriors or conquerors, but merely as transients. A great emigration occurred from the Greek mainland to the outlying shores around the Aegean, and the island of Cyprus assumed a major role as a crossroads for trade with the cultures of the Middle East. All this transmigration had the effect of making the entire Aegean area essentially a "Greek sea."

THE ARCHAIC GREEK WORLD

The time from approximately 800 to 480 B.C. is called the "archaic period" in order to contrast this phase of development in Greek civilization from a more vigorous cultural advancement called the "classical period" which occurred in the middle third of the fifth century B.C.

Early in the archaic period, a great population explosion occurred, as nomads from the north continued to filter into the Greek peninsula and surrounding Aegean coastal areas. Sometimes the immigrating peoples forced indigenous peoples from their homes, causing them to emigrate to other areas, often across the seas. Sometimes, the immigrants themselves simply moved on. In any case, the rocky, mountainous Greek peninsula could not support the numbers of people who sought to live there. Thus, the population of Greece spread outward, throughout not only the Aegean area but beyond, around the Mediterranean. Especially after the development of the city-state around 800 B.C., emigration often included traders and mercenary soldiers. After the greatest period of population growth—that is from approximately 750 to 600 B.C.—Greek settlements had been established along the coasts of Asia Minor and the Black Sea and as far west as Italy, Sicily, Libya, France, and Spain.

THE POLIS

The Greek city-states that developed at the beginning of the archaic period were already well-established and functioning by the time recorded history began, but we do know, at least, that they did not all spring up simultaneously. Each city, or polis, consisted of a collection of self-governing people. The Greeks referred to cities by the collective name of their citizens—thus, for example, Athens was "the Athenians." Each polis was surrounded by a group of villages and a rural territory, and each was self-governing, functioning as an independent state. No central, unifying government drew these cities together, and each polis developed its own ethos—that is, a sense of self. Some, like Athens, emerged as relatively peaceful, with a high esteem for the arts and philosophy. Others, such as Sparta, were militaristic and seemingly indifferent to high culture.

All the cities formed their social orders on distinct class structures: some people were free and others were slaves. Among free males there existed a clear demarcation between those who were citizens and those who were not: only citizens could participate in political decision-making, own land, or serve in wars. But access to citizenship could alter according to the city's circumstances at a given time.

Physically, the polis was formed of two cities: a lower city, in which the people lived, and a high city, or acropolis, an elevated place in the center of the city occupied by the temples of the gods. This practice was little different from the ways in which towns developed in the Middle Ages, when the cathedral was built on the highest elevation in the center of a city to symbolize the centrality and elevation of the Christian church. The citizens of the Greek polis owned the city, including the acropolis, and the pantheon of gods was more often a focus of civic pride than of reverence.

Originally, the typical polis had an organization similar to the tribal structure brought down from the north by the invaders, whose tribes were governed by an aristocracy or council of leading families. Typically, the leading landowners were part of such an aristocracy, and, occasionally, a polis might have a "king," like that of the ancient Minoans or Mycenaeans. Power in the polis actually belonged, however, to the landowners and tribal leaders, and the concept of a king gradually faded away, and was replaced by a group of elected magistrates.

In the seventh and sixth centuries B.C. the aristocracy went into decline, giving rise to a new degree of freedom. As in the Middle Ages, the rise of trade and the increasing wealth of the merchant class siphoned power from the landowners. In addition, military tactics changed from chariot-fighting, which could be dominated by aristocrats, to large armies of foot soldiers formed of regular citizens. This change in military tactics involved the perfection of the phalanx.

The phalanx was a long row of infantrymen, packed shoulder to shoulder to form a solid, moving wall behind large shields with spears and swords protruding. Battles were more like shoving matches between two phalanxes than the wild hand-to-hand fighting we might imagine. In reality, the only individuals vulnerable to much sword-hacking were individuals at the extreme left of the phalanx. These men—their swords typically in their right hands—were vulnerable to the sword of the soldier on the right end of the opposing phalanx, who, with his right arm free, could slash around the shield to the exposed left shoulder of his opponent. A phalanx of strong, well-armored fighters provided a virtually unstoppable military machine for which even chariots and horses were no match.

As the polis developed, land, money, and military service became powerful qualifications for political power. Farmers, merchants, and craftsmen who could afford to buy weapons—each member of the army was self-armed—demanded inclusion in political decision-making. Often, tyrants—that is, spokesmen for the citizenry and quasi-rulers—arose from the ranks of the military.

By the end of the sixth century B.C. these unique Greek poleis were scattered throughout the Aegean and Mediterranean area. Although they did not match the cities of Egypt, Mesopotamia, or even Minoa or Mycenae in wealth and splendor, they contained thriving populations living in simple houses who, as a group, built impressive temples, theatres, and stadiums.

We look back on the Greek poleis and call them "democracies," seeing them as the forebears of our own "democratic" form of government. They were, of course, far from democratic in the modern sense of the word, for only native-born, free, adult males of a specific economic standing were citizens, and so had any voice in government or in the great philosophical debates of thinkers such as Socrates, Plato, or Aristotle. Nevertheless, the polis was a democracy in that the rule lay in the hands of the many and not in the hands of a few or, as in the monarchies of Ancient Egypt and Mesopotamia, in the hands of a god king.

2.5 Wrestlers, from a statue base, c. 500 B.C. Marble, 12¼ ins (31.8 cm) high. National Archeological Museum, Athens.

THE HELLENES

There was a unifying spirit among these independent poleis of Greek derivation—they saw themselves as "Hellenes." All the different peoples of the area—for example, the Ionians, Dorians, and Aculians—had a common language, which, although old, had only recently developed a written form. The earliest surviving Greek written characters are found on a jug dating from 725 B.C. These characters appear to be adapted from Phoenician script, one example of the many outside influences, especially Middle Eastern, that helped to shape Greek culture.

The Hellenes used a common calendar, which dated from the first Olympic games in 776 B.C. These games embodied much more than a mere sporting event—they represented life's struggles ("athletics" is a Greek word, meaning contest or struggle), and they symbolized the joy that can be found in toil and cost. The contests were undertaken for the honor of competing, and victory was regarded as a sufficient prize. But although the victors gained nothing more than a simple wreath of wild olive leaves, the citizens of a victorious athlete's polis often complemented the simple prize with more lucrative ones such as free meals for life. Only men and boys could compete in the five-day festival of the Olympic games, held every four years, at Olympia. They competed in the nude—married women were forbidden even to attend the games—and the principal event was a foot race to honor Zeus, king of the gods (see the discussion on religion on page 63). Later, boxing, wrestling (Fig. **2.5**), other field sports, and chariot racing were added. The first day of the Olympic festival witnessed peripheral events, such as poetry readings and art exhibitions, and the third day was reserved for solemn religious sacrifices at the altar of Zeus.

The Ancient Greeks pointed with pride to some of the external roots of their culture, but, most importantly, this

TECHNOLOGY: PUTTING DISCOVERY TO WORK

The Olive Press

Often, one of the interesting things about the record of history is not its claims, but the fact that particular individuals are recorded as having invented particular pieces of technology, and the Greeks had a great regard for technological innovation. The status of the technician in Greece was raised high—much more so than in neighboring Asiatic countries—and an interest in technology was respectable, with inventors being regarded as benefactors.

As Greek civilization spread through the Aegean and Mediterranean during the archaic age, trade became increasingly important. One of the few products that Greece, with its mountainous terrain and poor soil, could produce in sufficient abundance to export was olive oil, which, together with wine and pottery, became their principal export. Manufacturing oil in quantity required technological advances in the presses by which olive oil is produced. Initially, the oil was extracted in a simple beam press illustrated in relief sculpture and vase paintings, but later, pulleys and screws worked the beam to press the oil (Fig. **2.6**).

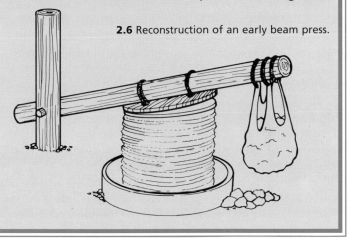

2.6 Reconstruction of an early beam press.

THE PERSIAN WAR

One such invasion came from the then largest and most powerful empire in the western half of Eurasia, the Persians. Built by Cyrus the Great in the middle of the sixth century B.C., the Persian Empire stretched from the eastern Mediterranean to the River Indus and from the Caucasus Mountains to the Arabian Sea. The Persians had conquered Babylon, Mesopotamia, and Egypt. Unlike his barbarian father Cyrus, Darius I had a more enlightened vision of power. He built roads and canals, divided his empire into twenty sub-areas called satrapies, and built splendid palaces in his capital cities of Persepolis and Susa. However, like any emperor, he could not tolerate rebellion, and when trouble arose in the Greek city-states of Ionia in 499 B.C., he moved to quash it. The result was what the Greeks called the great Persian War.

The revolt began in the trading city of Miletus, but the Ionians were no match for the Persians, and the revolt was soon crushed. The city of Athens responded to a plea for help, and that response prompted Darius to set his face to mainland Greece to punish the upstarts in 490 B.C. Darius drew his fleet ashore near the plain of Marathon, northeast of Athens, and 20,000 Persians and Medes out-numbered the Athenians two to one. The Athenian phalanx charged at the dead run, but the center broke and the Persians poured through. However, the vulnerable flanks of the Persian phalanx were turned by the aggressive Athenians, and, as a result, the Persians were forced to withdraw to their ships in disarray.

Darius died before he could take retributive action, and his son, Xerxes I, spent the next decade preparing for a new invasion of the Greek mainland, which set the stage for the great classical era of Athens, which we will trace in the next chapter.

RELIGION

The Greek mind was an earthy one, and Greek thought and religion centered on this life, rather than on the one to come. Ancient Greeks may often have looked for meaning in the order of the stars, but there, as on earth, the human mind was "the measure of all things."

At the core of Greek religion was a large family of superhuman gods. Their history in myth had been traced by the poet Homer in the *Iliad*. Greek religion had no holy books or scriptures. The stories of the gods were well known, however, through oral tradition and through writings such as Hesiod's *Theogony*. These gods were called "Olympian" because they dwelt on the mythical (and also real) Mount Olympus. All were descended from a pair of older gods: Uranus, representing the heavens, and Gaia, representing the earth. But their genealogies were the sub-

diverse group saw a commonality in their language that, despite the independent status of each polis, made them all Hellenes, and that unified them against other cultures that might try to invade them.

jects of so many varied myths that, although central to Greek religion, they are confusing, and, to some degree, confused. In addition to the central family of gods, the Greeks worshipped local deities who were thought to preside over certain human activities and to protect various specific geographical features such as streams and forests.

Unlike the Egyptians and Mesopotamians, the Greeks represented their gods in human terms, sometimes superior to humans, sometimes worse than us. This is a radical departure from, for example, the gods of Assyria and Babylonia, and the implication is clear: if the gods can be like humans, humans can also be god-like. Thus, an intimacy existed between the gods and their human companions, and life on earth for the Greeks was similar to that of the gods.

Homer had elaborated many of the often bizarre relationships of the gods in the Olympic pantheon, and some of the gods took shape from earlier religions of the Minoans and Mycenaeans, which may account for what often are confusing traits and characteristics.

In the Greek pantheon, Zeus, the sky god, functioned as the king of the gods on Mount Olympus. He hurled thunderbolts and presided over councils of gods. Endowed with a rapacious sexual appetite, Zeus sired both gods and mortals. Hera, Zeus' wife—and also his sister—functioned as the patron of women, who appealed to her for help. In legend, she also spent a good deal of time trying to keep an eye on her philandering husband. Zeus' two brothers, Poseidon and Hades, ruled the rest of the universe: Poseidon ruled the seas, waters, and earthquakes; while Hades ruled the underworld and land of the dead. Zeus had twin children, Apollo and Artemis, who symbolized the sun and the moon, respectively. Apollo represented the intellect and reason while Artemis was patroness of childbirth and wild creatures (Fig. **2.7**).

Zeus' other children included Athena, goddess of wisdom and patron of the city of Athens. She sprang, fully developed, from the head of Zeus, and was worshipped as a virgin goddess. Ares was the god of war, who engaged in an incestuous and adulterous liaison with his half-sister Aphrodite, goddess of love and beauty, who was married to another of Zeus' sons, Hephaestus, the god of craftsmen. According to legend, Hephaestus was both ugly and lame. Another son of Zeus, Hermes, served as the gods' messenger and patron of merchants and thieves. Zeus' sister Hestia protected the hearth in the Greek home.

Two other important deities headed large cults. Demeter, sister of Zeus, was goddess of the harvest, whose power made the earth fertile and crops grow. Initiates from all over Greece traveled to Eleusis, a small village in Attica, to worship her in quiet dignity and to join her cult with its promise of immortality. In contrast, Dionysus was the god of wine and reveling, and his devotees participated wildly in search of rejuvenation and rebirth. His annual ceremonies in Athens gave birth to the festivals of drama we will study in the next chapter.

PHILOSOPHY

The age of great Greek philosophers was yet to come, but during the archaic period the groundwork was laid for rationalism and intellectual acuity that would blossom in the fifth century B.C. The word philosophy means "love of wisdom," and its practice developed into searches for the meaning and significance of the human condition. In the archaic period philosophy first turned away from its roots in religion and began to apply reason to the discovery of the origins of the universe and the place of human beings in it.

In deference to the great philosopher of the Greek classical age yet to come, succeeding generations have called the philosophers of the archaic period the pre-Socratics, a term that does not refer to any specific philosophic system, of which there were several during the archaic period. Undoubtedly, the best known and, arguably, the most important was the system of philosophy developed by Pythagoras and called Pythagoreanism. In his search for truth, Pythagoras concluded that mathematical relationships were universal—that is, that there were universal constants that applied throughout life. For example, his deduction of what we call the Pythagorean theorem postulates that the square of the hypotenuse of a right-angled triangle equals the sum of the squares of the other two sides. We see this as a mathematical given, but Pythagoras rationalized that this mathematical truth

2.7 The Pan Painter, Attic Red Figure Krater showing Artemis Shooting Actaeon, c. 470 B.C. 16 3/4 ins (42.5 cm) high. Museum of Fine Arts, Boston.

revealed the larger, universal truth about the cosmos: that the universe has a single reality existing apart from substance. He called this the "harmony of spheres." He further believed that all living things were related. Beyond his philosophical contributions, his mathematical inquiries deduced the numerical relationships among musical harmonies, his research in this area forming the basis of contemporary musical practice that divides a musical scale into an OCTAVE or eight tones.

Another important school of pre-Socratic philosophy was that of the atomists. Led by Leucippus and Democritus (c. 460 B.C.), this system believed that the universe is an ultimate and unchangeable reality based on atoms—that is, small "indivisible" and invisible particles. A second quality of the universe was "the void" or nothingness. Of course, we recognize both the term and the definition of "atom" as a part of the twentieth-century physical science of quantum mechanics.

Other pre-Socratic schools included the materialists, headed by Thales of Miletus (c. 585 B.C.), who believed that water was the primary element underlying the changing world of nature. A century later, another materialist, Empedocles of Acragas (c. 495 B.C.) postulated that the elements of nature consisted of fire, earth, air, and water. Combined (love) and separated (war and strife), they accounted for the progress of creatures and of civilizations.

CRITICAL REVIEW below

A CRITICAL REVIEW

We look back to the Ancient Greeks as the source of the democratic spirit on which the United States is based. This system of government grew from the concept of the polis. Although we see many differences between democracy then and now, there are many similarities, especially with the time in which the United States was founded. Perhaps the remarkable thing about the peoples called the Hellenes was the fact that they were able to find a common ethos. After all, even the geography of the countryside mitigated against their unification.

From the dawn of history, the Greeks revealed traits of rationalism and intellectual acuity. This led to philosophic inquiry and a number of schools of thought. Review the three schools of pre-Socratic philosophy:

In what ways does the system of government of the polis resemble that of the United States, both now and in the past?

What were the factors that allowed or contributed to the common cultural ethos of the Hellenistic peoples in this period?

Of the three schools of pre-Socratic thought, which is closest to your own view of things? Explain why.

A CRITICAL LOOK

We have arrived at the cultural birth of the Western tradition. Art, architecture, literature, and music reveal themselves as PROTOTYPES. As we read the next section, we will recognize things we have seen before—not in history books or in museums, but on the streets of our own towns. That is what prototypes are: the original ideas or forms on which later ideas and forms are based. For example, Ancient Greek architectural styles enjoyed a resurgence during the Renaissance and again in the Neoclassical era—indeed they are still employed, albeit playfully, in the 1990s.

In this section we will learn additional vocabulary that is specific to the artistic style of the time—for example, terms such as protogeometric and DORIC.

Explain the characteristics fundamental to the three styles of vase painting.

Describe the nature of Greek music.

Identify and describe the characteristics of the Doric architectural order.

Describe the plot, characters, tone, and language of Homer's Iliad.

ART

VASE PAINTING

PROTOGEOMETRIC STYLE Our earliest impressions of art during the "dark ages" between 1200 and 800 B.C. are given by the only artifacts that have survived: pots or vases. Whether the ornamentation on the objects qualifies as an art form is arguable; moreover, the term "vases" is somewhat misleading. Unlike modern fine-art ceramics, which are objects intended to convey beauty and comment on reality, these pots were designed to serve exclusively utilitarian purposes. They were cups, jugs, and vessels for storing and carrying water, wine, and oil. Vase painting was thus, at best, a minor art form among the Greeks.

Nevertheless these vessels do provide some insights into their time. The earliest examples, which date from around 1000 B.C., fall into a category known as "protogeometric," a term that simply means "earliest forms of geometric." During this time, artists made use of bold, simple designs consisting mostly of circles and semicircles (Fig. **2.8**). The patterns are symmetrically balanced although the execution, while finely detailed, is somewhat haphazard. For example, the semicircles at the top of the AMPHORA in Figure **2.8** are irregularly spaced: they overlap in one place, touch in another, and are separated by a gap in a third. Nonetheless, the overall composition here and elsewhere reveals a concern for rational order and for fine detail. The quality of the potter's technique is also quite high. The vases are wheel-thrown, and exhibit an exceptionally smooth surface. Decoration was applied by brush while the vase was turned on the wheel, or, in the case of the circular motifs, with a pair of compasses.

2.8 Protogeometric amphora, c. 950 B.C. 21¾ ins (56 cm) high. Kerameikos Museum, Athens.

GEOMETRIC STYLE Within the next two centuries, vase painting progressed to its full geometric phase. Figure **2.1** shows a geometric amphora in which the circular design of the protogeometric style has been replaced by linearity, using zigzags, diamonds, and the meander or maze pattern. The vessels themselves are more intricate in shape and larger in size. Some examples are nearly six feet (1.8 meters) high—so large, in fact, that they had to be constructed in sections.

Virtually every space on the vase is filled. The decoration is composed in horizontal bands not unlike the registers found in Egyptian painting. When it appears, the human form is depicted in silhouette, with the head, legs, and feet in profile while the torso faces forward. This stylization is also very similar to the Egyptian. In general, geometric vase design expresses absolute symmetry.

ARCHAIC STYLE Figure representation remained two-dimensional until the middle of the sixth century B.C. Depiction was restricted to full profile, or a full-frontal torso attached to legs in profile. The head, shown in profile, contained a full-frontal eye. Fabric was stiff and conventionalized. But by 500 B.C. artists were attempting to portray the body in a three-quarter position, between profile and full frontal. At the same time, a new feeling for three-dimensional space developed, and artists began to depict eyes more realistically. Fabric began to assume the drape and folds of real cloth. All these characteristics mark vase painting of the sixth century B.C., and they typify the various stages of the archaic style.

Individual vase-painters' styles differed greatly from each other. We know some of these artists from their signatures. Others have been assigned names based on the subject or the location of their work. The Gorgon Painter (Fig. **2.10**) was named after the Gorgons that decorate his work. In this example of the sixth-century style, the design is arranged in graduated registers, with an intricate and lovely geometric design as a focus on the middle band. The painter

The Dipylon Vase

The Dipylon Vase (Fig. **2.9**), from slightly later in the eighth century B.C. than figure **2.8**, was found in the Dipylon Cemetery in Athens. This pot and others like it served as grave monuments. Holes in the bottom allowed liquid offerings to filter down into the grave.

The vase in Figure **2.9** shows the body of the deceased lying on a funeral bier, surrounded by mourners. Also depicted on the vase is a funeral procession with warriors on foot and in chariots drawn by horses. Every human and animal figure in this complex design suggests a geometric shape and clearly represents a stylized approach, harmonizing with the other elements on the vase. Although recognizable and narrative in purpose, the figures appear as just another type of ornamentation within the larger context of the overall design. They follow the convention, noted on p. 66, of portraying the torso frontally while the head and legs are in profile; turning the head to the rear would denote a figure in motion.

One of the amazing features of this vase is the amount and intricacy of detail that occupies every inch of its surface. Another important point is the organization of that detail into carefully balanced horizontal bands, each displaying a different geometric pattern. With only a few shapes, the artist has created a tremendously detailed painting with a subtle and sophisticated balance and focus. The dark, wide bands on the base and at the bottom of the bowl ground the design and help the viewer to focus on the story of the dead person. The patterns at the top and bottom of the vase are completely different, and yet they seem harmonious. Also notable is the balanced

2.9 Dipylon Vase, Attic geometric amphora, eighth century B.C. 3 ft 6⅝ ins (1.08 cm) high. Metropolitan Museum of Art, New York (Rogers Fund, 1914).

juxtaposition of straight lines and curves: the snake-like design and circles sit quite naturally alongside rectangles and triangles.

Lydos is responsible for one of the largest surviving terracotta KRATERS (bowls for mixing wine and water).

We can see the development of the archaic style toward the classical in a SKYPHOS painted by Makron in the early fifth century B.C. (Fig. **2.11**). Makron painted nearly all the vases signed by the potter Hieron, and in this example the delicate folds of the fabric reflect his idealization of line and form. He tells the story of Paris and Helen with graceful rhythms and repetitions of form tempered by careful variation.

The work of the painter Douris spans the years 500 to 470 B.C. Over thirty vases survive with his signature and more than 200 others in the same style are believed to be his work. Figure **2.12** illustrates Douris' use of rhythm and his skill in animating figures.

The works of Makron and Douris clearly illustrate the new fashion for red-figure vases (see below). Painters discovered that figures were more lifelike when they appeared in the natural red color of the terracotta, with the background filled in in black. At first, the change from black-figure to red-figure was tentative. Some vases appeared with red-figure work on one side and black-figure on the other. Douris made the transition completely, and his graceful and careful rendering of the human form moves toward realism.

RED- AND BLACK-FIGURE POTTERY Attic pottery can be divided into two types—black-figure and red-figure. In

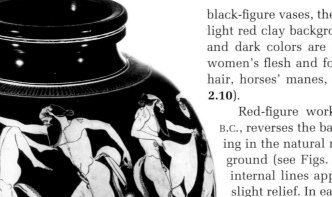

2.10 (*left*) Attic bowl showing Perseus and the Gorgons, early sixth century B.C. 36½ ins (93 cm) high. Louvre, Paris.

2.11 (*below*) Skyphos by Hieron, painted by Makron, showing Paris abducting Helen, 500–480 B.C. 8½ ins (21.5 cm) high. Museum of Fine Arts, Boston (Francis Bartlett Donation).

2.12 Douris, psykter showing dancing satyrs, c. 500–480 B.C. 11 ⅜ ins (28.7 cm) high. British Museum, London.

black-figure vases, the design appears in black against the light red clay background. Details are incised, and white and dark colors are added. White tends to be used for women's flesh and for old men's beards. Red is used for hair, horses' manes, and for parts of garments (see Fig. **2.10**).

Red-figure work, which first appears around 530 B.C., reverses the basic scheme, with the figures appearing in the natural red clay against a glazed black background (see Figs. **2.11** and **2.12**). Contours and other internal lines appear in glaze and often stand out in slight relief. In early red-figure work, incision is occasionally used for the contours of the hair, with touches of white and red. Other techniques that appeared in the fifth and fourth centuries B.C. include the use of PALMETTES and other motifs impressed in the clay and covered with black glaze.

SCULPTURE

Stone and metal are more durable than pottery, and sculpture often surpasses all other art forms in its survival of the centuries. However, Greek sculpture does not exist

OUR DYNAMIC WORLD

Native American Culture

When we speak of Native American art and culture, we speak of a variety of cultures and styles. In North America alone, no fewer than ten general cultural areas exist. Mexico and Central America add more. The history of native peoples in Mexico and Central America emerges on either side of a dividing line created by the European invasions of the late fifteenth and early- to mid-sixteenth centuries. Art is thus labeled as either pre-Columbian—before Columbus—or post-Columbian. South America was home to a wide variety of tribes, and the artistry of these diverse peoples encompassed weaving, metalsmithing, and pottery as major arts. Probably the focal point of South American Indian art is Peru, because it was the territory of the Incas.

Native American artists, like all artists, developed their own set of conventions, which are quite different from the artistic conventions of Western culture. Many of the subtleties of Native American art emerge from the culture itself, and such art portrays not only visual qualities, but also emotional and psychological qualities. All works of art are not of equal qualitative value, but judging the quality of works of art from different cultural traditions often requires different criteria. Those who do not come from a Native American cultural heritage may never, probably cannot ever, fully engage a work of art from this tradition.

However, in many respects, Native American art is the same as Western art, Chinese art, or any other art: it is an expression of a human perception of reality manifested in a particular medium and shared with others. Within the Native American culture exist a wide variety of expressions, approaches to materials, and general styles, but among many tribes there is no specific word that is equivalent to the word "art." In Native American culture in general, however, art is anything that is technically well done or well done in the end result. The effect might be magical or it might be power. The concept of "artist" is simply someone who is better at a job than someone else. Only a few Indian tribes—for example, the Northwest Coast, Mayan, and Inca—had a group of professionals who earned a living by producing what we would call art.

The earliest identifiable art in Mexico comes from the Olmec people—called the "rubber people"—and can be dated to approximately 1000 B.C. These people carved a number of subjects—for example, the delicate, baby-faced figure shown in Figure **2.13**. This finely carved figurine has a characteristic turned-down mouth, a facial feature that is a common characteristic of Olmec sculpture of this period. Even though much of the body is missing, we can see that the carefully carved details on the green-gray stone effigy make a powerful statement.

2.13 Fragment of carved stone figurine; Olmec-style head with trace of red paint inlay. Xochipala, Guerrero, Mexico, 1250–750 B.C., 3 × 1 ins (7.6 × 2.5 cm). National Museum of the American Indian, Smithsonian Institution.

in great quantity, and it is unfortunately more than likely that some of the greatest examples have been lost to humanity forever.

ARCHAIC STYLE

Most of the free-standing statues in the archaic style are of nude youths, and are known as kouroi. (The term means, simply, "male youth," and the singular form is KOUROS.) More than 100 examples have survived. All exhibit a stiff, fully frontal pose. The head is raised, eyes are fixed to the front, and arms hang straight down at the sides, with the fists clenched. The emphasis of these statues is on physicality and athleticism. The shoulders are broad, the pectoral muscles well developed, and the waist narrow. The legs show the musculature of a finely tuned athlete with solid buttocks and hardened calves. Nevertheless, these figures are clearly not realistic. The sculptor seems over conscious of the block of stone from

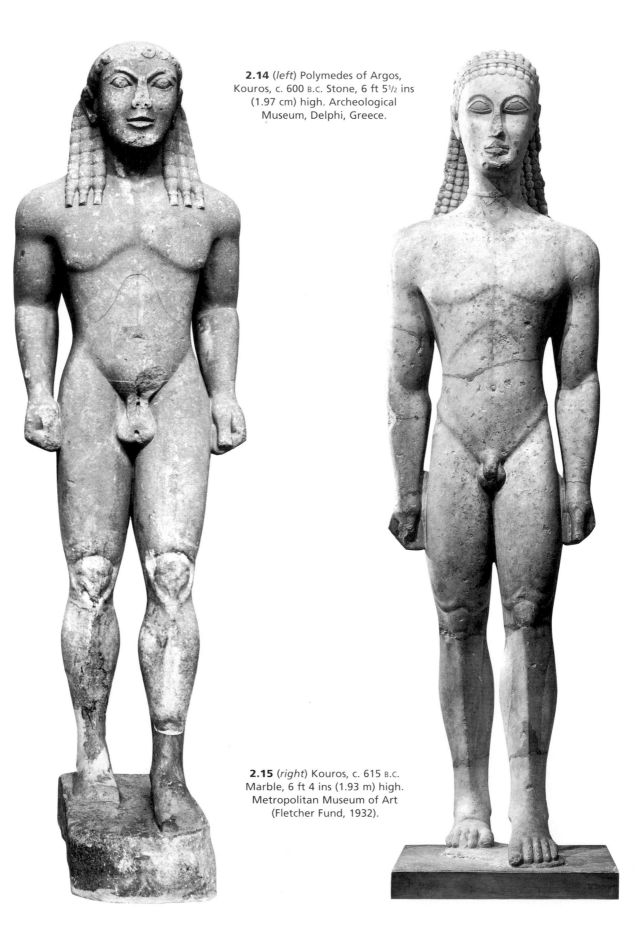

2.14 (*left*) Polymedes of Argos, Kouros, c. 600 B.C. Stone, 6 ft 5½ ins (1.97 cm) high. Archeological Museum, Delphi, Greece.

2.15 (*right*) Kouros, c. 615 B.C. Marble, 6 ft 4 ins (1.93 m) high. Metropolitan Museum of Art (Fletcher Fund, 1932).

which the figures have been cut. Features are simplified, and the posture, despite the movement of one foot into the forward plane, is rigid. In spite of these limitations, however, these works represent a sculptural innovation. They are the first examples of truly free-standing sculpture. By freeing the statue of any support, the artist is able to represent the human form independently of any non-living matter. This accomplishment prepares the way for later, more successful representations of living beings.

Most of the kouroi were sculpted as funerary and temple art. Many of them were signed by the artist: "So-and-so made me." Whether the statues were intended to represent humans or gods—they are most definitely not portraits of individuals—is debatable. The fact that all are nudes is perhaps a celebration of the physical perfection of youth and of the marvelous nature of the human body. The kouroi may also represent, more directly, the naked athletes who took part in the games loved by the Greeks. The Greeks explained the practice of competing in the nude by telling the story of a runner who dropped his loin cloth and, thus unimpeded, won the race. Other more symbolic explanations of the nudity of these statues have been offered, but no one view has prevailed.

Two significant characteristics are exemplified by the kouros from around 600 B.C. shown in Figure **2.14**. First is the fact that although there is an obvious attempt by the sculptor to depict the human figure in a fairly realistic form, the figure does not represent a particular person. Rather, it is a stereotype, or a symbol, and an idealization, perhaps of heroism. But it does not depict ideal human form. The sculpture lacks refinement, and this is a characteristic that helps to differentiate the archaic from the classical style.

The second characteristic lies in the attempt to indicate movement. Even though the sculpture is firmly rooted, the left foot is extended forward. This creates a greater sense of motion than if both feet were side by side in the same plane, yet the weight of the body remains equally divided between the two feet, as we saw in Egyptian sculpture.

The striking similarity of form and style among the kouroi can be seen when we compare Figure **2.14** with the statue in Figure **2.15**. There are the same physical emphases, the same frontality and the same slight departure from the horizontal plane, with the left feet forward. The stylized treatment of the hair is nearly identical, except that one has the curls pushed back behind the ears, while the other wears his hair over the shoulders. In both statues the kneecaps are curiously over-articulated. Nevertheless, the kouroi differ in proportion and in facial details.

The kouros had a female counterpart in the kore (plural korai, meaning "maidens"). These figures are always fully dressed, and in other ways too the kourai show far more variety than the kouroi. Some of these dif-

2.16 Kore, c. 510 B.C. Marble. 21½ ins (54.6 cm) high. Acropolis Museum, Athens.

ferences may stem from variations in regional dress, but clearly the sculptor's interest lies in the treatment of that dress, in the technical mastery required for the accurate depiction of cloth in stone. As in Egyptian sculpture, much of the rendering remains decorative rather than representational, but occasionally the sculptor achieves more than mere decoration.

Figure **2.16** shows a typical kore. In this delicate and refined portrayal, the sculptor seems to be reaching beyond the world of mortals, perhaps to depict an eastern goddess or queen. In contrast to the kouroi, the carving of this statue shows a lightness of touch and delicacy, not only in the anatomical features, but also in the precise folds of the robes, the finely detailed jewelry, and the stylized hair. These elements combine to give the statue a greater degree of verisimilitude than the kouroi we have examined.

In comparison with Figure **2.16**, the kore shown in

2.17 Kore in Dorian peplos, c. 530 B.C. Marble, 4 ft (1.22m) high. Acropolis Museum, Athens.

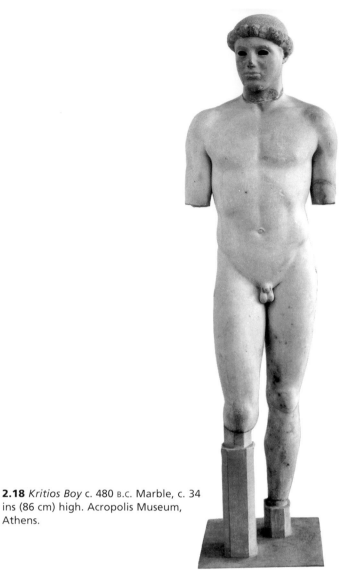

2.18 *Kritios Boy* c. 480 B.C. Marble, c. 34 ins (86 cm) high. Acropolis Museum, Athens.

ered the principle of weight shift—that is, the way in which the body parts position themselves around the flexible axis of the spine. The *Kritios Boy* is the first known portrayal of this important principle, and in it we can discern the beginnings of the classical style.

ARCHITECTURE—THE DORIC ORDER

The archaic period witnessed the building of temples in a new adaptation of the post-and-lintel structure. The style employed imposing vertical posts or columns capped by heavy lintels and a PEDIMENTED roof, and it was probably drawn from elements of Egyptian, Mycenaean, and pre-archaic Greek structures—for example, the FLUTED or vertically grooved column was used in Egypt at the Temple of Zoser, Saqqara, nearly two thousand years before its appearance in Greece. The style of these temples was called Doric after one of the Hellenic peoples, the Dorians, and it seems to have been well established by 600 B.C. Although the style itself changed over time, the early version had a cumbersome appearance, with thick

Figure **2.17** lacks detail, but it thereby achieves cleaner more graceful lines. Although anatomical details are disguised by the heavy fabric, the body, with the waist naturalistically emphasized, is convincingly present beneath the robes. The kore's smile exhibits more personality than the blank stare of many archaic statues, and the extension of the left arm forward into space indicates a new interest in movement outside the main block of the statue.

By the early fifth century B.C. the stiffness of the archaic style had begun to modify. The human form began to be portrayed with subtlety and to display movement. The transition began with the *Kritios Boy* (Fig. **2.18**), named for its presumed sculptor. Here is a statue in which the body truly stands at rest. The artist has discov-

2.19 Reconstruction drawing of the west front of the Temple of Artemis, Corfu. [After Rodenwaldt.]

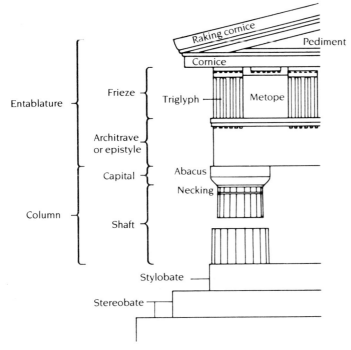

2.20 The Doric order.

2.21 Corner of the "Basilica," Paestum, Italy, c. 550 B.C.

columns and blocky, oversized capitals. Many of its characteristics came from earlier wooden buildings. We can sense the qualities and details of the order by examining a reconstruction drawing of the west front of the Temple of Artemis at Corfu (Fig. **2.19**). In this example, tapering columns sit directly on the STYLOBATE or uppermost element of the foundation. The fluted SHAFT, the tubular main trunk of the column, tapers inward as it rises. The shaft leads to a flared ECHINUS, a round collar-like cushion between the shaft and a square ABACUS: the slab at the top of the column on which the ARCHITRAVE, or bottom portion of the lintel, rests (Fig. **2.20**). Above the ENTABLATURE we can see a FRIEZE or band of relief elements known as triglyphs and metopes (pronounced meh-toe-PEE). Above the frieze rest two CORNICES. One is horizontal and the

other rises at an angle creating a triangular space called a PEDIMENT, which was often filled with relief sculptures (see Figs **3.11** and **3.12** in the next chapter).

The best-preserved temple from this period is the "Basilica" at Paestum (Fig. **2.21**). It is called the Basilica or meeting hall, although it was dedicated to the goddess Hera. Here, the flaring of the columns is exaggerated and the capitals seem unduly large, as if the architect were afraid that the lintels of the architrave would collapse if not supported along their length. The PROPORTION or relationship of the width of the columns to their height gives the Basilica a squat appearance with none of the grace of its classical successors.

MUSIC

Although we cannot play any Greek music because we simply do not know how to interpret the surviving records, we do know that music played a fundamental role in Greek life and education, and in Greek mythology, music had tremendous power to influence behavior. The

2.22 Attributed to the Eucharides painter, amphora showing Apollo playing a lyre and Artemis holding an aulos before an altar, c. 490 B.C. 18 ½ ins (47 cm) high. Metropolitan Museum of Art, New York (Rogers Fund, 1907).

gods themselves invented musical instruments, and the deities and heroes of Greek legend played them to remarkable effect. Apollo played the lyre, and Athena, the flute. Achilles, Homer's great hero of the *Iliad*, played proficiently.

Surviving records tell us that Greek music consisted of a series of MODES, the equivalent of our scales. Each mode—for example, the Dorian and Phrygian—had a name and a particular characteristic sound, not unlike the difference between our major and minor scales, and the Greeks attributed certain behavioral outcomes to each mode. Just as we say that minor scales sound sad or exotic, the Greeks held that the Dorian mode exhibited strong, even warlike, feelings, while the Phrygian elicited more sensual emotions.

We have a fairly good picture of what Greek musical instruments looked like from vase paintings. Figure **2.22** illustrates the aulos, a double-reed instrument, and the lyre, a stringed instrument. The Greeks were particularly fond of vocal music, and instruments were used principally to accompany vocal music. The lyrics of songs have survived, and these include songs to celebrate acts by the various gods, from whom some mortal had gained special favor.

LITERATURE

Homer, whose work we examine in more detail at the end of this chapter, is probably the best known of the ancient Greek poets, but he was by no means the only one. The growth of individualism in Greece produced a new literature: personal lyric poetry. Ancient lyrics, anonymous and often intended for use in rituals, had been concerned with experiences common to all. But by the end of the seventh century B.C. poets appeared along the Ionian coast who tell us their names, and sing of themselves, their travels, military adventures, political contests, homesickness, drinking parties, poverty, hates, and loves.

SAPPHO

The lyric poet Sappho, who was born around 615 B.C., lived all her life on the island of Lesbos. She gathered around her a coterie of young women interested in poetry, and who may have been worshippers of the cult of Aphrodite. Many of Sappho's poems are written in honor of one or other of these young women. Sappho was married, and had a daughter, Cleïs. Other than these few facts, we know nothing certain about her, although she has inspired numerous legends.

God's Wildering Daughter
Sappho

God's wildering daughter deathless Aphrodita,
A whittled perplexity your bright abstruse chair,
With heartbreak, lady, and breathlessness
Tame not my heart.

But come down to me, as you came before,
For if ever I cried, and you heard and came,
Come now, of all times, leaving
Your father's golden house

In that chariot pulled by sparrows reined and bitted,
Swift in their flying, a quick blur aquiver,
Beautiful, high. They drew you across steep air
Down to the black earth:

Fast they came, and you behind them. O
Hilarious heart, your face all laughter.
Asking, What troubles you this time, why again
Do you call me down?

Asking, In your wild heart, who now
Must you have? Who is she that persuasion
Fetch her, enlist her, and put her into bounden love?
Sappho, who does you wrong?

If she balks, I promise, soon she'll chase,
If she's turned from gifts, now she'll give them.

And if she does not love you, she will love,
Helpless, she will love.

Come, then, loose me from cruelties.
Give my tethered heart its full desire.
Fulfill, and, come, lock your shield with mine
Throughout the siege.

Sappho's poems are MONODIES on the theme of love. The lyrics are very personal; typically they celebrate some important event in the lives of those around her, often a bridal ceremony or wedding night. Their tone is emotional and frank, their language simple and sensuous. Her words and imagery depend on sound for many of their effects. As a result, translation into a language without the sounds and rhythmic character of Greek profoundly diminishes her verses. Most of the works exist only in very brief fragments of a few words or phrases. Yet at least one of the longer fragments, "He Seems to be a God, that Man," was much admired and imitated by later poets. In it Sappho gazes at a young bride sitting and laughing next to her bridegroom and is overcome with emotion.

HESIOD

Born at the end of the eighth century B.C., Hesiod was the son of an emigrant farmer from Asia Minor. He depicts this hard life in his poem *Works and Days*. Hesiod's lesson is that men must work, and he sketches the work that occupies a peasant throughout the year, recounting how an industrious farmer toils and how work brings prosperity, in contrast to the ruin brought about by idleness. He captures the changing seasons and countryside with vivid word pictures. He also describes life at sea, and concludes with a catechism detailing how people should deal with each other. His style is similar to Homer's, but his subject matter is quite different, for rather than telling of heroes and gods, Hesiod dwells on the mundane and mortal.

Hesiod's most famous work, however, is the *Theogony*, in which he traces the mythological history of the Greek gods. He describes the rise of the earth out of chaos, the overthrow of the Titans by Zeus, and the emergence of each god and goddess. Scholars attempting to understand Greek art and religion have found this work invaluable as a source of information.

A CRITICAL REVIEW

This section of the chapter has given us not only important concepts that form the basis for Western culture, but also additional important terms that enhance our understanding of art in general. Just as in Mesopotamia and Ancient Egypt, we find here a clearly demarcated style of art. Style, as we know, represents a recognizable use of the basic elements of each artistic discipline so that works by one or several artists reveal who made it. Style is like a fingerprint or a DNA sample. Perhaps more importantly, style reveals not only the who, but also the why of art. In the Introduction we asserted that art was a view of human reality, and style is the reflection of how artists see human reality, because they make a conscious choice to make their figures realistic or not, heavy or light in mass, and so on. That choice reveals the way in which artists feel and think about their world and, therefore, portray it in their art work.

Thus, we now have an arsenal of materials by which we can approach, recognize, and analyze the artistic things with which we come in contact daily. Our eye should tell us that there are clearly identifiable approaches—for example, to the human figure—that we can place in a cultural framework such as Ice Age, Mesopotamian, Egyptian, or Greek, and we can also use some fairly sophisticated terminology to describe what we see.

Also in this section, we introduced art from the same time in history from another part of the world—North America.

Describe the Doric order of architecture and define its composite parts—for example, stylobate, and so on.

Define kouros and develop a comparative analysis of at least three of the works illustrated in this book.

Find an example of architecture in your town that uses the Doric style as its prototype. Write an extended paragraph comparing the building you found with the original Doric style.

Describe the characteristics of Native American art and compare these with the art of Egypt, Mesopotamia, the Aegean, and Archaic Greece.

SYNTHESIS

The Iliad of Homer

Homer's *Iliad* and *Odyssey* created the mythical history that later Greeks accepted as their historic heritage. It took the dark and unknown past and created in a literary, originally oral, form a cultural foundation for an entire people. It told of heroes and described the gods. It depicted places and events, and it did so in a form that represented a supreme artistic achievement: epic poetry.

The ideals that dominated the early years of the first millennium B.C. found their way into the books of the Old Testament and numerous other writings. Nothing better synthesizes the early Greek mind and soul, however, than the singular mythology of the *Iliad* and the *Odyssey*. Both poems deal with minor episodes in the story of the battle of Troy, which ended, with the destruction of the city, in about 1230 B.C. These poems became the basic texts for every schoolboy in ancient Greece, and they have influenced Western literature ever since.

The plot of the *Iliad* describes a quarrel between Achilles, the greatest warrior of the Greeks, and Agamemnon, the commander-in-chief of the Greek army. This story is told against the backdrop of the siege of Troy. The heroes are types, not real people, and their characters were established in legend long before they were described in this epic poem.

When the action opens, the Greeks have been besieging Troy for nine years, trying to rescue Helen, wife of Agamemnon's brother Menelaus, from Paris, one of the sons of the Trojan King Priam. The time span covered in the poem is about forty days, during which Homer develops events on the battlefield and behind the lines of both adversaries. From his descriptions, an elaborate evocation emerges of the splendor and tragedy of war and the inconsistencies of mortals and gods. Here is an extract from Book XX:

So these now, the Achaians, beside the curved ships
were arming around you, son of Peleus, insatiate of
battle, while on the other side at the break of the
plain the Trojans armed. But Zeus, from the many-
folded peak of Olympos, told Themis to summon all
the gods into assembly. She went everywhere, and
told them to make their way to Zeus' house. There
was no river who was not there, except only Ocean,

there was not any one of the nymphs who live in the
lovely groves, and the springs of rivers and grass of
the meadows,
 who came not.   10
These all assembling into the house of Zeus cloud
 gathering
took places among the smooth-stone cloister walks
 which Hephaestus
had built for Zeus the father by his craftsmanship
 and contrivance.
So they were assembled within Zeus' house; and the
 shaker
of the earth did not fail to hear the goddess, but
 came up among them
from the sea, and sat in the midst of them, and
 asked Zeus of his counsel:
"Why, lord of the shining bolt, have you called the
 gods to assembly
once more? Are you deliberating Achaians and
Trojans? For the onset of battle is almost broken to
 flame between them."
In turn Zeus who gathers the clouds spoke to him in
 answer:
"You have seen, shaker of the earth, the counsel
 within me,   20
and why I gathered you. I think of these men though
 they are dying.
Even so, I shall stay here upon the fold of Olympos
sitting still, watching, to pleasure my heart.
 Meanwhile all you others
go down, wherever you may go among the Achaians
 and Trojans
and give help to either side, as your own pleasure
 directs you,
for if we leave Achilleus alone to fight with the
 Trojans
they will not even for a little hold off swift-footed
 Peleion.
For even before now they would tremble whenever
 they saw him,
and now, when his heart is grieved and angered for
 his companion's
death, I fear against destiny he may storm their
 fortress."   30
So spoke the son of Kronos and woke the incessant
 battle,

and the gods went down to enter the fighting, with
purposes opposed.
Hera went to the assembled ships with Pallas Athene
and with Poseidon who embraces the earth, and
with generous
Hermes, who within the heart is armed with astute
thoughts.
Hephaestus went the way of these in the pride of his
great strength
limping, and yet his shrunken legs moved lightly
beneath him.
But Ares of the shining helm went over to the
Trojans, and with him Phoibos of the unshorn hair,
and the lady of arrows
Artemis, and smiling Aphrodite, Leto, and
Xanthos.   40
Now in the time when the gods were still distant
from the mortals,
so long the Achaians were winning great glory, since
now Achilleus

showed among them, who had stayed too long from
the sorrowful fighting.
But the Trojans were taken every man in the knees
with trembling
and terror, as they looked on the swift-footed son of
Peleus
shining in all his armor, a man like the murderous
war god.
But after the Olympians merged in the men's
company strong Hatred, defender of peoples, burst
out, and Athene bellowed
standing now beside the ditch dug at the wall's
outside and now again at the thundering sea's edge
gave out her great cry,   50
while on the other side Ares in the likeness of a dark
stormcloud
bellowed, now from the peak of the citadel urging
the Trojans
sharply on, now running beside the sweet banks of
Simoeis.

CHAPTER THREE

GREEK CLASSICISM AND HELLENISM

AT A GLANCE

The Classical World
The Persian War
The Age of Pericles
The Peloponnesian War
Philosophy
Literature: The Platonic Dialogues
  OUR DYNAMIC WORLD: Philosophy and
    Religion in East Asia
History and Science
The Classical Style
  MASTERWORK: Myron—Discus Thrower

Architecture
  MASTERWORK: The Parthenon
Theatre
  PROFILE: Aeschylus
  MASTERWORK: Sophocles—Oedipus the
    King
  OUR DYNAMIC WORLD: The Nok Style of
    Africa
Music

The Hellenistic Age

Alexander and the Spread of Hellenistic
  Culture
Theatre and Literature
Philosophy and Religion
  TECHNOLOGY: Hero's Steam Turbine
Hellenistic Style
  OUR DYNAMIC WORLD: Qin Dynasty
    Realism—Terracotta Warriors

Synthesis: From Idealism to Realism
  Prometheus and Hecuba

3.1 The Parthenon, Athens, 447–438 B.C.

A CRITICAL LOOK

To begin this chapter, we will examine what we now call the "Classical World"—that is, the world of the Athenian Greeks of the fifth and fourth centuries B.C. The first three short sections of this treatment explain three important historical "events" that formed the crucible from which Western culture emerged. The first of these is the Persian War, to which we referred in the last chapter. The second is the brief period of prosperity after the Persian War, known as the Age of Pericles or the golden age, in which the city-state of Athens reached its cultural and political zenith. The third event is the Peloponnesian War during which Athens' bright light was extinguished.

What specific factors gave Athens the opportunity to become the power and the cultural center that emerged during the Age of Pericles?

In what ways did Athens and Sparta differ, and how was Sparta able to effect its defeat of Athens?

THE CLASSICAL WORLD

THE PERSIAN WAR

As we have seen, the Persians, defeated at Marathon in 490 B.C., spent the next ten years regrouping under Xerxes I and preparing for another invasion of the Greek mainland. That invasion took place in 480, when an army of perhaps as many as 60,000 men proved unstoppable, completely overrunning northern Greece. It must have been a frightening spectacle: Medes and Persians clad in leather breeches and fishtail iron jerkins, with short, powerful bows; Assyrians in bronze helmets and carrying long lances; Arabs in flowing robes; and Ethiopians in leopard and lion skins. A coalition army headed by the Spartans battled valiantly, at a narrow northern pass named Thermopylae—the Hot Gates—which has gone down in history largely because a traitor revealed to the Persians how to take the defenders from the rear. As the Persian army moved steadily south, its fleet sailed north against southern Attica. Athens was taken and destroyed, and ultimate victory for the Persians seemed a certainty.

B.C.	GENERAL EVENTS	LITERATURE & PHILOSOPHY	VISUAL ART & ARCHITECTURE	THEATRE & MUSIC
500	Persian invasion Delian League Greek revolt against Darius Battle of Marathon		Eucharides *Charioteer* (**3.8**) Douris, kylix (**3.7**) Myron, *Discus Thrower* (**3.10**)	
450	Pericles		Parthenon (**3.1**, **3.11**, **3.12**) Acropolis (**3.18**, **3.19**, **3.20**) *Riace Warrior* (**3.14**)	Aeschylus Sophocles
400	Athenian navy destroyed by Sparta	Herodotus Sophocles Thucydides Socrates	Mausoleum, Halicarnassus (**3.13**) Polyclitus, *Lance Bearer* (**3.9**) Propylaea (**3.22**) Temple of Athena Nike (**3.23**) Nereid Monument	Aristophanes Euripides
300	City-states defeated by Philip II Alexander the Great Invasion of Persia Death of Darius	Hippocrates Plato Aristotle Demosthenes Zeno the Stoic Epicurus Euclid	Praxiteles (**3.15**, **3.16**) Lysippus, *Scraper* (**3.17**)	Theatre at Epidaurus (**3.26**, **3.27**)
200	Roman defeat of Pyrrhus Battle of Mylae	Pentateuch translated into Greek	*Dying Gaul* (**3.33**)	Theatre at Ephesus *Hydraulos*
100			*Nike of Samothrace* (**3.30**) Temple of Olympian Zeus (**3.34**) *Laocoön and his Two Sons* (**3.31**)	

Timeline 3.1 Greek Classicism and Hellenism.

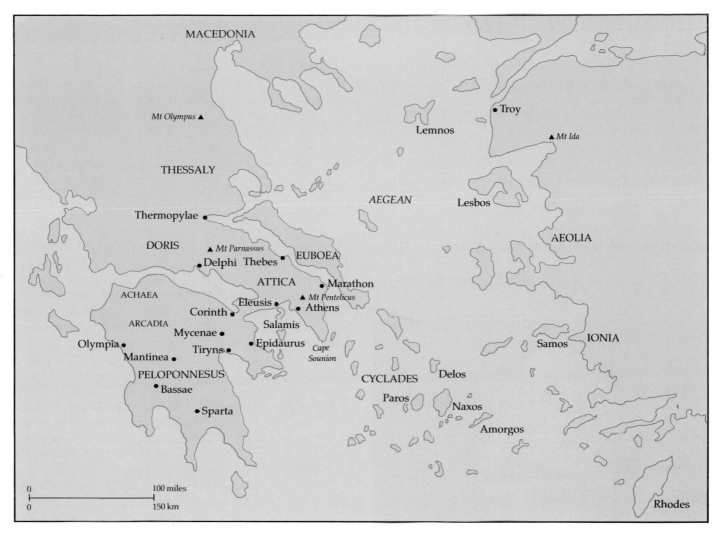

Map 3.1 Ancient Greece.

The Greeks were, however, fighting on territory they knew well, they had brilliant leaders, and they were motivated by the desire to save their homeland. For years the Athenian Themistocles had championed the Greek navy, and hundreds of new triremes (Fig. **3.2**) had been built. These long, oar-driven warships, manned by disciplined citizen-sailors, took to the sea against the Persian fleet. The critical battle came off the port of Athens, near the small island of Salamis, where the triremes massed against the Persians, ramming them as Greek warriors swarmed aboard. The battle of Salamis was a Greek triumph, totally destroying the Persian fleet and leaving the Persian army unsupported.

The Persian army wintered in Thessaly, and in 479 it marched south again. Under Spartan command, the Greek army emerged victorious at the critical battle of Plataea. The beaten Persians withdrew, never again to set foot in Greece. The Persian War did not end for another thirty years, but after the battles of Salamis in 480 and Plataea in 479 B.C., the "war" consisted largely of annual raids by the Greeks on coastal lands of the Persian empire.

3.2 Reconstruction of a Greek trireme.

THE AGE OF PERICLES

Claiming to be the saviors of Greece, the Athenians set about liberating the rest of the country. Several city-states banded together with Athens to form the Delian League in 478 B.C. The League took its name from the Ionian island of Delos, where the group met and stored its money. Delos was the site of the shrine of Apollo, and such sanctuaries were always chosen as treasuries so that the god would guard them. The states made a contract, and the signatories agreed to follow a common foreign policy and to contribute ships and/or money, as Athens deemed necessary. Athens contributed the most money and commanded the fleet. What followed was a systematic libera-

3.3 Kresilas, *Pericles*, Roman copy after original of *c* 440 B.C. Marble, Vatican Museum, Rome.

tion of the Greek cities around the Aegean, and the conquest of some islands populated by non-Greeks. The Delian League became, in fact, a highly prosperous Athenian empire.

The destruction of Athens, the victory over the Persians, and the formation of the Delian League helped to transform the young democracy of Athens, with its thriving commerce, unique religion, and inquisitive philosophies, into a culture of immense artistic achievement. The ruined city had to be rebuilt, and the spirit of victory and heroics prevailed. The Delian treasury, moved to Athens by Pericles, was used to help finance the immense costs of reconstruction.

Athens had witnessed a succession of rulers, and an interesting form of democracy had gradually emerged. Historians estimate that when Pericles came to power, in 461 B.C., the population of Athens was approximately 230,000 people. About 40,000 of these were free male citizens; 40,000 were Athenian women; 50,000 were foreign born; and 100,000 were slaves. Athenian democracy, however, allowed only free male citizens to vote, and the tyrant, or ruler, wielded considerable power. This power emanated principally from ownership of land. Private estates provided not only for the tyrant's individual welfare, but also for the horses and arms necessary to make him a leader in warfare. The Greek tyrants seem in general to have been especially benevolent. They were not necessarily aristocrats, and their claims to leadership were often based on their popularity among the citizens.

The central factor in Greek politics remained the sanctity of the polis, or city. More than an organized conglomeration of people, the polis was also a community, which was aware of the interests of the whole group as opposed to individual interest.

By the fifth century B.C., Athens was the richest of the Greek city-states. Greek law had been reformed by the great Athenian lawmaker Solon, and after 508 B.C. constitutional changes created a complex of institutions that became the foundations of an almost pure form of democracy. All political decisions were made, in principle at least, by a majority vote of the citizens. Conditions were now right for an age of high cultural achievement. By historical standards, the golden age of Athens was very brief—indeed, it lasted less than half a century—but that middle third of the fifth century B.C. was one of the most significant periods in Western civilization.

The tyrant Pericles (Fig. **3.3**) dominated Athenian politics between 450 and 429 B.C. A descendent of the old aristocracy, he flourished under the new democracy. The Athenian historian Thucydides wrote that Pericles was enormously popular and known for his financial integrity. He clearly had a vision of Athenian greatness that he was able to bring to fruition, and under his leadership Athens boomed. Trade flourished, as the Athenian port of Piraeus bustled with ships and a thriving commerce in wine and olive oil. Employment was high because after its sack by the Persians, Athens had to be rebuilt. This coming together of Delian money, high spirits, and visionary leadership gave Athens life and prosperity. As we shall see, philosophers such as Socrates disputed in the agora, a meeting and marketplace at the foot of the Acropolis, Aeschylus and Sophocles wrote for the Theatre of Dionysus on the opposite slopes of the Acropolis from the agora, and the great sculptor Phidias worked on the columns of the new temple of Athena, the Parthenon, on the top of the Acropolis.

THE PELOPONNESIAN WAR

Although they had joined forces to defeat the external threat of the Persians, the Greeks, with their independent city-states, never really coexisted peacefully, and toward the end of the fifth century B.C. that contentiousness led to a war of attrition between Athens and Sparta that effectively brought to a close the golden age of Athens. The Peloponnesian War, which began in 431 B.C., constituted a clash between two completely opposite ways of life.

If Athens was a cultured society, democratic, and artistic, Sparta represented the old ways of warriors, courage, militarism, and oligarchy. Sparta was ruled by a council of elders, and its males were required to live in barracks, as soldiers, until they were thirty years old. In reality, every citizen had to be a soldier, because Sparta's agriculture depended on the labor of the subject peoples, who far outnumbered the Spartans. In order to keep the population subdued, it was essential for Sparta's men to remain militarily expert. Spartans were, in consequence, the best soldiers in all of Greece.

Sparta's militaristic character caused it to seek dominance over all of its neighbors in the Peloponnese, the large peninsula of southern Greece, and it therefore maintained and enforced among these subjugated poleis an alliance called the Peloponnesian League. Conflict between the Peloponnesian League, which was dominated by Sparta, and the Delian League, which was dominated by Athens, seemed inevitable, especially after Athens began to meddle in the affairs of Sparta's allies. The war rumbled on for more than a quarter century.

Athens seemed destined to be quickly overpowered. Its military might consisted of its navy—which had dispatched the Persian fleet and cut off the Persian army—but unlike the Persians, the Spartan army was not an army away from its home, and Sparta, located inland in the center of the peninsula, was impervious to Athenian ships. Athens, on the other hand, could not match the land power of the formidable Spartan army. In addition, in the second year of the war, the city was ravaged by a plague, among whose victims was Pericles. The war, now in the hands of lesser leaders, dragged on, its savagery damaging the whole peninsula.

In 404 B.C. the Spartans were victorious. Athens and the Athenians were humiliated, losing their navy and being forced to watch their empire collapse. Sparta made Athens tear down the defenses that guarded and connect-

A CRITICAL REVIEW

The euphoria of victory and the need to rebuild its physical structure gave Athens a perfect opportunity to become the "cradle of Western civilization." Once the euphoria began to wane and events turned sour during the Peloponnesian War, however, Athens' place in the sun was eclipsed—at least from the standpoint of political control and influence. Yet despite its lapse as a world power, its cultural importance continued, and, as we shall see in the next chapter, Athenian architectural, artistic, and intellectual influence helped to reshape the great empire of Rome. Thus, despite a humiliating defeat by the Spartans, Athens, not Sparta, continued to be the predominant cultural force in the world.

The elation of victory and the need to rebuild its infrastructure gave Athens a tremendous opportunity and resulted in one of the most important periods of human history. The euphoria soon gave way to pessimism and the demoralizing effects of the Peloponnesian War. There may be a parallel between those times and what happened in Europe and America after World War II and in America throughout the Vietnam era.

Given the complete defeat of Athens by Sparta and their different ways of life and philosophy, but the continuing influence of Athenian culture, some people conclude that such circumstances prove that artistic culture is more important than power and conquest. Do you agree or disagree with such a view and why?

Speculate on the kinds of social conditions that are necessary for a culture to flourish and to have a lasting positive impact on the future.

CRITICAL
REVIEW
p. 83

CRITICAL
LOOK
above

A CRITICAL LOOK In the next sections we continue our examination of the classical world by considering its intellectual life. We focus on philosophy, particularly the philosophical approach known as sophistry, before turning to three intellectual giants of Western civilization—Socrates, Plato, and Aristotle. This will be followed by one of Plato's dialogues, *Phaedo*, and a discussion of history and science.

In what ways is sophistry a skeptical philosophy?

In what specific ways are the techniques and principles of Socratic, Platonic, and Aristotelian philosophies alike or different?

---

ed Athens to its port, and also put Athens under the control of a council of conspirators called the Thirty Tyrants.

Although Sparta achieved political dominance, it did not assume any kind of cultural leadership nor much long-lasting influence. Athens regained its freedom almost immediately, and although it was politically weakened and its role as a political power was diminished, its intellectual and aesthetic dominance continued to flourish. Peace was short lived, however, as battles raged on well into the fourth century until another power, a rough people from the north, the Macedonians, conquered all of Greece—Athenians and Spartans alike.

PHILOSOPHY

HUMANISM AND INTELLECTUALISM

The classical Greeks laid great emphasis on human rationality and the intellect. However, such an emphasis did not preclude a profound respect for the irrational and the mysterious. The Greeks recognized oracles and omens. They made pilgrimages to the shrines of Apollo's oracle at Delphi and at Didyma and there solicited advice which, if not always lucid, was respected. Numerous religious cults celebrated the cycle of the seasons and encouraged the fertility of the earth by performing mysterious and secret rites. Greek dance and drama developed from these rites, and belief in the supernatural and the darker forces of human irrationality lies close to the heart of the great classical tragedies.

Philosophy was an important discipline in Greek culture. A keen mind and a desire to answer life's critical questions were considered noble qualities. Under Pericles, philosophers such as Thales, Anaximander, and Heraclitus had great influence. They wrestled with questions such as "What is the basic element of which the universe is composed?" [Water.] "How do specific things emerge from the basic elements?" [By "separating out."] "What guides the process of change?" [The universe is in a constant flow. Nothing is; everything is becoming.]

SOPHISTRY: THE DISTRUST OF REASON

HUMANKIND: "THE MEASURE OF ALL THINGS" The middle of the fifth century B.C. was the end of a cycle of constructive activity and the beginning of a period of criticism and skepticism. All established beliefs and standards, whether religious, moral, or scientific, came under fire. Reason, it was argued, had led only to deception. The agonies of the Peloponnesian Wars, combined with a new awareness that the value systems of other cultures seemed to work just as well as the value system of Athens, gave rise to the adoption of realism, as opposed to idealism, and relativism, as opposed to absolutism.

Skepticism emerged in an Athens torn by disputes and ruled by a form of democracy that depended on persuasion and practicality. Debating skills were thus an absolute necessity, and these conditions produced teachers of rhetoric. Those who championed this new utilitarian art of persuasion were called Sophists or "wise ones." They were well versed in rhetoric, grammar, diction, and logical argument, as well as in behind-the-scenes intrigue, and the Sophists' star began to rise. They set up schools, and charged high fees for their services—a most unethical act according to traditional Greek thinking.

Placing themselves at the disposal of the highest bidder, the Sophists became servants of the rich and enemies of the masses. Conservative Athenian elders were aghast at the way the Sophists seemed to infect the youth of the city with irony and cynicism. Most of these teachers were non-Athenians, and they were also accused of spreading foreign "broad-mindedness." They supposedly taught their students how to win an argument at all costs and by whatever means, although whether all Sophists were unscrupulous is a matter of some debate. Certainly Protagoras, the great Sophist philosopher, escaped such charges, although his approach to morality deals more with appearances than with belief. Virtue, morality, and truth, the Sophists held, were relative to circumstance.

In his treatise *On the Gods*, Protagoras indicates that one "cannot feel sure that they [the gods] are, or that they are not, nor what they are like in figure, for there are many things that hinder sure knowledge, the obscurity of the subject and the shortness of human life." He then amplifies this religious doubt into a denial of any absolute truths at all. The individual person is "the measure of all things, of things that are that they are, and of things that are not that they are not." Truth is therefore relative and subjective. What appears true to any given person at any given moment is true, and what appears as real is real so far as any one person is concerned. But one such truth cannot be measured against another.

It was not the Sophists, however, but Socrates, Plato, and Aristotle who laid the philosophical base of classical Greek thinking, especially as it applied to the arts.

SOCRATES, PLATO, AND ARISTOTLE

SOCRATES Socrates (c. 470–399 B.C.) called himself the "gadfly" of Athens. He did not hesitate to condemn the Sophists for their lack of belief in a universal moral and intellectual order, but he also opposed many of the traditional values of Athens. He called on Athenians to examine their own lives and to think seriously about the real meaning of life. Sitting in the agora, or marketplace, he questioned everyone who passed by about subjects ranging from justice to art. He had no qualms about cornering a judge and asking him to explain justice, or in forcing an artist to define art, and was passionate in his defense of the right of individuals—including himself—to speak freely. He gathered around him young people, challenging them to examine their lives, and discussing with them how society should be organized and how life should be lived. For Socrates, the unexamined life was not worth living.

At the center of Socrates' thinking lay the psyche: the mind or soul. This, he believed, was immortal and much more important than the body, which perished. It was the responsibility of every individual to raise their psyche to its highest potential—that is, to fill it with knowledge acquired through rigorous debate and contemplation of abstract virtues and moral values. He believed that knowledge created virtuous behavior, and that those who did evil did so because they did not have knowledge—evil-doing was clear evidence of lack of knowledge.

As Plato reveals in his dialogues (see the extract from *Phaedo* on page 87), Socrates' method was to question his students, and an inability to answer revealed the deficiency of their learning. His rigor was particularly upsetting to the elders of Athens who, in the years following the Peloponnesian War, believed Socrates to be a disruptive element in society, and many found evidence of blasphemy and even treason in his public arguments. In 399 B.C. Socrates was arrested for impiety and corrupting youth. He was tried by a jury, found guilty, and sentenced to death by drinking a cup of poisonous hemlock.

One of his mourners, a young man named Plato, was so moved by the apparent injustice of Socrates' death that he dedicated his life to immortalizing his teacher and explaining his philosophy.

PLATO Plato was born in Athens in 427 B.C., two years after the death of Pericles, and he grew up during the years of the Peloponnesian War, which brought an end to the Athenian Empire. His family belonged to the old Athenian aristocracy, but it escaped the financial ruin that befell many Athenian aristocrats, and managed to give him a good education. He emerged a thoroughly well-rounded individual, a good athlete, and with experience of painting, poetry, music, literature, and drama. He received military training and fought in the wars. Although well suited and well connected enough for a career in politics, Plato turned instead to philosophy and fell more and more under the influence of the teacher Socrates.

After Socrates' execution for "corrupting Athenian youth," Plato concentrated entirely on philosophy. Anti-Socratic feeling ran high in Athens, and for ten years Plato found it expedient to live outside the city, writing many of the early dialogues during this period. Much of his aesthetic theory can be found in these dialogues, which follow Socrates' customary question-and-answer format.

Plato invented aesthetics as a branch of philosophy, and Western thought has been profoundly influenced by his metaphysical approach to the philosophy of art. We find in Plato's dialogues a clear, though not very systematic, theory of art and beauty.

For Plato, art derived primarily from the skill of knowing and making, or techne. Techne was the ability of an artist to be in command of a medium, to know what the end result would be, and to know how to execute the artwork to achieve that result. The fundamental principles of techne were measurement and proportion. Standards of taste—what is good and what is beautiful—could not be considered unless the work was correct in proportion and measure.

Plato's theory of beauty and the creation of beauty, or art, rests on his concept of imitation. According to Plato, the artist imitates the Ideal that exists beyond the universe. Indeed, the universe itself is only an imitation of ideas, or unchanging forms. This point is crucial to all Platonic thought, yet it is a difficult one. To simplify a complex notion, ideas, or forms, are reality. Everything on earth is an imitation of reality. Ideals are thus not thoughts conceived by an individual human mind (or a divine one). Forms are rather the objects of thought. They exist independently, no matter whether, or what, we think of them.

The arts are practiced to create imitations of forms. Plato mistrusted the arts, and especially drama, however, because the individual artist may fail to understand the ultimate reality, and may instead present merely an "appearance of perceivable nature." Therefore, art must be judged by the statesman, who "envisages the human community according to the Ideas of justice, the good, courage, temperance, and the beautiful."[1] In the end, what is proper as art depends upon the "moral ends of the polis."

In addition to possessing technical ability and the ability to know and imitate Ideas, the artist must have a third quality, artistic inspiration. No one can ascend to the highest levels of artistry without divine inspiration and assistance. Plato calls artistry a form of "divine madness."

ARISTOTLE Born in 384 B.C., Aristotle (Fig. **3.4**) did not have Plato's advantages of birth. His family was middle class, and his father was court physician to Amyntas of Macedon, grandfather of Alexander the Great. Aristotle was orphaned when he was quite young, and gained a home and his education through the generosity of a family friend. When he was eighteen years old he became a student at Plato's ACADEMY where his affectations and self-absorption caused some trouble with the school's authorities. After Plato's death, Aristotle left the Academy and married. Around 343 B.C. he gained a favorable position as tutor to Alexander the Great. Aristotle sought to teach Alexander to revere all things Greek and despise anything barbarian—that is, non-Greek.

When Alexander acceded to the throne in 336 B.C., Aristotle returned to Athens to set up his own school, the Lyceum. Over the next twelve years he produced a prolific outpouring of writings as well as research in physics, astronomy, biology, physiology, anatomy, natural history, psychology, politics, ethics, logic, rhetoric, art, theology, and metaphysics. Aristotle's "is probably the only human intellect that has ever compassed at first hand and assimilated the whole body of existing knowledge on all subjects, and brought it within a single focus."[2]

3.4 Aristotle.

Aristotle's major work on the philosophy of art is the *Poetics*. There he maintains that all the arts imitate nature, and that imitative character is rooted in human psychology. For Aristotle, the end of artistic creation determines the appropriate means for its realization. In order to assess the excellence of a work, we must determine whether the work has a perfection of form and a soundness of method that make it a satisfactory whole. The elements of composition must display symmetry, harmony, and definition.

Aristotle's theory differs considerably from Plato's. Plato insists that artistic imitation, especially tragedy, fuels the passions and misleads the seeker of truth. Aristotle, by contrast, believes that the arts repair deficiencies in nature and that tragic drama in particular makes a moral contribution. Therefore the arts are valuable and justifiable. Aristotle rejects Plato's notion of the centrality of beauty and erotic love, as well as his metaphysical idealism. He sees beauty as a property of an artwork rather than its purpose, whereas for Plato the search for beauty is the proper end of art. He does agree with Plato "that art is a kind of *techne*, and that the most important human arts, such as music, painting, sculpture, and literature are imitative of human souls, bodies, and actions."[3]

The purpose of art, however, is not edification, nor the teaching of a moral lesson. The purpose of art is to give pleasure, and to the degree that it does that, it is good art. The pleasure Aristotle refers to comes when art excites our emotions and passions. These are then purged in response to the art and our souls lighten, delighted and healed. High art makes us think, of course, but the highest art must produce this CATHARSIS, or purging effect.

Art can also provide entertainment for the lower classes, who, he maintains, are incapable of appreciating high art properly. It is better that they enjoy some kind of art than none at all, and they are entitled to this pleasure. Thus, Aristotle's aesthetics encompassed both the higher and the lower arts.

LITERATURE: THE PLATONIC DIALOGUES

Perhaps the greatest of Plato's dialogues is the *Republic*, in which Socrates seeks answers to the question "What is justice?" and describes the ideal society. The *Apology*, another of Plato's dialogues, gives his version of the speech Socrates gave in his own defense at his trial. Socrates was accused, and found guilty, of corrupting the youth of Athens and of believing in gods of his own devising rather than the gods of Athens. *Phaedo* concludes the story of Socrates' trial and death, and the dialogue presents his final hours as reported by Phaedo, a

Phaedo

And now, O my judges, I desire to prove to you, that the real philosopher has reason to be of good cheer when he is about to die, and that after death he may hope to obtain the greatest good in the other world. And how may this be, Simmias and Cebes, I will endeavor to explain. For I deem that the true votary of philosophy is likely to be misunderstood by other men; they do not perceive that he is always pursuing death and dying; and if this be so, and he has had the desire of death all his life long, why when his time comes should he repine at that which he has been always pursuing and desiring?

Simmias said laughingly: Though not in a laughing humor, you have made me laugh, Socrates; for I cannot help thinking that the many when they hear your words will say how truly you have described philosophers, and our people at home will likewise say that the life which philosophers desire is in reality death and that they have found them out to be truly deserving of the death which they desire.

And they are right, Simmias, in thinking so, with the exception of the words "they have found them out"; for they have not found out either the nature of that death which the true philosopher deserves, or how he deserves or desires death. But enough of them:—let us discuss another matter amongst ourselves. Do we believe that there is such a thing as death.

To be sure, replied Simmias.

Is it not the separation of soul and body? And to be dead is the completion of this; when the body exists in herself, and is released from the soul, what is this but death?

Just so, he replied.

There is another question, which will probably throw light on our present enquiry if you and I agree about it:—Ought the philosopher to care about the pleasures—if they are to be called pleasures—of eating and drinking?

Certainly not, answered Simmias.

And what about the pleasures of love—should he care for them?

By no means.

And will he think much of the other ways of indulging the body, for example, the acquisition of costly raiment, or sandals, or other adornments of the body? Instead of caring about them, does he not rather despise anything more than nature needs? What do you say?

I should say the true philosopher would despise them.

Would you not say that he is entirely concerned with the soul and not with the body? He would like, as far as he can, to get away from the body and to turn to the soul.

Quite true.

In matters of this sort philosophers, above all other men, may be observed in every sort of way to dissever the soul from the communion of the body.

Very true.

Whereas, Simmias, the rest of the world are of opinion that to him who has no sense of pleasure and no part in bodily pleasure, life is not worth having; and that he who is indifferent about them is as good as dead.

That is also true. What shall we say of the actual acquirement of knowledge?—Is the body, if invited to share in the inquiry, a hinderer or a helper?

I mean to say, have sight and hearing any truth in them? are they not, as the poets are always telling us, inaccurate witnesses? and yet, if even they are inaccurate and indistinct, what is to be said of the other senses?—for you will allow that they are the best of them?

Certainly, he replied.

Then when does the soul attain truth?—for in attempting to consider anything in company with the body she is obviously deceived.

True.

Then must not true existence be revealed to her in thought, if at all?

Yes.

And thought is best when the mind is gathered into herself and none of these things trouble her—neither sounds nor sights nor pains nor any pleasure,—when she takes her leave of the body, and has as little as possible to do with it, when she has no bodily sense or desire, but is aspiring after true being?

Certainly.

And in this the philosopher dishonors the body; his soul runs away from his body and desires to be alone and by herself?

That is true.

Well, but there is another thing, Simmias: Is there or is there not an absolute justice?

Assuredly there is.

And an absolute beauty and absolute good?

Of course.

But did you ever behold any of them with your eyes?

Certainly not.

Or did you ever reach them with any other bodily sense?—and I speak not of these alone, but of absolute greatness, and health, and strength, and of the essence and true nature of everything. Has the reality of them ever been perceived by you through the bodily organs? or rather, is not the nearest approach to the knowledge of their several natures made by him who so orders his intellectual vision as to have the most exact conception of essence of each thing which he considers?

Certainly.

And he attains to the purest knowledge of them who goes to each with the mind alone, not introducing or intruding in the act of thought sight or any other sense together with reason, but with the very light of the mind in her own clearness, searches into the very truth of each; he who has got rid, as far as he can, of eyes and ears and, so to speak, of the whole body, these being in his opinion distracting elements which when they infect the soul hinder her from acquiring truth and knowledge—who, if not he, is likely to attain to the knowledge of true being?

What you say has a wonderful truth about it, Socrates, replied Simmias.

And when real philosophers consider all these things, will they not be led to make a reflection which they will express in words something like the following? "Have we not found," they will say, "a path of thought which seems to bring us and our argument to the conclusion, that while we are in the body, and while the soul is infected with the evils of the body, our desire will not be satisfied? For the body is a source of endless trouble to us by reason of the mere requirement of food; and is liable also to diseases which overtake and impede us in the search after true being; it fills us full of loves, and lusts, and fears, and fancies of all kinds, and endless foolery, and in fact, as men say, takes away from us the power of thinking at all. Whence come wars, and fightings, and factions? Whence but from the body and the lusts of the body? Wars are occasioned by the love of money, and money has to be acquired for the sake and in the service of the body; and by reasons of all these impediments we have no time to give to philosophy; and, last and worst of all, even if we are at leisure and betake ourselves to some speculation, the body is always breaking in upon us, causing turmoil and confusion in our enquiries, and so amazing us that we are prevented from seeing the truth.

It has been proved to us by experience that if we would have pure knowledge of anything we must be quit of the body—the soul in herself must behold all things in themselves; and then we shall attain the wisdom which we desire, and of which we say that we are lovers; not while we live, but after death; for if while in the company of the body the soul cannot have pure knowledge, one of two things follows—either knowledge is not to be obtained at all or, if at all, after death. For then, and not till then, the soul will be parted from the body and existing herself alone. In this present life, I reckon that we make the nearest approach to knowledge when we have the least possible intercourse or communion with the body, and are not surfeited with bodily nature, but keep ourselves pure until God himself is pleased to release us. And thus having got rid of the foolishness of the body we shall be pure and hold converse with the pure, and know of ourselves the clear light everywhere, which is none other than the light of truth. For the impure are not permitted to approach the pure." These are the sort of words, Simmias, which true lovers of knowledge cannot help saying to one another and thinking. You would agree; would you not?

Undoubtedly, Socrates.

But, O my friend, if this be true, there is great reason to hope that, going whither I go, when I have come to the end of my journey, I shall attain that which has been the pursuit of my life. And I therefore go on my way rejoicing, and not I only, but every man who believes that his mind has been made ready and that he is in manner purified.

Certainly, replied Simmias.

And what is purification but the separation of the soul from the body, as I was saying before; the habit of the soul gathering herself from all sides out of the body; the dwelling in her own place alone, as in another life, so also in this, as far as she can;—the release of the soul from the chains of the body?

Very true, he said.

And this separation and release of the soul from the body is termed death?

To be sure, he said.

And the true philosophers, and they only, are ever seeking to release the soul. Is not the separation and release of the soul from the body their especial study?

That is true.

And as I was saying at first, there would be a ridiculous contradiction in men studying to live as nearly as they can in a state of death, and yet repining when it comes upon them.

Clearly.

And the true philosophers, Simmias, are always occupied in the practice of dying, wherefore also to them the least of all men is death terrible. Look at the matter thus:—if they have been in every way enemies of the body and are wanting to be alone with the soul, when this desire of theirs is granted, how inconsistent would they be if they trembled and repined instead of rejoicing at their departure and that place where, when they arrive, they hope to gain that which in life they desired—and this was

OUR DYNAMIC WORLD

Philosophy and Religion in East Asia

At a time roughly parallel to the rise of Greek philosophy—that is, at the end of the archaic period in Greece—and of the Hebrew prophets, classical philosophy and thought was developing in China, and the Buddha lived in India. Chinese philosophy, which focused on humankind as a social and political animal, was distinctly humanistic in tone, in contrast to the divine philosophies of India and parts of the Mediterranean world. Philosophers helped to strengthen the historical-mindedness of China by using the past as a model for the present, and amid this movement came the establishment of a classic canon of Chinese literature—that is, a set of books associated with the Confucian tradition called *The Five Classics*.

Confucius (551–479 B.C.), who was probably the first professional teacher and philosopher in China, was recognized as the greatest of all teachers and philosophers. His work, the *Analects*, contains his answers to questions prefaced by "The Master said." However, his thought tends to be on a more pragmatic plane than the intellectual pursuits of Socrates or Plato, and his primary interest seems to have been politics. He proposed a return to the ancient way, in which persons must play their proper, assigned roles, subject to authority, but he nevertheless viewed government as a fundamentally ethical problem. He held that a ruler's virtue, rather than his power, yielded contentment in the people, and his aim was to convince rulers to pursue ethical principles, thereby becoming China's first moralist and the founder of a great ethical tradition.

In contrast to Confucianism, Taoism, or "The Way," taught the independence of the individual. Taoism was a philosophy of protest of the common individual against despotic rulers, and of the sensitive intellectual against the rigidity of the Confucian moralists. If Confucianism was pragmatic, Taoism was mystical.

Closely related to another Indian religion, Brahmanism, Buddhism was a system of philosophy and ethics founded by the Buddha (563–483 B.C.) (Fig. **3.5**). With less formalism and a greater emphasis on self-denial than Brahmanism, the "four noble truths" of Buddha are: existence is suffering; the origin of suffering is desire; suffering ceases when desire ceases; the way to reach the end of desire is to follow the "noble eightfold path," which comprises right belief, right resolve (to renounce carnal pleasure, harm no living creature, and so on), right speech, right conduct, right occupation or living, right effort, right contemplation or right-mindedness, and right ecstasy. The final goal of the religious man is to escape from existence into blissful nonexistence—*nirvana*. Individuals are made up of elements that existed before they were born, that separate at death, and that may be recombined in a somewhat similar fashion after death. It is from this chain of being that humans seek to escape by religious living.

3.5 Teaching Buddha from Sarnath, Gupta, fifth century A.D. Sandstone, 5 ft 2 ins (1.58 m) high. Sarnath Museum, India.

wisdom—at that same time to be rid of the company of their enemy. Many a man has been willing to go to the world below animated by the hope of seeing there an earthly love, or wife, or son, and conversing with them. And will he who is a true lover of wisdom, and is strongly persuaded in like manner that only in the world below he can worthily enjoy her, still repine at death. Will he not depart with joy? Surely he will, O my friend, if he be a true philosopher. For he will have a firm conviction that there, and there only, he can find wisdom in her purity. And if this be true, he would be very absurd, as I was saying, if he were afraid of death.

Quite so, he replied. [...] he arose and went into a chamber to bathe; Krito followed him, and told us to wait. So we remained behind, talking and thinking of the subject of the discourse, and also of the greatness of our sorrow; he was like a father of whom we were being bereaved, and we were about to pass the rest of our lives as orphans. When he had taken the bath and his children were brought to him—(he had two young sons and an elder one); and the women of the family also came, and he talked to them and gave them a few directions in the presence of Krito; then he dismissed them and returned to us.

Now the hour of sunset was near, for a good deal of time had passed after his bath, but not much was said. Soon the jailer, who was the servant of the Eleven, entered and stood by him, saying:—To you, Socrates, whom I know to be the noblest and gentlest and best of all who ever came to this place, I will not impute the angry feelings of other men, who rage and swear at me, when, in obedience to the authorities, I bid them drink the poison. Indeed, I am sure that you will not be angry with me; for others, as you are aware, and not I, are to blame. And so fare you well, and try to bear lightly what must needs be—you know my errand. Then bursting into tears he turned away and went out.

Socrates looked at him, and said: I return your good wishes, and will do as you bid. How charming the man is: since I have been in prison he has always been coming to see me, and at times he would talk to me, and was good to me as could be, and now see how generously he sorrows on my account. We must do as he says, Krito, and therefore let the cup be brought, if the poison is prepared: if not, let the attendant prepare some.

Yet, said Krito, the sun is still upon the hilltops, and I know that many a one has taken the draught late and after the announcement has been made to him has eaten and drunk, and enjoyed the society of his beloved; do not hurry—there is time enough.

Socrates said: Yes, Krito, and they of whom you speak are right in so acting, for they think that they will be gainers by the delay; but I am right in not following their example, for I do not think that I should gain anything by drinking the poison any later; I should only be ridiculous in my eyes for sparing and saving a life which is already forfeit. Please then do as I say and not to refuse me.

Krito made a sign to the servant, who was standing by; and he went out, and having been absent some time, returned with the jailer carrying the cup of poison. Socrates said: You, my good friend, who are expert in these matters, shall give me directions how I am to proceed. The man answered: You have only to walk about until your legs are heavy, and then to lie down and the poison will act. At the same time he handed the cup to Socrates, who in the easiest and gentlest manner, without the least fear or change of color or feature, looking at the man with all his eyes, Enchekrates, as his manner was, took the cup and said: What do you say about making a libation out of this cup to any God? May I, or not? The man answered: We only prepare, Socrates, just so much as we deem enough. I understand, he said, but I may ask the gods to prosper my journey from this to the other world—even so—and so be it according to my prayer. Then raising the cup to his lips, quite readily and cheerfully drank off the poison. And hitherto most of us had been able to control our sorrow; but now when we saw him drinking, and saw too that he had finished the draught, we could no longer forbear, and in spite of myself my own tears were flowing fast; so that I covered my face and wept, not for him, but at the thought of my own calamity in having to part from such a friend. Nor was I the first; for Krito, when he found himself unable to restrain his tears, had got up, and I followed, and at that moment Apollodoros, who had been weeping all the time, broke out in a loud and passionate cry which made cowards of us all. Socrates alone retained his calmness: What is this strange outcry? he said. I sent away the women mainly in order that they might not misbehave in this way, for I have been told that a man should die in peace. Be quiet then, and have patience. When we heard his words we were ashamed, and refrained our tears; and he walked about until, as he said, his legs began to fail, and then he lay on his back, according to the directions, and the man who gave him the poison now and then looked at his feet and legs; and after a while he pressed his foot hard, and asked him if he could feel; and he said, No; and then his leg, and so upward and upward, and showed us that he was cold and stiff. And he felt them himself, and said: when the poison reaches the heart that will be the end. He was beginning to grow cold about the groin, when he uncovered his face, for he had covered himself up and said—they were his last words—he said: Krito, I owe a cock to Asclepius: will you remember to pay the debt? The debt shall be paid, said Krito; is there anything else? There was no answer to this question; but in a minute a movement was heard and the attendant uncovered him; his eyes were set, and Krito closed his eyes and mouth.

Such was the end, Enchekrates, of our friend; concerning whom I may truly say that of all the men of his time whom I have known he was the wisest and justest and the best.

HISTORY AND SCIENCE

The Greek intellect probed the mysteries of this world as well as the more ethereal realms that were the domain of the philosophers. Before the fifth century B.C., accounts of the past were part of an oral tradition, more myth than fact, but at this time, history—which derives from *historia*, meaning inquiry—became a written form, put together from careful research. The first to view history as a specialized discipline was Herodotus (c. 484–430 B.C.), and

he wrote nine great volumes called *History of the Persian Wars*. The change from telling the narrative story in the form of epic or lyric poetry to relating it in a new descriptive form, earned Herodotus the title of "Father of History."

Although he was not an historian in our sense of the word—his writing tends to be filtered through the personalities of the people involved and he often invented inspiring speeches for kings and generals—he retained a neutrality and freedom from patriotic bias. He described the war in colorful detail, seeking to show how human beings, in this case Greeks and Persians, settled their differences by resorting to arms, and he made full use of his tremendous powers of observation and recorded as much information as he could unearth, including conflicting points of view. He also examined the reliability of his sources and presented them so that his readers could draw their own conclusions about their veracity. However, he did not shy away from drawing his own conclusions about the causes of events. He believed that the present had its causes in the past, and his analysis of the Persian War concluded that the Greeks defeated the Persians because the Greeks were morally right and

A CRITICAL REVIEW

Socrates believed that an unexamined life was not worth living. He taught not by lecturing but by asking questions of his students. Would you like to be a student of Socrates or would you rather sit in class and let the professor lecture to you, providing you with the answers? Think about what Socrates means by "the unexamined life" and how the two techniques just noted help or interfere with true learning and critical thinking. Socrates' technique places more demands on the student to think critically rather than merely to memorize what the professor says. In the long run, which technique provides for better education? Or, do they both have a place?

For Plato, "reality" existed not in our world, but in a world of forms. Our world was merely an "imitation" of reality. Aristotle did not have the same aesthetic viewpoint as did Plato. Plato was skeptical about artists' abilities to reflect truth correctly, while Aristotle believed that the arts could repair deficiencies in nature.

We tend to think of history as a fairly straightforward and objective telling of specific events, but even so, we often find that one historian's "view" of a particular period is quite different from another's. This is especially true when historians try to "interpret" the events that they report on or when they look back on historical events from some time in the future rather than recording them soon after they happened.

What constitutes reality for you? Is it just what you can see, smell, taste, and touch, or does it include a larger sphere that includes what you believe in but cannot prove? Explain the confines of your "reality."

Contrast Plato's and Aristotle's viewpoints on drama, on beauty as a purpose for art, and on the purpose of art in general.

Explain why you believe that it is or is not possible to write "objective" history.

the Persians were morally wrong. The moral fault in the Persians lay in their HUBRIS, or excessive pride and ambition. There was also a religious undertone to Herodotus' judgment, for he believed that the gods supported justice and truth and would insure the victory thereof.

Thucydides (died c. 401 B.C.), who wrote a history of the Peloponnesian War, took history in a more subtle and thoughtful direction. He shared Herodotus' passion for the truth, and, although he had been an Athenian commander in the war, he dispassionately lists the foibles, follies, and errors made by the Athenians. Although it should be borne in mind that Thucydides was exiled from Athens for his failure as a naval commander early in the contest, his writing does not include self-justification. Rather, it is an unbiased compilation that strives to reveal human motives in ordinary events in order to draw a larger picture of history. His object was to instruct his readers so that they would be armed with knowledge when events of the past recurred—not in simplistic but in similar ways—in the future.

Greek intellects also turned to science and the natural world. Although they often erred in their observations, they also gave us many of our basic theories. Euclid's elements of geometry, for example, remained a standard text well into the twentieth century, and physicians still begin their careers by reciting the "oath" of the Greek physician Hippocrates. Greek astronomers recognized that the earth was a sphere, and they even calculated its size and distance to the sun and moon through mathematics and trigonometry.

CRITI REVI p. 91

CRITICAL LOOK above

A CRITICAL LOOK

In the next section we begin an examination of one of the basic "styles" in art—that is, the "classical" style. The next few pages consider painting and sculpture, and we will look at several fundamental ways in which the classical style is distinguished from other styles.

Who are the major sculptors of the Greek classical style, and how did that style progress in its development? Be specific in identifying the traits that differentiate "late" classical style from its antecedents.

THE CLASSICAL STYLE

Throughout history, people have sought rationality, intellectual challenge, and order from chaos. But the existence of emotion and intuitive feeling cannot be denied, and the struggle between intellect and emotion is one of the most significant problems in human existence. Although the two forces are not mutually exclusive, the conflict between them has been a theme of Western art.

The fifth-century Athenians recognized this struggle. Indeed, Greek mythology tells a story that demonstrates the Periclean belief in the superiority of the intellect over the emotions. Marsyas, a mortal, discovered an aulos discarded by the goddess Athena. (An aulos is a flute-like musical instrument associated with the wild revelries of the cult of Dionysus: see Fig. **2.22**.) With Athena's aulos, Marsyas challenged the god Apollo to a musical contest. Apollo, patron of the rational arts, chose the lyre as his instrument, and he won the contest, symbolizing the dominance of intellect over emotion.

VASE PAINTING

Fifth-century Athenian vase painting reflects some characteristics of earlier work, including the principally geometric nature of the designs. This indicates the continuing concern for form and order in the organization of space. What distinguishes the classical style in vase painting (our only visual evidence of Greek two-dimensional art of this period) from earlier styles is the new sense of idealized reality in figure depiction.

Such realism reflects a technical advance as well as a change in attitude. Many of the problems of foreshortening (the apparent decrease in size as an object recedes in space) had been solved. As a result, figures have a new sense of depth. The illusion could be strengthened in some cases by the use of light and shadow. Records imply that mural painters of this period were extremely skilled in realistic representation, but we have no surviving examples to study. The limited scope of vase painting does not, unfortunately, allow us to assess the true level of skill and development of the two-dimensional art of this period. Vase painting does demonstrate, however, artists' concern for formal design—that is, logic and balance in the organization of space.

In the fifth century B.C. many of the most talented artists were engaged in sculpture, mural painting, and architecture. Nonetheless, vase painters like the Achilles painter continued to express the idealism and dignity of the classical style. In the LEKYTHOS shown in Figure **3.6**, a quiet grandeur infuses the elegant and stately figures. The portrayal of the feet in the frontal position is significant, reflecting the new skill of foreshortening.

By the end of the fifth century B.C., vase painters had begun to break with the convention we have seen in Egyptian and Mesopotamian art of putting all the figures

THE CLASSICAL WORLD **93**

along the base line: spatial depth was sometimes suggested by placing some figures higher than others. But it was not until the end of the next century that this convention was completely abandoned.

We generally use the word "style" to refer to form, rather than content, but often the two cannot be separated. As the forms of classicism became more individualized and naturalistic, its subject matter broadened to include the mundane, as well as the HEROIC. We find some early examples of this in vase painting. The KYLIX in Figure **3.7** shows women putting away their clothes. The graceful curves and idealized forms of the classical style are still present, but the subject matter is clearly taken from everyday life. The implications of this apparent change are not entirely clear. Perhaps the domestic rather than ceremonial nature of vases of this kind accounts for the humbler subject matter.

Appeal to the intellect was the cornerstone of the classical style in all the arts. In painting, as well as in other disciplines, four characteristics reflected that appeal. Foremost is an emphasis on the formal organization of the whole into structured, balanced parts. A second characteristic is idealization: the intentional portrayal of things as better than they are, in order to raise them above the level of common humanity. For example, the human figure is treated as a perfect type rather than as a flawed individual body. A third characteristic is the use of convention, and a fourth is simplicity. (This term means freedom from unnecessary ornamentation and complexity; not merely lack of sophistication.)

3.7 Attributed to Douris, red-figured kylix showing two women putting away their clothes, c. 470 B.C. Diameter 12½ ins (31.7 cm). Metropolitan Museum of Art, New York (Rogers Fund, 1923).

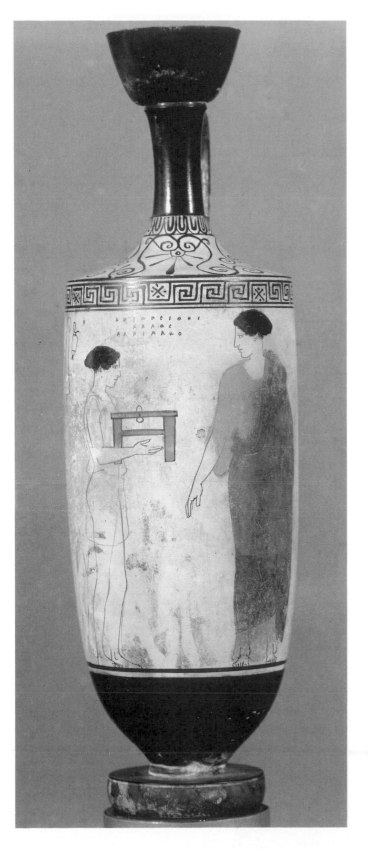

3.6 The Achilles painter, white ground lekythos from Gela(?), showing a woman and her maid, 440 B.C. 15 ins (38.4 cm) high. Museum of Fine Arts, Boston (Francis Bartlett Fund).

SCULPTURE

Styles do not start on a given date and end on another, even when they are as local and limited as those of the small city-state of Athens during the rule of Pericles. Although much of what we can surmise about Greek classical sculpture is actually based on inferior copies made at a later time, we know that the Greek classical style, especially in sculpture, was continually in a state of change. One artist's works differ from another's even though, in general, they reflect the four basic characteristics of classicism. In classical sculpture, the humanism of Greek philosophy is reflected in the idealism of vigorous, youthful bodies that make a positive statement about the joy of earthly life.

From early in the fifth century B.C. we find an example of bronze sculpture representative of the new, developing classical style. The *Charioteer* from Delphi (Fig. **3.8**) records a victory in the games of 478 or 474 B.C. The figure is elegantly idealized, with subtle variation of the sleeves and drapery folds. The balance departs from absolute symmetry: the weight is slightly shifted to one leg, and the head turns gently away from the center line. The excellent preservation of this statue allows full appreciation of the relaxed control of the sculptor.

However, the age of Greek classical style properly began with the sculptors Myron and Polyclitus in the middle of the fifth century B.C. Both contributed to the development of cast metal sculpture. (The example in Figure **3.9** is a marble copy of a bronze original, as is also Figure **3.10**.) In his *Lance Bearer* (*Doryphorus*), Polyclitus is reputed to have achieved the ideal proportions for a male athlete: the *Lance Bearer* thus represents *the* male athlete, not *a* male athlete. The body's weight is thrown onto one leg in the *contrapposto* stance. The resulting sense of relaxation, controlled motion, and the subtle play of curves made possible by this simple device are hallmarks of Greek classical style.

The east pediment of the Parthenon once contained marvelous sculptural elements (Figs **3.11** and **3.12**). The

3.8 (*far left*) *Charioteer*, from the Sanctuary of Apollo, Delphi, c. 478 or 474 B.C. Bronze, life-size. Archeological Museum, Delphi, Greece.

3.9 (*left*) Polyclitus, *Doryphorus* (*Lance Bearer*). Roman copy after a bronze original of c. 450–440 B.C. Marble, 6 ft 6 ins (1.98 m) high. Museo Archeologico Nazionale, Naples, Italy.

MASTERWORK

Myron—Discus Thrower

Myron's best-known work, the *Discus Thrower* (or *Discobolus*) (Fig. **3.10**), exemplifies the classical concern for restraint in its subdued vitality and subtle suggestion of movement coupled with balance. But it also expresses the sculptor's interest in the flesh of the idealized human form. This example of the *Discus Thrower* is, unfortunately, a much later marble copy. Myron's original was in bronze, a medium that allowed more flexibility of pose than marble. A statue, as opposed to a relief sculpture, must stand on its own, and supporting the weight of the marble on a small area, such as one ankle, poses a significant structural problem. Metal has greater TENSILE STRENGTH (the ability to withstand twisting and bending), and thus this problem does not arise.

In *Discovery of the Mind: The Greek Origins of European Thought* Bruno Snell writes: "If we want to describe the statues of the fifth century in the words of their age, we should say that they represent beautiful or perfect men, or, to use a phrase employed in the early lyrics for purposes of eulogy: 'god-like' men. Even for Plato the norm of judgment still rests with the gods, and not with men."[4] Even though Greek statuary may take the form of portraiture, the features are idealized. Human beings may be the measure of all things, but in art the individual is raised above human reality to the state of perfection found only in the gods.

Myron's representation of an athlete competing in an Olympic event brought a new sense of dynamism to Greek sculpture. It captures a dramatic moment, freezing the moving figure in the split second before the explosive release of the discus, achieving confliction of opposing forces. Myron's composition draws its tension not only from the expectation of the impending force, but also in the dramatic intersection of two opposing arcs: one created by the downward sweep of the arms and shoulders, the other by the forward thrust of the thighs, torso, and head.

As is typical of Greek free-standing statues, the *Discus Thrower* is designed to be seen from one direction only. It is thus a sort of free-standing, three-dimensional "super-relief." The beginnings of classical style represented by celebration of the powerful nude male figure are an outgrowth of what is known as the "severe style." Myron was trained in this style, and the suggestions of moral idealism, dignity, and self-con-

3.10 Myron, *Discobolus* (*Discus Thrower*), c. 450 B.C. Roman marble copy after a bronze original, life-size. Museo Nazionale Romano, Rome.

trol in the statue are all qualities inherent in classicism. However, the *Discus Thrower* marks a step forward, in the increasing vitality of figure movement, a process we can trace from the frozen pose of the archaic kouros of Polymedes of Argos (see Fig. **2.14**), through the counterpoised balance of the *Kritios Boy* (see Fig. **2.18**), to Myron. Warm, full, and dynamic Myron's human form achieves a new level of expressiveness and power. It is fully controlled and free of the unbridled emotion of later sculpture such as the *Laocoön* (see Fig. **3.31**). For Myron, balanced composition remains the focus of the work, and form takes precedence over feeling.

3.11 The *Fates*, from the east pediment of the Parthenon, c. 438–432 B.C. Marble, over life-size. British Museum, London.

group of *Three Goddesses*, or *Fates*, is now on display in the British Museum in London. (This group of sculptures is known as the "Elgin Marbles" [pronounced EL-ghin] after Lord Elgin, who removed them from the Parthenon between 1801 and 1803 and took them to London. British possession of these treasures is a continuing controversy between Britain and Greece.) Originally, this group formed part of the architectural decoration high on the Parthenon. There, its diagonal curvilinearity would have offset the straight lines, and strong verticals and horizontals, of the temple. The scene depicted on this pediment was an illustration of the myth of the birth of Athena, patron goddess of Athens, from her father Zeus' head. Also from this east pediment is the figure of Dionysus

3.12 *Dionysus* (*Heracles* (?)), from the east pediment of the Parthenon, c. 438–432 B.C. Marble, over life-size. British Museum, London.

(sometimes thought to be Heracles) shown in Figure **3.12**.

We can learn much from these battered but superb figures. What strikes us first is the brilliant arrangement of the figures within the geometric confines of the pediment. This triangular design encloses curving lines that flow rhythmically through the reclining figures, leading the eyes naturally from one part to the next. The treatment of the draperies of the female figures is highly sophisticated, for not only do the drape and flow of the stone fabric reinforce the simple lines of the whole, but they also reveal the perfected human female form beneath, demonstrating once again the classical goal of depicting not what is real, but what is ideal. These, and the Dionysus, are forms raised beyond the merely specific and human, to the level of symbols, as is appropriate to their intended position on a temple.

Even in their repose, these figures show grace and subtle movement: the counterthrust of tension and release is carefully controlled. This formal restraint is made more evident when we compare these figures with those of a later style in Figure **3.13**. The composition here is more open, its movement less fluid, and the geometric groups of figures jerk the eye between sections of the work, rather than leading.

Perhaps the most impressive sculptural finds of recent years are the two statues discovered in 1972 in the seabed off the coast of Riace, in southern Italy. Figure **3.14** shows one of these masterpieces, which are known as the *Riace Warriors*. The statue has been restored, but it shows the bone and glass eyes, silver teeth, and copper lips and nipples that would have adorned many ancient Greek bronzes. The simplicity with which the imposing musculature is portrayed, and the confident handling of

3.13 Scopas(?), Battle of Greeks and Amazons, from the east frieze of the Mausoleum, Halicarnassus, 359–351 B.C. Marble, 35 ins (88.9 cm) high. British Museum, London.

3.15 Praxiteles, *Cnidian Aphrodite*, probably Hellenistic copy of fourth-century B.C. original. Marble, 5 ft ½ in (1.54 m) high. Metropolitan Museum of Art, New York (Fletcher Fund, 1952).

3.14 Phidias(?), *Riace Warrior*, fifth century B.C. Bronze with bone, glass-paste, silver and copper inlaid. 6 ft 6⁴/₅ ins (2 m) high. Museo Nazionale, Reggio Calabria, Italy.

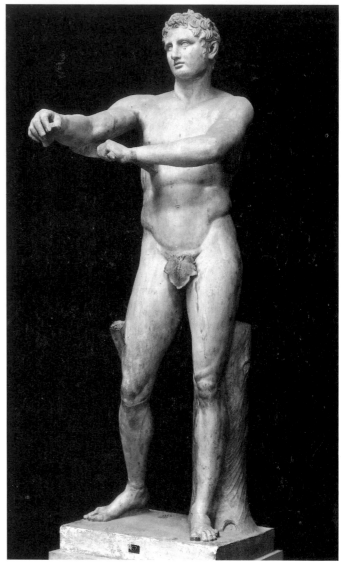

3.16 (*left*) Praxiteles, *Hermes and Dionysus*, c. 340 B.C. Marble, about 7 ft (2.13 m) high. Archeological Museum, Olympia, Greece.

3.17 (*above*) Lysippus, *Apoxyomenos* (*Scraper*), Roman copy, probably after a bronze original of c. 330 B.C. Marble, 6 ft 9 ins (2.06 m) high. Vatican Museums, Rome.

the CONTRAPPOSTO mark the work of a great sculptor of the mid-fifth century B.C. Some scholars even claim that the statues can be identified as part of a set of thirteen sculpted by Phidias, dedicated to the Athenian victory at Marathon in 490 B.C. They were probably shipwrecked around the first century B.C., on their way to Rome, having been plundered from Greece.

LATE CLASSICAL STYLE

Sculpture of the fourth century B.C. illustrates clearly the changes in attitude characteristic of late classicism. Among other innovations was the representation of female nudity. Praxiteles is famous for the individuality and delicacy of his treatment of his subjects, such as the earliest female nude, the *Cnidian Aphrodite* (Fig. **3.15**). (Note that this is again a copy; the original has never been found.) His work looks inward in a way that differs from the formal detachment of earlier sculptors evident in the *Dionysus* (see Fig. **3.12**), for example. Originally, Aphrodite rested her weight on one foot: her body sways to the left in the famous Praxitelean S-curve. Strain on the ankle of the sculpture was minimized by the attachment of the arm to drapery and a vase.

The elegance of Praxiteles' work can also be seen in the *Hermes and Dionysus* (Fig. **3.16**). Although this marble statue may be a copy, it nonetheless exhibits fine sub-

tlety of modeling and detailed individuality.

From the late fourth century, the sculpture of Lysippus, a favorite of Alexander the Great, displays a dignified naturalness and a new concept of space. His *Apoxyomenos* (*Scraper*) (Fig. **3.17**) illustrates an attempt to depict the figure in motion, in contrast to the poses we have seen previously. The subject of the *Scraper* is mundane—an athlete scraping dirt and oil from his body. The proportions of the figure are even more naturalistic than those of Polyclitus (see Fig. **3.9**), but the naturalism is still far from complete.

CRITICAL REVIEW below

A CRITICAL REVIEW

We might summarize classical principles as those that emphasize form over feeling or intellect over emotion. We often characterize people in the same way, even describing ourselves as more rational than emotional, or vice versa. Another way to describe these differing emphases is to label them as COGNITIVE or AFFECTIVE. Cognitive skills stress those of rational knowing, while affective skills stress those of intuition. Some popular books have been written on the function of the brain in such processes, and we now know that the left side of the brain controls our cognitive functions, and the right side of the brain controls our affective functions. Most people tend to be more adept with one side of the brain than with the other.

How would you describe yourself? Are you a right- or left-brain person? That is, do you tend to be more adept at performing logical tasks or do you do better with intuitive tasks? Would you classify yourself as "mathematically" inclined or "artistically" inclined? Is there any advantage to being one or the other?

A CRITICAL LOOK

In the next section, we meet some forms that will look very familiar to us. "Classical" architecture is as old as the Greeks and as new as the most contemporary "postmodern" building we pass everyday on our way to and from home. We will divide classical architecture into three separate orders, and we should learn to differentiate among them: even though, as we shall see, one of the orders is really not classical, but a later style. This section also contains some technical, architectural terminology.

Memorize the terminology and the parts of buildings to which they refer.

Understand how the Parthenon and other examples noted exemplify the characteristics of classical style.

ARCHITECTURE

CRITICAL LOOK above

Existing examples of Greek architecture offer a clear and consistent picture of the basic classical style, and nothing brings that picture so clearly to mind as the Greek temple. H.W. Janson makes an interesting point in *A Basic History of Art* when he suggests that the crystallization of the characteristics of a Greek temple is so complete that when we think of one Greek temple, we think of all Greek temples. Even so familiar a structure as a Gothic cathedral does not quite do this, because, despite the consistent form of the Gothic arch, it is used in such diverse ways

that no one work can typify the many.

The classical Greek temple has a structure consisting of horizontal blocks of stone laid across vertical columns. This is called "post-and-lintel" structure. It is not unique to Greece, but the Greeks refined it to its highest aesthetic level. Structures of this type have some very basic problems. Stone has no great tensile strength, although it is high in COMPRESSIVE STRENGTH (the ability to withstand crushing). Downward thrust works against the tensile qualities of horizontal slabs (lintels) but for the compressive qualities of the vertical columns (posts). As a result, columns can be relatively delicate, whereas lintels must be massive.

MASTERWORK

The Parthenon

On the summit of the Acropolis at Athens (Figs **3.1** and **3.18**) stands the Parthenon, the greatest temple built by the Greeks and the prototype for all classical buildings thereafter. When the Persians sacked Athens in 480 B.C., they destroyed the existing temple and its sculpture. And when Pericles rebuilt the Acropolis later in the fifth century B.C. Athens was at its zenith, and the Parthenon was its crowning glory. The Parthenon (Figs **3.19** and **3.20**) exemplifies Greek classical architecture. Balance is achieved through geometric symmetry, and the clean, simple lines represent a perfect balance of forces holding the composition together. For the Greeks, deities were only slightly superior to mortals, and in the Greek temple, deity and humanity met in an earthly rendezvous. This human-centered philosophy is reflected by the scale of the temple.

In plan, the Parthenon has short sides slightly less than half the length of the long sides. Its interior, or naos, which is divided into two parts, housed a 40-foot (12-meter) high ivory and gold statue of Athena. The temple is peripteral—that is, it is surrounded by a single row of columns. The number of columns across the front and along the sides of the temple is determined by a specific convention. The internal harmony of the design rests in the regular repetition of virtually unvaried forms. All the columns appear alike and to be spaced equidistantly. But at the corners the spacing is adjusted to give a sense of grace and perfect balance, while preventing the monotony of unvaried repetition.

All the elements are carefully adjusted. A great deal has been written about the "refinements" of the Parthenon—those features that seem to be intentional departures from strict geometric regularity. According to some, the slight bulge of the horizontal elements compensates for the eye's tendency to see a downward sagging when all elements are straight and parallel. Each column swells toward the middle by about 7 inches (18 centimeters), to compensate for the tendency of parallel vertical lines to appear to curve inward. This swelling is known as ENTASIS. The columns also tilt inward slightly at the top, in order to appear perpendicular. The stylobate is raised toward the center so as not to appear to sag under the immense weight of the stone columns and roof. Even the white marble, which in other circumstances might appear stark, may have been chosen to reflect the intense Athenian sunlight.

Vitruvius, the Roman architect, is the earliest known commentator to describe these adjustments as "aesthetic," but some scholars now believe that practical concerns also played a role. According to Janson, the theory that they are optical corrections does not

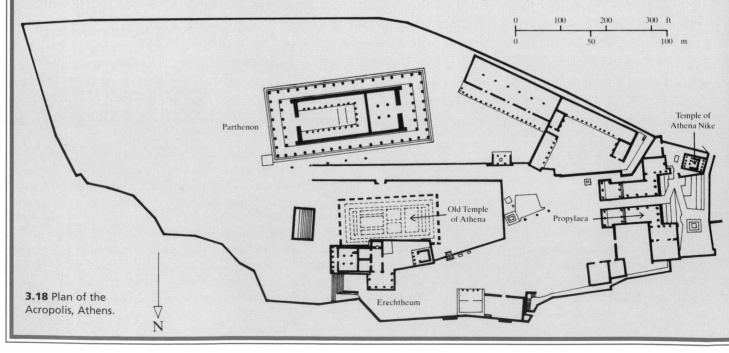

3.18 Plan of the Acropolis, Athens.

Parthenon

Old Temple of Athena

Propylaea

Temple of Athena Nike

Erechtheum

N

work. If that were the case, he says, we would be unable to observe them except by careful measurement. But because they can be seen, they were meant to be seen, and to add to the harmonious quality of the structure.

In a single structure the Parthenon exhibits the classical characteristics of convention, order, balance, simplicity, and grace.

3.19 Ictinos and Callicrates, the Parthenon, Acropolis, Athens, from the northwest, 447–438 B.C. Marble.

3.20 The Parthenon, frieze on the west cella, c. 440 B.C.

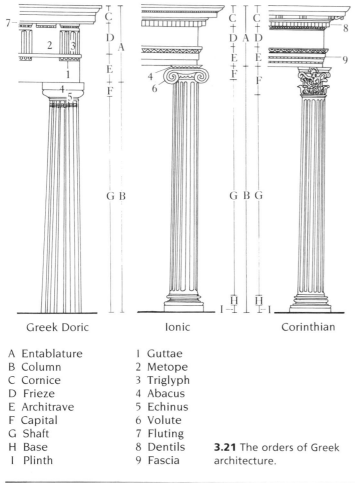

Greek Doric   **Ionic**   **Corinthian**

A	Entablature	I	Guttae
B	Column	2	Metope
C	Cornice	3	Triglyph
D	Frieze	4	Abacus
E	Architrave	5	Echinus
F	Capital	6	Volute
G	Shaft	7	Fluting
H	Base	8	Dentils
I	Plinth	9	Fascia

3.21 The orders of Greek architecture.

This structural system allows for only limited open interior space. This was no great problem for the Greeks, because their temples were built to be seen and used from the outside. The Greek climate does not drive worshippers inside a building. Thus, exterior structure and aesthetics were the primary concern.

Greek temples used three orders, Doric, IONIC, and CORINTHIAN. The first, as we noted in the last chapter, is archaic in origin, although it was modified and used in classical style. The second, is classical; the third, though of classical derivation, is of the later, Hellenistic style that we will examine further on in this chapter. As Figure **3.21** shows, simplicity was important to the Greek classical style, and the Doric and Ionic orders maintain clean lines even in their capitals. The Corinthian order has more ornate capitals. Taken in the context of an entire building, this detail may not seem significant. But columns, and particularly their capitals, are convenient ways of identifying the order of a Greek temple. Differences are also apparent in column bases and the configuration of the lintels, but the capitals tell the story at a glance. The earlier of the two classical orders, the Doric, has a massive appearance compared with the Ionic. The Ionic column, with its round base, is raised above the baseline of the building. The flutings of the Ionic order, usually twenty-two per column, are deeper and more widely separated

3.22 The Propylaea, Athens, from the west, c. 437–432 B.C.

3.23 Temple of Athena Nike, Acropolis, Athens, (?)427–424 B.C.

than those of the Doric, giving it a more delicate appearance. Ionic capitals consist of paired spiral shaped forms, known as VOLUTES. The Ionic architrave, or lintel, is divided into three horizontal bands, which diminish in size downward, creating a sense of lightness, unlike the massive Doric architrave.

The structure that serves as the entrance portal to the Parthenon is one of the most imposing monuments on the Acropolis. The Propylaea (Fig. **3.22**) was begun soon after the Parthenon was finished. It combines Doric and Ionic elements—two Doric temple-like FAÇADES are linked by an Ionic COLONNADE—in a design of some complexity which accommodates the awkward, sloping site. Work on the project was interrupted by the onset of the Peloponnesian Wars, and the building was never completed.

A final example of classical architecture takes us slightly beyond the classical period of the late fifth century B.C. Although no inscriptional information or other evidence provides a certain date for the Temple of Athena Nike (Fig. **3.23**), this little Ionic temple probably dates from the last quarter of the century. The pediments contained sculptures, but none of these has survived. What remain are sculptures from the frieze. The battle of Marathon of 490 B.C., the Athenians' greatest victory over the Persians, is the subject matter for the frieze on the south side of the temple. It is "the only known example

in temple sculpture of a conflict from near-contemporary rather than legendary history".[5] The battle had apparently assumed a legendary status even by 420 B.C.

THEATRE

In contrast to sculpture and painting, which used more-or-less realistic images to portray the ideal, Greek classical theatre pursued the same ends through quite different means. The theatre of Periclean Athens was theatre of convention. In theatre of illusion, scenic details are realistically portrayed. Stage mechanics do not hamper the playwright in the theatre of convention, however, and the audience will accept a description in poetic dialogue, without demanding to see it. Imagination is the key to this kind of theatre. Greek dramatists found that, free from the need to create an illusion of reality, they were better able to pursue the lofty moral themes fundamental to the Greek perception of the universe. Although we have some extant play texts from this era that indicate what and how the playwright wrote, we do not know the specifics of how that work became theatre—that is, how it was produced. Nevertheless, we can try to envisage a production based on descriptions in the plays themselves and on other literary evidence.

CRITICAL REVIEW p. 104

CRITICAL LOOK p. 104

A CRITICAL REVIEW

Another definition of the term "classical" is "traditional" or "enduring." Having studied just a few examples of Greek classical architecture, we can see clearly why such a definition applies. Throughout history, the Greek classic style of architecture has been imitated, and we even find it in the pediments and columns suggested by the most modern buildings of our time. The style is so obvious that we probably do not need even to remember the characteristics that define it to recognize it. Nonetheless: find at least three examples of Greek classical architecture in your community and on your campus. Obviously, these are not Greek classical buildings, because they were built after the Greek classical period, but you will easily recognize some basic characteristics of the Greek classical style in them.

The buildings you chose may be described by some other stylistic label—for example, Greek Revival or Georgian. These are classically imitative styles that we will examine later, but you are correct: they are reflective of Greek classical style.

What specific characteristics of classical style do these buildings exhibit—for example, a pedimented post-and-lintel porch with Ionic, Doric, or Corinthian columns? Do these buildings have the same proportions of height, width, and length that we saw in the Parthenon and other examples in this chapter?

A CRITICAL LOOK

In the next section we will meet another important Greek contribution to Western art—the theatre. This is our first examination of this form of artistic expression, and we will consider what makes theatre into theatre, rather than, say, literature. We will discuss Aristotle's aesthetic analysis of tragedy and learn how his labeling of the elements of a tragic play can help us to investigate any theatrical performance. Then, we will meet four important playwrights: Aeschylus, Sophocles, Euripides, and Aristophanes. We will also pause to note how the plays of the classical period were produced, including an assessment of their stage settings and costumes. Finally, we will be introduced to Greek music—at least, to the very little we actually know about it.

In the next section we will also take a detour to Africa to examine a particular style of sculpture from that continent.

Recognize the parts of the theatre building and apply the proper descriptive terminology to it—for example, ORCHESTRA, SKENE, and theatron.

Describe the role of music in Greek society and how our contemporary musical expressions might fill the same role.

What evidence exists to suggest that Africa had early connections with the rest of the world?

How did the Nok artists represent reality?

Theatre productions in Ancient Greece were part of three annual religious festivals: the City Dionysia, the Rustic Dionysia, and the Lenaea. The first of these was a festival of tragic, and the last, of comic plays. The City Dionysia took place at the Theatre of Dionysus in Athens. Contests held at these festivals were begun in 534 B.C., before the classical era. Although we do not have most of the plays themselves, we do know the titles and the names of the authors who won the contests, from the earliest to the last. From inscriptions we know that three playwrights figured prominently and repeatedly as winners.[6] They were Aeschylus, Sophocles, and Euripides. All the complete tragedies we have were written by these playwrights—seven by Aeschylus, seven by Sophocles, and eighteen by Euripides.

Playwrights entering the contests for tragedy or comedy were required to submit their plays to a panel of presiding officers, who selected three winners for production. The early classical plays had only one actor, plus a chorus. At the time of selection, the playwright was assigned the chief actor and the patron who paid all the expenses for the production. The author was also director, CHOREOGRAPHER, and musical composer, and often played the leading role as well.

AESCHYLUS

At the time the *Kritios Boy* (see Fig. **2.18**) was created, Aeschylus, the most famous poet of Ancient Greece, began to write for the theatre. He wrote magnificent tragedies of high poetry and on lofty moral themes. For example, in *Agamemnon*, the first play in the *Oresteia* trilogy, Aeschylus' chorus warns that success and wealth are insufficient without goodness.

> Justice shines in sooty dwellings
> Loving the righteous way of life,
> But passes by with averted eyes

> The house whose lord has hands unclean,
> Be it built throughout of gold,
> Caring naught for the weight of praise
> Heaped upon wealth by the vain, but turning
> All alike to its proper end.[7]

Aeschylus poses questions that we still ask, such as, how responsible are we for our own actions? how subject are we to uncontrollable forces? His characters are larger than life, to be read as types rather than individuals, in accordance with the contemporary emphasis on the ideal. Yet in their strivings, as in their flaws, they are also undeniably human. Aeschylus' casts for his early plays consist of one actor and a chorus of fifty, conforming to the convention of the time. He is credited with the addition of a second actor, and, by the end of his long career, a third actor had been introduced and the chorus had been reduced to twelve.

Aeschylus' plays appeal strongly to the intellect. Aristophanes, the master of Greek comedy, has Aeschylus, as a character in *The Frogs*, defend his writing as an inspiration to patriotism, to make people proud of their achievements. This is a high appeal, not a low one—

PROFILE

Aeschylus (c. 525–456 B.C.)

Aeschylus (pronounced ES-kih-luhs) was the first and perhaps the greatest classical Greek tragedian. Together with Sophocles and Euripides, he is one of only three Ancient Greek playwrights whose works have survived, and although he wrote fewer plays and won fewer contests than Sophocles, his contributions to the development of theatre are enormous. His contributions to dramaturgy and production make him, if not the greatest writer, then certainly the most important person in Western theatre history. He was instrumental in establishing tragedy as a genre, and some have referred to him as "the creator of tragedy." According to Aristotle, Aeschylus was responsible for adding the second actor to tragic performance.

Born into an aristocratic family, he fought in the important battles of Marathon and Salamis (between the Greeks and the Persians), and his firsthand knowledge of battle infuses his works, which illumine the miseries—not the glories—of war. Apart from a few documented travels to as far as Sicily, little else is known of the life of this major figure in Western lit-

erature and theatre. It is known that he won his first contest in 484 B.C., winning at least thirteen first prizes at the major festivals. His victory total increased to twenty-eight after his death because he was granted the singular honor of being allowed to compete through posthumous revivals. He may have written as many as ninety tragedies and satyr plays, although only eighty titles are known and only seven tragedies have survived.

The characters in Aeschylus' are "types" in the classically idealized mold. He treats history loosely and seeks to describe a broad religious view underwritten by patriotic exultation. He always remains within the controlled formality of the classic viewpoint, with its focus on intellect (form) as opposed to emotion (feeling), and he writes in an exalted style, using vocabulary that is clearly linked to the epic and lyric traditions of Homer (see p. 76). He handles the problems of evil and divine justice grandly and powerfully, and although his style may seem foreign to us, his questions and insights are not.

to the intellect rather than the emotions. Aeschylus lived through the Persian invasion, witnessed the great Athenian victories, and fought at the battle of Marathon, and his plays reflect this experience.

SOPHOCLES

Sophocles' career overlapped with that of Aeschylus. With *Oedipus the King*, his personal career reached its peak at the zenith of the Greek classical style. Sophocles' plots and characterizations illustrate a trend toward increasing realism similar to that in classical sculpture. The move toward realism did not involve any illusion of reality onstage, however, and even Euripides' plays, the least idealistic of the Greek tragedies, are not realistic as we understand the word.

Sophocles was certainly a less formal poet than Aeschylus, however. His themes are more human, and his characters more subtle, although he explores the themes of human responsibility, dignity, and fate with the same intensity and high seriousness that we see in Aeschylus. His plots show increasing complexity, but within the formal restraints of the classical spirit.

Sophocles lived and wrote after the death of Pericles in 429 B.C., and he experienced the shame of Athenian defeat. Even so, his later plays did not shift toward the emotionalism and interest in action we noted in sculpture. Classical Greek theatre consisted mostly of discussion and narration. The stories often dealt with bloodshed, but, though the play might lead up to the violence, and action was resumed when it was over, it is important to note that blood was never seen to be shed on stage.

EURIPIDES

Euripides was younger than Sophocles, although both died in 406 B.C. They did, however, compete with each other, despite the fact that their works have quite different styles. Euripides' plays carry realism further than any other Greek tragedies and deal with individual emotions rather than great events. His language, though still basically poetic, has greater verisimilitude and much less formality than that of his predecessors. Euripides also experiments with, or ignores, many of the conventions of his theatre, relying less heavily on the chorus.[8] He explores the mechanical potential of scenery shifting.[9] He also

---

MASTERWORK

Sophocles—Oedipus the King

The story of Oedipus is one of the great legends of Western culture. It has permeated our literature and even found its way into Freudian psychology in the term "Oedipus complex," which denotes an unnatural love of a son for his mother. When Sophocles used the legend in *Oedipus the King*, the story was familiar to all Athenians. In fact, it had also formed the basis for plays by Aeschylus and Euripides. However, Sophocles' treatment can arguably claim the title of the world's greatest tragedy.

The action moves from one moment of dramatic tension to another, rising in pyramidal form to its climax. The protagonist, or central character, Oedipus, starts with no knowledge of his true identity. Slowly he discovers the truth about himself and the terrible deeds he has unknowingly committed: the murder of his father and marriage to his mother. However, his tragedy lies in the discovery of his guilt, rather than in the heinous acts themselves.

In *Oedipus*, Sophocles explores the reality of the dual nature we all share. He again poses the eternal question, can we control our destinies or are we the pawns of fate? In exploring this question, he vividly portrays the circumstances in which one's strengths become one's weaknesses. Oedipus's HAMARTIA, or tragic flaw, is the excessive pride, or hubris, which drives him to pursue the truth, as a king—or a man—should, only to find the awful answer in himself.

Although the play is a tragedy, the message is one of uplift and positive resolution. (This type of structure is more fully described in the section below on Aristotle's theory of tragedy.) When Oedipus recognizes his own helplessness in the face of the full horror of his past, he performs an act of contrition: he blinds himself, and then exiles himself. As grotesque as this may seem, it nevertheless releases Oedipus onto a higher plane of understanding. The chorus chants, "I was blind," while seeing with normal eyes, and Oedipus moans, "I now have nothing beautiful left to see in this world." Yet, being blind, Oedipus is now able to "see" the nobler, truer reality of his self-knowledge.

questions the religion of the day in his plays. They are more TRAGICOMEDIES than pure tragedies, and some critics have described many of them as MELODRAMAS.[10] He was also less dependent on the chorus.

Plays such as *The Bacchae* reflect the changing Athenian spirit and dissatisfaction with contemporary events. Euripides was not particularly popular in his time, perhaps because of his less idealistic, less formal, and less conventional treatment of dramatic themes and characters. Was he perhaps too close to the reality of his age? His plays were received with enthusiasm in later years, however, and they are unquestionably the most popular of the Greek tragedies today.

ARISTOTLE'S THEORY OF TRAGEDY

We cannot leave the discussion of Greek theatre without noting Aristotle's analysis of tragedy. His ideas are still basic to dramatic theory and criticism, despite the fact that they have often been misunderstood and misapplied over the past 2,400 years. Drawing principally on Sophocles as a model, Aristotle laid out in the *Poetics* the six elements of tragedy. In order of importance they are: (1) plot, which includes exposition, discovery, reversal, point of attack, foreshadowing, complication, climax, crisis, and DÉNOUEMENT, where events are brought to a conclusion; (2) character; (3) thought; (4) diction; (5) music; and (6) spectacle.

Here we find further evidence of the classical focus on intellect, form, idealism, convention, and simplicity. Plot, in tragedy, is far more than the simple story line. For Aristotle, plot creates the basic structure of the play, just as form is the cornerstone of classical design. The parts of plot give shape to the play with a beginning (exposition), a middle (complication), and an end (dénouement), ensuring that the audience understands the progress of the drama. Additional points in the plot include discoveries, in which characters learn about themselves and others; foreshadowing, in which the playwright alerts the audience to future action; reversals, in which fortunes change; and crises, in which tension is created and characters grow. The point of attack and the climax are special forms of crises which respectively begin and end the complication section of the play.

Aristotle uses character to mean the force that drives the individuals in the play, that is, the psychological make-up that determines the way they respond to a situation. Thought is the intellectual content of the play. Diction is the words of the script, as opposed to music, which consists of all the aural elements of the play, including the way in which the actors speak the words. Finally, spectacle includes all the visual elements of the production.

Tragedy, for Aristotle, is a form of drama in which a protagonist goes through a significant struggle which ends in disaster. However, the protagonist is always a heroic character, who gains a moral victory even in physical defeat. Tragedy therefore asserts the dignity of humanity, as well as the existence of larger moral forces. In the end, tragedy is a positive experience, which evokes a catharsis, or purging, of pity and fear in the audience.

ARISTOPHANES

Tragedies were not the only works produced in the theatre of the classical era in Athens. The Athenians were extremely fond of comedy, although no examples survive from the Periclean period. Aristophanes (c. 450–c. 380 B.C.), of whose plays we have eleven, was the most gifted of the comic poets. His comedies of the post-classical period, such as *The Acharnians*, are highly satirical, topical, sophisticated, and often obscene. Productions of his comedies are still staged, in translation, but as the personal and political targets of his invective are unknown to us, these modern productions are mere shadows of what took the stage at the turn of the fourth century B.C.

COSTUME

If the plays of the Greek classical style treated lofty themes with theatrical, poetic language, the style of the productions displayed no less formality, idealism, and convention. The larger-than-life characters were portrayed by actors, always men, in larger-than-life, conventionalized costumes. Actors and chorus wore bright robes whose colors conveyed specific information to the audience. The robes were padded to increase the actor's size; height was increased by thick-soled boots called *kothurnoi*, and large masks whose fixed, conventionalized expressions were readily identified by the sophisticated and knowledgeable audience (Fig. **3.24**). Height was further increased by an *onkos*, a wiglike protrusion on top of the mask.

THEATRE DESIGN

Scholars do not agree about the exact layout of the classical Greek theatre building and the precise nature of the acting area and scenery. But we can summarize some of the architectural and archeological speculation, bearing in mind that it is only speculation.

The form of the Greek theatre owes much to its origins in the choral dances associated with the worship of Dionysus. In 534 B.C. Thespis is reported to have introduced a

3.24 Greek statuette of a tragic actor, wearing a mask and a rich costume.

OUR DYNAMIC WORLD

The Nok Style of Africa

For thousands of years, African artists and craftsmen have created objects of sophisticated vision and masterful technique. The rich cultural history of the African continent, which traded with the Middle East and Asia as early as A.D. 600, is documented by Chinese T'ang Dynasty coins found on the maritime coast of East Africa. Climate, materials, and the nature of tribal culture meant that much African art was doomed to extinction; only a small fraction remains. Nonetheless, what has survived provides evidence of a rich vision, which varies from culture to culture, and whose style runs from abstract to naturalistic. Its purposes range from magical to utilitarian, portraying visions of human reality that individuals from other cultural traditions may be ill-equipped to understand.

During the first millennium B.C., on the Jos plateau of northern Nigeria, the Noks, a nonliterate culture of farmers, entered the Iron Age and developed an accomplished artistic style. Working in terracotta, these artists produced boldly designed sculptures (Fig. **3.25**). Some works represent animals in naturalistic form, while others portray life-sized human heads. Although they are stylized—with flattened noses and segmented lower eyelids, for example—each work reveals individualized character: facial expressions and hairstyles differ from work to work. Curiously, the unusual combination of human individuality and artistic stylization makes the works powerfully appealing. Probably, these heads are portraits of ancestors of the ruling class, because the technique and medium of execution seem to have been chosen to insure perma-

3.25 Head from Jemaa, c. 400 B.C. Terracotta, height 10 ins (25 cm). National Museum, Lagos, Nigeria.

nence and for magical rather than artistic reasons. This Nok style was seminal to several other West African styles.

single actor to these dances. In 472 Aeschylus added a second actor, and in 458 Sophocles added a third. Throughout its history the Greek theatre was composed of a large circular orchestra—the acting and dancing area—with the vestige of an altar at its center, and a semicircular *theatron*—auditorium or viewing place—usually cut into or occupying the slope of a hill. Since the actors played more than one role, they needed somewhere to change costume, and so a *skene*—scene-building or retiring place—was added. The process by which the *skene* developed into a raised stage is somewhat obscure.

The earliest theatre still in existence is the Theatre of Dionysus on the south slope of the Acropolis. It dates from the fifth century B.C., and is where the plays of Aeschylus, Sophocles, Euripides, and Aristophanes were

3.26 Plan of the theatre at Epidaurus, Greece, c. 350 B.C.

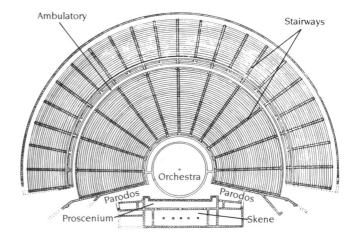

3.27 Polyclitus the Younger, theatre at Epidaurus, Greece, c. 350 B.C. Diameter 373 ft (114 m), orchestra 66 ft (20 m) across.

staged. Its current form dates from a period of reconstruction work around 338–326 B.C. The theatre at Epidaurus (Figs **3.26** and **3.27**) is the best preserved. It was built by Polyclitus the Younger in about 350 B.C. Its size demonstrates the monumental character the theatre had assumed by that time. The orchestra measures 66 feet (20 meters) in diameter, with an altar to Dionysus in the center. The auditorium, comprising slightly more than a semicircle, is divided by an AMBULATORY about two-thirds of the way up, and by radiating stairways. All the seats were of stone, and the first or lowest row consisted of seats for the dignitaries of Athens, which had backs and arm rests, some decorated with relief sculptures.

The design of theatres undoubtedly differed from place to place but time has removed most examples from our study. The many theories about how Greek theatre productions worked, how scenery was used, and whether or not a raised stage was present, make fascinating reading, and the reader is encouraged to explore the area in detail elsewhere.

MUSIC

Few examples of Ancient Greek music survive from any era—a handful of fragments with no clue as to how they were supposed to sound. Thanks to vase paintings and literature, however, we can at least speculate on the classical Greek theory of music and about its tone quality, or TIMBRE.

The lyre and the aulos were the instruments basic to Greek music, and each had a significant role in pre-classical ritual. In the classical era the lyre and the aulos were used as solo instruments and as accompaniment.

The spirit of contest popular among the Greeks apparently extended to instrumental and vocal music. As with all the arts, music was regarded as essential to life, and almost everyone in Athens participated. Perhaps the word "dilettante," or lover of the arts, would best describe the average Athenian. Professionalism and professional artists, however, were held in low esteem, and Aristotle urged that skill in music stop short of the professional. Practice should develop talent only to the point where one could "delight in noble melodies and rhythms," as he says in the *Poetics*. He also discouraged excessive complexity.

We should not infer too much from such an observation: complexity for the Ancient Greeks would no doubt still be simplicity by our musical standards. It appears reasonably clear, for instance, that all Greek music of this era was MONOPHONIC. "Complexity" might therefore mean technical difficulty, and perhaps melodic ornamentation, but not textural complication. Whether that would have been contrary to the classical spirit we do not know, but a specific reaction against complexity did occur some time after 325 B.C., and it is from the Hellenistic era that our only remnants of Greek music come.

It is possible to glean some information about the purpose of music from contemporary literature. Aristotle said that music should lead to noble thought, but some music in the Greek repertoire certainly led the other way. Rituals in praise of the god Dionysus were emotional and frenetic, and music played an important role in these. We can assume that the calls for restraint and pursuit of the ideal indicate that at least some music was of an intellectual nature.

If Plato's *Republic* can be taken as an accurate guide, Greek music seems to have relied on convention. Most of the performances in Periclean Athens appear to have been improvised, which may seem at odds with formal order. However, "improvisation" should not be interpreted here as spontaneous or unrehearsed. The Greeks had formulas or rules concerning acceptable musical forms, and a system of scales, or modes, for nearly every occasion. So the musician, though free to seek the momentary inspiration of the Muses—the mythological sisters who presided over the arts—was constrained by all the conventions applicable to the occasion.

The reliance on form that characterized classical style was reflected in music through its relationship to mathematics. Greek classicism exemplified an orderly, formal, and mathematical approach to reality. Pythagoras taught that an understanding of numbers was the key to an understanding of the entire spiritual and physical universe. Those views, expressed in music, as well as the other arts, led to a system of sounds and rhythms ordered by numbers. The intervals of the musical scale were determined by measuring vibrating strings. The results yielded relationships which even today are fundamental to Western musical practice: 2:1 = an octave; 3:2 = a fifth; 4:3 = a fourth. Since the characteristics of vibrating strings are constant, this aspect of Greek music, at least, is comprehensible.

CRITI
REVI
below

A CRITICAL REVIEW

If you go to Greece, you can visit many ancient theatres, some of which are still in use, and you may even have an opportunity to attend a production of a play by one of the playwrights we have discussed in this chapter. If you are in Athens, you can visit two ancient theatre sites on the slopes of the Acropolis, the later of which is still used for productions and concerts. A short journey will take you to Epidaurus, and there you can sit in the ancient theatre just as it appears in our illustration. The remarkable thing about this theatre—aside from its tremendous size—is the clarity of its acoustics: you can try these out for yourself if you visit there. Even if you do not go to Greece, you may have the opportunity to see a live production or video tape of a modern production of one of the playwrights we have studied. You may find the poetic language a little awkward at first, but you will quickly adapt. What you will find entrancing are the deeper, human issues that these plays explore. The form of the production should also lead you to ask some critical questions. Our movies, plays, and television dramas are all "realistic"—that is, they look, sound, and feel as though they might be happening right next door to people whom we would recognize as our neighbors and friends. Greek classical plays do not look, sound, or feel like this. They keep us separated emotionally from the action and the characters—which means that we respond differently to the drama, and the playwrights intended this.

Is there any benefit to being kept at "arm's length" from a drama? Does it really offer us a better opportunity to "see" the playwright's point with more objectivity?

Do you enjoy dramas more if you are able to become emotionally involved in them—that is, with characters just like you—or do you prefer a more "intellectual" approach, in which by recognizing that the characters are clearly symbols rather than fully drawn humans, you can explore the larger issues raised by the play?

What are the effects of "realism" versus "theatricality" in the presentation of human action? What about graphic violence on the stage and screen?

A CRITICAL LOOK

In the next few pages, we trace the circumstances that, perhaps as much as any others, spread Greek culture through the Western world. Rarely does an individual like Alexander the Great occur in history. His accomplishments, and the fact that his teacher was Aristotle, gave Greek thought and culture a hold on the Western world that went far beyond that of Athenian Greece of the golden age.

The theatrical staple of the Hellenistic Age seemed to be comedy. In philosophy the idealism of classicism ended and was replaced by a series of philosophies that vied for supremacy.

Explain how the Macedonian conquest and that of Alexander affected Greek thinking and created a "Hellenistic" world.

Contrast "Old" and "New" comedy.

Differentiate the characteristics of cynicism, skepticism, stoicism, and epicureanism.

THE HELLENISTIC AGE

ALEXANDER AND THE SPREAD OF HELLENISTIC CULTURE

Earlier in the chapter we noted that peace finally came to the Greek peninsula after the Macedonian conquest. The conquest came under the powerful King Philip II, who had seized the throne of Macedon in the middle of the fourth century. He assembled and trained a powerful army of Macedonians, conquered his neighbors, and became involved in the tangled alliances of the Greeks. In 338 B.C., at the battle of Chaeronea, Philip and his army routed the combined army of Athens and Thebes.

Two years later Philip was assassinated by his own men, and his son, Alexander, ascended the throne as king and commander. A pupil of Aristotle, Alexander proved to be not only an able king and general, but also a man of sophisticated vision. Unlike his father, he was more interested in a world order than in mere conquest and pillage. His rule began with a twelve-year expedition in which he led an army, one quarter of which was Greek, into Asia. Yet, the brilliant twenty-two-year-old carried Greek—that is, Athenian—culture further afield than ever before. According to legend, when he reached Asia—Alexander cut the Gordian knot tied by King Gordius of Phrygia. An oracle had foretold that whoever could untie the knot would be the next ruler of Asia—Alexander simply cut it with his sword and then defeated the Persian king, Darius III, at the battle of Issus. From there, Alexander led his forces against the city of Tyre in Syria, and pressed on to Egypt where, in the delta of the Nile, he founded Alexandria, one of the most influential and important cities in the Hellenistic world. A second defeat of Darius and the subsequent sacking of his capital, Persepolis, led to Alexander's installation as successor to the Persian

throne. After pushing as far as the River Indus in India, Alexander's army balked, and so, after following the Indus south to the Indian Ocean, Alexander returned across the great desert and ended his odyssey in Babylon. According to legend, when Alexander the Great could find no more worlds to conquer, he sat down and wept. In any case, his destiny fulfilled, Alexander died of a sudden fever in Babylon at the age of thirty-three (Fig. **3.28**). He had married a Persian princess, declared himself a king and a god, and founded twenty-five Greek city-states. Along the way, his soldiers married native women and established Greek customs, trade, administration, and artistry throughout half of Asia.

Under the Alexandrine, or Hellenistic, Empire, which stretched from Egypt in the west to the Indus in the east, civilization and the arts flourished, and the influence of Hellenistic art continued for centuries after the fall of the empire to the Romans.

The success of Alexander's conquests depended to a great extent on his forceful personality. On his death, the empire began to crumble as regional fragmentation and struggles for power marked the post-Alexandrian Hellenistic world. Nevertheless, the creation of so vast an empire fostered an internationalism of culture that persisted into, and was strengthened under, the Roman Empire. Commerce flourished, and international communication carried Greek thought and artistic influence to all parts of the known world. Intercultural relationships blossomed: Buddhist sculpture in India, for example, shows signs of Greek influence, and the European pantheon of gods began to reflect Eastern emotionalism. Athens, thus, remained an important center for ideas and cultural accomplishments, in spite of the weakness of its commercial and military power.

The source of Hellenistic culture was Alexandria, which was, at this time, the greatest city in the world and was endowed with phenomenal wealth. Legally it was a Greek city "by" not "in" Egypt. Brilliant writers and new literary forms emerged, and the Ptolemies patronized sci-

3.28 *Alexander Sarcophagus*, c. 310 B.C. Marble, 6 ft 4½ ins (1.94 m) high. Archeological Museum, Istanbul, Turkey.

ence and scholarship. Royal funds paid for many splendid buildings, including an enormous library, which became the focal point of the Hellenistic intellectual world.

THEATRE AND LITERATURE

The period from roughly the fourth century B.C. to the Roman infiltration, about 250 B.C., is called the Hellenistic period. This was a time for great expansion for the threatre in Greece, and evidence exists of theatres at Epidaurus, Megalopolis, Thoricus at Attica, Eretria at Euboea, Piraeus, and Syracuse in Sicily, as well as at Athens. The general plan of the theatres did not change, but the *skene* frequently was two stories tall. After the chorus disappeared, in later Hellenistic times, a stage as

high as twelve feet (3.6 meters) was not unusual.

In this period, comedy was the staple of the theatre. Only five, incomplete, plays by Menander (c. 343–c. 291 B.C.) survive, but the characteristics of his style are fairly clear. In this "New" Comedy, in contrast to the "Old" Comedy of Aristophanes, the biting political invective is gone, although the action is still bawdy. The situations are pleasant and domestic, and for the most part superficial and without satire. Religion no longer played a central role in the theatre, and, as we have noted, the chorus disappeared entirely.

Non-dramatic literature flourished, especially in Alexandria. The Ptolemies' support of the museum and library lured poets as well as scholars, and a variety of forms was pursued—for example, poetry, history, essays, and biography. A new form, the pastoral, which was developed by the poet Theocritus (c. 310–250 B.C.), focuses on rural scenes—for example, farmers and shepherds—and treats the subject with idealization and artificiality. Perhaps his works appealed because they played on the nostalgia of the readers, reminding them of the quiet country life that they had left for the hustle and bustle of the cities. Theocritus also wrote in a form called the idyll, which drew poetic pictures of common, everyday life and its affairs.

PHILOSOPHY AND RELIGION

Four schools of thought vied for philosophical supremacy in the Hellenistic period. These were cynicism, skepticism, stoicism, and epicureanism. Led by Diogenes (c. 412– c. 323 B.C.), the Cynics taught that humans are animals and that the good life lay simply in satisfying their animal needs. Since those needs can be troublesome, however, a wise person will have as few needs as possible but will disregard any social conventions that stand in the way of his own satisfaction. In other words, if a person wanted nothing, then he could lack nothing. The Cynics had little use for society as an organizing principle, believing that it stood in the way of individual freedom and

independence, and they therefore isolated themselves as much as possible from society. Needless to say, cynicism had little appeal either to the masses or the aristocracy.

Followers of Pyrrho of Elis, the Skeptics, asserted that nothing was certain and that the senses were completely unreliable as sources of knowledge. Ultimately, the only certainty was that truth was unachievable. They questioned everything and admitted the truth of nothing. For the skeptic, everything was relative. Universal doubt ruled their world. Less popular, even, than cynicism, skepticism did make inroads in later times, particularly during the Roman era.

Stoicism, founded by Zeno, held that humans were the incarnation of reason or *logos*, which produces and directs the world and gave a spark to the individual soul in the form of rationality. The good life was defined as that which follows reason, wisdom, and virtue, but the only way to achieve these goals lay through renunciation and asceticism. The Stoic tended to leave everything to God and to accept whatever came his way. Once this state of mind was achieved, it was possible to disregard public

TECHNOLOGY: PUTTING DISCOVERY TO WORK

Hero's Steam Turbine

When Ptolemy became ruler of Egypt he proclaimed himself king and gave himself the name Soter, or Savior. Despite a somewhat exaggerated view of his own importance, Ptolemy established what was essentially a research institute by founding the Museum at Alexandria, the library of which was to become the most famous in the world. The museum attracted scholars from around the Hellenistic world to teach and to learn. One of these was Hero, whose tutor, Strato, had been a contemporary of Aristotle at the Lyceum in Athens. Hero compiled a textbook of engineering and invented a number of useful pieces of equipment, including a water clock. From his written account, it is clear that he gave a great deal of thought to maintaining an even flow of water into the mechanism so that it would keep accurate time. His steam turbine (Fig. **3.29**), which depended on the expansion of air and the vaporization of water when heated, could probably have been developed further to provide a useful source of power, but the machine appears to have been regarded merely as an entertaining toy.

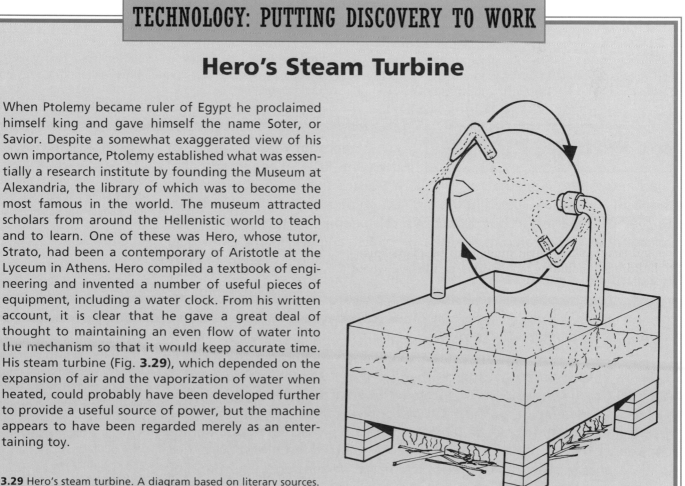

3.29 Hero's steam turbine. A diagram based on literary sources.

opinion, misfortune, and even death—that is, one approached life with apathy. Stoicism maintained that happiness was the ultimate goal of the individual. It also stressed the importance of the senses in perceiving underlying moral law and the divine plan for the world. In the end, the Stoics perceived an ideal state, guided by *logos* and law, that included all humanity regardless of race, sex, nationality, or social standing. Stoicism proved a popular philosophy, especially among intellectuals and political leaders. Essentially stoicism was an optimistic viewpoint that stood in strong contrast to the pessimism of the other philosophies of the time.

Epicurus (c. 342–270 B.C.) led Epicureans to a life of strict quietude. They concluded that human beings consisted of a temporary arrangement of atoms that dissolved at death. Because everything was temporary, the good life was simply an untroubled one. Wisdom dictated that one should avoid entanglements, maintain good health, tolerate pain, and accept death without fear. Epicurus founded a school in Athens, and his pupils, including women and slaves, gathered to discuss ideas. Epicureans believed that the senses could be relied upon to give an accurate picture of reality and that the mind functioned as a storehouse for those observations. Free will allowed humans to reach moral conclusions based on ethical constructs.

Hellenistic times were uncertain times, and human confidence in the ability to control anything waned. At such times, people tend to develop a belief that fate will do whatever fate will do and to adopt pietistic religious beliefs—that is, beliefs in which emotionalism takes the place of intellectualism or rationalism. In the Hellenistic world, a variety of mystery cults emerged from the East and from Egypt. The cult of Dionysus, god of revelry and wine, was particularly appealing in Greece proper. To unite Egyptians and Greeks, Ptolemy I, founder of the Alexandrian Museum, invented a new god Serapis, who became popular throughout the Hellenistic world. Another powerful mystery cult that spread throughout the Mediterranean world and, later, because one of the most antagonistic forces met by the early Christians was the cult of Isis. Originating in Egypt in the eighteenth century B.C., Isis was a nature goddess, who became the prototype for all goddesses. In Egyptian mythology she was the faithful wife and sister of Osiris and mother of Horus. After Osiris was slain by their brother, Set, and his body scattered in pieces, Isis gathered the pieces together; Osiris was then restored and became ruler of the dead. The legend symbolized the sun (Osiris) overwhelmed by night (Set), followed by the birth of the sun of a new day (Horus) from the eastern sky (Isis). Thus, it was a religion that emphasized resurrection after death: one of the characteristics that put it into direct conflict with Christianity. Isis was universal mother and mistress of all magic, and her cult prevailed until the middle of the sixth century A.D. Probably, the appeal of the mystery cults lay in their mystery—that is, in secret initiation rites that gave the member a special status and, thus, satisfied a universal need to belong.

CRITI REVIE below

A CRITICAL REVIEW

Today, philosophy as a mode of inquiry has little of the impact that it had in the past. Nonetheless, the characteristics that we find in the four schools of thought discussed in the last section do represent ways of thinking that still operate in our world. We call people, on the basis of their philosophical temperament, skeptics or cynics, and we might even hear someone described as a sophist, although the epicureans seem to have lapsed from our vocabulary.

What elements of cynicism, skepticism, stoicism, and epicureanism can you find in yourself or the people you know?

A CRITICAL LOOK

Sculpture and architecture, being visual and very durable, point out to us the psychological and aesthetic changes that followed the collapse of Athenian Greek classicism. Its replacement as an artistic style—reflective of the Alexandrine empire in which it took root—is called Hellenism, and in it we will find a definite shift of temperament. Finally, across the globe and at the same time, remarkable achievements occurred in Chinese sculpture. They are all the more striking because of the circumstances surrounding their discovery, as we shall see.

What artists created works in the Hellenistic style of sculpture and architecture, and what are their characteristics?

What similarities tie the Qin Dynasty warriors to the sculptures of the Hellenistic age?

3.30 *Nike of Samothrace* (*Winged Victory*), c. 190 B.C. Marble, 8 ft (2.44 m) high. Louvre, Paris.

HELLENISTIC STYLE

SCULPTURE

The Hellenistic style in sculpture continued to dominate the Mediterranean world until the first century B.C. As time progressed, it began to reflect an increasing interest in the differences between individual humans. Hellenistic sculptors turned away from idealization, often toward PATHOS, trivia, even banality, or flights of technical virtuosity. These characteristics appear in Figures **3.30**, **3.31** and **3.33**. The *Dying Gaul* (Fig. **3.33**) is a powerful expression of emotion and pathos. This Roman copy

CRITICAL LOOK p. 114

3.31 Hagesandrus, Polydorus, and Athenodorus, *Laocoön and his Two Sons*, first century A.D. Marble, 8 ft (2.44 m) high. Vatican Museums, Rome.

3.35 The west front of the Altar of Zeus, from the temple at Pergamon (restored), 197–159 B.C. Pergamonmuseum, Staatliche Museen, Berlin.

in this style was designed to produce an overpowering emotional experience. Begun by the architect Cossutius for King Antiochus IV of Syria, this is the first major Corinthian temple. Its elaborate detail pushed its completion date into the second century A.D. under the Roman emperor Hadrian. The ruins can only vaguely suggest the size and richness of the original building, which was surrounded by an immense, walled precinct.

One center of Hellenistic power in Asia Minor was the city of Pergamon. Here, we find an example of Hellenistic style that ranks as one of the major accomplishments of the time. It was, in fact, considered to be one of the wonders of the then-known world. The Altar of Zeus from the temple at Pergamon (Fig. **3.35**) was excavated in pieces beginning in 1873 and reassembled in a painstaking process that took more than fifty years. The altar was built by King Eumenes II as a means to glorify the king and to impress he Greek world with Eumenes' contribution to the spread of Hellenism by his victories over the barbarians. The great frieze of the altar stands more than seven feet (2.1 meters) tall and runs for more than 450 feet (137 meters) around the entire perimeter of the building. The frieze represents a radical departure from the design concept of the classical Greek temple. For example, in the Parthenon the colonnade serves as a part

of the structure, supporting the entablature, which, in turn, elevates the frieze into a position of ethereal space and sustains the pediment and roof. In the Altar of Zeus, the frieze stands independently on a podium consisting of five steps. The colonnade retains no structural reason for being and becomes, rather, a unifying design device to give a boundary to the frieze.

The sculptures of the frieze narrate a typical battle between gods and giants, but the gods—now less potent in religious thought—symbolize qualities of good; the giants represent malevolent natural forces such as earthquakes and floods, and the portrayal symbolizes the struggle between the forces of light and the forces of darkness. An entire pantheon of gods is depicted, including Zeus, Helios the sun god, Hemera the winged goddess of the day, Artemis, and Heracles. Below the frieze we find the names of the sculptors who executed this magnificent work.

The technical details of the frieze are nearly as interesting as the power of its scale and the intricacies of its proportion. Throughout, great care was given to surface texture. Cloth, saddles, belt buckles, and flesh have been patiently finished to create textures of the real objects. Also of note is the depth of the relief. The cuts slant inward and nearly separate the forms from the background. To the eye, the figures appear fully dimensional. In this display of high emotion and technical virtuosity we find none of the restrained order, idealization, and simplicity of the classical style.

A CRITICAL REVIEW

We have seen a dramatic shift from the idealized types of the classical style to the realistic individualism of the Hellenistic style, and we also have seen a shift in historical circumstances. Although we may draw conclusions about the connections between the two, however, we should do so carefully. One of the questions art always raises is its relationship to the context in which, or from which, it rises. Is art a mirror of its time? Does disturbing art represent disturbing times? You might wish to speculate on this question with regard to the times and the art we have just examined in this chapter—that is, classicism and Hellenism and the historical and philosophic framework around them. You might wish to look around you to see if you can substantiate your viewpoint in today's context and art. Nevertheless, one thing that does emerge from this—and indeed from every chapter in this text—is that the reason we give art various stylistic labels is because art represents different ways of expressing the reality of the universe in which we live.

Write an extended paragraph in which, referring only to the artists' use of the compositional element of line (see the Introduction), you compare Laocoön and his Two Sons with Discobolus.

Write an extended paragraph in which you compare the characteristics of classicism and Hellenism, using the Parthenon and the Temple of the Olympian Zeus as examples.

SYNTHESIS

From Idealism to Realism—
Prometheus and Hecuba

In examining Athenian art in this chapter, we have been able to compare the various art forms of classical and Hellenistic Greece, to isolate some shared themes, and to draw some general conclusions about them. Thus, the work of synthesis is largely done. It may be more useful here to focus on the process of change in Greek culture instead. In particular, we can see how much change occurred over a brief time in a single discipline, the theatre. To do this, we will use two plays that bracket the classical period in Athens: Aeschylus' *Prometheus Bound* and Euripides' *Hecuba*.

According to legend, Prometheus frustrated the plans of Zeus by giving fire to a race of mortals whom Zeus sought to destroy. Here is classical Greek idealism at work: through reason, application, and vision, human beings can defy the gods and win. They are capable of nobility and infinite improvement. As punishment for his presumption, however, Zeus has Prometheus chained to a rock. In Prometheus' justification of what he did, he suggests that humankind, through technology and reason, can have dominion over nature.

Prometheus is a play unusual even for Aeschylus in its heavy dependence on dialogue and character, and in its lack of action. The hero is motionless, chained to a rock. Nothing happens. There is only conversation between a parade of different people, through which the playwright reveals character and situation.

In this extract, the scene is set for an exchange between Force, Violence and Hephaestus, the fire god. Violence does not speak, however, as there are only two actors. Force presents the situation:

Far have we come to this far spot of earth,
This narrow Scythian land, a desert all untrodden.
God of the forge and fire, yours the task
The Father laid upon you.
To this high-piercing, head-long rock
In adamantine chains that none can break
Bind him—him here, who dared all things.
Your flaming flower he stole to give to men,
Fire, the master craftsman, through whose power
All things are wrought, and for such error now
He must repay the gods; be taught to yield
To Zeus' lordship and to cease
From his man-looking way.

Through speeches such as these, the characters are revealed—Force as a villain, and Hephaestus as a weak but kindly fool. After Force, Violence, and Hephaestus exit, Prometheus appears. He may have been revealed on a low wagon, called an *eccyclema*, which was rolled out from the central door of the *skene*. He speaks:

O air of heaven and swift winged winds,
O running river waters,
O never numbered laughter or sea waves,
Earth, mother of all, eye of the sun, all seeing,
On you I call.
Behold what I, a god, endure for gods.
See in what tortures I must struggle
Through countless years of time.
This shame, these bonds, are put upon me
By the new ruler of the gods.
Sorrow enough in what is here and what is still to
    come.

And so the myth unfolds itself in high poetry as Prometheus discourses with the chorus, a group of kindly sea-nymphs, with Hermes, with Ocean, a humorous old busy-body, and with Io, an ephemeral creature. When the dialogue has run its course, Prometheus declaims:

An end to words. Deeds now,
The world is shaken,
The deep and secret way of thunder
Is rent apart.
Fiery wreaths of lightning flash.
Whirlwinds toss the swirling dust.
The blasts of all the winds are battling in the air,
And sky and sea are one.
On me the tempest falls.
It does not make me tremble
O holy Mother Earth, O air and sun,
Behold me. I am wronged.[11]

Prometheus is an idealistic exploration of human capacity, achievement, and power, written as the height of the golden age of Athens approached. Euripides' play *Hecuba*, on the other hand, is a bitter tragedy of the interrelationships between those who rule and those who obey. It was written at a time when failure of leadership had dragged Athens downward through a long war of attrition with Sparta. Here again the playwright deals with myth, in this case, the story of the sack of Troy.

Two separate events are related, giving the plot an episodic character. Hecuba is the wife of Priam, king of Troy, whose city has at last fallen to the Greeks. She endures first the slaughter of her daughter Polyxena by the Greeks, then she discovers the body of her son, Polydorus, who has been murdered by Polymestor. Each of these events takes her one step further from grief and nearer to despair. She seeks the help of the Greek king, Agamemnon, in her quest for revenge on Polymestor, but receives only pity and the question, "What woman on this earth was ever cursed like this?" Hecuba replies in language less poetic and more realistic than that of Prometheus:

There is none but goddess Suffering herself.

But let me tell you why I kneel
At your feet. And if my suffering seem just,
Then I must be content. But if otherwise,
Give me my revenge on that treacherous friend
Who flouted every god in heaven and in hell
To do this brutal murder.

At our table
He was our frequent guest; was counted first
Among our friends, respected and honoured by me,
Receiving every kindness that a man could meet—
And then, in cold deliberation killed
My son.

Murder may have its reasons, its motives,

But this—to refuse my son a grave, to throw him
To the sea, unburied!...

See me whole, observe
My wretchedness—

Once a queen, now
A slave; blessed with children, happy once,
Now old, childless, utterly alone,
Homeless, lost, unhappiest of women
On this earth...[12]

Step by step she moves inevitably toward her final acts of atrocity. The play focuses on how she is forced to yield, one at a time, her values, her self-respect, and "the faith which makes her human." Underlying the play is a stark condemnation of the logic of political necessity. When faced with power over which she has no control, she pleads the case of honor, decency, the gods, and moral law. All these appeals fail. As despair destroys her humanity, she passes beyond the reach of judgment. The chorus condemns the tragic waste of war and questions the necessity and logic of imperialism. Finally, Euripides attacks the gods themselves. Even if they exist, he implies, their justice is so far removed from humans that it has no relevance.

The transition from idealism, form, order, and restraint to greater realism and emotion represented by these two plays parallels the changes we have seen in painting, sculpture, and architecture. In all the arts, the idealization of classicism turned to the realism of succeeding styles; restraint gave way to emotion, and form gave way to feeling.

CHAPTER FOUR

THE ROMAN PERIOD

AT A GLANCE

Roman Civilization

The Etruscans

The Roman Republic
Military Expansion
The Roman Civil War
The Visual Arts and Architecture
Theatre
Philosophy and Religion

The Roman Empire
Augustus
Pax Romana
Roman Law
Philosophy
Religion
Two-dimensional Art
Sculpture
  OUR DYNAMIC WORLD: Han Dynasty Painting

Architecture
  MASTERWORK: The Pantheon
  TECHNOLOGY: Cement
Music
Literature
  PROFILE: Vergil

Synthesis: Augustus—Classical Visions

4.1 *Gemma Augustea* (detail of the crowning of Augustus), early first century A.D. Onyx cameo, whole cameo 7½ × 9 ins (19 × 23 cm). Kunsthistorisches Museum, Vienna.

When we speak of the "classical world" as the foundation of the Western tradition, we often mean not only the brief but critical period of the golden age of Athens but also the entire period from 485 B.C. in Greece, through the Hellenistic Age of Alexander, and into the several hundred years of the Roman Empire as well. As we shall see, the Romans adapted the existing and prevailing Greek culture, making contributions of their own, which, through the centuries, have merged with the Greek to create an expanded vision of classicism that, at varying times and in varying ways, the Western world has seen as its foundation.

Like other identifiable cultures, the Roman culture rose from its own roots on the Italian peninsula, first among the Etruscans and then from within the Roman Republic. We therefore begin with the part of the system that would become the trunk of what we call Western culture.

How did the Roman Republic expand and, eventually, come to an end?

What characteristics marked Roman Republican art and architecture?

What dramatic forms were popular in Republican Rome, and what were their characteristics?

ROMAN CIVILIZATION

The Romans conquered their world. By A.D. 70 they had destroyed the temple at Jerusalem (see page 162) and colonized Britain, thereby spreading their pragmatic version of the Hellenistic Mediterranean civilization to the Iron Age peoples in north and west Europe. Under Augustus, Roman culture drew its inspiration from Greek classicism, and in that spirit glorified its capital city, its emperor, and the empire. At the opening of the Christian era the Augustan period forms a plateau, linking the Roman Republic and Empire, but a slide into chaos and ultimate extinction followed over the next 300 years. In contrast to the temples, art, and ideas of the Greeks, the Romans left us practical things—roads, fortifications, viaducts, planned administration, and a sophisticated yet robust legal system. These provide us with the foundations for our own society. Roman culture represents the final and, for us, the most historically important flowering of classical civilization.

THE ETRUSCANS

The civilization that would become the Roman one arose at the same time as that of Ancient Greece. By the sixth century B.C. the Etruscan invaders who had come out of Asia by way of Greece dominated the Italian peninsula. The Etruscans brought to their new land a militaristic and practical society, an ANTHROPOMORPHIC conception of the deities, and arts roughly equivalent to those of archaic Greece, whose style had influenced them (Fig. **4.2**). Roman legend held that Rome was founded in 753 B.C. by Romulus, an orphan, who, with his twin brother Remus,

had been suckled by a wolf as the boys' foster-mother. One Etruscan religious cult revered wolves, and this legend is taken as further evidence that Roman civilization had Etruscan roots.

Despite the rich archeological record left by the Etruscans, little is known about them as a people. There are several hypotheses about where they came from. They probably migrated from Asia at the end of the Hittite Empire, joining with groups occupying the Italian peninsula perhaps as early as 1000 B.C. It is clear that they had an advanced culture—metallurgy had been developed as early as the tenth century B.C.—and they were also literate and had an alphabet much like the Greek one. Politically and economically, they were organized as a group of wealthy city-states governed by kings. One of these cities, at the southern edge of Etruria (the region for which the Etruscans are named), was Rome. Although small, Rome occupied an important location as a convenient bridging point across the River Tiber.

Toward the end of the sixth century B.C. Rome joined with other Latin cities in instigating a revolt against Etruscan domination. In 509 B.C., according to Roman tradition, the last Etruscan king was expelled from Rome. This set the Romans on a 900-year course that would lead them to all corners of the then known world. Etruscan influence continued, however, and it was largely due to that influence and its inherited links with Greece that the Romans carried forward the classical ideas that continue to permeate the Western approach to life today.

THE ROMAN REPUBLIC

Once free of Etruscan domination, the Romans developed a republican form of government that lasted until the first

4.2 Etruscan warrior supporting a wounded comrade, early fifth century B.C. Bronze, height (without base) 5¼ ins (13.4 cm). Metropolitan Museum of Art, New York (Rogers Fund, 1947).

century B.C. This political stability provided important continuity for other Roman institutions. The motto "S.P.Q.R."—*Senatus Populusque Romanus* (the Roman Senate and People)—reflected the early Roman political and social order, and remained the watchword of Roman society until Imperial times. It meant that sovereignty rested in the people themselves, and not in any particular form of government. In many ways the Roman Republic functioned as a democracy. Decisions affecting society were made at a series of assemblies, which all citizens attended to express their will. The Senate, on the other hand, conducted the actual business of government, including the passage of legislation and the supervision of elected magistrates. Over the centuries, the greatest issues affecting Roman society were played out as dramas between the people and the Senate.

The Senate itself was an hereditary institution composed of an assembly of the heads, or *patres*, of old families and, later, of wealthy members of the citizenry, or *plebs*. The Senate's 300 members therefore represented old and new money, power, and social interest. It was a self-renewing OLIGARCHY. The two most important officers

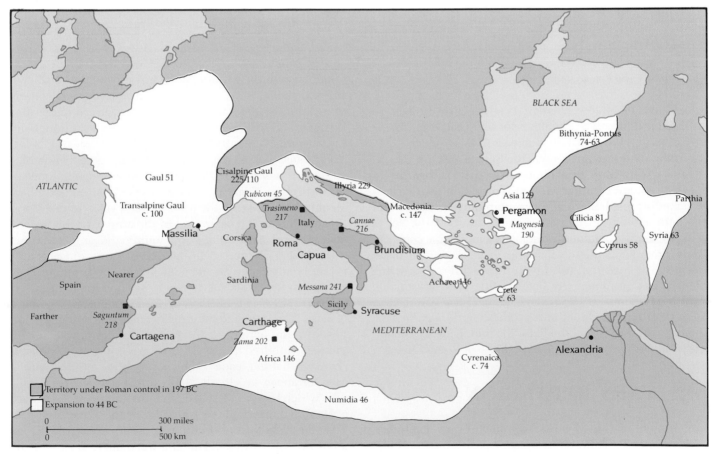

Map 4.1 The Roman Republic, showing important battles and dates (B.C.) that areas came under dominion.

	GENERAL EVENTS	LITERATURE & PHILOSOPHY	VISUAL ART & ARCHITECTURE	THEATRE & MUSIC
753 BC	Founding of Rome Etruscan culture			
500	Roman revolution		Etruscan warrior (4.2)	*Phylakes* farces
400	Gauls invade Rome		*Hermes* (4.5)	Mime
300	Roman Republic Roman conquest of western Greece First Punic War Second Punic War	Stoicism of Chrysippus		Development of Roman comedy Plautus
200	Marius Third Punic War	Middle Stoa Diogenes	Pantheon (4.20, 4.21, 4.22) Temple of Fortuna Virilis (4.8) Temple of Olympian Zeus (4.7)	Terence First stone theatres in Rome
100	Julius Caesar elected consul Julian calendar Battle of Actium Augustus	Roman Late Stoa Horace Seneca Vergil	Villa at Boscoreale(4.4) *Portrait of an Unknown Roman* (4.6) Vitruvius *Lady Playing the Cithara* (4.3) Augustus (4.15, 4.27, 4.28) Trajan's Column (4.16, 4.17) *Ara Pacis* (4.31)	Pantomime invented
AD 100	Roman Empire Destruction of Temple of Jerusalem Eruption of Mount Vesuvius	Livy Epictetus Juvenal Apuleius New Testament Marcus Aurelius	Forum of Augustus (4.29, 4.30) *Hercules and Telephos* (4.12) Colosseum (4.19, 4.23) Arch of Titus (4.24) Collegium of Augustales	
200		Plotinus	Sarcophagus (4.18)	
300	Split between Rome and Byzantium		Head of Constantine	

Timeline 4.1 The Roman period.

who ruled the state were the *consuls*, who were elected by the representative assemblies for one-year terms, at the end of which they became members of the Senate.

In Rome the rich ruled via the Senate and the general citizenry were little more than peasants. By the third century B.C. the division between aristocrat and peasant had widened appreciably, the former growing in riches and the latter sinking further and further into poverty. Yet as long as Rome remained reasonably small, the constitutional framework of the Republic held the social order together. It warded off revolution while permitting change and provided the body politic with reasonably well-trained leaders who knew how, above all else, to keep the Republic functioning and alive. It was, in fact, the internal stability of the Republic that made expansion possible, bringing about the next phase of Roman history.

MILITARY EXPANSION

Roman expansion was based on military conquest. Through conquest Rome assumed a position of political

dominance in the Hellenistic world during the third and second centuries B.C. (Map **4.1**) The internationalization of culture, evident in Hellenic times, grew under the Romans. Later, Rome would extend its control throughout Europe and eventually as far as the British Isles.

Because Roman expansion and conquest depended on strong military power, the Roman army became a powerful institution. Every male citizen who held property had an obligation to serve for up to sixteen years in the army, if conscripted. The basic unit of the army was the legion, composed of 5,000 men. Apparently the only occasion during the early period on which the army did not successfully discharge its responsibilities occurred in 390 B.C., when the Gauls succeeded in sacking Rome itself.

By 272 B.C. the Romans had conquered western Greece. Then they took on Carthage, the other major power of the period, in the first of the Punic wars. Over the next hundred years, in three great stages, Rome and Carthage battled each other for control of the whole Mediterranean world. It was during the second Punic war, which began in 218 B.C., that the Carthaginian general Hannibal marched his legions over the Alps into Italy. The end of the second Punic war in 202 B.C. left Rome in a position of advantage and at a watershed.

Rome had the choice either to consolidate order and security in the west by ridding itself of the Carthaginian threat or to expand toward the east. The Romans chose to move eastward, hoping to gain new riches from the conquered territories. The outcome, though unforeseen, was to leave Rome overlord of the entire Hellenistic world. But with the third Punic war, which began in 149 B.C., Rome also accomplished its other objective: within three years Carthage was destroyed.

THE ROMAN CIVIL WAR

The continuous state of war on the borders of the Roman provinces, as well as the practical requirements for effective government, led to an increase of power and authority in the hands of the Roman Senate and a decrease in the participation of ordinary citizens. Unlike Athens, Rome had very little commerce or industry, and the quality of life in Rome came to depend directly upon the wealth of conquered regions brought back to Rome as spoils.

The greatest danger to Rome did not lie in foreign wars, however, but in the threat of civil war. Conquests had made the Romans rich, and the *proconsuls* who governed the provinces took advantage of their positions, the availability of cheap land, slaves, and tribute money. Corruption was a temptation few could resist. They built vast estates and, in general, abused the poor, who became poorer. Rome itself became a Mecca for the rich and poor alike, and the widening gap between the two increased tension and bitterness among the masses. This was exacerbated by the violent excesses of generals who, having conquered the hinterlands, returned home with their armies intact. The result was a period of upheaval, which lasted from approximately 133 to 31 B.C. and which brought the Roman Republic to a close.

During this time a succession of men attempted leadership. Marius was the first of these. Then came a power struggle in the late first century B.C. from which the dictator Sulla emerged, to be followed by Pompey.

In 59 B.C. Marius' nephew Julius Caesar (Caesar was the family name) was elected consul. During a five-year campaign against the Gauls, he kept a close watch on Roman politics. Corruption, intrigue, and murder were disfiguring public life and discrediting the Senate. Having returned to Italy in 49 B.C. he declared war on Pompey by crossing the River Rubicon, which marked the limit of his province. By 44 B.C. he had returned to Rome in triumph, to be voted dictator for life. His life was cut short only days later, however, on 15 March 44 B.C., at the hands of assassins in the Senate.

One of Caesar's most lasting achievements was the invention of the Julian calendar, in which the year has 365 days, with an additional day every four years. The new calendar was used from 1 January 45 B.C.

THE VISUAL ARTS AND ARCHITECTURE

WALL PAINTING

Very little Roman painting has survived. Most of what survives appears to have been done in bright colors, in FRESCO—that is, painting on wet plaster that becomes a permanent part of the wall surface—and much of that art was an outright copy of Greek classical and Hellenistic work. Many Greek artists and craftspeople were brought to Rome, and it was they who produced most early Roman art, so it is not surprising that Roman painting reflected classical and Hellenistic themes and styles, although certain uniquely Roman qualities were added. The illustrations that appear in this chapter may not be typical of Roman painting. They are, however, typical of what survives.

One of the characteristics common to Roman painting is an insistence on naturalistic figure depiction, such as we witnessed in Hellenistic style. In the painting of the *Lady Playing the Cithara* (Fig. **4.3**) naturalistic detail

4.3 *Lady Playing the Cithara* c. 50 B.C. Wall painting, 6 ft 1½ ins (1.87 m) square. Metropolitan Museum of Art, New York (Rogers Fund, 1903).

4.4 Bedroom of a villa at Boscoreale, Italy, showing painted decorations, c. 50 B.C. Wall painting, average height 8 ft (2.44 m). Metropolitan Museum of Art, New York (Rogers Fund, 1903).

merges with an everyday subject matter. From this illustration we get a taste of Roman clothing, hair style, accessories, and furniture. The ornately turned legs of the chair and the gold embossing indicate careful and skilled craftsmanship as well as opulence. Notice how carefully and naturalistically the folds of the fabric are rendered, but notice, too, how careless the artist has been in the treatment of perspective. The legs and back of the chair have been drawn without regard to the way lines and shapes actually recede into the distance. Nonetheless, this fresco is a formally composed picture, fitting its imposed boundary.

Roman wall painting may combine landscape representation with painted architectural detail (Fig. **4.4**). Often, the outdoor view appears as a panoramic vista seen through a TROMPE L'OEIL window. Rooms painted in this style reflect the tastes of late Republican aristocratic society. They took as their models the opulence and stylishness of the late Hellenistic princely courts, which were still influential around the Mediterranean.

Scenes from Greek mythology were very popular in Roman wall decoration, and it is possible that the treatment of subject matter in wall painting had some relationship to the painting of scenery in the theatres. The Roman architectural historian Vitruvius (first century A.D.) indicates in his book *De Architectura* that wall painters imitated theatrical scenery for tragedies, comedies, and satyr plays. Different styles prevailed in the different genres, and examples of each may be seen in surviving Roman wall paintings. Tragic scenery depicted columns, pediments, statues, and palace decor. Comic scenery portrayed private dwellings with balconies and windows. Satyric scenery illustrated trees, mountains, and rustic scenes. If the villa at Boscoreale (see Fig. **4.4**) does indeed reflect theatrical scenery, it seems clear that

4.5 *Hermes*, Roman copy of a Greek work of c. 400 B.C. Marble, 5 ft 11 ins (1.8 m) high. Metropolitan Museum of Art, New York (Gift of the Hearst Foundation, 1956).

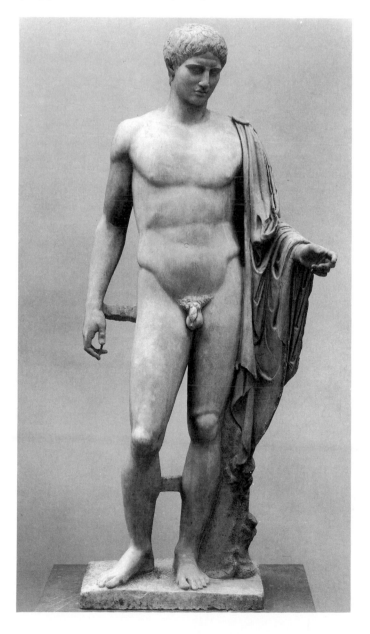

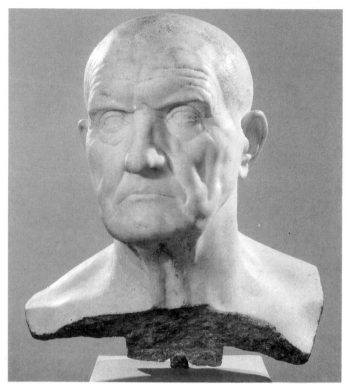

4.6 *Portrait of an Unknown Roman*, first century B.C. Marble, 14³/₈ ins (36.5 cm) high. Metropolitan Museum of Art, New York (Rogers Fund, 1903).

all three types are represented. The left panel seems satyric, the center panel tragic, and the right panel comic.

Mystery cults, especially that of Dionysus, were fashionable, and are represented in various manifestations in wall paintings, particularly in the so-called Villa of the Mysteries, which is located just outside the boundaries of the city of Pompeii.

SCULPTURE

Not all Roman art was an imitative reconstruction of Greek prototypes, although some Roman statues do fit this category. Figure **4.5** illustrates a Roman copy of a Greek statue of Hermes dating back to c. 400 B.C. It would have represented to the Romans not only a mythological subject, but also the qualities of the earlier Hellenic era.

Some Roman sculpture, however, expresses a vigor that is uniquely Roman. Scholars do not always agree on what particular works of Roman sculpture mean or on why they were made. For example, the *Portrait of an Unknown Roman* (Fig. **4.6**) dates from a time when Hellenistic influence was becoming well established in Rome. It is tempting to attribute the highly realistic representation of this work to the same artistic viewpoint that governed Hellenistic style and to conclude that it is a copy of a Hellenistic work. An important Etruscan-Roman religious practice undoubtedly had a stronger influence, however. Portraits were an integral part of household and ancestor worship, and wax death masks were often made and kept by the family to remember a loved one. Wax is not a substance ideally suited for immortality, and it is possible that the bust in Figure **4.6** was made from a death mask. There may be more to this portrait, however, than mere accuracy. Some scholars point to an apparent emphasis on certain features which reinforces the ideas of ruggedness and character.

ARCHITECTURE

Given the practicality of the Roman mind, it is not surprising to find that a distinctive Roman style is most evident in architecture. The clarity of form we found in the post-and-lintel structure of the classical Greek temple is also present in the Roman arch, but while in Greek architectural composition the part is subordinate to the whole, in Roman architecture each part often carries its own significance. The result is that we can usually surmise the appearance of a whole structure from one element.

Little survives of the architecture of the Republican period, but the use of Corinthian features and the graceful lines of what remains suggest a strong Hellenistic influ-

4.7 Temple of the Olympian Zeus, Athens, 174 B.C.–A.D. 130.

4.8 Temple of Fortuna Virilis, Rome, late second century B.C. Stone.

ence. There are notable differences, however. Hellenistic temples were built on an impressive scale (see Fig. **4.7**, Temple of the Olympian Zeus). Classical Greek temples were smaller, and Roman temples were smaller still, principally because Roman worship was mostly a private rather than a public matter.

Roman temple architecture employed ENGAGED COLUMNS—that is, columns partly embedded in the wall—and as a result, Roman temples lacked the open colonnades of their Greek counterparts, and this gave them a closed, slightly mysterious atmosphere. The Temple of Fortuna Virilis (Fig. **4.8**), which dates from the second century B.C. is the earliest well-preserved example of its kind. Greek influence may be seen in the delicate Ionic columns and entablature, but Etruscan elements are also present in the deep porch and in the engaged columns that are necessitated by the wide CELLA, or main enclosed space. (The one-room cella departs from the Etruscan convention of three rooms.) The Romans needed more spacious interiors than the Greeks, because they used them for displaying trophies from military campaigns, as well as to house the image of the deity.

THEATRE

The Romans loved entertainment, particularly drama, and their drama, for the most part, occupied the opposite end of the intellectual spectrum from classical Greek theatre. Roman theatre was wild, unrestrained, lewd, and highly realistic. Accounts of stage events suggest that very little was left to the audience's imagination. Actors wore various masks, and grotesquely padded costumes. Three important dramatic forms prevailed: *phlyakes* farce, Roman comedy, and MIME. Probably the earliest was the *phlyakes* farce, which may be traceable to Greek origins in Sicily as early as the fifth century B.C. The *phlyakes*—the name derives from the word for "gossips"—had an earthy style. Its themes parodied mythology and, later, burlesqued tragedy. Little literary evidence exists about the *phlyakes*, but a considerable number of vase paintings testify to its existence and character. If such evidence can be taken at face value, the *phlyakes* was bawdy, with actors suggestively padded and extravagantly masked. These farces seem to have used a raised stage consisting of a rough wooden platform with a simple background, and doors for entrances and exits. Curtains masked the area below the stage.

As Roman comedy developed in the third and second centuries B.C., it borrowed much from Hellenistic comedy, with its large theatres, high stages, and elaborate scene buildings (see Chapter 3). The Romans were receptive to the new comedy of Menander, assimilating it quickly, and the importation of this Greek comedy led to the rise of two of Rome's most important playwrights, Plautus (c. 254–184 B.C.) and Terence (c. 185–159 B.C.).

The twenty plays by Plautus that survive provide a picture of a playwright who was principally a translator and adaptor. He copied Greek originals, changing the locations to Rome and inserting details of Roman domestic life. His characters were types, not individuals: the braggart soldier, the miser, the parasite, and the wily but mistreated slave. With their slapstick humor and "sight gags," Plautus' plays are full of farcical energy and appeal directly to the emotions, not to the intellect. They are not particularly well written, but they work well enough on stage.

Terence, who was better educated than Plautus and a more literary writer, enjoyed the support of a wealthy patron. In his six extant plays he appears to be a dramatist capable of drawing universal situations and characters. Like Plautus, he had a great influence on the theatre of later ages, but he was not particularly popular with Roman audiences, perhaps because he did not use banality and buffoonery.

The third form of Roman theatre, the mime, may in fact have been older than the other two forms, but it did not achieve prominence in Rome until the time of the empire. Mimes dealt with low life, and appealed to all classes of Romans. Some mimes were adventures, and some ridiculed Christianity, particularly the rite of baptism. Consequently they found little favor with the Christian community and early Christian writers condemned the obscenities of the mimes, noting that adultery actually took place on stage. While that may be an exaggeration, the style of Roman theatre in general clearly was anticlassical. Idealization, formality, simplicity, and intellectual appeal were not among its characteristics.

Theatre fulfilled an important social function in keeping the minds of the masses off their problems. Yet it also served as a forum in which the general public could address grievances to the bureaucracy. When an official of the state had betrayed his trust, when a wrong had been suffered, or when an impropriety of state had become flagrant, the bite of Roman satire could be fierce, direct, and penetrating.

PHILOSOPHY AND RELIGION

Rome assimilated much of its philosophical thought from the Greeks and the Hellenistic world, and it was particularly receptive to Stoicism. For the Stoic, reason, or *logos*, governed the world, and the Great Intelligence was god. Specific guidelines for goodness and nobility gave order to life. The main tenets of Stoicism were acceptance of fate and duty, and the kinship of all people. The latter idea gave to Roman law the goal of providing justice for everyone, and this was one of Rome's great contributions to subsequent Western culture. Essentially, however, Stoicism was deterministic. The Great Intelligence controlled all things, and a person could do nothing but submit to this greater will.

The philosophy of Stoicism followed a wandering course over the years. It traced its roots back to the Greek philosopher Zeno of Citium (334–262 B.C.). Then, it dealt primarily with a scheme of salvation and a way of life—that is, a definition of human happiness and a means of attaining it. By 280 B.C. the Stoic philosophy had fallen under the charge of Chrysippus, who redefined it, giving it a form that would be unchanged for as long as Stoicism remained vital. Called the Old Stoa, this period witnessed a modification of some of the more extreme tenets, and a thrust that resulted in the Romans turning Stoicism into a religion.

On its way to Rome, Stoicism passed into the hands of Diogenes of Babylon in the second century B.C., a period known as the Middle Stoa. Diogenes brought Stoicism to Rome in 156–155 B.C., and he lectured on his philosophy, favorably impressing the Romans. The fate of Stoicism finally, however, depended on the skills of Panaetius and Posidonius in the early first century B.C. Under them it lost much of its cynicism, became more cultured and universal, and more attuned to the Roman spirit. Panaetius adopted Aristotle's definition of virtue as a "golden mean," and espoused the belief that material goods might not only be a means to right living, but could also be pursued as an end in themselves. An emphasis on temperance, propriety in daily life, and the performance of daily duty made Stoicism even more attractive to the Roman way of thinking.

As a result of the work of Panaetius and Posidonius, Rome became the home of Stoic philosophy and Stoicism entered its Late Stoa. The worldliness and common sense of the Romans made it into a mellow, urbane, and tolerant set of beliefs, and freed it from intellectual and moral dogmatism.

The earliest divinities of Rome were nature-spirits who dwelt in trees, in springs, and on hilltops. In addition to Jupiter (Zeus), the sky-spirit, Saturnus, a spirit of agriculture, and Mars, a spirit of agriculture and of war, there were gods of the home—for example, Janus, god of the doorway, and Vesta, goddess of the hearth-fire. No shrine was regarded with greater veneration than that of Vesta, where the sacred fire was kept burning. The round base of the shrine can still be seen in the Roman Forum.

As Rome's influence spread outward and interreacted with other cultures, other divinities took their place in the Roman pantheon, in some cases displacing and in other cases merging with earlier Roman gods and goddess. In time, the gods of Rome were identified with the gods of Olympus and assumed their functions while retaining their Roman names. In 500 B.C. a great temple was dedicated to the triad, Jupiter, Juno, and Minerva, the equivalents of the Greek gods Zeus, Hera, and Athena.

During the Republican era, what was now a Greco-Roman religion became more and more a religion of the state. As such, it was subordinated to political aims and intended to secure for the state the protection of the gods and the aversion of their ill-will. By the first century B.C. religion in Rome had slid into benign neglect, and temples and festivals were, for the most part, ignored.

CRITI REVIE below

A CRITICAL REVIEW

The idea of participatory government, as opposed to a monarchial or dictatorial one, now arises for the second time in our study. In both cases, the forum for this type of government was a small and relatively homogeneous citizenry. As life and population became more expansive, complicated, and diverse, the governmental form itself became problematical—or so it seems. Compare Periclean Athens, the Roman Republic, and contemporary United States, speculating in each case on the relationship between population size, cultural diversity, and the effectiveness of participatory democracy.

In what ways does Roman Republican art and architecture reflect a Grecian or Hellenistic heritage?

Find at least one example of Roman influence in contemporary American architecture and describe its relationship to its prototype.

A CRITICAL LOOK

Now we move to the Rome with which we are most familiar—that is, the Roman Empire: the Rome of Augustus Caesar; the Rome that dominated the Western world, Israel, and Judah; the Rome of Pontius Pilate, St Peter, and St Paul. Remarkably, the Roman genius for organization created a system that, although it certainly did not foster a cultural ethos like that of the Hellenes, nonetheless worked efficiently enough to insure that, under a single government, the world knew relative prosperity and peace. Central to the *Pax Romana* was the Roman judicial code and its sense of justice and equality under the law. In addition, the Roman Empire witnessed more intangible things, in the form of philosophy and religion.

Identify by time period and note the effects of Augustus Caesar's reign and the Pax Romana.

Describe the philosophies of Seneca, Marcus Aurelius, Epictetus, and Plotinus.

THE ROMAN EMPIRE
AUGUSTUS

CRITICAL LOOK above

If anyone had hoped that the assassination of Julius Caesar would bring about the return of Republican rule, they must surely have been disappointed, for the political turbulence simply continued. Caesar's assassins and his old commanders battled for control, while orators like Cicero labored to save the old Republic. In the end, Julius Caesar's great nephew and adopted son Octavian—known to history as Augustus Caesar—out-maneuvered and out-fought everyone.

The year after his uncle's death, Octavian and his allies of the Caesarian faction joined forces in an alliance called the Second Triumvirate. By means of intrigue and threat, they coerced the Senate into granting them—and

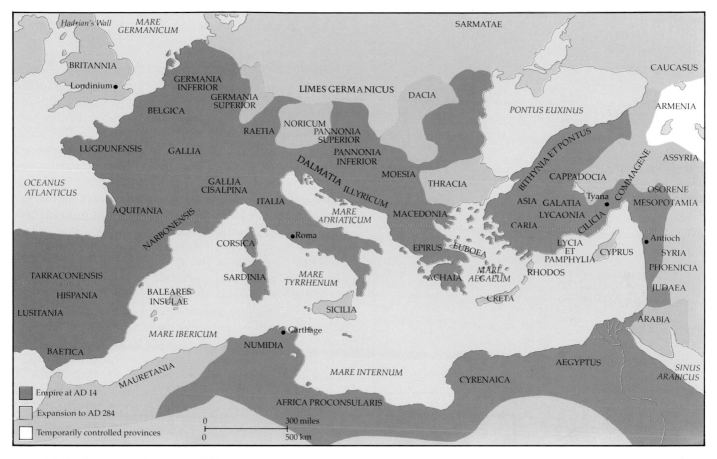

Labels on map:
Hadrian's Wall, *MARE GERMANICUM*, SARMATAE, CAUCASUS, BRITANNIA, GERMANIA INFERIOR, GERMANIA SUPERIOR, LIMES GERMANICUS, DACIA, ARMENIA, *PONTUS EUXINUS*, Londinium, BELGICA, NORICUM, RAETIA, PANNONIA SUPERIOR, ASSYRIA, LUGDUNENSIS, GALLIA, PANNONIA INFERIOR, CAPPADOCIA, COMMAGENE, *OCEANUS ATLANTICUS*, GALLIA CISALPINA, *DALMATIA*, *ILLYRICUM*, MOESIA, THRACIA, ASIA, GALATIA, Tyana, OSORENE, MESOPOTAMIA, AQUITANIA, NARBONENSIS, ITALIA, *MARE ADRIATICUM*, MACEDONIA, LYCAONIA, CARIA, CILICIA, CORSICA, Roma, EPIRUS, EUBOEA, LYCIA ET PAMPHYLIA, CYPRUS, Antioch, SYRIA, TARRACONENSIS, SARDINIA, *MARE TYRRHENUM*, ACHAIA, *MARE AEGAEUM*, RHODOS, PHOENICIA, HISPANIA, BALEARES INSULAE, *CRETA*, JUDAEA, LUSITANIA, *MARE IBERICUM*, SICILIA, ARABIA, BAETICA, NUMIDIA, Carthage, AEGYPTUS, *SINUS ARABICUS*, MAURETANIA, *MARE INTERNUM*, CYRENAICA, AFRICA PROCONSULARIS

Legend:
Empire at AD 14
Expansion to AD 284
Temporarily controlled provinces
0   300 miles
0   500 km

Map 4.2 The Roman Empire A.D. 14–284.

their legions—the power to restore peace to the Roman state. In the battle of Philippi, in northern Greece in 42 B.C., Octavian and his allies defeated the conspirators who had assassinated Julius Caesar. However, peace was not at hand. Octavian split with his former allies, especially with Mark Antony, who was now Cleopatra's lover. In a climactic naval battle at Actium in 31 B.C. Octavian defeated Mark Antony. Antony's death and Octavian's victory effectively ended the Roman Civil War. In the thirty-seventh poem in his first book of *Odes*, the poet Horace wrote in response: *Nunc est bibendum nunc pede libero pulsanda tellus!* ("Now is the time for drinking, now, with unshackled foot, for dancing!") Octavian took power, and Horace hailed him as "Caesar," which, for the first time, became an honorific title.

Gaius Julius Caesar Octavianus held both military command (*imperium*) and tribunician power (spokesperson for the people); he was both chief priest (*pontifex maximus*) and first citizen (*princeps*). He was also politically astute enough to adorn reality with palatable outward forms, replacing democracy with autocracy in a way that did not antagonize the public. He called on the services of culture, religion, literature, architecture, and the visual arts to help create a new picture of the world, with the result that there was a politically inspired aesthetic revolution, which led to the legalization of absolute power. In 27 B.C. Octavian formally divested himself of all authority. In response, the Senate and the people promptly gave it back to him, voting him the title Augustus (the Fortunate and Blessed). Although he was never officially "emperor" of Rome at all, within four years he had assumed complete power—including the right of veto over any law. The Republic was formally dead.

During the forty-five years that Augustus ruled (31 B.C.–A.D. 14), the Senate and popular assemblies continued to meet. However, the election of consuls, proconsuls, tribunes, and other officials required his blessing, the Senate was filled with Augustus' friends, and the popular assemblies seem to have lost all political function. As commander of the armies, he ruled all the vast territories of an empire that reached to the Rivers Rhine and Danube in what is now Germany. He commanded in the name of his uncle, Julius Caesar, and on the basis of his own military victories, claiming that he brought peace and order after a century of civil wars. He rebuilt temples to the Olympian gods, the "divine" Julius Caesar, and to "Rome and Augustus." He built roads, bridges, and aqueducts, established a sound currency, nurtured honest government, and maintained peace, which lasted nearly two hundred years.

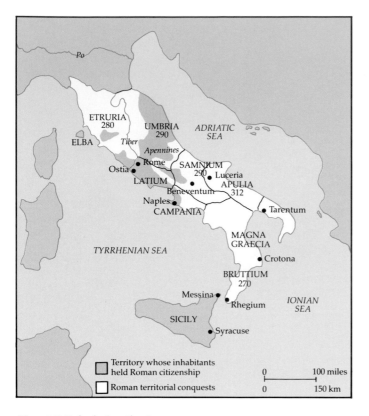

Map 4.3 Italy during the Roman Empire A.D. 14–284, showing date (B.C.) conquered.

PAX ROMANA

"The Roman Peace" (*Pax Romana*) brought under a single government a huge geographical area (Map **4.2**). The Augustan heritage was carried forward during the first and second centuries by a number of excellent emperors—for example, Claudius, Trajan, Hadrian, and Marcus Aurelius. The city of Rome spread out across its "seven hills" (Fig. **4.9**) and Roman citizenship was granted to the peoples of Italy (Map **4.3**) and the far-flung provinces, which meant that they were equal to their conquerors and could serve in the army, the bureaucracy, and higher levels of government. Roman administration and Roman law kept order, prosperity, and peace intact. The Roman administrative system developed a closely supervised hierarchy of professional officials, who made the machinery of day-to-day living work for the people. At its height, the Roman Empire covered more than 3 million square miles (7.78 million square kilometers): just slightly less than the size of the United States of today. The population was approximately 80 million. The entire empire was linked by a system of roads reaching out from a central hub at Rome. Wherever the Romans went, they took their

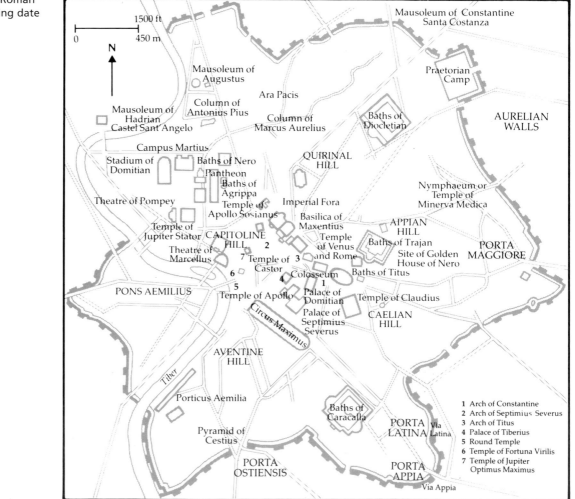

4.9 Imperial Rome.

culture. Roman theatres, for example, were built in Orange, France, and Sabratha in North Africa.

The age was not entirely free of calamities and tyrants—in the modern sense of the word. Along with good emperors came the insane Caligula and Nero, who crucified Christians and drove Gaul to revolt. It was a time in which anyone who took up arms against Rome had their right hand severed as punishment. It was a time in which thousands of citizens thronged to the Colosseum in Rome and amphitheatres throughout the empire to watch gladiatorial contests to the death and public executions of criminals. Overall, however, it was a time of peace and prosperity (Fig. **4.10**).

The best of times ended at the end of the reign of Marcus Aurelius (A.D. 161–180), called the Stoic emperor (see page 136). In A.D. 180 the army seized power and, to all intents and purposes, central authority in Rome collapsed. Emperors came and went, largely at the whim of the army. Standards of living declined precipitously as the population moved from the countryside to cities that became bloated by the poor living on public charity. Taxes rose and the middle class shrank. New pressures along the borders further destabilized the empire. Although, as we shall see in the next chapter, the empire survived for another century, with a brief resurgence under Diocletian and Constantine, Rome was in its death throes as an empire.

ROMAN LAW

Probably the most influential concept developed by the Romans in any field was the technique for deciding how general laws could be applied to specific cases (jurisprudence). This question was dealt with by legal experts—jurisconsults—who were not part of the state machinery, but who had special knowledge of the meanings of laws. Judges were able to choose only from opinions they submitted; the jurisconsults, in effect, became the lawmakers.

Thus a knowledge of the law and a body of expert opinion on its interpretation was established and handed down. Legal knowledge replaced family and position as a requisite for the practice of law.

Roman law was transformed from a set of isolated instances into a legal system by applying philosophical methods to legal cases: drawing out similarities and differences between them. General principles could thus be

4.10 Scale model of ancient Rome. Museo della Civiltà Romana, Rome.

laid down. These showed how laws should be applied consistently, thereby making the law predictable and the same for all.

PHILOSOPHY

SENECA

The changes wrought on Stoicism by the Romans and the general nature of the times are illustrated by the writings of the Roman philosopher, dramatist, and statesman, Seneca (8 B.C.–A.D. 65). "Austere and somewhat sactimonious by nature, he was given to deploring human weakness and to bewailing the vanity and wickedness of the world, from which he professed himself to await impatiently release in a happier home beyond the grave."[1] He was not, however, averse to success in his own life. His business sense was shrewd, and he was tireless in his attempts to increase the considerable fortune he had inherited. While the Epicureans deprecated wealth, Seneca staunchly defended the "righteousness of great wealth" in his philosophical sermons. He believed that reason was bankrupt, and late Stoicism saw sentimental and moral needs as sufficient grounds for religious convictions.

MARCUS AURELIUS AND EPICTETUS

By the time of Augustus Caesar (63 B.C.–A.D. 14), Stoicism had gained popularity among the masses as well as the upper classes, by accepting popular religion as an allegory of the truth. But by the time of Nero (A.D. 37–68), who sought to suppress all freedom of thought, Stoicism, which propounded free inquiry and discussion, had fallen on hard times. It was seen as a threat to the state, and many of its leaders were executed or exiled.

Stoicism reemerged as a central doctrine under the Stoic Emperor Marcus Aurelius (A.D. 121–80), who, along with the slave Epictetus, gave final definition to the revived philosophy. The *Discourses* and the *Manual* of Epictetus and the *Meditations* of Marcus Aurelius show us a somewhat old-fashioned Stoicism, leaning toward austerity and concerned mainly with moral and religious rules of behavior. Stoicism now appealed to the moral sense rather than to the intellect, and it turned people to the "way that led to happiness and peace." Salvation lay in cultivating independence from external circumstances, enriching oneself by religious sentiment, and having faith in "an assurance that all is for the best." Central to the thinking of both Marcus Aurelius and Epictetus was the idea that all people are the "children of one Father." Thus, everyone, regardless of age or status, should be loved uncritically, as one loves one's family.

Above all, the world was seen as rationally ordered.

Everything was an expression of a divine reason. Death was the end of the individual, merging each of us with that from which we sprang, and reuniting our reason with the *logos* of which it was a part. Death was therefore to be neither feared nor desired: it was merely to be accepted. After Marcus Aurelius' death, however, Stoicism lost ground to the emerging Christianity.

PLOTINUS: BEAUTY AND SYMBOL

Plotinus (c. 205–270) was an Egyptian-born philosopher and the greatest exponent of the neo-Platonist school: that is, a partial return to Platonic doctrines with additions from Stoic and Epicurean teachings.

According to Plotinus, beauty in art and nature reflect a unified universe—individual beauty is a reflection of harmony in the universe and a higher "reality" on which all experiences of beauty depend. As a result, artists' products are valuable because they are symbols of a higher order of existence. Plotinus was the first philosopher to treat art in a comprehensive manner. In the *Ennead*, Plotinus uses dance as a symbol of how nature has harmony and exists as a "living whole." He also reasons that a universal "Good" is the source of all "Beauty"; artworks—that is, man-made objects of beauty—thus imitate the universal "Beauty" and, in so doing, imitate the "Good." In addition, the arts are able to perfect the incomplete beauty of natural objects. As a result, for Plotinus, artworks occupy a special place in human experience because they form a bridge between incomplete natural objects and the universal concept of beauty, and, therefore, good: art raises the mind to a higher moral plane. An artwork can thus be seen as symbolic in two senses: it symbolizes the natural world, but perfected; and it symbolizes ultimate reality in the only way comprehensible to human minds.

RELIGION

By the end of the first century A.D. the most formidable religious cult in the empire was the Persian mystery-cult of Mithra, which took root in Rome and was carried by the Roman legions to the far corners of the empire. Roman monuments to Mithra can be found at the borders of Scotland, the shores of the Black Sea, and the frontiers of the Sahara Desert in Africa. Mithraism particularly appealed to soldiers, for it encouraged military virtues, imposed severe self-discipline, abstinence and control of the passions, and imparted a sense of brotherhood. Mithra was not the supreme god in Mithraism; rather, he was the mediator between an unknowable and unreachable god who dwelt in eternal spheres and a suffering and struggling human race.

A CRITICAL REVIEW

Augustus Caesar was one of the cleverest politicians of all history. In addition to knowing how to manipulate public opinion in order to achieve his own ends, he knew the power of art and literature in shaping a public persona and public opinion. As we will see, he used art and literature to invent not only his own aura but that of Rome itself. Nonetheless, he was also a skillful ruler, and under his direction the Roman Empire maintained peace and stability while Rome was rebuilt into perhaps the most magnificent city on earth.

In the area of philosophy and religion, Stoicism witnessed a rebirth and expansion, and Plotinus revived Platonic philosophy—neo-Platonism—focusing on symbol and beauty. At the same time as Christianity was rising, so was a similar Persian cult called Mithraism.

Describe Augustus Caesar's contributions to the Roman Empire and compare him with any contemporary politicians or national leaders whom you believe have shown similar prowess.

Compare Mithraism to other religions with which you may be familiar.

4.11 The prophet Mithra, from Dura-Europos, c. A.D. 245. National Archeological Museum, Damascus, Syria.

Mithra is pictured as constantly engaged in a struggle against the powers of evil (Fig. **4.11**). He had been compelled to catch a bull and, after a struggle, to slay him. From the body of the slaughtered bull came all plants and useful animals. Dogs, scorpions, and other creatures were considered malevolent, and it was with these creatures that Mithra did battle. Mithra also presided over the judgment of souls after death and guided them to their celestial homes, where he received them like children returning from a long voyage. Although Mithra was the god of light, his worship was carried on in underground temples. Those who sought membership of the cult were required to endure a long, painful course of preparation, after which the initiate took an oath called *sacramentum*. The initiate was eventually allowed to participate in a sacred rite in which a loaf of bread and a cup of wine and water were placed before the priest, who pronounced a sacred formula over it. By partaking of the mystical food, the neophyte gained power to combat evil spirits and to gain immortality.

CRITICAL REVIEW above

TWO-DIMENSIONAL ART

Although it is less well known than Pompeii, the city of Herculaneum provides us with excellent examples of wall painting from the Roman Empire period, which were preserved by the ash and lava of Mount Vesuvius' cataclysmic eruption in A.D. 79. In these works, as well as in works from Pompeii, we see that, as in wall painting from the Republican era, brightly colored frescos were the order of the day. These works also share the naturalism of their predecessors. The wall painting *Hercules and Telephos* (Fig. **4.12**) uses highlight and shadow to create marvelously rendered flesh and musculature as well as intricately detailed fabric in the Hellenistic style. Here

CRITICAL LOOK p. 139

4.12 *Hercules and Telephos*, Roman copy of a Greek work of the second century B.C. Wall painting from Herculaneum, 5 ft 7½ ins (1.71 m) high. Museo Archeologico Nazionale, Naples, Italy.

4.13 Wall decoration, c. A.D. 70-79. Wall painting, room dimensions 14 ft 2 ins × 13 ft 4 ins (4.32 × 4.06 m). Collegium of the Augustales, Herculaneum, Italy.

A CRITICAL LOOK

If we walk the streets of Rome today we see a curious amalgam of the old and the new. The Colosseum's tattered remains rise shakily above a heavily traveled thoroughfare, and across the street we can walk quietly through the remains of the Roman Forum. In other places, we can stand on the sidewalk and look down into the remains of the Empire and marvel at how high the current street is above the level of the ground of 2,000 years ago. In other places, we see where Imperial ruins have simply been incorporated into the bricks and mortar of later construction to create a curious time-warp. However, wherever we go, we are aware that we are looking at the ruins of a great ancient city. Rome was not the only city of the Roman Empire, however, and to the south lie two cities whose unfortunate geographical position caused them to disappear under the lava and ash of Mount Vesuvius only to reawaken, as if frozen in time, more than a thousand years later to give us a clearer picture of life in the Roman Empire. As we study the art and architecture of the Roman Empire in the next section, we will see Rome and Herculaneum (pronounced hur-cue-LAY-nee-uhm) at their finest. We will also look (in the Our Dynamic World feature) at a great dynasty in China during the same period.

What were the characteristics of Roman painting and sculpture under the Empire? Identify and describe them.

What was Rome's contribution to classical architecture? Cite specific examples.

What was life like in China during the Han dynasty, and what were the characteristics of its two-dimensional art?

the subject matter is mythical and heroic: Hercules' discovery of the infant Telephos in Arcadia. Hercules, the dynamic figure on the right, reveals warm flesh and sinewy musculature, full of life and warmth. In contrast, the personification of Arcadia, the semireclining figure, seems distant and remote—as cold as a piece of sculpture. The lion is rendered with quick, rough brushstrokes, which stand in stark contrast to the smooth, delicate treatment of the doe in the lower left. Above Arcadia, a playful Pan with his pipes, shows an almost offhand treatment, as flippant as his smirk.

A second example from Herculaneum (Fig. 4.13) exemplifies the Roman taste for forceful colors and the painted "architectural structuring" of large areas. In later periods, the walls of houses, were decorated with paintings hung in frames. Here, paintings are a permanent part of the wall and are "framed" with painted architectural detail. This particular painting was a shrine devoted to the cult of the emperor, and the central panel, which depicts the introduction of Hercules into Olympus in the presence of Minerva and Juno, is a metaphor for the divinity of the emperor.

All the illustrations of Roman wall decoration in this chapter, whether of the earlier Republican or of the Imperial period, demonstrate the colorfulness of Roman interior design. The style of the painting is certainly theatrical, but it has a permanence, not only in that it forms an integral part of the wall, but also in that each panel contains an architecturally complete composition enclosed in a painted "frame." This approach is very different from that of later periods, in which pictures are separate framed entities, and can be moved from place to place.

SCULPTURE

The straightforward naturalism of the Roman Republic was modified during the Augustan period. Although Hellenistic influence had become strong by the late first century B.C., Greek classical influence always predominated in some quarters, but with a Roman—that is, a more practical and individual—flavor. By the time of the Empire, classical influence had gained precedence, returning sculpture to the idealized character of that of Periclean Athens. Augustus (Fig. 4.15) boasted that when he came to power, Rome was a city of sun-dried bricks, and that when he left it, it had become a metropolis of marble. Greek classical form in sculpture was revived and translated into vital forms for the Romans. The Greek concept of the "perfect body" held sway. It was common for a sculptor to copy the idealized body of a well-known Greek statue and add to it a highly realistic portrait head of a contemporary Roman. Other figures after the Greek style were similarly Romanized. A male nude might be draped in a toga; another might be made to represent Augustus in armor. The aesthetics of sculptural depiction

OUR DYNAMIC WORLD

Han Dynasty Painting

At almost the same time as the Roman Empire, the Han dynasty gave China a great empire in the East. They had much in common—both covered vast areas and contained tremendous populations, and in each power was concentrated in the hands of an emperor and an immense, centralized bureaucracy. Like Rome, China perceived itself as the only true civilization, surrounded by barbarians, and in both cases, a significant breakdown of authority occurred early in what we call the Christian era. Interestingly, both great empires knew of, and, indirectly, traded with, each other.

Unlike the scattered empire of the Romans, China under the Han dynasty was composed of a contiguous land mass and a relatively homogenous people, who shared a common heritage and who spoke a common language. In addition, the Chinese were more willing to accept an emperor than were the diverse and conquered peoples of the Roman Empire. Chinese culture was a family-centered culture in which the patriarch of the family "ruled," and in much the same sense, China viewed its emperors as "fathers" of an extended family, of which all Chinese saw themselves as members.

Much like Egyptian pharaohs and, as we shall see later, the Byzantine emperors, Han emperors ruled on the authority of the Mandate of Heaven. The divine right to rule more or less demanded a strong centralized monarchy, and the peace and prosperity that the Han provided gave China one of its most splendid periods. Also during this period, an idealized concept of women took shape that has continued to the present day. Chinese women's virtues were family virtues. Chinese women were expected to be devoted to their parents and, later, to their husbands. Their fundamental task was the nurturing of family and children, and fidelity, chastity, and modesty were considered ideal female virtues.

During the Han period, great accomplishments in scholarship and the arts occurred. Unfortunately, however, much of the artistic output has vanished, for the splendid palaces were made of wood, and the paintings that adorned the walls have crumbled with them. Literary evidence reveals that the subjects of Han dynasty painting were social and historical—that is, they dealt with everyday life rather than the

4.14 Lintel and pediment of tomb, Han dynasty, 50 B.C.–A.D. 50. Earthenware, hollow tiles painted in ink and colors on a white-washed ground, 29 × 80½ ins (73.8 × 204.7 cm). Courtesy, Museum of Fine Arts, Boston. (Denman Waldo Ross Collection.)

mythology of the gods. Three styles of painting exist-ed during that period of the Han dynasty that spanned the first century A.D. The first style was a rather formal and stiff style, very geometric and HIER-ATIC, in which the figures were flat and outlined. In contrast, the second style depicted lively action and deep space. The third was midway between the two previous styles, being more painterly and exhibiting movement and lively depictions of, for example, mythical beings, dragons, and rabbits. As can be seen in Figure **4.14**, a tile taken from the lintel and pedi-ment of a Han tomb, masterfully rendered figures are drawn with brushstrokes that suggest liveliness and movement. The figures appear in three-quarter poses, which gives the painting a sense of depth and action, and the active line, with its diagonal sweeps, adds to the sense of action. The poses of the people suggest character—that is, the psychology of the figure por-trayed—but although the use of pose and direction reflects a sophisticated approach and technique, the figures remain on the same baseline, with no sense of placement in deeper space.

4.15 Augustus in armor, Villa of Livia, Prima Porta, c. 20 B.C. Marble, 6 ft 8 ins (2.03 m) high. Vatican Museums, Rome.

thus remained Greek, with Roman clothing added. The pose, rhythm, and movement of the body originated in the past.

At this time much sculpture portrayed the emperor. Emperors had been raised to the status of gods, perhaps because in so far-flung an empire it was useful for people to revere their leaders as superhuman.

Other sculptures told the story of a leader's accom-plishments. Trajan's Column, erected in the Emperor's Forum, rose 128 feet (39 meters) above the pavement on an 18-foot (5.5-meter) base. Atop the 97-foot (30-meter) column stood a more than twice life-size statue of Trajan (Fig. **4.16**). (Trajan's statue was later replaced by a figure of St Peter.) Inside the column, a staircase winds upward

4.17 Trajan's Campaign against the Dacians, detail of Trajan's Column, A.D. 106-113. Marble, height of frieze band 4 ft 2 ins (1.27 m).

4.16 Apollodorus of Damascus, Trajan's Column and ruins of Basilica Ulpia, Rome. Trajan's Column, A.D. 106–113. Marble, height of base 18 ft (5.49 m), height of column 97 ft (29.57 m).

4.18 Roman sarcophagus, showing Dionysus, the Seasons, and other figures, c. A.D. 220–230. Marble, 7 ft 3¾ ins (2.23 m) long. Metropolitan Museum of Art, New York (Purchase, Joseph Pulitzer Bequest, 1995).

to the top. On the outside, from bottom to top, a spiral band of relief sculpture (Fig. **4.17**) depicts the campaign in which Trajan defended Rome. Trajan himself appears ninety times in the narration, each appearance marking the start of a new episode.

The sculpture relies on symbolism and convention. Water is represented by a waving line; mountains, by jagged lines. Proportions are not realistic, and perspective is irrational. However, the intent and effect are clear. Trajan's story unfolds in a form to be "read" by the man and woman in the street.

We have touched already on the death mask as Roman funerary art. The intricate relief sculpture which decorated Roman SARCOPHAGI shows the way that Roman art reflected private life. This type of sculpture emerged early in the second century A.D., when the practice of cremation fell out of favor. Marble sarcophagi were adorned with rich and varied relief decoration. There were three major centers of sarcophagus production—Athens, Asia Minor, and Rome—and sarcophagi were often exported before completion and finished at the site. Attic sarcophagi had decoration on all four sides, with scenes drawn from Greek mythology. They were typically carved in high relief, with a somber tone. Sarcophagi from Asia Minor had figures carved almost in the round, against a background of architectural detail. Roman sarcophagi were carved on three sides, with the fourth side designed to sit against a wall. The front typically showed a mythological scene, while the ends were carved with decorative motifs in low relief (Fig. **4.18**).

4.19 Colosseum, Rome, c. A.D. 70–82. Stone and concrete, 159 ft (48.5 m) high.

ARCHITECTURE

In the Augustan age at the beginning of the imperial period, Roman architecture, like contemporary sculpture, was refashioned in Greek style. This accounts to a large extent for the dearth of surviving buildings from previous eras since old buildings were replaced with new ones, in the new style. Temples were built on Greek plans, but the proportions were significantly different from those of the classical Greek.

The first through the fourth centuries A.D. brought what is now typically identified as the "Roman style." The most significant characteristic of this style is the use of the arch as a structural element, in ARCADES and TUNNEL and GROIN VAULTS. The Colosseum (Figs **4.19** and **4.23**), the best known of Roman buildings and one of the most stylistically typical, could seat 50,000 spectators. Combining an arcaded exterior with vaulted corridors, it was a marvel of engineering. The circular sweep of its plan and the curves of the arches are countered by the vertical lines of the engaged columns flanking each arch. The columns at each level are of different orders, and progress upward from heavy Doric columns, to Ionic ones, to lighter Corinthian ones at the top level.

Placed in the center of the city of Rome, the Colosseum was the site of gladiatorial games and other gruesome spectator sports. Emperors competed with their predecessors to produce the most lavish spectacles there. The Colosseum was a new type of building, called an AMPHITHEATRE, in which two semicircular theatres are combined, facing each other, to form an arena surrounding an oval interior space. Originally, a system of poles

MASTERWORK

The Pantheon

As its name suggests, the Pantheon (Figs **4.20**, **4.21**, and **4.22**) was built to honor all the gods. The structure brought together Roman engineering, practicality, and style in a domed temple of unprecedented scale.

Until the mid-nineteenth century, only two buildings had equalled the span of its dome, and during the Middle Ages, it was suspected that demons might be holding up the roof of this pagan temple. Around the circular interior statues of the gods stood in NICHES in the massive walls. Corinthian columns add grace and lightness to the lower level. Heavy horizontal moldings accentuate the feeling of open space under the huge dome. The dome itself is 143 feet (44 meters) in both diameter and height (from the floor to the OCULUS, or eye, the round opening at the top of the dome). The circular walls supporting the dome are 20 feet (6 meters) thick and 70 feet (21 meters) high. Square COFFERS on the underside of the dome give an added sense of lightness and reflect the framework into which concrete was poured. Originally the dome's

interior was gilded to suggest "the golden dome of heaven."

In both plan and CROSS-SECTION the Pantheon is designed on a perfect circle: the dome is a hemisphere (Fig. **4.21**). From the exterior, we see a simple, sparsely adorned cylinder capped by a gently curving dome. The entrance is via a porch in the Hellenistic style with graceful Corinthian columns. Originally the porch was approached by a series of steps and a rectangular forecourt, so what remains is only part of a larger, more complex original design.

Inside, both the scale and the detail are overwhelming, but the way in which practical problems have been solved is equally impressive. Support PIERS for the dome stand in niches that are alternately rectangular and rounded. The vault over each niche is designed to transfer the weight of the dome onto solid footings. Drains cut into the slightly concave floor of the building carry away any rain that falls through the oculus above.

What captures our immediate attention is the

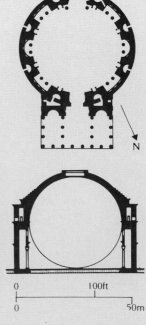

4.20 Pantheon, Rome, c. A.D. 118-128. Marble, brick, and concrete.

4.21 Plan and cross-section of the Pantheon, Rome.

4.22 Giovanni Paolo Panini, *Interior of the Pantheon*, c. 1740. Oil on canvas, 4 ft 2 ins × 3 ft 3 ins (1.27 m × 99 cm). National Gallery of Art, Washington D.C. (Samuel H. Kress Collection).

sense of space. In most Egyptian and Greek architecture, the focus is on mass—the solids of the buildings. Here, despite the scale and beauty of the solids, it is the vast openness of the interior that strikes us. This is Roman inventiveness and practicality at its best, yet the atmosphere of the building is not one of practical achievement but of sublimity.

How could the Romans build such a colossal structure? Some historians argue that the key lies in a new building technology made possible by concrete con-

taining a specific kind of cement newly developed near Naples. The secret, however, may lie in the mysterious rings around the dome. As a recent study at Princeton University suggests, they probably "perform a function similar to the buttresses of a Gothic cathedral.... The extra weight of the rings... helps stabilize the lower portion of the dome. Rather than functioning like a conventional dome, the Pantheon behaves like a circular array of arches, with the weight of the rings holding the end of each arch in place."[2]

4.23 Colosseum, interior. 616 ft 9 ins (188 m) long; 511 ft 10 ins (156 m) wide.

4.24 Arch of Titus, Roman Forum, Rome, c. A.D. 81. Marble. About 50 ft (15 m) high.

TECHNOLOGY: PUTTING DISCOVERY TO WORK

Cement

In their rapid conquests, the Romans learned quickly to appreciate and to copy other people's mechanical devices. The major contribution to technological development made by the Romans was probably their ability to absorb ideas and then to provide the administrative underpinnings to allow those ideas to be used to their fullest. Many technological practices are credited to Rome, but, in fairness, a large number of these had been invented and practiced elsewhere before the Romans acquired them. Even aqueducts, a much-vaunted Roman innovation, had seen predecessors in Greece, Assyria, Babylonia, Persia, and Egypt, and the same was true of drainage systems, which, as we noted, were part of the technology of Minoa. Roman roads were no better than those in Greece and Persia.

One of the truly original contributions of Rome to technology was the introduction of cement. In addition to its uses as a bonding material, the Romans discovered that it could be used in the making of concrete, which, when combined with a brick facing,

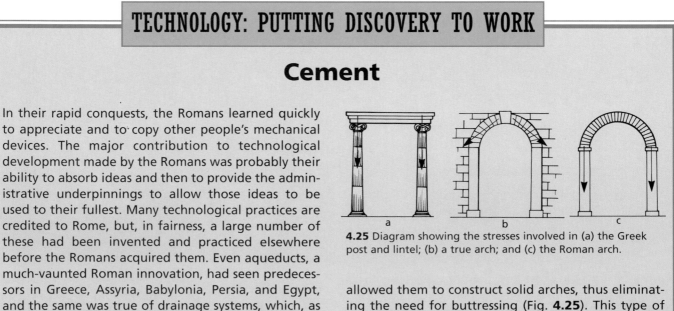

4.25 Diagram showing the stresses involved in (a) the Greek post and lintel; (b) a true arch; and (c) the Roman arch.

allowed them to construct solid arches, thus eliminating the need for buttressing (Fig. **4.25**). This type of arch was seen most frequently in the construction of aqueducts, but the development of the brick-and-concrete arch may also be considered a major Roman contribution to technology. Essentially, this consisted of a brick arch reinforced with a heavy infill of concrete. Once the concrete set, the arch became a vast lintel that exerted little lateral pressure. Thus, the pillars that supported it required no supporting buttresses.

and ropes supported awnings to shade spectators. The space below the arena contained animal enclosures, barracks for gladiators, and machines for raising and lowering scenery.

Roman triumphal arches are also impressive architectural monuments. The Roman classical style survives in a memorial to Titus, which was raised by his younger brother, Domitian. The Arch of Titus (Fig. **4.24**) was a political gesture of homage to the accomplishments of Titus and his father Vespasian during the conquest of Jerusalem. The reliefs on the arch illustrate allegories rather than actual historical events. Titus appears as *triumphator*, along with figures such as the *genius Senatus*, or spirit of the Senate, and the *genius populi Romani*, or spirit of the people of Rome. The richly and delicately ornamented FAÇADE of this arch, stands in marked contrast to its massive internal structure. This is an important characteristic of Roman architecture, which distinguishes it from Greek principles, in which the structure can always be seen.

CRITICAL REVIEW below

A CRITICAL REVIEW

The ruins of Rome, Pompeii, and Herculaneum tell us that life—at least for some—during the Roman Empire, especially during the great *Pax Romana*, must have been fairly pleasant. The mild Mediterranean climate, comfortable homes of marble, centered on an open courtyard and richly decorated with wall paintings would be inviting and comfortable, even by contemporary standards. Public displays of sculpture were everywhere, and the Roman inclusion of the arch as the centerpiece of architectural structures gave Rome and other cities of the Empire a majestic air. The fact that Augustus' vision focused on the solid proportions of classical Greece must have lent to Romans a sense of order and stability that seemed eternal. Of course, it was not—but then, neither were they. However, were they aware of the subtle changes taking place around the edges of their society? Were they able to compare it with what it once was? Were they able to grasp when the zenith had been reached?

It is moderately easy for us to look back from the vantage point of history and say, "Oh yes, that's what happened; that's where and when they went wrong." We know, of course, that it is not so easy to see things like that when you are in the middle of them. Look back at the Roman Empire and its art and consider:

What does the style of Roman architecture tell us about the worldview of its people?

Using the concepts of line, structure, proportion, and style, analyze the Roman Colosseum and compare it to the Greek Parthenon.

A CRITICAL LOOK

It remains for us to view, briefly, the arts of music and literature. Roman music pales in comparison to literature as we view it from the vantage point of history and the criteria of high culture. Were we to inject ourselves and our values into Roman society, we would conclude that music and, indeed, dance represented what we would call pop culture, while literature represented the educated classes, although we should not assume that the latter could not be found in audiences for the former, such was the egalitarian spirit of the Roman Empire. Vergil (also spelled Virgil) was Rome's Homer, except that he was a contemporary Roman rather than a mythical Greek. If you can, read an excerpt from the *Aeneid*, which you should endeavor to compare to the *Iliad*. Finally, in the Synthesis section, we will focus on the central force in the period, Augustus Caesar, and briefly note his visions.

Explain the characteristics of music and its role in Roman society.

Describe the main directions of Roman literature.

MUSIC

CRITICAL LOOK p. 147

Music was very popular among the Romans. Contemporary reports describe festivals, competitions, and virtuoso performances. Many Roman emperors were patrons of music, and Greek music teachers were popular and very well paid. Large choruses and orchestras performed regularly, and the *hydraulos*, or water organ, was a popular attraction at the Colosseum. The *hydraulos* was apparently so loud that it could be heard a mile away, and the fact that it provided "background music" for the spectacles in which Christians were fed to lions meant that it was banned from Christian churches for centuries.

Aristotle had deplored professionalism in the pursuit of music. Music, he believed, existed for its own aesthetic qualities and as a moral force in character development. It was a measure of intelligence. The pragmatic Romans did not see it this way. Professional dexterity and *virtuosity* were social assets, and meaningless accomplishments, such as blowing the loudest tone or holding the longest note, were rewarded with great acclaim. Musical entertainment did fulfill an important social and political function for the Romans, however. As more and more people flocked to Rome from conquered territories, the numbers of the poor grew. The state began to provide entertainments to keep them occupied and under control. "Bread and circuses" became the answer to the dissatisfactions of the poor and the oppressed, and music also played an important role. As a result, music became less an individual pastime and more an exclusively professional activity.

The Romans seem to have contributed little to musical practice or theory. They took their music direct from Greece after it became a Roman province in 146 B.C., adopting Greek instruments and theory. They did invent some new instruments, principally brass trumpets and horns for military use. As with most ancient music, we know that Roman music existed, and we understand a little of its theory, practice, and instrumentation, but we have no real conception of how it sounded, melodically or rhythmically.

By the end of the fifth century A.D. all mention of secular music had virtually disappeared. It must have existed, but we have no record of it.

PROFILE

Vergil (70–19 B.C.)

Rome's greatest poet, Publius Vergilius Maro, loved the rural countryside. He was born a peasant, and he focused the central force of his poetry on people. His writings also reveal his thorough education in Cremona, Milan, and Rome and the influence of the Epicureans and Stoics, who were central to the rhetoric and philosophy of his studies. Shy and retiring, he seems never to have participated in politics or the military; he was a poet first and foremost. Nevertheless, he kept in close contact with current events, and his works often reflect an overview of contemporary Roman life.

His first work, the *Eclogues*, brought him immediate recognition and access to the exclusive literary circles of Rome. The following years, 37–30 B.C., were spent writing the *Georgics*, and the remainder of his life was occupied by the *Aeneid*, which is to Rome what the *Iliad* and the *Odyssey* are to Greece (see page 76).

The twelve books of the *Aeneid* tell the story of Rome, and in them Vergil sought to hold up to his readers the qualities of Roman character and Roman virtues that had made the city great. The first six books tell the story of Aeneas' wanderings—as Homer had told of Ulysses' travels in the *Odyssey*—and the final six books set the scenes of battle—as Homer did in the *Iliad*. Further internal similarities exist as well.

Vergil's influence on literature and Western thought is probably greater than any other classical poet. His poetry reflects consummate skill in the use of diction, rhythm, and word music. Above all, he captures a quality of the human condition, elevated to a grand scale, with which every human being can identify. At the time of his death, Vergil was highly troubled by the imperfections he found in the *Aeneid*, and he wanted to burn it. However, the Emperor Augustus refused to allow the work to be destroyed and had it published, with some minor revisions, two years after the poet's death.

LITERATURE

The practical early Romans did not produce any remarkable literature. When literature as an art form did become reasonably popular, it was Greek slaves who nurtured it. The first literary works were imitations of Greek works, and they were written in Greek. Latin was initially considered a peasant language, with few words capable of expressing abstract notions. A Latin prose style and vocabulary for the expression of philosophical ideas had to wait for Cicero.

During the reign of Augustus, the poets Horace and Vergil were commanded to write verses glorifying the emperor, the origins of Rome, the simple honesty of rural Roman life, patriotism, and the glory of dying for one's country. Livy set about retelling Roman history in sweeping style. Vergil's *Aeneid*, an epic account of the journey of Aeneas from the ruins of Troy to the shores of Italy, far surpasses mere propaganda.

> Arms and the man I sing, who first made way
> Predestined exile, from the Trojan shore
> To Italy, the blest Lavinian strand.
> Smitten of storms he was on land and sea
> By violence of Heaven, to satisfy
> Stern Juno's sleepless wrath; and much in war.
> He suffered, seeking at the last to found
> The city, and bring o'er his fathers' gods
> To safe abode in Latium; whence arose
> The Latin race, old Alba's reverend lords,
> And from her hills wide-walled,
> imperial Rome.[3]

The influence of the lyric poets Horace, Vergil, and Livy on Western culture is difficult to overestimate. In the words of one commentator: "They are so much a part of us that we take their values for granted and their epigrams for truisms."[4] To the Emperor Augustus, they fully expressed the Roman tradition and Roman language. The three writers created a literature that distracted the upper classes from Greek "free thought" and made it easier for the Emperor to rally them to the "ancient Roman order" as represented in his person.

A moralizing Stoicism runs throughout the literature of the Augustan period. In poetry, this Stoicism was expressed through satire, which allowed writers to combine morality with popular appeal. Martial and Juvenal used satire to attack vice by describing it in graphic detail. Petronius produced satirical PICARESQUES of verse and prose that were as readable as Martial's and Juvenal's work, but free of their moralizing.

Finally, Apuleius and Lucan followed in the same tradition. Apuleius' *Golden Ass* is one of the earliest precursors of the novel. The author creates a fictional biography that describes how the central character is tried and condemned to death for the murder of three wineskins. He is brought back to life by a sorceress, but as he tries to follow her in the form of a bird, he is changed instead into an ass. The only cure for this affliction appears to be the procurement of some rose leaves, and in his search for these, he has bizarre and fantastic adventures.

SYNTHESIS

Augustus—Classical Visions

The aesthetic revolution at the start of the Roman Empire saw a shift in the purpose of art toward propaganda. One of the artistic ramifications of Augustus' new political order was the emergence of the NEO-ATTIC style.

Sculptural works, with their new emphasis on portraying the emperor, can be divided into three main types. These are differentiated by scholars primarily by hairstyle, while facial features remain recognizably the same. In the first type (Fig. **4.26**), before Octavian was made emperor, his hair is shown in realistic disorder. The second type (Fig. **4.27**) depicts the same man (now called Augustus) as emperor, with a more refined, nobler face and the hair divided into two strands above the right eyebrow. In the third type (Fig. **4.28**), the forelock is gone, and the hair is combed to the side.

The essence of Roman neo-Attic sculpture, however, is to be found in the statue of Augustus shown in Figure **4.15**. The portrait head of the Emperor sits on an idealized, youthful body like that Polyclitus made for his *Lance Bearer* (see Fig. **3.9**). Unlike the lance bearer, however, Augustus reaches outside his cube of composition-

4.29 Temple of Mars the Avenger, Forum of Augustus, Rome, from the south, dedicated 2 B.C. Marble facing over stone and concrete.

4.26 Octavian, copy of a type created in 31 B.C. Marble, 14⅝ ins (37.2 cm) high. Museo Capitolino, Rome.

4.27 Augustus, copy of a type created in 27 B.C. Bronze, 16⅞ ins (42.9 cm) high. British Museum, London.

4.28 Augustus, final type before 12 B.C. Marble, 12 ins (30.5 cm) high. Museum of Fine Arts, Boston (Gift of Edward W. Forbes).

4.30 Temple of Mars the Avenger, Forum of Augustus, reconstructed view.

the garlands, or swags, strung from ox-skulls represent peace, while the fact that they are composed of varieties of fruit which do not ripen together symbolizes the unending nature of this peace. The figures themselves, though their poses are perfectly natural, exude royal dignity and nobility, characteristics that Augustus sought to emphasize in the popular conception of himself. The whole altar, dedicated to peace, thus serves as an image of the golden age of Augustus—that is, an era of peace and prosperity whose source was the emperor himself.

Monumentality, symbolism, practicality, and a resurrection of Greek classicism adapted to Roman tastes—these are the hallmarks of the Augustan age. Taken together, they describe what we have come to know as Roman classicism, and they reflect the quintessence of Roman life, as the Romans themselves saw it.

al space, and the final effect is much less introspective and more dignified than that of its prototype.

The Forum of Augustus in Rome (Figs **4.29** and **4.30**) exemplifies monumental Imperial art at its classical grandest. In both its conception and its dimensions it speaks of greatness. Constructed from war booty, the Forum honors Mars the Avenger, to whom Octavian had made a vow during his wars against the assassins of Julius Caesar. The Forum's style reflects Augustus' view that in all the arts the Greeks had achieved perfection in the classical style. All this served to establish Augustus as the greatest among *summi viri*, or the greatest "among all the great men of Roman history."[5]

Finally, we turn to a "jewel" of Augustan classicism, the *Ara Pacis*, or Altar of Peace (Fig. **4.31**). It is representative of a movement toward a saturating symbolism, in which every detail was intended to convey meaning. Here, even apparently decorative elements are symbolic:

4.31 *Ara Pacis* (Altar of Peace), Rome, 13–9 B.C. Marble. Outer wall about 34 ft 5 ins × 38 × 23 ft (10.5 × 11.6 × 7 m).

CHAPTER FIVE

JUDAISM AND EARLY CHRISTIANITY

AT A GLANCE

The People of Israel
The Patriarchs
The Ten Commandments
Conquest and the Judges
The United Monarchy
The Divided Kingdom and Exile
The Post-exilic Period and Beyond
  PROFILE: Solomon
The Hebrew Bible
Jewish Art and Architecture
  MASTERWORK: The Temple of Jerusalem

Christianity
  OUR DYNAMIC WORLD: Shinto Sculpture in
    Japan
Jesus Christ and His Teachings
The Apostolic Mission
The Early Christian Church

Christianity and the Late Roman Empire
Diocletian and Constantine
The Barbarians

Late Roman and Early Christian Art
The Visual Arts and Architecture
Literature
Music
  TECHNOLOGY: Matches

**Synthesis: St Paul and the
  Westernization of Christianity**

5.1 The apse, S. Apollinare in Classe, c. A.D. 540–7. Ravenna, Italy.

A CRITICAL LOOK

At this point in our journey we must halt our forward momentum. So far we have been progressing in a more or less chronological fashion, but we must now backtrack, because during the Roman Imperial period, a different heritage—the Judeo-Christian—made a new and significant impact on Rome and on Western civilization. Judaism was already an important religion and culture in the Mediterranean, but out of it came a new religion, Christianity, whose spread throughout the Roman Empire profoundly changed the course of Roman and European history. To understand Judaism and Christianity, we must return to the Middle East, some two thousand years before Augustus Caesar, and work our way forward again.

Who were the central people in the history of Judaism, and what were their contributions?

What are the three parts of the Hebrew Bible, and what are their contents?

What did the Temple of Solomon look like, and what was its importance to Judaism?

In Chapter 2 we encountered a Semitic people who occupied part of Mesopotamia and interacted with the peoples of that ancient world, but there is much more to the story of Israel than that brief glimpse allows. The story of Israel is an unbroken chain of development from which came a new religion and perhaps the most fundamental force in the shaping of the Western world—that is, Christianity. Christianity overlaps the Roman Empire, and at the time that the Empire was in its nadir, Christianity was in its ascent. In actual terms, Christianity and the Roman Empire overlapped for nearly five hundred years, but it was not until the late third century that, as strong forces,

they intertwined significantly. Thus, it is now appropriate that in our chronological development of Western culture, we take up the subject of the final years of the Roman Empire and the development of Christianity.

In order to do so, however, we must backtrack not only through the previous three centuries of Rome to the Caesar Augustus who appointed King Herod of Judea and ordered all the world to be taxed, thus bringing Joseph and a pregnant Mary to Bethlehem, but also through history to a time in the second millennium B.C. when the "father of nations," Abraham, began a chain of events that led to Judaism, Christianity, and Islam.

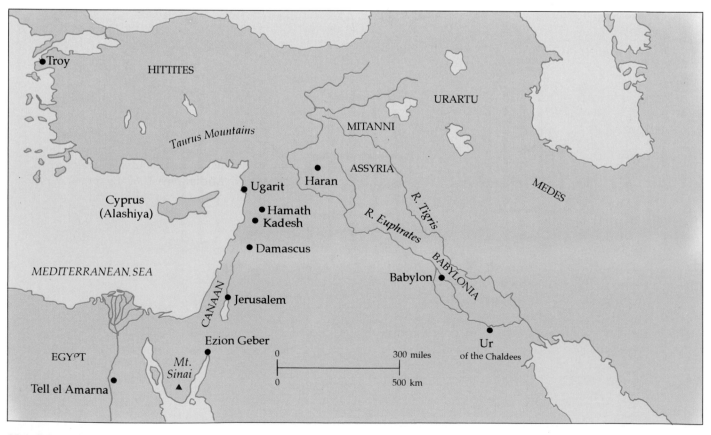

Map 5.1 Lands of the Bible.

THE PEOPLE OF ISRAEL

THE PATRIARCHS

ABRAHAM

The ancestors of Israel were semi-nomadic peoples from Mesopotamia. The Israelites traced their history back to a patriarch named Abram (later Abraham) who lived in "Ur of the Chaldees" in the second millennium B.C.

Abram took his wife and household from the heathen environment of Haran and traveled to Canaan. Canaan held a particular spiritual appeal to Abram, because he believed that the land there was suitable for the fulfillment of a destiny to which he had been appointed by God. Canaan was a secluded hill country, which made it possible for Abram and his people to practice their religion in relative peace and isolation. On the other hand, Canaan lay quite close to important trade routes of the ancient world, and was thus in a good position for spreading the new religion (Map **5.1**). Because they came from the other side of the Euphrates, Abram and his family were known as Hebrews, from a word meaning "the other side." Abram had a son, Isaac, through whose line of descent God's promises were seen to continue. As a boy, Isaac was nearly sacrificed by Abram at God's command (Fig. **5.2**).

MOSES

During the reign of Pharaoh Thothmes III, there arose a national liberator named Moses. During one particularly

5.3 Miniature from the *Golden Haggadah* (Spanish), fourteenth century. The Jews are portrayed leaving Egypt "with a high hand"—a Hebrew expression meaning "triumphantly," but here illustrated literally. British Museum, London.

cruel oppression, the Pharaoh ordered the slaughter of all Hebrew children. To avoid this, the mother of the infant Moses made a basket of bulrushes and set the baby afloat in the Nile near where Pharaoh's sister bathed. The princess found the baby, adopted him, and brought him up in the royal court. However, when Moses killed an Egyptian who was abusing an Israelite, he was forced to flee the country to Midian, east of Egypt, where he became a shepherd and was adopted by the wandering tribes of the area.

One day, while he was tending his flocks in the Sinai wilderness, he came to Mount Horeb, and there heard the voice of God coming from a burning bush that was not consumed by the fire. God ordered him to return to Egypt to deliver his brethren from bondage and lead them to the land of promise. Moses returned to Egypt in approximately 1450 B.C. The enslaved Hebrews soon recognized Moses' message as authentic, but convincing the ruling Pharaoh, Amenophis II, was another matter entirely. However, after a series of divine visitations, known as the ten plagues, Pharaoh's heart was softened and he allowed the people of Israel to depart from Egypt, by biblical reckoning, approximately 1447 B.C. (Fig. **5.3**).

5.2 *The Sacrifice of Isaac.* Mosaic. Beth-Alpha Synagogue.

	GENERAL EVENTS	LITERATURE & PHILOSOPHY	VISUAL ART & ARCHITECTURE	THEATRE & MUSIC
2000 BC	Patriarchs in Canaan			
1700	Jacob's descendants in Egypt			
1300	Exodus, covenant at Sinai	Decalogue		
1200	Invasion of Canaan Period of Judges			
1000	Saul David Solomon		Temple of Solomon (5.7–11)	
900	Divided Kingdom			
800	Isaiah			
700	Fall of Samaria			
600	Destruction of Jerusalem Exile First exiles return			
500	Completion of the Temple			
200	Judea under the Seleucids Maccabean rebellion			
100	Herod the Great Augustus Caesar Jesus Christ			
AD 100	St Paul Emperor Domitian	Synoptic Gospels	*Breaking of Bread* (**5.22**)	
200		Tertullian	Synagogue of Dura-Europos (**5.6**) SS. Pietro e Marcellino (**5.15, 5.23**)	
300	Emperor Diocletian Constantine Theodosius Barbarian invasions Council of Nicea Edict of Milan	St Augustine St Jerome St Benedict New Testament canon	Catacomb painting Baths of Diocletian (**5.25**) Basilica of Constantine (**5.26, 5.27**) St Peter's Basilica (**5.28**) *Good Shepherd* (**5.21**) *Chi-Rho* (**5.18**) Sarcophagus of Bassus (**5.24**)	Christian hymnody
400	Christianity a state religion Fall of Rome		Fuori le Mura (**5.29**)	

Timeline 5.1 Judaism and early Christianity.

Moses led his people from Egypt toward the Sinai wilderness by way of the Red Sea, which they crossed, by a miraculous parting of the waters, near Suez (Fig. **5.4**). Pharaoh had changed his mind, and the Egyptian army was in hot pursuit when they were swallowed up as the sea crashed in upon them. The result of the miracle gave Moses' people a greater sensitivity to divine promise and action and inspired their faith to new heights. The God of their fathers was seen as he who saved them from bondage and would spare them from the hands of their enemies.

THE SELECTION OF ISRAEL

In the third month after their escape from Egypt, the Israelites arrived at Sinai, a burning desert with steep cliffs and volcanic mountains. Here, they made a covenant with their God, Yahweh: He would be their God, and they would be his people. The Sinai covenant had its roots in Yahweh's covenant with Abraham, which, in turn, could be traced to the covenant with Noah, and, thereby, to a framework in which humanity, made in the image of God, must conform to the character

5.4 *Crossing the Red Sea*, c. A.D. 245. Fresco from the synagogue at Dura-Europos. National Archeological Museum, Damascus, Syria.

of God. Because God is a creating God, humankind must also create and work with God in maintaining and developing the work God had committed, in the creation of the world, into human care. Obedience to God must express itself in obedience to his moral law—that is, *justice* and *righteousness*. Thus, the selection of Israel as a people formed an important moment of universal history in the eyes of the Judaic tradition.

Ratification of God's covenant with Abraham came in a covenant with Israel at Sinai, expressed in the giving of the Ten Commandments.

THE TEN COMMANDMENTS
(Deuteronomy 5:6-21)

1. You shall have no other gods before me.
2. You shall not make for yourself a graven image, or any likeness of any thing that is in heaven above, or that is on the earth beneath, or that is in the water under the earth beneath, or that is in the water under the earth....
3. You shall not take the name of the Lord your God in vain....
4. Observe the sabbath day, to keep it holy, as the Lord your God commanded you....
5. Honor your father and your mother....
6. You shall not kill.
7. Neither shall you commit adultery.
8. Neither shall you steal.
9. Neither shall you bear false witness against your neighbor.
10. Neither shall you covet your neighbor's wife... or anything that is your neighbor's.

CONQUEST AND THE JUDGES

Immediately after the exodus from Egypt, neither Israel as a nation nor the nations that occupied the land of Canaan were ready for a Hebrew invasion and conquest. The Egyptian empire was still strong, and the land of Canaan contained several vassal kings of Egypt who were capable of banding together to resist such an invasion. As a people fresh from servitude, the Israelites had not yet progressed to a point of unification and cohesion, but were still an undisciplined, spiritually immature, and fractious group. They therefore wandered in the wilderness of Sinai for forty years, and although the route they took cannot be traced, it was circuitous and subjected them to the privation and hardship of the desert. That time of difficulty hardened Israel into a strong, disciplined nation, with well-inculcated spiritual values.

Under the leadership of Joshua, the people of Israel conquered Canaan and organized themselves into a relatively stable political and religious entity. A period of anarchy followed Joshua's death, and "every man did what was right in his own eyes" (Judges 17:6). Too weak to resist infiltration by bordering tribes, Israelites soon began intermarrying with outsiders and turning away from Yahweh to idolatrous religious practices. To counteract this defection from the covenant, a series of twelve "Judges" arose and set about liberating Israel from her enemies and recalling the nation to the worship of Yahweh. But the judges—for example, Deborah and Gideon—were more local tribal heros than national leaders, and by the time of Samuel, who had emerged as a judge, a new threat had arisen: the Philistines. In a devastating defeat, the Philistines succeeded in capturing the Ark of the Covenant, Israel's most sacred object. The shock of this defeat provided Samuel with the impetus needed to bring about further reforms and to achieve some sense of centralization, which led, in turn, to a great clamor for the appointment of a king. After initial resistance by Samuel and the careful delineation of the powers of the king, Saul was chosen by common consent of the people, and became probably the first constitutional king in history.

THE UNITED MONARCHY

Although he was unable to meet all the demands placed on him, Saul was able to free Israel from the Philistines and to unify the nation. It lay to David, however, to consolidate the monarchy. Samuel chose David as the instrument of Yahweh, and at first David was Saul's comforter and right arm, but he was also immensely popular with the people, which made Saul jealous and vengeful. In the ensuing struggle, David became king, and Israel's golden age began. He unified the tribes of Israel and extended the kingdom from Phoenicia in the west to the Arabian Desert in the east, and from the River Orontes in the north to the Gulf of Aqaba in the south. He ultimately captured the Canaanite stronghold of Jerusalem, where he established a national and religious capital in which his son, Solomon, built the great Temple.

THE DIVIDED KINGDOM AND EXILE

Following the death of Solomon, a dispute over succession split the nation into Northern and Southern Kingdoms, with Jerusalem remaining the capital of the Southern Kingdom. The division left the nation weakened, and in the eighth century B.C. the Northern Kingdom fell to the Assyrians. The period between Solomon and the Assyrian conquest of the Northern Kingdom, which was called Samaria, gave rise to the great prophet Isaiah. Subsequently, the exile and dispersion of the Northern peoples led to their being called the "Lost Tribes of Israel." In 587 B.C. the Babylonians conquered

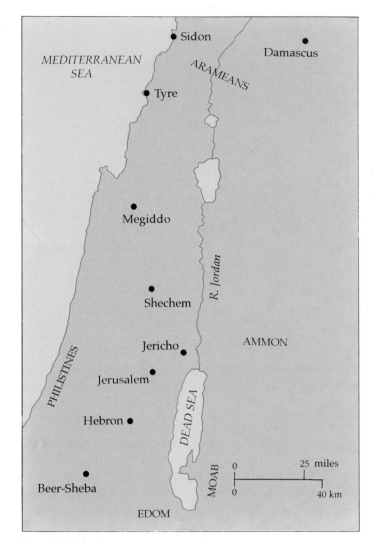

Map 5.2 Palestine.

the Southern Kingdom, now called Judah, destroyed Solomon's Temple, and carried the people into the Babylonian Captivity.

THE POST-EXILIC PERIOD AND BEYOND

At the end of the sixth century, Cyrus the Great led the Persian Empire to dominion in the Middle East. After conquering the Babylonians, Cyrus freed the Jews, as they were now called, and in 538 B.C. the first exiles were able to return from Babylon. In 515 the Temple was rebuilt, and the next hundred years witnessed the building projects and leadership of Nehemiah and Ezra. It was a time of spiritual revival and the renewal of religious rites and practices for the Jews, who believed that their God had rescued them. As a result, they established a theocracy—that is, a government ruled by those who are believed to

PROFILE

Solomon (c. tenth century B.C.)

Solomon, son of David and Bathsheba, ruled Israel for forty years during the second third of the tenth century B.C. In Hebrew the name meant "Yahweh's beloved," as indicated in the biblical book of Second Samuel, chapter 12, verse 25. While David still ruled, he affirmed his commitment to make Solomon his successor. The priest Zadok, with the assistance of the prophet Nathan, installed Solomon as co-regent until David's death, when Solomon's brother Adonijah sought Bathsheba's support in his request to marry Abishag, who had served David in his old age. Regarding this move as a threat, Solomon had Adonijah executed, and others, who were seen as accomplices, were expelled from Jerusalem.

Solomon effected a political consolidation of Israel and created administrative districts that cut across old tribal lines. He also expanded Israel's international affairs, and his empire included trade routes that linked Africa, Asia, Arabia, and Asia Minor. Solomon's political and commercial activities brought much wealth and a cosmopolitan sophistication to the kingdom, and his wisdom "surpassed the wisdom of all the people of the east, and all the wisdom of Egypt" (1 Kings 4:30, Hebrews 5:10). The Bible ascribes seven hundred wives to Solomon, including many whom he undoubtedly married as part of political alliances. Solomon's extensive building program included stone cities as well as fortifications, and in Jerusalem, he built an elaborate palace complex and a temple. His reign brought the promises made to the patriarchs of Israel to fruition. On the other hand, the influx of foreign practices marks the beginning of a religious decay that increased internal dissent and external enemies.

have special divine approval and direction. Although many exiles returned to their homeland, many did not, and these Jews, who remained outside their homeland, became known as Jews of the Diaspora—that is, the Dispersion.

During this time Judaism underwent a series of refinements, which included concerns about the end of the world—that is, eschatology—and prophecies about the coming of God and a day of judgment—that is, apocalypse. They looked for the coming of Messiah, who would lead them and bring peace and justice.

The leadership that descended on Israel came in the form of outside conquerors, however. In 332 B.C. Alexander the Great conquered the region, then in the second century B.C. Judah fell under a series of foreign rulers—for example, the Seleucids—until a brief uprising by the Maccabees under Judas Maccabeus brought a short period of independence around 165 B.C. Within a century, Israel fell under the rule of Rome. In 70 A.D., after an uprising in Jerusalem, the Romans sacked the city and destroyed the Temple. A small band of rebels held off the Romans for two years at a mountain fortress called Massada until it, too, fell in A.D. 73. The destruction of the Temple of Jerusalem meant the destruction of Israel and the Judaic nation.

THE HEBREW BIBLE

The word "bible" comes from the Greek word for book, and it refers to the town of Byblos, which exported the papyrus reed used for making books in the ancient world. The Jews compiled the history of their culture and religion into a collection of sacred writings called scriptures. The compilation grew from the oral traditions of the Hebrew people and took shape over a period of years as it was assembled, transcribed, and verified by state officials and scholars. The Bible has been handed down in a variety of forms. The Hebrew Bible, often called the Masoretic Text (MT), is a collection of twenty-four books written in Hebrew, with a few passages in Aramaic.

The earliest written Bible probably dates to the United Monarchy in the tenth century B.C. It is composed of an assemblage of history, songs, stories, and prophecy. After the Babylonian Captivity, in the fifth century B.C., Jewish religious leaders and scholars carefully scrutinized the body of writings and established a canon—that is, an officially accepted compilation—that was believed to be divinely inspired. The first canon consisted of the Torah or the Pentateuch, the first five books of the current Bible. The current Hebrew Bible was canonized by the Council of Jamnia in A.D. 90. It contained three parts: The Law (Torah), the Prophets, and the Writings.

During the Hellenistic period major centers of

Judaism existed in Syria, Asia Minor, Babylonia, and, particularly, in Alexandria, Egypt. Here, the Jewish Canon was translated into Greek and called the Septuagint, meaning "seventy" from the seventy scholars who were supposed to have worked on it.

THE TORAH

The Torah, meaning "the teaching," includes doctrine and practice, religion, and morals. It contains the books of Genesis, Exodus, Leviticus, and Deuteronomy. The commandments, in addition to the Decalogue, were designed

5.5 Joseph (maker, first name), Torah case from Damascus, Syria, 1565. Copper inlaid with silver, 32 ins (81.3 cm) high. Jewish Museum, New York.

to prepare Israel for a holy mission that the nation would be called upon to undertake in order to become "holy unto God." The preparation entails a separation from all that is opposed to the will of God and a dedication to his service. Thus, holiness meant religion and morality. In religion, the holiness of Israel meant abhorring idolatry and its associated practices, such as human sacrifice, sacred prostitution, divination, and magic. It also meant adopting a cult and ritual that were ennobling and elevating. In morals, holiness meant resisting the urges of nature that were self-serving and adopting an ethic in which service to others lay at the center of life. Consequently, the Torah, as given to Israel, prescribes two sets of laws that connect religion and morality—that is, belief and practice. In their positive nature, they are intended to carry a dynamism that can transform individuals and, therefore, societies. Disregard of the law, thus, becomes not an individual but a social offense.

Fundamental to moral law in the Torah are the two principles, mentioned earlier, of justice and righteousness. These lie at the heart of humankind's creative cooperation with God. Justice meant the recognition of six fundamental rights: the right to live; the right of possession; the right to work; the right to clothing; the right to shelter; and the right of the person, which includes the right to leisure and liberty and the prohibition to hate, avenge, or bear a grudge. Righteousness manifested itself in the acceptance of duties—for example, concern for the poor, the weak, and the helpless, whether friend or foe—and although possession of earthly goods was a right, it was also a divine trust.

The Torah constitutes the uniqueness of the religion of Israel (Fig. **5.5**). The distinct approach of the Torah to the conduct of human behavior is by way of the heart. It speaks to the mind concerning duties, but applies itself to the heart in terms of the perversities of vices and evil. Torah embraces all of life and, thus, becomes a means for strengthening the supremacy of holy will and bringing all life into relationship with serving God.

THE PROPHETS

The Prophets include the Former Prophets—that is, Joshua, Judges, Samuel, Kings—and the Latter Prophets—that is, Isaiah, Jeremiah, Ezekiel, and the twelve minor prophets. These books record the history of Israel and Judah and further develop Hebrew concepts of God, his nature, and the Hebrews' relationship to him. They tell the story of the conquest of Canaan, the Judges, and the United Monarchy, and describe the development of the theocratic state in the post-Babylonian Captivity period. Of course, this is more than history. The prophets speak with the authority of God. We tend to think of the word prophet as one who predicts the future, but such was not the case with the Hebrew prophets. The Prophets did speak of a coming time of peace and justice when Messiah came, but their principal message was one of reconciliation of the Hebrew people with their God. The prophets called upon the people of Israel to return to the ways of the covenant with God and pointed out exactly how they had fallen short of the expectations of that covenant. In a sense, the prophets were social critics. They admonished the people of Israel to remember the Law, which requires justice and decent treatment of the poor, and called on them to turn away from the self-indulgences of the current generation and to return to the compassionate behavior called for in the Torah.

Unlike the Levites—that is, the priestly tribe—whose divine function came as a result of their birth into the tribe of Levi, prophets were individuals called directly by God to preach his word to the nation. The life of a prophet was not an easy one, and prophets like Isaiah often resisted their initial calling. Accepting God's prophetic ministry often meant a violent death—railing against contemporary practice has never been popular.

THE WRITINGS

The writings, which contain a variety of literary forms, including poetry and apocalyptic visions, are made up of the biblical books of Psalms, Proverbs, Job, Song of Songs, Ruth, Lamentations, Ecclesiastes, Esther, Daniel, Ezra, Nehemiah, and Chronicles. The story of Job, for example, tells the story of a righteous man who is beset with calamity so that God can show Satan how a truly righteous man will respond to adversity. Satan maintains that a good man like Job is good only because he is blessed. Take away his comfort and he will curse God. The tale, like many, illustrates the qualities of righteous behavior more than it details the nature of God—although that is present as well. In the book of Ruth we learn of the qualities of love, devotion, and loyalty: "Where you go, I will go. And where you lodge, I will lodge. Your people shall be my people, and your God, my God; where you die, I will die, and there I will be buried. May the Lord do so to me and more also if even death parts me from you" (Ruth 1:16–17).

JEWISH ART AND ARCHITECTURE

VISUAL ART

The biblical injunction against graven images means that there is little significant Jewish sculpture or painting. Occasionally, however, the injunctions were relaxed sufficiently to allow decoration, and the assembly hall wall of the synagogue at Dura-Europos is one such example

(Fig. **5.6**). Dating to approximately A.D. 250, this richly detailed account tells the history of the Chosen People and their covenant with the Lord, and is an attempt to put into pictures the traditions previously restricted to words. Unlike most paintings, there appears to be no unifying relationship among the details of this decoration. Animals, humans, buildings, and cult objects are all exquisitely portrayed, but we find nothing that would tell us how they relate to each other. It is as if the artist assumed that the viewer would understand how these objects coalesce. Nevertheless, if the meaning is hidden, the execution is explicit, and we can find pleasure in the luster of the execution and the sophisticated depiction of details. Although it is less naturalistic than the Roman wall decoration we have previously examined, these depictions reveal a concern with PLASTICITY—that is, three-dimensional space. Human and animal forms are shaded and detailed in such a way as to give fullness to form and a sense of action and character.

5.6 *The Sacrifice of Conon*, from the assembly hall of the synagogue at Dura-Europos. A.D. 245–256. Mural. National Museum, Damascus, Syria.

MASTERWORK

The Temple of Jerusalem

The Temple of Jerusalem was the symbol of Israel's faith as early as its third king, Solomon, son of David (c. 1000 B.C.). Described in 1 Kings 5–9 the Temple of Solomon was primarily the house of the Lord God—Yahweh—as opposed to a place to which common people came to worship. In fact, the general populace had access to only the Temple courts and not to the inside of the structure itself. Even the clergy did not have free access to the building. The inner sanctum remained off limits to everyone except the chief priest, and to him only on the Day of Atonement. Although the public did not have access to the Temple, it was very much a public building in all senses, including politically and economically. Ancient Israel, although a monarchy, remained a theocracy, and the Temple played an important role in the organization and administration of the national community.

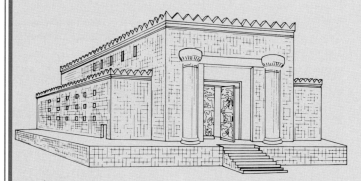

5.7 Reconstruction drawing of Solomon's Temple. The significance of the two bronze pillars is uncertain, but some scholars suggest that they may have represented the twin pillars of fire and smoke that guided the Israelites during their wanderings in the desert after the Exodus from Egypt.

5.8 Ground plan of the Temple of Solomon.

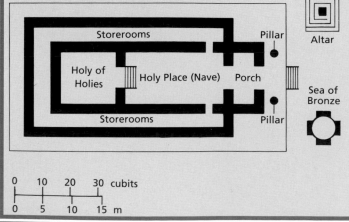

Two major rebuilding projects took place between its construction under Solomon and its ultimate destruction by the Romans in A.D. 70 (Fig. **5.9**), and we often find reference to the First, Second, and Third Temples. The Temple of Solomon is the First Temple, and we know it primarily from the description in 1 Kings 6-8 and a parallel account in 2 Chronicles 2–4. No trace of the first Jerusalem Temple exists archeologically. The basic shape of the Jerusalem Temple (Figs. **5.7** and **5.8**) was a rectangle subdivided laterally into three sections, each with the same interior width—20 cubits. The building was 60 cubits long and 30 cubits high. A cubit equals approximately 20.9 inches (53 centimeters), the Temple was, therefore, approximately 105 feet (32 meters) long, 35 feet (10.7 meters) wide, and 52 feet (15.8 meters) high. These are internal measurements given in 1 Kings, but the biblical book of Ezekiel gives a different set of dimensions—100 by 50 cubits—but these are probably external dimensions and include subsidiary rooms built around the Temple.

The Temple stood on a 6-cubit-high platform with a dominating entrance of huge wooden doors flanked by two bronze pillars, 18 cubits high, situated at the top of the ten stairs. The doors were decorated with carved palms, flowers, and cherubim—that is, guardian winged beasts sometimes shown with human or animal faces. To enter the Temple, one passed through the first of its three sections, variously referred to as a "vestibule," "porch," "portico," or "entrance hall." The second section of the Temple was its main or largest room, measuring 40 by 20 cubits and reaching a height of 30 cubits. The Hebrew word *hikhal* or *hekal* means that this room—the Temple's largest—was a "great house" or "holy place," and it signifies that the Temple was the "house of the Lord," an earthly dwelling place of the deity. A large, elaborate cypresswood doorway carved with cherubim and palm trees and overlaid with gold provided entry. Walls paneled with cedarwood exhibiting rich floral carvings had small rectangular windows at the top, through which light entered the space. In the room itself were various sacred furnishings—ten large golden lampstands, an inlaid table for priestly offerings, and a cedarwood altar covered with gold.

From a staircase behind the altar one entered the Holy of Holies, the most sacred part of the Temple.

5.9 Destruction of the Temple, a detail from the Arch of Titus, showing the menorah procession, A.D. 81. Marble, arch 47 ft 4 ins (14.43 m) high. Rome.

This was a windowless cubicle, 20 by 20 by 20 cubits, which contained the Ark of the Covenant, the symbol of God's presence, that the Jews had carried with them from the wilderness. The Ark was flanked by two large cherubim.

The symbolic nature of the Temple as a residence for God went beyond providing assurance to the Israelites that God was with them. Construction of the Temple was anticipated by David, who brought the Ark of the Covenant to Jerusalem and began assembling materials. Solomon gave great priority to completing the Temple. He assembled an enormous work-

5.10 The third (Herod's) Temple, 20 B.C. (reconstruction). Jerusalem, Israel.

5.11 Reconstruction of the third Temple.

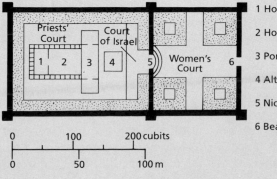

1 Holy of Holies

2 Holy Place (Nave)

3 Porch

4 Altar

5 Nicanor Gate

6 Beautiful Gate

force and completed the job in a remarkably short time: seven years.

Construction of the Temple coincided with the institution of the monarchy and the emergence of Israel, for the only time in its existence, as an independent and dominant political power in the region. Thus, the Temple symbolized not only the presence of the Lord God, but also Israel's very national identity.

The Temple was extended extravagantly by Herod beginning c. 20 B.C. (Fig. **5.11**), a reconstruction of which can be seen in Jerusalem (Fig. **5.10**).

MUSIC

References to music and dance occur frequently in the Jewish scriptures. Genesis 4:21 refers to those who play the "lyre and the pipe." In Exodus 15:20-21:

> Miriam the prophetess, the sister of Aaron, took a timbrel in her hand; and all the women went after her with timbrels and with dances.

And Miriam answered them, Sing ye to the Lord, for he hath triumphed gloriously; the horse and his rider hath he thrown into the sea.

The musicianship of David is documented in 1 Samuel 16:23. When King Saul was tormented, "David took the lyre and played it with his hand; so Saul was refreshed, and was well, and the evil spirit departed from him."

CRITIC REVIEW below

A CRITICAL REVIEW

Judaism followed a challenging course from the Patriarchs through the Judges to the Monarchy. The story is one of a people to whom God revealed himself, with whom he made a covenant, and whom he led to nationhood. The story centers on the constant struggle of humankind to follow its own dictates rather than those of a divine being, even one who performed mighty acts to show his power and his steadfast love of his chosen people. Although the creator of the universe was their king, the Hebrews clamored for a king of their own—a human king—and thus arrived the monarchy. There is much to find in the story of the Hebrews about theology and the emergence of monotheism, about the nature of revealed truth, about human obstinacy and self-will, and about the consequences of disobedience.

What does the word Diaspora mean, and how does it relate to Jewish history and religious thought?

Using two of the text illustrations as reference, describe how Jewish art and architecture reflect the tenets of Old Testament religion.

A CRITICAL LOOK

The study of Christianity has always centered on its mysterious central figure. In recent years, efforts have been made to draw conclusions about Jesus as an historical figure—a person—as opposed to the divine status he occupies in Christianity. In the next section, we will look at Jesus Christ and his teachings, at the fundamental characteristics of Christianity, and of the amazing spread of Christianity throughout the Roman Empire. In particular, we aim to: examine the relationship between Judaism and Christianity, especially the concept of the revelation of God to humankind; describe the core of Jesus Christ's message; and discover how the Apostles spread Christianity. This study will bring us back to the time in history we left at the end of Chapter 4.

Who were the early leaders of Christianity and what was the focus of their thoughts about the Church and the soul?

How did the reforms and actions of Diocletian and Constantine rejuvenate the late Roman Empire and affect the spread of Christianity?

Explain how Rome fell to the barbarians.

CHRISTIANITY

CRITICAL LOOK above

Rooted in Judaism's post-exilic Messianic hopes, Christianity arose in what its central personage and its later believers professed was God's intervention in human history to establish a new covenant to supplant the covenant established with Moses. Jesus of Nazareth was the Christ—Messiah. As Christianity spread through the Roman world after the death of Jesus, Christology became an important and divisive issue among Christians. Exactly what was the nature of Jesus Christ: Man or God or some combination? And what was the relationship of God, Christ, and the Holy Spirit, about whom Jesus preached? These and other fundamental concepts brought Judaism, Rome, and the Western world together in a manner that has shaped humankind in the two thousand years since.

OUR DYNAMIC WORLD

Shinto Sculpture in Japan

Unlike the monotheism of Judaism, Shinto, or Way of the Gods, Japan's indigenous religion, was a polytheistic nature cult without dogmas, scriptures, or images. What little we know of its development comes from burial practices. In the Kofun period, between the fourth and seventh centuries A.D.—at the same time as the late Roman Empire—the graves of rulers were surrounded by moats and topped by huge burial mounds. One burial site near Osaka covers nearly 277 acres (112 hectares) in area and rises to a height of 110 feet (33.5 meters). Around the tombs, Shinto devotees erected terracotta tubes called *haniwa*. These stood 2 feet (61 centimeters) tall and were topped with human figures or heads or figures of animals. Such figures are unique to Japan. Tradition indicates that they were substitutes for real humans who at one time had been slaughtered at the chieftain's funeral. The figure shown in Figure **5.12** reveals a highly stylized approach, much like the votive statues from Tel Asmar in Mesopotamia, but instead of widely expressive eyes, this figure's eyes are nothing more than slits. Nonetheless, the expressiveness in the facial features contrasts with the emotionless eyes and mouth. There is absolutely no attempt to portray anatomically correct details—the arms round smoothly from the shoulders like the handles on a vase—and whatever skill the maker may or may not have had appears irrelevant. These arms are not intended to look like arms, and the same may be said of the legs. However blousy the costume of the day may have been, there is no attempt to depict it accurately. The effect is one of exaggeration and stylization, done for visual effect. As in the pictograms of Japanese writing, the ebbing and flowing of curvilinear line is more important than attention to anatomy, although the bowed legs do create a curious center of attention. Unlike the carefully detailed naturalism of Roman wall painting and sculpture, Shinto sculpture of the period shows a logical simplicity that draws attention to materials and overall form rather than on internal compositional particulars. The overall effect reveals a love of rustic simplicity that is characteristic of Shinto, which eventually developed into the most sophisticated of aesthetic cults in Japan.

5.12 *Haniwa* figure, c. A.D. 300–600. Terracotta, c. 2 ft (61 cm) high. Musée Guimet, Paris.

JESUS CHRIST AND HIS TEACHINGS

What we know of Jesus Christ comes from later writings called the gospels, the first four books of the New Testament of the Christian Bible. Jesus' early life remains unknown. The gospel of St Matthew includes a long genealogy tracing Jesus' ancestry to King David, and provides a number of stories about Jesus' birth, the Wise Men, the flight to Egypt, the slaughter of the innocents, the return to Israel, and the residence in Nazareth, but these provide few details of Jesus' life. In the gospel of St Luke (Fig. **5.13**) we find a poetic narration of the birth and connection between Jesus and John the Baptist through their mothers, Mary and her cousin Elizabeth, and we find historical figures such as King Herod, Caesar Augustus, Quirinius, governor of Syria, and a specific reference to Caesar's "first" enrollment. Correlating Herod's actual death in 4 B.C., Augustus' reign, and Jesus' birth story, and accommodating changes and corrections to the calendar that have occurred since, we get a birth date for Jesus at somewhere around 4 B.C.

With the exception of the story of Jesus in the Temple as a youth, no further information is available about him until he began his public ministry when he was thirty years old. The gospel of St Mark is vague about whether Jesus was a carpenter—the reference could apply to Joseph, his father—and although he appears to have been a "teacher," no indication exists of his formal education. He had close associations with women, which would

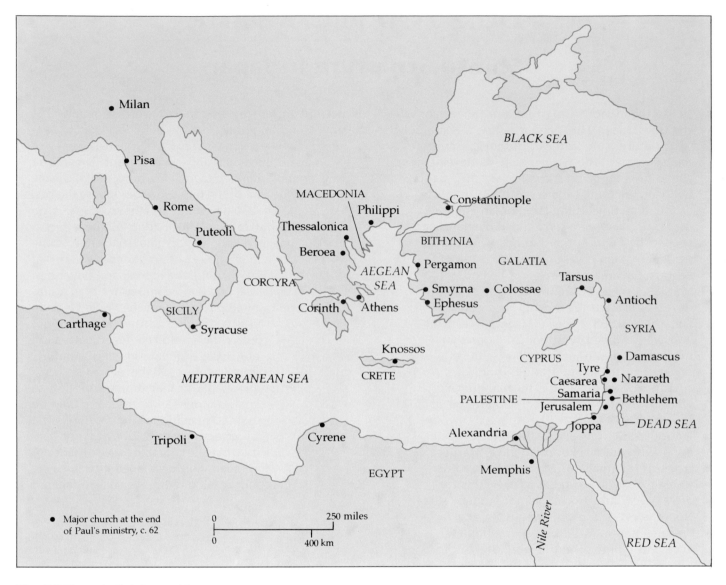

Map 5.3 The early Christian world.

have been unusual for a Jewish teacher at that time, and we conclude that he must have had a relatively normal and typical home life in his formative years.

The actual beginnings of Jesus' ministry are also vague. He was baptized by John the Baptist, whom the gospels portray as a harbinger of Jesus, and he shared John's message that the people of Israel must "repent" and return to the ways of God. During his ministry, Jesus called twelve disciples to share his teaching and healing ministry. The symbolic link with the twelve tribes of Israel undoubtedly was intentional.

The core of Jesus' teaching was the Kingdom of God. Although the significance of the Kingdom with regard to human activity is strong, Jesus used the symbol as a means for revealing God himself. Through it, Jesus evokes God's active involvement in saving humankind and in establishing a reign of justice and peace. Above all, it

reveals God's steadfast love and grace, which is offered to humankind without precondition. One of the most interesting aspects of this complex teaching is the step it takes away from conventional Jewish thought in regard to the judgment of God on the human race—the end of the world or the Time of Tribulation in Jewish theology—which it says has already begun. The central focus of Jesus' ethic is love, based on the Judaic commandment: "Thou shalt love the Lord thy God with all thy heart, soul, mind, and strength, and thy neighbor as thyself." The call for repentance, like that of the Old Testament prophets, presupposes that there is a tremendous distance between God and the daily life of his people. Hence, the need to repent, not just to polish up a few sinful acts, but to have a fundamental change of heart.

The gospels portray Jesus as a teacher, miracle worker, and friend of sinners (Fig. **5.14**). He goes out of his way to associate with the poor, the downtrodden, and the socially unacceptable. His ministry proclaims that such people, not the righteous, are the special objects of God's love and care.

Jesus' message was revolutionary—it drew the ire especially of the Jewish religious establishment, and the Romans who occupied Palestine had no sympathy for him. What he said and did—while not illegal either by Jewish or Roman standards—were cause for concern because they created unrest in the population. That, in first century Palestine, was dangerous, and the political authorities misunderstood Jesus' teaching and his motives and decided that he should be put to death. Pontius Pilate, the Roman procurator, wanted to take no risks on the issue and went along with the Jewish authorities. Jesus was arrested, interrogated by both Jewish and Roman authorities, condemned, and—in the Roman custom—crucified with other criminals on a hill called Golgotha (the place of the skull) outside the city of Jerusalem.

All four gospels indicate that on the third day after his death, Jesus rose from the dead and, at various times, appeared to his disciples—not as a spirit, but in a solid

5.14 Christ as Pantocrater, Kariye Church, Istanbul, Turkey.

body—before ascending into heaven. The resurrection becomes for Christians not only a miracle, but also God's redeeming act in the salvation of the world.

THE APOSTOLIC MISSION

Christianity spread principally because Jesus commanded his followers to carry on his commission from God. In the Synoptic Gospels—Matthew, Mark, and Luke—the charge is direct. After the Resurrection, Jesus appears to the disciples and tells them: "All authority in heaven and on earth has been given to me. Go therefore and make disciples of all nations, baptizing them in the name of the Father and of the Son and of the Holy Spirit, teaching them to observe all that I have commanded you" (Matthew 28:18a-20a). Implicit in this commission is the assumption that the Way, as the followers called themselves immediately after the resurrection, would spread beyond the confines of Judaism and include the Gentile world as well. Within a generation, the new name, Christian, had appeared, and an organized movement with appointed leaders took shape.

Critical to the spread of Christianity was its own written canon. Serious questions about exactly who Jesus was

5.13 St Luke, from the presumed St Augustine Bible, sixth century. Corpus Christi College, Cambridge, England.

5.15 *St Peter*, third-century A.D. wall-painting from a catacomb of SS. Pietro e Marcellino, Rome.

and what the faith entailed needed to be settled, and divisions within early Christianity were many. The Bible of the earliest Christians was the Old Testament—the Jewish Canon—and this was supplemented in Christian worship by oral apostolic accounts of the words of Jesus, interpretations of his person, and significance for the life of the Church. This was soon to change.

The books of the New Testament, which were later adopted as the Christian canon, were written within a period of less than one hundred years. They fall into four different literary forms. Four of them are "Gospels" because they tell the "good news" of Jesus Christ. Church history occurs in the Acts of the Apostles, which is an account of the spread of the Christian faith during the first thirty years after the Resurrection. Twenty-one of the books are letters written to various churches and individuals by the early evangelists. The last book of the New Testament (the book of Revelation) is an apocalypse—that is, a revelation of God's will for the future.

The earliest of the four gospels was written by John Mark around the year A.D. 70. According to tradition, John Mark was a disciple of the Apostle Peter (Fig. **5.15**). The

Gospels of Matthew and Luke use Mark as a source (each appeared ten to twenty years later than Mark), and because they have so much in common, they are called the Synoptic Gospels—from the Greek word *synopsis*, a seeing together. Unlike the Synoptics, which tell mainly of Jesus' public teaching and ministry, the Gospel according to John contains information concerning Jesus' early Judean ministry and extensive discussions with the disciples about the union of the Church with Christ. None of the parables of the Synoptics appear in John.

Much of basic Christian theology emerges from the letters section of the New Testament. Probably the most important promulgator of Christian thought was the apostle Paul, who shaped the eastern tone of Judaic Christianity into the logical, intellectual patterns of the Greek-thinking world of the Roman Empire.

The book of Revelation, or Apocalypse, closes the Christian scriptures, and its last chapters portray the fulfillment toward which the entire biblical message of redemption is focused. It contains powerful poetic imagery that appeals to the imagination. It represents a vision of its author, whose name was John. Probably, parts of the book were written before the fall of Jerusalem in A.D. 70, but the book apparently achieved its final form on the rocky island of Patmos, to which the author had been exiled by the Emperor Domitian (A.D. 81–96). Over the centuries the Revelation to John has proved to be one of the most difficult and inspiring representations of God ever written.

THE EARLY CHRISTIAN CHURCH

Like most emerging religions, Christianity felt an intense need to create institutions. Christianity was loosely organized and totally different in its theology from the religions around it. It needed a united front in order to grow and to make its way in a suspicious, pagan world. In the first centuries of its existence, Christians had shed each other's blood as various sects battled over questions of dogma, and this had to stop if the Church were to survive. In the thrust and counterthrust of all this, however, the emerging Church was a force coming together in a world that was mainly falling apart.

Why and how did Christianity survive? Its monotheism was an extension of the Jewish heritage. The historical immediacy of its founder and the doctrines he taught appealed to men and women of the late Roman and post-Roman periods. In its extreme simplicity on the one hand and its subtlety on the other, Christianity had a multifaceted appeal that made it acceptable to the most lowly and illiterate people as well as those of sophistication and schooling.

Little is known about the spread of Christianity through the Roman Empire. Conversions among the aristocracy and upper classes enhanced its chances of survival substantially, and by the end of the third century, Christians were numerous enough to count as a political force. Every city of consequence had a Christian community presided over by a bishop who was assisted by priests and deacons. Regarded as successors of the original apostles, bishops were chosen by their communities, and theological disputes were decided in councils of bishops.

Christianity encountered varying degrees of tolerance from the Roman state. In general, the Imperial government treated all the various religious practices in its diverse empire with an even hand. Occasionally, however, Christians suffered fierce persecution, mainly because they refused to worship the emperor as a divine being. In addition, their secret meetings and rites troubled the authoritarian government. Christians also abhorred violence and refused to serve in the Roman army, which was very difficult for the beseiged state to tolerate.

As we shall see, the last great persecution occurred under Diocletian in 303. Shortly afterward, Constantine transformed Christianity into a favored religion in the Roman state. According to the bishop Eusebius, Constantine reported that he had had a dream prior to the Battle of Milvian Bridge against his co-ruler, the tetrarch Maxentius, in which he was told to send his soldiers into battle carrying standards marked with Christian symbols. Constantine did so, won the battle, and was converted to Christianity. He later claimed that he was "brought to the faith by God to be the means of the faith's triumph." Christianity soon became the official religion of the empire.

Numerous privileges came with this new status. The Church could receive legacies, its clergy were exempt from taxation, and bishops were permitted to settle disputes of law in all civil cases in which a Christian was a party. In addition, the Church obtained the rights of sanctuary for its buildings—that is, they became places where a criminal was safe from arrest or punishment.

After Constantine's conversion, the Church began to build up its own administration, adopting a structure similar to that of the civil bureaucracy. By the fourth century, each province was divided into bishoprics, with an archbishop at its head. There was, however, no centralized administration for the whole Church comparable to the Imperial government. The bishops of the four great cities of Rome, Jerusalem, Antioch, and Alexandria claimed special privilege because the Church in each of those cities was founded by the apostles. Rome claimed supremacy both because it was founded by St Peter, to whom Jesus had entrusted the building of the Church, and because it was capital of the empire.

Yet the opportunities presented by the conversion of emperors to Christianity were to some extent offset by problems that stemmed from the same source. In return for championing the faith, the emperor expected the bishops to act as loyal servants of the Imperial crown. When theological disputes arose, the emperor often insisted on deciding the matter himself. For example, in the fourth century, the Arianist controversy broke out over the nature of the Son in the Christian Trinity of Father, Son, and Holy Spirit. In an attempt to quell the controversy, a new institution of Church government was established— the General Council. When the Council met in Nicea in 325, at its first convocation, it agreed on the doctrine that the Son was "of one substance with the Father." The issue of Jesus' divinity or humanity continued to flare up over the reigns of successive emperors—Constantine I, Constantius II, and, finally, Theodosius I, whose Council of Constantinople in 381 reaffirmed the doctrine of Nicea and put the issue to rest.

THE POPES

References to the primacy of Rome can be found as early as the letters of St Ignatius in 110 and St Irenaesis around 185. The claim of the medieval popes to exercise complete authority over all of Christendom was developed slowly, however. The bishops of Rome claimed supremacy because they were the heirs of St Peter and because their city was the capital. Other arguments included the sanctification of Rome by the blood of martyrs and its freedom from the contamination of the heresies that had touched other churches. Specific acknowledgement of Rome's supremacy by a Church Council first came in 344 from the Council of Sardica. The Council of Constantinople placed the bishop of Constantinople second after the bishop of Rome "because Constantinople is the New Rome." A series of strong and able bishops of Rome consolidated the move toward Rome's supremacy during the next century.

The argument put forward by the bishops of Rome in support of their case came to be known as the "Petrine theory," and perhaps its clearest formulation came from Pope Leo 1 (r. 440–61), a man with considerable administrative ability who played a significant role in civil affairs. Leo was twice called on by the emperor to negotiate with the leaders of the barbarian armies that invaded Italy in 453 and 455. Pope Leo insisted that he was "heir" of St Peter and that "Christ had appointed Peter to be head of the whole universal Church." He affirmed that because all other apostles were subordinate to Peter, all other bishops were subordinate to the bishop of Rome, who had succeeded to Peter's See at Rome. In fact, nearly all Western Christians came to acknowledge the pope of Rome as head of the whole Church. What remained unclear was the actual extent of his authority in temporal affairs and in affairs of Church governance.

EARLY CHRISTIAN THOUGHT

TERTULLIAN AND LEGALISM The study of medieval thought of the first millennium is really the study of Christian thought. In order to understand the men and women of the early Middle Ages—how they might have seen the universe, and how that viewpoint was translated into art—it is important to examine some of early Christian thought. Two of its most important thinkers were Tertullian and Augustine, and our examination focuses on them.

In the early years of the Middle Ages, the West depended for its culture on the East. Its art, literature, and philosophy tended to be derivative rather than original. On the other hand, the prevailing interests of the West differed significantly from those of the East. Reflecting the West's Roman heritage, they concentrated on the functional, practical, and ethical. Law and government, the sovereignty of the state, institutions and tradition, were social preoccupations, and they also affected Western Christianity. The functions and authority of the Church as an institution were of prime importance. Duty, responsibility, sin, and grace were all topics of great interest.

The theistic and cosmological problems that took precedence in the East seem to have caused far less concern in the West. The major theological conflicts occurred in the East, and the West almost automatically accepted the doctrinal decisions of the Eastern Church. In North Africa, however, in the Roman provinces of Africa, Numidia, and Mauritania, Eastern influence was less apparent than in Gaul and Italy. Particularly in the province of Africa, large numbers of Italian colonists had close ties to the provincial capital, Carthage, and thereby to Rome. By 200 Carthage boasted a strong and vital Christian Church, and from this community came Tertullian, the first of the Latin "Fathers."

Tertullian's main contributions to Christian thought lie in two areas. He founded the language of the Western Church, and he enunciated those aspects of its theology that marked a break with the East. His writings were highly influential, and continued to be so even after his defection to Montanism destroyed his standing as a Catholic Father.

Probably the most important of Tertullian's writings is an elaborate analysis of the soul. His arguments lean heavily on Stoicism. He believed that the soul has length, breadth, and thickness, and although it is not identical with the body, it permeates all its parts, with its center lying in the heart. The soul controls the body, using the body as it wills. Yet, the soul remains spiritual, not material. For Tertullian, spirit and matter were two substances, different in nature but both equally real. Spirit, being indivisible, was therefore indestructible.

His notion of God and the Trinity was based on legal concepts. When Tertullian says that God has three parts, he means that God is "three persons in the legal sense, that is, three persons who share or own in common one substance or property."[1] God is a personal sovereign, to whom all people are subject. Independent and omnipotent, God created the world out of nothing. On the question of one's proper relationship to God, Tertullian was precise in defining God as an authority figure whom one approaches with humility and fear. "The fear of man is the honor of God... Where there is no fear there is no amendment... How are you going to love unless you are afraid not to love?" Virtue is thus obedience to divine law springing from fear of punishment if the law is broken. In this and many other areas, Tertullian's legal training is clear. He also formulated an elaborate list of sins, including the seven deadly sins of idolatry, blasphemy, murder, adultery, fornication, false witness, and fraud.

By the time of Tertullian, the Church had begun to see this life as a mere probation for the life to come. Earthly life was without value in itself and possessed meaning only in that it provided the opportunity to lay up rewards in the life beyond the grave. Tertullian believed the supreme virtues were humility and the spirit of other-worldliness, by which Christians could escape the perils of this life and be assured of enjoying the reward prepared for the saints in heaven.

ST AUGUSTINE AND NEO-PLATONISM St Augustine (354–430) did not receive the sacrament of baptism until he was an adult. His mother, who was a Christian, believed that if he were baptized as a child, the healing virtue of accepting the faith would be destroyed by the lusts of youth. Nonetheless, after a period of skepticism, and adherence to Manichaeism—a philosophy that combined Christianity with elements from other religions of the time—he was baptized into the Christian faith. He later became Bishop of Hippo, in Asia Minor. A prolific writer, his works greatly influenced developing Christian thought. The *Confessions* and *City of God* are the best known of his works.

Apparently Augustine found great inspiration in the writings of Plotinus, but he was also highly influenced by Platonic and neo-Platonic thought. He recoiled from Tertullian's emphasis on the senses and the body, but shared Tertullian's belief in intuition as the source of knowledge concerning God, although Augustine's concept of intuition had an intellectual cast. The senses, he believed, give us unreliable images of the truth. Instead, our intuition, our affective thinking, has a certainty which springs from "the fact that it is of the very nature of reason to know the truth."[2] Knowledge is an inner illumination of the soul by God. Whatever we find intelligible is, therefore, certain. Knowledge comes from intuition and "confirms and amplifies the certainty of faith."[3]

Augustine argued that to doubt the existence of the soul is in fact to confirm its existence: in order to doubt we must think, and if we think, we therefore must be thinking beings, and therefore souls. Unlike Tertullian, Augustine thought the soul immaterial, that is, a purely spiritual entity. This spiritual character, as well as its immortality, is demonstrated by our power to grasp eternal and immaterial essences.

His concept of original sin, as developed in *City of God* led Augustine into a central role in the so-called Pelagian heresy. Pelagius and his followers opposed the concept of original sin. The doctrine of original sin, to which Augustine subscribed, held that all people are born to sin because of Adam's fall from grace when he disobeyed God in the Garden of Eden. Thus, we are "punished by being born to a state of sin and death, physical and spiritual, from which only Christ's passion and saving grace can redeem us."

Pelagius rejected the doctrine of original sin. He insisted that sin was purely voluntary and individual, and that it could not be transmitted, for, as he said, "Adam's fall affected neither the souls nor the bodies of his descendants." Every soul enters the world sinless, according to Pelagius, and becomes sinful by individual act. Death is a natural event having nothing to do with the fall. Thus, whereas Pelagius argued that people were bad if they did bad things, Augustine held that people were bad and therefore did bad things. The Pelagian heresy may have gained popularity from its consequences of possible salvation for the unbaptized, including those who had lived before Jesus.

Augustine also attacked the question of predestination and divine foreknowledge—that is, whether God's omniscience robs humans of free will. His conclusion, that free will is not a certainty, influenced many later contributors to the debate, which still continues among Christian theologians today.

Augustine's philosophy of art represents a radical shift from that of Plato and Aristotle, especially in the principles of art evaluation. Plato and Aristotle approach art from political and metaphysical points of view. Augustine approaches the subject from a Christian point of view. Scripture, not philosophy, is his guide. Augustine considers the production and consumption of art to hold the interest for the Church that Plato felt they held for the polis. The Christian and the pagan face the same questions about the function and purpose of art. Augustine, however, finds the answers in a strictly Christian context, in the teachings of scripture and tradition. For him, the answers are found in an understanding of God's relationship with the world, and in the mission of the Church in dealing with art. Augustine untiringly attempted to satisfy the requisites of faith while doing justice to the natural pleasures that art can provide.

Even when the basic conflict is resolved, Augustine still has a problem in the immediate sensuous gratification of art. Although "divine order and harmony" are reflected in nature and to a degree in art, "perceptual objects tie the senses down to earthly things and prevent the mind from contemplating what is eternal and unchanging."[4] Art and beauty are thus guides for the soul. Those arts that depend least upon the senses are the best mirrors of the divine order.

The best teacher of all, however, is scripture. Properly interpreted, scripture provides the most direct knowledge of God's purpose and order, although the arts can contribute to our understanding as well. As long as art agrees with the tenets of faith and reflects the harmony of divine creation, it is justified.

CHRISTIANITY AND THE LATE ROMAN EMPIRE

Christianity spread to Rome early in the first century, brought there by nameless individuals who benefited from the freedom of travel that existed throughout the Empire and were helped by the *Pax Romana*. While the Romans tolerated the Jews—despite their occasional rebellions in Palestine—Christians suffered continuously and, miraculously, grew stronger perhaps because of it.

DIOCLETIAN AND CONSTANTINE

The Roman Empire's crisis of the third century, which we discussed in Chapter 4, ended with the reforms brought about by two emperors, Diocletian and Constantine, who also changed the fortunes of Christianity. Diocletian (r. 284–305) was born in the Balkans and rose to power through the ranks of the Roman army. He was strong-willed, insisting on divine status, and he took the image of emperor to grandiose heights—whenever he was in the presence of his subjects, for example, he separated himself from them by a wall of curtains. His self-image must have reflected the larger-than-life portrait that was necessary for him to cope with all the problems of the far-flung Empire, in which anarchy was rampant, barbarians threatened every border, and the army turned rebellious.

Nonetheless, Diocletian attacked the problems with a creative and organized plan that, eventually—if temporarily—brought some stability and reasonable prosperity. He restructured the empire by installing a Tetrarchy, wherein imperial power was shared among four rulers: two senior Augusti supported by two junior Caesars. Diocletian reformed and strengthened the imperial bureaucracy, reformed taxation to effect greater equality, and attempted to control wages and prices. His most

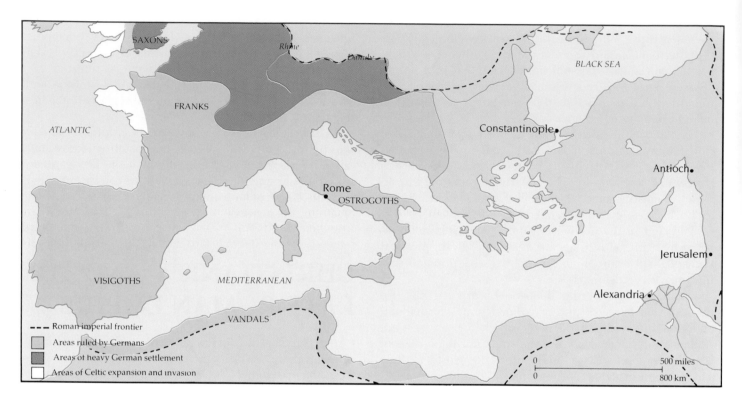

Map 5.4 Europe and North Africa in the late Roman period.

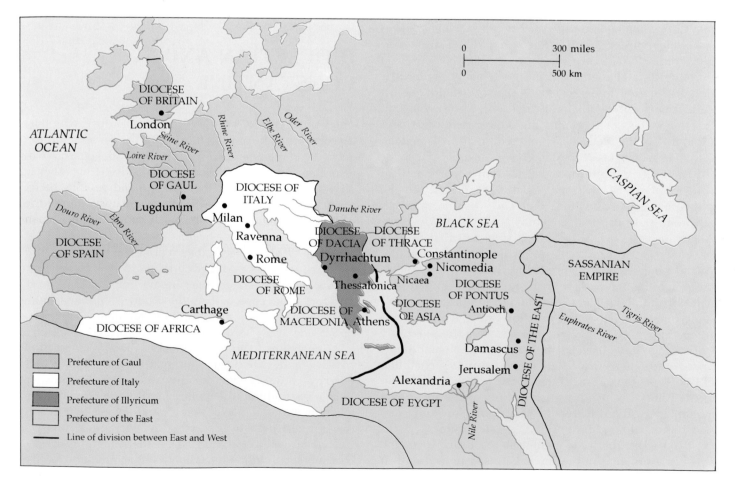

Map 5.5 The Roman Empire in the fourth century.

ambitious undertaking was to split the Empire into two halves, east and west, with each half administered by an Augustus and a Caesar. He also divided the provinces into dioceses. The cumulative effect of splitting the Empire and restructuring the provinces was to centralize the state and to create an awkward and increasingly large class of bureaucrats.

In his last years Diocletian embarked on a major persecution of the Christian church, whose expanding power he regarded as a threat to the hierarchy of the state. The persecution lasted for a period of eight years, extending beyond Diocletian's reign, which ended with his retirement in 305. The persecution, which was given official status by a series of edicts, was intended to eliminate Christianity altogether by forbidding Christians to worship, destroying their churches and books, and arresting their bishops. Anyone suspected of being a Christian was forced to make a sacrifice to the Emperor, which amounted to a repudiation of their faith, and failure to do so was punishable by death. In 311 the persecution ceased. Its purpose had been to stamp out Christianity, but its effect, by creating martyrs, was just the opposite. Christianity won many new converts on the strength of the faith of those who died rather than renounce.

The Tetrarchy collapsed after Diocletian, and a series of civil wars between the tetrarchs broke out. Eventually, Constantine (r. 306–337), son of one of the tetrarchs, fought his way to power as sole emperor of Rome, and carried Diocletian's reforms to even greater lengths. Constantine established two capitals—one in Rome, the other in Byzantium, later named Constantinople in his honor—thereby creating two Roman Empires, one in the West and one in the East. The latter lasted for another thousand years, the former for barely a century.

Constantine arranged an elaborate administrative system, split into four huge imperial prefectures, a dozen dioceses, and 120 separate provinces, which stretched from Britain to Egypt. He separated the civil bureaucracy from the army, which he reformed to strengthen the fron-

tiers, and in order to keep the Empire afloat financially, he levied a series of taxes that had the net effect of reducing many to near-slave status. One group, however, loved Constantine—the Christians. As we noted, he legalized the Christian church in Rome in 313, and it prospered under this new opportunity. Priests could be found in the army, and bishops at the imperial court. Constantine, who saw himself as defender of the faith, undertook an active campaign to increase the flock and to enhance its material welfare. When Constantine moved his capital to Byzantium, he rebuilt the old city as a Christian center, renaming it Constantinople, and filling it with Christian churches and monuments. All the following emperors were Christian, and the faith had an unshakable hold on all levels of society, from peasant to aristocrat, the bureaucracy to the army.

The cumulative effects of the reforms introduced by Diocletian and Constantine enabled Rome to survive for a century, but the benefits of Roman rule had reached a point at which most people in the Empire may well have welcomed the barbarian incursions that were to come.

THE BARBARIANS

The Roman Empire did not fall on a specific date. Throughout the third and fourth centuries, a gradual Germanization of the western provinces accompanied a reciprocal Romanization of the Germanic peoples. The Germanic tribes constantly pressed against the borders of the Empire, occasionally gaining a victory, but only to be pushed back by a fresh contingent of Roman troops. In the far northwest, the Angles and Saxons raided the coasts of Britain. On the lower part of the Rhine River, the Franks fought each other, some allied with Rome and others not. Frankish troops formed the backbone of Roman defenses along the upper Rhine against Germanic peoples there, while Germans defended Roman territory along the Danube. By the end of the fourth century, the Roman

A CRITICAL REVIEW

At this point, you may be asking what religion has to do with the direction in which we have been traveling and with our interest in the arts. Although some may see it differently, the course of Western culture, and especially its arts, from the time of Constantine until the eighteenth century (and perhaps longer) is closely intertwined with that of the Christian Church. Art history and Church history are, in many cases, inseparable. It seems, therefore, that a reasonably developed foray into Judaism and Christianity as major heritages helps us gain a fuller understanding of the cultural and creative expressions that we will examine as the book progresses.

Explain the relevance of the Petrine theory to the development of the Western Church.

Describe how Diocletian and Constantine shaped the late Roman Empire and the spread of Christianity.

A CRITICAL LOOK

We now move back into the stream of history we left at the end of Chapter 4 in order to expand our understanding of the Judaic-Christian tradition, which not only joined with but eventually flooded the Roman Empire, as the two came together. Early Christian and Roman art also began to intermingle, and we will see how the two cultures affected their creative experiences.

What were the primary characteristics of late Roman and early Christian visual art?

How did late Roman architecture utilize space, form, and scale to achieve its ends?

army had, to a large extent, become an army of barbarians, often led by barbarian officers.

Around the beginning of the fifth century, entire populations of Germanic peoples migrated into Roman territories rather than raiding them, and they established permanent settlements. At the same time, the Huns, a Mongolian people—"a race savage beyond all parallel," as one Roman historian put it—turned their attention from the borders of China to the Germanic peoples, and set off a further chain of migrations. The Visigoths, led by their greatest king, Alaric I, rose up in 396 and ravaged Greece. Alaric and the Goths turned on Italy in 402, only to be repulsed by a defending army under a Vandal general. By 406 Roman defenses had deteriorated considerably, and a mixed horde of Germanic peoples, mostly Vandals, surged into the empire and made their way through Gaul into Spain. Capitalizing on the situation, Alaric again attacked Italy and succeeded in sacking Rome itself in 410. He apparently had designs on Africa as well, but died before he could carry out his plans.

CRITICAL
REVIEW
p. 173

LATE ROMAN AND EARLY CHRISTIAN ART

THE VISUAL ARTS AND ARCHITECTURE

VISUAL ART

CRITICAL
LOOK
above

LATE ROMAN ART Roman visual art of the period continued the practice of Augustan times in the celebration of emperors. Diocletian's Tetrarchy was represented in sculptural solidity (Fig. **5.16**), with the figures clasping shoulders to further signify the steadfastness of imperial rule. The figures here are squat and stylized, as opposed to the naturalism of earlier Roman sculpture, although this may partly stem from the need to place this particular piece within the framework of the building to which it is attached, a feature found in later, Romanesque sculp-

5.16 Diocletian's Tetrarchy, fourth century. St Mark's Cathedral, Venice, Italy.

ture. The compactness of the composition does create a sense of solidity and immovability.

The exaggeration of anatomical form for symbolic effect may also be seen in a colossal bust of Emperor Constantine (Fig. **5.17**), a gigantic representation—the head is over 8 feet (2.4 meters) tall—exhibiting a stark and expressive realism that is countered by caricatured, ill-

proportioned intensity. Coming as it does after Diocletian's insistence on being worshipped as divine, the bust represents a returning awareness that people—even Roman emperors—are humans and not gods. Nonetheless, the Empire needed to see its emperor as something large enough to maintain order and prosperity. This likeness is not a portrait of Constantine—it is the artist's view both of Constantine's presentation of himself as Emperor and of the office of Emperor itself.

EARLY CHRISTIAN ART One of the major questions debated by Christians for nearly eight hundred years was whether or not to depict the figure of Christ. The first visual symbols of Christianity were symbolic rather than representational, and they stemmed from the fact that because they were members of a persecuted sect, Christians required some kind of arcane imagery that only they could identify. Perhaps the earliest Christian symbol was the *Chi-Rho* monogram—that is, a combination of the first two letters of the word *Christos* — *XP* —in Greek. We see an artistic elaboration of the sign in Figure **5.18**, which is taken from a fourth-century sarcophagus. The *Chi-Rho* symbol stands at the center of a Roman triumphal wreath and above a cross. Doves, a symbol of the Holy Spirit and a reference to Jesus' baptism by John the Baptist, surround the monogram, which indicates the triumph of Christ over death, as two Roman soldiers, present at the crucifixion sit below.

In addition to the *Chi-Rho*, Christians used a number of other visual symbols—for example, the fish and the lamb. The fish was a rebus—that is, a riddle composed of symbols suggesting the sound of the words they represent. The Greek word for fish, *icthus*, provided the initials for the formula "Jesus Christ Son of God, Saviour." The rebus of two curved, intersecting lines, created a means by which two Christians could secretly identify each other. One would trace a curve in the dirt. The other, if a

5.17 (*left*) Head of Constantine the Great (originally part of a colossal seated statue), A.D. 313. Marble, 8 ft 6³/₈ ins (2.61 m) high. Palazzo dei Conservatori, Rome.

5.18 (*right*) *Chi-Rho* monogram, detail of a sarcophagus, c. A.D. 340. Museo Pio Cristiano, Vatican Museums, Rome.

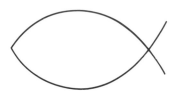

5.19 "The fish" rebus for "Jesus Christ Son of God, Savior." Early Christian symbol.

Christian, would respond to create the sign of the fish (Fig. **5.19**).

The lamb as a symbol referred to the metaphor used by John the Baptist, who described Christ as the "Lamb of God, which taketh away the sins of the world." Christ described himself as the "Good Shepherd" that "giveth his life for his sheep." The symbol of the lamb had been used in pagan art to represent benevolence or philan-

thropy, but it took a new meaning in Christianity and became one of the earliest artistic symbols in the faith (Fig. **5.20**). In this early depiction of the Trinity, the diadem and *chlamys* (a Greek mantle worn pinned at the shoulder) represent Christ the Son, the empty throne represents God the Father, and the dove represents the Holy Spirit. It is probable that in this depiction, the lambs symbolize the classic virtue of beneficence rather than Christ.

The same is true of a beautifully detailed statue entitled *The Good Shepherd* (Fig. **5.21**). According to some scholars, depictions such as this, based on the injunctions we noted earlier, were not supposed to represent Christ but acquired Christian meaning only from their context in Christian tombs. In this particular case, the influence of classical Greek sculpture is clear right down to the Praxitelean "S" curve that forms the axis of the figure. The dress is classic Greek, and the detailing is skillful and

5.21 *The Good Shepherd*, c. A.D. 300. Marble, 36 ins (92 cm) high. Vatican Museums, Rome.

5.22 *The Breaking of Bread*, late second century A.D. Wall painting in the catacomb of Priscilla, Rome.

5.20 The Throne of God as a Trinitarian image, probably Constantinopolitan c. A.D. 400. Marble 65²/₃ × 33 ins (167 × 84 cm). Stiftung Preussisches Kulturbesitz, Berlin-Dahlem, Germany.

5.23 Painted ceiling, fourth century A.D. Catacomb of SS. Pietro e Marcellino, Rome.

naturalistic, with the clothing hanging like real fabric rather than decoration.

The earliest Christian painting is found in the catacombs of Rome. The catacombs served as underground cemeteries, for both Christians and Jews avoided public burial places that were dedicated to pagan deities. In addition, belief in the resurrection of the body meant that early Christians eschewed cremation, which was the norm for ordinary citizens in Rome. Wall paintings similar to that seen in Figure **5.22** often had multiple meanings. This work, which depicts men and women sitting at table with bread and wine, could represent the early Christian "love feast" (*agape*), or it may represent Christ's first miracle—the wedding feast at Cana at which he turned water into wine. The obvious meaning was that of

the sacrament of Holy Eucharist—that is, the re-enactment of the Last Supper.

The catacombs reveal much about early Christian thought and communal spirit. An otherworldly outlook can be seen in the example shown in Figure **5.23** although here, again, the art itself has pre-Christian influences. In this case, the ceiling is divided into compartments, as we witnessed in earlier Roman wall painting (see Fig. **4.4**). However, the artist, who was of only modest ability, translates old forms into new meanings: the great circle represents the dome of heaven inscribed with the cross; the symbol of the good shepherd with a sheep on his shoulders, similar to the statue in Figure **5.21**, adorns the central panel; and the semicircular panels tell the story of Jonah. The standing figures represent members of the Church, their hands raised in prayer for divine assistance.

The spread of Christianity among the ruling classes in Rome gave rise to personal expressions in Christian art, as can be seen in the sarcophagus of Junius Bassus (Fig. **5.24**). Bassus was a prefect of the city of Rome, and his burial vault reflects a carefully designed, classically inspired creation. Two separate, elaborate arcades tell a variety of biblical stories, including those of the Hebrew children in the fiery furnace, the baptism of Christ, and the raising of Lazarus. The composition itself represents a sophisticated intricacy of high artistic quality. In the first place, the figures, although small, are carved with delicate attention to naturalistic detail. They stand away from

5.24 Sarcophagus of Junius Bassus, A.D. 359. Grottoes of St Peter, Vatican Museums, Rome.

the background, creating a sense of deep space between the COLONNETTES, and this gives each scene an individual identity, while the overall composition of the sarcophagus is maintained by the continuing linearity of the upper and lower architrave and the colonnade. Curiously, the heaviest architectural representation is on the top—that is, the post-and-lintel structure of the upper band looks heavier than the alternating arches and pediments of the lower band. One would expect the opposite. The detailing on the colonnettes also reveals the artist's skill. The middle scenes create a central axis, which is balanced by symmetrical treatments on either side. The central axis is identified by pairs of colonnettes, whose detailing differs from the two pairs that flank them. However, in order to create maximum variety and interest, the artist has reversed the angles of diagonal banding on these outer sets of colonnettes.

In addition, the scenes themselves balance thematically. For example, at either end of the lower register, we find an afflicted Job and St Paul being led to execution. These parallel treatments not only represent redemption through suffering but also refer to Christ's suffering for the redemption of humankind. Christ himself occupies the central focal points of both registers. On the bottom, he is shown in his triumphal entry into Jerusalem; on the top, he is enthroned between St Peter and St Paul. The enthronement signifies his regal triumph. Christ's feet rest on a canopy supported by the Roman sky god Coelus.

5.25 *Tepidarium of the Baths of Diocletian*, Rome, c. A.D. 298–305. (Converted by Michelangelo and others into the church of S Maria degli Angeli.)

ARCHITECTURE

By the third century A.D. Rome may have been in decline, but the opposite may be said for the ornateness of its architecture. Opulent buildings with excessive decoration arose throughout the Roman Empire, especially in Egypt, Syria, and Asia Minor, where Hellenistic architectural principles were revised to reflect Roman ideals—for example, axial symmetry (equality of form around a central axis) and logical sequence. Size and scale were the order of the day.

Even though much of the political power of the Empire was moving toward the East, Roman emperors still built their most lavish monuments in Rome. The best examples of Roman monumentality in architecture are the *thermae* or baths, and one of the most grandiose of these is the Baths of Diocletian (Fig. **5.25**). The interior proportions of the tepidarium or hall enclosed over 16,000 square feet (1,486 square meters). The space we see today has been diminished because of a later renovation that converted the building to a church and raised the floor by 7 feet (2.1 meters). In its original form, the tepidarium contained huge openings that made it possible to see into adjacent spaces. The walls and ceilings were covered with mosaics and marble, which reflected light entering the space through high windows, but the renovation replaced the reflective surfaces with plaster

and paint and closed in the openings. Nonetheless, we can appreciate the vastness of this work, which is supported by 50-foot-high (15-meter) columns of Egyptian granite, supported by eight huge concrete piers.

Another building based on the shape of the Roman baths, particularly that of Diocletian, is the Basilica of Constantine, whose scale exceeded even Diocletian's Baths. In its time, it probably was the largest roofed building in Rome (Figs **5.26** and **5.27**) but only the north aisle remains. The three groined vaults covering the NAVE and directing the thrust of force outward to four corners, made it possible to erect upper walls into which openings called CLERESTORY windows could be cut to allow light into the space. Thus, despite its tremendous size, the building must

5.26 Reconstruction drawing of the Basilica of Constantine (after Huelsen).

5.27 The Basilica of Constantine, Rome. c..A.D.310–20.

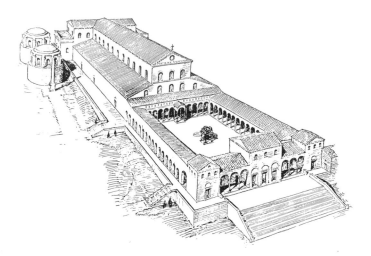

5.28 Old St Peter's Basilica, Rome, c. A.D. 333. Reconstruction by Kenneth J. Conant, Francis Loeb Library, Harvard University, Cambridge, MA.

5.29 Interior of San Paolo Fuori le Mura, Rome, late fourth century A.D. Engraving by Giovanni Battista Piranesi (1720–78).

have had a light and airy atmosphere. This detail of design was used extensively from the Middle Ages onward.

When Christianity became a state religion in Rome, an explosion of building took place to accommodate the need for places to worship. Previously, small groups of the faithful had gathered as inconspicuously as possible wherever it was practical and prudent for them to do so. Even had it been safe to worship publicly, there was no need for a building of any size to house so few people. Respectability changed all that.

Early Christian architecture was, like painting, an adaptation of existing Roman style. For the most part, churches took the form of the Roman BASILICA. We tend to think of the word "basilica" as referring specifically to Christian structures, as in St Peter's Basilica in Rome. The term originally referred to Roman law courts, whose form the first large Christian churches took.

The original basilica had a specific architectural design, to which Christian architects made some simple alterations. Roman basilicas had many doors along the sides of the building to facilitate entrances and exits. Church ritual required the altar to be the focal point, and so the entrance to the Christian basilica was moved to the end of the building, usually at the western end, to focus attention down the long, relatively narrow nave to the

altar at the far end. Often the altar was set off by a large archway reminiscent of a Roman triumphal arch, and elevated to enhance sightlines from the congregation, who occupied a flat floor space.

The basic structure of a basilica (Figs **5.28** and **5.29**) has two or four long, parallel rows of columns, or piers, surrounded by an outer wall that is separated from the columns by an aisle. The central space, or nave, was heightened by a clerestory and a beam or simple truss roof describing an isosceles triangle of fairly low pitch. Low-pitched roofs covered the side aisles. The basilica was reasonably easy to build, yielding a nave width of 70 or 80 feet (21 or 24 meters). In contrast to later church styles, the basilica was not monumental by virtue of its height, although its early association with the law courts gave it an air of social authority. Interior parts and spaces were clearly defined, and this form was stated in simple structural terms.

Another change occurred in the treatment of interior space as different from the exterior shell. In architectural design, there are two approaches to the interior-exterior problem. Either the exterior structure expresses and reveals the nature and quality of interior space and *vice versa*, or the exterior shell is just that—a shell—in many instances obscuring what lies inside. The basilica exemplified the latter style. Whether intentionally or not, it thus symbolizes the difference between the exterior world of the flesh and the interior world of the spirit.

LITERATURE

The literature of the late Roman Empire reflected a dispirited decline, parallel to that of the Empire in which it existed. Compared with earlier times, little of any quality was produced—there was no experimentation with new forms nor a major production of old forms—and it seemed as if the only writers whose outlook was to the future and optimism were the Christians.

The Bible, which was not widely available until 313, emerged as the most significant literature of the period. By the mid-second century, Irenaeus, a bishop of Lyon, had put forward a canon of twenty-one of the present twenty-seven books—the inclusion of Revelation raised considerable disagreement—and some books not at present in the Bible were often included. Church councils in Hippo (393) and Carthage (397) recognized the twenty-seven book canon.

Although the Bible speaks to Judaic and Christian religious needs, it also contains some of the most vibrant literature of all time. Certainly, its poetry is without peer, even though it comes to us in translation. Later, we will witness the epistolary form of Paul's letters, but one of the most beautiful hymns ever written is the Magnificat of Mary, which is found in the Gospel of St Luke. This is

Mary's response to God's plan for her to bear his son, and it is an example of the kind of obedience deemed righteous by both Jews and Christians. The passage is steeped in the Old Testament, and is especially akin to Hannah's song of praise in 1 Samuel 2:1–10. Some commentators have seen the Magnificat as a revolutionary document because it speaks of three revolutions of God. First, it speaks to a moral revolution, because God will scatter the proud in the plans of their hearts. A basic tenet of Christianity is the death of pride, and seeing oneself in the light of Christ is a death blow to pride. Second, it speaks to a social revolution: "He casts down the mighty—he exalts the humble." Prestige and social labeling have no place in the new covenant. Third, it speaks of an economic revolution: "He has filled those who are hungry... he sends away empty those who are rich." There is no room here for an acquisitive society—that is, one in which people are out for as much as they can get. What the Magnificat argues for is a society in which no one dares to have too much while others have too little.[5]

Thus, within this poetry, there is a powerful upheaval—a revolution of thinking that is as applicable today as it was two thousand years ago.

> Luke 1:46-56: And Mary said, "My soul magnifies the Lord, and my spirit has exulted in God, my Saviour, because he looked graciously on the humble estate of his servant. For—look you—from now on all generations shall call me blessed, for the Mighty One has done great things for me and his name is holy. His mercy is from generation to generation to those who fear him. He demonstrates his power with his arm. He scatters the proud in the plans of their hearts. He casts down the mighty from their seats of power. He exalts the humble. He fills those who are hungry with good things and he sends away empty those who are rich. He has helped Israel, his son, in that he has remembered his mercy—as he said to our fathers that he would—to Abraham and to his descendants forever."

MUSIC

As with almost everything else we have noted, music in the late Roman period reflected Roman decline and Christian ascension. Just as St Paul took the Judaic and Eastern mystical traditions of Christian thought and shaped them into the logical processes of the Greco-Roman world, so early Christian music began to combine the music of Jewish worship with forms from the classical heritage. Most of the music from the Greek, Hellenistic, and Roman traditions was rejected by the early Christian Church, while music that was cultivated simply for enjoy-

TECHNOLOGY: PUTTING DISCOVERY TO WORK

Matches

The year 577 marked the invention of an item that today we take for granted—the match. In 950, in a book entitled *Records of the Unworldly and the Strange*, the Chinese author T'ao Ku writes: "An ingenious man devised the system of impregnating little sticks of pinewood with sulfur and storing them ready for use. At the slightest touch of fire, they burst into flame." Actually, T'ao Ku was wrong. Matches were a Chinese invention, but credit must go to some impoverished court ladies, who, during a military siege in the short-lived kingdom of the Northern Ch'i, were so short of tinder that they could not start fires for cooking and heating. They therefore devised a means of making it possible to start fires in a more opportune fashion. As T'ao Ku indicates, they devised a means of impregnating little sticks of pinewood with sulfur. The marvelous invention was initially called a "light-bringing slave," but it rapidly became an article of commerce, and its name was changed to "fire inch-stick."

5.30 Pu Qua Workshop, *A Boy Selling Pipe Lighters and Matches*(?), c. 1790. Watercolor on paper, 14⅛ × 17¼ (36 × 44 cm). Victoria & Albert Museum, London.

ment together with any music or musical instrument associated with activities objectionable to the Church were considered unsuitable. The *hydraulos* (see p. 148), for example, was banned. On the whole, the music of the classical West was simpler than the more ornate elaborations of liturgical texts in the East, especially in congregations with a large Jewish contingent. The consequent intermingling of the two styles resulted in a rich pastiche of hymnody and liturgy that was both vocal and instrumental. There was, nevertheless, a deep suspicion of instrumental music in many quarters and an outright rejection of it in others, because it was reminiscent of pagan customs. Disapproval of Roman or Greek music did not reflect a negative attitude toward music itself as much as a need to break ties with pagan traditions.

There was also a reaction against the use of trained choruses, initially instituted to help lead congregations who were unfamiliar with the chanting of psalms. When trained choruses were used, the congregation tended to sing less and the chorus more. In turn, this led to more complex music, which church leaders eventually found undesirable. In 361 the Provincial Council of Laodicea ruled that each congregation could have only one paid cantor or performer. In responsorial PSALMODY the leader

sang a line of the psalm, and the congregation sang a second in response. The melody began with a single note for the first few words, changing for the final words to a HALF CADENCE. The congregation then sang the beginning of the response on the same note, concluding with a CADENCE. The early Church also used an ANTIPHONAL psalmody, in which singing alternated between two choruses.

We know that from earliest times music played a role in Christian worship, and because Christian services were modeled on Jewish synagogue services, it is likely that any music in them was closely linked to liturgical function. In Rome, Christian liturgy (literally, "the work of the people") included only chants and unaccompanied singing. In Antioch, however, a new form, HYMNODY, emerged via the Jewish synagogue and its songs. The hymn, a song of praise to God, quickly spread throughout the Christian world as part of the liturgy that comprised the worship service or Mass, in which the eucharist was the focus.

Hymns were introduced into the Western Church early in the fourth century. Some sources credit St Ambrose for this innovation, others credit Hilary, bishop of Poitiers. Early hymns had poetic texts consisting of several verses, all of which were sung to the same melody, which may have been taken from popular secular songs.

The hymns were mostly syllabic—that is, each syllable was sung on a single note—and they were intended to be sung by the congregations, not by a choir or a soloist. In style and content, early Church hymns tended to express personal, individual ideas, although other sections of the liturgy were more formal, objective, and impersonal.

Another type of Church music at this time was the *alleluia*, which presented an interesting contrast in style to the hymn. The *alleluia* was melismatic in style—that is, there were many notes for each syllable of text—and it was sung after the verse of a psalm. The last syllable of the word was drawn out "in gladness of heart." Eastern in influence and emotional in appeal, the *alleluia* came to the Christian service directly from Jewish liturgy.

A CRITICAL REVIEW

A major theme running through Christian doctrine and one that we see specifically in the biblical poetry of the Magnificat is that of obedience to God. Not only has such a concept proved difficult for devoted Christians, it is problematic in general, for it raises the question of the fundamental nature of the individual and of his or her "freedom" or "rights" to pursue individual happiness.

In the next chapter, we shall see that another of the major religions of the world, Islam, forbids the depiction of the human form altogether, not only the depiction of the deity. On the basis of the material in the section we have just studied, develop an extended paragraph on the issues involved in making lifelike pictures of God and Jesus. Divide your essay into two parts and argue both sides of the issue.

Write a short essay on the issue of individual freedom and obedience to authority. Authority in this case may be divine or secular, whichever you find more challenging as you pursue the goals in your own life. Explain somewhere in your essay your reactions to the manner in which Mary submitted to authority.

SYNTHESIS

St Paul and the Westernization of Christianity

In this section we look at one of the most influential Christian figures, St Paul (Fig. **5.31**). Although Constantine cleared the way for Christianity to proceed without overt persecution, it was undoubtedly St Paul who made it palatable to the more logical inclinations of the Roman Empire, whose heritage lay in Greek classical thought. Paul carried the Christian gospel into Greece, and his interpretation of the Christian message and the nature of Christ were singularly successful in adapting what, basically, was an Eastern, mystical religion into a Western, intellectual one. Because Paul represents the transition of Judaic-Christian culture successfully into the Greco-Roman culture, he provides us with a synthesis of how these two cultures coalesced, to the point that soon one would supplant the other. After studying this section, you should be able to describe the life of St Paul and to describe his contribution to the spread of early Christianity.

The Apostle Paul was the most effective missionary of early Christianity and its first theologian. He is sometimes called the "second founder" of Christianity, having written more than one-fourth of the New Testament and having been responsible for translating Christianity into terms that could be accepted by the Greek-thinking people of the Roman Empire. His theology emerges from the many letters he wrote to the young churches throughout Asia Minor and Greece, but his Letter to the Romans probably stands as the greatest systemization of Christian theology ever produced. Although generally not a systematic theologian, Paul uses the Letter to the Romans as a means for establishing Christian dogma. While acknowledging his theological debt to Judaism, including his concept of righteousness, his cosmology—that is, his philosophy about the origin and shape of the universe—reflect that of the Hellenistic world. His belief that improper participation in the Lord's Supper causes sickness and death is not unlike ideas found in some of the Hellenistic cults. Above all, however, Paul is a biblical theologian, and his basic purpose was to interpret the revelation of the God of the Old Testament in the death and resurrection of Jesus Christ.

One of the central premises in Pauline theology is the concept of justification through faith. He presents this view in the Letters to the Romans and Corinthians, in which he argues that God moved first to save humankind and that nothing that humans can do—except believing in Jesus Christ as Lord—can earn them salvation. Also central to Paul's thinking is a kind of apocalyptic mysticism—that is, an emphasis on the coming of the end of history. In this view, Paul accepts and affirms the ultimate triumph of God over evil.

All of this rests, of course, on the assumption that Jesus is Lord and Messiah, and, because Messiah has come, the end is at hand. The decisive event has occurred in the crucifixion and resurrection of Christ, and the cross becomes a central force in Paul's Christology—that is, his definition of Christ. Through the crucifixion, God reveals his love for humankind and uses it as a propitiation for all sin. However, Paul's theology includes God's judgment. Humankind has failed to follow the word of God and lives enslaved by sin, which leads to death. The Law is insufficient for redemption. Only God's grace, with its consequent gift of righteousness, can lead to eternal life. In Christ, God reveals his mercy to those who respond in faith.

Paul's theology is far more complex than this brief description can encompass, but his systematic explanation of who Christ is and what God intended in Christ has underpinned Christian thought and belief for nearly two thousand years. Paul explained his theology in a series of occasional letters written to specific local churches undergoing specific local problems. They were intended to be read to the entire congregation and are structured according to the letter-writing standards of the day. They begin with an introductory salutation, followed by a statement of thanksgiving, then comes the main body of the letter, which addresses the major points of concern. Paul first treats questions of doctrine, then he uses persuasive exhortation in order to move the congregation to the action he desires of them, before ending the letter with a statement of his travel plans, a greeting, and benediction.

Paul's favorite form is the Hellenistic discourse known as the diatribe. In this argumentative structure, the correspondent raises a series of questions and then answers them. Because Paul dictated his letters, their style is often awkward and, occasionally, difficult to comprehend. Complex sentences, which never seem to end, are not infrequent, and thoughts are often truncated or expressed in incomplete sentences. When they are placed in the framework of contemporary practice, his cultural assumptions sometimes cause problems—for

5.31 St Paul, early twelfth century. Tempera on wood, Os de Tremp, Spain.

example, his comments in the Letters to the Corinthians about restricting the role of women. Scholars and clerics have been dealing with these issues for two millennia, but it is important to remember that the letters were written to address specific circumstances in specific locations. It has, for example, been suggested that the comments about women in Corinthians were made in response to the fact that some women in Corinthian society were especially disruptive, and applying Paul's comments in general distorts their original intention.

The letters were arranged in their current form after their collection toward the end of the first century. They represent the heart of Christian doctrine as it was shaped into canon by the early Church, and it is through Paul's inspiration and interpretation that the Christian world has viewed the events described in the Gospels and chronicled in the Acts of the Apostles.

THE FIRST LETTER OF PAUL TO THE THESSALONIANS

During his second missionary journey, Paul, accompanied by Silas and Timothy, went to Thessalonica, the capital of Macedonia, where, for three successive Sabbaths, he preached in the Jewish Synagogue, proclaiming Jesus as Messiah and using scripture to prove the necessity of Jesus' death and resurrection. Many Jews, including recent Hellenistic converts to Judaism, were converted to Christianity by Paul, and as a result the leaders of the synagogue accused him of sedition, making it necessary for Paul and Silas to be spirited out of town by their friends. Concerned for the young Christian community in Thessalonica, which had been deprived of its leadership, persecuted by the synagogue, and subjected to some scurrilous attacks on Paul's character, motives, and authority, Paul sent Timothy to strengthen and encourage the Thessalonican church. When Timothy returned with good news about the faith and loyalty of the Christians in Thessalonica, Paul wrote the first letter to that congregation. He expresses his gratitude and joy at their perseverance, exhorts them to Christian conduct, and answers two questions that concerned them: Is a Christian deprived of the blessings of the kingdom if he dies before the second coming of Christ? and When will Christ come in glory?

The earliest of Paul's correspondence, the letter was written from Corinth around A.D. 50.

CHAPTER SIX

BYZANTIUM AND THE RISE OF ISLAM

AT A GLANCE

Byzantium
Justinian
Reorganization of the Eastern Empire
The Isaurian Emperors and Iconoclasm
From Rise to Fall (867–1453)
Byzantine Intellectualism

The Arts of Byzantium
  MASTERWORK: The Harbaville Triptych
  OUR DYNAMIC WORLD: Chinese Theatre

The Rise of Islam
The Religion of Islam
  PROFILE: Muhammad
The Spread of Islam
Islamic Style in the Arts

**Synthesis: In Praise of the Emperor
The Mark of Justinian**
  PROFILE: Anthemius of Tralles
  TECHNOLOGY: Spanning Space with
    Triangles and Pots

6.1 Empress Theodora and attendants, c. 547. Detail of wall mosaic. San Vitale, Ravenna, Italy.

title of the "first crusader." Before his death, however, the Empire was already facing its next challenge from the Arabs, who conquered Syria, Egypt, North Africa, and Armenia. The following decades were the darkest in Byzantine history. Threats from Lombards, Slavs, Arabs, and Bulgars effectively reduced the Empire to an enclave centered on Constantinople (Map **6.1**).

It was not until the advent of the Isaurian emperors in 717 that Byzantium recovered, but critical changes resulted. All political power was invested in the military leaders. Latin was replaced by Greek, and literary forms began to take on Eastern characteristics. Orthodox Christianity, with its emphasis on monastic retreat from worldly life, strengthened its hold on public affairs. In all areas of life, the breach with the Roman legacy widened. Out of all this arose a truly Eastern and enduring empire, militarily strong and efficiently organized.

THE ISAURIAN EMPERORS AND ICONOCLASM

The task of stabilizing the Eastern Empire fell to the first oriental rulers to take control. These were the Isaurian emperors, who ruled from 717 to 867. They had originally come from the distant mountains of Anatolia. The first ruler of the Isaurian dynasty, Leo III, finally drove the Arabs from Constantinople in 717. His successor, Constantine V, re-established control over important territories in Asia Minor, and fortified and consolidated the Balkan frontier. As they tried to minimize internal strife, the Isaurians concerned themselves with administrative order and the general welfare of their subjects. The bureaucracy of the Empire thus became more closely associated with the imperial palace.

An even briefer legal code, called the *Ecloga*, replaced Justinian's *Corpus*. The *Ecloga* limited the traditional authority of the Roman *paterfamilias*, the male head of the household, by increasing rights for women and children. This was a concept new to Christian society: marriage was no longer a dissoluble human contract, but, rather, an irrevocable sacrament. The oriental punishment of mutilation replaced the death penalty in criminal justice, reflecting at least some concern for rehabilitation.

The period of Isaurian rule saw violent conflict within the Christian Church, however. The causes of this conflict, known as the "iconoclastic controversy," have been variously interpreted. In the preface to the *Ecloga*, the emperor's duties were cast in terms of a divine mandate

> Since God has put in our hands the imperial authority…we believe that there is nothing higher or greater that we can do in return than to govern in judgment and justice those who are commited by Him to our care.[1]

In his self-appointed role of king-priest, Leo III entered the controversy, which concerned the use of ICONS in the Eastern Church. Icons, or images, depicting the saints, the blessed Virgin, and God himself, by now occupied a special place in Orthodox churches. From the sixth century onward, these paintings and mosaics had been extremely important in Orthodox worship and teaching, but in the eighth century, their use was questioned, and those who were opposed to them maintained that icons were idols—that is, they had become objects of worship in themselves, perverting the worship of God. They demanded the removal of icons, and on many occasions they used force to impose their will, hence the name "iconoclast," or "icon-destroyer."

Leo III favored the iconoclasts, and, in 730, issued a proclamation forbidding the use of images in public worship. One reason for the edict appears to have been Leo's belief that the Arab invasions and volcanic eruptions at the time indicated God's displeasure with Orthodox practices. The iconoclast movement reached its peak under Constantine V and was formally approved by the council of bishops in 754. Over the next century icons remained at the center of controversy, and their use ebbed and flowed, depending on the current emperor. Gradually, however, the "iconophiles," or "icon-lovers," gained ground. Persecution was relaxed, and on the first Sunday of Lent in 843, a day still celebrated as an Orthodox feast-day, icons were permanently restored to their place in Eastern worship.

The resolution of the iconoclastic struggle and the establishment of a united empire under Charlemagne in the West in 800 finally set Byzantium on its own course. By the time of the Emperor Theophilus (829–892), the Byzantine court rivaled any in the world. The University of Constantinople was reorganized, in about 850, by Caesar Bordas, and it became a great intellectual center. The triumph of the iconophiles in 843 united the Orthodox Church, and strengthened its influence and character. The 150 years that followed the reign of Theophilus were a period of great prosperity and brilliance.

FROM RISE TO FALL (867–1453)

Nothing in the West during this period remotely resembled the splendor and sophistication of Byzantium. In the East, unlike the West, religious and secular life were closely intertwined. The visual arts flourished, and the subject matter was almost without exception religious. The Church calendar was inseparable from the court calendar. Moreover, the spectacle of court and Church ritual had a theatrical splendor, which reinforced the majesty of the empire and the place of the emperor as the vice-regent of God. Even the emperor's public appearances were

	GENERAL EVENTS	LITERATURE & PHILOSOPHY	VISUAL ART & ARCHITECTURE	THEATRE & MUSIC
330	Constantinople founded	Early hagiography	Theodosian obelisk (**6.10**)	Christian hymnody established
400	Eastern and Western Empires split Fall of Rome		Narrative Christian art	
500	Reign of Justinian	History developed Justinian legal code Procopius of Caesarea Anthemius of Tralles Isidorus of Miletus	*Barberini ivory* (**6.11**) San Vitale, Ravenna (**6.1, 6.6, 6.27,** **6.28, 6.29, 6.32**) St Sophia (**6.30, 6.33, 6.34, 6.35, 6.36**) Mosaics (**6.3, 6.4, 6.5**)	
600	Isaurian rulers Leo III repulses Moslems Death of Muhammad Alexandria and Carthage taken by Moslems		Silk textile art (**6.9**) Dome of the Rock (**6.23, 6.24**) Great Mosque, Damascus (**6.25, 6.26**)	Disappearance of formal theatre performance
800	Charlemagne unifies Western Empire End of Iconoclast struggle		*Raising of Lazarus* (**6.8**) *Vision of Ezekiel* (**6.7**) *Virgin and Child* (**6.13**) *Harbaville Triptych* (**6.12**)	*Kanones*
1000	Comneni rulers Moslem conquest in west Africa	Revival of Platonism Michael Psellus Prodomic poems	Emergence of hieratic style St Theodosia (**6.16**) St Luke and the Virgin (**6.17**)	Turkish *Orta Oinu*
1200	Constantinople sacked by Frankish invaders Crusades		St Mary Pammakaristos (**6.18**) *Dormition of the Virgin* (**6.2**)	
1453	Fall of Constantinople to the Ottoman Turks			Exodus of actors

Timeline 6.1 Byzantium and the rise of Islam.

Map 6.2 The empire of Justinian I.

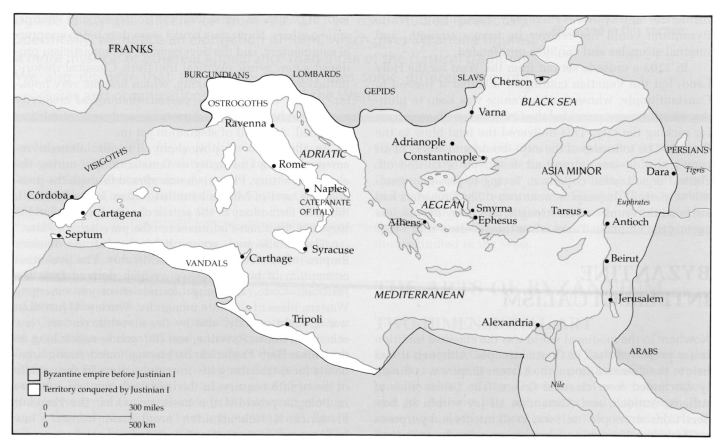

6.2. *Dormition of the Virgin* (detail), 1258–64. Fresco. Church of the Trinity, Sopoćani, Yugoslavia.

By the eleventh century, Byzantine style had developed a hierarchical formula for wall painting and mosaics. There was reduced emphasis on narrative. The Church represented the kingdom of God, and as one moves up the hierarchy, one encounters figures ranging in form from human to the divine. The placing of figures in the composition depended upon religious, not spatial, relationships. The representation of figures is in no way illusionistic: it is strictly two-dimensional, but the style is elegant and decorative. In twelfth- and especially in thirteenth-century art, this style intensifies, detailed with architectural backdrops, flowing garments, and elongated but dynamic figures (Fig. **6.2**). The fourteenth century produced small-scale, crowded works that are highly narrative. Space is confused by irrational perspective, and

6.3 A seated "philosopher," early sixth century. Floor mosaic, Imperial Palace, Istanbul, Turkey.

styles developed and where they came from are unresolved. The expansion of artistic forms from those appropriate to the constrained spaces of late Roman Christian churches to those better suited to the vast wall surfaces of new Byzantine churches posed problems that took time to resolve. The development of this new narrative Christian art dates back to the mid-fifth century, but early attempts at the depiction of religious ideas can be traced to the third and fourth centuries.

The content and purpose of Byzantine art was always religious, although representational style underwent many changes. Classical standards slipped with the decline in enlightened patronage and skilled craftsmanship. The ostentation of the Imperial court influenced artistic style, and Christ and the saints were depicted as frozen in immobile poses and garbed in regal purples. Lacy ornamentation corrupted what was left of classical purity in the sixth century.

The period of Justinian marks an apparently deliberate break with the past. What we describe as the distinctly "Byzantine style," with its characteristic abstraction and its focus on feeling rather than form, began to take shape in the fifth and sixth centuries. (If the classical Hellenistic tradition survived at all, it was only as an undercurrent.) The style of some works in which the realism of the depiction appears to predate the work itself has caused some confusion over dating. Throughout the seventh century, classical realism and decorative abstraction intermingled in Byzantine art.

6.4 Eagle and serpent.

6.5 Border, detail of head.

figures are distorted, with small heads and feet. The effect is of intense spirituality.

MOSAIC Covering a period of a thousand turbulent years, Byzantine art contains a complex repertoire of styles. When Constantine established his capital at Constantinople, a group of artists and craftsmen, trained in other centers, was already there. When these people set to work on Constantine's artistic projects, they naturally rendered their subjects in a manner quite different from the Roman style.

One of the earliest examples of two-dimensional art is a MOSAIC floor in the Imperial Palace of Constantinople. Mosaic was a characteristic Byzantine medium, and Figures **6.3**, **6.4**, and **6.5** show examples whose finely detailed execution allows for an essentially naturalistic style. The mosaics depict figures, buildings, and scenes, unconnected with each other, presented against a white background. The grandeur and elegance of these works reveal Greek classical influence. Although the figures are fairly naturalistic, the absence of background and shadow indicates that pictorial realism was neither intended nor important. Rather, each figure has a mystical, abstract feel that is clearly unclassical.

The palette is rich and varied. The fragment shown in Figure **6.5** is representative of one important develop-

6.6 *Emperor Justinian and his Court*, c. 547. Wall mosaic, San Vitale, Ravenna, Italy.

the treatment of space, with its crowded figures, its concentration on the surface plane, and lack of realistic linear perspective, is entirely Byzantine.

Figure **6.9** shows the use of figure reversal and repetition, similar in character to the Mesopotamian designs discussed in Chapter 1, now adapted to a particularly suitable medium, woven textiles. The central, repeated figure of the design is probably Samson, whose struggle with a lion is recounted in the Old Testament Book of Judges. The borders are composed of representational and geometric elements, and the whole design gains force from the bold colors.

SCULPTURE

Sculpture developed in the same historical context as the two-dimensional arts. Early works include sculptural vignettes illustrating Old and New Testament themes of salvation and life after death. For two centuries or so, the old art of Roman portrait sculpture held sway. But by the end of the fourth century, styles had begun to change. In Figure **6.10**, the base of an obelisk set up by Theodosius I, the frontal poses of figures, the ranks in which they are grouped, and the large, accentuated heads reflect oriental influence. Oriental and classically inspired works existed alongside each other in this period. Large-scale sculpture virtually disappeared from Byzantine art after the fifth century. Small-scale reliefs in ivory and metal continued in abundance, however. The clear-cut, precise style of Greek carving later became an outstanding characteristic of Byzantine sculpture. As in painting, sculpture took a classical turn after the iconoclastic struggle, but with an added awareness of the spiritual side of human beauty.

Ivory, traditionally a precious material, was always

6.11 *Barberini Ivory*, showing a mounted emperor, c. 500. Ivory, 13¹/₂ × 10¹/₂ ins (34.1 × 26.6 cm). Louvre, Paris.

6.10 Base of the Theodosian obelisk, c. 395. Marble, about 13 ft 11 ins (4.2 m) high. Hippodrome, Istanbul, Turkey.

very popular in Byzantium. The number of carved works in different styles provides evidence of the various influences and degrees of technical ability in the Eastern Empire. Many of the ivories are diptychs, that is, in two panels. The *Barberini Ivory* (Fig. **6.11**) is a work of five separate pieces, one of which is missing. At the center, an emperor is depicted on horseback. To the side is a consul in military costume, and above is a bust of Christ with winged victories on either side. The long panel at the bottom depicts Gothic emissaries on the left side and emissaries from India on the right; interestingly, the latter are portrayed carrying elephant tusks—the source of the artist's material. The rounded features and brilliant high-relief technique are typical of the period. The portrait of the emperor is individualized and recognizable. Later ivories show a more delicate elegance and a highly finished style.

The only known Byzantine free-standing sculpture in ivory is the tenth-century *Virgin and Child* (Fig. **6.13**). The drapery falls exquisitely and the surface is highly finished. The facial features, hands, and torsos display characteristic hieratic elongation.

The Harbaville Triptych

The tenth and eleventh centuries have left us the greatest number of ivory objects, many decorated with small, elegant reliefs. In secular art, ivory caskets covered with minute carvings were the most popular form. Byzantine ivory carvers of the time showed remarkable ease and skill in imitating classical models. The same technique was used for small-scale reliefs of religious subjects, which cover an extensive variety of content and style. The *Harbaville Triptych* (Fig. **6.12**) is an exquisite example.

The TRIPTYCH was probably intended as a portable altar or shrine. The two wings folded shut for traveling, across the center panel. In the top center Christ is enthroned and flanked by John the Baptist and the Virgin Mary, an arrangement known as *deesis*, where these two plead for mercy on behalf of all humanity. Five of the apostles appear below. The two registers of the central panel are divided by an ornament repeated, with the addition of rosettes at the bottom border, and three heads in the top border. On either side of Christ's head appear medallions depicting angels holding symbols of the sun and moon. The figures have hieratic formality and solemnity, yet the depiction exhibits a certain softness that may result from a strong classical influence.

The figures stand on a plain, flat ground, ornamented only by the lettering of their names beside the heads. The side wings contain portraits of four soldier saints and four bishop saints. Between the levels are bust-length portraits of other saints. All the saints wear the dress of various civilian dignitaries. The triptych thus aligns the powers of Church and State, within the hierarchical formula of Byzantine art: each personage has his or her own place in the divine hierarchy, with Christ at the top.

This work and others from the same period belong to a class of works known as "Romanus," after a plaque in the Bibliothèque Nationale in Paris that shows Christ crowning the Emperor Romanus IV and his Empress Eudocia. The works of this Romanus school of ivory carvers are identifiable by style, of course, but they have a particular ICONOGRAPHIC peculiarity as well. The cross in Christ's NIMBUS, or halo, shows the usual rectangular outline, but a pearled border has been added to both cross and nimbus. Similarly fine workmanship is found in the mosaics and painting of the time, and, in fact, stylistic developments in the ivories were closely associated with those in painting.

6.12 The *Harbaville Triptych*, interior, late tenth century. Ivory, 9¹⁄₂ ins (24.2 cm) high, central panel 5⁵⁄₈ ins (14.2 cm) wide. Louvre, Paris.

6.13 *Virgin and Child*, tenth century. Ivory, 12⁷⁄₈ ins (32.5 cm) high. Victoria & Albert Museum, London.

LITERATURE

The literature of Byzantium is often thought of as Greek literature. That is true of the majority of Byzantine literary works, and certainly of the literature coming out of Constantinople. But the Eastern Empire of Byzantium was not confined to Constantinople. The literature of the Empire in fact includes works in Latin, Syriac, Coptic, Church Slavonic, Armenian, and Georgian.

Byzantine literature in Greek, however, does comprise a vast quantity of works. Much from the early period has unfortunately been lost, and much remains unpublished, in manuscript form. Most of Greek Byzantine literature is on religious subjects, and much of it is hagiographic—that is, covering the life stories of saints and other religious figures. In addition, there are sermons, liturgical books, poetry, theology, devotional works, scriptural commentaries, and so on. Of the thousands of volumes that have survived, only a few hundred are secular.

To understand Byzantine literature, we need to know something about Byzantine aesthetic taste, which was quite different from our own. Modern readers do not obtain much pleasure from Byzantine literature, because we expect to find quite different qualities in what we read: we like originality of thought and expression. Educated Byzantines did not wish to be surprised. They liked clichés. Where we value clarity and directness, they admired elaboration and verbiage.

The Greek language itself had gone through several stages: an epic stage (the language of Homer and Hesiod); a literary stage (the Attic of the fifth and fourth centuries B.C.), and a New Testament Greek stage, which Byzantine scholars considered decadent. Sensitive to the rhetorical excesses of the past, churchmen admired only humble Byzantine speech and rejected "the fine style of the Hellenes," which they compared "to the proverbial honey that drips from the mouth of a whore." They would have considered that using the epic meters of the past was "an insult to Christ and the apostles."³ As a result, each generation of Byzantine authors resisted the influence of its predecessors, going directly to ancient models. Many Byzantine works, therefore, exist in a sort of stylistic vacuum, without an acknowledged author, without contemporary references, and without place.

Byzantine literature falls into three principal genres. The first is historiography. This is not the history we speak of when we refer to a chronicled record of events, which was a separate activity in Byzantium. Historiography is, rather, a specific literary genre, related to rhetoric. It is written in ancient Greek, in imitation of ancient models, and interprets events and their influence on each other. As Theophanes Continuatus wrote: "The body of history is indeed mute and empty if it is deprived of the cause of actions." Probably the best known of the

Byzantine historiographers was Procopius of Caesarea. His broad, sweeping narratives, which were known for their objectivity and accuracy, were modeled on the work of the Athenian historian Thucydides.

The bulk of Byzantine literature belongs to the second genre, hagiography. Many of these texts on the lives of the saints survive, most of them written in ecclesiastical Greek. They consist of anecdotes about the saints, as well as full life-histories, which had been preserved by Egyptian monks. The anecdotal accounts were first circulated by word of mouth, then collected in books. The stories told of supernatural deeds attributed to monks, and stressed the moral precepts they followed in their lives. The first "life" was written by Athanasius of Alexandria (c. 360) about St Anthony. Principally designed to praise the behavior of its subject, a "life" usually follows a specific rhetorical format. The writer first proclaims embarrassment at undertaking a task so great; then the birthplace (if it is worthy of note) or the nation in which the subject was born is described and praised; next comes a description of the family, but only if it is glorious; then the subject's birth and any miraculous signs accompanying it, real or invented, are noted; finally, in carefully organized subdivisions, physical appearance, education, upbringing, deeds, and so on, are described. This outline, or SCHEMA, made it easy to develop biographies of saints about whom little was known or who may never have existed. The "lives" are interesting and readable, if somewhat predictable, and they provided heroes and heroines for the medieval world. Written in simple language, they were intended for as wide an audience as possible.

The third genre was literature written in the vernacular, or language of the common people. The earliest works of this sort, the Prodromic poems, date to the first half of the twelfth century. They are attributed to the court poet Theodore Prodromos, although they may have been written by several authors.

These poems employ a popular verse-form based on fifteen syllables and are written as complaints directed to the Emperors John II and Manuel I and other members of the Comneni family. One of the poems tells the story of a hen-pecked husband; another, the story of the father of a large family who cannot make ends meet on his small salary. These works are largely humorous, although their tendency to monotony and repetition often mars the effect of the slapstick and the coinage of bizarre words. Romances of chivalric knights, maidens, witches, and dragons in the fashion of the Western Empire were also popular. Epic poems that told heroic tales of the eastern border between Byzantium and the Arabs in the ninth and tenth centuries also found favor.

Much of Byzantine literature, however, is solemn, even somber in mood. Its writers seem most at home with themes of calamity, death, and the precariousness of human existence.

THEATRE AND MUSIC

The Byzantines were undoubtedly familiar with theatre. Ruins of Hellenistic theatres have been found throughout the Eastern Empire. Justinian's wife, Theodora, was an actress, and theatrical spectacles surrounded the life of the Imperial court. There are references to an exodus of actors and playwrights from Byzantium at the time of the Turkish conquest.

But what of theatre itself? The period between the fall of Rome and the late Middle Ages witnessed the virtual extinction of theatre in both East and West, except in its most rudimentary form. The Byzantine preference for artistic anonymity might account for the absence of dramas, and the literature of Byzantium certainly excluded drama from its priorities. In a society dominated by the Christian Church, the kind of debased spectacles popular in the late years of the Roman Empire were undoubtedly frowned upon. Such was the moral tone of the time that senators were barred by law from marrying actresses: Justinian had to change this law in order to marry Theodora. *Scaenici*, as theatre productions were called, continued into the sixth century in the West, and we hear of professional actors in Byzantium as late as the seventh century, but after that formal theatre performances seem to have disappeared. As one commentator puts it, "In the East problems more serious soon set people thinking of things sterner than merry supper-parties with groups of dancing girls."[4]

Throughout the Middle Ages, critical remarks to the effect that it was "better to please God than the actors" suggest that some form of performance art continued, however, and it is not unlikely that this was also the case in Byzantium. Mime, and some form of pantomime, were probably the only forms of theatrical activity during this period.

Twelfth-century Turkish theatre would almost certainly have been influenced by Byzantine practice. Evidence of its character is provided by the Turkish *Orta Oinu*, which consisted of simple plays that were acted in the open, with minimal scenery. Popular theatre in Byzantium may well have followed this course. During the latter period of the Eastern Empire, the aristocracy seems to have satisfied its dramatic inclinations with spectacles involving the actual members of the Imperial court.

Before reaching Europe, the Christian Church spread throughout Asia Minor, accumulating musical elements on its way. Byzantium appears to have acquired much of its musical heritage from the monasteries and churches of Syria, where the development of antiphonal psalmody and the use of hymns originated. Clear evidence of hymn singing can be found in the New Testament, both in the Gospels and in the letters of Paul and James, and in the writings of Pliny the Younger in Bithynia and Asia Minor in the second century. Some early Christian hymns were

OUR DYNAMIC WORLD

Chinese Theatre

Just as the dogmas of Confucianism shaped Chinese culture, Confucianism also gave shape to early Chinese drama at the time that East was separating from West in Rome. Tradition holds that Confucius put to death an entire troupe of actors who took part in a play that violated his teaching. Taoism also provided important building blocks for the theatre in China. As a result, we can find in some Chinese drama the mystical leanings of Taoism, in which the exploration of relationships between individuals and society reflects an intuitive, emotional drift, with great imagination and flights into fantasy.

One significant characteristic of Chinese drama that emerged from these roots concerned women on stage. Women in China were subject to severe restrictions and were forbidden to act in the theatre, and until the twentieth century, all female roles in Chinese theatre were played by men. These portrayals mimicked the teetering style of walking that resulted from the practice of footbinding among the upper classes, and utilized a device called *tsai jiao* to keep the actor "on point"—in the balletic sense—throughout the performance.

Although legend documents the presence of actors and clowns and a dramatic form known as the Peking play as early as the nineteenth century B.C., the traditional founding of Chinese theatre came in the seventh to tenth centuries A.D., during the Dang dynasty, when the Emperor Minghuang established the Pear Garden Conservatory for the training of professional actors.

"On stage" in Chinese theatre means "center stage." When an actor exits, he merely moves to an area away from center. Although he remains in full view of the audience, by convention he is not there, and so he can do whatever tasks need to be done, from drinking tea to adjusting his costume. All entrances occur from stage left, and all exits from stage right.

Costume and makeup play a significant and symbolic role in Chinese theatre. Color, especially, portrays emotion and social standing. Yellow means royalty. Dark crimson is reserved for military personages, as well as for barbarians. Red also connotes loyalty. Black symbolizes the poor and the fierce. Green stands for virtue. White represents the old, the very young, and the bereaved. Color also distinguishes character types. We can get an impression of the subtlety, complexity, and depth of Chinese drama and its audience relationships when we realize that costume is used to make very specific and detailed statements about character, with perhaps as many as three hundred combinations of headdresses, shoes, and other costume items per character—all of which would be understood by the audience.

Chinese theatrical costume, like its scenery, does not attempt to depict historical accuracy. Styles and periods mix freely so as to create dramatic effect and reinforce nuances. Nuance and inflection form important parts of Chinese philosophy and language, and the same is true for theatre. Chinese costume is similar to Classical Greek costume (see Fig. **3.24**) in that rank and station are indicated through the use of padding and *kothurnoi* or thick-soled boots. The American movie form, the Western, was not unlike Chinese drama in its use of costume. In the former case, the "good guys" wore white hats, and the "bad guys" black ones. In Chinese theatre, the good guys wear square hats, and the bad guys, round ones.

6.14 Chinese theatre performance in progress.

probably sung to folk melodies. Thus there seem to have been both Eastern and Greek influences on early Christian music.

Although no music manuscripts survive from this period, the strong traditions of the Greek Orthodox, Russian, and other Eastern Churches still preserve what must be a flavor of the Byzantine chants that served as their models. Based on Syrian melodies and incorporating short responses between verses of the psalms, an independent hymnody gradually developed. Byzantine hymns had an elaborate structure, which stood in contrast to the simple hymns of the Western Church.

One type, developed in the eighth to tenth centuries, was based on sixth-century hymns and was called *kanones*. Its texts were commentaries based on passages from the Bible. Its melodies, also not entirely original, were constructed on a principle common to Eastern music but were unfamiliar in the West. Rather than building a new melody from the tones in a scale, Eastern singers constructed melody out of a series of short given motifs, which they chose and combined. Some motifs were designed for beginnings, some for middles, some for endings, and some for links. There were also standard ornamental formulas, and originality in performance depended on the combination, variation, and ornamentation of the motifs. Byzantine music had eight forms, or *echoi*. These *echoi* played a fundamental part in the development of Western music. Our knowledge of them is limited, however, by the fact that in the Byzantine Church music was passed on by oral tradition for centuries before being written down.

Undoubtedly Eastern music had a contemplative, even mystical, character and a degree of complexity that was quite in keeping with the character of Eastern thought.

ARCHITECTURE

The architecture of the early years of the Eastern Empire was dominated by the personality and objectives of the Emperor Justinian. It was an age in which royal patronage encouraged artistry, but the arts clearly reflected the source of that encouragement. Justinian's purpose was to glorify Justinian, and, in a remarkably creative way, the arts and architecture of the age succeeded in doing just that. The results of his efforts can be seen both in the West

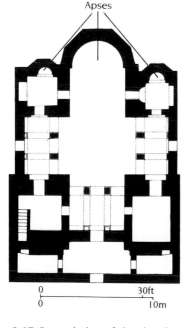

6.15 Ground plan of the church of St Clement, Ankara.

6.16 St Theodosia, Istanbul, Turkey. c. 1000.

(see Fig. **6.6**) and in the East (see Figs **6.30**, **6.33–6.36**).

6.17 Churches of St Luke and the Virgin, Stiris, Turkey, eleventh century.

6.18 St Mary Pammakaristos, Istanbul, Turkey, thirteenth century.

The period from the sixth century until the beginning of the ninth was, as we have seen, characterized by external and internal struggles. But out of this turbulence emerged the Byzantine state and, eventually, a high Byzantine culture.

After Justinian's death, the construction of public churches all but ceased. The palace was the only important building project. Yet the churches that were built at this time became models for later Byzantine architecture. The general form of these early churches, such as that of St Clement in Ankara, consists of a central dome and a group of three APSES at the east end (Fig. **6.15**). The entire space describes a cross-in-square layout, which, again, can be seen in later churches. The cross-in-square is outlined on the ground plan: look outward from the center to the end of each of the transverse arms, the lower arm of the nave, and the upper arm just to the edge of the circular apse at top center.

The churches constructed in the two or three centuries after St Clement's employed the classical principles of harmony among their parts, and composition to express human aspirations (Fig. **6.16**). The three apses just described point toward the viewer, and the dome above the central pavilion is visible at the top. The church's vertical striving and precise symmetry give it an elegant solidity. Delicate, arched niches and grilled windows tend to counter the heaviness of the walls.

As Byzantine power waned, the vigor and scale of new church construction reduced. The ground plans became smaller, and in partial compensation, height was increased. Greater emphasis was also placed on the appearance of the exterior, with decorative surface treatment of the brickwork or masonry of the walls (Figs **6.17** and **6.18**). Another characteristic of later church building was the addition of churches or chapels to existing ones, creating very different forms from the organized massing of the single-domed church. The elaborate detail and frequent changes of plane that these additions created give us a fascinating surface with which to interreact, as the Churches of St Luke and the Virgin illustrate. Here, verticality or upward striving line is much less apparent—the strength of horizontal elements and the shorter apses give the impression that the building is much more squat.

The interiors of these churches are elegant, jewel-like, sumptuous, glowing with color, and heavily decorated. They are reached through NARTHEXES, and sometimes side porches, that create a spatial and visual transition from the outside world to the interior. The spaces of the church flow smoothly from one to another and are carefully designed to meet liturgical needs. A deep, vaulted SANCTUARY and apse house the altar. Chambers adjoin the apse on either side. Just beyond the eastern columns a screen painted with icons stands across the sanctuary. The entire effect of the mosaic-covered vaults, elaborate ecclesiastical vestments, chants, ancient rites, and incense sought to create for the worshiper the spiritual and physical sense of another world—one central to Byzantine life.

CRITICAL REVIEW below

A CRITICAL REVIEW

In the material we have just studied, several important stylistic features have been described. We are now able to identify and explain a style meaning "holy" or "sacred" and account for the formula in wall painting in which progression upward moves from humankind to the divine.

Explain what scholarly evidence suggests the presence of Byzantine theatre.

Describe the characteristics of the Barberini Ivory and other works of art.

A CRITICAL LOOK

In the next section we will examine another of the world's great religions—Islam. As part of that examination, we will study its basic precepts, learn about the life and beliefs of Muhammad, its founder, and analyze several products of its creative spirit. Islam is a world-wide religion.

What are the basic precepts of the Islamic religion and how did it spread after Muhammad's death?

THE RISE OF ISLAM

THE RELIGION OF ISLAM

The Islamic tradition springs from the religion of Islam, of which Muhammad was the prophet. The latest of the three great monotheistic religions, it drew upon both Judaism and Christianity, and it is now one of the world's most populous religions. Islam's largest communities are in the Middle East, North Africa, Indonesia, Bangladesh, Pakistan, India, and the former Soviet Union.

When Muhammad, the prophet of Islam, was called to preach, the conditions included great suffering among the poor—notably in the city of Mecca in southwestern Arabia. Most of the people worshiped a variety of gods and prayed to various idols and spirits. Muhammad taught that there was only one God and that this God requires people to make Islam—that is, submission—to him.

Muhammad began preaching in Mecca around A.D. 610, but, as noted in the Profile on p. 207, that follows, his teachings were not immediately accepted. However, by the time of his death in 632 he was acknowledged as Prophet. His companions preserved his revelations and combined them to form the holy book of the Muslims, the Koran. The word Koran means "recitation," and Muslims consider the Koran to contain the words of God himself, spoken to Muhammad by an angel. Parts of the Koran resemble the Hebrew Bible and contain many stories about the prophets who appear in the Old Testament. The Koran also has stories from the New Testament about Jesus, whom it calls the "Word of God." The strictures of the Koran prohibit usury, games of chance, and the consumption of pork and alcohol. Like the Bible, it forbids lying, stealing, adultery, and murder, but it does not require "an eye for an eye." Instead, the offender can pay "blood money" and is urged to seek forgiveness. The Koran permits slavery but urges that slaves be treated with kindness and freed. Polygamy—up to four wives—is

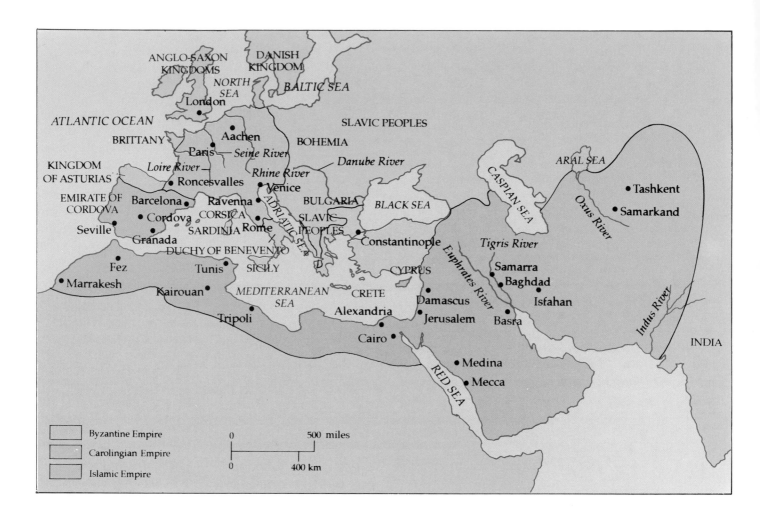

Map 6.3 The Byzantine, Carolingian, and Islamic Empires c. 814.

permitted under some conditions.

In the religion of Islam, there is one absolute and all-powerful God, known as Allah. He is the creator of the universe, and is just and merciful. God desires that people repent and purify themselves so that they can attain Paradise after death. God communicates with the human race through prophets, and the predecessors of Muhammad were the Old Testament prophets and Jesus. Muhammad was the last of the prophets. Muslims respect Muhammad, but they do not worship him.

Like Judaism and Christianity, the Islamic faith teaches that parents should be honored, orphans and widows protected, and charity given to the poor. It proclaims faith in God, kindness, honesty, industry, courage, and generosity. An Islamic wife has rights against her husband to protect her from abuse. Islam also teaches that life on earth is a period of testing in preparation for an afterlife. Angels keep a record of individual good and bad deeds, and God's justice determines a person's reward. Death is the gateway to eternal life, and at the last day, judgment will occur. The record book of each individual will be

placed in the right hand of those who will go to heaven and in the left hand of the wicked who will go to hell. The description of the agonies and tortures of hell are similar to those in the Bible, while heaven is a garden with flowing steams, delicious fruit, richly covered furniture, and beautiful maidens.

Five duties are prescribed for every Muslim, the last being that he must, if he can, once in his life make the pilgrimage, or Hajj, to Mecca. This last provision has made the pilgrimage the greatest in the world and a great unifying force in Islam. The other duties are profession of God and the prophethood of Muhammad, prayer, almsgiving, and fasting.

Muslims pray five times daily: at dawn, noon, in the afternoon, in the evening, and at nightfall. A crier or muezzin (pronounced myoo-EZ-in) announces prayer time from a tower, or minaret, in the mosque, the Muslim place of worship, meaning a place of kneeling. Noon prayer is expected to be performed in the mosque. Immediately before prayer, Muslims wash their face, hands, and feet. Friday is a day similar to the Jewish Sabbath and the Christian Sunday. During prayer, the leader faces Mecca, and the men stand in rows behind him, with women standing behind the men. Prayers

PROFILE

Muhammad (c. 570–632)

The name Muhammad means Praised One, and there are several common spellings of the name, including Mohammed and Mahomet. Muhammad was born in Mecca, but his father died before he was born, and his mother died shortly thereafter. Raised under the guardianship of his grandfather and, later, his uncle, Muhammad lived for a while with a desert tribe tending sheep and camels. Tradition maintains that he went with his uncle on caravans throughout Arabia and to Syria.

When he was twenty-five years old, Muhammad went to work for a wealthy widow named Khadija, who was fifteen years older than he was and whom he later married. They had two sons and four daughters, and although the sons died young, one of the daughters, Fatima, married Ali, son of Abu Talib. Many Muslims trace their ancestry to Muhammad through his daughter in a genealogy called the Fatamid dynasty.

When Muhammad was thirty-five years old and living in Mecca, a flood damaged the most sacred shrine, the Kaaba. Because of his moral excellence, Muhammad was selected to put the sacred stone back into place. The angel Gabriel later appeared to Muhammad in a vision and called him to serve as a prophet to proclaim God's message to his people. Although he was at first unsure of the vision, he was convinced of its validity by his wife, who became his first disciple. However, no further visions occurred, and Muhammad grew disheartened. Then, Gabriel appeared again and told him: "arise and warn, magnify thy Lord...wait patiently for Him."

Muhammad began to preach periodically in public, and, at first, most of the people who heard him ridiculed him. But he gained a few followers, including a rich merchant named Abu Bakr, which gave him confidence and standing in the community. He continued preaching in Mecca until both his wife and son-in-law died, but the people of Mecca persecuted him for his claims and attacks on their way of life. In A.D. 622, therefore, he fled to Medina in the north. That emigration is called the *Hegira*, and Muslims date their calendar from this year. In Medina he found a welcome, and most of the population became his followers. He eventually became both head of a religion and a political leader—his religious message became law, and he made a variety of changes in the legal system and customs to conform to the precepts of Islam.

At first it seems as though Muhammad expected Christians and Jews to recognize him as a prophet. He was benevolent to them and decreed that Jerusalem was to be faced in prayer. However, a conspiracy among Jews in Medina and Muhammad's enemies in Mecca caused him to drive them from the city and to organize a strictly Muslim society. In order to recognize the independence of the religion, he decreed that from that time onward his followers face Mecca in prayer, a practice still observed.

The Meccans attacked Medina several times, although without success, and in 630 Muhammad and his followers turned the tables. They attacked Mecca and successfully occupied the city, destroying all the idols in the Kaaba, and turning it and the area around it into a mosque. In a gesture of reconciliation, Muhammad offered to pardon the people of Mecca, who accepted Islam and acknowledged Muhammad as a prophet. The two cities of Medina and Mecca became the sacred cities of the religion. Muhammad died in Medina two years later, and his tomb is in the Prophet's Mosque in Medina.

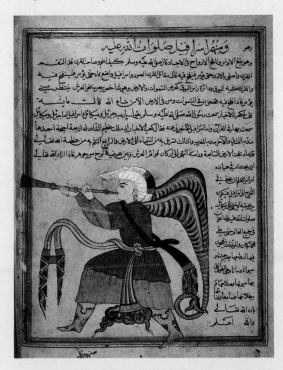

6.19 The Archangel Gabriel. British Library, London.

include bowing from the hips and kneeling with one's face to the ground. Friday prayers include a sermon. Islam does not have an organized priesthood—any virtuous and able Muslim can lead prayers—but most mosques have an imam, or leader, who is the chief officer of the mosque and leads the people in prayer.

Early in its history, Islam split between the Sunnites and Shiites, and this split has persisted. The original split was over the caliphate, which was the crowning institution of the theocratic structure of Islam—that is, the placement of both religious and political leadership in the hands of a single ruler. The caliphs were the successors, or deputies, of Muhammad, and their claim to authority rested on their descent from the families of the Prophet or his early associates. Although secularism has modified the unity somewhat, in theory the civil law in Muslim countries is not separate from religious law; religion governs all aspects of life. There have developed some four different systems of interpretation of the law in Sunnite Islam, all regarded as orthodox. Islamic philosophy is in effect part theology; rationalism and mysticism both grew up in Islam, but were equally absorbed.

THE SPREAD OF ISLAM

Islam spread rapidly throughout the Middle East and North Africa in the seventh and eighth centuries, beginning with conquests launched from Mecca and Medina (Map **6.3**). After Muhammad's death, the Caliph Abu Bakr and his successors encouraged jihad, or holy war, in order to expand the faith's sphere of influence. Within a century, an Islamic empire stretched from northern Spain to India, engulfing much of the Byzantine and Persian empires, and the Muslims threatened to overrun Europe until they were defeated by Charles Martel at the Battle of Poitiers (Tours) in 732.

A religion that was originally spread "by the sword," Islam's appeal lay in its openness to everyone. It stresses the brotherhood of the faithful before God, regardless of race or culture, although the Arab warriors who started out to conquer the world for Allah, did not expect to make converts of conquered peoples—they expected the unbelievers to be obedient to them, the servants of the One True God. The Koran was not translated into any languages because it was dictated by God to Muhammad in Arabic. Converts were expected to become Arabs, and they had to submit to the social and

6.20 Symbol of Islam on Pakistan's national flag.

legal precepts of the Muslim community (Fig. **6.20**). As a result, the conquering Arabs resisted the usual fate of conquerors—being absorbed into the culture of the conquered.

During the early Middle Ages in Europe, the Muslims were responsible for transmitting much of the classical knowledge of the ancient world. They were proficient mathematicians and scientists, as well as artists, writers, and architects.

ISLAMIC STYLE IN THE ARTS

VISUAL ART

Theoretically, all human and animal figures are prohibited from Islamic art, but in reality, images are widespread: the only prohibition seems to have been on those objects intended for public display. In the courts of the caliphs, for example, images of living things were commonplace. They were considered harmless if they did not cast a shadow, were small in scale, or appeared on everyday objects.

A continuity of visual art seems to have occurred during the early years of Islam through the illustration of scientific texts. The Arabs obtained manuscripts from Byzantium, and were tremendously interested in Greek science. The result was a plethora of texts translated into Arabic. Illustrations from original Greek works also were copied. Typical of the illustration drawn in Arab manuscripts is a pen-and-ink sketch, perhaps from a Mesopotamian manuscript of the fourteenth century (Fig. **6.21**). The drawing has a clear presentation, with many of the strokes seeming to act as accents. The lines flow freely

6.21 Al-Qasim ibn 'Ali al-Hariri, *Maqamat al-Hariri* (a book of stories), 1323. Mesopotamian manuscript, Oriental Collection, British Library, London.

6.22 Unknown illustrator, *The Ascension of Muhammad*, 1539–43. Persian manuscript. Oriental Collection, British Library, London.

worship." The reference in the Koran was later expanded upon: Muhammad ascended from Jerusalem under the guidance of the Angel Gabriel, rising through seven heavens and meeting Adam, Abraham, Moses, and Jesus before coming into the presence of God.

The images in the painting are fascinating. Muhammad rides a curiously oriental centaur—a mythological beast with a horse's body and the head of a man. The surrounding angels have oriental faces, and the composition seems to divide along the diagonal axis—also similar to some oriental works. The crescent-shaped figures appear to swirl in an elliptical path around Muhammad, and the artist shows a sophisticated color composition by carrying the predominant colors of one section into another section—for example, the white of the clouds carries into the upper parts of the painting in small details of trim and in the lighter flesh tones; reds that provide an encircling motif in the upper portion are carried into the lower section where they accent rather than dominate.

LITERATURE

Probably the most familiar Islamic literature, aside from the Koran, is a collection of tales called *The Arabian Nights* or *The Thousand and One Nights*. These tales accumulated during the Middle Ages, and as early as the tenth century they were part of the oral traditions of Islam in the Near East. Over the years more tales were added, including a unifying device called a frame-tale, which placed all the separate stories within a larger framework. By around 1450 the work had assumed its final form.

The frame-tale recounts the story of a jealous Sultan who, convinced that all women were unfaithful, married a new wife each evening and put her to death the following morning. A new bride, Shaharazad, or Scheherazade, gained a reprieve by beginning a story on her wedding night and artfully maintaining the Sultan's curiosity. She was able to gain a reprieve for one thousand and one nights—during which she produced three male heirs—after which the Sultan abandoned his original practice. The tales capture the spirit of Islamic life, its exotic setting, and sensuality. Although no particular moral purpose underlies the stories, there is a moral code within the fantasies. The tales cover a variety of subjects and range from fact to fiction. They include stories of camel trains, desert riders, and insistent calls to prayers. They are supernatural, aristocratic, romantic, bawdy, and satiric.

ARCHITECTURE

The first major example of Islamic architecture did not appear until A.D. 691, when work began on the Dome of the Rock in Jerusalem (Fig. **6.23**). Built near the site of the Temple of Solomon, it was begun by Islamic emperors

in subtle curvilinear movements to establish a comfortable rhythm across the page. In very simple line, the artist is able to capture human character, thus showing a strong observational ability. The witty flavor of the drawing goes far beyond mere illustration.

Even before Islam, Arab traders had penetrated the Far East, and as a result Chinese influence can be seen throughout the Middle East. This is particularly true in the emergence of religious subjects for visual art. The Mongol rulers were very familiar with the Buddhist tradition in Chinese art, and brought that interest to Islamic art—ignoring their predecessors' reluctance to pictorialize Muhammad. Thus, in the fourteenth-century painting that depicted narratives about Muhammad became quite common. Chinese influences are strongly at work in an Islamic manuscript illustration from sixteenth-century Persia. *The Ascension of Muhammad* (Fig. **6.22**) tells the story from the Koran, in which Muhammad ascends into Paradise after "a journey by night...to the remote place of

6.23 Dome of the Rock, Jerusalem, late seventh century A.D.

who were direct descendants of the Prophet's companions. Shaped as an octagon, it was designed as a special holy place—not an ordinary mosque. Inside, it contains two concentric ambulatories, walkways, surrounding a central space capped by the dome. The mosque sits on a site revered by Jews as the tomb of Adam and the place where Abraham prepared to sacrifice Isaac. According to Muslim tradition, it is also the place from which Muhammad ascended into heaven. Written accounts suggest that it was built to overshadow a sacred temple of similar construction on the other side of Jerusalem—the Holy Sepulchre. Calif Abd al-Malik wanted a monument that would outshine the Christian churches of the area, and, perhaps, the Kaaba in Mecca. The exterior was later decorated with the glazed blue tiles that give the façade its dazzling appearance; the inside glitters with gold, glass, and mother-of-pearl, in multicolored mosaics. A detail of the richly intricate mosaics of the Dome of the Rock in Jerusalem can be seen in Figure **6.24**. This symmetrical pattern in deep red and gold, highlighted with accents of white and purple, illustrates the skill and delicacy which Muslim artists brought to this form. Undoubtedly, the Dome of the Rock was intended to speak to Christians as well as Muslims, distracting the former from the splendor of Christian churches. Inside the mosque is an inscription: "The Messiah Jesus Son of Mary is only an apostle of God, and His Word which he conveyed into Mary, and a Spirit proceeding from Him. Believe therefore in God and his apostles and say not 'Three.' It will be better for you. God is only one God. Far be it from his glory that He should have a son."

6.24 Details of mosaic decoration, Dome of the Rock, Jerusalem, Israel, A.D. 691–692.

6.25 Great Mosque, Damascus, Syria. Courtyard looking west, c. 715.

6.26 Details of mosaic decoration, Great Mosque, Damascus, c. 715.

Another excellent example of Islamic architecture is the Great Mosque of Damascus (Fig. **6.25**). When the Muslims captured Damascus in 635, they adapted the precinct of a pagan temple, which had been converted into a Christian church, into an open-air mosque. Seventy years later, al-Walid demolished the church and set about building the largest mosque in Islam. The only feature of the original buildings left standing was the Roman wall, although the four original towers were metamorphosed into the first minarets, from which the faithful were called to prayer. Unfortunately, the centuries have not been kind to the Great Mosque. Sacked a number of times, much of the splendor of its lavish decorations has been lost. However, some of its grandeur can be seen in the arcaded courtyard, with fine, gold-inlaid detailing visible in the returns of the arches (see Fig. **6.25**). Inside, colorful mosaics (Fig. **6.26**) express great subtlety of detail and texture. These works rank among the most accomplished of mosaics and were probably produced by Byzantine craftsmen.

A CRITICAL REVIEW

Islam traces its heritage back to the Jewish Patriarch Abraham and Jesus plays a prominent role in the Islamic view of the end of the world. That being the case, we need to speculate why there has been so much friction among these three religions.

Islam, Judaism, and Christianity rest on the premise of "revealed truth"—a set of holy scriptures in which the single God of the universe is claimed to have revealed his nature and his will directly to an individual or individuals who have, then, passed that revealed truth on to others.

How does the art of Islam reflect the teachings of Muhammad's version of "revealed truth?"

Return to Chapter 5, examine the Temple of Solomon, and, using the elements of line, structure, and proportion, compare it with the Dome of the Rock.

SYNTHESIS

In Praise of the Emperor—the Mark of Justinian

Our Synthesis material for this chapter comes from the individual who tried to reunite the Eastern and Western Empires. Like Augustus Caesar, he saw art as a way of perpetuating his image as an emperor, although a Christian one. We draw the synthesis by examining two great edifices, the church of San Vitale in Ravenna and the monumental Hagia Sophia, Church of St Sophia, in Constantinople. We have to imagine the Church of St Sophia without its four minarets. These were added after the Muslims conquered Byzantium and converted the building to a mosque. Today St Sophia is a museum, and there is no picture that can prepare you for the breath-taking nature of its scale. After nearly fifteen hundred years, its dome still represents one of the greatest engineering feats of human history. Thus, these two edifices, one in the East and one in the West—reflecting the persona of the emperor who would reunite East and West and altered by Islamic minarets—give us a closing overview of Byzantium, the crossroads of Europe and

Asia, Roman Catholicism, Eastern Orthodoxy, and Islam.

The portraits of Justinian that appear in mosaics—such as that in Figure **6.6**—reveal a man who does not look like an emperor. He was of average height and build, and had dark hair and a ruddy complexion. He was clean shaven, and every portrait shows a slight smile. However, despite his unexceptional appearance, he was a brilliant thinker who possessed enormous talents. He apparently liked the role of emperor and played it to the hilt, but he seems to have been likeable, in spite of his vigor and arrogance.

San Vitale in Ravenna (Figs **6.27** and **6.28**) is the major Justinian monument in the West. It was probably built as a testament to the power of Orthodoxy in the declining kingdom of the Ostrogoths.

The church consists of two concentric octagons (see Fig. **6.28**). The hemispherical dome, 100 feet (30 meters) above the floor, rises from a drum above the inner octagon, which is pierced with windows that flood the inte-

Anthemius of Tralles (c. sixth century)

It may seem strange to include a profile about someone like Anthemius of Tralles (pronounced an-THEE-mee-us), about whom virtually nothing is known. However, the fact that we know his name at all is a testament to the vision and profound quality of his architectural work. During this period of history, individual artists—especially architects—did not gain fame. Their work was an expression, usually religious, that glorified God, the emperor, or the Church, and individualism, as we know it, in artistic work had ceased. However, we know of Anthemius. First of all, he was a mathematician and the author of *Concerning Remarkable Mechanical Devises*, a treatise on burning glasses that recorded the mathematical function of the directrix.

Anthemius' lasting fame, however, came as a result of his design for what was at the time, and still

remains, one of the greatest architectural accomplishments of history—the church of St Sophia in Constantinople. Commissioned by the Emperor Justinian, Anthemius designed a building that, according to Justinian's court historian, Procopius, "through the harmony of its measurements... is distinguished by indescribable beauty." Inasmuch as Anthemius was a mathematician, it does not surprise us to discover that Anthemius and his partner, Isidorus of Miletus (also a mathematician), based the design for St Sophia on a sphere standing upon a circle. To Anthemius, architecture was the "application of geometry to solid matter," and his designs brought to Constantinople an entirely new approach to architecture by showing an inventive structure of form that stood entirely outside the Roman tradition. Such a departure reveals a profound intellect and great courage.

6.27 San Vitale, Ravenna, Italy, 526–547. Interior, looking east.

6.28 Plan and transverse section of San Vitale, Ravenna, Italy.

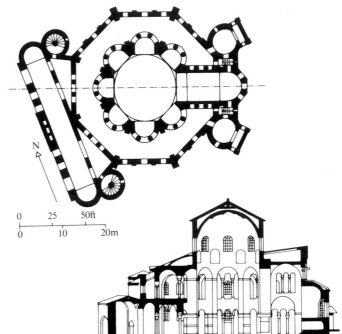

6.29 *Abraham's Hospitality and the Sacrifice of Isaac.* Wall mosaic, San Vitale, Ravenna, Italy.

rior with light. Below, eight large piers alternate with columned niches to define precisely the central space and to create an intricate, many-layered design. The narthex is placed at an odd angle. There are two possible explanations for this: the practical one is that the narthex paralleled a then-existing street; a more spiritual one is that the narthex was so designed in order to force worshipers to reorient themselves on entering, thereby facilitating the transition from the outside world to the spiritual one.

On the second level of the ambulatory was a special gallery reserved for women—a standard feature of Byzantine churches.

The internal spatial design is intricate. The visitor experiences an ever-changing vista of arches within arches, linking flat walls and curved spaces. All the aisles and galleries contrast strikingly with the calm area under the dome. The clerestory light reflects off the mosaic tiles with great richness. In fact, new construction techniques in the vaulting allowed for windows on every level and opened the sanctuary to much more light than had previously been possible.

The sanctuary itself is alive with mosaics of the Imperial court and of sacred events. The difference in style between two mosaics in the same church is particularly fascinating. *Abraham's Hospitality and the Sacrifice of Isaac* (Fig. **6.29**) demonstrates what is, by Byzantine standards, a relaxed naturalism. The mosaic showing Justinian and his court (see Fig. **6.6**), on the other hand, demonstrates the orientalized style, more typically Byzantine, with the figures posed rigidly and facing forward. The mosaics clearly link the church to the Byzantine court, reflecting again, the connection of the emperor to the Faith, of Christianity to the State, and, indeed, the concept of the "Divine Emperor." Justinian (see Fig. **6.6**) and Theodora (see Fig. **6.1**) are portrayed very much like Christ and the Virgin. The two mosaics face each other behind the high altar of San Vitale. In Figure **6.6** the emperor has a golden halo with a red border, he wears a regal purple robe, and he is shown presenting a golden bowl to Christ, who is pictured in the SEMIDOME above the mosaic (see Fig. **6.27**).

If San Vitale praises the emperor and Orthodoxy in the West, St Sophia, is a crowning monument to his achievement in the East (Figs **6.30**, **6.33–6.36**). Its architect, Anthemius, was a natural scientist and geometer from Tralles in Asia Minor. St Sophia is characteristic of the Justinian Byzantine style in its use of well-rehearsed Roman vaulting techniques combined with Hellenistic

6.30 Anthemius of Tralles and Isidorus of Miletus, St Sophia, Istanbul, Turkey, 532–537.

TECHNOLOGY: PUTTING DISCOVERY TO WORK

Spanning Space with Triangles and Pots

The ingenuity of human achievement is often revealed in the subtleties of invention that have allowed architects to create great open spaces under remarkably heavy materials such as stone and cement. We have seen this in the great dome of the Pantheon of Rome, and now we see it in what is still the largest dome ever created, St Sophia in Constantinople. It is a reminder that what was best in the West came from the uninterrupted Roman building tradition of that city. In 537, at a time when Western Europe was at its most barbaric, Justinian's great brickwork cathedral was dedicated. What made it remarkable was the invention of a device to transfer the weight of a great dome downward—not on a cylindrical tub as was the case of the Pantheon—but through the use of a triangular device called a PENDENTIVE (Fig. **6.31**) to the corners of a square tower, 180 feet (55 meters) above the ground. Dedicated to the Divine Wisdom, St Sophia illustrates the sublime ingenuity of humankind.

In another of Justinian's marvels, as we have noted, Byzantine influence and technological creativity reflects itself in the church of San Vitale in Ravenna (Fig. **6.32**). Here, in order to compensate for the potentially crushing weight of a

6.32 Façade of San Vitale, Ravenna, Italy.

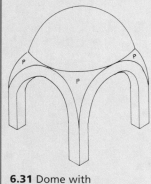

6.31 Dome with pendentives (P).

solid dome, the architect used hollow earthenware pots for construction. Thus, space was enclosed without utilizing a base so cumbersome as to ruin the aesthetic considerations of lightness and beauty. Whether in soaring domes or towers that reach 110 stories into the air, technological inventiveness has always lain at the heart of new dimensions in architecture. None has superseded the marvels of Byzantium, where, in addition to unsurpassed domes, stone was jointed with such precision that some buildings did not require mortar.

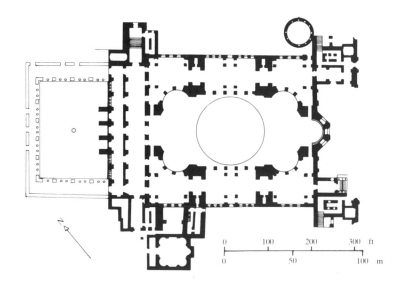

principles of design and geometry. The result is a building in an orientalized, antique style.

Built to replace an earlier basilica, St Sophia was for a long time the largest church in the world. It was completed in only five years and ten months, between 532 and 537. The speed of the work, together with Byzantine masonry techniques, in which courses of brick alternate with courses of mortar as thick as, or thicker than, the bricks, caused great weight to be placed on insufficiently dry mortar. As a result, arches buckled, and buttresses had to be erected almost at once. The additional effects of two earthquakes caused the eastern arch and part of the dome itself to fall in 557.

6.33 Plan of St Sophia, Istanbul, Turkey.

6.34 St Sophia, Istanbul, interior.

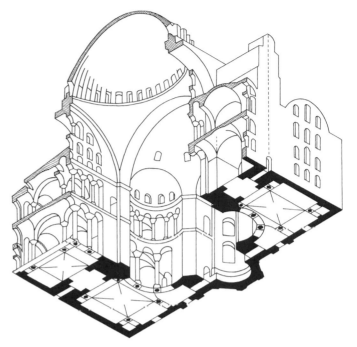

6.35 Axonometric section (perspective view) of St Sophia, Istanbul, Turkey.

6.36 Capitals in St Sophia, Istanbul, Turkey.

The flatness of a dome so large—110 feet (33.5 meters) in diameter—remains unique, and the delicate proportioning of the vaults that support such great weight is also remarkable. Basic to the conception is the elevated central area, with its picture of heaven in the dome and its large, open, and functional spaces. The building could hold large numbers of worshippers in a transcendental environment, where thoughts at once rise to a spiritual sphere. "It seemed as if the vault of heaven were suspended above one," wrote Procopius.

The capitals of the columns in St Sophia (see Fig. **6.36**) illustrate a style that is totally Byzantine. The deeply undercut ornament shows originality and technical mastery. Classical elements, such as volutes and leaves like those on Corinthian capitals, are subsumed into the vigorous decoration. This is in no way a dilution of classicism, but the birth of a new style. Justinian's other buildings show work of the same type, but that in St Sophia represents the highest quality.

Justinian's reign inaugurated the style called "Byzantine," blending traces of previous styles, Eastern and Western, to form a new style. The hieratic art from the reign of Justinian expresses the relationship between God and the State. With the emperor governing by, and for, the will of God, all reality—political, philosophical, and artistic—became spiritualized.

CHAPTER SEVEN

THE EARLY MIDDLE AGES

AT A GLANCE

The Middle Ages

The Medieval Church
Devils and Division
The Roman Papacy
Monasticism
  PROFILE: Pope Gregory I

Charlemagne's Empire

Feudalism
Feudal Lords
Serfs and Women
  TECHNOLOGY: The Viking Ships

The Ottonians

The Visual Arts
Manuscript Illumination and Sculpture
Romanesque Style in Architecture and
  Sculpture
  MASTERWORK: The Bronze Doors of
    Hildesheim Cathedral

OUR DYNAMIC WORLD: Igbo-Ukwu

Music
Sacred Music
Secular Music

Literature

Theatre

Synthesis: The Carolingian Renaissance

7.1 Scenes from the life of St Paul, from the Bible of Charles the Bald, c. 875–877. San Paolo Fuori le Mura, Rome.

ROMANUMQ SOLUM LINQUIT LOCA SCA PETENDO · INSTRUITUR TALI REDIMENS ELEMENTA MAGISTRO

PLACUIT · IN ROREM COGITOS FATERI · PAULAM CUM PROLE DOCET QUIBUS IN MAX PI
NON M HIEROSUM CONFERRI DONA SUPERNA · GRATEM DIFFUSUM FIDEI DONUM DUPLICAVIT

ARCHIS CUM NETRAS LIBRATUM CLAM COS IS DISCIPLA NESIRAT LABOR TRAN MILLI HABENDA
HIER ALICOS EBURNEA TEMPLA IUDAEUM NEMUS QUOD FATENS IN VIT NOSTRIS

SERAT IN PRESS DATO LUMINE LUSTRANS MOX AFER LIMEN LINQUO QUOD SID

A CRITICAL LOOK

We are about to examine the period of time that produced the currently popular medieval chant. As we will see, this period is part of a thousand-year epoch (which will take us three chapters to finish) that is foreign to, and yet strangly like, our modern era. After the introductory passage, we look again at the Christian Church, because it was the prevailing force in the Western world at the time. We will see how it gave shape to society and kept alive intellectual traditions that might otherwise have perished. However, first, we must look more closely at the years we call the Middle Ages, because, although we put a single label on that millennium, it was made up of some very distinct periods and artistic styles.

What were the divisions of the Middle Ages, and what were their characteristics?

What was the role of the Christian Church in the events of the time?

What were the characteristics of medieval monasticism?

THE MIDDLE AGES

We have come to use the name the Middle Ages for the period that began with the fall of Rome and closed with the Renaissance in Italy. Although we must not regard particular dates as indicating specific beginnings and ends of periods or artistic styles, we can see a relative changing of conditions and attitudes that helps us to draw relative parameters on history, and, in so doing, assists us in keeping our chronological bearings. From roughly the late fifth century to the early eleventh century it seemed that humankind had crept into an enclosed world of mental and physical isolation and self-protection, but there are divisions within this large expanse of time. For example, the years from approximately 200 to the middle of the sixth century are often called Early Christian. We have already looked at part of this period, and we will continue our examination in this chapter. The term Dark Ages is occasionally used to describe the two hundred years between 550 and 750. The Carolingian and Ottonian period occurred from 750 to 1000; the Romanesque, from 1000 to 1150; and the High Gothic, from 1150 to 1400. The late Gothic period from 1300 to 1500 overlaps High Gothic, and was a time of transition during which the flower of the Renaissance was beginning to bloom. This chapter will take us from approximately 500 to 1150, or from the Dark Ages through to the artistic style called Romanesque.

As we saw in Chapter 3, Periclean Athens represented a consolidation of diverse forces that created a cohesive civilization, but the early Middle Ages was a period of dissolution. Indeed, the Western world disintegrated into a chaotic confusion and, to a large degree, spiritual and intellectual darkness. The time from the fall of Rome until the beginning of the Gothic period was, for many, a time of fear and superstition. For Christians, who had little to hope, save that beyond this life lay the promise of heaven for those who obediently followed the teachings of the Catholic Church, it was "a vale of tears," but, in

monasteries and convents throughout Europe, literacy, learning, and artistic creativity were nurtured. It was widely believed that the end of the first millennium would bring the Second Coming of Christ, and many of the works of the period are filled with a deeply moving, intuitive vision.

The thousand years between the fifth and the fifteenth centuries have been called the Middle Ages or medieval period on the theory that nothing—or worse than nothing—happened between the classical perfection of Greece and Rome and the revival of classical humanism in the fifteenth century. We shall use the terms as convenient labels, but not as value judgments. Furthermore, in an overview such as this, we must remember that there are always specific exceptions to any general summary, and this is especially true of a world as fragmented as that of the Middle Ages.

Pessimism and disillusionment had increased in ancient Rome, and this mood, summed up in a well-known epitaph—"I was not; I was; I am not; I care not"—continued into the Middle Ages. Civic, secular government had all but ceased to exist. When Constantine I founded the second capital of the Roman Empire at Constantinople, he set in motion a division that became permanent in 395. In the West, the cloak of internationalism, which had loosely united the Mediterranean world since Alexander, fell apart. It became a case of "every locality and every people for themselves."

As we noted in previous chapters, since the turn of the Christian era, the Roman Empire had been attacked from without, while decaying from within. The Goths, the Huns, the Visigoths, the Vandals, and the armies of Islam threatened and pierced the perimeters of the Empire. The Western world was in a state of continual change. As one people imposed against another, the victim turned upon its neighbor on the other side. Nations as we know them did not exist. Borders changed from day to day as one or another people wandered into the nebulously defined territory of its neighbors, bringing confusion and war.

	GENERAL EVENTS	LITERATURE & PHILOSOPHY	VISUAL ART & ARCHITECTURE	THEATRE & MUSIC
400	End of Roman occupation of Britain Sack of Rome by Goths Visigoths begin conquest of Spain Clovis, king of Francs			
500	Justinian I Birth of Muhammad Gregory I, the Great St Augustine to England	*Book of Pastoral Care*		Gregorian chant
600	Sutton Hoo burial ship Alexandria taken by Muslims Buddhism established	Lindisfarne Gospels (7.8)		Troubadours
700	Charles Martel in France Pepin, king of Francs	*Beowulf* Gospel of Godescalc (7.21) Dagulf Psalter (7.25)		
800	Charlemagne Earliest dated book printed in China Death of Alfred the Great	Gospel of St Médard (7.22) Lorsch Gospels (7.26) Carolingian Renaissance *Song of Roland*	Palatine Chapel, Aachen (7.27, 7.28)	
900	Monastic reform from Cluny Sung dynasty in China (until 1279)		Gero crucifix (7.10)	Notker Balbulus
1000		*Niebelungenlied*	Hildesheim Cathedral (7.11) St Sernin (7.12, 7.13) Cluny (7.15, 7.16, 7.17) Autun Cathedral (7 19) Ste-Madeleine (7.20)	Guido of Arezzo

Timeline 7.1 The early Middle Ages.

THE MEDIEVAL CHURCH

DEVILS AND DIVISION

The devil, as a symbol of the powers of darkness and evil, was a strong force in medieval thinking, and the Church manipulated those fears as it sought, often fanatically, to convert the pagan world of the early Middle Ages. The promise of heaven and the prospect of the fires of hell were constant themes of the times. Ever-present devils and demons fostered a certain fascination as well as fear—as we shall see in medieval theatre, for example, the devil often had the best part.

Nevertheless, the Church played an important stabilizing role in this often desperate and frenzied world. It provided a source of continuity, and, as its influence spread, medieval philosophy turned from the acceptance of human beings as the measure of all things to regarding God as the measure of all things. Led by the Church, the Western world slowly came to believe that death promised a glorious life in the hereafter, at least for a select few.

The Church was itself divided, however, and it did little to reduce the isolation and ignorance of its followers. Very early, the clergy separated into two groups, one consisting of the regular clergy, monks, and others who preferred to withdraw into a cloistered life—a lifestyle that greatly appealed to many intellectuals as well—and the other consisting of the secular clergy—that is, the Pope, bishops, and parish priests who served in society at large. The overall effect of this division was to confine learning and philosophy to monasteries, and to withhold intellectual activity from the broader world. Inquiry among both groups was rigidly restricted. Detailed and unquestioned dogma was deemed essential to the Church's mission of conversion—and, indeed, to its very survival—and as a result, the medieval world was one of barricades, physical, spiritual, and intellectual. Each man, woman, and institution retreated behind whatever barricade he, she, or it found safest.

THE ROMAN PAPACY

In the sixth century, Italy faced an uncertain future. Although Rome no longer ruled a secular empire, the primacy claimed by its bishops gave Rome a potential position of great importance in the Christian world. Such a possibility, however, was clouded by two significant factors. One was the barbarism that still held sway in the western provinces. The other was the complex theocracy of the East, where the emperors were both secular and sacred rulers.

In response to yet another quarrel over doctrine, Pope Gelasius (492–496) drew up a new formulation of the roles of priests and kings in the government of the Christian world. The world, he said, was ruled by two powers, the sacred authority of the priesthood and royal power. The responsibilities of the priesthood were the greater, however, because priests had kings within their pastoral charge. The problem was further complicated by Justinian's grand designs for a unified empire (see Chapter 6). Justinian had not the slightest intention of yielding to the Roman bishops in matters of religion if it were politically inconvenient for him. By the middle of the sixth century it appeared likely that the Roman Church and its Pope would simply become tools of Byzantine Imperial policy. Rome appeared to have been demoted to a peripheral status as a mere center of Catholic Christianity, with little actual power or influence.

Rome was rescued from potential demise by one of the greatest pontiffs in the history of the Roman Church, Gregory I (the Great), who was pope between 590 and 604. Gregory showed great abilities as a ruler and teacher that significantly affected numerous aspects of the Church and its history, as well as many political and social matters in Rome. His land reforms and his administration of estates that had been given to the Church revitalized Church income, relieved famine, and provided money for churches, hospitals, and schools. His influence spread from Rome to the rest of Italy and beyond. One of the most important tasks he undertook was the sponsorship of St Augustine in his mission to convert England in 597. The most significant of Gregory's written works was his *Book of Pastoral Care*, in which he spoke idealistically of the way a bishop should live and how he should care for his flock.

As a result of Gregory's efforts, Rome regained its position of primacy among the Western Christian Churches. Despite the long-term results of Gregory's actions, he did not himself consider that he was building for the future. He believed that the Second Coming of Christ was near, and he merely did what he thought had to be done in what little time remained. Thus it was unintentionally that he built a base for an enduring Church and a dominant papacy of wealth and great prestige.

MONASTICISM

Seeking refuge from the temptations and tribulations of the medieval world, monks, nuns, some aristocrats, and others sought refuge behind the walls of perhaps the most typical example of medieval life—the monastery and the convent—which were outposts of order and charity. Often, too, they were well-organized and productive centers of agriculture. Monasteries and nunneries were established in the centers of non-Christian populations as means of converting pagans to Christianity. If monastery life offered an escape from some of the tribulations of the secular world, it did not permit an escape from rigor and hard work. Pious men and women of the monastic communities combined labor in the fields with religious thought, meditation, prayer, and other activities, such as copying sacred scripts and creating beautiful manuscript illuminations. Monks, who took vows of poverty, chastity, and obedience, renouncing all worldly goods, family life, and the pleasures of the senses, owned nothing—not even their own wills. They were subject to a strict discipline under the authority of the abbot and the will of God (Fig. **7.2**).

Within the walls of the monastery, everything that was necessary for bodily and spiritual existence was provided, and the objective of the monastery was to be fully independent from all secular authority and life. In the

7.2 Monks in choir. Illustration from Cotton Domitian. A XVII, folio 122v. British Library, London.

PROFILE

Pope Gregory I, the Great (540–604)

Nothing is known about Pope Gregory's early years and education. He rose to the position of prefect of the City of Rome, but left politics and founded the Monastery of St Andrew in Rome. Pope Pelagius II sent Gregory to Constantinople—then the seat of Roman Imperial government—as ambassador, and his experiences and the contacts he made over six years in that position proved invaluable. When Pelagius died in 590, Gregory was elected pope when he was fifty years old.

One of the major difficulties confronting the new pope lay in the conflict over the Roman ideology of emperor as divinity on earth. In such a scheme, the pope was merely another patriarch. While he had served as ambassador in Constantinople, Gregory had gained a realistic understanding of the political situations of the day, and he recognized the delicacy of the pope's rela-

7.3 Pope Gregory I, the Great (540–604).

tionship to the secular, imperial government. Gregory wisely turned his attention to Western Europe, a domain that lay outside imperial jurisdiction, where he could push the claim of the supremacy of the Church of Rome without any interference from Constantinople.

One of his major missionary achievements was the conversion of England, which began in 597 with the mission of St Augustine. Gregory also supported St Benedict, leading to the development of Benedictine monasticism. His extraordinary administrative abilities brought most of Europe and North Africa under Roman papal authority, and he provided the driving force in the unification of much of Church doctrine and practice, exercising in all these ways a tremendous influence throughout the Western world.

monastery, a fine example being the great monastery at Cluny (see Figs **7.15**, **7.16**, and **7.17**), the ascetic world and the secular world often rubbed shoulders, however. In addition to clerics and contemplatives, Cluny, for example, often harbored criminals seeking refuge from secular authorities.

Life for the Cluniac monk exemplified life in the cloistered communities of Europe in general. Religious contemplation alternated with other religious duties, and the abbey church witnessed prayer and worship day and night. Prayers were held according to the appointed hours of liturgy, running from sunrise to sunset in a form similar to the following:

2:00 a.m. Rise
2:10–3:30 Nocturns (matins) The first office of prayer
3:30–5:00 Individual study and contemplation
5:00–5:45 Lauds (morning prayer)
5:45–8:15 Prime (an office of prayer); private reading; Mass; or breakfast, depending on the season
8:25–2:30 Work, separated by the offices of Tierce, Sext, and None (third, sixth, and ninth hours)

2:30–3:15 Dinner
3:15–4:15 Private reading and contemplation
4:15–4:45 Vespers; Compline (night prayers)
5:15–6:00 Retire for the night

The daily schedule, or *horarium*, changed somewhat for Feast Days and to allow for the longer days of the summer months.

Of course, in addition to religious activity, more practical matters needed attention. In the center of the monastery complex lay the CLOISTER, a covered arcade around a rectangular, open garden. An important part of the monastery was the refectory where monks ate their meals, and there was also a chapter hall where monks met to conduct their communal business. A dormitory lay close to the church.

Many monasteries were also centers for pilgrimages, and travelers as well as pious pilgrims came for veneration and overnight accommodation to those monasteries that contained sacred relics. A hospice, or guest house, provided lodging, especially for visitors during the pilgrimage season, and barns, stables, and places for blacksmithing were often among the components of a monastic community.

The way of the monk and nun was the way of asceti-

trade throughout the interior of Europe.

Charlemagne's reign was, as we noted, a brief ray of light in the Dark Ages. It succeeded in slowing—perhaps halting—the long decline of Europe, and it illumined a pathway whereby peace and prosperity might be restored. However, the heir to the Carolingian throne did not have Charlemagne's physical strength or his strength of will. Less than thirty years after his death, his grandsons divided the kingdom into three. The Carolingian era lasted until late in the ninth century, but, when it was over, Europe reverted to a divided and troubled condition waiting for strong kings—the true heirs of Charlemagne—to come onto the scene.

FEUDALISM

FEUDAL LORDS

Perhaps the main reason why centralized authority could not take hold in the early Middle Ages was a societal system called feudalism. The real political powers in Europe in the Dark Ages were the dukes, counts, knights, and other warrior lords, who were linked together in a loose confederation of units, each one small enough to be governed by one man. Because no powerful authority ultimately controlled the individual parts, the system encouraged bloodshed and warfare as feudal lords continually raided each other to increase their wealth and property.

Feudalism was a system of military service and land ownership that created a pyramid of political and military power. Under this system, the less powerful knights sought protection and economic support from more powerful knights who, thus, became their feudal lords, or seigneurs, and who required military service, money, and political support from their vassals. Although feudalism was based on a system of vassalage, by which barons were responsible to, or vassals of, kings, sufficient power to effect real control rarely existed at any level above the individual landholder. Thus, despotic rulers flourished.

The oath of fealty was performed at a solemn and symbolic ceremony. The vassal knelt, put his hands between those of his lord, and pledged allegiance to the lord, promising a certain number of days of military service each year and specific sums of money on occasions such as the knighting of the lord's son (Fig. **7.5**) or the marriage of the lord's daughter, or ransom for the lord himself if he were captured by his enemies. To complete the ceremony, the lord would present to the vassal a piece of earth or a sprig from a tree to symbolize the lord's grant of a fief—that is, a parcel of land including villages of serfs to work it.

7.5 The girding-on of swords, part of an increasingly formalized ritual associated with the making of a knight. MS D XI fol 134 vi. British Library, London.

SERFS AND WOMEN

Trapped at the bottom of this rigid social structure, and often in the middle of the bloodletting, were the common people, or serfs. Serfs were little more than slaves, who were attached to the land, worked for the local lord, and were subject to the lord's bidding. It was a life of ignorance and destitution, and one of total subservience to the manor's lord. Serfs did all the work of the manor, and in return paid the lord for the privilege. All law enforcement and punishment occurred within the manor, and no serf could marry without the lord's consent. In the strictest sense of the ancient world, serfs were not slaves, but they were bound to the land of the estate for life, and, bound to the land, they were bound to the lord of the manor for as long as the lord owned it. In return, the lord was obliged to provide guardianship for his serfs—that is, provide basic necessities and care for them in their old age, should they reach it.

Drudgery marked the daily life of the village. People lived in one-room, sparsely-furnished huts with earthen floors. They shared the hut with members of the family, chickens, and whatever other animals may have been theirs, and at night the entire family slept huddled together on straw bedding. In the spring, life took a decided turn for the worse, for typically the fall's harvest barely lasted the winter, and it was too early in the growing season for

7.6 Leprosy, from the manuscript *Miroir historial de Vincent de Beauvais*, trans. by Jean de Vignay, 1330–50. Bibliothèque Nationale, Paris.

TECHNOLOGY: PUTTING DISCOVERY TO WORK

The Viking Ships

While feudal Europe struggled and while Charlemagne was emerging as Holy Roman Emperor, the Vikings of Scandinavia were sailing as far as the shores of North America, preceding Columbus to the New World by more than six hundred years. Their means of transport was the Viking ship (Fig. **7.7**), and its construction and use prove that these hearty and hardy peoples were as skillful in their technology as they were warlike and adventurous. The vessel had a true keel, a single steering-oar with a tiller handle, well-raked—that is, angled—stem- and stern-posts, sixteen rowing ports cut into each side, and a square-sail rigged on a single mast amidships. Light and buoyant, they were called long-ships because their length was such a striking feature, exceeding the beam by more than five to one. In time, the Viking ships grew until they had thirty and even sixty oars to a side. It was in these large vessels that the Vikings made their raids, conquests, and far-reaching explorations to Russia and America.

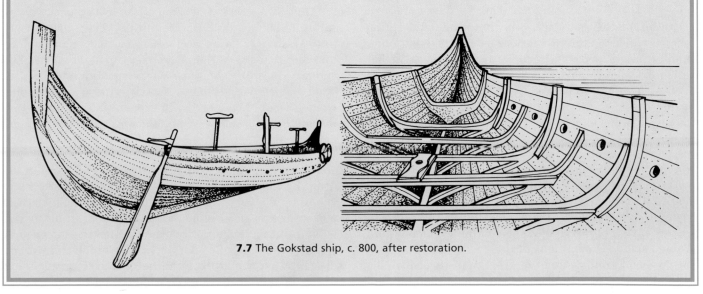

7.7 The Gokstad ship, c. 800, after restoration.

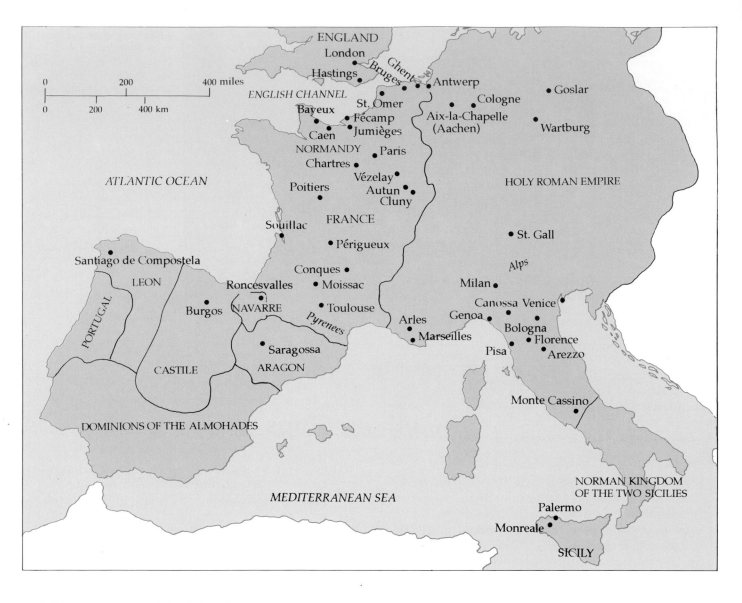

Map 7.2 Europe in the early twelfth century.

new crops to mature. As a result, starvation in the springtime provided a constant threat, as did raids by other, equally hungry, people who formed raiding parties of barbarians or other local barons. Disease was a constant companion, and there were no doctors (Fig. **7.6**). All told, the medieval serf could only resign himself to his fate and trudge on from day to day, hopeful that death would release him into a better condition. As Christianity spread, the terrors of "today" were endurable only in anticipation of reward in the life to come.

Women played a central role at every level of medieval society. In the manor house as well as the village hut, the family was the core of the social order, and among serfs, it also provided the central production unit. Women shared the burdens of daily existence, caring for children and animals and working small vegetable plots near the hut. They prepared food, made clothing, and

helped with the harvest. Their life expectancy was short.

On the other hand, women of the manor often shared ruling functions and responsibilities. The power structure, again, was based on the family, and one was born into the aristocracy. The system depended on inheritance and marriage, and because women could inherit, they often owned vast estates. As wives of feudal barons, women were often faced with the necessity of managing the manor in its entirety while the lord was away for long periods, fighting wars on behalf of his liege lord.

Women could also find individual identity and authority in the Church. If the burdens of secular life proved overpowering, women could "take the veil" by entering a convent. Wealthy women could establish their own convents and become a mother superior or abbess, wielding absolute authority over her subservient nuns. A woman who so devoted her life to the Church and worked diligently on behalf of it and her fellow humans could dream of sainthood—an honor bestowed by the Church after death—which would place her at the right hand of God for eternity.

THE OTTONIANS

The focus of Europe shifted to Germany in the tenth century when the pope crowned the German Emperors Otto I, II, and III. These Ottonians subsequently attempted to control the still struggling Church, and the resulting conflict between emperor and pope, along with the effects of the developing feudal and monastic systems, ensured Europe's continued political fragmentation.

The Ottonian emperors failed in their attempts to subjugate the growing Christian Church, however. By the eleventh century, the Church, and especially its monastic orders, had come to great power and wealth. Christianity had triumphed throughout Europe, and the threat of invasion from the perimeters had ceased. Religious fervor and fanaticism now resurfaced. More and more pilgrimages were made to sacred sites, and the crusades to liberate the Holy Land began. Trade started up again as the Italian ports of Venice, Genoa, and Pisa began to reclaim the trade routes of the Mediterranean. Towns and cities were growing, and a new middle class was emerging.

THE VISUAL ARTS

MANUSCRIPT ILLUMINATION AND SCULPTURE

Early Christian painting adopted local styles. The tomb paintings in the catacombs of Rome, the only safe haven for Christians, were, for example, Roman in style but incorporated Christian symbolism. Roman Christians were converted Roman pagans, and their paintings had a frankly practical intent. In its earliest phases, before Constantine, Christian painting was a secret art in a secret place, and its function was simply to affirm the faith of the follower on his or her tomb.

One often finds in early Christian painting a primitive quality; it is probably more a reflection of lack of technical ability than anything else. The need to pictorialize the faith was foremost. Artistic skill was not important.

Christian painting developed in several stages. From the beginning, it reflected the absolute belief in another, superior existence in which individual believers retained their identity. Painting was a tangible expression of faith. Later, it was used to make the rites of the Church more

---

A CRITICAL REVIEW

We tend to see feudalism as a social organization limited to a particular period of time in human history. Its manor-driven, local-centered life probably could not function today with our instant access to world events and lives that tend to be controlled by state and national governments and international trade. Although feudal organization may have disappeared, however, feudal thinking may not have. Is our world-view centered on ourselves and the events closest to us? Is there a local "manor" in our lives in whose service we toil in return for the promise of protection?

Identify some of the psychological and social aspects of feudalism that still exist. Are these helpful or harmful? Defend your case, and then defend the opposite side.

A CRITICAL LOOK

Debates often arise about questions like these: Does art really mirror its times, or is it purely a result of some internal necessity of the artist? Should art be useful or does it exist for its own sake? Keep these questions in mind in the next section, in which we examine the arts of the period. Among other things, we will be investigating: the role fulfilled by manuscript illustration and its compositional qualities; the psychological qualities of Romanesque sculpture and architecture; and the characteristics of secular music of the early Middle Ages and the important musical developments of the time.

What was the condition of the theatre in the early medieval period, and who were the important individuals associated with it?

Identify and explain the German hero-stories of the twelfth century.

vivid. Its final role was that of depicting and recording Christian history and tradition. Inherent from the start was a code of symbolism whose meaning could be grasped only by a fellow Christian.

As the Roman world first split and then fell apart, plunging the West into chaos, painting became once again a private art, more an intellectual pursuit than an inspiration to the faithful. A new and exquisite form of two-dimensional art emerged, not on canvases or church walls, but on the beautifully illustrated pages of scholarly Church manuscripts. By the time Christianity had sufficient status to come into the open, a dramatic change had occurred in the format of written texts. Rolls of papyrus had been replaced by more convenient and durable parchment pages bound together between hard, protective covers, known as a codex. Although scrolls continued to be used for special occasions throughout the Middle Ages, they were now made of stitched parchment.

The only illustrated manuscript of the New Testament in Latin to survive from this early period is a copy of the Gospels that probably came to England in 597 with St Augustine, the first Archbishop of Canterbury and a missionary from Pope Gregory the Great. (This Augustine is not to be confused with the earlier St

7.9 Hinged shoulder clasp from the ship burial at Sutton Hoo, England, seventh century. Gold decorated with garnets, mosaic, glass, and filigree. British Museum, London.

Augustine of Hippo.) Only two full-page miniatures survive, one of which (see Fig. **5.13**) shows St Luke and twelve scenes from his Gospel. It is a full-page frontispiece. We see the saint seated in the foreground within an arched border. In the sides of the frame are little compartments portraying events, including the story of the washing of feet, with an unbearded Peter. The rich colors and detailing of this miniature rival those of the wall mosaics and decorations of Byzantium. The artistic quality of the St Augustine Gospels is not very high, however, in that the figure proportions are inaccurate, the medium is handled loosely, and details are carelessly executed. Perhaps it was not considered worthwhile to send a more valuable book to the still largely heathen England.

Nonetheless, this work is an interesting example of an early picture cycle, and it typifies certain stylistic qualities that became more marked in medieval painting and sculpture. Compositions are close and nervous: figures bump against each other amid an atmosphere of frenetic energy. We feel a certain discomfort emanating from these "walled-in" and crowded scenes, which perhaps mirror the closed-in world of the medieval illustrator.

An Irish contribution to medieval manuscript illumination appears in Figure **7.8**. Here the figures are flat and almost ornamental, though they are precisely and delicately rendered. Highlight and shadow give a sense of depth in the curtain, and space is suggested by the oblique treatment of the bench. Accurate linear perspective is unknown to these artists. Colors are few and subtle. Of note here is the frontal treatment of the angel's eye, in contrast to the head, which is in profile. Outlining adds to the stylization. The picture is carefully composed, with both color and form controlled to achieve a pleasing balance.

From the fifth to the eleventh centuries, a tremendous wealth of artistic work emerged in several nontraditional areas. Life was generally in a state of flux throughout Europe in the early Middle Ages, and it was to ordinary

7.8 St Matthew, from the Lindisfarne Gospels, before 698. 13$\frac{1}{2}$ × 9$\frac{3}{4}$ ins (34.3 × 24.8 cm). British Library, London.

and portable media that nonmonastic nomadic people turned much of their artistic energy. Clothing, jewelry, and ships, for example, all exhibited the artistry of the Germanic, Irish, and Scandinavian peoples (Fig. **7.9**).

Emotionalism in art increased as the approach of the millennium sounded its trumpet of expected doom. The fact that the world did not end on 1 January 1001 reduced this feeling only slightly. Emotionalism was strengthened further by an influx of Eastern art into the Ottonian Empire, when Otto II married a Byzantine princess. A combination of Roman, Carolingian, and Byzantine characteristics typify Ottonian manuscript illustration. Despite the medieval crowding and an inherent appeal to feeling, such work testifies to the increasingly outward-looking approach of the early years of the second millennium.

Sculpture played only a very minor role in the centuries between the collapse of the Roman Empire and the rise of the Romanesque style in the eleventh century. The fact that the Old Testament prohibited graven images may have been partly responsible for this. The association of statuary with pagan societies, notably Rome, was fresh in the memory of the Church. Thus, when Christian sculpture emerged, it was largely funerary and not monumental. The earliest examples are all sarcophagi.

Some of the most beautiful sculptural work of the Christian era after Constantine resembles manuscript illumination in its small-scale, MINIATURE-like detail. Its restless, linear style is eloquent with emotion, and it is very precise in its detail.

7.10 *Gero crucifix*, 969–976. Oak, 6 ft 1⅝ ins (1.87 m) high. Cologne Cathedral, Germany.

Especially poignant is the *Gero crucifix* (Fig. **7.10**). The realism of the crucified Christ, whose downward and forward sagging body pulls against the nails, and the emotion with which it is rendered, are very compelling. The muscle striations on the right arm and chest, the bulging belly, and the rendering of cloth are particularly expressive. This work has a hardness of surface. The form is human, but the flesh, hair, and cloth do not have the soft texture we might expect. The face is a mask of agony, but no less full of pathos for that. An intense spirituality reflects the mysticism prevalent in the early Middle Ages. The *Gero crucifix* depicts a suffering Christ whose agony parallels the spirit of the times. This portrayal contrasts markedly with the *Christus Rex* crucifixes that became popular later and are frequently seen today, in which Christ on the cross is a victorious, resurrected King.

ROMANESQUE STYLE IN ARCHITECTURE AND SCULPTURE

As Charlemagne's Empire in the ninth century and then the tenth century passed, a new and radical style in architecture emerged. Unlike its counterparts in painting and sculpture, Romanesque architecture had a fairly identifiable style, despite its diversity. The Romanesque took hold throughout Europe in a relatively short period of time. When people of the Renaissance saw its curved arches over doorways and windows throughout Europe, they saw a style that was pre-Gothic and post-Roman— but like the Roman. Therefore, they called it "Romanesque." With its arched doorways and windows, this style was massive, static, and comparatively lightless, which seems further to reflect the barricaded mentality and lifestyle generally associated with the Middle Ages.

The Romanesque style nonetheless exemplified the power and wealth of the Church militant and triumphant. If the style mirrored the social and intellectual system that produced it, it also reflected a new religious fervor and a turning of the Church toward its growing flock. Romanesque churches were larger than earlier ones; we can see their scale in Figures **7.12** and **7.13**). St Sernin is an example of southern French Romanesque, and it reflects a heavy elegance and complexity we have not previously seen. The plan of the church describes a Roman cross, that is, a cross with the lower staff longer than the arms. The side aisles extend beyond the crossing to create an ambulatory, or walking space. This was so that pilgrims, most of whom were on their way to Spain, could walk around the altar without disturbing the service.

One additional change is worth noting. The roof of

The Bronze Doors of Hildesheim Cathedral

Of the Ottonian rulers, Otto II was the greatest patron of the arts. In the Church, that honor belongs to Bernward of Hildesheim, tutor of Otto III. During his years as bishop (993–1022), the city of Hildesheim became a center for manuscript painting and other arts. Bernward's patronage, however, was largely confined to the area of metalwork, in particular, the bronze doors of the Hildesheim Cathedral (Fig. **7.11**). These doors were cast by the *cire-perdue*, or LOST-WAX, process, which had been used for casting the bronze doors at Aachen two centuries earlier.

The building of the abbey church of St Michael at Hildesheim was part of Bishop Bernward's plan to make the town a center of learning. The doors for the south portal of St Michael's were completed in 1015 and they were probably installed before 1035. Apparently cast in one piece, Hildesheim's doors are the first in a succession of figured bronze doors throughout the Middle Ages and the Renaissance, a tradition that culminated in Ghiberti's *Gates of Paradise* for the baptistery in Florence (see page 322). The massive doors of Hildesheim also represent a return to larger scale sculpture that was to become typical of the Romanesque period.

The scenes portrayed on Bernward's doors tell biblical stories in a carefully arranged order. The number of scenes depicted—sixteen—is an example of medieval number symbolism. (Sixteen is the number of the Gospels multiplied by itself.) Reading from top to bottom, the scenes are paired, so that the left door

this church is made of stone, whereas earlier buildings had wooden roofs. As we view the magnificent vaulted interior, we wonder how successfully the architect reconciled the conflicts between engineering, material properties, and aesthetics. Given the properties of stone and the increased force of added height, did he try to push his skills to the edge, in order to create a breathtaking interior? Did he aim to reflect the glory of God or the ability of humanity?

Returning to the exterior view, we can see how some of the stress of the high vaulting was diffused. In a complex series of vaults, transverse arches, and bays, the tremendous weight and outward thrust of the central vault were transferred to the ground, leaving a high and

7.11 Doors of Hildesheim Cathedral, 1015. Bronze, 16 ft 6 ins (5.03 m) high. Hildesheim, Germany.

unfolds the Old Testament story of the fall, and the right, the New Testament story of the redemption. For example, *The Temptation of Adam and Eve* (third from the top, left), which depicts the fall from grace, is purposely aligned with the *Crucifixion* (third from the top, right), which illustrates the redemption of humankind. The scenes are highly reminiscent of manuscript illustration, and they tell their stories with a simple directness. In the fourth panel from the top on the left, an angry God reproaches Adam and Eve. His angry glare is heightened by his accusatory, pointing finger, and Adam and Eve cower under his condemnation. As the sinners try to shield their nakedness, Adam points to Eve, passing to her the blame for his transgression; she, in turn, looks downward, and with her left hand points an accusing finger at the serpent.

What is striking about all the scenes is the strong sense of composition and physical movement. Every set of images, against a plain background of open space, speaks forcefully in dumb show. The doors tell their story in medieval fashion, as a vivid but silent drama, effectively communicating the message of the Christian faith to a largely illiterate public. Replace these simple scenes with a clergy-actor, and you have the beginnings of liturgical drama (see the theatre section below). Just as the mystics of the Middle Ages understood communication through the intuition and nonrational emotions, so the artists of the period understood the raw power and effectiveness of the simple nonverbal image.

7.12 St Sernin, Toulouse, France, c. 1080–1120.

7.13 St Sernin, Toulouse, France, c. 1080–1120.

unencumbered central space. If we compare this structural system with post-and-lintel structure and consider the compressive and tensile properties of stone, we can see why the arch is superior as a structural device for creating open space. Because of the weight and the distribution of stress in this style, only very small windows were possible. So, although the fortress-like, lightless qualities of Romanesque architecture reflect the spirit of their time, they also had a practical explanation.

The tenth-century church of Cluny, known as Cluny II, inspired numerous buildings throughout the West in the eleventh century. When it became too small, a new church, Cluny III, was begun in 1088. It remained the largest church in Christendom until St Peter's in Rome

OUR DYNAMIC WORLD

Igbo-Ukwu

In west Africa, unlike in other parts of the world, the iron age came before the age of bronze, and by the end of the first millennium, African artisans used iron for making weapons, cult images, and agricultural tools. Celebrated in myth and ritual, the coming of iron, an indigenous metal, marked a significant development in African culture. Bronze had to be imported, and its use was, therefore, restricted to those who could afford it—that is, kings and priests—and its application was to objects of more limited scope and purpose. Nevertheless, surviving artifacts prove that African artists and artisans not only used but mastered bronze, and a remarkable example of that mastery is in a ritual water-pot found in the village of Igbo-Ukwu in eastern Nigeria (Fig. 7.14).

The level of skill achieved by ninth- and tenth-century Africans in this object is astounding. In the first place, it was cast using the sophisticated *cire perdue* (lost wax) method. This method involves the making of a wax model around which a mold is placed. The mold is heated, the wax melts and runs out of the mold, and the void is then filled with the molten metal that forms the finished work. This leaded bronze artifact has amazing virtuosity. The ritual water-pot stands enclosed in a net of simulated rope. The knots and delicate striations are perfect, and the graceful design of its recurved lines and flaring base by themselves are exquisite. This is a design and execution of immense sophistication of both technique and vision.

Other objects from this period are encrusted with brightly colored beads or created with delicate relief, miniature in scale, and showing intricate ornamental patterns. No one knows where the materials used for such items came from or how the artisans acquired the skill to work with them. They appear out of nowhere, with no artistic antecedents, and vanish just as mysteriously, with no subsequent development.

7.14 Roped pot on a stand, from Igbo-Ukwu, ninth to tenth centuries. Leaded bronze, height 12½ ins (32 cm). National Museum, Lagos, Nigeria.

was rebuilt in the sixteenth century. Although Cluny III (Figs **7.15**, **7.16** and **7.17**), was badly damaged during the French Revolution, we know that the nave, which had double aisles, the double transepts, and the choir with an ambulatory were all enormous in scale. The arcades of the nave had pointed arches, and the interior housed magnificent wall paintings. Protruding apses and numerous towers adorned the exterior.

The Norman Romanesque style of building, with its accent on rounded arches, was loosely based on the classical architecture of Roman times. It is, therefore, covered by the broad umbrella term, "Romanesque style." Norman style came to England from western Europe even before the Norman invasion of 1066 and flourished alongside the earlier Saxon architecture. Norman style, however, became firmly established in the flurry of building—especially church building and rebuilding—that followed the Conquest and continued until around 1190. Its impact was especially noticeable on the larger churches. Small parish churches adopted the changes more slowly.

Most Norman churches were built of stone cut into square blocks, although when stone was not readily available, bricks and cut flints were also used. In the Abbey Church of St Alban (Fig. **7.18**) bricks and cut flints from the ruined Roman city of Verulamium served for the building. The Roman bricks were thinner than our

7.15 (*top*) Transverse section of the nave, and west elevation of the great transept of the Abbey Church, Cluny III, France, 1088–1130.

7.16 (*middle*) Transverse section of the transept. Drawing by Kenneth J. Conant. Frances Loeb Library, Harvard University, Cambridge, MA.

7.17 (*bottom*) Exterior of southwest transept of Cluny III.

bricks—about the size and shape of paving stones. The massive walls and piers of St Albans—nearly 6 feet (1.8 meters) thick at the tower ceiling level—are constructed of rubble faced with Roman bricks. The walls of the nave were plastered over and painted white.

Norman arches were often decorated with carvings of various designs. At St Albans, the Roman brickwork proved too hard to carve and so the arches of the nave were brightly painted in typical Norman linear designs. Ribbed vaulting (see Introduction), which was introduced late in the Norman period, proved stronger and more attractive than groin vaulting. The earliest known Norman ribbed vaults appear in Durham Cathedral in England, and date from approximately 1095.

Like the architecture of the period, sculpture of the eleventh and early twelfth centuries is also called Romanesque. In the case of sculpture, the label refers more to an era than to a style. Examples of sculpture are

7.18 St Albans Cathedral, England, the nave facing east, c. 1280–90.

so diverse that we probably could not group them under a single label, were it not for the fact that most of them take the form of decorative elements attached to Romanesque architecture. We can, however, draw some general conclusions about Romanesque sculpture. First, it is associated with Romanesque architecture; second, it is heavy and solid; third, it is stone; fourth, it is monumental. The last two characteristics represent a distinct departure from previous sculptural style. Monumental stone sculpture had all but disappeared in the fifth century. Its reemergence across Europe at the end of the eleventh century over such a short period was remarkable. The emergence of sculptural decoration indicated at least the beginning of dissemination of knowledge from the cloistered world of the monastery to the general populace. Romanesque sculpture was applied to exteriors of buildings where the lay worshipper could see it and respond to it. The relationship of this artistic development to the increase in religious zeal among the laity was probably strong. In works such as the Last Judgment TYMPANUM of Autun (Fig. **7.19**), the illiterate masses could now read the message of the Church, an opportunity previously reserved for the clergy. The message of this carved scene is quite clear. In the center of the composition, framed by a Roman-style arch, is an awe-inspiring figure of Christ, Next to him, malproportioned figures writhe in various degrees of torment. The inscription of the artist,

7.19 Gislebertus, Last Judgment tympanum c. 1130–35. Autun Cathedral, France.

7.20 *The Mission of the Apostles* tympanum of central portal of narthex, 1120–32. Ste-Madeleine, Vézelay, France.

Gislebertus, tells us that their purpose was "to let this horror appal those bound by earthly sin." Evil was still central to medieval thought, and devils share the stage with Christ, attempting to tip the scales of judgment in their favor and gleefully pushing the damned into the flaming pit.

Another Romanesque tympanum comes from the central portal of the narthex of the abbey and pilgrim church of Sainte-Madeleine, Vézelay, in Burgundy (Fig. **7.20**). The story depicts the mission of the apostles and was especially meaningful to medieval Christians at the time of the crusades (see Chapter 8). Here the artist proclaimed the duty of every Christian to spread the gospel to the ends of the earth. At the center of the tympanum, a rather elongated figure of Christ spreads his arms, from which emanate the rays of the Holy Spirit, empowering the apostles, who carry the scriptures as tokens of their mission. Around the border is a plethora of representatives of the heathen world. The arch is framed by the signs of the zodiac and labors appropriate to the months of the year, stressing that the preaching of the faith is an on-going year-round responsibility without end.

Although revolutionary in its material, scale, and scope, Romanesque sculpture retains the emotional, crowded, nervous qualities of previous medieval works. The Romanesque style, a close cousin of its predecessors, marked the closing stages of a point of view that was about to be supplemented by another.

MUSIC

SACRED MUSIC

GREGORIAN CHANT

Around the year 500, a body of music called chant, or PLAINCHANT, was used in Christian services. This was vocal music, and it used a single melodic line, monophony, whose notes were kept relatively close together on the musical scale. The haunting, undulating character of early chant undoubtedly had Near Eastern origins. There were two types of chant settings: in one, called syllabic, each syllable of the chant was given one note; in the other, called MELISMATIC, several tones were sung on the vowel of one syllable. Chants were sung in a flexible tempo, with unmeasured rhythms following the natural accents of normal Latin speech. Early chant had a highly regular rhythm in which the duration of long and short notes was proportional—that is, one long note equalled two short notes in length.

Pope Gregory supervised the selection of melodies and texts he thought most appropriate and edited those selections for the musical setting of Church celebrations.

Plainchant style had become the basic music of the Church, and the melodies had to be given different texts appropriate for the Church year. In addition, there had to be a method of Latin singing appropriate for worship. Although Gregory did not by any means invent plainchant, his contributions were such that it acquired his name, and is today known as GREGORIAN CHANT.

Gregory's work filled a needed place in the contemporary Church. As it spread to North Africa as well as northern Europe, the Western Church developed a variety of regional variations in the liturgy. Had these been allowed to proliferate without restraint, the result would have been a loss of the common heritage that helped to unify Christendom. Principally because of Pope Gregory's efforts, plainchant remains to this day the traditional chant of the Roman Catholic Church. Although there were nearly three thousand melodies, the organization of the music of the Mass reflects Gregory's logical method. Having organized Church music, he became active in disseminating it throughout the West. The result of his efforts was not only the creation of an additional unifying force in the Church, but also the foundation of a basic universal musical language. Long after Gregory's death, Charlemagne, who acknowledged the spiritual rule of Rome, invoked Gregory's name in order to settle a dispute that had arisen between Italian and French singers at an Easter Festival.

SEQUENCES AND TROPES

In northern France, England, and Germany, music in the church took new directions. One of these directions was the addition of new words to the music and text of the plainchant. The result was called a sequence. Next, new music was added. Ordinary plainchant used one melody repeated with each verse, but the new sequences had a richer form, consisting of a single line followed by a variety of verse couplets, each having a different musical phrase and a repetition. More inventive than plainchant, this new "sequence" music for the first time acknowledged its composers—the German monk, Notker Balbulus of St Gall in Switzerland (d. 912), for example, claimed to have invented a number of sequences.

Other additions to the Mass led to a body of musical work that was given the name TROPE. A sequence was a trope, but there were other forms as well. For example, the *Kyrie* text of the Mass is "Lord have mercy on us," but using a trope, the text might become: "Lord, Almighty Father, Giver of Light and Life, have mercy upon us." Sometimes the new words were squeezed into the original music. At other times new music was added as well. The importance of the tropes, which to us do not seem to be much of a change at all, is that they led to the development of a kind of church musical drama, by the same name, which we will study in Chapter 8 (p. 272).

SECULAR MUSIC

The Middle Ages also witnessed a growth in secular music. As might be expected, secular music used vernacular texts—that is, texts in the language of the common people, as opposed to the Latin of church music. The subject matter mostly concerned love, but other topics were also popular. Secular music probably owed much to the dance pantomime of Roman times, whose performers were eventually expelled from cities and forced to become wandering bands of entertainers. A strong link probably exists between the traditions of the pantomime and the poet-musicians of later medieval Europe—*trouvères* in northern France, troubadours in southern France, and minnesänger in Germany. These wandering minstrels created and performed vocal music as they traveled throughout the countryside. Apparently, most of their music was monophonic and unaccompanied, like church music, but they also sang with some form of musical accompaniment. Medieval secular song was probably mostly STROPHIC—that is, composed of several stanzas that were sung to the same melody.

Musical instruments of this era included the lyre, the harp, and a bowed instrument called the vielle or fiedel—that is, the viol, or fiddle. The psaltery, which was similar to a zither, the lute, the flute, the shawm, which was a reed instrument like an oboe, trumpets, horns, drums, and bagpipes were all popular. Small, portable organs were also popular, despite the instrument's unpleasant associations with the Roman persecution of Christians, and the organ eventually found its way into the medieval church.

In the ninth or tenth century, a new compositional and radically different texture appeared—POLYPHONY—which brought more than one melodic line into musical composition. Early polyphonic compositions were called organa—the singular is ORGANUM—and in the earliest polyphonic forms, the rhythmic component of music remained free and unstructured. As melodic lines gained freedom from each other, however, necessity dictated that some type of rhythmic structure be employed to coordinate them, and at the very end of this era, a new rhythmic notation emerged called mensural notation. This made it possible to indicate the precise duration of each tone.

LITERATURE

It seems clear that in the early Middle Ages—with the notable exception of the Carolingian court—the politically powerful cared little for culture, and for the most part could neither read nor write. Thanks to the efforts of the monastic community, and particularly the Benedictine monks, however, important books and manuscripts were preserved and copied. St Benedict (c. 480–c. 550) was one of the few great scholars of the Dark Ages.

The Muslims had come into contact with Greek culture when they invaded Egypt, and they brought it with them to Spain, where literature flourished. The schools they set up in Cordoba studied Aristotle and Plato alongside the Koran. Toledo and Seville were also centers of learning. It was biblical literature, however, that became the central focus during the early Middle Ages.

St Jerome (c. 342–420) was a contemporary of St Augustine of Hippo, and his writings assumed a position of primary importance in the last years of the Roman Empire. St Jerome was familiar with the classical writers, and the style of the scriptures seemed somewhat crude to him. He had a dream, however, in which Christ reproached him and accused him of being more a Ciceronian than a Christian. As a result, Jerome resolved to spend the rest of his life in the study of the sacred books. He made a famous translation of the Bible into Latin, and assisted by Jewish scholars, he also translated the Old Testament from the Hebrew.

The other major literary accomplishment of the early Middle Ages, one with a completely different subject matter, was the German *Niebelungenlied* ("Song of the People of the Mists," meaning the dead). These early hero-stories of northern peoples, which took their final shape in southeast Germany c. 1200, are a rich mixture of history, magic, and myth. There are ten complete and twenty incomplete manuscripts of the *Niebelungenlied*, folk tales of thirty-nine adventures, commencing with that of the hero Siegfried, son of Siegmund, King of the Netherworld. Wagner used this and other stories from the cycle as sources for his operas.

The favorite Old English epic, *Beowulf* (c. 725), is the earliest extant poem in a modern European language. Composed by an unknown author, it falls into separate episodes that incorporate old legends. The poem is written in unrhymed alliterative verse. Its three folk stories center on the hero, Beowulf, and his exploits against the monster Grendel, Grendel's mother—a hideous water hag—and a fire-breathing dragon.

We will discuss another popular poem, the *Chanson de Roland* or "Song of Roland," which tells of Charlemagne, in the Synthesis section at the end of the chapter.

THEATRE

Scholars used to argue that theatre ceased to exist in the Western world for a period of several hundred years. That viewpoint is no longer widely held, and two pieces of evidence certainly suggest that theatrical productions continued. One is the presence of the wandering entertainers we have already noted. In this tribe of entertainers were mimists, jugglers, bear baiters, acrobats, wrestlers, and storytellers. The propensity of human beings for acting out or mimicking actions and events is too compelling to deny its existence amid the entertainments we know existed in this era. We do not know, however, how such entertainments were presented during the early Middle Ages. They may have consisted simply of the acting out of a story silently or the reading of a play script, rather than the formal presentations we call "theatre."

Our second piece of evidence, however, proves more conclusively that theatre existed. Writings from North Africa argue that there was a continuation of the mime there and it is probable that if it still existed in North Africa, it also existed in Europe. Sisebert, King of Spain in the seventh century, refers to the popularity of *ludi theatrici* or old Roman festival plays, at marriages and feasts, adding that members of the clergy should leave when these were performed. In France in the ninth century, the Council of Tours and the Council of Aix-la-Chapelle ruled that the clergy should witness neither plays nor the obscenities of actors. These railings of the Church against the theatre certainly suggest that it existed. Charlemagne added his powerful backing in defense of the clergy by ruling that no actor could wear a priest's robe under penalty of corporal punishment or banishment. This edict has been taken by some as evidence of theatrical presentation and also, perhaps inaccurately, as evidence of the beginnings of liturgical drama. If this were the case, the prohibition would imply the use of actors other than the clergy in church drama. In the tenth century, the German nun Hrosvitha is known to have written six plays based on comedies by Terence. We do not know if Hrosvitha's plays were performed, but if they were, the audience would have been restricted to the other nuns in the convent.

We are sure, however, that liturgical drama began as an elaboration of the Roman Catholic Mass, probably in France. These elaborations were called tropes, and they took place on ceremonial occasions, especially at Easter, the dramatic highlight of the Church year. Records at Winchester in southern England dating from the late tenth century tell of a trope in which priests acted out the discovery of Jesus' empty tomb by his followers on Easter morning.

The first dramatic trope was the "Quem Quaeritis trope." The earliest Easter trope dates from 925, and the dialogue was:

> *Angels*: Whom seek ye in the tomb, O
> Christians?
> *The Three Marys*: Jesus of Nazareth, the crucified, O Heavenly Beings.
> *Angels*: He is not here, he is risen as he foretold. Go and announce that he is risen from the tomb.

So theatre, along with all the other arts, except dance, was adopted by the Church and became an instrument of God in an age of faith and demons.

A CRITICAL REVIEW

In this section, amid the discussion of medieval art, we studied a bronze water pot from Igbo-Ukwu in eastern Nigeria, Africa. In Igbo-Ukwu we find an artistic vision and technique that are as sophisticated and accomplished as any we have yet experienced. Using the artistic compositional qualities of line, mass, and texture, analyze and compare the Igbo-Ukwu pot with the bronze doors at Hildesheim Cathedral.

Citing specific examples from the text, describe the qualities of Romanesque style in architecture and sculpture.

Identify and describe early polyphonic musical compositions.

SYNTHESIS

The Carolingian Renaissance

One way to view a synthesis is to see it as the bringing together of various elements into some form of unified statement. On few occasions in history have individuals been able to put their individual temperament on so many aspects of society and art as did Charlemagne. His reign was so all-encompassing and his interest in all the aspects of life so wide that the word "renaissance" has been applied to the time of his rule. As we will see, the Carolingian renaissance had its limits, but, given its time and circumstances, it truly was remarkable.

When Pepin III died in 768, he was succeeded by his two sons, Charles and Carloman. Carloman died three years later, and Charles, denying the succession of

Carloman's infant sons, acquired for himself the entire Frankish Empire. Carrying on the work of his father and grandfather, Charlemagne set about subduing the Frankish peoples and other tribes throughout Europe. He ruled over a vast empire of many nations, and became protector of Pope Leo III in Rome. On Christmas Day in the year 800, as Charlemagne knelt in prayer

7.21 St Mark and St Luke, from the Gospel Book of Godescale, 781–783. Vellum, 12¼ × 8¼ ins (31.1 × 21 cm). Bibliothèque Nationale, Paris.

7.22 St Mark, from the Gospel Book of Saint Médard of Soissons, early ninth century. Paint on vellum, 14³/₈ × 10¹/₄ ins (36.5 × 26 cm). Bibliothèque Nationale, Paris.

7.23 The crypts at St-Germain, Auxerre, France, ninth century.

before the altar in the old church of St Peter, Pope Leo suddenly placed a crown on his head, and the people acclaimed him as emperor.

Perhaps his greatest contributions to European civilization lay in his support of education, reform of the Church, and cultivation of the liberal arts. Under the leadership of Alcuin of York, scholars were assembled from all parts of the West to reunite the scattered fragments of the classical heritage. The Carolingian renaissance—or *renovatio*, as it was called—represents the hinge, as it were, on which the ancient world turned into the Middle Ages. The classical revival initiated by Charlemagne was part of his attempt to revive the Roman Empire.

MANUSCRIPT ILLUMINATION AND WALL PAINTING

Carolingian manuscript illuminations are striking examples of early medieval painting. As an official court art, book illumination was promoted by the king, his relatives, associates, and officers of state. One exemplary product of the time was the Gospel Book of Godescale (Fig. **7.21**). The models for this work were probably Byzantine: the evangelists have lean, bearded faces, and the cloth of their garments reveals a rudimentary attempt at modeling, with little attention to realism, merely light and dark stripes representing the highlight and shadow of the folds. Unlike the Gospel Book of Godescale, the Gospel Book of Saint-Médard of Soissons (Fig. **7.22**) displays a definite classicism in its arches complete with columns, intricate architecture, and frames adorned with CAMEOS and pictures containing tiny figures. Nonetheless, there is a confusion in the plethora of detail and a crowded nervousness that is characteristic of medieval work.

Wall paintings were a highly original feature of Carolingian art and architecture. Although few examples remain, it seems clear that Carolingian palaces and churches were brightly painted in a style not unlike that of the Romans. For example, three-dimensional architectural detail is presented in a highly realistic fashion on a two-dimensional surface. Large frescoes depicting the history of the Franks were also typical. In many cases, the inscriptions accompanying these frescoes reflect the scholarship of Alcuin and others. The lifesize figures of several bishops of Auxerre found in the crypts there (Fig. **7.23**) show a great deal of originality. Clearly the mural painters of the period possessed great skill and imagination. In the segment depicting the stoning of St Stephen (Fig. **7.24**), all of the important vertical lines of the painting conform to a mathematical formula based on a grid created from the half-square in which the arch bordering the painting is framed.

7.24 *The Stoning of St Stephen at the Gate of Jerusalem*, ninth century. Wall painting. Crypts of St-Germain, Auxerre, France.

7.25 (*left*) Cover of the Dagulf Psalter, showing David in various scenes, 783–95. Ivory, each leaf 6⅝ × 3¼ ins (16.8 × 8.3 cm). Louvre, Paris.

7.26 (*opposite*) Back of the Lorsch Gospels, showing the Virgin and Child between Zacharias and John the Baptist, c. 810. Ivory, 15⅛ × 10⅝ ins (38.4 × 27 cm). Victoria & Albert Museum, London.

SCULPTURE

The works of the palace school at Charlemagne's court also reflect an effort to revive classical style by copying sculpture from the late antique period. Classical influence continued to be nurtured, perhaps because Charlemagne's political opposition to the Byzantine Empire led him to reject its artistic style as well. The so-called *Statuette of Charlemagne* (see Fig. **7.4**), for example, clearly imitates a classical model.

It is, however, the ivories of this period that most clearly show both the classicizing trend and the artistry of the time. Although derived from antique models, these works are highly individual. The ivory covers of the Dagulf Psalter (Fig. **7.25**) bear a close resemblance to Roman work. Commissioned as a gift for Pope Adrian I, the figures and ornamentation on this cover are stilted and lifeless. There is little attempt at creating three-dimensional space, although the figures themselves appear in high relief. Composition in each panel appears to be organized around a central area, to which interior line directs the viewer's eye. This focus is reinforced by the direction in which the figures themselves are looking. The scenes are crowded, but not frenetic. The figures have strange proportions, almost dwarf-like, with heavy rounded heads, long torsos, and short legs. Hairstyles reflect the late Roman Imperial period.

The ivory cover of the ninth-century Lorsch Gospels (Fig. **7.26**), on the other hand, is an exact replica of a

7.27 Detail of the parapet railings in the Tribune of the Palatine Chapel, Aachen, Germany, 792–805.

sixth-century design. The images in the upper register, the layout, and the rounded faces in the figure depiction clearly show its kinship with the *Barberini Ivory* (see Fig. **6.11**). The Roman arches in each of the three middle panels testify to the classical derivation of the Lorsch Gospels. In the center panel sits the Virgin Mary, enthroned, with the infant Christ and surrounded by saints. The face of the Christ child is that of a wise adult, a common medieval practice. Encircled in the top register and flanked by heraldic angels, the risen Christ appears. In the lower register are scenes from the nativity. So the Gospel cover reads chronologically from birth to Resurrection in hierarchical fashion.

Architecture, like painting and sculpture, was ruled by the political goals of the Carolingian court. It is also clear that the artists of the period were capable of reproducing capitals and friezes from classical antiquity accurately, as Figure **7.27** illustrates. Charlemagne carefully chose bishops for his kingdom who would assist in the building program he envisaged, and almost immediately new construction began across the empire. Large-scale building in the period was short-lived, however, despite its bold conception.

CAROLINGIAN DESIGN

No serious attempt at architectural design was made until the rule of Charlemagne. Charlemagne's renaissance included architecture, and he returned to his capital, Aachen, or Aix-la-Chapelle, from visits to Italy not only with visions of Roman monuments, but also with a belief that majesty and permanence must be symbolized in impressive architecture.

The realization of these dreams, however, was tempered by some of the difficult facts of life that stand between builders and their completed works. Charlemagne took as his model the church of San Vitale in Ravenna (see Figs **6.27**, **6.28** and **6.32**), which had been built by Justinian in the Byzantine style. All Charlemagne's materials, including columns and bronze gratings, had to be transported over the Alps from Italy to Aachen in Germany. Skilled stonemasons were few and far between, but the task was, nevertheless, accomplished and the design of Charlemagne's Palatine Chapel is still dominant and compelling today (Figs **7.28** and **7.30**), despite later alterations to the building. Charlemagne also encouraged the building of monasteries and apparently developed a standard plan for their design that was used, with local modifications, throughout his Empire.

It was the Palatine Chapel at Aachen (Fig. **7.27**), built to be Charlemagne's tomb-house, that became the jewel in his crown. A further illustration of the interior (Fig. **7.28**) reveals the grandeur and style of this building. Designed by a Frankish architect, Odo of Metz, the

7.28 View into the octagonal interior of the Palatine Chapel, Aachen, Germany, from the Tribune.

Palatine Chapel has very little of the spatial subtlety of San Vitale, however. There is less mystery, and the space itself seems more constricted, with the emphasis on verticality rather than openness. The rounded arches and thick, rectangular pillars that support the dome create massiveness, which cannot be offset by slender, decorative columns. Part of the building's sense of massiveness comes from its heavy material: rubble faced with stone for the vaults. Charlemagne's throne was placed in the first gallery above the door and looked down and across the central space to the altar.

During Charlemagne's reign, then, we find a true renaissance, modified as it may have been to serve the grand design and political ambitions of the emperor. The recreation of antiquity in the arts and humanities

made visible and intelligible the dream of a resurrected Roman Empire, with Charlemagne at its head.

SONG OF ROLAND

The court of Charlemagne included singer-poets, whose poems were extremely popular. These professional storytellers produced fantastic legends and romances, such as the *Song of Roland*, and although this old epic French poem probably dates to around 1100, it tells of the Carolingian times and so, we include it here. Its author was probably a Norman poet named Turold, whose name is mentioned in the last line of the poem. It is the story of the historical battle of Roncesvalles, which was fought in 778 between the armies of Charlemagne and the Saracens of Saragossa in the Pyrenees mountains between France and Spain. In reality, the battle was little more than a skirmish against the Basques, but the poet turns the event into a heroic encounter on the level of the Greek battle of Thermopylae, which we studied earlier.

In style, the poem is direct and sober. It focuses on the clash between the recklessly courageous Roland and his more cautious friend Oliver, a conflict that illustrates divergent views of feudal loyalty.

The poem begins as Charlemagne, having conquered all of Spain except Saragossa, receives overtures from the Saracen king. In response, Charlemagne sends the knight Ganelon to negotiate peace terms, but, Ganelon, Roland's stepfather, is angry because Roland proposed him for the dangerous task, and he conspires with the Saracens to achieve Roland's death. On his return to Charlemagne's camp, Ganelon insures that Roland will command the rear guard of the army as it withdraws from Spain. As the army crosses the Pyrenees, the rear guard is surrounded at the pass of Roncesvalles by an overwhelming Saracen force.

The headstrong Roland, preoccupied with valor, rejects his friend Oliver's advice to blow his horn and summon help from the rest of Charlemagne's army. The battle ensues, and the valiant French soldiers fight until only a handful remain alive. Finally, the horn is sounded, but it is too late to save Oliver or Roland, who was fatally wounded in error by a blow from a blinded Oliver. However, it is not too late for the arriving army to avenge the heroic vassals.

When Charlemagne returns to France, he breaks the news to Aude, Roland's fiancée and Oliver's sister, who falls dead at the news. The poem ends with the trial and execution of Ganelon.

CHAPTER EIGHT

THE HIGH MIDDLE AGES

A T   A   G L A N C E

The Social Order of the High Middle Ages
The Rise of Cities
The Middle Class
  TECHNOLOGY: A Better Horse Collar
Feudal Monarchs and Monarchies
Chivalry

The Christian Church
Reform in the Christian Church
St Bernard of Clairvaux and Mysticism
The Crusades

Philosophy and Theology
The Rise of Universities
Abelard and Realism
St Thomas Aquinas and Aristotelianism
  PROFILE: St Francis of Assisi

Literature
Courtly Romances
Dante and the Divine Comedy

Gothic Style
Architecture
  MASTERWORK: Salisbury Cathedral

Sculpture
Painting
  OUR DYNAMIC WORLD: Buddhism in Japanese Art

Music
Ars Antiqua

Theatre

Synthesis: Suger and the Abbey Church of Saint-Denis

8.1 Giovanni Pisano, Pulpit, begun 1297. Marble, Sant' Andrea, Pistoia, Italy.

A CRITICAL LOOK

The period known as the High Middle Ages witnessed demonstrable changes in four areas: cities, the middle class, feudal monarchs and monarchies, and a code of conduct called chivalry. As we look at the material in the next section, we will sense a profound change taking place in Europe, not only in its institutions but also in the way it viewed matters both earthly and eternal. Several reforms affected the Christian Church: the rise of mysticism, and the Crusades, which attempted to liberate the Holy Land from the Muslims.

How did the rise of cities and an emerging middle class change the political power structure of the era?

In what ways did the code of chivalry change the roles of women?

Explain the Crusades as political, military, and religious projects.

Humanity in the late Middle Ages seemed to undergo a spiritual and intellectual revival that had a profound influence on the creative spirit. A vigorous growth of towns and cities accelerated the pace of life, and as the focus of wealth and power shifted from the feudal countryside, the new universities in the cities replaced monasteries as centers of learning. In the Gothic cathedral, the mystery of faith was embodied in the mystery of space, which was flooded by colored light streaming in through stained-glass windows. The austere and fortress-like massiveness of the Romanesque style was transformed, and the human spirit seemed to blossom as attention shifted from the oppressive wrath of God to the sweetness and mercy of the loving Savior and the Virgin Mary.

THE SOCIAL ORDER OF THE HIGH MIDDLE AGES

THE RISE OF CITIES

In the year A.D. 1000 Europe consisted of stone fortresses on hills and muddy huts in cramped villages. Two centuries later, the world had been transformed. This transformation of medieval society sprang largely from the resurgence of cities, for which three main factors were responsible—agricultural improvements, population

	GENERAL EVENTS	LITERATURE & PHILOSOPHY	VISUAL ART & ARCHITECTURE	THEATRE & MUSIC
1000	Leif Ericsson discovers North America St Stephen king of Hungary Normans in southern Italy			Guido of Arezzo Pérotin Léonin
1050	Norman Conquest of England Pope Gregory VII Carthusians founded Domesday Book compiled Cistercians founded	Lanfranc Anselm		
1100	First Crusade Henry I of England Investiture Controversy Civil War in England	Peter Abelard		Mystery, miracle, and morality plays *Ars antiqua*
1150	Emperor Frederick Barbarossa Henry II of England Second Crusade Carmelites founded Thomas à Becket murdered Third Crusade	St Bernard of Clairvaux	Abbey Church of Saint-Denis (**8.7**, **8.8**, **8.28**, **8.29**, **8.30**)	Troubadours and *jongleurs* Courtly tradition
1200	Fourth Crusade Magna Carta in England Franciscans founded Albigensian Crusade	St Francis of Assisi Thomas Aquinas Roger Bacon Duns Scotus Dante Psalter of St Louis Douce Apocalypse	Chartres Cathedral (**8.11**, **8.12**, **8.13**, **8.14**, **8.18**, **8.19**, **8.20**) Notre Dame (**8.9**, **8.10**) Amiens Cathedral (**8.17**) Salisbury Cathedral (**8.15**, **8.16**)	Minnesänger Adam de la Halle

Timeline 8.1 The High Middle Ages.

growth, and the revival of trade.

Primitive as the manor system of feudalism was, it did produce a number of important agricultural improvements. One of these was a three-field system of crop rotation. Others included the heavy wheeled plow for more effective tilling, windmills for grinding grain, and the horse collar.

After the year 1000 the amount of land under cultivation increased tremendously. An increase in the food supply meant an increase in the general population of Europe. However, the primary cause of the rebirth of cities was revival of trade in the eleventh, twelfth, and thirteenth centuries. Soldiers returning from the crusades brought tales of the East and of marvelous fabrics and goods that caught the fancy of nobles and commoners alike.

Merchant and craft guilds—that is, trade associations of dealers in, or makers of, particular products from cloth to metals—dominated trading cities. As time progressed, cities developed independent political authorities—for example, magistrates and city councils although these political authorities were elected only by business peo-

ple. However, the component character of the city was established. At its heart lay the doers of business—crafts guilds, their masters, assistants, and apprentices; merchants who required stevedores, porters, and muleteers, and so on. In addition, priests, students, lawyers, runaway serfs, and others were drawn to the city in search of protection and employment. The city offered a new hope of escape from slavery to the land, and thousands flocked there.

THE MIDDLE CLASS

As the commercial class grew richer, it also gained power, filling—amid changing values—a vacuum between nobility and peasantry. However, no order gives up power easily, and struggles, sometimes violent, pitted burgher against nobleman. The crusades had ruined many feudal landholders, and a taste of potential power and wealth strengthened the resolve of the "middle-class" citizens. However they needed a more dynamic society than feudalism could offer, so they threw their weight and power into strengthening monarchies that favored them. Thus,

---

TECHNOLOGY: PUTTING DISCOVERY TO WORK

A Better Horse Collar

In the Middle Ages, the horse came into its own as a technological tool. Horsepower was the most universally available source of power known to humankind, although in the medieval period, the horse was seen primarily as a means of carrying knights and their retinue. However, the horse offered potential for both transportation and agriculture. The first horse harnesses unsuccessfully used the ox yoke as a model, but horses do not have the prominent and powerful shoulders of the ox. The next step consisted of a breast-band, which held the harness down by means of a strap passing between the legs to a girth-band. This device chaffed the horse, and, when heavy loads were pulled, the breast-band caused choking pressure on the horse's neck and windpipe. Even the ingenious Romans had not been able to invent a useful means for hitching a horse to wagon or

plow. In the twelfth century, however, three main improvements occurred. Shafts, which could be attached well down the breast-band, came into common use. Next, traces—that is, side straps or chains to connect the animal to what it is pulling—served in the same way as shafts to bring the pressure to the middle of the breast-band, and made it possible to use horses in file, as opposed to side by side. However, the most important invention was that of the padded horse-collar. This stiff apparatus replaced the breast-band and made it possible for the horse's power to be multiplied by as much as five times over the old method. Thus, the horse came into its own as a technological device. Modern horse carts were developed in France, and the horse replaced the ox for pulling plows and carriages. As a result, effective agriculture and land-based trade were just a step away.

8.2 Two-wheeled cart, from the Luttrell Psalter.

an emerging middle class played a vital role in the emerging social order that would see more centralized administration, stabilization, and rudimentary democracy.

FEUDAL MONARCHS AND MONARCHIES

The explosion of economic activity led to the reestablishment of centralized power in the hands of medieval kings. Under their aegis a new form of government itself evolved. It included political institutions that continued to develop until modern times. In the end, modern bureaucratic government is the grandchild of the monarchies of the Middle Ages. The basic problem for the medieval monarch was the need to replace feudal law with royal law and to tax what amounted to a nation. For such problems to be solved, compromises had to be made, and where the monarchies were most successful—in England and France—the monarchs paid for their growing power by granting rights to representative bodies that spoke for the primary classes of medieval society—that is, the nobility, the Church, and the wealthy new cities and towns.

Some monarchs were more successful than others at statecraft. Probably the most notable of the medieval monarchs was Duke William, the Bastard of Normandy, who invaded and conquered England in 1066, thus gaining for himself the name William I the Conqueror (1066–87). His conquest brought a more developed French feudalism to backward Anglo-Saxon England. As King of England he gave the country greater centralized government than it had ever known, and under his successors, Henry I and Henry II, England developed its system of common law, the royal council, and the exchequer (treasury). By the end of the twelfth century, England had the strongest monarchial government in Europe.

France had two significant monarchs during the High Middle Ages. The first was Philip Augustus (1180–1223). Although not particularly inspiring physically, Philip proved to be France's most successful medieval monarch. At the summit of the feudal system, like William the Conqueror, he used his position to gain power over the nobility and to develop an effective, independent royal administrative system that included a strengthened legal system. Unlike William I of England, Philip Augustus did not conquer any foreign lands. However, he did conquer rebellious feudal barons in the south of France, and he won from Henry II of England parts of western France that had been under English rule since the time of William the Conqueror. Thus, under his rule, France tripled in size, and France replaced the Holy Roman Empire as the most powerful entity in Europe.

The strong but pious Louis IX (1215-70), who reigned from 1226, gave France the prestige of a saint in its royal lineage. Although Louis did not hesitate to increase royal power, to issue royal edicts without consultation, or to tamper with the legal system, he possessed great strength of character and medieval Christian virtue. He had such a reputation for justice, which he often meted out sitting under an oak tree, that he was known as Louis the Just. Among the acts for which he was canonized only thirty years after his death was the washing of lepers' feet. His saintly life did much to solidify his power over the devoutly religious French people.

CHIVALRY

Society was still feudal throughout Europe in this period. The Carolingian and Ottonian Empires had suggested that a wider stability and order were possible. But life remained polarized in a rigid class system. The clergy and nobility ruled, and the serf labored. In between, there was a vacuum. Gradually, as we have seen, this vacuum came to be filled by the town and the town guild. When this happened, another new age was born.

At the same time, another medieval phenomenon was born of a change in attitude that permeated society and the arts. Feudalism was a masculine, "men-at-arms" code of behavior. But by the twelfth century, a distinctly feminine point of view ruled ethics and personal conduct—that of chivalry and the courtly tradition. Men were away from their homes or castles for long periods of time, whether they were off trading or off warring, and it fell to women to run their households and control domestic matters and manners. If Eleanor of Aquitaine (1122–1204) is a representative example, women managed this very well. Society thus took on a gentler, more civil tone than under the rough code of feudalism, and elaborate codes of conduct and etiquette emerged, which culminated in "courts of love."

We may speculate that the code of chivalry was a practical and euphemistic way of glossing over illicit love affairs while husbands were away. Most aristocratic marriages were arranged for political convenience anyway, while those of the lower classes had economic advantage as their goal.

More important than its impact on morals was the impact of the courtly tradition on religious philosophy. The early Middle Ages were fixated on devils and death, faith notwithstanding. As time passed, however, we find a warmer feeling, a quality of mercy. Christ the Savior and Mary, his compassionate mother, became the focal points of the faith. This change in viewpoint is reflected very clearly in the arts of the time.

It is interesting to note that, although chivalry introduced a more "feminine" ethos into the High Middle Ages, and although some very important women, like Eleanor of Aquitaine emerged, in general, women proba-

8.3 French knights, commanded by King Louis XI, taking the Egyptian city of Damietta during the Seventh Crusade (1249). MS Fr. 13568. Fol. 83. Bibliothèque Nationale, Paris.

THE CHRISTIAN CHURCH

REFORM IN THE CHRISTIAN CHURCH

The development of Western culture, including its artistic institutions in the late Middle Ages, was profoundly affected, if not controlled, by the Christian Church. By the middle of the eleventh century, the Church had become very powerful.

Although the tenth-century Church had become feudalized and corrupt, with many of its secular clergy seeking only wealth and power, this corruption did not go unchallenged. Cries for reform came loudest from the monasteries. The founding of the Abbey of Cluny by William of Aquitaine in 910 signaled the start of a major reform movement. The strict discipline and high moral

bly lost many of the independent opportunities and positions of authority they had earlier enjoyed.

In its earliest formulation, chivalry meant mostly the virtues of war—that is, courage, skill with weapons, fairness to one's foes, and loyalty to one's liege lord (Fig. **8.3**), However, under the guidance of medieval women, the chivalric code, as we have just noted, turned to a code of courtly love. The truly chivalrous knight was encouraged to protect women *and* to love, serve, and revere a particular lady, although from afar. Nonetheless, women paid for the services of minstrels and troubadours, and these wandering entertainers were suited to the tastes of their benefactresses. They composed and sang songs of love, praising knights who served their ladies well.

standards of Cluny's Benedictine monks and abbots made Cluny a model of reform, and its influence spread across Europe.

While monastic life was successfully reformed to its original standards, however, the secular clergy changed their behavior very little. Feudal lords and the lesser nobility appointed priests and bishops, often choosing the highest bidder. Bishoprics were treated as family property, and the secular clergy, many of whose priests were married, did not place a high priority on their religious duties.

Conditions were ripe for reform, and the reformers vehemently attacked the evils of the secular clergy. Circumstances changed in 1046 under Emperor Henry III of Germany. Henry championed the cause of the reformers, and in 1049 he appointed Pope Leo IX, who ruled until 1054. During those five years, Leo introduced a brilliant ecclesiastical reorganization, including the creation of a body of cardinals. Creation of the rank of cardinal made it possible for the papacy to exercise control over those bishops who had been named by lay rulers. After a series of synods in Rome, Leo made a personal tour of the empire, during which he publicized his reforms. As he put them into practice, he both consolidated his program and rid the clergy of many of its most offensive bishops.

Conflict between papacy and laity over the investiture of ecclesiastical office was not solved so easily, however. At the heart of the matter lay the issue of the basis of royal authority. The resulting struggle became known as the "Investiture conflict." Through a series of negotiated settlements with the various monarchs of Europe, the relationships between nobility and clergy, and clergy and papacy, were stabilized. The outcome was a compromise in which kings gave up their ancient claims to represent God's will in appointing senior clergy. They did continue to nominate bishops, but they had greater difficulty in presenting candidates considered unsuitable by the Church. From the twelfth century onward, the quality of ecclesiastical appointments improved substantially.

The papacy emerged from the conflict with greatly enhanced prestige, and the importance of the Church in medieval affairs, artistic and otherwise, continued to grow.

ST BERNARD OF CLAIRVAUX AND MYSTICISM

Many new religious orders were founded during this period. The Virgin Mary assumed a new importance in religious life, and the cult of Mary Magdalene spread through Europe. A key figure in the changing religious thought was a young nobleman, Bernard of Clairvaux (1090–1153), who entered the order of Cîteaux, the most influential new monastic movement of the twelfth century.

Bernard was an enthusiast, perhaps even a fanatic, having no doubt in his own mind that his views were correct. He entered into eager combat with anyone who disagreed with him, and those individuals included the most influential clerics and philosophers of the times, men such as the scholar and theologian Peter Abelard, the monk and abbot, Suger, of Saint-Denis, and the entire order of Cluny. At the same time, Bernard could show great patience and common sense. He treated his monks with patience and forgiveness, and reportedly turned down the Duke of Burgundy's request to become a monk by saying that the world had many virtuous monks but few pious dukes.

His religious teaching set a new tone for twelfth-century Christianity through its emphasis on a more mystical and personal sense of piety than had existed previously. In his writings he described a way of "ascent to God," consisting of four stages of love by which a soul could gain union with God. In his sermons for the common people, he treated more ordinary themes and vividly retold familiar stories from the New Testament. Rather than treating Jesus, Mary, and the apostles as remote images, Bernard described them as living personalities. Bernard's preaching was an important stimulant for the spread of the Mary cults.

Bernard's popularity and leadership proved an important stimulant also for the growth and spread of the Cistercian order. In the 38 years between 1115 and Bernard's death in 1153 the order went from five houses to 343. By the end of the thirteenth century that number had doubled. The number of monks in each house was large too, with some approaching 700 monks.[1]

THE CRUSADES

Many of us have the notion that the Crusades featured knights in shining armor setting out on glorious quests to free the Holy Land from Infidels. The Crusades were far from a romantic quest, however. Instead, they illustrate clearly a new and practical energy and optimism in Europe in a new millennium and a new era. A strengthened Church leadership emerged from the period of the crusades.

As early as the tenth century, popes had led armies against the Saracens in Italy. By the end of the eleventh century, the Church was able to put forward several reasons why a Christian army might march against the Muslims. Constantinople had been rescued from the Turks, and a healing of the east-west schism seemed possible. Furthermore, pilgrimages to the Holy Land as a form of penance had become increasingly popular in this age of religious zeal, and the safety of these pilgrims was ample reason for interference by the popes. A more practical benefit closer to home was the removal of troublesome nobles from the local scene. An opportunity came in 1095 at the Council of Clermont. When envoys of the eastern emperor Alexius Comnenus supposedly asked Pope Urban II for aid, Urban set about mounting a crusading army. The response to his call was astonishing. Thousands came forward to take up the cross. Men, women, and children—even those who were disabled—clamored to take part, and the aforementioned nobles also went riding off to war.

The reasons for the First Crusade went beyond its political and military objectives. Its impetus came from the religious enthusiasm of those who made up the crusading army. These people were ready to make significant sacrifices for their faith. The idea of a Crusade generated such a tremendous emotional response that even the Pope could not control it. Itinerant preachers heralded an upcoming Crusade in their revival meetings. No one cared about the practical problems—it was an act of faith

and piety. The infidels would scatter in fear before the banner of the cross. The walls of fortresses would tumble down like those of Jericho.

The First Crusade, which ultimately led to the capture of Jerusalem and a bloody massacre, wound its way through Hungary, Greece, Constantinople, Syria, Nicea, the southern coast of Asia Minor, Edessa, and Antioch (Map **8.1**). Beset by infighting and other self-inflicted problems, the Crusaders stumbled onward. When they finally conquered Jerusalem, even more problems appeared. What was Jerusalem to become? Was it to be a secular kingdom or Church property, like Rome? How was it to be defended? Most of the Crusaders rushed home after their pilgrimages, however, and the wide-ranging Christian conquests proved virtually indefensible. As time went on, closer and closer association with the local people led any Christians who stayed on to adopt the customs of the country. Very little was settled, and no centralized authority was set up. By 1144 the Muslims had reunited and the Christian state was under

Map 8.1 Europe at the time of the First Crusade.

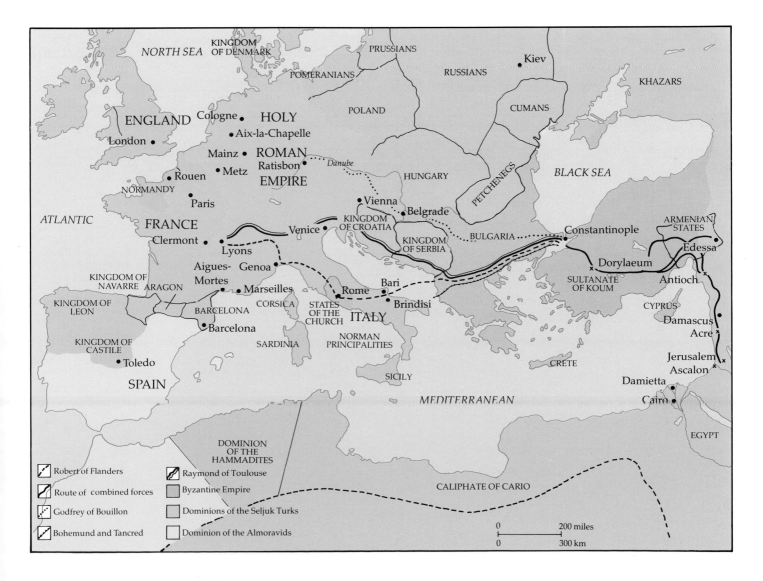

siege. Edessa fell, sending shock waves through Europe. The clamor for another crusade coincided with the reform movement of St Bernard of Clairvaux. The Second Crusade set out in 1147, but ended in disarray and defeat. After that, Europe lost its enthusiasm for such ventures, for a generation.

In the interim, the Muslims gathered their forces and set about driving out the Christians. On 3 October 1187, led by Saladin, the Muslims conquered Jerusalem, ending eighty-three years of Christian rule. Again the news shocked Europe, and again the Pope took the opportunity to attempt to make peace among warring nobles in Europe. Henry II of England and his son Richard, Philip Augustus of France, and Frederick Barbarossa of Germany all took up the cross. Well-planned, well-financed, and led by the most powerful rulers of Europe, the Third Crusade set off in high spirits, with high expectations. But one disaster after another befell the crusaders, and by 1189, only Richard and Philip were still in the field. Their major accomplishment was the capture of Acre after a two-year siege. Philip then returned home to make trouble for Richard, now Richard I of England, as France and England resumed hostilites; Richard did succeed in agreeing a truce with Saladin, which allowed pilgrims to enter Jerusalem safely. Another chapter in the conflict of politics and religion had come to a close.

CRITICAL REVIEW p. 255

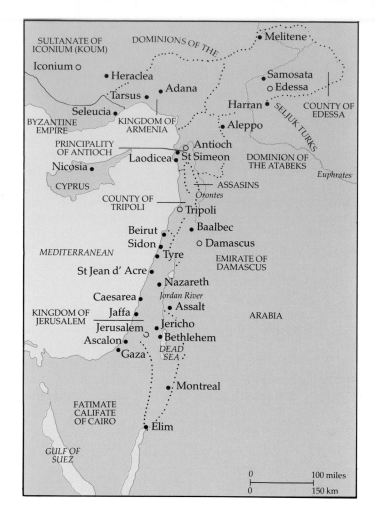

Map 8.2 Areas of the Crusades.

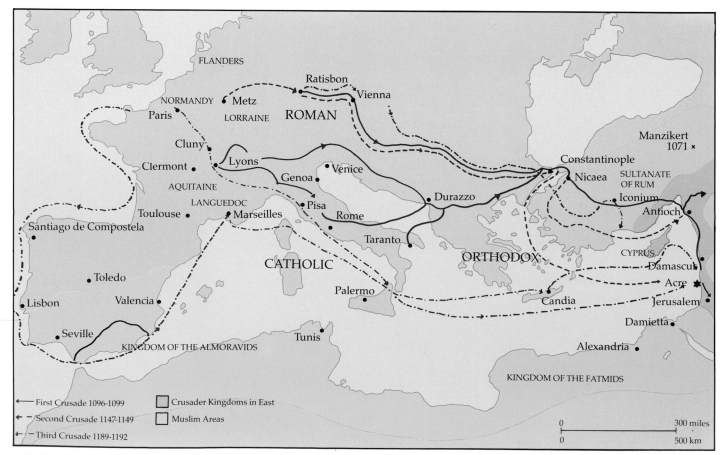

First Crusade 1096-1099
Second Crusade 1147-1149
Third Crusade 1189-1192

Crusader Kingdoms in East
Muslim Areas

Map 8.3 The Crusades.

A CRITICAL REVIEW

If we could boil life down to its basest element, that element might be the desire to control: our own lives, the actions of those around us, general events, and so on. The story of the Middle Ages has at its center the attempts to control society and all its aspects. In an age such as our contemporary one, we find the issue of separation of Church and State—that is, keeping the State free from the "Church"—a controversial one. In the Middle Ages, the struggle had a different twist: the local secular rulers wanted to oversee the Church, which, in turn, wanted its own overarching control.

Mysticism has manifested itself in many ways during the last few years, as it did in the High Middle Ages. What evidence—for example, the charismatic movements in Christianity—can you find of its presence in contemporary society?

A CRITICAL LOOK

Philosophy, theology, and literature during the High Middle Ages shaped the ideas and directions of intellectual and cultural life even as they do in our own day. This was a time of flux. The barricades were coming down and light was flowing into every corner of human existence.

This was the time when universities were born. It was also a time when the tenets of Christian faith were remolded and shaped by individuals like Abelard and St Thomas Aquinas.

Literature brought us a new genre, called "courtly romances," and a major poet named Dante.

Be sure that you understand the term "humanism" as it applies to the Middle Ages.

Compare and contrast the philosophies of Abelard and Aquinas.

Explain what is meant by "courtly romances."

PHILOSOPHY AND THEOLOGY

The twelfth century has often been called an "age of humanism." The wave of religious enthusiasm that swept Europe from the second half of the eleventh century to the middle of the twelfth coincided with a burst of cultural activity and a zestful interest in learning. The writers of the twelfh century seem more like real persons—much more so than those of the earlier Middle Ages. There was a revival of classical literary studies, a vivid feeling for nature in lyric poetry, and a new naturalism in Gothic art. With these exciting intellectual and ecclesiastical developments, new humanist or "personalist," elements in religious devotion, theology, and philosophy also took hold.

This environment bred new philosophies. As we shall see, St Thomas Aquinas built a philosophical structure that accommodated divergent points of view. Dante suggested a new mix of views in the *Divine Comedy*. Aristotle was rediscovered and introduced throughout Europe. As intellectual walls broke down, light and fresh air flooded into Western culture. New freedoms, new comforts, both physical and spiritual, and a new confidence in the future pervaded every level of society. Thirteenth-century philosophy reconciled reason and revelation, the human and the divine, the kingdom of heaven and the kingdom on earth. Each took its place in a universal, harmonious order of thought.

THE RISE OF UNIVERSITIES

Many universities gained their charters in the twelfth and thirteenth centuries—for example, Oxford University in England, the University of Salamanca in Spain, the University of Bologna in Italy, and the University of Paris in France (Fig. **8.4**). Many had existed previously in association with monasteries, but their formal chartering made the public more aware of them.

Medieval universities were not like today's institutions. They had no buildings or classrooms, instead they were guilds of scholars and teachers who gathered their students together wherever space permitted. Students

8.4 Medieval scholars studying in Latin, Hebrew, and Arabic at a school in Sicily, c. 1200.

came from all over Europe, for example, to hear the lectures at the University of Paris by teachers like William of Champeaux (1070–1121) and, later, Peter Abelard. University life spawned people with trained minds who sought knowledge for its own sake and who could not accept a society that walled itself in and rigidly resisted any questioning of authority. In Paris, by the late twelfth century, the arts became a prelude to the study of theology.

The rise of universities at this particular time came as a result of a number of factors. As we previously mentioned, this was a time of rediscovery and publication of many of the texts of the classical world, especially works by Aristotle, which came to the West through Muslim sources in Spain. There was also a large amount of mathematical and scientific material coming to the attention of European scholars, again, largely through contact with Muslim scholars. In addition, for example in Bologna, legal studies received new impetus. All of this, coupled with the exploding population of the new cities and the consequent complexity of life, created a demand for a new, intellectual class who could bolster the cultural and socioeconomic foundations of medieval society.

ABELARD AND REALISM

Peter Abelard (1079–1142) has become a figure of both philosophy and romance. His life-long correspondence and late-in-life love affair with Héloïse accounts for the romantic element. As for the philosophy, he studied with William of Champeaux and with Roscellinus, but he disagreed with the conclusions of each of his masters. Abelard denied that objects are merely imperfect imitations of universal ideal models to which they owe their reality. Instead, he argued for the concrete nature of reality. That is to say, objects as we know them have real indi-

viduality which makes each object a substance "in its own right."

Abelard went beyond this, to argue that universals do exist, and comprise the "Form of the universe" as conceived by the mind of God. These universals are patterns, or types, after which individual substances are created and which make these substances the kinds of things they are.

Abelard has been called a "moderate realist," or, sometimes, a "conceptualist," even though that term is usually applied to later teaching. His views were adopted and modified by St Thomas Aquinas, and in this revised form they constitute part of Roman Catholic Church dogma today. Abelard believed that philosophy had a responsibility to define Christian doctrine and to make it intelligible. He also believed that philosophers should be free to criticize theology and to reject beliefs that are contrary to reason.

Abelard regarded Christianity as a way of life, but he was very tolerant of other religions as well. He considered Socrates and Plato to have been "inspired." The essence of Christianity was not its dogma, but the way Christ had lived his life. Those who lived prior to Jesus were, in a sense, already Christians if they had lived the kind of life Christ did. An individual act should be understood as good or evil "solely as it is well or ill intended," he argued in his treatise *Know Thyself*. However, lest anyone excuse acts on the basis of "good intentions," Abelard insisted that there should be some sort of standard for judging whether intentions were good or bad. Such a standard existed in a natural law of morality, "manifested in the conscience possessed by every man, and founded upon the will of God." When opinions differed over the interpretation of the law of God, he said, each person must obey his or her own conscience. Therefore, "anything a man does that is against his own conscience is sinful, no matter how much his act may commend itself to the consciences of others."[1]

ST THOMAS AQUINAS AND ARISTOTELIANISM

The rediscovery of Aristotle in the thirteenth century marked a new era in Christian thought. With the exception of Aristotle's treatises on logic, called the *Organon*, his writings were inaccessible to the West until the late twelfth century. Their reintroduction created turmoil. Some centers of education, such as the University of Paris, forbade Aristotle's metaphysics and physics. Others championed Aristotelian thought. Their scholars asserted the eternity of the world and denied the existence of divine providence and the foreknowlege of contingent events. In the middle were thinkers such as

PROFILE

St Francis of Assisi (1181/2–1226)

Francis (Fig. **8.5**) was baptized Francesco di Pietro di Bernardone (pronounced fron-CHAY-scoe dee pee-AY-troe dee bur-nahr-DOE-nay), the son of a cloth merchant. He learned to read and write Latin as a child and later learned to speak some French. In 1202 he participated in the war between Assisi and Perugia, was taken prisoner, and held for nearly a year. On his release, he was seriously ill, but he recovered and sought to serve in the army again in late 1205. However, after a vision told him to return to Assisi and await a call to a new kind of knighthood, he devoted himself to solitude and prayer in order to know the will of God. This began his conversion, which consisted of a number of episodes. He renounced material goods and family ties and embraced a life of poverty.

Although he was a layman, he began to preach the gospel. He attracted a number of disciples and devised a rule of life for them, based on the Gospel of Matthew: "Take no gold, nor silver, nor money in your belts, no bag for your journey" (Matthew 10:9–11). When the number of disciples, called friars, reached twelve, they went to Rome, where Pope Innocent III gave his blessing to their rule of life. This event, on 16 April 1209, marked the formal beginning of the Franciscan order. The Franciscans

8.5 Cimabue, *Enthroned Madonna with St Francis* (detail), 1280. Fresco, lower church of San Francisco, Assisi, Italy.

preached in the streets and, gradually, the order grew and spread throughout Italy.

Perhaps the most powerful experience of Francis' life occurred in the summer of 1224 when he went to the mountain retreat of La Verna to celebrate the feast of the Assumption of the Virgin and to prepare for St Michael's day with a forty-day fast. He prayed that he might know how best to please God. Opening the Gospels to find an answer, he came three times to the Passion of Christ. Then, as he prayed, he saw a figure coming toward him from heaven. It had the form of a seraph and smiled at him. Francis felt both joy and deep sorrow because of Christ's crucifixion. He understood that by God's providence he would be made like the crucified Christ through conformity of mind and heart. After the vision was over, Francis was marked with the stigmata of the Crucified—Francis' body actually showed marks on his body resembling the wounds on the body of Christ. Francis tried to hide the marks for the remainder of his life. He lived for only another two years, and was blind and in constant pain. After his death, his stigmata were announced to the order by letter. One of the most venerated religious figures of his time, he was made a saint on 15 July 1228.

Albertus Magnus, who, though orthodox in their acceptance of the traditional Christian faith, regarded the rediscovery of Aristotle in a wholly positive light. Magnus' first pupil was Thomas Aquinas (1227–74).

In his youth, Aquinas joined the newly formed mendicant Order of Preachers, the Dominican Order. This led him to Paris to study with Magnus, who was the master teacher of the Dominicans. A prolific writer, Aquinas produced philosophical and theological works and commentaries on Aristotle, the Bible, and Peter Lombard. His most influential works are the *Summa contra Gentiles* and the *Summa Theologiae*. Aquinas, like Magnus, was a modernist, and he sought to reinterpret the Christian system in the light of Aristotle—in other words to synthesize Christian theology and Aristotelian thought. He believed

that the philosophy of Aristotle would prove acceptable to intelligent men and women, and, further, that if Christianity were to maintain the confidence of educated people, it would have to come to terms with and accommodate Aristotle. Aquinas was a very devout and orthodox believer. He had no wish to sacrifice Christian truth, whether to Aristotle or any other philosopher.

In dealing with God and the universe, Aquinas carefully defined the fields of theology and philosophy. Philosophy was limited to whatever lay open to argument, and its purpose was to establish such truth as could be discovered and demonstrated by human reason. Theology, on the other hand, was restricted to the "content of faith," or "revealed truth," which is beyond the ability of reason to discern or demonstrate, and "about which there can be no argument." There was, nonetheless, an area of overlap.

Aquinas concentrated upon philosophical proofs of God's existence and nature. The existence of God could be proved by reason, he thought, and Aristotle had inadvertently done just that. The qualities to which Aristotle reduced all the activities of the universe become intelligible "only on the supposition that there is an unmoved ... self-existent ... form of being whose sheer perfection sets the whole world moving in pursuit of it."

LITERATURE

COURTLY ROMANCES

The change in outlook that accompanied the code of chivalry brought with it a new, popular form of poetry called the romance. These were long narratives whose subjects were knights and ladies. The name itself, like Romanesque, comes from a later age that mistakenly thought that these poems sought to imitate Roman literary forms. Chivalric and sentimental, the romance often drew its subjects from legends of ancient Troy and, most popularly, from Celtic legends of King Arthur and the knights of the Round Table.

Perhaps the first treatment of Arthur and Camelot came from Chrétien de Troyes (c. 1148–c. 1190). In this prototype, the simple story we know from the musical *Camelot*, is elaborated though many episodes and complicated with religious and courtly themes. In the end, Lancelot rescues Guinevere but, *en route*, suffers through misadventure after misadventure, from which he learns humility in order to love Guinevere with absolute obedience. The fact that Chrétien clearly parallels Lancelot's adventures with the suffering and death of Jesus, gives the work a disturbing character that borders on sacrilege. Also troubling for many is the moral neutrality with which the author treats Guinevere's adultery—a deadly sin in the eyes of the medieval Church. That Chrétien's perspective was unacceptable to some can be seen in a later, English, version of the story, Thomas Mallory's *Le Morte d'Arthur*, in which the collapse of Arthur's court was blamed directly on Lancelot and Guinevere's passions.

DANTE AND THE DIVINE COMEDY

Undoubtedly, the greatest poet of the age was Dante Alighieri (1265–1321). Dante wrote a few lyric poems and told the story of his passion for his unattainable love, Beatrice, in *La Vita Nuova*, but the *Divine Comedy* was

---

DANTE'S *COMEDY*

HELL
The Anteroom of the Neutrals
Circle 1: The Virtuous Pagans (Limbo)
Circle 2: The Lascivious
Circle 3: The Gluttonous
Circle 4: The Greedy and the Wasteful
Circle 5: The Wrathful
Circle 6: The Heretics
Circle 7: The Violent against Others, Self, God/Nature/and Art
Circle 8: The Fraudulent
Circle 9: The Lake of the Treacherous against kindred, country, guests, lords, and benefactors

PURGATORY
Ante-Purgatory: The Excommunicated/The Lazy/The Unabsolved/Negligent Rulers
The Terraces of the Mount of Purgatory
1. The Proud
2. The Envious
3. The Wrathful
4. The Slothful
5. The Avaricious
6. The Gluttonous
7. The Lascivious
The Earthly Paradise

PARADISE
1. The Moon: The Faithful who were inconstant
2. Mercury: Service marred by ambition
3. Venus: Love marred by lust
4. The Sun: Wisdom; the theologians
5. Mars: Courage; the just warriors
6. Jupiter: Justice; the great rulers
7. Saturn: Temperance; the contemplatives and mystics
8. The Fixed Stars: The Church Triumphant
9. The Primum Mobile: The Order of Angels
10. The Empyrean Heavens: Angels, Saints, The Virgin, and the Holy Trinity

8.6 The structure of Dante's *Divine Comedy*.

the major work of his life. Its description of heaven, hell, and purgatory is a vision of the state of souls after death told in an ALLEGORY—that is, a dramatic device in which the superficial sense is accompanied by a deeper or more profound meaning. It works on several levels to demonstrate the human need for spiritual illumination and guidance. On a literal level, it describes the author's fears as a sinner and his hopes for eternal life. On deeper levels, it represents the quandaries and character of medieval society faced with, for example, balancing classicism and

Christianity. Part of Dante's significance lies in the fact that he elevated vernacular Italian to the status of a rich, expressive language that was suitable for poetry. It was no longer necessary for writers to use Latin.

Dante, an aristocrat, was educated in both classical and Christian works. As with many Florentine office-holders and literati, Dante suffered exile when his political allies fell from power. In 1301 he was banished from Florence for life. During the years of his exile, in which he suffered deprivation and poverty, he composed *The Comedy* (*Commedia*). Actually, Dante gave the work a particularly personal title: *The Comedy of Dante Alighieri, A Florentine by Birth but not in Behavior.* He called it a comedy because, according to him, it had a happy ending and was written in the language of the people. Recognition of the superb character of the work caused later admirers to affix the word "Divine," which has remained since.

The poem is divided into three book-length parts, detailed in Figure **8.6**.

In the *Comedy* Dante narrates his fictional travels through three realms of the Christian afterlife, beginning on Good Friday 1300. For the first two parts of the journey, he is accompanied by the Roman poet Vergil, from whose work *The Aeneid* Dante drew considerable inspiration. Vergil represents human reason and the classical culture. In the first part, Dante descends into Hell, where he hears the damned tell of their sins against God and moral law. In the second part, Dante stands in Purgatory, where lesser sinners do penance while awaiting their entrance into heaven. In Purgatory, Vergil turns over Dante's guidance to Beatrice (Italian for "blessing"), Dante's symbol of the eternal female and of spiritualized love and Christian culture. She also represents divine revelation, and is, therefore, superior to Vergil. She guides Dante into Paradise, where he finds the souls of the saved divided into three groups: lay people, the active, and the contemplative. Nine categories of angels inhabit the closest circles to the throne of God.

As occurs often in medieval arts, Dante's *Comedy* contains symbolic numbers. The structure of the work breaks into one hundred cantos. The first canto serves as an introduction, and the three major parts each have thirty-three cantos. Three is a common symbol for the Christian Trinity (Father, Son, and Holy Spirit). The poem is written in a three-line verse form called *terza rima*, which uses an interlocking rhyme scheme in three-line stanzas—for example *aba, bcb, cdc, ded*, and so on, ending in a rhymed couplet. Multiples of three occur in the nine regions, plus a vestibule of Hell and Purgatory. Paradise contains nine heavens plus the highest heaven (*Empyrean*). In Hell, the damned are divided into three groups: those who sinned by incontinence, by violence, or by fraud. In Purgatory, those who wait are divided in three ways depending on how they acted in relation to love. Paradise contains nine categories of angels.

CRITICAL REVIEW below

A CRITICAL REVIEW

As early as the twelfth century humankind began to have an interest in themselves as individuals: individuals who had some further purpose on earth than merely to go on dutifully enduring with no greater purpose than to get through this "vale of tears" and into the eternal happiness of heaven that waited beyond the grave. People began to see themselves as being important and as having a connection with the world of the past. New "personalist" or humanist elements entered devotion, theology, philosophy, and literature, and together with new directions in intellectual life came the formal introduction of great centers of learning, called universities. These reintroduced the classical past, brought to the West mainly through the Muslim conquest of Spain and the resulting contact of Muslim and Western scholars.

In the Middle Ages, symbolism played an important role not only in theology but in art as well.

In what ways do the concepts of Abelard's "universal truths" still exist?

Does your concept of the universe include universal truths or do you believe that truth is relative? Explain whatever point of view you hold and contrast it with the opposite.

Explain the symbolism in the structure of Dante's Comedy.

A CRITICAL LOOK

Like the Greek temple, Gothic archi-tecture—particularly the Gothic cathedral—has come to symbolize an entire era and to form an important prototype for building not only churches but also other structures in our contemporary world. Gothic sculpture tends to be an extension of the buildings on which it appears, and Gothic two-dimensional art, magnificent though it is, tends to be hidden in the pages of the relatively few manuscripts produced during the time. Nonetheless, they share a specific set of characteristics in their use of line, form, balance, and unity. Gothic style is very much a part of its environment and in architecture it can be seen as a synthesis of that environment.

Note the changes from the Romanesque that can be seen in the development of Gothic style. Be sure that you know what these are— that is, what attitudes, reflections, and general characteristics differentiate Gothic style from its prede-cessor, and what marks early Gothic from late Gothic style.

GOTHIC STYLE

ARCHITECTURE

CRITICAL LOOK above

Although Gothic style in architecture took many forms it is best exemplified by the Gothic cathedral. In its synthe-sis of intellect, spirituality, and engineering the cathedral perfectly expresses the medieval mind. Gothic style was widespread in Europe, but like the other arts it was not uniform in application, nor was it uniform in date. Initially a very local style, on the Ile de France in the late twelfth century, it spread outward to the rest of Europe. It had died as a style in some places before it was adopted in others. The "slipping, sliding, and overlapping" pat-tern of artistic development fully applies to Gothic archi-tecture.

The cathedral was, of course, a Church building whose purpose was the service of God. However, civic pride as well as spirituality inspired the cathedral builders. Local guilds contributed their services in financ-ing or in building the churches, and guilds were often memorialized in special chapels and stained-glass win-dows. The Gothic church occupied the central, often ele-vated, area of the town or city. Its position symbolized the dominance of the universal Church over all human affairs, both spiritual and secular. Probably no other architectural style has exercised such an influence across the centuries. The story of the Gothic church is an intri-cate and fascinating one, only a few details of which we can highlight here.

The beginnings of Gothic architecture can be pin-pointed to between 1137 and 1144, in the rebuilding of the royal Abbey Church of Saint-Denis (see Synthesis sec-tion, p. 275) near Paris (Figs **8.7** and **8.8**). There is ample evidence that Gothic style was a physical extension of philosophy, rather than a practical response to the struc-tural limitations of the Romanesque style. That is, Gothic

theory preceded its application. The philosophy of the Abbot Suger, who was advisor to Louis VI and a driving force in the construction of Saint-Denis, held three main points. Harmony, the perfect relationship of parts, is the source of beauty; divine light is a mystic revelation of God; and space is symbolic of God's mystery. The com-

8.7 Exterior of the Abbey Church of Saint-Denis, near Paris, 1137–44.

8.8 Interior of the Abbey Church of Saint-Denis.

8.9 Notre Dame, Paris, flying buttresses, 1163–1250.

8.10 Notre Dame, Paris, west front, 1163–1250.

positon of Saint-Denis and subsequent Gothic cathedrals clearly expressed that philosophy. As a result, Gothic architecture is more unified than Romanesque. Gothic cathedrals use refined, upward-striving lines to symbolize humanity's upward striving to escape the bounds of earth and enter the mystery of space (the kingdom of heaven).

The pointed arch is the most easily identifiable characteristic of this style. It represents not only a symbol of Gothic spirituality, but also an engineering practicality. The round arch of the previous era places tremendous pressure on its keystone, which then transfers thrust outward to the sides, but the pointed arch redistributes the thrust of downward force in more equal, controllable directions. It controls thrust by sending it downward through its legs, and it makes design flexibility possible. The Gothic arch also increases the sense of height in its vaults. Some have said that Gothic structure actually made increased heights possible, but this is not quite correct. Some Romanesque churches had vaults as high as those in Gothic churches. It is the possibility of changing the proportion of height to width that increases the apparent height of the Gothic church.

Engineering advances implicit in the new form made possible larger clerestory windows, which let in more light. And more slender ribbing placed greater emphasis

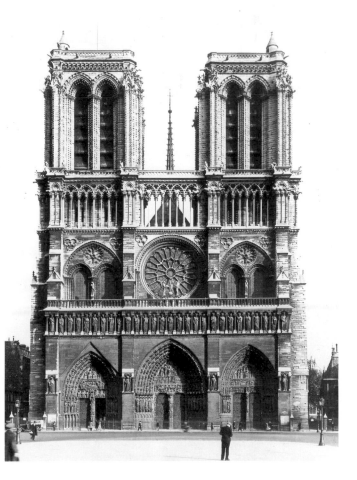

on space, as opposed to mass. On the exterior, the outward thrust of the vaults is carried gracefully to the ground through a delicate network of ribs, vaults, and FLYING BUTTRESSES (Fig. **8.9**). Every detail of the decorative tracery is carefully integrated into a system that emphasizes mysterious space.

Three examples characterize Gothic style and illustrate the marvelous diversity that existed within it. The four-square power of Notre Dame de Paris (Fig. **8.10**) reflects the strength and solidity of an urban cathedral in Europe's greatest city of the age. Its careful design is highly mathematical—each level is equal to the one below it, and its three-part division is clearly symbolic of the Trinity. Arcs (whose radii are equal to the width of the building) drawn from the lower corners meet at the top of the circular window at the second level. The effect of this design is to draw the eye inward and slowly upward. The exterior structure clearly reveals the interior space, as it did not in Romanesque buildings.

Chartres Cathedral (Fig. **8.11–14**) stands in remarkable contrast. Chartres is a country cathedral that rises above the center of a small city. Just as its sculptures

8.11 Chartres Cathedral, France, west front, 1145–1220.

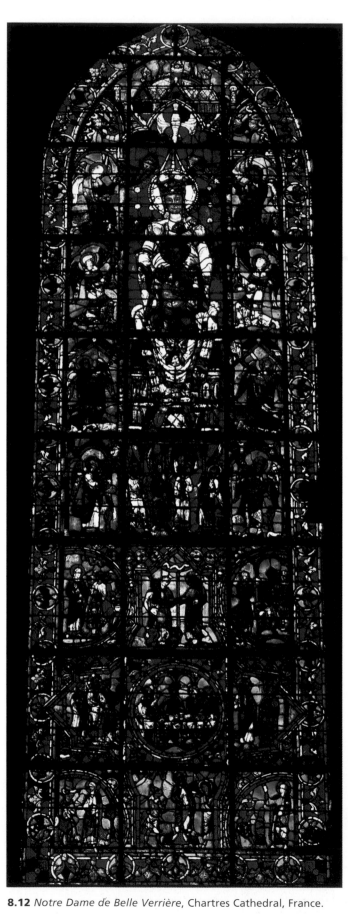

8.12 *Notre Dame de Belle Verrière*, Chartres Cathedral, France.

illustrate a progression of style (see Figs **8.18** and **8.20**), so does its architectural design. At first glance we wonder why its cramped entry portal is so small in comparison with the rest of the building. The reason is that Chartres was not built all at once. Rather, it was built cumulatively over many years, as fire destroyed one part of the church after another. The main entry portal and the windows above it date back to its Romanesque beginnings. The porch of the south transept (Fig. **8.13**, the portal holding the statues of the warrior saints) is much larger and more in harmony with the rest of the building.

Our biggest question, however, concerns the incongruity of the two unmatched spires. Again, fire was responsible. The early spire, on the right illustrates faith in its simple upward lines rising, unencumbered, to disappear at the tip into the ultimate mystery of space. The later spire is more ornate and complex—the eye travels up it with increasing difficulty, its progress halted and held by decoration and detail.

A major difference between the Gothic style and the Romanesque lies in the fenestration. Gothic-style walls are pierced by windows that take the form of sparkling jewels of stained glass, such as the *Notre Dame de Belle Verrière* ("Our Lady of the Beautiful Window") of Chartres Cathedral (Fig. **8.12**). Stained-glass windows replaced the wall paintings of the Romanesque and the mosaics of the Byzantine style. Their ethereal, multicolored light further mysticized the spiritual experience of the medieval worshiper. Light now became an additional property for artistic manipulation and design. The loveliness and intricacy typical of the art of medieval stained

8.13 Chartres Cathedral, France, south transept porch, c. 1205–50.

8.17 Amiens Cathedral, France, west front, c. 1220–59.

hand, carries its portals upward to the full height of the lower section. In fact, the lines of the central portal, which is much larger than the central portal of Notre Dame, combine with the lines of the side portals to form a pyramid whose apex penetrates into the section above. The roughly similar size of the portals of Notre Dame reinforces its horizontality, and this is what gives it stability. Every use of line, form, and proportion in Amiens reinforces lightness and action. Everything about the appearance of Notre Dame reinforces stability and strength. One design is no better than the other, of course. Nevertheless, both cathedrals are unquestionably Gothic, and the qualities that make them so are easy to identify.

The importance of stained-glass windows in Gothic cathedrals cannot be overemphasized. They carefully control the light entering the sanctuary, and the quality of that light reinforces a marvelous sense of mystery. With the walls of the Romanesque style replaced by the space and light of the Gothic style, these windows take the place of wall paintings in telling the story of the gospels and the saints.

8.18 Chartres Cathedral, France, jamb statues, west portal, c. 1145–70.

SCULPTURE

Gothic sculpture again reveals the changes in attitude of the period. It portrays serenity, idealism, and simple naturalism. Gothic sculpture, like painting, has a human quality. Life now seems to be more valuable. The vale of tears, death, and damnation are replaced by conceptions of Christ as a benevolent teacher and of God as awesome in his beauty rather than in his vengeance. There is a new order, symmetry, and clarity. Visual images carry over a distance with greater distinctness. The figures of Gothic sculpture are less entrapped in their material and stand away from their backgrounds (Fig. **8.18**).

Schools of sculpture developed throughout France. Thus, although individual stone carvers worked alone, their links with a particular school gave their works the character of that school. The work from Reims, for example, had an almost classical quality; that from Paris was dogmatic and intellectual, perhaps reflecting the role of Paris as a university city. As time went on, sculpture became more naturalistic. Spiritual meaning was sacrificed to everyday appeal, and sculpture increasingly

8.19 Chartres Cathedral, France, central tympanum, west portal, c. 1145–70.

reflected secular interests, both middle class and aristocratic. A comparison of the figure of Christ in the central tympanum at Chartres (Fig. **8.19**) with that in the Vézelay tympanum (see Fig. **7.19**) illustrates this point. At Chartres, Christ has a calm solemnity, in contrast to the emotion-charged, elongated, twisting figure at Vézelay.

Compositional unity also changed over time. Early Gothic architectural sculpture was subordinate to the overall design of the building. As later work gained in emotionalism, it began to claim attention on its own (Fig. **8.20**).

The sculptures of Chartres Cathedral, which bracket nearly a century from 1145 to 1220, illustrate clearly the transition from early to High Gothic. The attenuated figures of the JAMB statues in Figure **8.18**, from the middle of the twelfth century, display a relaxed serenity, idealism, and simple naturalism. They are an integral part of the portal columns, but they also emerge from them, each in its own space. Each figure has a particular human dignity

8.20 Chartres Cathedral, France, jamb statues, south transept portal, c. 1215–20.

despite its idealization. Cloth drapes easily over the bodies. Detail is somewhat formal and shallow, but we now see the human figure beneath the fabric, in contrast to the previous use of fabric merely as a surface decoration.

As human as these saints may appear, this quality is even more pronounced in the saints' figures from less than a century later (see Fig. **8.20**). Here we see the characteristics of the High Gothic style, or Gothic classicism. These figures have only the most tenuous connection to the structural elements of the building. Proportions are more lifelike, and the figures are carved in subtle S-curves rather than as rigid perpendicular columns. The drape of the fabric is much more natural, with deeper and softer folds. In contrast to the idealized saints of the earlier period, these figures have the features of specific individuals, and they express qualities of spirituality and determination.

The content of Gothic sculpture is also noteworthy. Like most Church art, it was didactic, or designed to teach. Many of its lessons are straightforward. Above the main doorway of Chartres Cathedral, for example, Christ appears as a ruler and judge of the universe, along with a host of symbols of the apostles and others (see Fig. **8.19**). Also decorating the portals are the prophets and kings of the Old Testament. These figures proclaim the harmony of secular and spiritual rule, and thus suggest that the kings of France are spiritual descendants of biblical rulers—a message much like that of San Vitale, built by Justinian at Ravenna.

Other lessons of Gothic cathedral sculpture are more complex and less obvious. According to some scholars, much of this art was created according to specific conventions, codes, and sacred mathematical calculations. These formulas govern positioning, grouping, numbers, and symmetry. For example, the numbers three, four, and seven (which often appear as groupings in compositions of post-Gothic periods) symbolize the Trinity, the Gospels, the sacraments, and the deadly sins (the last two both number seven). The placement of figures around Christ shows their relative importance with the position on Christ's right being the most important. These codes and symbols, consistent with the tendency toward mysticism, and finding allegorical and hidden meanings in holy sources, became more and more complex.

PAINTING

In the twelfth and thirteenth centuries, traditional fresco painting returned to prominence. Manuscript illumination also continued. Two-dimensionality flowed from one style into another without any clearly dominant identity emerging. Because this period is so closely identified with Gothic architecture, and because painting found its primary outlet within the Gothic cathedral, however, we need to ask what qualities identify a Gothic style in painting. The answer is not as readily apparent as it is in architecture and sculpture, but several characteristics can be identified. One is the beginnings of three-dimensionally in figure representation. Another is a striving to give figures mobility and life within three-dimensional space. Space is the essence of Gothic style. Gothic painters and illuminators had not mastered perspective, and their compositions do not exhibit the spatial rationality of later works. But if we compare these painters with their predecessors of the earlier medieval eras, we discover that they have more or less broken free from the frozen two-dimensionality of earlier styles. Gothic style also exhibits spirituality, lyricism, and a new humanism. In other words, it favors mercy over irrevocable judgment. Gothic style is less crowded and frantic—its figures are less entangled with each other. It was a changing style with many variations.

The Gothic style of two-dimensional art found magnificent expression in manuscript illumination. The Court Style of France and England is represented by some truly exquisite works. The Psalter of St Louis (Fig. **8.21**) was produced for King Louis IX of France in about 1250. It was a lavish book containing seventy-eight full-page pictures of scenes from the Old Testament. The figures are gracefully elongated and delicate. Set against gold backgrounds, the compositions are carefully balanced and, while somewhat crowded, show a relaxed comfort in their spatial relationships. Precision and control charac-

8.21 *Gideon's Army Surprises the Midianites*, from the Psalter of St Louis, c. 1250. 4³/₄ × 3⁵/₈ ins (12.1 × 9.2 cm). Bibliothèque Nationale, Paris.

8.22 *St John on Patmos*, from the Douce Apocalypse, before 1272. 12¹/₂ × 8⁵/₈ ins (31.75 × 21.9 cm). Bodleian Library, Oxford, England.

terize the technique. Colors are rich. Human figures and architectural details are blended in the same manner that church sculpture both decorated and became a part of its architectural environment.

The artists who made these works were professionals living in Paris. They were influenced by Italian style, and they clearly had a new interest in pictorial space, which begins to distinguish them from their medieval predecessors. This Parisian style, in turn, influenced English manuscript illumination. Figure **8.22** of *St John on Patmos* was painted for Edward, son of Henry III, and his wife Eleanor of Castile. The elongated figures and small heads reflect the French court influence, as does the heavy drapery. The English painters, however, frequently altered their French models, giving them more angular treatment of the folds and exaggerated poses and even expressions.

The same characteristics can be seen in Figure **8.23**, *David Harping*. The curious proportions of face and hands, as well as the awkward linear draping of fabric juxtaposed against the curved forms of the harp and chair, create a sense of tension. The layout of the background screen is almost careless. The upward curving arcs at the top are intended to be symmetrical, but their lack of symmetry is reinforced by the imprecision of the diamond shapes. A touch of realism appears in the curved harp string which David is plucking. A rudimentary use of highlight and shadow gives basic three-dimensionality to cloth and skin, and although it is out of balance in its interior space, the figure does not appear to crowd the borders. It has space in which to move.

CRI
REV
belo

8.23 *David Harping*, from the Oscott Psalter, c. 1270. 7⁷/₈ × 4³/₈ ins (20 × 11.1 cm). British Library, London.

A CRITICAL REVIEW

Earlier in the chapter we noted that mysticism became an important part of the life of the High Middle Ages. Perhaps nothing symbolizes that mysticism better than the Gothic cathedral and its associated sculptural decoration. We asserted that Gothic cathedrals were the perfect synthesis of spirituality, engineering, and intellect of the time. What does this assertion mean? Is there something innately religious about Gothic architecture? After all, it has remained a popular style for places of worship right up to the present day, and particularly during the nineteenth century.

Find an example of a church or other building in your community that uses the Gothic style as its inspiration. Describe that building and explain how the Gothic influence manifests itself in it.

What is there about the Gothic style that gives it its sense of mysticism?

A CRITICAL LOOK	Music and theatre in the twelfth and thirteenth centuries—like all

art—had particular qualities tying them to the era.

What are ars antiqua; organum; ballades and rondeaux?

The theatre of the time gave us a unique combination of depiction and convention called the mansion stage.

The story of the Abbey Church of Saint-Denis, which is included in the Synthesis section, is an important look at the very first Gothic cathedral, in which the essence of the Gothic style can be found.

MUSIC

Paris was the center of musical activity in the twelfth and thirteenth centuries. Perhaps in response to the additional stability and increasing complexity of life, music now became more formal in notation and in structure, and also it increased in textural complexity. Improvisation had formed the basis of musical composition. Gradually musicians felt the need to write down compositions—as opposed to making up each piece anew along certain melodic patterns every time it was performed. As a result, in the late Middle Ages "musical composition" became a specific and distinct undertaking.

Music was often transmitted from performer to performer or from teacher to student. Standardized musical notation now made it possible for the composer to transmit ideas directly to the performer. The role of the performer thus changed, making him or her a vehicle of transmission and interpretation in the process of musical communication.

As the structure of musical composition became more formal during this period, conventions of RHYTHM, harmony, and mode (similar to our concept of KEY) were established. Polyphony began to replace monophony, although the latter continued in chants, hymns, and other forms during this time.

ARS ANTIQUA

Each of these developments contributed so distinctly to music that modern scholars refer to the mid-twelfth and thirteenth centuries as *ars antiqua*, or the "old art." In the fourteenth century, music underwent notable change, and came to be described as *ars nova*, or "new art."

Music of *ars antiqua* was affected by the same change of attitude as two-dimensional art and sculpture—a more rational, as opposed to emotional, underlying approach

and feeling. A number of forms typify twelfth- and thirteenth-century music. Among these are organum, an early sacred form of music, sung in Latin. At first organum used two parallel melodic lines, based on a plainsong theme, moving in exactly the same rhythm, and separated by a fixed interval. Later, a third or fourth voice was added. By the twelfth century the various voices were no longer restricted to singing parallel lines. The plainsong melody remained in long notes in a low voice, as the basis of the music structure. Meanwhile the upper voices had more interesting, freely flowing lines to sing.

Alongside organum existed secular songs such as BALLADES and RONDEAUX. These were vernacular songs in set forms, usually easy to listen to and direct in appeal. Some were dancelike, often in triple meter. The tradition of the troubadour and the wandering entertainer continued, and the courtly approach found in music and poetry an exquisite forum for its love-centered philosophy. But the most important new form of the thirteenth century was the MOTET, whose name probably derives from the French word *mot*, meaning "word." As in organum, the motet used a plainsong melody in long held notes in a low voice, while upper parts were more elaborate. Motets were written not only for the Church, but also for secular use, with the upper voices singing nonreligious words over the plainsong.

THEATRE

Probably because of their relationship to the Church, major movements in the arts in the twelfth and thirteenth centuries were reasonably unified and widespread. Although local diversity was common, styles were generally alike. The theatre was no exception. As the Middle Ages progressed, drama associated with the Church followed the example of painting and included more and more Church-related material. Earliest Church drama, that is, the trope, was a simple elaboration and illustra-

8.27 The Valenciennes Mystery Play, 1547. Contemporary drawing. Bibliothèque Nationale, Paris.

parade. Each wagon carried the set for a specific part of the play cycle. Many of these wagons were very elaborate, two stories tall, and curtained for entrances and exits like a modern theatre. In some cases, a flat wagon was combined with an elaborate background wagon to provide a playing area. This type of production was mostly used in cities where narrow wagons were needed to negotiate narrow streets. At intersections where there was more space, wagons were coupled and crowds gathered to watch a segment of the play. When the segment finished, the wagon moved on, and was shortly replaced by another wagon, which served as the setting for another short play in the cycle.

SYNTHESIS
Suger and the Abbey Church of Saint-Denis

Between 1135 and 1137, Suger, abbot of Saint-Denis, began to rebuild the royal abbey church. That undertaking changed architecture for all time. The ancestry of every Gothic church in the world—including the recently completed Episcopal "National" Cathedral in Washington D.C.—owes its existence to it. Unlike any other artistic style, the beginning of Gothic style can be pinpointed to the planning and construction of this one building.

As we have seen, Suger lived in a rapidly changing world, in which developing royal authority brought about trade, commerce, expanding towns and cities, and a broadening sense of security. Humankind was challenged to discover and develop individual powers of reasoning, and the Church gave assurance that love and understanding would lead to salvation. These conditions produced a new confidence and hope, unlike the pervading belief of the Romanesque world, and new ways were found to express human faith in the Christian universe.

Suger, a man blessed with personal charm and great talent, was abbot of Saint-Denis from 1122 to 1151. He was born in 1081 in humble circumstances, but by the time he died, he was known as "father of his country." He entered the abbey as an oblate in 1091 at the age of ten. In those days it was usual for humble people, burdened with too many children, to give or vow a child to a monastery in return for access to education and a career. Suger was a student at Saint-Denis for more than ten years, during which time he read voraciously, studying the archives of the charters and other documents of the abbey. By the time he was twenty-five, his talent had been recognized, and he began public life as a representative of Adam, abbot of Saint-Denis, at the Council of Poitiers in 1106. A year later, at the consecration of La Charité-sur-Loire by Pope Paschal II, he successfully argued before the pope the abbey's case for independence from the Bishop of Paris. Demonstrating his administrative abilities, he rose to become deputy of the abbey's priory of Berneval in Normandy, finally becoming abbot in 1122.

Immediately thereafter, Suger was immersed in the controversy surrounding Peter Abelard (see page 256), who had entered Saint-Denis as a monk after his humiliating mutilation in Paris in 1119. Abelard had offended the abbey community by questioning its identification

with the first-century Dionysius (Denis, in French), who had been converted by St Paul in Athens (Acts 17:34) and who was considered to be the apostle who had brought Christianity to France. Furious at the aspersion, Abbot Adam had Abelard thrown into prison, but he escaped and took refuge with the Count of Champagne. Adam refused to release Abelard from his vows and threatened excommunication. This was the situation when Adam died, and Suger became abbot. On the advice of the king's councillor, Suger allowed Abelard to retire to a place of his own choosing, provided that he remain a monk of Saint-Denis, but thereafter, he ignored Abelard and his troubles, concerning himself instead with the affairs of administration, and, finally, with the reconstruction of the abbey church.

Suger was a champion of the monarchy, which he invested with religious significance. The abbey church of Saint-Denis benefited from Suger's politics and from its own history. It was the shrine of the apostle of France, the sacred protector of the realm, and the chief memorial of the Carolingian dynasty: Charlemagne and his father Pepin had been consecrated there, and it was the burial place of Charles Martel, Pepin, and Charles the Bald. Suger wanted to make the abbey the spiritual center of France, a center of pilgrimage and the center of religious and patriotic emotion. To meet such ends, the church needed to be enlarged. His chronicles of the planning and goals of that project have given us a clear picture of the nature and scope of Gothic architecture itself.

In reality, none of the individual elements of Saint-Denis was completely new. Apses with radial chapels had been built as early as St Sernin (see Figs **7.12** and **7.13**). However, at Saint-Denis, the plan allowed space to flow around them, uninterrupted by walls (Fig. **8.28**). Pointed arches and ribbed vaults also had been used before, but never in such a way that the heaviness of Romanesque style was transformed into the lightness of slender supports and bearing walls that occurred here. The revolution represented at Saint-Denis was one of structural relationships rather than of forms. It took existing ideas and transformed them into something new and enduring.

An additional revolution occurred in the transformation of the interior. As Suger wrote, the entire church shone "with the wonderful and uninterrupted light of most luminous windows, pervading the interior beauty."

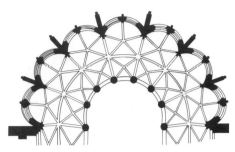

8.28 Plan of the ambulatory and radiating chapels of choir at Saint-Denis, Paris, 1140–44.

The architectural forms seem graceful and weightless, and the windows cease to be openings and become translucent walls in themselves. All this is possible because of the accommodation of the active thrust of the high arches through buttresses. The weight of the whole structure is transferred through them, and, thus, the interior space becomes open and clean, and the structural system is visible only from outside.

The result is a new dimension, a new spirit. Suger's emphasis was on strict geometric planning and a search for luminosity. Suger continually insists that his design

8.29 Reconstruction of the west façade of Saint-Denis as envisaged by Abbot Suger. Drawn by Gregory Robeson.

placed the highest value on harmony—that is, the perfect relationship among parts in terms of mathematical proportions—as the source of beauty. Harmony for Suger represents the "Divine Reason" by which the universe has been constructed. The light that floods the interior is "Light Divine," a mystic revelation of God's spirit.

In preparing for the reconstruction of Saint-Denis, Suger visited artists throughout Europe. These included bronze founders, jewelers, and enamel workers from the valleys of the Rhine and the Meuse, masons and stonecarvers from Normandy, Burgundy, and southwestern France, mosaicists from Italy, and many masters of stained glass from various regions. The abbot believed that the church should offer attainment of outward splendor, spectacles offered to God and humankind, and light to lead the dull mind from the material to the immaterial, and that he was translating a godly philosophy into stone, glass, precious metals, and jewels. He summoned the best artists and artisans, and his administrative skills made it possible to handle the finances to attract the best. He guaranteed funds that put no limitations on their work, so an international gathering of artists and craftsmen translated Suger's ideas.

Normally, the construction of medieval churches began at the eastern end so that services could be conducted as soon as possible. Suger began his construction at the west end—that is, the entrance façade itself. The façade at Saint-Denis, unlike that of many churches, is not merely an exterior embellishment. The Norman towers are set back on the entrance bays so that they become an integral part of the western structure (Fig. **8.29**). The bays have two stories with upper chapels, which function independently from the rest of the building. This is symbolic of royal, secular authority, as distinct from the authority of the church, which is presided over by the clergy at the high altar and chapels at the eastern end of the building.

The triple portals of the west façade were one of the new features. The three arches with one larger, central arch suggest the triumphal arches of Constantine in Rome, which Suger certainly had seen. Roman writers describe the emperor passing in triumph through the arch as an act of purification on the way to becoming deified. Thus, the idea of purification on entry through the portal of the church's façade seems clear in this application. Suger refers to the church's dedication and indicates that there was "one glorious procession of . . . three men" who left the church through a single door. The three bishops, acting as one, proceeded to perform the dedication of the three doors in a single act and then re-entered the church through a single door. The reference to the numbers one and three is clearly a reference to the Christian Trinity, in the sense that we found it in Dante's *Comedy*.

The dominant theme at Saint-Denis is the Last Judgment tympanum above the central western door (Fig. **8.30**).

Christ the Judge dominates everything. He reveals his two natures as Son of God and Son of Man. As judge, Christ summons the dead to appear from the grave, which is depicted in the lintel below his feet. He is also depicted at the moment of his crucifixion with out-stretched arms and his right side bared showing the mark of the spear. Surrounding the central figure are angels, trumpeting the awakening of the dead, scenes of heaven and hell awaiting the blessed and the damned, and the Apostles, seated together to represent the Last Judgment. They are conversing with each other in their role as teachers.

In sum, Suger and the Abbey Church of Saint-Denis represent the age: old elements and orders emerging

8.30 The tympanum of the west portal, west façade, Saint-Denis. (All heads are nineteenth-century restorations.)

into new establishments and attitudes as enclosure breaks forth into space and light.

Remarkably, in this chapter we have witnessed something that has never happened before or since—the emergence of a magnificent and lasting style from a single aesthetic, spiritual, intellectual, and engineering conceptualization: a crystallization that represents a true synthesis. The Abbey Church of Saint-Denis sums up the High Middle Ages because it represents the beginning of the single vision that dominated the age: the Gothic style. It also illustrates a point we have considered before—that is, the importance of a single human being in turning great historical events.

CHAPTER NINE

THE LATE MIDDLE AGES

AT A GLANCE

The End of the Middle Ages
Secularism and Transition
The Hundred Years' War
PROFILE: Joan of Arc
The Secular Monarchies
The Plague
Economics and Industrialization
Religion and the Great Schism
TECHNOLOGY: Keeping Time

Literature
Petrarch and Boccaccio
PROFILE: Geoffrey Chaucer
Froissart's Chronicles

Art and Architecture
Late Gothic Architecture
Late Gothic Sculpture
Painting
MASTERWORK: Van Eyck—The Arnolfini
Marriage

Music
Ars Nova
OUR DYNAMIC WORLD: Noh Theatre of Japan

Theatre

**Synthesis: The Late Gothic
Temperament in England**

9.1 Salisbury Cathedral, England, from the southwest, begun 1220.

A CRITICAL LOOK

The struggle between Church and State that occurred in the late Middle Ages broke the hold of the Roman Catholic Church on the general social order and created an increasingly secular society.

At the same time, war, disease, and economics changed the basic conditions of human life. In the next sections we will see how society in Europe moved into a new era and discuss in detail a war that reflected rising national interests that were occurring during the time. We will encounter several interesting personalities and watch as feudalism and Church authority took a back seat to the emerging secular monarchs who ruled over large, nationally homogeneous populations that were beginning to approximate to what we recognize as "countries." Finally, we watch as nearly one-half of the population of Europe was wiped out by plague.

Enumerate and explain the effects of the Plague and the Hundred Years' War on the late Middle Ages.

Explain how the rise of secular monarchies changed the way society was organized.

Describe the Great Schism and its effects on Europe and religion.

THE END OF THE MIDDLE AGES

SECULARISM AND TRANSITION

By the fourteenth century, revelation and reason, and God and the State, were considered to be separate spheres of authority, neither subject to the other. Such a separation, of what had previously been the full realm of the Church, was the beginning of secularism—that is, a rejection of religion and religious considerations. Individual nations—rather than feudal states or holy empires—had arisen throughout Europe, although it would be misleading to say that religion and matters of State were entirely divorced. As we shall see, they intermingled freely when it was convenient; but they clashed severely when questions of power and authority were at stake. However, amid the conflict of secular and Church interests, two events had a catastrophic impact on Europe. The year 1338 marked the beginning of what was called the Hundred Years' War, and, early in that, the plague (1348–51) further disrupted the relative prosperity of the High Middle Ages. During this time, secular arts gradually gained prominence, respectability, and significance, reflecting a shifting emphasis rather than an outright reversal of values.

Medieval people believed that misfortune was a divine punishment for their sins. The difficulties experienced between 1300 and 1500 landed across the shoulders of Christian Europe like "the scourge of God." Disaster struck at all parts of society, and as war and disease laid waste the land, economic depression plunged living conditions to new lows, especially after the relative peace and prosperity of the High Middle Ages of the previous two centuries. In many ways, it marked an end of an era, a time of transition to a world that emerged thereafter with a completely different spirit and manner of looking at the universe. In tune with matters of faith, therefore, the time could be seen as a closing of one door

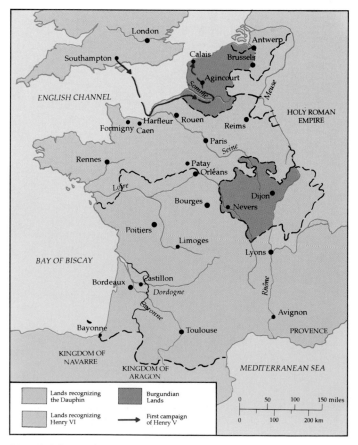

Map 9.1 France in 1429.

	GENERAL EVENTS	LITERATURE & PHILOSOPHY	VISUAL ART & ARCHITECTURE	THEATRE & MUSIC
1300	Papacy to Avignon Ashikaga period in Japan Hundred Years' War begins	Dante *Book of Hours of Jeanne d'Evreux*	Cimabue (**9.14**) Duccio (**9.15**) Giotto (**9.16, 9.17**) Pisano (**9.13**) Ely Cathedral (**9.27**) Exeter Cathedral (**9.25**) Wells Cathedral (**9.26**) Salisbury Cathedral (**9.1**) Lincoln Cathedral (**9.29**) Hallenkirchen Florence Cathedral (**9.8**) Gloucester Cathedral (**9.30, 9.31**) Milan Cathedral (**9.9**) Doge's Palace (**9.10**)	
1350	Black Death or plague in Europe Battle of Poitiers Conquests of Tamerlane (Timur) in Asia Ming Dynasty in China (until 1644)		Lorenzetti (**9.18**)	Philippe de Vitry
1375	Hanseatic League controls Baltic Union of Denmark, Norway, and Sweden (until 1448) Mechanical clocks	Petrarch Boccaccio Chaucer Froissart	Sluter (**9.12**)	de Machaut *Ars nova* Noh theatre in Japan
1400	Joan of Arc		van Eyck (**9.20**) van der Weyden (**9.21**)	

Timeline 9.1 The late Middle Ages.

and the opening of another. To the people who followed, it was a door to better times: a modern world.

THE HUNDRED YEARS' WAR

The Hundred Years' War really lasted more than one hundred years. It consisted of an intermittent struggle between England and France which involved periodic fighting over the question of English fiefs in France (Fig. **9.2**), fighting that had begun in the twelfth century. The series of on-going battles concerning a number of issues, including the rightful succession to the French crown, traditionally began in 1337 and lasted until 1453.

As we saw in the last two chapters, medieval feudalism and the growing sense of centralized authority had more to do with liege loyalties than with any established national borders. In fact, "borders" as we know them were non-existent, except as one powerful individual might, by virtue of feudal allegiances, enforce them. Once gained, properties were inherited by successive generations who might or might not retain them. In the medieval world,

9.2 Jean de Wavrin, *Chroniques d'Angleterre*, showing cannons used as siege weapons, fifteenth century. Bibliothèque Nationale, Paris.

Joan of Arc (1412–31)

It is fair to say that Christianity was the heart of medieval European culture, and the life and death of Joan of Arc (Fig. **9.3**) illustrates that circumstance poignantly. Born in a small village in northeastern France, St Joan was a pious but illiterate woman growing up in the middle of the Hundred Years' War. When she was seventeen years old, she began to hear heavenly voices telling her to save her country from the unending ravages of war. With childlike belief and obedience, she left home and family and traveled to the court of King Charles VII. The king was a particularly uninspiring presence—and, at the time, uncrowned—but somehow Joan was able to pick him

out of the hundreds of his courtiers. Her simple faith and straightforwardness convinced the unhappy monarch that she should be allowed to join the French army, which was massing for a major battle with the English.

Her presence among the troops lifted their morale and inspired them to victory after victory, from breaking the siege at Orléans to the battle of Reims. After the victory at Reims, Charles was formally crowned at the cathedral there in 1429. Victories inspired by The Maid, as she was universally called, provided a focus for the French, who rallied to the support of the newly crowned and anointed king. After Charles' coronation, Joan ceased hearing her voices. That for her, meant that her mission had ended, and she wished to return home. The king, however, recognized the powerful symbol that she represented and kept her in his service, sending her to lead the French troops marching on Paris, which was still held by the English. The attack failed, and Joan was captured by England's Burgundian allies and sold to the English. She was tried for witchcraft by an ecclesiastical court subservient to the English, found guilty, and burned at the stake in Rouen in 1431.

Although her public career lasted only two years, half of which was spent in prison after her capture, Joan remains one of the most potent symbols of the age: mystical, charismatic, faithful, courageous, and enigmatic. Although she did not actually command troops, she knew exactly when and where to make her appearance felt in order to inspire and turn the tide of battle. She believed completely in her voices— St Catherine and the archangel Michael—and obediently followed their commands, regardless of the circumstances. In many ways, this obedience to the faith was typical of the times. She said that her voices called her a "daughter of God," and no one questioned the powers that drove her, although the English called her "a disciple and limb of the Fiend."

9.3 Joan of Arc (1412–31).

one king might, in fact, be the vassal of another king if the first king inherited land that lay within the claim of the second king. Such was the condition of Europe, and such was the situation that had existed in England and France since William I, the Conqueror, who was Duke of Normandy, had conquered and become king of England in 1066. William's successor English kings laid claim to portions of France, and marriages and other alliances

complicated the picture. The ensuing conflict was called the Hundred Years' War.

As in modern warfare, medieval wars occasionally consisted of massed armies pitted in battles, a victory in which might prove decisive. More often, however, they consisted of sieges of important fortified cities, which were not only lengthy but expensive to both parties (see Fig. **9.2**). For approximately twenty-seven years from 1337 the English kept a military presence in France, but did not gain much territory in the process, although they won some battles—for example, at Crécy in 1346 and Poitiers (1356). The French then offered a settlement to the English in terms of full sovereignty over lands formerly held.

Between 1380 and 1413 internal power struggles in both countries reduced—but did not entirely eliminate—the broader conflict, and in 1413, the English King Henry V decided to take advantage of a relatively chaotic situation in France, resulting from disputes over kingly succession, and renewed English claims on the French throne. An alliance with one contingent of the feuding French, the Burgundians, gave the English effective control of Aquitaine and all of France north of the River Loire, including Paris.

The turning point came in 1429 when, inspired by Joan of Arc, the French broke the English siege of Orléans (see Profile, p. 282). When the English became embroiled in the War of the Roses at home, France conquered Normandy and Aquitaine, and by 1453, Calais remained as the only English territory in France, and that was relinquished in 1458. The end of the Hundred Years' War heralded the end of English adventurism on the Continent and contributed to a new sense of national identity in western Europe.

THE SECULAR MONARCHIES

Amazingly, both France and England seem to have emerged as more stable countries as a result of the Hundred Years' War. In France the period following the Hundred Years' War saw the establishment of a strengthened absolute monarchy, which reached its zenith under Louis XIV in the seventeenth century.

In England at this time there were disputes and a power struggle between the kings and an increasingly influential Parliament. During the war in France, the English population was torn by civil strife and rebellion, and because the kings were not particularly strong monarchs, Parliament had an edge in the struggle. The population was turning against the papacy, and Parliament took advantage of its new powers to pass laws restricting papal power in England. Things changed somewhat after the Wars of the Roses with the institution of a new dynasty in 1485. The Tudor dynasty, founded by Henry VII (1485–1509), placed the king and Parliament in less of an adversarial relationship, and managed to avoid most of the issues that had caused friction between previous kings and the legislative body. As a result, England experienced a new centralization of monarchial power, and Henry's political acumen moved Parliament to an increasingly peripheral role. In the end, England emerged with as strong a central monarchy as had been established in France.

THE PLAGUE

Known as the Black Death, the catastrophic plague that ravaged Europe between 1348 and 1350, was a combination of bubonic and pneumonic plagues. The epidemic, which eventually claimed more than 25 million lives, originated in China, carried to Europe probably by traders, as the first cases of the disease occurred in the Crimea, then spreading to Mediterranean ports in Sicily, North Africa, Italy, Spain, and France, before being carried into the European continent and England. Although it officially came to an end after three years, outbreaks continued to recur for the next fifty years.

There seemed to be no logic to the devastation brought by the disease. Some areas—for example, Milan and Flanders—suffered little, while others, like Tuscany and Aragon, were decimated. Those areas with the densest populations—for examples, large cities and monasteries—suffered most. Neither rank nor station offered sanctuary—kings, queens, princes, and archbishops, felt the sting of the plague's effects as much as peasants and merchants. In total, nearly one-third of the entire population of Europe died from the disease in the three-year period. By 1400, for example, the population of England had declined to one-half of what it had been a century before, and chroniclers estimated that a thousand English villages were completely wiped out.

The effects of the plague were many. Commerce slumped temporarily, but more importantly, the death of so many people made cultivation of land nearly impossible. In order to stay afloat, many landowners had to begin to pay wages and to substitute money rents in lieu of labor services. The shortage of workers thus led to an increase in wages for both peasants and artisans and tended to break down the stratification of society that had previously existed.

ECONOMICS AND INDUSTRIALIZATION

The drastic reduction of population that resulted from wars and the plague changed the basic shape of the European economy. Wages went up, production went down, and the cost of goods spiraled upward. Consumers and landowners suffered from the inflationary pressures of increased wages, encouraging many landowners to turn to less labor-intensive use of their lands, such as raising sheep rather than growing crops. Governments across Europe attempted to control the situation by imposing price and wage controls, and in Germany, a group of cities called the Hanseatic League formed economically protective alliances.

The precarious living conditions fomented violent

9.4 Banking scenes, miniature from *De septem vitiis*, Italian, late fourteenth century. British Museum, London.

class struggles, and conflicts between peasants and landowners, or between craft guilds and merchants often spread into anticlerical outbursts, as well. The Church occupied a privileged position—not only did it pay no taxes, but the clergy benefited through the payment of tithes—and was widely resented. Although social unrest accomplished little—those protesting had little power and were easily subdued by a well-armed officialdom— the unheavals ultimately created a better standard of living for everyone. Workers earned higher wages, merchants benefited from higher prices, and landowners profited from new uses of their resources. There also emerged a new class of entrepreneurs, who established more effective business practices and encouraged innovation and mechanization (Fig. **9.4**). The textile industry, for example changed significantly. Previous textile centers, like Flanders, were cut off from their sources and

faced new competition from Germany and Poland, while England stopped exporting raw wool and began to export finished cloth.

In many spheres—mining, metallurgy, printing, and shipbuilding, for example—industry became more efficient because of the switch from labor-intensive practices to technology. Demand for iron products—especially weapons, armor, and horseshoes—provided a spur to that industry. Rag paper, which had been invented by the Chinese and perfected by the Arabs, was manufactured in Spain and distributed widely, and this, combined with the invention of moveable type in the fifteenth century, drastically changed the course of events in Europe. Printing and publishing industries arose, profoundly affecting literature and education. Of course, these developments depended on the extent of the devastation caused by the plague in particular areas. In some places— for example, Germany and eastern Europe—the plague had little effect, and the old feudal order remained as strong as it had ever been.

RELIGION AND THE GREAT SCHISM

By the end of the Great Plague it was not uncommon to find religious penitents walking along the roads, flagellating each other and prophesying the end of the world. It was the time of the dance of death, with skeletal figures leading knights, burghers, and peasants to the grave. The increasing secularism in government, which separated the Church from the European monarchies, did not diminish the weight of medieval Christianity on the lives of individuals. The simple faith of someone like Saint Joan stood side by side with the fanaticism of the Inquisition, and the burning of witches and heretics. Pogroms against Jews and the persecution of all individuals believed to be in league with Satan were common. Charged with maintaining the purity of Christian thought, the Holy Office of Inquisition used any means necessary—including torture—to obtain confessions from all those accused of heresy. Anyone found to be an enemy of Christ and unrepentant was given over to the civil authorities to be burned alive.

These excesses went hand in hand with sincere and deep, mystical faith among the laity. By this time the creeds of the Christian Church were well established and much more elaborate than the simple virtues of Pauline Christianity—that is, faith in Christ, hope of salvation, and charity towards one's fellow human beings—for example, there were seven deadly sins of: pride, greed, envy, sexual self-indulgence, violence, laziness, and gluttony. Religious duties were essential. The sacraments brought the Church into the events of everyday life, bap-

TECHNOLOGY: PUTTING DISCOVERY TO WORK

Keeping Time

The measurement of time presented humankind with tremendous difficulties until the late Middle Ages. Records of time were among the earliest uses of writing, and the Egyptians had established a relatively accurate calendar by 3500 B.C., but for primitive people, work began at sunrise and ended at dusk, and the divisions of time between were of little interest. A seasonal calendar, on the other hand, was of prime importance. The first attempt to divide daylight into units was probably the shadow-clock, which was developed in Egypt around 1450 B.C., with later developments including water clocks and sandglasses. It was not until the thirteenth century, however, that mechanical clocks were invented to bring consistent accuracy into the telling of time. The first mechanical clocks (Fig. 9.5) were driven by falling weights, and spring-driven mechanisms, which made watches possible, came into being in the fifteenth century.

The accurate measurement of time must be based on some repetitive movement that occurs with complete regularity. The earliest mechanism,

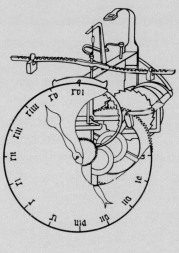

9.5 Early alarm clock, c. 1390.

called a verge, had a pair of pallets attached to an oscillating arm, which engaged alternately with cogs on a wheel rotated by a falling weight. The earliest surviving clock of this type, in Salisbury Cathedral (see page 265), dates from around 1386. Although it worked perfectly satisfactorily, the verge was friction-driven and not, therefore, wholly accurate. The spring made it possible to construct more compact mechanisms, but required a device to compensate for the diminishing force of the spring as it uncoiled. This problem did not exist with weight-driven mechanisms, because the force exerted by the weight at the end of the descent is the same as at the beginning. To compensate, spring-driven mechanisms employed a fuse—that is, a conical drum with a helical groove—cut so that, as the spring uncoiled, the connecting cord exerted greater pressure on the shaft.

Early clocks often had only a single hand to indicate the hours. Soon, however, a face to indicate quarter hours became common, as did a minute hand.

---

tism, confirmation, marriage, and death. The sacraments also provided penance and absolution for sins, conferred spiritual powers on ordained clergy, and celebrated the communion of believers with their savior in the central Christian mystery of the Mass.

In the fourteenth century, the papacy fell to its nadir. This was a time in which the once mighty and independent popes came under the influence of the French kings, who moved the papal see to Avignon in southern France. The office of pope was humiliated under the force of the French monarchs and further weakened by what is called the Great Schism in 1378. During the Schism, groups supporting diverse claimants to the throne fought each other, and for several decades, there were two and even three aspirants to the papacy, each excommunicating the others in what bewildered lay people saw as a complete degradation of the Church. In 1417 the Council of Constance, convened by the Holy Roman Emperor, deposed three pretenders and reunified the papal see at Rome.

The tragedy of what was called the Babylonian Captivity—a term paralleling the Avignon papacy with the Hebrews' captivity in Babylon—and the Great Schism brought increased demands for reform, especially to free the papacy from the control of French monarchs. In England between approximately 1320 and 1384, the reformer John Wycliffe sought to cleanse the church of its worldliness. He argued for abolition of all church property, the subjugation of the Church to secular authority, and the denial of papal authority, although his greatest achievement was the inspiration of a scholarly translation of the first Bible in English. Wycliffe's followers were branded as heretics, and were persecuted and punished by the secular authorities. Wycliffe's influence was felt as far away as Bohemia by way of reformers in the Holy Roman Empire who had met him at Oxford. In the hands of pietistic Christians and evangelical preachers and theologians such as John Huss (c. 1369–1415), the reform movement spread. Huss, to whom modern-day Moravian Brethren trace their heritage, accepted some of Wycliffe's teachings and rejected others. He was present at the

A CRITICAL REVIEW

The Great Schism reminds us of the all too human nature of those who undertake leadership in any institution. The nobility or goodness of the institution itself seems irrelevant when humans struggle for power, and the person in "control" often appears to be more important than the institution.

Although the United States has been spared the ravages of plague, some areas must deal with traumatic repopulation and economic devastation like that of the Middle Ages—for example, the inner cities and "one industry" communities whose factories have closed down.

Search the newspapers or your memory and identify two recent examples in which noble institutions have been affected by the struggle for power and control.

Find and describe a recent economic situation that parallels the economic and industrial plight of Europe after the plague.

A CRITICAL LOOK

We now turn to literature, architecture, and visual art. We are in a transitional period leading to a great burst of individuality called the Renaissance, but we will again see marked changes in the way humans saw and represented their universe in art, and we will recognize something new: we begin to deal with individual artists whose names we know. Because of the new focus on humans as people, we need to give extra attention not only to style but to artists themselves.

Identify the works of Petrarch, Boccaccio, Froissart, and Chaucer and explain their general characteristics and themes.

Describe the characteristics of late Gothic art and architecture in northern Europe and contrast it with that of Italy.

CRITICAL REVIEW above

Council of Constance, but his views were seen as heretical and condemned, and he was burned at the stake by the authorities. His martyrdom inspired his followers, many of whom were wealthy nobles, and they, in turn, used his beliefs as a vehicle for Czech nationalism against the German emperors and the Roman Church.

LITERATURE

PETRARCH AND BOCCACCIO

CRITICAL LOOK above

It is fair to say that the late Middle Ages—especially the fourteenth century—provide a transition between medieval thought and the Renaissance that was to come, and as we shall see as we study the material that follows, in literature especially we find the stirrings of ideas that are more Renaissance than medieval. In the fourteenth century, Italian writers like Petrarch and Boccaccio began to develop the works of ancient writers in a new way. They borrowed ideas, stories, figures of speech, and general style, and tried to recreate ancient poetic and prose styles. In so doing, they provided a more penetrating investigation and analysis of ancient literature and art than their medieval predecessors had achieved, and the result was an ordered plan, integrated structure, symmetry, and lofty style, which fourteenth-century writers believed represented a classical type of beauty. Various rules were laid down—for example, the epic must begin in the middle of the plot, must contain supernatural elements, and must end with a victory for the hero. The Italian model had a strong influence on Spanish, French, English, and German literature.

PETRARCH

The Italian poet Petrarch (1304–74), who created the sonnet form and who wrote in both Latin and his native Tuscan dialect, is a key figure in the transition from medieval to Renaissance thought. His writings are very different from those of Dante, for example, and are filled with complaints about "the dangers and apprehensions I have suffered." Contrary to what he wrote, however, he

PROFILE

Geoffrey Chaucer (c. 1340–1400)

Born in London, Geoffrey Chaucer (pronounced CHAW-sir) came from a prosperous family of vintners who were occasionally connected to the King's court (Fig. **9.6**). We know little of his education, although we do know that he learned Latin and French.

Although we know him as a writer, he appears mainly to have been a successful government employee with a long career as courtier, diplomat, and public servant. In 1359 he was captured and held for ransom while on a military expedition to France. He married in 1366. He traveled in Spain, and entertained in song, stories, and music at the court of the king of England, traveling to France and Italy on the king's business between 1369 and 1372. Possibly on the last of these trips to Italy, he encountered the works of Dante and Boccaccio, and these probably influenced his poetry, especially *The Canterbury Tales*.

Between 1374 and 1386, he created three major works: *The House of Fame*, *The Parliament of Fowls*, and *Troilus and Criseyde*. His best known work, *The Canterbury Tales*, was written over a period of years, mostly after 1387. The large scheme for this work included a band of thirty pilgrims on a journey from the Tabard Inn in Southwark, a suburb of London, to the shrine of Thomas à Becket in Canterbury and back again. Each pilgrim was to tell two stories when going and two while returning, but the final work included only twenty-four stories, some of which remain unfinished. The tales are funny, satirical, ironic, insightful, and individualistic in character development; some are philosophical, some are thoughtful, and others are serious. Altogether, they paint a broad portrait of fourteenth-century life and expectations. The framework resembles that of Boccaccio's *Decameron*, with which Chaucer was familiar, but Chaucer's cultivated irony and robust comedy are unprecedented.

9.6 Geoffrey Chaucer (c. 1340–1400).

enjoyed the favor of the great men and women of his day. He flourished at the papal court at Avignon. Petrarch was unable to reconcile his own conflicting aspirations and interests into a workable existence: he desired solitude and quiet, but was continually active. Although he adored being a celebrity, he attacked the superficiality of the world around him and longed for the monastic life. His love sonnets to Laura may also be addressed to the laurel wreath awarded in classical Greece to an outstanding poet.

Petrarch's real love was learning, for which he earned the title "Father of Humanism," and he made a significant impact on those who followed. He rejected medieval philosophy and also found science wanting as a way toward

a "happy life." He had a passion for classical literature and Roman antiquity, but although he was a classical scholar, his religious thought was thoroughly medieval. He felt guilty about admiring the things learned from pagan philosophers, and he could not accept Dante's connection between the good of this world and that of the next. He rejected the intellectual tradition of the Middle Ages but clung tenaciously to its moral code.

BOCCACCIO

Giovanni Boccaccio (1313–75), a life-long friend of Petrarch, was, in contrast, a man of the world. Much of his early work was inspired by, and dedicated to, his consuming passion, Fiammetta, but this was completely overshadowed by the *Decameron*, which was completed in 1358. In the framing tale, ten young people flee from the plague in Florence in 1348 to sit out the danger in the countryside. To amuse themselves, they tell one hundred stories over a fourteen-day period. The first tale from Day One tells of a lively day spent in witty conversation. Days Two and Three are tales of adventure. Day Four presents unhappy love, and Day Five treats the same subject in a somewhat lighter vein. Day Six returns to the happiness of Day One, and Days Seven, Eight, and Nine cover laughter, trickery, and license. Day Ten ties the foregoing themes together in a conclusion. In total, the *Decameron* extols the virtue of humankind, proposing that to be noble, one must accept life as one finds it, without bitterness. Above all, one must accept the responsibility for, and consequences of, one's own actions.

FROISSART'S CHRONICLES

A popular genre of literature during this period was the medieval chronicle. A chronicle is history told in a "romantic" way, and in the contemporary language of the country. The *Chronicles of England, France, and Spain* by the French writer Jean Froissart (c. 1333–c. 1400) is an outstanding example of this genre. Froissart's work covers the history of the fourteenth century and the wars between England and France. It was not written as a factual account but, in the words of its author, "to encourage all valorous hearts and to show them honorable examples."

ART AND ARCHITECTURE

LATE GOTHIC ARCHITECTURE

We should be aware by now that broad categorizations about places as diverse as Europe and time-spans as broad as two hundred years do not always apply uniformly. In Germany, for example, Gothic style in architecture took much longer to gain a foothold than in other parts of Europe, and most characteristic of the German interpretation of Gothic style is a form known as the hall church or *hallenkirche*, in which the aisles and the nave are the same height, unlike the more traditional Gothic style, in which the nave is high and the aisles lower in order to allow for clerestory windows in the nave. The *hallenkirche* approach is, in reality, similar to Romanesque. The large hall choir added to the church of St Sebald in

Nuremberg (Fig. **9.7**) is a typical example. Here graceful bundles of columns rise toward pointed arches, flaring outward at the last second into a series of ribs. Space is light and airy, with tall lancet windows adding delicacy to the feeling of openness that results from the slender columns and seemingly unimpeded space. The tone of the design is simple. Nothing interrupts the eye as it travels up the unadorned vertical line to narrow vaults that belie the unencumbered expanse below.

In Italy we find another variation on the Gothic theme in the Florence Cathedral or *Duomo* (Fig **9.8**). Although the architect's primary concern was an impressive interior, our view of this church tends to focus on the impressive dome (see Fig. **10.7**), which was added later by the Renaissance architect Brunelleschi in an imitation of classical forms appended to medieval structures. Brunelleschi's dome rises 180 feet (55 meters) into the air and its height is apparent both from the outside and inside. If we compare it with the Pantheon (see Fig. **4.22**), Brunelleschi's departure from tradition becomes clearer. The dome of the Pantheon is impressive only from the inside of the building because its exterior supporting

9.7 Choir of church of St Sebald, Nuremberg, Germany, 1361–72.

9.8 Nave and choir, Florence Cathedral, Italy, begun 1296.

was completed only in 1910. Its flamboyance lends the façade a lightness that the somewhat horizontal sprawl of the building would not otherwise achieve. Needlelike spires reach above the roof line to lift the spirit from earth into the mystery of space.

Gothic style was also used in secular buildings, and we capture glimpses of this late application, typical of the spirit of the age, in Venice, where a unique version of the style developed in the fourteenth century and was used in particular for nonreligious buildings. One of the most delightful examples is the Doge's Palace (Fig. **9.10**), which represents a direction in architecture developed specifically for the palaces of the rich and powerful merchant class. Begun in the 1340s, the palace was designed to serve as a large meeting hall for the *Maggior Consiglio*, the elective assembly of the Republic of Venice. Remarkable for this period is the building's sense of openness and tranquility, and the absence of features for fortification reflects the relative peace that the republic enjoyed at the time. The solidity of the upper storeys above the open colonnades gives an almost top-heavy appearance, and the rather squat proportions of the lower arcade detract from the delicacy of the overall design, while the Gothic arches are combined with the eastern

structure is so massive that it clutters the visual experience. The phenomenal height of Brunelleschi's dome is apparent because the architect has hidden the supporting elements, such as girdles and lightweight ribbing. The result is a clear statement that visual experience is foremost, and structural considerations are subordinate. Thus, the dome becomes related to a work of sculpture.

As we look at Florence Cathedral from any angle on the exterior, we recognize little that would identify it with the Gothic style—there are no flying buttresses and rather than great stained-glass windows, we find only solid walls inlaid with geometric marble patterns that match a Romanesque baptistery, a separate building that sits just opposite the main entrance. However, as we move inside, we are greeted by Gothic arches (see Fig. **9.8**), perhaps less serene than we have become accustomed to, but Gothic nonetheless. There is a sense of coldness and decorative solemnity here. Horizontal banding breaks the clean flow of line up the supporting columns, separating the design into what seems almost awkward proportions. The sense of space becomes horizontal rather than vertical.

On the other hand, Milan Cathedral (Fig. **9.9**), the largest of Italy's Gothic churches, is, with its delicate traceries, pure late Gothic. Although it was begun in 1386, it

9.9 Apse of Milan Cathedral, Italy, begun 1386.

influence seen in the patterning of the brickwork. The result illustrates a particularly Venetian inventiveness seen often in the city, as European and Moorish influences intermix.

LATE GOTHIC SCULPTURE

In general, we may say that Gothic sculpture took the traditional themes of Christian art and gave them emotional appeal, and toward the end of the thirteenth century, that tendency was applied to objects designed to enhance private worship. This type of object is often called *Andachtsbild*, because Germany played a leading role in its development, and it was best exemplified by the PIETÀ, which derives from the Latin word *pietas*, meaning "pity" and "piety," whose main visual representation was a grieving Virgin Mary holding the dead Christ in her arms. The pietà offers a symmetrical balance to the Madonna and child depictions that were always popular, although nothing in scripture suggests that the Virgin Mary ever held the body of the crucified Christ in her arms. This tragic scene—full of deep emotion—is a complete invention of the time. The emotion typical of this genre of sculpture stands out poignantly in a German pietà from the early fourteenth century (Fig. **9.11**). In a move away from the emerging realism we have seen previously, in this work realism takes a back seat to powerful emotion, which is achieved through stylization and exaggeration. The forms of Mary and Jesus look remarkably like puppets, and Christ's wounds are exaggerated to grotesque proportion for emotional effect. The work is clearly asking the viewer to identify with the horror and grief that the Mother of God must have felt.

The exploration of reality that we find in the pietà can be seen in the north of Europe, where it reached a climax around the year 1400. It was called the International style, and its greatest exponent was the Flemish sculptor Claus Sluter (c. 1350–1405), who worked for the Duke of Burgundy in Dijon. Sluter carved a number of works reminiscent of the monumental sculpture on cathedral portals. However, his works are much larger and command a presence not found in earlier Gothic works, like the portal sculptures from Chartres (see Figs **8.18** and **8.20**). In the earlier works, the figures spring from the context of the doorway and are confined by the space it allows, emerging, as we saw, three-dimensionally but clearly part of the context. Sluter's work, as seen at the portal of the Chartreuse de Champol at Dijon (Fig. **9.12**) command the space. The figures seem to be affixed to the portal rather than growing from it. They are large, bold, and nearly

9.12 Claus Sluter, portal of the Chartreuse de Champol, Dijon, France. 1385–93. Stone.

9.11 *Pietà*, early fourteenth century. Wood, height 34½ ins (87.5 cm). Provinzialmuseum, Bonn, Germany.

full-round. The dynamic quality of the work is intensified by the fact that the figures of Duke Philip the Bold and his wife, who are accompanied by their patron saints, turn inward to direct complete attention on the central figure of the Madonna. Thus, rather than a series of separate jamb statues, like those at Chartres, this grouping forms a single statement—it is a single work composed to highlight a central focal area.

In sculpture as in architecture, Italy stood apart from the Gothic style found in the rest of Europe. Although the Gothic emotionalism we have previously noted is present, the figures of Italian Gothic sculpture have a more classical sense than their northern counterparts. Figures have a roundness that has been tied not only to classicism but also to Byzantium. We can see this tendency in the work of Giovanni Pisano (c. 1250–c. 1320), the son of the famous Tuscan sculptor, Nicola Pisano (c. 1225–c. 1284) whose works reflect the same tendencies. On visits to the Cathedral at Pisa, care must be taken to note which Pisano's works one is viewing. Nicola carved a pulpit in the Baptistery; his son, a pulpit in the cathedral proper, and it is this work that draws our attention here (Fig. **9.13**). Done in marble, Giovanni's figures reflect a slenderness and flowing line that is much less classical than had strongly influenced Italian art. The "neo-Byzantine" style, or "Greek manner," prevailed in Italy throughout the thirteenth century, and when the Gothic style of northern Europe mixed with the "Greek manner," it produced a revolutionary approach exemplified by Giotto, as we shall see.

CIMABUE Among the artists of the Greek manner, one of the most famous was Cimabue (pronounced chee-mah-BOO-ay), who may have been Giotto's teacher. Cimabue (c. 1250–c. 1302) created very large tempera panels. Tempera is a painting medium in which egg yolk acts as a binder for the pigment, and it was usually applied to panels that had been prepared with a coating of gesso], a smooth mixture of ground chalk or plaster and glue. An application of gold leaf and an underpainting in green or brown preceded the application of the tempera paint.

9.13 Giovanni Pisano, pulpit, 1302–10. Marble. Pisa Cathedral, Italy.

his father's. It is much more a reflection of the elegance found in Gothic sculpture in Paris during the late thirteenth century. Giovanni's figures have much greater depth of dimensionality, in which the space becomes as important as the forms themselves. The figures are not packed together, but spaced so that we can see the background that frames them. In addition, they are so free within their context that their dramatic effect is heightened by an increase in light and shade created by the extreme contrast between foreground and background.

PAINTING

ITALY

The end of the thirteenth century produced an outburst of creative activity in Italy that was destined to influence painting in the future. When the Fourth Crusade conquered Constantinople in 1204, it reinvigorated a Byzantine influence in Italian painting that had stayed alive throughout the medieval period, even though it never went north beyond Italy's borders to the rest of Europe, although, of course, the art of northern Europe

9.14 Cimabue, *Madonna Enthroned*, c. 1280–90. Tempera on wood, c. 12 ft 7½ ins × 7 ft 4 ins (3.84 × 2.24 cm). Uffizi Gallery, Florence, Italy.

Cimabue's panels were larger than anything that had been attempted in the East, and they further differed from Byzantine works in the severity of their design and expression. The very form of *Madonna Enthroned* (Fig. **9.14**) embodies an upward-striving monumentality, and the gabled shape is quite unlike anything done in Byzantium. Designed for the high altar of the church of Santa Trinita, the work rises over 12 feet (3.7 meters) in height. Its hierarchical design places the Virgin Mary at the very top center, surrounded by angels, with the Christ Child supported on her lap. Below her elaborate throne, four half-length prophets display their scrolls.

The verticality of the composition is reinforced by rows of inlaid wood in the throne and by ranks of angels rising, one behind the other, on either side. The figures in the top rank bend inward to reinforce both the painting's exterior form and the focus on the Virgin's face. The delicate folds of the blue mantle and dark red robe, which are highlighted with gold, encircle the upper torso, drawing attention to the Madonna's face and to the child. In a convention appropriate to the theology of the time, the Christ Child is depicted as a wise and omniscient presence, with a patriarchal face older than his infant years. The clean precision of the execution gives the work a fineness and lightness that recall the exquisiteness of Byzantine mosaics.

DUCCIO A quarter century later, the Italian artist Duccio (c. 1255–c. 1319) portrayed the same subject matter in a similar scheme but with significant differences (Fig. **9.15**). Duccio (pronounced DOO-chee-oh) softens the frozen, Byzantine linearity of Cimabue—his roundness of form and treatment of fabric reflecting Roman characteristics—and gives it a three-dimensionality that is Gothic. The tender emotion exchanged between mother and child stands in contrast with Cimabue's formal, outward stares of the principal figures. The Sienese called this painting the *maesta* or "majesty," thus identifying the Virgin's role as Queen of Heaven. Unlike Cimabue's vertical composition, Duccio's work flows outward in a horizontal format, increasing the size of the celestial court and adding small compartments with scenes from the lives of Christ and the Madonna. The composition itself reflects a new treatment of space, giving us the sense that the figures are enveloped by space rather than sitting on the front edge of a two-dimensional plane.

GIOTTO Despite the advances of Cimabue and Duccio, it remained for Giotto (c. 1266–1336/7) to take far bolder and more dramatic steps. Perhaps less close to the Greek manner than his predecessors, Giotto (pronounced JAH-toe) undertook wall painting on a monumental scale. He also painted in tempera on panel. Giotto's treatment of the same subject as Duccio and Cimabue—that is, *Madonna Enthroned* (Fig. **9.16**)—gives us another means by which we can learn to identify the subtleties of style that differentiate one artistic vision from another. In the

9.15 Duccio, *Madonna Enthroned*, center of the *maesta altar*. 1308–11. Tempera on panel, height 6 ft 10¹/₁ ins (2.1 m). Museo dell' Opera del Duomo, Siena, Italy.

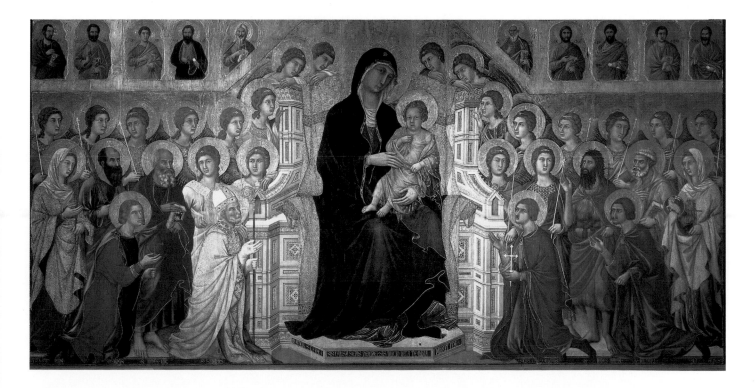

first place, we find in Giotto's treatment a greater simplification of the subject matter and supporting details. The central focus is even more human, warm, and three-dimensional than in the two earlier works, and it has a sense of drama, heightened by the fact that Giotto's viewpoint is lower than Duccio's or Cimabue's—that is, the viewpoint of the observer relative to the space in the painting. An innovation is that the actual confines of the painting are defined more by the figures than by the architectural details, and although such a perspective tends to lessen the depth of space, it nevertheless gives a more dynamic quality to it. The figures come to life for the viewer, as Giotto's genius gives painting a previously unknown liveliness that brought painting to a par with sculpture.

Giotto did not attempt merely to transfer Gothic sculpture into paint. Rather, by creating what amounted to an entirely new treatment of space, he gave the surface of the painting a new appearance. In the past, composition tended to lead the eye from one specific detail to another. Giotto, on the other hand, takes our eye and allows us to grasp the entire work at one time, and the composition has an inner unity achieved by strong, simple groupings of figures. The throne, based on Italian Gothic architecture, encloses the Madonna and cuts her off from the background. In another innovation, Giotto takes great pains to create a fake texture in the colored

9.16 (*above*) Giotto, *Madonna Enthroned*, c. 1310. Tempera on panel, 10 ft 8 ins × 6 ft 8 ins (3.3 × 2 m). Uffizi Gallery, Florence, Italy.

9.17 Giotto, *The Lamentation*, 1305–06. Fresco, 7ft 7ins × 7ft 9ins (2.31 × 2.36m). Arena Chapel, Padua, Italy.

marble surfaces. The creation of false textures had not been used in painting since early Christian times, and Giotto's reintroduction of this approach attests to his familiarity with ancient Roman wall paintings, similar to those we studied in Chapter 4.

This new sense of space, three-dimensionality, and mobility are clear in Giotto's masterpiece *The Lamentation* (Fig. **9.17**). The figures are skillfully grouped in a simple, coherent scene. Giotto's fabrics retain a decorative quality from an earlier time, but they also show an increased realism. Although the figures are crowded, they still seem free to move within the space. For all its emotion and intensi-

9.18 Pietro Lorenzetti, *The Birth of the Virgin*, 1342. Panel painting, 6 ft 1½ ins × 6 ft ½ in (1.87 × 1.84 m). Museo dell' Opera Metropolitana, Siena, Italy.

ty, the fresco remains human, individualized, and controlled. What makes the fresco so compelling, is Giotto's unique mastery of three-dimensional space. He employs atmospheric PERSPECTIVE—that is, the use of haze and indistinction to create a sense of distance—for the background, but unlike other painters, who created deep space behind the primary focal plane, Giotto brings the horizon to our

stemmed from a new development in painting media—oil paint. The versatile properties of oil paints gave Flemish painters new opportunities to vary surface texture and brilliance, and to create far greater subtlety of form. Oils allowed the blending of color areas because they remained wet and could be worked on the canvas for a while. Egg tempera, the earlier medium, dried almost immediately upon application.

Gradual transitions between color areas made possible by oil paints allowed fifteenth-century Flemish painters to refine AERIAL PERSPECTIVE—that is, the increasingly hazy appearance of the objects farthest from the viewer. This helped them to control this most effective indicator of deep space. Blending between color areas also helped them achieve realistic MODELING, or light and shade, by which all objects assume three-dimensionality. Without highlight and shadow, the appearance of realistic relief disappears. Early fifteenth-century Flemish painters used sophisticated light and shade, not only to heighten three-dimensionality, but also to achieve perceptual unity in their compositions. Pictures without consistent light sources or without natural shadows on surrounding objects create very strange effects, even if they depict individual forms very realistically. The new skill in creating realistic three-dimensionality separated fifteenth-century Flemish style from the Gothic style and tied it to the Renaissance.

"The prince of painters of our age," was the way one of his contemporaries described Jan van Eyck (c. 1390–1441), whose work advances the new naturalism of the age. Although little is known about his life, he seems to have been an active and highly placed functionary of the Duke of Burgundy. On one of his trips in the duke's service, van Eyck visited Italy, where he met Masaccio and other Florentine artists. Without doubt van Eyck was one of the greatest artists of any age, and he brought a new "reality" to painting.

Although slightly different in style from van Eyck's work, Rogier van der Weyden's *The Descent from the Cross* (Fig. **9.21**) displays softly shaded forms and three-dimensionality. Its surface realism is quite unlike that of Gothic style. Carefully controlled line and form create soft, undulating S-curves around the borders and diagonally through the center. The painter explores the full range of the color spectrum, from reds and golds to blues and greens, and the full extent of the value scale from dark to light. Composition, balance, and unity are extremely subtle. The figures are depicted almost in the manner of statues, yet the shallow drapery folds exhibit a nervous broken linearity.

The striking feature in this painting, however, is its individualized presentation of human emotion. Each character displays a particularized reaction to the emotion-charged situation. These figures are not types—they are individual people so fully portrayed that we might expect to encounter them on the street.

CRIT REVI p. 29

9.21 Rogier van der Weyden, *The Descent from the Cross*, c. 1435. Oil on panel, 7 ft 2⁵/₈ ins × 8 ft ⁷/₈ ins (2.2 × 2.46 m). Prado, Madrid.

A CRITICAL REVIEW

However bleak it may have been, life under the monolithic control of feudal lords and a central Church must have been fairly simple and straightforward. As society changed during the late Middle Ages, things got more complicated, and, as if to mirror the life around it, art reflected that increased complication with an emerging ornateness.

Compare Chartres Cathedral with Milan Cathedral.

Explain the term Andachtsbild and its application to late Gothic sculpture.

A CRITICAL LOOK

We close this chapter with music and theatre, and a Synthesis consisting of a glimpse of the Gothic spirit in England. The theme of increased complication that we have just noted continues in these investigations as well. The Synthesis section, which draws together various arts in one location, gives us an additional personal view of the mental attitude of people at this time, and we may find their outlook rather surprising, given the terrors occurring around them.

What is meant by ars nova? Identify and describe the works of its major proponent as noted in this section.

In what ways did theatre reflect its social and religious contexts?

MUSIC

ARS NOVA

The fourteenth century saw a distinct change in musical style. This new style was called *ars nova* or "new art," and it drew its name from the title of a book by Philippe de Vitry (1291–1361). Music of the *ars nova* was more diverse in its harmonies and rhythms. Harmony consisted of two parallel melodies (tones one and five in the musical scale—parallel fifths) that created the bare, haunting sound characteristic of medieval chant, but this was used less frequently than passages of parallel thirds and sixths, which sound more harmonious to modern listeners. In the fourteenth century, rhythmic developments were quite complex. Subdivisions of the pulse of a piece created the illusion that the pulse was variable, and this created a richness of rhythmic invention that remained unparalleled until the twentieth century. Perhaps the most popular *ars nova* rhythmic device was the hemiola, meaning "one-and-a-half," which describes an arrangement of pulse subdivisions, first in threes and then in twos. It creates a series of patterns similar to:

```
>   >   >  >  > >   >   >  >
123 123 12 12 12 123 123 12 12 12
```

Ars nova was predominantly a secular movement. The characteristics of its rhythmic vibrancy did not meet the Church's expectations for worship, and early in the century, the Church forbade any musical elaboration of the Mass that might alter the character of the chant, and this had the effect of stifling polyphonic development in sacred music. The secular impetus continued, however, and, indeed, found its way into the church in instrumental accompaniment for the solo voice and in increased use of instrumental music.

GUILLAUME DE MACHAUT

The "new art" in music put France in a central position in European music, and the first great exponent of *ars nova* was the French composer Guillaume de Machaut (1300–77). A priest, poet, and composer, he served King John of Bohemia, who had two courts: one at Prague and one at Paris. Machaut's music in the new style had a smoothness and sweetness, as well as making increasing use of polyphony. He also used a new structural form that allowed him to give his compositions unity of style. One of the features Machaut used to achieve unity was isorhythm, in which phrases are repeated in their rhythm, but not necessarily in their melody. He also used short fragments of melody to create unity. This technique provided the structural underpinnings for his Mass for four voices written c. 1364, and it is the earliest known complete polyphonic setting by one composer. Throughout the Middle Ages, music for the Mass had been compiled from a variety of sources, mostly anonymous, rather than composed as a unified whole, and distributed to the singers and instrumentalists. The idea of one person composing an entire Mass was something new, and it marked a significant change in the application of music in the Mass. In addition, because his music had a fundamental

OUR DYNAMIC WORLD

Noh Theatre of Japan

Japan's two great dramatic forms, Noh and Kabuki, both originated from religious rituals dating to the late eighth and early ninth century, when dramatic devices were used as teaching tools by Buddhist monks. In much the same way as the medieval miracle, mystery, and morality plays that we noted in Chapter 8, the dramatizing of religious ritual in Buddhism slowly became more and more secularized, found its way out of the sanctuary, and gained in popularity. The results were seen as dramatic forms that were performed in markets as well as temples.

Japanese Noh drama took its fundamental shape in the fourteenth century. It represented the most significant and original literary and performing art development of the Ashikaga period. A highly conventionalized art form, Noh drama grew out of two sources: simple dramas based on symbolic dances performed to music at the imperial court, and similar mimetic performances popular with the common people. Its final form is credited to a Shinto priest, Kan'ami, and his son, Seami. They also founded one of the hereditary lines of Noh performers, the *Kanze*, who still perform today.

Noh drama is performed on a simple, almost bare stage and, like classical Greek tragedy (see Chapter 3), uses only two actors. Also, as in classical Greek drama, actors wear elaborate masks and costumes (Fig. **9.22**),

and a chorus functions as a narrator. Actors chant the highly poetic dialogue to orchestral, musical accompaniment. All the actions suggest rather than depict, which gives the drama its sense of stylization and conventionality, and symbolism and restraint characterize both acting and staging.

The subjects of Noh drama range from Shinto gods to Buddhist secular history, but they usually concentrate on the more popular Buddhist sects. The tone of the plays tends to be serious—appealing to the intellect—and to focus on the spirit of some historical person who wishes salvation but is tied to this earth by worldly desires. The plays are usually short, and an evening's performance encompasses several plays interspersed with comic burlesques called *Kyogen* ("crazy words"). Almost all of its canon of approximately 240 scripts come from the fourteenth century, with more than a hundred written by Seami alone.

Noh plays can be classified, in general, into five types—plays about the gods, warriors, women, spirits or mad persons, and demons. Traditionally, an evening's performance included all five types, performed in the order noted, but contemporary practice, however, has shortened the program to two or three. Although Noh drama is performed today and is extremely popular, it remains primarily a fourteenth-century form.

9.22 Performance at the Noh Theatre of the Kongo School, Kyoto.

9.23 An example of a cadence.

smoothness and consonance, he was able to use dissonance as an emotional effect. For example, as the words of the Mass describe the crucifixion, the composer underscores them with discordant notes, thereby creating not only beauty but emotional expressiveness.

Machaut also represents the end of the troubadour tradition, and many of his surviving works are secular poems, often with music. Here, also, there is a new approach to music. His characteristic texture was that of a solo voice with two instrumental parts forming an accompaniment. Each of his phrases comes to a definite end, called a cadence. Some of these are simple, and some are quite ornamental, as an example from one of his *virelais* illustrates (Fig. **9.23**).

Machaut was an inventive craftsman to whom the sound of the music mattered as much as its structure. His watchwords were beauty and feeling, and he once indicated that words and music without true feeling were merely false.

THEATRE

The characteristics of theatre we noted in the last chapter continued throughout the late medieval period. Theatre is often a static art, far more resistant to change than the other arts, which tend to evolve around the vision of a single artist. Theatre, more a group expression, gets caught in its own inertia, and that, certainly, was the case in the late Middle Ages. However, one of the most enduring plays, which is still performed and enjoyed in modern times, came out of this era. No one knows for certain when it originated, because it circulated through the oral tradition before it was finally put into print. Nonetheless, the most famous play of this era—indeed, of the entire Middle Ages—is *Everyman*. It is an anonymous morality play in which the hero undertakes a journey to his death. He seeks the company of all those earthly things on which he has counted—for example, Fellowship, Kindred, and Goods—but each of these things, which is personified as a character in the allegory, refuses. Beauty, Strength, Discretion, and Five Wits desert him as he approaches the grave. Good Deeds alone accompanies him to his fate.

SYNTHESIS

The Late Gothic Temperament in England

In England, as in the rest of the medieval world, the Catholic Church was the center of the spiritual community and, at least partly, of the secular community as well. It was a time of expanding horizons, a time of greater openness. Individual national characteristics crept into each corner of the European world, and in England, the changing styles and pervasive humor of the English peasant found their way into art.

Peasant restiveness led to a revolt against Richard II, which came to be known as Wat Tyler's rebellion. The attitudes behind that uprising are vividly expressed in the *Second Shepherd's Play*, part of a passion play, the Wakefield Cycle, whose folk spirit is typically English.

9.24 *Drôlerie*, from the Psalter of Alfonso, 1284. British Library, London.

Hilarious farce exudes from the invented story of Mak, who steals a sheep and hides it in his wife's bed. This is followed by the journey of the shepherds to the manger to see the Christ Child. A one-act play, this masterpiece of English farce is full of comic characterizations drawn very realistically. Mak, the sheep stealer, lives by his wits in the hard world and when under pressure simply brazens it out.

Throughout the play the characterizations remain consistent. One of the interesting features of the *Second Shepherd's Play* is the way in which location and "reality" are invented. In the last episode, the very English shepherds journey to Bethlehem—apparently not far from England. Throughout the play is a sense of wonder, of medieval faith—mystical and unquestioning. Amid the farce, though, the shepherds grumble amusingly about social injustice and the inequalities of domestic life. Mak complains about poverty, and yet all of his complaints, misbehavior, harsh words and bad weather seem to melt into the mystery of the nativity. In the end, everything leads to the necessity of redemption from suffering, sin, and evil.

Medieval English humor found another outlet in manuscript illumination, in a form known as *drôlerie*, which began to appear in the margins of books in the thirteenth century. From these illuminations comes a wealth of information on contemporary costume, customs, social behavior, musical instruments, and even a few individual eccentricities. They show a taste for exaggerated, elongated forms and a love of lavish decorations. These margin drawings also found their way into religious books, for example the Psalter of Alfonso (Fig. **9.24**).

The Gothic spirit found expression in church building here as elsewhere. The architecture of the period between 1280 and 1375 is called the Decorated style. During this time, English buildings evolved exuberant forms that anticipated late Gothic styles in Germany and France.

In Exeter Cathedral (Fig. **9.25**) we see the decorative effect in every detail. Moldings multiply and the ribs of the vaulting proliferate and project boldly. At Wells Cathedral (Fig. **9.26**), eleven ribs spring from each bay boundary, giving an overwhelming richness of linear form and a complex interplay of light and shade. At Wells, four so-called STRAINER ARCHES appear between the

9.25 Exeter Cathedral, England, interior looking toward the east, 1280–1350.

9.26 Wells Cathedral, England, arches of crossing, 1338.

9.27 Ely Cathedral, England, interior and lantern of crossing tower, 1323–30.

CHAPTER TEN

THE EARLY RENAISSANCE

AT A GLANCE

The Renaissance

The Renaissance Viewpoint
Antiquity Revisited and Measured
Humanism
Neo-Platonism
  PROFILE: Niccolò Machiavelli
Capitalism
Discovery
The Papal States
Italian City-states
  TECHNOLOGY: Flywheels and Connecting
    Rods

**The Beginnings of Renaissance
  Architecture**
Brunelleschi

Sculpture
Donatello
Ghiberti

Painting
Masaccio
  MASTERWORK: Masaccio—The Tribute
    Money

OUR DYNAMIC WORLD: The Ming Dynasty in
  China

Music
Music in Renaissance Florence
The Spread of the Renaissance Style

Theatre

Synthesis: Florence in the Quattrocento

10.1 Andrea Mantegna, detail of the ceiling of the Camera degli Sposi, 1474. Fresco. Ducal Palace, Mantua, Italy.

A CRITICAL LOOK

For some reason, humans like things to fit into neat boxes with defined edges. History rarely obliges us, however, even though scholars have done their best to make it easy for students by rounding things off into centuries and by inventing labels to summarize eras. We have seen this in the last three chapters, which, for convenience, we called the Middle Ages, although, as we noted, the period covered a lot of time and a diversity of ideas, events, and artistic styles. But why did we call them "middle"? That word suggests that they occurred between two other "ages," and implies, if subtly, that whatever they were between must have been more important. The next three chapters will help to explain the implications inherent in the phrase "Middle Ages."

In the first sections of this chapter we will try to understand what, at least to some, seemed like a "new" age.

What does the word "Renaissance" imply, and what are some of the complications that arise in trying to define it?

What was the Renaissance view of antiquity, and how did the philosophies of humanism and neo-Platonism figure in that view?

THE RENAISSANCE

The Renaissance was explicitly seen by its leaders as a rebirth of our understanding of ourselves as social and creative beings. "Out of the sick Gothic night our eyes are opened to the glorious touch of the sun," was how Rabelais expressed what most of his educated contemporaries felt. At the center of Renaissance concerns were the visual arts, and these new ways of looking at the world soon spread to the performing arts as well. Florence, the crucible of the Renaissance in Italy, was called the "New Athens," and it was here that the fine arts, or "liberal arts," were first redefined as art, in contrast to their status as crafts in the Middle Ages. Now accepted among the intellectual disciplines, the arts became an essential part of learning and literary culture. Artists, architects, composers, and writers gained confidence from their new status and from the technical mastery they were achieving (Fig. **10.2**). For the first time, it seemed possible not merely to imitate the works of the classical world, but to surpass them.

The word "Renaissance" has many meanings, its most literal translation being "rebirth." But a rebirth of what? Does "Renaissance," like "Gothic," imply one artistic style, or can it include many similar styles? Is it an historical term or a philosophical one? Is it merely a natural extension of forces from the previous period? Definitions of the Renaissance have been debated for centuries. The word certainly describes a new sense of self and self-awareness felt by western European people, who had come to see themselves as no longer part of the Middle Ages. But deciding where and how the Renaissance began, and what specifically it was is as difficult as answering the question of where and how it ended—if it ended at all. For

example, in the middle of the nineteenth century, a Swiss historian, Jacob Burckhardt, began what is formally known as Renaissance studies. He maintained—thus agreeing with fifteenth-century Italians—that an actual rebirth of ideas began in the 1400s after centuries of stagnation, and asserted that in Italy during the fourteenth century there was a new spirit of inquiry and understanding in which the classical world of Greece and Rome again became the inspiration for a superior civilization.

However, many scholars in the mid-twentieth century felt that Burckhardt's viewpoint was overly simplistic, and that the period was nothing more than a natural extension of the previous times—that is, the clear break identified by Burckhardt had not occurred. As we noted in the previous chapters, parts of Italy never lost sight of their classical heritage and were in tune with the classical traditions kept alive in Byzantium. To the scholars who disagreed with Burckhardt, the apparent change that took place in the fifteenth century was more of a shift in cultural and educational emphasis than it was a new discovery of the past. In addition, the Renaissance, rather than being a monolithic period, was really three or more periods, each with its own circumstances and—to a large degree—its own characteristics. That is, we can identify the early Renaissance, particularly that occurring in Florence; a High Renaissance, specifically in Rome and Venice; and a Renaissance that occurred outside Italy, particularly in the northern European states, and that was highly influenced by—or at least related to—the Protestant Reformation.

In the last thirty years a third viewpoint has emerged, which attests that the word "Renaissance" is strictly an educational and artistic label and is not particularly applicable to politics and society at large. According to this viewpoint, any label like "Renaissance" does not do

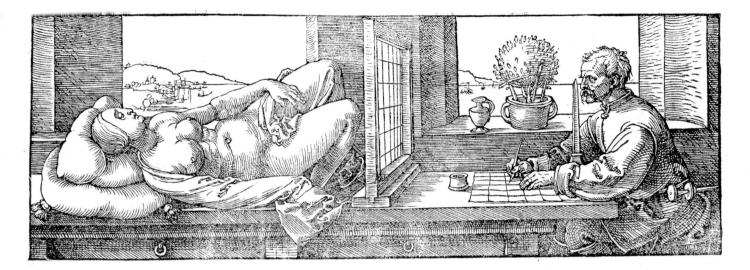

10.2 Albrecht Dürer, *Alberti's Veil*, 1525, from Dürer's *Perspective and Proportion*. Engraving. British Museum, London..

justice to the complex issues and circumstances that arose in such a diverse area as Europe over a period as long as two hundred years.

We can understand this last viewpoint when we consider that the period of the Renaissance—by anyone's definition—encompassed from approximately 1400 to about 1600, and that as we noted in Chapter 9, the years from 1400 to 1500 in some parts of Europe—including Italy—were medieval in spirit and culture. Thus, in the opening century of the Renaissance, we find both Gothic art, which ended in some places before it began in others, and a renewed or at least revitalized interest in classical antiquity, but we also find new explorations and scientific discovery, dramatic changes in religion and philosophy, innovation in politics and economics, and revolutionary developments in artistic styles, including movements like Mannerism.

Whatever the circumstances, the word Renaissance, as an historical or philosophical concept, broadly describes an age in which enlightenment brought humanity to the threshold of a world view increasingly similar to our own. We will examine the Renaissance in three chapters divided along the lines we have just described—that is, the early Renaissance in this chapter, the High and late Renaissance and Mannerism in Chapter 11, and the Renaissance in the North in Chapter 12.

The Renaissance was an age of conflict and inquisitiveness, vitality, and change. It is often compared with the early and mid-twentieth century, and the two ages do have at least one thing in common: then, as now, people saw themselves in a particularly favorable light in comparison with those who preceded them in history, although such a view may have passed as the twentieth century in America draws to a close.

THE RENAISSANCE VIEWPOINT

ANTIQUITY REVISITED AND MEASURED

In the Renaissance, as in other times, attitudes and events are interrelated in complex ways, and if certain aspects of society—for example, politics, religion, and the arts—are treated separately, as they are in these chapters, it does not mean that they were isolated from each other.

The revived interest in antiquity that is normally associated with the Renaissance was not its first revival. As seen in Chapter 7, Charlemagne had already rekindled an interest in antiquity, and indeed, in some quarters, such an interest had never been extinguished. For example, as we also noted, the German nun, Hrosvitha, had access to Terence and used his works as models for her plays, and scholars had studied Aristotle in the late Middle Ages. However, the fifteenth-century interest in classical antiquity was more intense and widespread than before, and Renaissance men and women felt that they had found kindred spirits in the Greeks and Romans. They were, after all, interested in things of this world. The Roman emphasis on civic responsibility and intellectual competence helped revivify the social order, and there was a desire to reinterpret the ancient writings, which many believed had been corrupted in the service of Church dogma.

Aristotle's work offered an appealing balance of active living and sober reflection, and the Greeks of Periclean Athens gave an idealized model of humankind that could, for example, be expressed in painting and sculpture. These ideals of nobility, intellect, and physical perfection led to new conceptions of what constituted

	GENERAL EVENTS	LITERATURE & PHILOSOPHY	VISUAL ART & ARCHITECTURE	THEATRE & MUSIC
1375	Pope returns to Rome Beginning of Western Schism Peasants' Revolt in England Switzerland independent	John Wycliffe		Confrérie de la Passion Mummeries
1400	Henry IV of England Henry V of England John Hus Battle of Agincourt		Masaccio (**10.18, 10.20**)	
1420	Henry the Navigator		Brunelleschi (**10.7–10, 10.14**) Ghiberti (**10.15, 10.16, 10.17**) Donatello (**10.11, 10.12, 10.13, 10.31**)	Dunstable Dufay Binchois
1450	Hundred Years' War ends Cosimo de Medici Lorenzo de Medici	Pico della Mirandola Petrarch Boccaccio	Fra Angelico (**10.21**) Alberti (**10.6**)	
1475	Spanish Inquisition begins	Machiavelli	Mantegna (**10.1, 10.28**) Leonardo (**10.19**) Uccello (**10.22**) Botticelli (**10.23, 10.27**)	des Prés

Timeline 10.1 The early Renaissance.

beauty. As scholars pursued an understanding of classical art and architecture, they became enamored of measuring things. "True proportions" were revealed when *De Architectura* by the Roman architect Vitruvius was rediscovered in 1414. Scientific curiosity and concern for detail led to a fascination with anatomy, and scientific investigation led to a new system of mechanical perspective. All this measuring and codifying produced a set of rules of proportion and balance, and unity, form, and perfect proportion were codified as a set of laws, to which Michelangelo, as we shall see shortly, objected strongly.

HUMANISM

The roots of humanism can be traced back to the slowly developing separation of organized religion and the State in the fourteenth century. Its specific origins can be found in Italy in the writings of Petrarch around 1341. Petrarch is a key figure in the transition from medieval to Renaissance thought, and, as we noted in Chapter 9, his writings are very different from those of Dante. He rejected medieval philosophy and found the science of the time wanting as a way toward a "happy life." Although he had a passion for classical literature and Roman antiquity, he clung to the religious thought of the Middle Ages. He felt guilty about admiring the things learned from pagan philosophers, and he found Dante's connection between the good of this world and that of the next impossible. On the other hand, his real love of learning made him reject the intellectual tradition of the Middle Ages for which he was given the title Father of Humanism. From Italy,

Petrarch's ideas spread throughout the Western world.

Humanism as a philosophy was not, as some have ventured, a denial of God or faith. Rather, it was an attempt to discover humankind's own earthly fulfillment, and was perfectly expressed in the biblical idea: "O Adam, you may have whatever you shall desire." The medieval view of life as a vale of tears, with no purpose other than preparing for salvation and the afterlife, gave way to what was viewed as a more liberating ideal of people playing important roles in this world.

Concern for diversity and individuality had emerged in the late Middle Ages, when expanding horizons and the increasing complexity of life provoked a new debate about human responsibility for a stable moral order and for the management of events. Such a discussion yielded a philosophy consistent with Christian principles, which focused on the dignity and intrinsic value of the individual. Human beings were both good and ultimately perfectible. They were capable of finding worldly fulfillment and intellectual satisfaction. Humanism developed an increasing distaste for dogma, and embraced a figurative interpretation of the scriptures and an attitude of tolerance toward all viewpoints.

NEO-PLATONISM

When Constantinople fell to the Ottomans in 1453, an influx of Byzantine scholars carrying with them precious manuscripts made Italy a center for the study of Greek literature, language, and philosophy, especially of Platonic and neo-Platonic philosophy. Cosimo de Medici established the Platonic Academy at one of his villas near Florence, and, under the direction of Marsilio Ficino

PROFILE

Niccolò Machiavelli (1469–1527)

Italian political philosopher, statesman, poet, playwright, and thinker, Niccolò Machiavelli (pronounced nee-COE-loe mah-kee-ah-VAY-lee) earned an undeserved unsavory reputation because of his insights on political power and human nature. Born into a wealthy and important Florentine family, Machiavelli was taught from an early age "to do without before he learned to enjoy," as he later wrote. His father—the poorest member of the family—had been disbarred from any public office, and as a result, Niccoló had less education than he might otherwise have received, and certainly less than his abilities demanded. Although he did attend the local school, he remained essentially self-taught through reading the books in the family's extensive library.

When he was twenty-nine years old, he held an important public appointment as secretary to the magistracy—that is, the agency that directed foreign affairs and defense. At the time, Europe, especially Italy, was in political turmoil, and during much of the time that Machiavelli spent in public office, Florentine political policy centered on the conquest of Pisa. He therefore spent a great deal of his time traveling to various Italian city-states on diplomatic missions, through which he gained significant firsthand information about military tactics. He came to know the Italian rulers, spending many weeks with the unscrupulous Cesare Borgia, and thus becoming an eyewitness to Borgia's vicious handling of those who stood in his way. Machiavelli also traveled to France and Germany, where he learned about the political institutions of those countries.

In 1512 the Medici family returned from exile to power in Florence, and Machiavelli lost his public position. He was accused of complicity in an ill-conceived coup attempt, and was imprisoned and tortured. On his eventual release, his movements and residence were severely restricted, and so, living in poverty and unhappiness, he retired to a small property he had inherited from his father in San Caciano. Forbidden to enter politics, this genius, who had previously reorganized the Florentine military and introduced conscription, began to write. By 1513 he had completed his most famous and influential work, *The Prince*, and other works followed over a thirteen-year period. In 1526, following another exile of the Medicis, Pope Clement VII restored Machiavelli to favor. He died a year later in Florence.

10.3 Niccolò Machiavelli (1469–1527).

The Prince represents Machiavelli's political theory. Written in the form of advice to a new ruler, it tells how to found a state and to maintain himself in power. The blunt nature of the maxims have given Machiavelli a reputation for immorality but many find in his theories merely a sense of the reality of humans and their political situations. These theories do not deal with life as it should be; rather, within the framework of their objectives, they describe life as Machiavelli saw it. It seems likely that he was not the cold, cynical, and irreligious man he is often accused of being. Above all, his theories seek the good of the public. He dreamed and hoped for the ideal prince who could rescue and restore Italy from the conflagration in which the times and the people of those times had embroiled it. The prince to whom Machiavelli directs his theoretical advice would have to deal with human nature and harsh realities as Machiavelli found them in Renaissance Italy.

SCULPTURE

DONATELLO

The essence of European sculpture in the early Renaissance can, once again, best be examined by looking to fifteenth-century Florence. The early Renaissance sculptors had developed the skills to create images of great VERISIMILITUDE, but their goal was not the same as that of the Greeks, who idealized the human form. Renaissance sculptors found their ideal in individuality—the glorious individual, even if not quite the perfect individual—and sculpture of this style presented a particularly clear-eyed and uncompromising view of humankind: complex, balanced, and full of action.

While relief sculpture, as we shall see, found new

10.12 Donatello, *Equestrian Monument to Gattamelata*, 1445–50. Bronze, c. 11 × 13 ft (3.4 × 4 m). Piazza del Santo, Padua, Italy.

10.11 Donatello, *David*, dated variously 1430–40. Bronze, 5 ft 2¼ ins (1.58 m) high. Museo Nazionale del

ways of representing deep space through the systematic use of scientific perspective, free-standing sculpture, long out of favor, now returned to dominance. Scientific inquiry and an interest in anatomy were reflected in sculpture as well as painting. The nude, full of character and charged with energy, reappeared for the first time since ancient times. The human form was approached layer by layer, through an understanding of its skeletal and muscular framework, and even when clothed, fifteenth-century sculpture revealed the body under the surface.

The greatest masterpieces of fifteenth-century Italian Renaissance sculpture came from the unsurpassed master of the age, Donatello (1386–1466). A contemporary of Ghiberti, Donato de Niccolò Bardi, known later as Donatello, saw life and reality in terms much different from his predecessors and contemporaries. He did not share Brunelleschi's concern for proportion, nor did he share Ghiberti's sense of line. He was fascinated by the optical qualities of form and by the intense inner life of his subjects, and, as a result, produced amazingly dramatic and forceful works. His new approach is seen vividly in the statue of *St George* (Fig. **10.13**). Carved for a guild of armorers and sword makers, who could not afford a work cast in bronze, *St George* was intended to look very different from the way we now see it in the Bargello Museum. Originally, the figure bore evidence of the products of the guild—that is, a helmet and jutting sword—which were attached to the statue by holes drilled in the back of the head and a socket attached to the

10.13 Donatello, *St George*, 1415. Marble, 3 ft 7½ ins × 2 ft 3 ins (109 × 67 cm). Museo Nazionale del Bargello, Florence, Italy.

right hand. Nevertheless, as it now stands the figure reveals a tautness of line in the pointed shapes of the shield, armored feet, and drapery. The facial expression reflects a human quality of realism—not idealism. Sensitivity, reflectiveness, and delicate features make this figure a hero of everyday proportions and not a god-like warrior out of mythology. This is humanism at work in art, illustrating how flesh and blood people react in crisis.

Over the next twenty years Donatello's style was refined, and from that refinement came his magnificent *David* (Fig. **10.11**), the first free-standing nude since classical times, although, like most classical figures, *David* is partially clothed. The figure exhibits a return to classical *contrapposto* stance in its refined form, but the armor and helmet, and the bony elbows and adolescent features, invest him with a highly individual presence. The work symbolizes Christ's triumph over Satan, and the laurel crown on the helmet and the laurel wreath on which the work stands allude to the Medici family, in whose palace the statue was displayed in 1469.

Perhaps Donatello's greatest achievement is the *Equestrian Monument to Gattamelata* (Fig. **10.12**). In this larger than life monument to a deceased general, we see the influence of Roman monumental statuary, and, in particular, the statue of *Marcus Aurelius on Horseback*, but Donatello creates a unique concentration on both human and animal anatomy. The viewer's focus is directed not to the powerful mass of the horse, however, but to the overpowering presence of the person astride it. The triangular composition anticipates the geometric approach to sculpture in the High Renaissance.

GHIBERTI

Relief sculpture, like painting, offered a new means of representing deep space through a systematic use of scientific perspective. Among the most ambitious sculptural projects in this medium we find not only a scriptural tale, but a human one as well in the doors of the Baptistery of the Cathedral of Florence. The entire project consisted of three sets of doors. One set, showing the life of John the Baptist, had already been completed by Andrea Pisano. Two more remained, illustrating the Old and New Testaments. In 1401 the Opera, the Board of Works, of the Baptistery conducted a competition for the east doors. Seven sculptors were chosen to compete, including Filippo Brunelleschi and Lorenzo Ghiberti (1381?–1455), a contemporary of Donatello. The award went to Ghiberti, who was only twenty years old at the time, and the disappointment and humiliation of the defeat caused Brunelleschi to abandon sculpture for the rest of his life, although, as we have seen, his devotion to architecture made such abandonment fortuitous for history. We are fortunate in that the models submitted by both Brunelleschi and Ghiberti have been saved (Figs **10.14** and **10.15**). The subject is the sacrifice of Isaac by his father, Abraham, at the Lord's command, and both reliefs explore the same moment—that is, Isaac is kneeling on the altar with Abraham ready to put the knife to his throat. The archangel intervenes, and the ram that the Lord provides as a substitute sacrifice is clearly visible. The two servants and the ass drinking water from a rock are also present. The theme of both works is the divine intervention that delivers the Chosen People from catastrophe, including the substitute victim and the miraculous appearance of water.

Brunelleschi's treatment of the subject (see Fig. **10.14**) is full of lifelike detail, from the scrawny, screaming boy to the dramatic imposition of the angel, who grabs the wrist of Abraham at the very last moment. Abraham twists the boy's head melodramatically. There is high drama here, but the rhythms seem awkward and disjointed. Line moves in fractured angles, refusing to carry through the work and, thus, create the overriding symmetry and balance we see in Brunelleschi's architecture.

Ghiberti's story, on the other hand, flows with sweeping curves, drawing its emotion from inference rather than contortion (see Fig. **10.15**). Abraham reaches around his son and grasps him by the left shoulder. The boy gazes expectantly at his father, while the angel remains in the heavens, not touching the obedient patriarch. The emphases are spiritual rather than physical, while the overtones of the work give us a sequence of curvilinear rhythms in which the principal axis runs across the diagonal to provide energy and tension. The way in which the two artists treat the human figure provides a further contrast. Brunelleschi uses anatomically correct details awk-

10.14 Filippo Brunelleschi, *Sacrifice of Isaac*, 1401. Gilt bronze, 21 × 17½ ins (53 × 44 cm). Museo Nazionale del Bargello, Florence, Italy.

10.15 Lorenzo Ghiberti, *Sacrifice of Isaac*, 1402. Gilt bronze, 21 × 17¹/₁ ins (53 × 44 cm). Museo Nazionale del Bargello, Florence, Italy.

wardly, while Ghiberti infuses them with what scholars called *natura naturata*—that is, transfigured nature. Ghiberti was trained as a painter and had not yet joined any guild—especially not the metalworkers' guild, the Arte della Seta—but his handling of the metal is profound and sophisticated. The project occupied Ghiberti from 1403 until 1424, and in the process, the Opera changed its mind about the subject matter, and Ghiberti found himself faced with the task of depicting the New Testament. The subject of Abraham and Isaac had to wait for the third set of doors.

The north doors are made up of twenty-eight quatrefoils arranged in seven rows of four. Each quatrefoil was enclosed in a frame, whose margins display a variety of animal and vegetable life, including branches, foliage, fruit, insects, lizards, and birds. At each of the forty-eight intersections is a head of an Old Testament prophet in its own tiny quatrefoil. Each one is different, and they portray a variety of emotions, from serenity to agitation. The bottom two rows show the four evangelists and the Four Fathers of the Church. New Testament scenes, beginning with the Annunciation, begin above these.

Perhaps the major breakthrough of Renaissance art came in the discovery of principles for depicting perspective mechanically and, thus, naturalistically. Attributed to Alberti, this new means of spatial representation pro-

10.16 Lorenzo Ghiberti, *The Story of Jacob and Esau*, panel of *The Gates of Paradise*, c. 1435. Gilt bronze, 31¼ ins (79.4 cm) square. Baptistery, Florence, Italy.

10.17 Lorenzo Ghiberti, *The Gates of Paradise*, 1424–52. Gilt bronze, c. 17 ft (5.2 m) high. Baptistery, Florence, Italy.

duced a visually convincing and attractive means of depicting objects in space and imbuing them with qualities that gave their relationship to the distant horizon rationality. Alberti's theories profoundly influenced the art not only of his own time but thereafter, and one of those influenced by him from 1425 was Ghiberti. The principal sculptural example is *The Gates of Paradise* or the east doors of the Baptistery of the Cathedral of Florence (Fig. **10.17**). Commissioned in 1425, these great doors bore ten scenes, originally twenty-four. Gone are the Gothic quatrefoils and consistent bronze background. Each square is totally gilded, and the sculptor is free to use each as if it were the canvas of a painting. In so doing, Ghiberti employs Alberti's elements of perspective to bring to relief sculpture a totally new sense of deep space.

The title of the doors apparently comes from the fact that they open on the *paradiso*, the area between the Baptistery and the entrance to the cathedral. Michelangelo is said to have remarked that the doors were worthy to be the Gates of Paradise, and the name stuck.

Each panel depicts an incident from the Old Testament. The perspective is so rational and the relief so defined, that the scenes take on a remarkable sense of space in which the picture plane seems almost to be fully round and free of the background. For example, in *The Story of Jacob and Esau* (Fig. **10.16**) Ghiberti created beautiful surfaces with delicate and careful detail, and used receding arcades to portray depth and perspective. Every detail is exact, and the bold relief of these scenes took Ghiberti twenty-one years to complete.

MASTERWORK

Masaccio—The Tribute Money

Masaccio's perception of the universe exploded into life in the decoration of the chapel of the Brancacci family in the Church of Santa Maria del Carmine in Florence. Late Renaissance artists such as Michelangelo came to view these frescoes and to study the new art developed by Masaccio.

The most famous of these frescoes is *The Tribute Money* (Fig. **10.18**). Its setting makes full use of the new discovery of linear perspective, as the rounded figures move freely in unencumbered deep space. *The Tribute Money* employs continuous narration, where a series of events unfolds across a single picture. Here Masaccio depicts a New Testament story from Matthew (17:24–27). In the center, Christ instructs Peter to catch a fish, whose mouth will contain the tribute money for the tax collector. On the far left, Peter takes the coin from the fish's mouth; on the right he gives it to the tax collector. Masaccio has changed the story somewhat, so that the tax collector appears directly before Christ and the Apostles, who are not "at home," but in a landscape of the Arno Valley. Masaccio's choice of subject matter may relate to a debate over taxation going on at the time in Florence. A contemporary interpretation of the fresco held that Christ had instructed all people, including clerics, to pay taxes to earthly rulers for the support of military defense.

The presentation of the figures in this fresco is remarkably accomplished. They are like "clothed nudes," dressed in fabric which falls like real cloth. Weight and volume are depicted in an entirely new way. Each figure stands in classical *contrapposto*

stance, and although the sense of motion is not particularly remarkable, the accurate rendering of the feet and the anatomically correct weight distribution make these the first painted figures to seem to stand solidly on the ground. The narrative, like that on the Hildesheim Cathedral doors, comes across through pantomimic gestures and intense glances. Nonetheless, the figures do encapsulate an astonishing energy and reality. Comparing these figures with those of Botticelli, later in the chapter, we will see that while Botticelli reveals form and volume through line, Masaccio uses the play of light and shade on an object—that is, by modeling. The key to this is the artist's establishment of a source for the light, inside or outside the painting, which strikes the figures. That source might be the sun or a candle, for example, but the artist must then render the objects in the painting so that all highlights and shadows occur consistently as if caused by that single light source. Masaccio does not include a light source in the fresco itself; instead, he uses a window in the nearby chapel to act as a light source, and the highlights and shadows are rendered accordingly (compare Rembrandt's *The Night Watch*, Fig. **13.28**). In addition, the figures form a circular and three-dimensional grouping rather than a flat line across the surface of the work. Even the halos of the apostles appear in the new perspective and overlap at odd angles.

Any expectation of historical accuracy in works of art was unknown to both Masaccio and Botticelli. Masaccio's setting is local and his figures are clothed in Italian Renaissance costume. Until the eighteenth

PAINTING

MASACCIO

Tommaso di Giovanni, better known as Masaccio (1401–29), joined the painter's guild in Florence in 1422, where he worked for four years, before moving to Pisa for two years, and then to Rome, where he died, probably of malaria, in 1429. The hallmark of Masaccio's invention and development of a "new" style lies in the way he employs deep space and rational foreshortening or perspective in his figures. In collaboration with the Florentine artist Masolino (c. 1383–c. 1432), Masaccio was summoned in 1425 to create a series of frescoes for the

Brancacci Chapel of the Church of Santa Maria del Carmine in Florence. Among these works were Masaccio's acknowledged masterpiece, *The Tribute Money*.

Masaccio's works have a gravity and monumentality that make them larger than life-size. The use of deep perspective, plasticity, and modeling to create dramatic contrasts gives solidity to the figures and unifies the paintings. Atmospheric perspective enhances the deep spatial realism. Figures are strong, detailed, and very human. At the same time, the composition carefully subordinates the parts of the painting to the whole.

The maturation of Masaccio's style can be seen in a second work, *The Holy Trinity* (Fig. **10.20**, p. 326), which is in the Church of Santa Maria Novella in Florence. Here, Masaccio states the central doctrine of Christianity in a

10.18 Masaccio, *The Tribute Money*, c. 1427. Fresco (after restoration 1989), 8 ft 4 ins × 19 ft 8 ins (2.54 × 5.9 m). Santa Maria del Carmine, Florence, Italy.

century, history was considered irrelevant to art. The apostles appear as Florentine "men in the street," and they have sympathetic and human features.

Compositionally, the single vanishing point, by which the linear perspective is controlled, sits at the head of Christ. We shall see this device for achieving focus again in Leonardo da Vinci's *The Last Supper* (Fig. **10.19**). In addition, Masaccio has rediscovered aerial perspective, in which distance is indicated through diminution of light and blurring of outlines. We can also see Masaccio's skill in handling landscape as well as figures. There is a previously unknown skill and seldom rivaled grandeur about this. As one art historian describes it:

> The background is filled with soft atmosphere. Misty patches of woodland are sketched near the banks. Masaccio's brush moves with an ease and freedom unexampled in Italian art since ancient Roman times. It represents not hairs but hair, not leaves but foliage, not waves but water, not physical entities but optical impressions. ... Each stroke of Masaccio's brush, in fact, is equivalent to a separate reflection of light on the retina.[1]

full-frontal, single vanishing point perspective rendering, which places the crucified Christ at the center of the statement. The fresco uses the viewer's eye level as the horizontal line, and the coffered barrel vault of the painted niche therefore recedes dramatically, as if we were gazing up into actual three-dimensional space. The linear angles of the T-shaped cross and the body and outstretched arms of Christ stand in dramatic juxtaposition to the rounded arch of the architectural frame and the ceiling of the vault itself. Masaccio carries the blood red colors of the architrave and cornice down through the arch, its capitals, the undergarment of God, and the figures at the lower corners, thereby achieving a unification and central focal area by virtue of this encirclement of color. The symbolism reflects the dead Christ (*Christus mortus*), sacrificed for humankind by God, who stands behind His son, steadying the cross with His hands while staring out at the rest of the universe. The dove of the Holy Spirit floats between the heads of Father and Son. Mary, the mother of Christ, looks out at us and gestures to us, indicating the sacrifice of her son. St John, the only disciple present at the Crucifixion, looks on, lost in the mystery. The figures at the lower corners, outside the niche, may be contemporary Florentines, and their coloration gives Masaccio a way of interjecting diagonal line to increase the sense of dynamics in the work. Black robes tie Mary and the feminine figure together, as do the red robes of the gentleman and St John. Thus, two, crossing, implied diagonals join at the feet of Christ.

The entire painting is executed with deliberate con-

10.19 (*above*) Leonardo da Vinci, *The Last Supper*, c 1495–98. Mural painting, 15 ft 1⅛ ins × 28 ft 10½ ins (4.6 × 8.56 m). Santa Maria della Grazie, Milan, Italy.

10.20 (*left*) Masaccio, *The Holy Trinity*, c. 1426–7. Fresco, 21 ft 10½ ins × 10 ft 5 ins (6.67 × 3.17 m). Santa Maria Novella, Florence, Italy.

cern for verisimilitude. Even the nails of the cross protrude according to the perspective of the chapel. Each body part is rendered with precise anatomical detail and accuracy.

THE HERITAGE OF MASACCIO

However revolutionary and important Masaccio may have been in retrospect, his influence on his contemporaries appears to have been relatively modest. His ideas did, however, strike a spark in some—for example, Fra Filippo Lippi and Fra Angelico—and Italian painting moved in the 1430s, 1440s, and 1450s toward a more common Renaissance style, called the second Renaissance style. This was the era of the Medicis, as we will see at the end of this chapter. The time was one of humanistically oriented patrons of art who commissioned buildings, statues, portraits, and altarpieces to fit their new classical tastes. The laws of Florence forbade luxury and display in personal finery, but the tone was set for a new life of ease and grace.

FRA ANGELICO Fra Angelico (c. 1400–55) lived a life of piety and humility. He was born Guido di Pietro and appears to have become an accomplished painter before taking vows in the Dominican Order as Fra Giovanni da

Fiesole. Once he had become a monk, he served his order as a prolific artist in San Domenico, Fiesole, and in San Marco, Florence. Eventually, he became prior of San Marco, and before his death he was widely known as "the angelic painter"—hence the name by which we know him, Fra Angelico. We have such a wealth of work from this amazing monk that it is difficult to choose one as illustrative. However, his *Annunciation* appears to be his most popular and best known, and, since we have told the story in this book (see Chapter 5), we will examine it (Fig. **10.21**). The work dates to the 1430s and was created as the altarpiece for San Domenico, Cortona. It now hangs in the Museo Diocesano in Cortona.

A portico of slender Corinthian columns provides the setting as the angel comes to Mary. The delicacy of the columns and the simplicity of the capital details lend delicacy and classical appropriateness to the simple faith and obedience of the Virgin. Angelico divides the canvas into thirds. The arches on the picture plane occupy two-thirds of the work; the receding arcade occupies the remainder. Mary is seated on a chair decorated with gold brocade, and the angel, genuflecting before the seated presence, enters the portico. Fra Angelico prints the angel's words on the canvas so that they appear to come out of his mouth, running from left to right. Mary's reply—"Behold the handmaiden of the Lord; be it unto me according to thy word" (Luke 1:38)—is written upside down, so that it must be read from Mary toward the angel. The dove of the Holy Spirit floats directly above Mary's head under a blue star-filled ceiling. The prophet Isaiah looks down from a medallion above the column that separates the two figures. The garden at the left is a symbol of Mary's virginity and also represents the Garden of Eden, from which a weeping Adam and Eve are being politely expelled at the rear. There is logic to the inclusion of the Eden scene here, because, according to Christian prophecy and doctrine, Christ would become the "new Adam" and Mary would be the second Eve.

The figures of Adam and Eve are fully clothed in the garments God gave them, and the entire scene lacks the dramatic power we have seen before. Fra Angelico's figures are rendered three-dimensionally, but barely. The highlight and shadow contrasts remain subdued, and the scene takes on an ethereal lightness as Mary crosses her hands over her breast in acceptance of God's request. Nonetheless, the rendering speaks of plasticity—however refined—even if the celebrated human anatomy of Renaissance depiction does not show through the clothing. There is deep space here, as the arcade recedes to a vanishing point on an imagined horizon drawn across the center of the picture. Fra Angelico has captured the spiritual beauty of the moment with a simple and delicate use

10.21 Fra Angelico, *Annunciation*, altarpiece for San Domenico, Cortona, c. 1434. Panel, 5 ft 3 ins × 5 ft 11 ins (1.6 × 1.8 m). Museo Diocesano, Cortona, Italy.

of line, form, and color. The perfectly drawn hands of the angel, for example, give us a taste of the mastery of medium and execution that accompany the profound simplicity of the story.

PAOLO UCCELLO   Another important exemplar of the second Renaissance style is Paolo di Dono, known as Paolo Uccello (1397-1475), whose work is representative of the fascination with the new understanding of perspective that dominated this period. Unlike Fra Angelico, Uccello was not very prolific, even though he lived to a ripe old age. He occasionally received important commissions, but he apparently preferred to study perspective rather than pursue serious works. His earliest dated painting is a colossal fresco in the Cathedral of Florence, done in 1436 as a commission from the Opera del Duomo. In 1445 he received a commission from the Medicis for a work that once decorated the end wall of a bedroom in the Medici Palace. *The Battle of San Romano* was a three-paneled work, which was, in total, more than 34 feet (10 meters) long and 6 feet (1.8 meters) high, and it now resides in three separate museums: the Uffizi in Florence, the Louvre in Paris, and the National Gallery in London. In the work, Uccello shows off his obsession with perspective. In Figure **10.22** we can appreciate the dedication to three-dimensionality and deep space that make this work highly representative of the second Renaissance style. The panels were designed to create a continuous

10.22 Paolo Uccello, *The Battle of San Romano*, c. 1456. Tempera on wood, 6 ft 1 in × 10 ft 7¾ ins (1.82 × 3.17 m). National Gallery, London.

panorama of combatant horses, men, and weapons on a relatively flat picture plane, which is separated from the deep space of the background by a row of trees. In a manner similar to Chinese landscape, in which the middle ground disappears leaving only foreground and background, this strangely static battle takes place. However plastic the rendering may be—for example, the horses seem almost round—Uccello seems incapable of infusing the scene with dramatic, lifelike energy, and what remains is a frozen time, as opposed to a dynamic moment such as that brief pause before the release of the discus that we noted in *Discobolus* in Chapter 3. To paraphrase one scholar, these are toy people, who do not bleed or actually wound each other. The perspective is perfect, but there is no energy or tumult of battle here. The broken lances on the ground have fallen to form a perfect perspective grid, either parallel to the picture plane or receding to a single, central vanishing point. Nonetheless, there is psychological insight, for the faces have depth and humanity. The picture also provides fascinating details beyond the rigidity of the composition— for example, the dog's pursuit of a rabbit, and the peasants, who are apparently unaffected by the battle and calmly bring grapes to a wine press.

LYRICAL POETRY IN PAINTING

BOTTICELLI By the last third of the fifteenth century, most of the originators of Renaissance art were dead. Florence had been briefly visited by Leonardo Da Vinci, whose work—including that done in Florence—belongs to a category that we will pursue in the next chapter. The essences of the new art were well known and well established, and it was now time for further exploration in other avenues. One of these avenues turns inward, toward the life of the spirit and in its search creates a lyrical expression, more poetic than anything we have seen thus far. Outward reality is often ignored in favor of more abstract values, and classical intellect is often cast aside (despite use of classical subjects) for a more emotional introspection. This tradition undoubtedly is best expressed in the paintings of Sandro Botticelli (c. 1445–1510). The linear quality of *La Primavera* or *Spring* (Fig. **10.23**) suggests an artist apparently unconcerned with deep space or subtle plasticity in light and shade. Instead, the forms emerge through outline. The composition moves gently across the picture, through a combination of gently undulating curved lines, with focal areas in each grouping. Mercury, the Three Graces, Venus, Flora, Spring, and Zephyrus—each part of this human, mythical

composition—carry their own emotion: contemplation, sadness, or happiness. The subject matter is apparently classical and non-Christian, but, in fact, the painting uses allegory to equate Venus with the Virgin Mary. Beyond its immediate qualities, the painting has a deeper symbolism, relating also to the Medici family, the patron rulers of Florence.

Botticelli's figures are anatomically quite simple. There is little concern with detailed musculature, and although the figures are rendered three-dimensionally and shaded subtly, they seem almost weightless, floating in space without anatomical definition.

In a fascinating portrayal of a rather ugly mythological tale, Botticelli painted one of his most familiar works, *The Birth of Venus* (Fig. **10.27**, p. 332). The story depicts the mythical birth of Venus from the sea, which had been fertilized by the severed genitals of Uranus. It is an allegory symbolizing the birth of beauty in the minds of humankind with ideas fertilized by divinity. Yet, out of this myth, Botticelli creates a lyrical and poetic picture of grace and beauty. Venus rises from a rather artificial sea

10.23 Sandro Botticelli, *La Primavera* (*Spring*), c. 1478. Tempera on panel, 6 ft 8 ins × 10 ft 4 ins (2.03 × 3.15 m). Uffizi, Florence, Italy.

OUR DYNAMIC WORLD

The Ming Dynasty in China

In 1368 the Ming Dynasty was proclaimed by a former peasant who led a revolt against the Mongolians. By the end of the century, all of China had been liberated, and a major policy of public works had been introduced. By the end of the sixteenth century, capitalism existed in small pockets throughout China, although the central government tried to restrict its emergence. At the same time, an official policy of population control was established. As China rediscovered its former prosperity, it spread its influence again throughout southeast Asia from Mongolia to Vietnam. Culture as well as goods were exported, but the emperor's lack of interest in seafaring and Japanese pirates took their toll on China's outward expansion. European incursion occurred at the same time, first from the Portuguese and then the Dutch. Industrial development and prosperity tended to undermine both China's agrarian foundations and the privileges of the aristocracy and its bureaucracy. Dissatisfaction spread among the peasants of the countryside and among city-dwellers, and this led to internal conflicts, which, heightened by a new threat from Mongolia, brought down the Ming Dynasty in 1644.

During the nearly three centuries of the Ming Dynasty, the style of Chinese art changed dramatically. Although subject matter remained constant, ostentation, detail, and dramatic presentation increased, and we can see these qualities in a work by Lu Chi entitled *Winter* (Fig. **10.24**). Here, strong contrasts, copious detail, hard color edges, and conflicting diagonals create strong action, exaggeration, and intensity. The curvilinear treatment of line instills a broad, sweeping, and, yet, reasonably soft dynamic, while open spaces and hard-edged outlining impart power and substance to the work. At the same time, an immense amount of delicate detail—for example, in the pheasant, the blossoms, and some of the smaller branches—is captured within the openness of the painting. Thus, the contrasts—that is, lights and darks, hard edges and curved lines, broad spaces and delicate details—create a curious mystery and opulence that are quite different from anything found in Western art or in previous Chinese art.

Opulence is also the theme of imperial architecture of the period. The third Ming emperor, Yongle, moved his capital from Nanjing to Peking in 1417. In a lust for ostentatious display, he laid out his new

10.24 Lu Chi, *Winter*, c. 1500. Hanging scroll, ink and color on silk, 5 ft 9 ins (1.75 m) high. National Museum, Tokyo.

palace according to Zhou Dynasty ritual, which indicated that the Son of Heaven, as the emperor was known, should rule from three courts. Consequently, a 15-mile (24-kilometer) wall was constructed to surround the courts separating the three great halls of state, which were built with wooden columns and

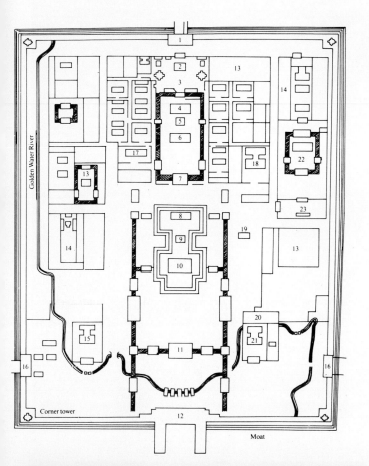

beams and wide roofs of glazed yellow tiles, a color reserved for imperial buildings (Fig. **10.25**). The outer gate to the capital enters into the first courtyard across a bridge over the Golden Water River (Fig. **10.26**). The white bridge and river railings blend harmoniously with the pavement of the courtyard and stand in charming contrast to the red columns and golden roof tiles of the buildings. An even larger courtyard stands beyond the Gate of Supreme Harmony. The scale and detail of these spaces and buildings more than met the emperor's desire to outshine the splendor of buildings that had so impressed Marco Polo that he described them as "so vast, so rich, and beautiful that no man on earth could design anything superior."

10.25 Plan of the Imperial Palace, Peking.
1. Gate of Divine Pride; 2 Pavilion of Imperial Peace;
3 Imperial Garden; 4 Palace of Earthly Tranquility; 5 Hall of
Union; 6 Palace of Heavenly Purity; 8 Hall of the Preservation
of Harmony; 9 Hall of Perfect Harmony; 10 Hall of Supreme
Harmony; 11 Gate of Supreme Harmony; 12 Meridian Gate;
13 Kitchens; 14 Gardens; 15 Former Imperial Printing House;
16 Flower Gate; 17 Palace of the Culture of the Mind; 18 Hall
of the Worship of the Ancestors; 19 Pavilion of Arrows;
20 Imperial Library; 21 Palace of Culture; 22 Palace of Peace
and Longevity; 23 Nine Dragon Screen.

10.26 The first courtyard of the Imperial Palace, Peking, with
the outer gate on the left, 1420, later restored.

10.27 Sandro Botticelli, *The Birth of Venus*, c. 1482. Tempera on canvas, 5 ft 8³/₄ × 9 ft 3¹/₂ ins (1.72 × 2.78 m). Uffizi Gallery, Florence, Italy.

and perches on a floating sea shell. The very picture of innocent beauty, perfect in form, delicate in tone, and naive in expression, she stares innocently out at nothing in particular, covering herself modestly with her hands and long, golden hair. Her weight seems to be suspended not in or even on the shell, but she is held in place almost magically by unseen forces, as the wind gods blow her to shore, where she will be robed by the waiting figure of Hour. Flowers float in the air, and the entire scene defies the trends of the Renaissance style we have previously explored. There is no deep space here. The background of water does not recede; rather, it piles upward just behind the picture plane, the waves suggested by V-shaped white lines. Nonetheless, the delicacy of line and form and the curvilinearity of line give us a profound statement, however mono-dimensional its space may be.

10.28 Andrea Mantegna, *St James Led to Execution*, c. 1455. Fresco. Ovetari Chapel, Church of the Eremitani, Padua, Italy (destroyed 1944).

BEYOND FLORENCE Of course, there was more to the early Renaissance than Florence. The work of the great Italian master, Andrea Mantegna (1431–1506), illustrates the period in the north of Italy. *St James Led to Execution* (Fig. **10.28**) presents us with a breathtaking example of early Italian Renaissance monumentalism. Here the forces of scale, CHIAROSCURO, perspective, detail, unity, and drama are overpowering. Much of the effect of this work is created by the artist's placement of the horizon line—that is, the assumed eye level of the viewer—below the lower border of the painting. Thus, we look up at sharply realistic buildings receding down a curving street and figures that tower above us as if we were peering at them from a manhole. Mantegna's classical knowledge is clear from the details of the triumphal arch and the soldiers' costumes. In his handling of perspective, however, he deliberately sacrifices the strict accuracy of mechanical reality for dramatic effect.

CRITICAL REVIEW below

A CRITICAL REVIEW

Understanding Renaissance art means understanding the work of its artists. It means being able to look at the work of one artist and compare its qualities with that of other artists of the same or other periods and of other styles. For example, we should be able to point out the characteristics that differentiate the east and north doors of the Baptistery of the Florence Cathedral. We should be able to describe specific qualities that represent Renaissance art and architecture, identify the individual artists who contributed to the tradition, and explain how, within the artworks themselves, the artists applied those innovations.

We saw in this section another Our Dynamic World feature, in which we described part of the most familiar of the Chinese art periods, the Ming dynasty, whose painting and architecture look quite different from those of the Florentine Renaissance. What qualities account for these differences?

Describe the qualities and characteristics of Donatello's David and compare them with Donatello's other works examined in the text.

Compare the characteristics of Botticelli's Spring and The Birth of Venus to Masaccio's The Tribute Money.

A CRITICAL LOOK

In two relatively brief sections on music and theatre, we mark some additional qualities of Renaissance art. In the music section, like that of architecture, sculpture, and painting, we distinguish among the work of individual artists as well as identify general characteristics. Theatre is little more than a footnote in this particular time, although the qualities present in fifteenth-century French theatre helped to spawn some completely new genres. At this stage, however, we need only describe some of the more general qualities.

Explain the qualities of Flemish music.

Describe the "ideal sound" of Renaissance music indicated in the text.

Identify the most famous French farce of the fifteenth century.

MUSIC

MUSIC IN RENAISSANCE FLORENCE

Although Florentine accomplishments in music did not compare with those elsewhere, the existence of the Academy and its interest in things classical encouraged much speculation and interest among the scholars of Florence, and music had an important role in Florentine life. Lorenzo de Medici founded a school of music that attracted performers from all over Europe, and music triggered the emergence of a new genre, theatre dance. The supervisor of the Academy, Marsilio Ficino, had a profound interest in the music of the Greeks and the role of music in society as expressed in the writings of Plato and Aristotle, who saw the Greek values of music as contributing to the highest moral order. Ficino tried to reconstruct at least the metrical if not the modal character of classical Greek and Roman music.

ICAL LOOK bove

THE SPREAD OF THE RENAISSANCE STYLE

It is, however, to the north of Europe that we must turn to capture the changes in music that occurred as Italian ideas spread out of Italy to influence the remainder of Europe in the early days of the Renaissance.

Music historians are not of one mind in labeling the style of this place and time. Some use the term "Franco-Flemish," while others reserve that term for a later, sixteenth-century development, preferring to call fifteenth-century Flemish composers the "Burgundian School." Like their Italian counterparts, the Dukes of Burgundy were active patrons of the arts, and the painter Jan van Eyck, for example, benefited greatly from their patronage. As part of their courtly entourage, the dukes retained a group of musicians to provide entertainment and chapel music. Musicians were frequently imported from elsewhere, thus contributing to the cosmopolitan character of the Burgundian courts and disseminating Burgundian influence throughout Europe.

Flemish composers were widely educated and thoroughly aware of the world around them. In their Masses and motets, they made significant contributions to the development of FOUR-PART HARMONY. They gave greater independence to the lower lines, in particular. The bass part was independent for the first time, and this became a typical feature of this style of composition. By the end of the Renaissance, it was normal for all parts to imitate each other using consistent, measured rhythm. They came together only at the ends of sections for cadences, the musical equivalents of punctuation marks, so that, for the first time in history, Flemish music used a true four-part texture.

Guillaume Dufay and Josquin des Prés were the most prominent composers to work in this style. Dufay (1400–74) had been a member of the Papal Chapel at Rome and Florence, and he had traveled extensively throughout Europe. Thus he brought to Flanders a wealth of knowledge and experience. Within his lifetime, he was hailed as one of the great composers of the era. He wrote prolifically, and a wealth of his work has been published in modern editions. His style is striking for its relative straightforwardness as compared with the complexity of much late Gothic music. Dufay's sacred motets, based on the chant *Salve regina*, formed the basis for numerous later polyphonic settings of the Mass. He also wrote many secular songs in the standard medieval forms, such as rondeaux and ballades, of which about eighty have survived.

Patronage and secular influence on music continued.

The printing press enabled music, like the written word, to be transmitted easily. More music than ever before was composed, and people started to identify composers as individuals. They strove to achieve an "ideal" sound, by which they meant four or more voice lines of similar and compatible timbres (as opposed to the contrasting timbres of earlier periods). Small groups of singers on each part replaced the earlier soloists. Composers concentrated on making each work a unified whole. The practice of combining texts in different languages within one piece died out. Much more attention was given to the relationship of music and text, and clarity of communication became one of the objectives of music. According to the values of the day, the ideal vehicle for musical communication was an unaccompanied vocal ensemble. These characteristics are exemplified in the works of Josquin des Prés (1450–1521).

Like Dufay, Josquin was trained in Milan, Rome, and Florence, among other places, and he brought to Flanders an equally rich but somewhat later Renaissance heritage. He was compared to Michelangelo, and called the "father of musicians." He wrote about seventy secular songs of a light, homophonic nature similar to the style popular in Italy at the time, but his chief contribution lay in the area of polyphonic development, as seen in his Masses and motets. Imitation became an important structural feature. For each group of words, a short musical theme would be presented in one voice and then be restated—that is, imitated—in the other voices. The overlapping of phrases wove a wonderful mesh of sound. From time to time this would be interrupted by chordal sections in which the voices moved together. Another structural device he sometimes used in motets was the repetition of sections of music. Thus, in *Memore esto verbi tui*, an opening section (A) is followed by new material (B), and is then restated in the third section (A). This became known as ABA form.

Compared to the music of the previous era, Josquin's is more flowing, with more varied rhythms, and the general sound is fuller and richer. Above all, emotion begins to shine through, so that the listener can immediately tell the difference between a religious work of rejoicing or penitence.

A sense of the quality of Renaissance music in the early fifteenth century is given by a French poem of about 1440. It refers to the English composer John Dunstable (c. 1385–1453) and comments on the "English countenance" that helped to make European music so "joyous and bright" with "marvelous pleasantness." Humankind had found a note of optimism in a period that was devoted to living enjoyably. Certainly there were troubles, but God and his mortal children had a fairly comfortable and comforting relationship.

THEATRE

The early Renaissance was almost exclusively a time of visual art and architecture. As we have noted, we remember a few composers, whose works are rarely played, and we remember even less about the remaining performing arts—that is, theatre and dance—though their time was only a few short years away. In terms of theatre, the newly developed science of visual perspective led to amazing scenic accomplishments, and no less a figure than Niccolò Machiavelli dabbled in playwriting. His play *Mandragola* or *The Mandrake* is still produced, if for no other reason than it is one of the few existing plays of any quality to be written during the Renaissance period. Elsewhere, theatre continued its inertia to change. For example, in France the *Confrérie de la Passion*, a professional theatre company, under license from Charles VI, continued to produce mystery plays in France throughout the fifteenth century. Their cycle of plays representing *Le Mystère du Vieil Testament* (*The Mystery of the Old Testament*) consisted of 44,325 verses and took twenty performances to complete. *Le Mystère du Nouveau Testament* (*The Mystery of the New Testament*) consisted of 34,574 verses. A third cycle, *Les Actes des Apôtres*

(*The Acts of the Apostles*), rounded out the *Confrérie*'s repertoire and took forty days to present in its entirety.

But the French also developed a new secular form, the *sottie*, which was made up of short theatrical entertainments woven into the yearly festivals of the Feast of the Ass and the Feast of the Fools. These festivals originated partly in pagan rites, and were bawdy burlesques of the Roman Catholic Mass. A person called the "bishop," "archbishop," or "pope of fools" celebrated a mock Mass with a great deal of jumping around, buffoonery, and noise. Participants wore strange costumes (or nothing at all), and the entire affair was accompanied by much drinking. One of the most popular of the *sotties* written for the Feasts, Pierre Gringoire's *Jeu du Prince des Sots* (*Play of the Prince of the Fools*), was produced in Paris in 1512 at the request of Louis XII to inflame the populace against Pope Julius II.

At the same time a more substantial French theatrical form also emerged—the farce. This secular genre was fully developed as a play form. The farce was performed as an independent production, in contrast to the *sottie*, which was a between-the-acts entertainment. The most famous of the French farces of this period was *Maître Pierre Pathélin* (1470), and it is still occasionally produced today.

SYNTHESIS

Florence in the Quattrocento

If you walk through the streets of Florence today, you are able to see almost all the important cultural accomplishments of the Renaissance, which had its beginnings here in the fifteenth century, a century the Italians called the Quattrocento—that is, simply, the 1400s. Almost everywhere you go, you can look up and see Brunelleschi's great dome above the Duomo. You can walk around the Baptistery and marvel at Ghiberti's doors or across the famous Ponte Vecchio bridge to the rather humble looking Santa Maria del Carmine church and gaze in awe at Masaccio's *The Tribute Money* in the Brancacci Chapel. In fact, there is hardly any church that does not contain some masterpiece of the Quattrocento, and a day in the Uffizi Gallery will leave you numb.

But Florence is and was more than a living museum. It is and was a city as human and individualistic as its Quattrocento humanist philosophy. If we are to understand these magnificent works as something other than artifacts, we must know something about Florence in the Quattrocento: a city of people who were probably not much different from you or me in their needs and desires. Who were the Florentines of the Quattrocento and how did they come to be the world's most famous and productive culture?

In the very early Middle Ages, the *piazza* or town center consisted of a mass of small houses and public

buildings. In the fourth century, the church of Santa Reparata was built over the foundations of an older building, and three centuries later a Baptistery was added, and the area began to be the center of Florentine religious life. Santa Reparata became a cathedral in 1128, but it quickly outgrew its size, as its role and importance grew greater as Florence's population continued to increase. In 1289 the Commune decided to enlarge the cathedral as part of a massive building project that involved new and more extensive city walls, a new Prior's Palace (now the Palazzo Vecchio), and alterations to other existing buildings and churches. Wishing the city to be new but harmonious, the city fathers hired one man, Arnolfo di Cambio, to direct and coordinate the work. A great architect and sculptor, he demolished houses, raised the level of the piazza, and began to build the new cathedral, for which he planned a dome and external decoration to match the Baptistery. He died in 1302, but the work continued with the construction of the bell tower under the direction of Giotto (see Chapter 9). With a population of approximately 50,000, Florence now stood on the threshold of the Quattrocento (Fig. **10.29**).

10.29 Francesco Rosselli, *View of Florence*, c. 1490. Watercolor after an engraving. Museo dell' Opera del Duomo, Florence.

A population of 50,000 may not seem large by today's standards, but at the time, Florence was the most populous city in Europe. Before the Great Plague it had a population of 100,000, and at the time, London and Paris contained roughly 20,000 people each. Florence was a city founded on commerce, and at the heart of its political and commercial life lay the guilds, which ruled the city. The guilds were self-regulating and subject to a single political party, the Guelph party. However, it was a democracy, and one that was far more advanced than Europe had seen since Pericles.

Despite almost constant war and tribulation, during the first quarter of the Quattrocento Florence acquired the ports of Pisa and Livorno, important inland cities like Arezzo and Cortona, and controlled all of Tuscany, from Lucca to Siena. It was the time of Masaccio, Donatello, Ghiberti, and Brunelleschi, but the source of greatest pride to the Florentines was its republicanism. The city's constitution was designed to spread political power among a large group of responsible citizens, and it contained legal devices to prevent political parties from developing or a single family from becoming dominant. "Liberty is equal to all," wrote Bruni in 1428.

COSIMO DE MEDICI

Notwithstanding the city's constitution, a mere six years later, Cosimo de Medici (1389–1464), a middle-aged banker with scholarly tendencies returned to Florence from a year's exile in Venice, and he received a welcome from the city, a welcome that Machiavelli saw almost in military terms. Cosimo was saluted as the benefactor of the people and the father of the country (Fig. **10.30**). The impossible had happened—a single, previously unremarkable, family created a party and produced a leader whose legacy, although occasionally interrupted, produced a hereditary chain of almost absolutist power.

The Medici were a family of bankers with bases in Venice, Rome, and Naples. Cosimo's father, Giovanni, had become chief papal banker in Rome in 1413, and by 1420, he had become predominant. Giovanni did not wish to appear politically ambitious, however, and he kept a reasonably low profile, although he had served in the *signoria* (an elected ruling body) and as a Florentine representative in Venice and Rome. Skillfull and clever, Giovanni built the Medici fortune and laid its power base while staying in the good graces of the population. On Giovanni's death in 1429, his entire inheritance went to Cosimo, whom Giovanni had married to the daughter of the reputable Bardi family.

Cosimo's scholarly qualities did much to endear him to the people of Florence and to mitigate any rough edges of political intrigue and ambition. He was a patron of art—a trait he learned from his father, who had been on the panel that chose Ghiberti to design the

10.30 Cosimo de Medici (1389–1464).

Baptistery doors and who had been instrumental in hiring Brunelleschi to design the dome of the Duomo, with sculptural additions from Donatello. He also donated the money to build the Duomo's sacristy.

By the time of Giovanni's death the Medici interests were actively pursued by a Medici political party formed on various branches of the family and bolstered by its wealth and careful marriages with several poorer, but more prestigious families. Although family pride and advancement were more or less a hallmark of the age and certainly a reminder of feudal times, the actual fostering of family interests in political terms ran foul of Florentine law. For example, it was illegal to solicit votes, and other practices, if less problematical, were nonetheless corrupt. Again, for example, the Medicis did everything they could to put their own family members in positions of political power; they offered loans to members of the party who were in financial difficulty; and they offered advice on financial and legal matters, all actions that were just within the law. Opposition to the Medicis came from a larger but less unified old guard of the city.

In 1433 those who were opposed to the Medicis

managed a one-vote majority in the *signoria*, and Cosimo was summoned and imprisoned. The opposition tried valiantly to have him condemned to death as a traitor who planned to overthrow the government, but instead Cosimo was banished to Padua for ten years. In August 1434 the *signoria* election produced a pro-Medici majority, which promptly relinquished all power of the signoria to an open assembly of all Florentine males, called a *parliamento*, asking it to steer the city out of its present crisis. This was ostensibly a democratic device to allow the people to act in the face of political deadlock, but worked to tilt the power directly to one side or the other. In this case, power went to the Medici, and Cosimo returned in triumph, barely ten months after his original sentence.

Cosimo proved to be a new kind of leader, who drew his power from banking and his political principles from the Roman Republic. He had never been in war, and he had no royal blood or famous ancestors. All his influence came from his extensive banking interests, but through these he was able to make his city prosperous. He was also a learned man, and he founded an Academy for the study of Plato, whose head was Masilio Ficino. He actively supported the arts, and artists such as Donatello were free to pursue their new artistic style, one that, in Donatello's case, progressed from the *St George* and

10.31 Donatello, *Mary Magdalen*. c. 1455. Wood, painted, 6 ft 3¼ (1.88 m) high. Museo dell' Opera del Duomo, Florence, Italy.

David we considered earlier to the modernly expressionistic portrayal of *Mary Magdalen* (Fig. **10.31**). He also collected Roman coins and prints, and loved gardening.

For thirty years, until his death in 1464, Cosimo de Medici was the most influential man in Florence. His wealth increased through the banks that he opened throughout Italy and Europe. Although he was under some pressure to assume complete power in Florence, as he undoubtedly could have done, he remained an ordinary citizen all his life. He held high office often, but no more often than any other leading citizen.

PIERO DE MEDICI

Cosimo's son, Piero (1418–69), inherited his father's fortune, palace, and villas, and it seemed likely that he would inherit his father's influence as well. However, to the Florentines of the time, the inheritance of a position that had depended so much on the personal qualities of Cosimo was not a foregone conclusion, and it appeared, two years later, that Piero would follow his father into exile. For the next five years, he lived in his father's shadow and was destined to shrink in the light of his even more famous son, Lorenzo. Nonetheless, he did manage to overcome a Florentine constitutional crisis in 1465–6 and thus make sure that the Medici were given the opportunity to become a dynasty of princes.

Nicknamed *Il Gottoso*, the Gouty, Piero inherited his father's uricemia and, crippled and bedridden much of the time, he was carried about in a litter. Despite his unimpressive appearance, he remained a man of no mean accomplishment in many ways. He had been thoroughly educated, and had mastered Latin. He collected manuscripts, coins, and cameos, and, even before his father's death, had become a significant patron of art. Thus, whereas Cosimo built, Piero decorated. It is, for example, speculated that Piero ordered Uccello's battle scenes for the Medici palace (see Fig. **10.22**). He was perhaps petty and spendthrift, but he proved an active and helpful patron.

When it was audited the Medici bank proved to be seriously over-extended, because Cosimo had patiently overlooked many debts in order to gain political advantage. When Piero, needing to retrench, called them in, it created a storm of resentment. Florence was in something of financial panic because of the wars between Venice and the Turks, which had compromised important Florentine trade with Venice and the eastern Mediterranean, and Piero's retrenchment was seen— unfairly perhaps—as a threat. Even his own son, Lorenzo, complained of his father's temperament and its cost in friends. Voices of discontent were heard, including cries for open elections to the *signoria* and a broadened base of those eligible. The deference accorded Cosimo in similar circumstances did not extend to his son.

However, Piero weathered the storm, showing skill and resolution, and actually emerged even more influential as the controlling voice in Florentine governmental decisions. By his death in 1469, however, many were thinking of change because Piero's heir, Lorenzo, was only twenty and was of unknown character.

LORENZO DE MEDICI

While the Florentines respected Cosimo and accepted Piero, they felt more affection for Lorenzo (1449–92). He had a natural charm and dashing style, which appealed to the people of Florence, and was a well-educated youth, fluent in the classics, who loved art as well as sport (Fig. **10.32**). Although it was still a democracy at heart, Florence gave Lorenzo an influence that occasionally upset the balance of the State. His period of influence coincided with a military threat from Naples and Rome and with economic decline, which hit the Medicis hard personally, forcing Lorenzo to close branches of the bank in Milan and Bruges. Lorenzo moved to strengthen Florence's government and did so by resurrecting his grandfather's idea of a Senate. As a result, a Council of Seventy assumed power in Florence, its members holding their position for life. Although Lorenzo proposed the council, the Florentines themselves approved it, hoping that it would provide a decision-making body that would prove equal to the needs of the times.

One of the council's first acts was to institute progressive taxation, which hit the rich very heavily. Lorenzo's taxes amounted to double those disproportionate taxes that Cosimo had paid. Looking back on Lorenzo's place in the political scheme of Florence, one finds that, even though he was sometimes called a "tyrant," there were real limits to his power. He certainly had considerable personal influence—his diarist described him as a man who "with a single gesture was able to bend all the other citizens to his will"—but he seems never to have stepped beyond constitutional bounds. When another plot to assassinate him was uncovered in 1481, however, the *signore* passed a law making any attempt on Lorenzo's life a crime against the state.

Perhaps the most important factor in his rise to power was the role he inherited in foreign policy. Good personal relationships with other rulers had been one of his grandfather's strengths, and it was misjudgment in this area that led to Lorenzo's son's exile in 1494 and the family's temporary decline. Lorenzo had met and favorably impressed many heads of state in Italy, a large number of whom assumed that Lorenzo had more power than, in fact, he did. He had to tread a delicate path in all his relationships, both domestic and foreign, and his

10.32 Lorenzo de Medici (1449–92).

diplomacy was often hampered by his insecure position as a banker. The family's political prestige made it uniquely liable to requests from rulers for loans, and although his fortunes were not totally dependent on the bank, Lorenzo had less access than his father or grandfather to free money by which to extend his influence. His whole political career was marked by intrigues and difficult situations—including major confrontations with Pope Sixtus IV.

Lorenzo the man, as distinct from Lorenzo the politician, now draws our attention, however. He undertook a staggering range of activities, in addition to his political activities—he ran the largest international bank in Europe, managed four country estates and a townhouse, planted botanical gardens, raised cows, bred race horses, looked after his children's education, did charitable work for the church, read Plato, bought art, played the lyre and the organ, possessed a theoretical and practical knowledge of architecture, and wrote music and poetry. Some of his friends thought that he was a better poet than Dante and Petrarch, because, as a Platonist, he had a deeper insight into the nature of love and reality.

A CRITICAL LOOK We recognize terms such as Renaissance and High Renaissance as the names of historical periods of great importance. When we use the word Renaissance, which, of course, includes the High Renaissance, we are defining a historical period by the nature of the art and ideas of that time. Perhaps with the exception of the nineteenth century, which is often called the Age of Industry, the human perception of its history has always focused on those avenues of understanding called the humanities, which we identified in the Introduction. No one would discount the importance of the way in which humankind keeps itself alive materially—that is, business, medicine, science, and so on—but when humans recall their journey through time, they identify blocks of time by art and ideas rather than by materialistic pursuits.

The period we are about to study remains one of the high points of Western culture, perhaps outranking even the classical period in Athens, and if it does outrank the golden age of Athens, it may be because of the quality of individual genius we find in it, particularly Michelangelo and Leonardo da Vinci. To make such an assertion again highlights one of the fundamentals of the Renaissance—individual humans count, and they count in the here and now.

In the opening sections of this chapter, we will study some events and individuals that contributed to the expanding world of the sixteenth century. You should be able to: identify these individuals and explain their contributions.

Explain the relationships between the Ottoman Turks, the Italian Wars, the Papal State, and the Golden Age of Spain as they affected events in the sixteenth century.

THE HIGH RENAISSANCE

As important and revolutionary as the fifteenth century or Quattrocento was, the high point of the Renaissance came in the early sixteenth century as papal authority was re-established and artists were called to Rome. The importance of this brief period, occurring from approximately 1508 until 1527 in Rome and exemplified by Michelangelo and Raphael, has led scholars to call it the High Renaissance. However, as we shall see, it began earlier in Florence with the work of a man very much ahead of his time: Leonardo da Vinci. It also involved locations other than Rome—for example, the great city of Venice where artists such as Titian and Tintoretto were active.

Especially important to an understanding of High Renaissance is a new concept—the concept of genius. In particular, we might argue that everything done in the visual arts in Italy between 1495 and 1520 was subordinate to the overwhelming genius of two men, Leonardo da Vinci and Michelangelo Buonarotti. In fact, such was the achievement of these two men that many have argued that the High Renaissance in visual art was not a culmination of earlier Renaissance style but a new kind of art entirely.

Whatever may be the case, by 1500 the courts of the Italian princes had become centers of cultural activity and important sources of patronage. Machiavelli, who thought the leaders of these centres soft and effeminate, and accused them of deliberately living in an unreal world. However, the Italian courtiers needed artists, writers, and musicians to pursue their lofty ideals of beauty, whether real or unreal. They now regarded the arts of the early Renaissance as vulgar and naive, and they demanded a more aristocratic, elegant, dignified, and lofty art, and this accounts, at least in part, for the new style found in the works of playwrights and painters. The wealth of the popes and their desire to rebuild and transform Rome on a grand scale also contributed to the shift in style and the emergence of Rome as the center of patronage. Music came of age as a major art form, finding a great patron in Pope Leo X. Ancient Roman sculptural and architectural style was revived. There were also important discoveries of ancient sculptures, such as the *Apollo Belvedere* and the *Laocoön* (see Fig. **3.31**), and because the artists of this period had such a rich immediate inheritance of art and literature from the early Renaissance, but felt that they had developed even further, they considered themselves to be on an equal footing with the artists of antiquity. Their approach to the antique in arts and letters was, therefore, different from that of their early Renaissance predecessors. So was their world.

	GENERAL EVENTS	LITERATURE & PHILOSOPHY	VISUAL ART & ARCHITECTURE	THEATRE & MUSIC
1450	Louis XI of France Charles the Bold, Duke of Burgundy Ferdinand and Isabella of Spain Caxton's printing press			
1475	Wars of the Roses in England Henry VII of England Diaz sails round Cape of Good Hope Columbus discovers West Indies		Leonardo (11.8, 11.9, 11.10) Michelangelo (11.13, 11.14, 11.15, 11.16, 11.31, 11.34, 11.36, 11.37) Bramante (11.23, 11.35) Lescot (11.24)	commedia dell'arte Teatro Olimpio
1500	Brazil discovered Henry VIII of England Suleiman I, the Magnificent Jesuits founded	Ariosto Castiglione Rabelais	Raphael (11.17, 11.18, 11.29, 11.38) Titian (11.19) Palladio (11.25) Bronzino (11.21)	Peruzzi Serlio
1550	Inquisition	Philip Sidney	Tintoretto (11.20) da Bologna (11.22)	Lassus Palestrina Victoria Byrd Gibbons

Timeline 11.1 The High Renaissance and Mannerism.

SOUTHERN EUROPE IN THE SIXTEENTH CENTURY

THE EXPANDING WORLD

In July 1497 Vasco da Gama sailed from Lisbon, Portugal, with two well-armed ships, a smaller and faster ship for scouting, and a storeship. In November 1497 he rounded the Cape of Good Hope, the southern tip of Africa, and spent Christmas on the east African coast, which he christened Natal. By May of 1498 he had reached India, where he found people living in rich principalities and used to trading with Persian and Arab merchants. Despite difficulties, he managed to load his ships with spices and precious stones and to return to Portugal. Although he lost half his fleet and men on the way, he proved beyond doubt that a sea route to India existed and that it could be exploited practically and profitably. Less than a year later, Pedro Alvares Cabral left Portugal with fifteen heavily armed ships and 1,500 men, determined to make Portugal a major trading power in the Indian ocean. However, on his way down the coast of Africa, he sailed too far west and ended up on the coast of Brazil, which he promptly claimed for Portugal. From there, he sailed east again, and in September 1500 arrived in Calcutta, where he established a trading post. Portugal's entry into the spice trade did not happen smoothly, for the Arab traders who had laid previous claims did not give up their posi-

tion peacefully. However, by 1515 Portugal dominated the main spice-producing region of the world, and Portuguese sailors found their way to Ceylon and beyond, to Japan as well. In the wake of the traders were Christian missionaries, and in 1559 a Jesuit mission was welcomed to the Japanese imperial capital at Kyoto. In 1569 a powerful Christian convert gave the Jesuits the town of Nagasaki, which became their major base. By the end of the century, there were over 300,000 Christians in Japan, and although Portuguese attempts to gain entry into China were not successful, by the mid-sixteenth century, Portugal had established a tremendous commercial empire stretching across four continents.

After Christopher Columbus had shown the way, the rate of exploration of the world grew rapidly. By 1500 the Antilles islands had been discovered and nearly a thousand miles of the South American coast had been explored. Twelve years later, there were major European settlements in the West Indies, Hispaniola, Cuba, Jamaica, and Puerto Rico. Large grants of land were made to individuals, who were supposed to be responsible for the well-being of the natives. All too often, however, the desire for profit took precedence over any humanitarian concerns, and the natives were forced not only to provide labor to the landholder but to pay tribute as well.

Among those who descended on the Americas were restless men and ex-soldiers looking for easy wealth and fame. Such a man was Vasco de Balboa, who, after leading a revolt against the governor of a new settlement on the coast of South America, set out up the coast and, crossing the Isthmus of Panama, sighted the Pacific Ocean in 1515.

Also among the footloose adventurers of the time was

In a few short years, therefore, curiosity and individual self-confidence had taken humankind to the furthest reaches of the planet to explore and exploit it for the benefit of the kingdoms of Europe. The full implications of the fact that the world was, indeed, round fell upon Renaissance men and women in 1522 when Magellan completed his three-year voyage around the world. It is easy for us to minimize the impact of these events on the general view of reality held at the time, but the discovery of an immense world in a heliocentric universe proved catastrophic for many, whose views of humanity and of God were compatible only with an earth-centered universe.

11.4 Suleiman I, the Magnificent (1494–1566). British Library, London.

THE OTTOMAN TURKS

In essence, the powers of Europe in the early sixteenth century were disunited and in conflict. The Ottoman Turks, on the other hand, represented a united and formidable fighting force. Their major asset was a well-disciplined army, which struck fear into the hearts of the opposition, but the army also showed one of the major tenets of the Turks—toleration. Most of the peoples in the Ottoman Empire were Jewish or Christian, and they were left to the unhindered practice of their own religions, provided that they paid tribute money for the sultan's military campaigns and turned over their male children to his service. The conscripted children were raised as Muslims, trained for the army, and then sent throughout the Empire.

The sultan to whom fell this dynamic and, perhaps, over-extended empire was Suleiman I, the Magnificent (1494–1566). He succeeded his father in 1520 and became one of the greatest rulers of the sixteenth century (Fig. **11.4**). He was a warrior, but also a cultured and learned man, a lover of the arts, and a law-giver. One of his first acts as sultan was to demand tribute from young King Louis II of Bohemia and Hungary. When Louis refused, Suleiman invaded Hungary and captured Belgrade. In a later offensive in 1526, the Turks defeated Louis' forces at Mohacs, and reached the border of the Hapsburg Empire. Louis was drowned in the fight, and Suleiman prepared to assault the Hapsburg capital, Vienna. The Turks were beaten back, and the onset of winter, overextended Turkish supply lines, and trouble elsewhere caused the Turks to retreat, and in 1533 to agree to a truce. Because of renewed conflict over the succession to the throne of the buffer state of Transylvania, the Turks succeeded in consolidating their hold on the Balkans and two-thirds of Hungary. By the middle of the century, the Ottoman Empire was secure, and by the time Suleiman died in 1566, it extended unbroken from the Black Sea to the Persian Gulf. Despite continued conflicts with the Hapsburgs and with Spain, the Ottoman Empire changed little in the rest of the century.

THE ITALIAN WARS

The political circumstances of Europe in the sixteenth century were too complicated for our limited discussion here. By the end of the Quattrocento, for example, the Italian states were totally disunited and, thus, ripe for outside intervention if not outright conquest. Venice refused to give assistance to Naples, which was under attack from Charles VIII of France, although Piero de Medici offered help from Florence. This venture, however, was extremely unpopular among the Florentines, and

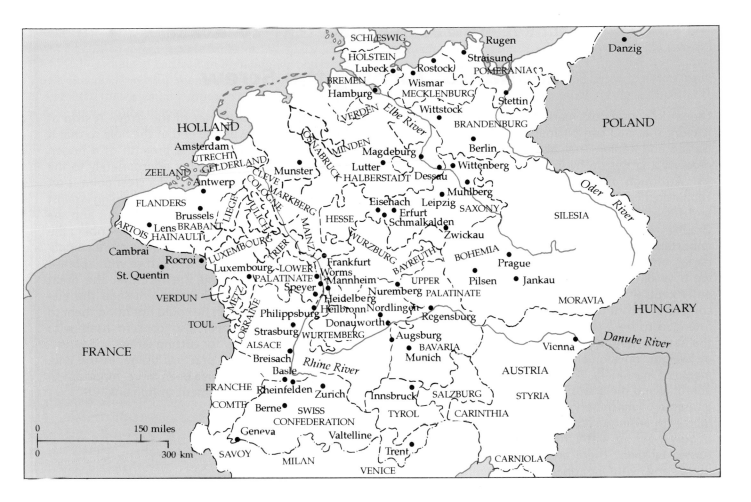

Map 11.1 The Holy Roman Empire.

they drove out Piero and called on Savonarola to save them. Savonarola had thought that Charles had been sent by God, but the brutality of the French soldiers soon convinced him otherwise, and he pleaded with Charles to move on. Charles turned on Rome, where some of the French cardinals wanted the French army to depose Pope Alexander VI, a Borgia. Charles was more interested in setting up a secure line to the throne of Naples than he was in entering a religious conflict, and so he accepted the pope's support and entered Naples unopposed in 1495. Charles realized that in the interests of his own personal safety he should leave Naples and return to France, leaving an occupying force in place. As he attempted to pass through the Duchy of Milan, his forces were attacked and almost defeated, but they managed to fight their way through a mountain pass to safety. The French troops who were left in Naples soon found themselves the victims of syphilis and constant attacks from a new invading force—the Spanish.

The relative ease with which the French had marched through Italy had made it clear that the city-states of the Italian peninsula were ripe for the picking, and the recurring conflicts between France and Spain over the next two centuries often had Italy in the middle. The intrigues and alliances that resulted are legion, and they include the

story of Cesare Borgia, who was established by his father, Pope Alexander VI, as temporal ruler of the Papal States, which gave the Borgia family a base from which they could establish themselves as independent princes.

THE PAPAL STATES

Having been a plaything of the great powers of Europe, the Church wished to secure independence by increasing its temporal and political strength. It looked for leadership not among saints and scholars, but among administrators and politicians, seeking worldly men of powerful personality and toughness who could make quick decisions. The power of the Papacy began to grow through worldly measures—such as war and diplomacy—and that reinforced the need for popes who could maintain such dominions. Popes such as Alexander VI and Julius II came to power. Alexander VI, whose lusts were repellant even in an age renowned for toleration, proved a hardknuckled diplomat and an excellent administrator in the dogged pursuit of policies that he believed were necessary for the Church—that is, temporal power expressed

that, unlike his father, he would succeed in dominating the entire Western world. It did not happen.

The growing Protestant powers of Europe allied themselves against him: England under Elizabeth I, the French Huguenots, and the Netherlands. As we shall see in Chapter 12, the cause was as much political as religious. Although Philip had some military successes, especially against the Turks, his critical battles were failures—for example, the attempted invasion of England that led to the catastrophic defeat of the Spanish Armada (Fig. **11.7**).

11.7 Hendrik Cornelisz Vroom, *The Sea Battle*, c. 1600. Oil on canvas, 3 ft 1¼ ins × 5 ft 1⅛ ins (91 × 153 cm). Landesmuseum Ferdinandeum, Innsbruck, Austria.

His attempts to crush the revolt in the Netherlands ended in 1609 with Dutch independence. Thus, in one generation, the most powerful empire in the world went from ascendancy to eclipse, and by the end of the sixteenth century, Spain had gone from a Golden Age into an insignificant footnote to subsequent European history.

A CRITICAL REVIEW

Some of the material we have just studied sounds like a repetition of the struggles for control we have been watching since the fall of the Roman Empire. However, there is a new player in the European scene— the Ottoman Empire, which made inroads into the heart of Europe that even the great charge of the Islamic invaders of the eighth century could not achieve. We have seen how the Church of Rome fought to maintain itself centerstage in the drama of European history, and we have also watched as the horizons of the European world began to expand and seen how that expansion affected the balance of power in Europe.

Many people take the view that this is the period in which the pursuit of power, wealth, and fame destroyed and enslaved much of the world outside Europe. Was this era one of progress, great ideas, and advances for the individual, or was it far less noble and more destructive?

Describe how the Portuguese and Spanish explorations changed the sixteenth-century world.

Explain how the actions of the Ottoman Turks, Charles V of Spain, and the popes affected Italian life during the sixteenth century.

In a short essay, explore both sides of this argument.

A CRITICAL LOOK

In the next section, we can ponder the larger question of art and its context. We look at the magnificent accomplishments of the artists of the time and place them in the context of political events. If art is the mirror of its time, how do these artistic accomplishments reflect the social and political environment that gave them birth? In addition, we will read about great masters who worked in Rome, and then we will change the scene and go to Venice. Finally, we will look briefly at a trend in visual art that emerged after the Spanish invaded Rome and the High Renaissance came to an end. As always, we need to differentiate among stylistic characteristics and to recognize individual accomplishments in painting and sculpture.

Describe and compare the contributions, characteristics, and qualities of the visual art of Leonardo da Vinci, Michelangelo, and Raphael.

Explain the Mannerist movement and analyze the works of its proponents described in the text.

THE VISUAL ARTS

THE HIGH RENAISSANCE

TICAL LOOK above

High Renaissance painting sought a universal ideal achieved through impressive themes and styles. Tricks of perspective or stunning renditions of anatomy were no longer enough. Figures became types again, rather than individuals—god-like human beings in the Greek classical tradition. Artists and writers of the High Renaissance sought to capture the essence of classical art and literature without resorting to copying, which would have captured only the externals. They tried to emulate rather than imitate. As a result, High Renaissance art idealizes all forms and delights in composition. Its impact is one of stability without immobility, variety without confusion, and definition without dullness. High Renaissance artists carefully observed how the ancients borrowed motifs from nature, and then set out to develop a system of mathematically defined proportion and compositional beauty emanating from a harmony of parts. This faith in harmonious proportions reflected a belief among artists, writers, and composers that the world of nature, not to mention the universe, also possessed perfect order.

This human-centered attitude also included a certain artificiality and emotionalism that reflected the conflicts of the times. High Renaissance style departed from previous styles in its meticulous composition, which was based almost exclusively on geometric devices. Compositions were closed—that is, line, color, and form kept the viewer's eye continually redirected into the work, as opposed to leading the eye off the canvas—and the organizing principle of a painting was usually a geometric shape, such as a central triangle or an oval.

LEONARDO DA VINCI

The work of Leonardo da Vinci (1452–1519) has an ethereal quality which he achieved by blending light and shadow, a technique called SFUMATO. His figures hover between reality and illusion as one form disappears into another, with only the highlighted portions emerging. In *The Madonna of the Rocks* (see Fig. **11.8**), Leonardo interprets the doctrine of the Immaculate Conception, which proposed that Mary was freed from original sin by the Immaculate Conception in order to be a worthy vessel for the incarnation of Christ. Mary sits in the midst of a dark world and shines forth from it. She protects the Infant Christ, who blesses John the Baptist, to whom the angel points. The gestures and eye direction create movement around the perimeter of a single central triangle outlined in light. Leonardo takes the central triangle and gives it enough depth to make it a three-dimensional pyramid of considerable weight. Light and shade are delicately used, even though the highlights and shadows do not flow from a consistent light source. The portrayal of rocks, foliage, and cloth displays meticulous attention to detail.

It is difficult to say which of Leonardo's paintings is the most admirable, but certainly *The Last Supper* (see Fig. **10.19**) ranks among the greatest. It captures the moment at which the apostles are responding with disbelief to Christ's prophecy that "one of you shall betray me." Leonardo's choice of medium proved most unfortunate because, unlike fresco, his own mixtures of oil, varnish, and pigments were not suited to the damp wall. The painting began to flake, and was reported to be perishing as early as 1517. Since then it has been clouded by retouching, defaced by a door cut through the wall at Christ's feet, and bombed during World War II. Miraculously, it survives.

11.8 (*above*) Leonardo da Vinci, *The Madonna of the Rocks* (*Virgin of the Rocks*), c. 1485. Oil on panel, 6 ft 3 ins × 3 ft 7 ins (1.91 × 1.09 m). Louvre, Paris.

11.9 (*above right*) Leonardo da Vinci, *Virgin and Child with St Anne*, 1508–10. Oil on panel, 5 ft 6¹/₈ ins × 4 ft 3¹/₄ ins (1.68 × 1.3 m). Louvre, Paris.

11.10 (*right*) Leonardo da Vinci, *Mona Lisa*, c. 1503–05. Oil on panel, 30 × 21 ins (76.2 × 53.3 cm). Louvre, Paris.

In *The Last Supper*, human figures, not architecture, are the focus. Christ dominates the center of the painting. All lines, actual and implied, lead outward from his face, pause at various subordinate focal areas, reverse direction at the edges of the work, and return to the central figure. Various postures, gestures, and groupings of the disciples direct the eye from point to point. Figures emerge from the architectural background in strongly accented relief; it is surprising how much psychological drama the mathematical format allows. Yet, despite the drama, the mood in this work and others is calm, belying the turbulence of Leonardo's own personality and his times.

Leonardo reverts to the pyramid as the basis of the composition in his *Virgin and Child with St Anne* (see Fig. **11.9**). The Virgin Mary sits on the lap of her mother,

PROFILE

Michelangelo (1475–1564)

Sculptor, painter, architect, and poet, Michelangelo was one of the world's greatest artists. Born Michelangelo Buonarroti, he came from a respectable Florentine family in the village of Caprese, where his father was a government agent. He had a standard classical education, and when he was twelve years old he was apprenticed to the Florentine painter Domenico Ghirlandajo. Even before his apprenticeship had ended, Michelangelo turned away from painting to sculpture, and he gained the attention of Florence's ruler, Lorenzo de Medici, The Magnificent, who invited the young Michelangelo to stay at his palace. During these early years, Michelangelo became a master of anatomy.

In 1494, after the Medicis fell from power, Michelangelo traveled. He spent five years in Rome and enjoyed his first success as a sculptor with a life-sized statue of the Roman wine-god Bacchus. He carved his magnificent *Pietà*—that is, the dead Christ in the lap of his mother—when he was twenty-three years old (see Fig. **11.15**), and this larger-than-life-sized work established him as a leading sculptor of his time.

He returned to Florence for four years in 1501, and there met Leonardo da Vinci. Both artists were commissioned to work on large battle scenes for the walls of the city hall. Leonardo never finished his scenes, and Michelangelo's are lost, and we know of them only through sketches and copies made by other artists. What this mural did show was Michelangelo's extreme skill in rendering human anatomy. According to some sources, during this time Michelangelo learned from Leonardo how to depict flowing and active movement in the human form, and the style developed during these years in Florence stayed with him for the rest of his life.

By 1505 Michelangelo was back in Rome, beginning a series of grand, large-scale works under the patronage of Pope Julius II. Over the next forty years he struggled unsuccessfully to complete the first of these colossal endeavors, Pope Julius' tomb. The second, the Sistine Chapel in the Vatican (Figs **11.12** and **11.13**)

11.11 Michelangelo (1475–1564).

became Michelangelo's most famous work, with *David* (see Fig. **11.16**) a close second.

Between 1515 and 1534 he was back in Florence, working for the Medicis, who had returned to power. There, he designed and sculpted tombs for two Medici princes and began the Medici chapel in which the tombs were placed. He left Florence and the unfinished chapel in 1534. Returning to Rome, he painted the fresco *The Last Judgment* for Pope Paul III on the altar wall of the Sistine Chapel, and the pope appointed him supervising architect of St Peter's Church in Rome. Earlier in this period he designed a square for the civic center of Rome, which symbolized Rome as the center of the world.

During the last years of his life his religious faith deepened, and he produced not only the complicated and somber frescoes of the Pauline Chapel in the Vatican but also a considerable amount of poetry. Among the few sculptural works attempted in his late years was a *pietà*, now in the Cathedral of Florence, which he designed for his own tomb. After his death in 1564, his body was returned to Florence for burial.

Michelangelo's ideal was the full realization of individuality—a reflection of his own unique genius. He epitomized the quality of *terribilità*, a supreme confidence that allows a person to accept no authority but his or her own genius. Critical of his own work, he was jealous of Raphael, disliked Leonardo, and clashed constantly with his patrons, yet in his letters he expresses a real sympathy and concern for those close to him. His works reveal a deep understanding of humanity and reflect his neo-Platonic philosophy. He captures the Platonic idea of potential energy, imprisoned in the earthly body, and he believed, as did Plato, that the image from the artist's hand must spring from the idea in his or her mind. The idea is the reality, and it is revealed by the genius of the artist. The artist does not create the ideas, but finds them in the natural world, which reflects the absolute idea: beauty. Thus, to the neo-Platonist, when art imitates nature, it reveals Truths hidden within nature.

St Anne. St Anne becomes the apex of the triangle whose right side flows downward to the Christ Child, who embraces a lamb, symbolic of his sacrificial death.

The famous *Mona Lisa* (see Fig. **11.10**, p. 352) was painted at about the same time as the *Virgin and Child with St Anne*. We are drawn to this work not so much by the subject as by the background. As if to emphasize the serenity of the subject, and in common with the *Virgin and Child with St Anne*, the background reveals an exciting mountain setting, full of dramatic crags and peaks, winding roads which disappear, and exquisitely detailed natural forms receding into the mists. The composition is unusual in its treatment of the full torso with the hands and arms pictured, completing the unity of the gentle spiral turn. Three-quarters of the figure is pictured, not just a bust. This marked a new format in Italian portraiture and provided a model which has been followed ever since. The result is a larger, grander, and more natural portrait, in keeping with the new sense of human dignity implicit in Renaissance idealism.

MICHELANGELO

Perhaps the dominant figure of the High Renaissance was Michelangelo Buonarroti (1475–1564). Michelangelo was entirely different in character from Leonardo. Leonardo was a skeptic, while Michelangelo was a man of great faith. Leonardo was fascinated by science and natural objects. Michelangelo showed little interest in anything other than the human form.

Michelangelo's Sistine Chapel ceiling (see Figs. **11.12**, **11.13** and **11.14**) perfectly exemplifies the ambition and genius of this era. Some scholars see in this monumental work a blending of Christian tradition and a neo-Platonist view of the soul's progressive ascent through contemplation and desire. In each of the triangles along the sides of the chapel, the ancestors of Christ await the Redeemer. Between them, amid *trompe l'oeil* architectural elements, are the sages of antiquity. In the corners, Michelangelo depicts various biblical stories, and across the center of the ceiling he unfolds the episodes of Genesis. The center of the ceiling captures the creation of Adam at the moment of fulfillment (see Fig. **11.14**). The human forms display sculpturally modeled anatomical detail. God stretches outward from his angels to a reclining, but dynamic Adam, awaiting the divine infusion, the spark of the soul. The fingers do not touch, but we can anticipate the electrifying power of God's physical contact with a mortal man.

The Sistine Chapel ceiling creates a breathtaking

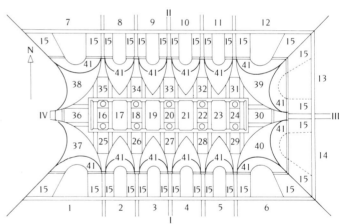

11.12 Diagram of the Sistine Chapel ceiling. **I** South wall with scenes from the life of Moses (1–6) **II** North wall with scenes from the life of Christ (7–12) **III** East wall with entrance (13–14) **IV** West wall with Last Judgment (1534–41) **15** Window niches with 24 portraits of the first popes **16** God separates Light and Darkness **17** God Creates the Sun and the Moon and the Plants on Earth **18** God Separates the Water and Earth and Blesses his Work **19** Creation of Adam **20** Creation of Eve **21** Fall of Human Race and Expulsion from Paradise **22** Sacrifice of Noah **23** The Flood **24** The Intoxication of Noah **25** Libyan Sibyl **26** Daniel **27** Cumaean Sibyl **28** Isaiah **29** Delphic Sibyl **30** Zechariah **31** Joel **32** Eritrean Sibyl **33** Ezekiel **34** Persian Sibyl **35** Jeremiah **36** Jonah **37** The Brazen Serpent **38** The Punishment of Haman **39** David Slaying Goliath **40** Judith with the Head of Holofernes **41** Lunettes above the windows with portraits of the ancestors of Christ and scenes from the Old Testament.

11.13 Michelangelo, Sistine Chapel ceiling, 1508–12. Fresco. Vatican, Rome.

11.14 Michelangelo, *The Creation of Adam*, detail from the Sistine Chapel ceiling, 1508–12. Fresco. Vatican, Rome.

visual panoply. It is impossible to get a comprehensive view of the entire ceiling from any point in the chapel. If we look upward and read the scenes back toward the altar, the prophets and sibyls appear on their sides. If we view one side as upright, the other appears upside down. These opposing directions are held together by the structure of simulated architecture, whose transverse arches and diagonal bands separate the painted vault compartments. Nudes appear at the intersections and tie the composition together because they can be read either with the prophets and sibyls below them or with the Genesis scenes, at whose corners they appear. We thus see a prime example of the basic High Renaissance principle of composition unified by the interaction of component elements.

Michelangelo broke with earlier Renaissance artists in his insistence that measurement was subordinate to judgment. He believed that measurement and proportion should be kept "in the eyes." This rationale for genius to do what it would, free from any pre-established "rules," enabled him to produce works such as *David* (see Fig. **11.16**), a colossal figure and the earliest monumental sculpture of the High Renaissance. Its impact on the viewer is as over-powering today as it was then.

In contrast to the energy of *David* is the quiet simplicity of the *Pietà* (see Fig. **11.15**). This is the only work Michelangelo ever signed. Here High Renaissance triangularity contrasts with what many believe to be a late medieval subject matter and figure treatment. The size of

the Madonna compared to Jesus reflects the cult of the Virgin characteristic of the late medieval period.

Beyond these considerations, however, lies the absolute perfection of surface texture. Michelangelo's polish has so enlivened the marble that it seems to assume the warmth of real human flesh. Skin becomes

11.15 Michelangelo, *Pietà*, 1498–99. Marble, 5 ft 9 ins (1.75 m) high. St Peter's, Rome.

MASTERWORK

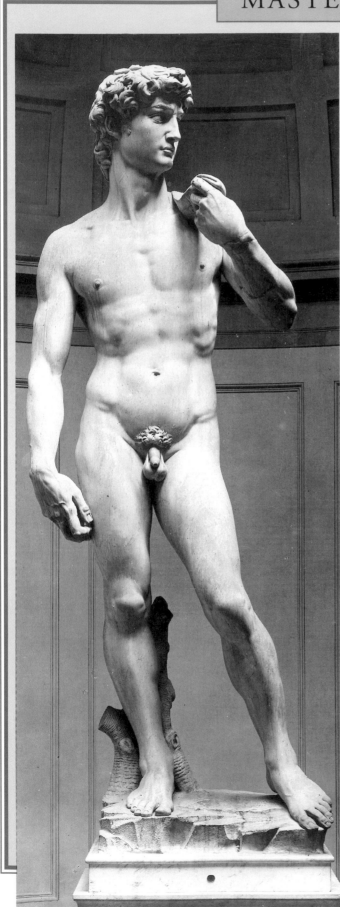

Michelangelo—David

Towering some 18 feet (5.5 meters) above the floor, Michelangelo's *David* awesomely exemplifies *terribilità*. This nude champion exudes a pent-up energy, as the body seems to exist merely as a non-Platonic earthly prison for the soul. The upper body moves in opposition to the lower. The viewer's eye is led downward by the right arm and leg, then upward along the left arm. The entire figure seeks to break free from its confinement through thrust and counter-thrust.

Much of the effect of the *David*—the bulging muscles, exaggerated rib cage, heavy hair, undercut eyes, and frowning brow—may be due to the fact that these features were intended to be read from a distance. The work was originally meant to be placed high above the ground on a buttress for Florence Cathedral. Instead, the city leaders, believing it to be too magnificent to be placed so high, put it in front of the Palazzo Vecchio. It also had to be protected from the rain, since the soft marble rapidly began to deteriorate.

The political symbolism of the work was recognized from the outset. The *David* stood for the valiant Florentine Republic. It also stood for all of humanity, elevated to a new and superhuman power, beauty, and grandeur. However, its revolutionary "total and triumphant nudity," which reflected Michelangelo's belief in the divinity of the human body, kept it hidden from the public for two months. When it did appear, a brass girdle with twenty-eight copper leaves hung around the waist.

Inspired by the Hellenistic sculptures he had seen in Rome. Michelangelo set out in pursuit of an emotion-charged, heroic ideal. The scale, musculature, emotion, and stunning beauty and power of those earlier works became a part of Michelangelo's style. In contrast to the Hellenistic approach, in which the "body 'acts' out the spirit's agony" (compare the *Laocoön*, by Hagesandrus, Polydorus, and Athenodorus shown in Figure **3.31**), *David* remains calm and tense.

11.16 Michelangelo, *David*, 1501–4. Marble, 14 ft 3 ins (4.34 m) high. Academy, Florence.

even more sensuous in its contrast to rough stone. Cloth has an exquisite softness, and the expressive sway of drape reinforces the compositional line of the work. Emotion and energy are captured within the contrasting forces of form, line, and texture.

RAPHAEL

Raphael (1483–1520) is generally regarded as the third painter in the High Renaissance triumvirate, although it has been argued that he did not reach the same level of genius and accomplishment as Leonardo and Michelangelo. In *The Alba Madonna* (Fig. **11.17**), the strong central triangle

11.17 Raphael, *The Alba Madonna*, c. 1510. Canvas (originally oil on panel), diameter 37¼ ins (94.5 cm). National Gallery of Art, Washington D.C. (Andrew W. Mellon Collection).

11.18 Raphael, *The Deliverance of St Peter*, 1512–14. Fresco. Stanza dell'Eliodoro, Vatican, Rome.

appears within the geometric parameters of a TONDO, or circular shape. The tendency of a circle to roll (visually) is counteracted by strong, parallel horizontal lines. The strong baseline of the central triangle is described by the leg of the infant John the Baptist (left), the foot of the Christ Child, the folds of the Madonna's robes, and the rock and shadow at the right. The left side of the central triangle comprises the eyes of all three figures and carries along the back of the Child to the border. The right side of the triangle is created by the edge of the Madonna's robe, joining the horizontal shadow at the right border.

Within this formula Raphael depicts a comfortable, subtly modeled, and idealized Mary and Christ Child. The textures are soft and warm, and Raphael's treatment of skin creates an almost tactile sensation—we can almost discern the warm blood flowing beneath it, a characteristic relatively new to two-dimensional art. Raphael's figures express lively power, and his mastery of three-dimensional form and deep space is unsurpassed.

In *The Deliverance of St Peter* (Fig. **11.18**) Raphael again accepted the challenge of a constraining space. To accommodate the intrusion of the window into the semicircular area of the wall, Raphael divided the composition into three sections representing the three phases of the miracle of St Peter's escape from prison. The intense light shining from the center section emphasizes the expressiveness of this depiction.

TITIAN AND TINTORETTO: THE HIGH RENAISSANCE IN VENICE

Tiziano Vecellio, known in English as Titian (1488?–1576), made one of the most crucial discoveries in the history of art. The art historian Frederick Hartt describes it this way: "He was the first man in modern times to free the brush from the task of exact description of tactile surfaces, volumes, and details, and to convert it into a vehicle for the direct perception of light through color and for the unimpeded expression of feeling."[1] This new type of brushwork is present in the *Assumption of the Virgin* (Fig. **11.19**) but is restricted to the background. Long before he died, he used the technique on entire paintings, and so did most other painters in Venice.

Part of Titian's unique technique lay in the way in which he built up pigment from a reddish ground through many layers of glaze, which lent warmth to all the colors of the painting. The glazes were used to tone down colors that the artist believed were too demanding and to give depth and richness to the work. Glazing made many of the colors and shadows seem "miraculously suspended." If Titian himself is a reliable source, he may have used as many as thirty or forty layers of glaze on a single painting.

Assumption of the Virgin exudes an almost fiery glow from the underpainting, and our eyes are led upward from the base of the picture, where our eye level is, to a

11.19 Titian, *Assumption of the Virgin*, 1516–18. Panel, 22 ft 6 ins × 11 ft 10 ins (6.9 × 3.6 m). Santa Maria Gloriosa dei Frari, Venice, Italy.

hovering Madonna lifted up on a cloud by a host of PUTTI or cherubs. Above her, emerging from a flaming yellow and orange sky, boiling in undulating brushstrokes and angelic faces, is the figure of God. The circular sweep of the painting's arched top and the encircling angels separate the Virgin from the outstretched hands of the apostles by compositional psychology as well as space, which is almost breached by the raised arm of the foreground figure.

As Titian grew old, the Venetian School produced another claim for leadership in Jacopo Robusti, called Tintoretto (1518–94), who took his name from his father's trade as a dyer. In many respects, Tintoretto bridges the time from Renaissance to baroque. It is said that Tintoretto worked in Titian's studio as a boy until Titian saw one of his drawings and ejected him from his house, never to return. Nonetheless, Tintoretto always admired Titian. He was impetuous as an artist and a man. For example, when he was competing for the commission for

11.20 Tintoretto, *St Mark Freeing a Christian Slave*, 1548. Oil on canvas, 13 ft 10 ins 18ft ⅛ in (4.15 × 5.41 m). Academy, Venice, Italy.

painting the ceiling of the Scuola San Rocco in Venice, Tintoretto reportedly sneaked into the school in the middle of the night and affixed his full-scale painting to the ceiling. That and other impetuous acts did not endear him to everyone, but his behaviour succeeded in gaining important commissions, which he finished with tremendous speed. It was, in fact, that spontaneous rapidity that characterized his style—he worked rapidly and with great passion, capturing the essences of the forms in opposition to the careful detail of others.

Darkness seems always to dominate the tone of his paintings, because he began his works with a dark underpainting, and the resulting tone can be seen in his first masterpiece, *St Mark Freeing a Christian Slave* (Fig. **11.20**). This depiction tells the story of the legend of a slave of a French knight who slipped away to go to Alexandria to venerate the bones of St Mark. When he returned, his master decided to punish him by gouging out his eyes and breaking his legs with hammers. However, St Mark descends from heaven and intercedes to end the torment and free the slave, whom we see at the base of the painting in dramatic chiaroscuro and perspective foreshortening. Broken hammer handles lie around him and, in a curious counterpoint to the line of the

painting, extend upward in the hands of the turbaned executioner. The golden cape of St Mark draws the eye powerfully and makes the viewer acutely aware of the disjointed emotionalism of the composition as a jumble of figures, formed from broken lines and competing colors, and throws the surface of the work into turmoil. This twisted and turning whirlpool effect of figures around a central point appears in many of Tintoretto's works, and gives them their characteristic frenetic appearance. Despite the darkened underpainting, the colors are vibrant and gleaming. Faces reflect deep human emotion and psychological insight. Originally intended as a ceiling painting in an octagonal space, the strong diagonal figures run parallel with or at right angles to the corners,

MANNERISM

Papal patronage had assembled great genius in Rome at the turn of the sixteenth century. It had also ignited and supported a brilliant fire of human genius in the arts. The Spanish invasion and sack of Rome doused the flame of Italian art in 1527 and scattered its ashes across Europe, contributing to the disillusionment and turmoil of reli-

11.25 Palladio, Villa Rotonda, Vicenza, Italy, begun 1567–69.

11.23 Donato Bramante, the Tempietto, authorized 1502, completed after 1511. San Pietro in Montorio, Rome.

11.24 Pierre Lescot, exterior façade of the Square Court of the Louvre, Paris, begun 1546.

Francis I. The Lescot wing of the Louvre (Fig. **11.24**) has a discomfiting design of superficial detail and unusual proportions, with strange juxtapositions of curvilinearity and rectilinearity. Here we find a continuation of decorative detail applied to exterior wall surfaces in the Renaissance fashion. However, careful mathematical proportions have been replaced by a flattened dome and dissimilar treatments of the shallow arches. The helmet-like dome stands in awkward contrast to the pediment of the central section and wears a sort of crown, perched nervously on top. The relief sculptures of the top level of the central section are far too large to be comfortable in their architectural context.

In this same period, another style sprang up that would significantly influence later eras. Andrea Palladio (1518–80) designed villas and palaces which reflected his clients' individuality and pride in their worldly possessions. The Villa Rotonda in Vicenza (Fig. **11.25**) shows strong classical influences, combining Greek and Roman details. The porticos carry free-standing Ionic columns, and the dome is reminiscent of the Pantheon. The rooms of the villa are arranged symmetrically around the central rotunda. Palladio's mathematical combination of cubes and circles is characteristic of the Renaissance, but he has cleansed the exterior surfaces of detail, placing the decorative sculpture above, in anticipation of baroque treatments. Palladio explained his designs in *Four Books on Architecture*, which were highly influential in establishing canons later used in various "revival" periods. Thomas Jefferson's Monticello in the United States is one such example (see Fig. **14.20**).

THE PERFORMING ARTS

MUSIC

Josquin des Pres continued to compose into the early sixteenth century, but it was a new time politically and musically. After Josquin's death, new composers came to the fore and new music centers developed. Although the sack of Rome by Charles V destroyed the city, its musical traditions survived, and the Papal chapel continued as one of the central musical forces in Europe. Venice, whose powers also diminished, witnessed a burst of creative activity in music, which coincided with her achievements in painting, that created a specifically Venetian musical tradition of great importance. The leading composers after Josquin adopted his techniques and developed them, inventing new techniques and genres that transformed the sound of music. Parody of old forms became common, as did new methods for expressing meaning. A separate genre of instrumental music—that is, separate from literary associations or dance—also

emerged, and from the second quarter of the sixteenth century came distinctly national styles of music. However, a central theme of Franco-Flemish music continued, and two of its major figures were Adrian Willaert and Nicolas Gombert. In addition, the use of movable type made it possible to print music by single impression, and this had a significant effect on the way music was distributed and the nature of the audience it reached.

Nicolas Gombert (c. 1500–56) was master of choirboys in the chapel of Charles V and one of the most astute composers of his time. He wrote in a new style, which avoided pauses and used harmony and imitation. His polyphonic lines consisted of long phrases, filled with clever syncopations that kept the motion flowing smoothly. Apparently Gombert had little concern for expression, in that his musical lines developed almost without regard for the placement of text accents, and his style is marked by harsh dissonances.

The music of Adrian Willaert (c. 1490–1562) rests strongly on the use of parody, but he also began to explore the expressive possibilities that occur when music fits the words both in form and meaning. He became increasingly aware of the benefits of perfect union between melody and text, and this is particularly the case in the Italian Madrigal. Willaert proved highly sensitive to the demands of poetry in his compositions, and as chapelmaster at St Mark's in Venice, he mastered musical declamation and observed strict rules, by which his compositions, according to Gaspar Stocker in 1570, offered to singers "greatest pleasure and no difficulties at all as far as the words are concerned." Stocker was referring to Willaert's collection of motets and madrigals entitled *Musica Nova* (*New Music*), in which many of the twenty-seven motets are settings of Old Testament texts or liturgical sequences, and the twenty-five madrigals are settings of sonnets by Petrarch. Like the composer, the pieces are quite restrained, but his intention and skill at projecting the meaning of the text in music is remarkable. Thus, the "new" element is the composer's care in treating the words in the midst of the moving sound that was characteristic of the music of the time. Undoubtedly, he was the most influential composer of the time, and the influence of Italian humanism encouraged him to seek a perfect marriage between poetry and melody. He excelled in every genre and reflects the Renaissance's admiration of universality.

As we noted, the sixteenth century also gave rise to national styles of music, among which was a particularly identifiable French style, which arose among composers in and around Paris. It was characterized by elegant simplicity and rational spirit, and it is graceful and straightforward, with charming melodies that follow closely the rhythms of the words. In the second quarter of the sixteenth century, Parisian composers leaned toward poetry that did not have fixed rhythms, and their structural for-

LITERATURE

The sixteenth century witnessed the climax and close of what amounted to an Italian monopoly in Renaissance literature. The influence of the Italian Renaissance spread to the rest of Europe, reaching France in the middle third of the century and England in the last third of the century. The common factor everywhere was imitation of the classics. In Italy the writers of the High Renaissance were apparently indifferent to the tragic social and political events to which they bore witness. In the last chapter, we noted something of Machiavelli's view—that of limited hope—but others reacted with bland unconcern and ironic humor. Most, like Castiglione, chose to ignore what was going on. However, it is reasonably clear that after the Spanish sack of Rome in 1527, literature, with perhaps the exception of Torquato Tasso, slipped into mediocrity.

BALDASSARE CASTIGLIONE

In essence, the Renaissance state was monarchial. In fact, the whole movement of the Renaissance was toward monarchial government, as we have seen in France and Spain and will see in England in Chapter 12. In Italy, it may have seemed less so, but it was nonetheless the case in the petty duchies and principalities, and the gentlemen and ladies of the Renaissance were courtiers. The Conte Baldassare Castiglione (1478–1529) was himself the perfect courtier (Fig. **11.29**), and his book *Il Cortegiano* or *The Courtier* became a universal guide to "goodly manners" and "civil conversation" of the court of the Duchy of Urbino. In effect, he was the arbiter of courtly behavior for all of Europe. In this influential work, Castiglione suggests, through an imagined dialogue, a picture of an artistically ordered society, in which cultivated Italians regard social living as a fine art.

Castiglione was raised at the court of Duke Sforza of Milan. He studied Greek, Latin, and Italian poetry, music, painting, and horsemanship. As his portrait reveals, he was a handsome, intelligent man, who entered the service of the Duke of Urbino in 1504, thereby entering an environment with a fabulous library that was the rendezvous of European scholars and artists. As a diplomat, he visited England, became an advisor of Pope Leo X, and papal nuncio of Pope Clement VII to the court of the Holy Roman Emperor Charles V. When the Emperor's troops sacked Rome, Castiglione became the subject of numerous rumors of treason.

The particular character of the book lies in the realistic manner in which the conversations are handled and the way in which the various opinions of the participants are introduced. Above all, *The Courtier* propounds the

11.29 Raphael, *Count Baldassare Castiglione*, 1514. Oil transferred from wood to canvas, 2 ft 9¾ ins × 2 ft 3½ ins (82 × 66 cm). Louvre, Paris.

humanist's ultimate ideals—of men and women of intellectual refinement, cultural grace, moral stability, spiritual insight, and social consciousness. It provided a model of the ideal Renaissance society, but its values are timeless: true worth is determined "by character and intellect rather than by birth."

LUDOVICO ARIOSTO

A second major literary figure of the time was Ludovico Ariosto (1474–1533). Ariosto was a courtier of the House of Este at Ferrara, and was in the civil and diplomatic service, as well as court poet. Classically trained, he wrote most of his work in Latin until he was twenty-five years old. His father died when he was twenty-six, and he assumed responsibility for providing for his four brothers and five sisters. He spent fourteen years as confidential secretary to Cardinal d'Este, and during this time he traveled throughout Italy on political missions. In 1518 he entered the service of the cardinal's brother, the Duke of Ferrara, eventually becoming the duke's director of entertainment. Under Ariosto's supervision, the court enjoyed pageants and dramatic productions, Ariosto himself designing the theatre and scenery and writing a number of the plays. Ariosto lived to see the sack of Rome and the tragic changes that occurred in Italy in the first quarter of the fifteenth century. As early as 1505 he began his masterpiece, *Orlando Furioso*, forty cantos (sections) of which were published in 1516. He continued to revise the work, which became one of the most influential poems of the Renaissance, for nearly thirty years. *Orlando Furioso* (*Roland in a Mad Fury*) is a romantic epic—its forty-six cantos total over 1,200 pages—of "Loves and Ladies, Knights and Arms.... Of Curtesies, and many a Daring Feat." Ariosto depended heavily on the Greco-Roman tradition of Homer and Vergil and borrowed incidents, character types, and rhetorical devices, such as the catalogue of troops and extended simile. Designed for a sophisticated audience, it employs an ottava rima (a stanza of eight lines rhyming abababcc), and it has a polished, graceful style. It became a best-seller throughout Europe.

Orlando Furioso captivated its sixteenth-century readers with its elements of the supernatural trips to the moon, allegorical incidents that taught modesty and chastity, and romantic adventure. However, the characters are shallow and two-dimensional, for Ariosto made no attempt to probe the depths of human behavior or to tackle important issues. Nonetheless, individual incidents are worked out with care and carried through to a climax, after which the next is taken up, and all the loose threads are tied together at the end. *Orlando Furioso* served the Renaissance as a model of the large-scale narrative poem that was written with technical skill, smoothness, and the gracefulness typical of the classics.

A CRITICAL REVIEW

Rather than the wide sweep of relatively homogeneous style, which we have noted in earlier chapters, we are now experiencing a diversity of individualized styles. In architecture we saw three works by three individuals in three styles.

Gombert and Willaert represented a new approach to music.

Theatre caught the Renaissance spirit and adopted, by creating the effect of deep space on a shallow stage, the visual display representative of the perspective tricks of earlier Renaissance painters. It also had a completely distinctive theatrical form.

Compare the structure, balance, and application of detail seen in Bramante's Tempietto, Lecot's Louvre, and Palladio's Villa Rotonda.

Describe and compare their works.

Describe the characteristics of commedia dell 'arte.

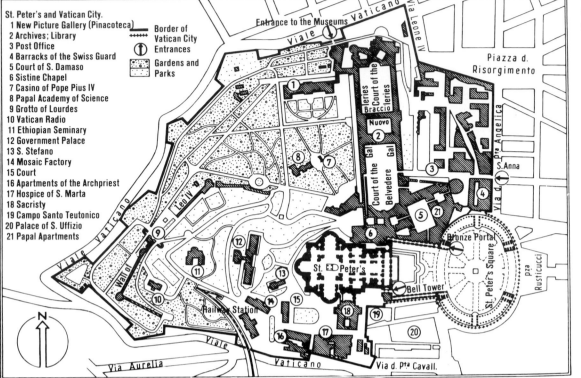

11.32 Plan of the Vatican and St Peter's, Rome.

St. Peter's and Vatican City.
1 New Picture Gallery (Pinacoteca)
2 Archives; Library
3 Post Office
4 Barracks of the Swiss Guard
5 Court of S. Damaso
6 Sistine Chapel
7 Casino of Pope Pius IV
8 Papal Academy of Science
9 Grotto of Lourdes
10 Vatican Radio
11 Ethiopian Seminary
12 Government Palace
13 S. Stefano
14 Mosaic Factory
15 Court
16 Apartments of the Archpriest
17 Hospice of S. Marta
18 Sacristy
19 Campo Santo Teutonico
20 Palace of S. Uffizio
21 Papal Apartments

Border of Vatican City
Entrances
Gardens and Parks

11.33 (*above*) Gian Lorenzo Bernini, statues on the colonnade of St Peter's Square, Rome, colonnade designed 1657.

11.34 (*right*) Michelangelo, Sistine Chapel, Vatican, Rome, showing the ceiling (1508–12) and *Last Judgment* (1534–41).

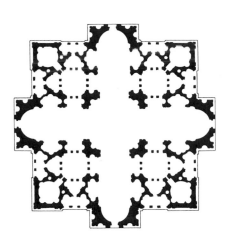

11.35 Bramante's design for St Peter's, 1506.

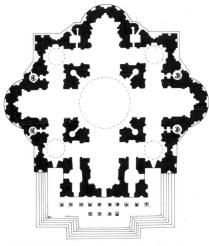

11.36 Michelangelo's design for St Peter's, 1547.

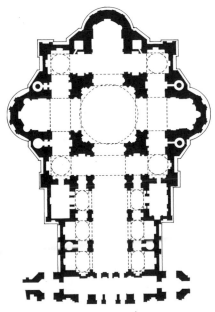

11.37 Plan of St Peter's as built to Michelangelo's design, with alterations by Carlo Maderno, 1606–15.

11.38 Raphael's Loggia, Vatican, Rome, c. 1516–19.

Palace apartments. Based on Raphael's study of ancient Rome and its buildings, the Loggia's theme is one of delight in seemingly inexhaustible inventiveness. Flowers, fruit, vegetables, bizarre animal figures, and winged putti appear throughout. On the ceiling vault is a series of frescoes devoted to Old Testament themes called *Raphael's Bible*. Raphael's *The Deliverance of St Peter* (see Fig. **11.18**) is also found in these apartments.

The Vatican is a rich complex that fully reflects its times and the power and wealth of the Church and the papacy. Perhaps its crowning jewel is the Sistine Chapel (see Figs **11.12**, **11.13**, and **11.14**), with its magnificent ceiling. But the ceiling is only part of a whole. It is the entirety of the Sistine Chapel (Fig. **11.34**) that is a supreme recreation of classical harmony.

CHAPTER TWELVE

RENAISSANCE AND REFORMATION IN NORTHERN EUROPE

A T   A   G L A N C E

The Reformation
The Background
Erasmus and Christian Humanism
Martin Luther
Ulrich Zwingli and Zurich
John Calvin and the New Jerusalem

Science and the Intellect
The Scientific Revival

TECHNOLOGY: Naval Artillery
Michel de Montaigne

The Visual Arts and Architecture
Germany
The Netherlands
France
OUR DYNAMIC WORLD: Ming Dynasty
Porcelain

Music
Germany
France

Synthesis: The Great Age of the Tudors
PROFILE: Christopher Marlowe
MASTERWORK: Marlowe—Doctor Faustus

12.1 Lucas Cranach the Younger, *Martin Luther and the Wittenberg Reformers* (detail), c. 1543. Oil on wood, 27⅝ × 15⅝ (70 × 40 cm). Toledo Museum of Art, Toledo, Ohio.

A CRITICAL LOOK

When we survey the religious map of the world today, we find that in many parts of the world the Roman Catholic Church represents a small minority of those people who call themselves Christian. The pain and separation of the Reformation remain as strong a schism in Christianity as they were in the sixteenth century. Divisions between Protestants and Catholics have been eased by the ecumenical movement of the last twenty-five years, but some Protestant denominations are as anti-Catholic as ever.

As we will see, the Reformation was a complex affair, often religious, but equally often political, in nature, that went far beyond the simple corruptions of the Roman hierarchy during the Renaissance and revealed some truly profound divisions involving important issues of dogma. The Reformation gave us the shape of today's Christianity.

What were the conditions—political and religious—that led to the Protestant Reformation?

What were the basic theological and dogmatic contentions of Erasmus, Luther, Zwingli, and Calvin?

What were the political circumstances that resulted from religious reforms in Germany and Switzerland?

THE REFORMATION

THE BACKGROUND

In this chapter we turn our attention to the north of Europe and examine roughly the same time in history that we pursued in Chapter 11—that is, the sixteenth century. What we are about to see represents a confluence of economic, political, and religious conflicts that, for ease of reference, we call the Reformation. It took place at the same time as the Renaissance period and represented the most shattering and lasting blow the Christian Church has perhaps ever experienced. Of course, it did not just appear out of the blue, but was, rather, the climax of centuries of sectarian agitation—in the fourteenth century, for example, English cries for reform and resentment of papal authority led to an English translation of the Bible. But reform and separation are worlds apart, and it is important to realize that the Reformation did not begin as an attempt to start a new branch of Christianity, but as a sincere attempt to reform what were perceived as serious religious problems.

The Roman Church had always been dominated by Italy, and it had responded to the diverse and unique political climate of the Italian peninsula—for example, to the events we witnessed in Chapter 11 and to the emerging ideas of the Renaissance—with an increasing worldliness and political intrigue that was of great concern to many, especially in Germany. Throughout Roman Catholic Europe, the huge body of clergy had amassed considerable tax-free wealth, much of which came from the sale of indulgences—that is, the selling of forgiveness—a practice that was, as we shall see, particularly repugnant to a monk named Martin Luther. In addition,

secular governments chafed at the Church's tax-free wealth, and the injury was compounded by the fact that the Church taxed the secular sector heavily. Thus, the furor of the Church's response to Luther quickly turned into a battle that was, in many places, as much a political struggle as a theological schism. Popular resentment of central ecclesiastical authority was widespread, and there was enough political stability, even in areas still essentially feudal, to resist domination by Rome.

In addition, many people found existing Church dogma indefensible. As we noted in Chapter 9, some opposition occurred earlier than Luther's among the followers of John Huss, and as we will see, John Calvin's *Institutes of the Christian Religion* affected mid-sixteenth-century Switzerland. In addition, a break with Rome—political rather than religious—occurred in England under Henry VIII, and resulted in the confiscation of all Roman Church property in the Act of Dissolution. Bloody conflicts between Protestants and Catholics laid the groundwork for conditions that led a group of emigrants to the shores of North America less than a century later. The discord of religious rebellion became more clamorous as various Protestant groups arose, some more dogmatic and intolerant than others, and some Protestant groups even persecuted others, while radical groups such as the Anabaptists suffered at the hands of Protestants and Catholics alike.

Although no direct cause-and-effect relationship exists between the revolution in the Church and the emotional disarray in the visual arts—for example, the characteristics of an emerging Mannerism that we witnessed in Chapter 11—the Reformation, coinciding as it does with the end of the High Renaissance and the beginnings of new styles in the visual and performing arts, is an important aspect of the complex events of the Renaissance.

	GENERAL EVENTS	LITERATURE & PHILOSOPHY	VISUAL ART & ARCHITECTURE	THEATRE & MUSIC
1500	Pope Leo X Francis I of France Erasmus Luther		Dürer (**12.8, 12.9, 12.10, 12.11**) Grünewald (**12.12, 12.13**) Altdorfer (**12.14**) Bosch (**12.15**) Clouet (**12.21**)	Claudin de Sermisy Frescobaldi
1525	Peasants' War Ivan IV (the Terrible) of Russia Henry VIII of England Copernicus Dissolution of the monasteries in England	Thomas More (*Utopia*)	Holbein (**12.2**) Cranach (**12.3**) Hilliard (**12.26**)	
1540	Calvin in Geneva Zwingli	Montaigne	Bruegel (**12.16, 12.17, 12.18**)	
1550	Edward VI of England			Shakespeare Marlowe

Timeline 12.1 Renaissance and Reformation in northern Europe.

Map 12.1 A contemporary map of Europe in the 1590s.

A CRITICAL REVIEW

As seems clear from contemporary events in the United States, politics and religion are hardly ever easy to separate. It is too easy to put labels on people, regarding those who openly mix their religion into the political process as "fanatics" or those who insist on absolute separation as "Godless," as some in our society do. Part of the Reformation of the sixteenth century had to do with questions of the mix of civil and religious authority, and the theocracies of Switzerland illustrate the solution proposed by some who wanted separation from the authority of the Roman Church. In places such as Germany things were less certain. Some areas remained loyal to Rome, while others found it more expedient in a more secular realm to do away with Roman authority. In England, there was no Reformation in the strict sense of the word, merely a semantic argument over who was head of the Church. Even today there is a strong Anglo-Catholic strain in the Church of England and its communions, including the Episcopal Church in the United States.

How do Erasmus' views constitute Christian Humanism, and how did that philosophy develop and spread throughout Europe?

On what issues did Luther base his attempts to reform Catholicism?

What circumstances led to Zwingli's rebellion, and what were his dogmatic and theological stands?

What did Calvin believe, and what influences did his beliefs have on Europe and America?

A CRITICAL LOOK

From our viewpoint we can see that the sixteenth century was a complex one. Remember that what we are studying in this chapter happened at the same time as the events we studied in the last chapter. In addition, a new force was rising in the world—the force of science. In the next section, we will examine the thoughts and accomplishments of those individuals who revived science and redirected intellectual endeavor during the century. As you study this material:

Identify and explain the contributions of Vesalius and Copernicus to the revival of science in the sixteenth century.

Explain the ways in which the ideas of Michel de Montaigne contributed to the intellectual changes of the late Renaissance.

of such crusading faith fueled religious revolutions across Europe, and it spread to the Huguenots in France and the Dutch Reformed church in the Netherlands. Its successors could be found in English Puritans, such as Oliver Cromwell in the seventeenth century, and the fiery Scottish Presbyterian followers of John Knox. It even spread across the Atlantic ocean to the early Puritan settlers of America.

Calvin's ultimate influence went beyond the bounds of religion to economics. His call for a capitalistic spirit based on unceasing labor in gainful pursuits for the glory of God may well have inspired the disciplined, rigorous drive that made Calvinist Huguenots and Puritans among the most successful businessmen in France and England, respectively. It has been suggested that Calvinism may have been an important cause in the growth of the capitalist system in the West.

SCIENCE AND THE INTELLECT

THE SCIENTIFIC REVIVAL

Into the religious upheaval of the late Renaissance and its human-centered universe burst the frightening revelations of scientific discovery. The spirit of inquiry was particularly concerned with astronomy, and in 1530 Copernicus transformed the world and humankind's perception of itself, its universe, and its God by formulating a heliocentric—sun-centered—theory of the universe. Although it was not immediately accepted, Copernican theory was devastating to those whose view of reality

TECHNOLOGY: PUTTING DISCOVERY TO WORK

Naval Artillery

A major technological change in the fifteenth century was the improvement of cannons and the development of lighter weapons, which, in particular, benefited naval artillery. However, the evolution of naval artillery depended on another peculiar factor on board ship. The first cannons, which were iron, were placed on a wooden cradle, and sailing ships were able to carry these cannons because they had space along the decks. Cannons were placed in a pivoting form (Fig. **12.7A**) attached to the framework of the bulwarks. These small-caliber guns were used to attack personnel on the deck and castles of an enemy

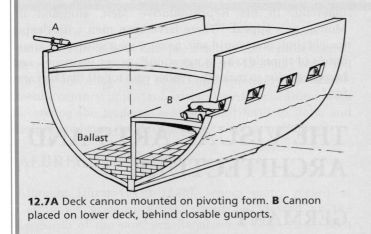

12.7A Deck cannon mounted on pivoting form. **B** Cannon placed on lower deck, behind closable gunports.

ship, but they were not sufficiently powerful to damage the hull of a ship. The tops of ships could be equipped with as many as 200 cannons, and such large numbers often proved of great menace to the crew and the rigging. Larger caliber cannons that were capable of attacking the hulls of ships, demolishing their tops, and sinking them, were so heavy that placing them on the deck or castles made the ships unstable. Sailing vessels are stable only when their weight topside is compensated for by ballast in the hold. Heavy cannons on deck would have required massive amounts of ballast.

At the beginning of the sixteenth century, the plan of merchant ships was altered to produce a warship capable of supporting the weight of the artillery, counterbalanced by ballast. Around 1500 a man from Brest named Descharges had the idea of placing the cannon on a lower deck and opening gunports for the artillery. Positioning guns in this way shielded them from the firing of lighter deck cannon on an opposing ship (see Fig. **12.7B**). Thus, the end of the sixteenth century marks a turning point in naval warfare, and eighty-eight years later, one of the most significant naval battles of all time—that is, the defeat of the Spanish Armada by the English—brought this development to a new level of importance.

---

placed humankind as the ultimate being in an earth-centered universe.

The sixteenth-century scientific revival, which came hard on the heels of religious reformation, revealed itself in two different forms represented in two different books, both published in 1543. Both books and their authors, however dissimilar, had a decisive impact on the scientific movement. The first was *On the Fabric of the Human Body* by a Fleming, Andreas Vesalius (1514–64). Its significance lies in its descriptive reporting and skillful illustrations, which render the structures of the human body in space in a way that represents the first step towards photographic realism in science. Vesalius was a precocious young man who showed great speed and facility in getting a tremendous amount of material into print within six years. He was an ambitious and popular teacher at the University of Padua, which at the time was becoming increasingly important as a center for the teaching of medicine, and his impact on science was as the founder of a method of investigation—for nearly two hun-

dred years, all discussion of how living organisms worked was founded on anatomy. Vesalius greatly improved the range and precision of knowledge of the structure of the human body. He had explored the body more thoroughly than anyone before, and that exploration proved to be an essential foundation for the rational physiology that followed in the seventeenth century.

The second book to be published in 1543, *On the Revolutions of the Celestial Orbs*, was by the Pole Nicholas Copernicus (1473–1543), and it was a work of philosophy and technical mathematics. Copernicus was an ecclesiastical administrator who had nurtured his great idea for nearly forty years. He did not make observations himself and did not use others' observations, nor did he aim at predictive accuracy. When the book was published, Copernicus was a dying man, already famous but with little in print. His impact lay in the way he exploited a great new principle—that in the system of the heavens there is a perfect reciprocity between sun-centered systems and earth-centered systems. Copernicus believed in a sun-cen-

12.9 Albrecht Dürer, *The Four Horsemen of the Apocalypse*, c. 1497–98. Woodcut, 15²/₅ × 11 ins (39.2 × 27.9 cm). Museum of Fine Arts, Boston (Bequest of Francis Bullard).

ticular quality. The picture is created by building up individual lines, formed when the artist cuts into the block of wood, leaving only exposed edges to which ink will be applied and then pressed onto the paper. Dürer shows remarkable skill in creating lines of tremendous delicacy, which combine into a poignantly complex picture. Notice in particular his treatment of the horses—Death rides an emaciated old nag, while the other three horsemen are astride powerfully muscular steeds. The power of the print emerges from both its technical and aesthetic aspects—the complexity of the linear expression of the woodcut gives the work some of its frenetic quality, but powerful diagonal sweeps add to the composition, as does the raw emotional terror of the human elements.

Another print from the same series, *St Michael Quelling the Dragon* (Fig. **12.10**), shows the same inspiration of St John's awesome visions. Again, we find great power in the black and white linear print. In some ways, its limited size—15³/₄ x 11¹/₈ inches (39.5 x 28.5 centimeters)—adds to the dynamics of the work, compressing the

12.10 Albrecht Dürer, *St Michael Quelling the Dragon*, from the *Apocalypse* series, c. 1497–8. Woodcut, 15³/₄ × 11¹/₈ (39.5 × 28.5 cm). Die Heimlich Offenbarung Iohannis, Nuremberg, Germany.

the Apocalypse (Fig. **12.9**), for example, and its medieval preoccupation with superstition, famine, fear, and death typify German art of this period, and it places Dürer at the pivot point between medieval and Renaissance styles. *The Four Horsemen of the Apocalypse* is the fourth work in a series of woodcuts. This print presents a frightening vision of doomsday and the omens leading up to it, as described in the Revelation of St John, the last book of the Bible. In the foreground, Death tramples a bishop, and working toward the background, Famine swings a scales, War brandishes a sword, and Pestilence draws a bow. Underneath, trampled by the horses' hoofs, lies the human race. The crowding and angularity of shapes are reminiscent of late Gothic style, and yet the perspective foreshortening and three-dimensionality of figures reflects the influence of the Italian Renaissance. We can read human character and emotion in the faces of the figures, which humanize them and give them a sense of reality and a proximity to life that adds depth to the meaning of the work.

The technique of the woodcut gives the work its par-

12.11 Albrecht Dürer, *Four Apostles*, Oil on wood, each panel 7 ft 2 ins × 2 ft 6 ins (215 × 76 cm). Altepinakothek, Munich, Germany.

raw energy of the piece into such a small space that it appears almost to cry out for explosive emotional relief. Compared to the sprawling frescoes of the Italian Renaissance masters, it seems minuscule, but that reduction in SCALE in no way detracts from either its vision or its technical perfection. If anything, its scale enhances both.

Dürer's last major work was a painting entitled the *Four Apostles* (Fig. **12.11**). It is a diptych—that is, two panels—portraying John and Peter in the left panel and Mark, who was not an apostle, and Paul in the right. The panels were originally intended as the wings of a triptych, of which the central panel would show the Madonna and Child with saints. However, the effects of the Reformation made such a rendering impossible in Nuremberg in 1526, and so the piece was never completed. When Dürer presented the panels to the city council, he gave them inscriptions of Luther's translation of the New Testament that warned all who read them not to confuse human error for the will of God. Dürer enthusiastically supported the Lutheran Reformation, agreeing with Luther's views on papal supremacy, but he found equally repugnant some of the extreme positions of those Protestants who advocated radical experiments, including polygamy and communism.

MATTHIAS GRÜNEWALD

Matthias Grünewald (c. 1475–1528), Dürer's contemporary, was deeply affected by Luther's reformation. His real name is believed to have been Mathis Gothardt Neithardt, and the name "Grünewald," by which he will always be known, was given to him by his first biographer, the seventeenth-century writer Joachim von Sandrart. As well as an artist, Grünewald was also an architect and hydraulic engineer. Unlike Dürer, he never went to Italy, but because he was implicated in the peasants' rebellion, he fled to Halle in Saxony, where he died. Second only to Dürer among Germany's great artists, Grünewald, unlike Dürer, remained relatively faithful to earlier traditions. He apparently knew of Dürer, and some of Dürer's influence can be seen in Grünewald's work. For example, the figure of the Virgin in the Isenheim altarpiece (Fig. **12.12**) recalls a famous watercolor by Dürer. Nonetheless, although Grünewald retains the emotional expressiveness of the medieval period, he did learn how to handle space and perspective and how to treat flesh from the Italians of the Renaissance. The Isenheim altarpiece, Grünewald's greatest work, was painted between 1512 and 1515 for the church of the Hospital of Saint Anthony in Isenheim near Colmar, France. It takes the form of an elaborate series of painted wings for a carved wooden shrine. The *Crucifixion* occupies the outermost wings and is visible when the altarpiece is closed. The picture's tragic intensity is amplified by the stark roughness of the cross itself: two freshly hewn logs. We can feel the weight of the body of Christ and the agony of pain in the grotesquely upraised fingers and the bending of the crossbar under the weight of the inert body of the dead Christ. Everything about the rendering puts us in mind of the torment of such a death—the arm bones seem almost torn from their sockets, and the crown of thorns, unlike the neat circular arrangements often depicted, is a misshapen mass of thorns thrust down over the entire head. Christ's face is a ghastly grayish-green: the pallor of death. The body is a mass of scars and scratches exuding deep red drops of blood, and the feet have been punctured by a giant spike.

The figure of Christ is surrounded by John the Baptist, above whose pointing finger appear the words "He must increase, but I must decrease" (John 3:30). Next to John stands the Lamb of God, holding a cross and pulling a chalice to its breast. Mary Magdalene throws herself at the feet of the cross, while St John the Evangelist holds the Virgin Mary who has fainted from grief. Grünewald sets the figures of the scene in stark contrast to a greenish-black sky. The emotionalism of the painting must have

12.12 Matthias Grünewald, *Crucifixion*, central panel of the Isenheim altarpiece, c. 1513–15. Oil on wood, 8 ft × 10 ft 1 in (2.44 × 3.07 m). Unterlindenmuseum, Colmar, France.

12.13 Matthias Grünewald, *The Meeting of St Anthony and St Paul the Hermit*, c. 1513. Oil on wood, 8 ft 10 ins × 4 ft 8¼ ins (2.65 × 1.41 m). Unterlindenmuseum, Colmar, France.

been particularly moving to the patients of the hospital who were brought before it daily and who must have recognized in it the message that Christ understood their suffering because of the extreme nature of his own. In this painting, Grünewald has raised the grotesque to the level of the tragic and, as a result, has created a painting of great appeal and beauty.

One of the wings of the shrine reveals to us another of Grünewald's expressive masterpieces, *The Meeting of St Anthony and St Paul the Hermit* (Fig. **12.13**). The figure of St Anthony is a portrait of the Abbot of Isenheim, Guido Guersi, whose coat of arms appears below the figure. The figure of St Paul is a portrait of Grünewald himself. This part of the rotating altarpiece would have been revealed on feast-days, while other stages would be revealed on Sundays and weekdays. It also contains depictions of the Temptation of St Anthony, the Nativity, and the Resurrection. In *The Meeting of St Anthony and St Paul the Hermit*, we again find examples of Grünewald's technical mastery and emotional content. Notice the hand of St Paul. Its exquisite gesture carries such expressiveness that it stands as a complement to the agony expressed in the hands of Christ in the *Crucifixion*. In the case of the *Meeting*, Grünewald amplifies the expression of the work by placing its central figures in front of a fantastic landscape of contorted exotic vegetation and animal forms.

ALBRECHT ALTDORFER

Similar to Grünewald in imaginative power was the painter Albrecht Altdorfer (1480–1538). Born in Regensburg, a beautiful Bavarian city on the Danube, Altdorfer had a special gift and affinity for landscape. In his most famous painting, *Battle of Alexander and Darius on the Issus* (Fig. **12.14**), we find the ancient battle between Darius III of Persia and Alexander the Great in 333 B.C. depicted as if it were a modern battle, probably the Battle of Ravenna in 1512 or the Battle of Parvia in 1525. What is most striking in this particular work is the fact that Altdorfer has painted thousands of individual soldiers in a space barely 5 feet (1.5 meters) high and 4 feet (1.2 meters) wide.

In contrast with some of the massive perspectives of the Italian Renaissance that we have examined, Altdorfer takes us up high for our perspective vantage point, and from this elevated viewpoint, we get a bird's eye glimpse of the solid mass of soldiers coming towards us out of a fantasy landscape that recedes without benefit of atmospheric perspective to the edge of the earth, whose very

12.14 Albrecht Altdorfer, *Battle of Alexander and Darius on the Issus*, 1529. Oil on wood, 5 ft 3¼ ins × 4 ft (1.58 × 1.20 m) Altepinakothek, Munich, Germany.

curvature we can see, almost as if we were astronauts gazing at earth from space. Our eyes are free to drift from point to point, for there is very little in the subject of the painting—that is, the battle—to hold our attention. A few fluttering flags create focal points, but the human element is lost in the swarm of thousands of indistinguishable bodies. Much more interesting than the human spectacle, massive though it is, is the glorious landscape and its rugged mountains, alpine lakes, swirling clouds, and glowing sunrise. A tablet with a lengthy Latin inscription and unfurling pennant floats over the scene, hung theatrically and magically in the sky. The stunning effect of the overall work stems from its absolute graphic clarity and accuracy. Each detail emerges crystal clear from foreground to background, and the perspective depiction of castles and armies winding away from us is nothing short of remarkable.

THE NETHERLANDS

HIERONYMUS BOSCH

Around 1500 the tradition began by Jan van Eyck (see Chapter 9) diminished as ideas were brought to the Netherlands, with trade, from Italy. It became a period of crisis and change for painters, and both the grand style of the High Renaissance and the emotional Mannerist movement that followed made strong inroads into the art of the country. However, the two greatest painters of the time in the Netherlands seem to have remained solidly apart from the styles of sixteenth-century Italy. The first of these painters was Hieronymus Bosch (c. 1450–1516). His fantastic works are all we know about him, and we do not even know when they were painted. Bosch has been an intriguing figure to modern individuals for a number of reasons. First, as we noted, is the total lack of information about him as a human being. Second, is the amazing likeness of his work to the images of the twentieth-century Surrealists whom we will meet in Chapter 17. Third, is the fact that his imagery lends itself to fascinating psychological probing and speculation. Fourth, the complexity and imagery of his most famous work *The Garden of Earthly Delights* (see Fig. **12.15**) has fueled almost feverish rumors of some connection with heretical sects. However, what little evidence there is suggests that Bosch was an orthodox Roman Catholic, and we do know that his work was admired by the Catholic monarch, Philip II of Spain.

Bosch was clearly a man of tremendous imaginative powers. Had that not been the case, he could not have created the truly fantastic depictions present in *Garden of Delights*. What we see in this illustration is the central panel of a three-panelled work. The left panel, called *The Creation of Eve*, is a fairly straightforward portrayal, but,

12.15 Hieronymus Bosch, *The Garden of Earthly Delights*, triptych, left panel *Garden of Eden*, centre panel *The World Before the Flood*, right panel *Hell*, c. 1505. Side panels 86 × 36 ins (218.5 × 91.5 cm), centre panel 86 × 76 ins (218.5 × 195 cm). Prado, Madrid.

like the central panel, it contains images that might remind us of Dr Seuss. However, the large central panel, measuring more than 7 feet (2.1 meters) by more than 6 feet (1.8 meters), takes us into a much more complex and mystifying world. Without exaggeration, we could probably spend the remainder of this book trying to describe each of the little scenarios present in this portrayal. Bosch's choice of color alone would lead us into a miasma of analysis and speculation. The vibrant pinks played against darkened blues draw the picture together and give emphases that run throughout. Of course, the figure groupings fascinate, too. They consist of youthful, thin, muscle-less individuals frolicking naked amid gigantic fruits, clams, fish, and so on. Other animals parade in line around the work. Although no explicit sexual activity is shown, the images are clearly erotic and have sexual connotations in several languages. But what is probably most arresting about the work is the collection of strange "machines" like the one that sits in the center of the lake in the background. What could Bosch have had in mind here? Is he depicting a paradise in which everyone may freely engage in their sexual fascinations, or is he making a statement about earthly life wherein sexual desire is the central force in human thought? One reading of the painting is a condemnation of erotic activity—but all the while one wonders about Bosch's obvious fascination with it.

PIETER BRUEGEL THE ELDER

The second Netherlandish painter of note is the sixteenth-century master, Pieter Bruegel the Elder (c. 1525/30–69). After traveling extensively in Italy, when he developed a deep love for the beauty of the southern Italian countryside as well as a mastery of Italian painting styles, and France in the 1550s, Bruegel worked in Antwerp and Brussels. A close follower of Bosch, he was influenced by Bosch's pessimism and fantasy, and although his work avoided the nudes of Renaissance Italian art, it captured its harmony of space and form and infused it with a northern European perspective on life. We can see the Italian influence in the colorful *Landscape with the Fall of Icarus* (Fig. **12.16**). The painting tells the story of Icarus, who, against the advice of his father, flew so high that the wax of his wings was melted by the sun. Icarus was a popular symbol in Italian art partly because it represented unbridled ambition and partly because it gave artists an opportunity to depict the human body in flight or falling. In Bruegel's portrayal, Icarus is hardly more than a sidebar. In fact, were it not for the title of the painting, we probably would barely notice him at all. His only manifestation in the painting is his legs, about to submerge with the rest of him under the water at the lower right. Instead, Bruegel gives us a warm and comfortable depiction of a farmer plowing his field, a singing shepherd, and an elegant ship, its sails billowing in the freshening breeze. Mountains the color of huge icebergs reach into a bright sky at the far horizon, and, as in Altdorfer's *Battle* (see Fig. **12.14**), we see the earth's cur-

12.16 Pieter Bruegel the Elder, *Landscape with the Fall of Icarus*, c. 1554–5. Oil on panel (transferred to canvas), 2 ft 5 ins × 3ft 8¹/₈ ins (74 × 112 cm). Musées Royaux des Beaux-Arts, Brussels.

12.17 Pieter Bruegel the Elder, *The Triumph of Death*, c. 1562–4. Oil on panel, 3 ft 10 ins × 5 ft 3³/₄ (1.17 × 1.62 m). Museo del Prado, Madrid.

12.21 Jean Clouet, *Francis I*, c. 1525–30. Tempera and oil on wood, 38¼ × 29½ ins (96 × 74 cm). Louvre, Paris.

(Fig. **12.21**), done between 1525 and 1530, shows a self-indulgent, calculating character—Francis was, in fact, notorious for his sexual affairs—but the likeness is stiff and formal, with the same kind of distorted, mannered appearance that we saw in Bronzino's *Portrait of a Young Man* (see Fig. **11.21**). The line and form of the foreground clashes with the decor of the background, and the brocade and stripes of the costume lead the eye downward to focus on the king's left hand, which seems to toy nervously with his poniard.

MUSIC

GERMANY

Unlike Zwingli and Calvin, who either removed music from worship entirely or severely limited its use, Martin Luther saw music as an integral part of liturgical worship. As we saw, the hallmark of the Reformation was the primacy of the Word of God, as revealed in the Bible, which was to be heard, obeyed, and incorporated into daily life.

The Swiss reformers distrusted music because it had a power of its own that they believed could subvert the Word of God. Music also had secular connections—often with immoral connotations—that made Zwingli and Calvin nervous. Luther, on the other hand, saw music in a more positive light and believed that it could be used for the glorification of God. He found in music a connection to the prophets, whom he believed used music to proclaim truth through psalms and song.

The Lutheran Reformation, therefore, brought many changes to Church music. Even after the separation, Lutheran music continued to have many Roman Catholic characteristics, including some Latin texts and plainsong chants. However, the most important contribution to the Lutheran Reformation was the chorale. Contemporary hymns, many of which date back to Martin Luther for both text and tune, illustrate this form. Our four-part harmonies are a later modification, although the recent edition of the Lutheran Book of Worship attempts to return to the early chorale form. Originally, the chorale was a single melody, stemming from the chant or folk song, and a text. Congregational singing was in unison and without accompaniment. The liturgical experience that developed in Lutheran churches, particularly in Wittenberg under Luther's leadership, contributed a rich and varied combination of Latin and German, traditional monody and contemporary polyphony, the music of Catholic and Lutheran composers, and choral and organ music, all held together by congregational hymnody.

Lutheranism also contributed a considerable body of polyphonic choral settings, many from Luther's principal collaborator Johann Walter (1496–1574). These settings vary tremendously in style and source, some being based on German *Lieder* (secular songs) and some on Flemish motets. Polyphony, a complex texture, is not, however, ideal for congregational singing, and polyphonic settings were uniformly reserved for the choir. By the end of the sixteenth century, Lutheran congregational singing had changed again, with the organ being given an expanded role. The congregation sang the melody, but was no longer unaccompanied—an organ played harmonic parts.

Also in Germany in the late fifteenth century the Renaissance spirit, with its secular traditions, produced polyphonic *Lieder*. These predominantly three-part secular songs provided much of the melodic basis for the church hymns of Lutheranism after the Reformation. Heinrich Isaac (1450–1517) was probably the first and most notable German *Lied* composer of this era. A prolific musician, his diverse background, which included living at various times in Italy, the Netherlands, and France, gave his work an international flavor. He and other composers of *Lieder* adapted folk songs into polyphonic settings. The frequent usage and refashioning of this type of composition can be seen in one of Isaac's most famous works, "Innsbruck, I Must Leave Thee." The song was originally a folk love song, but Isaac changed the song into a polyphonic piece with words by the Emperor Maximilian. Later, he used the melody in his own sacred work, the *Missa Carminum*. The song then became widely known in another adaptation under the sacred title, "O World, I Now Must Leave Thee." Even Johann Sebastian Bach used the *Innsbruck Lied* in the *St Matthew Passion*.

FRANCE

Paris retained its importance as a musical center for centuries. In the fifteenth century the French Chapel Royal employed some of the greatest musicians, and by the mid-sixteenth century, a new French style of music had emerged. In the late 1520s, again thanks to mass printing, vast quantities of music, written by composers living and working in and around Paris and representing a markedly different style, began to appear. The two greatest French composers of the time were Claudin de Sermisy (c. 1490–1562) and Clement Janequin (c. 1485–c. 1560). In the 1530s and 1540s they were associated with a new kind of chanson (song), known as the Parisian chanson, which represented a genre that perfectly captured the elegant simplicity and rational spirit of French musicians.

Many of Sermisy's chansons are short, graceful, straightforward, lyrical pieces with charming melodies that closely follow the texts they set. We see the simplicity of his composition in a song like *Tant que vivray* (Fig. **12.22**), a setting of a poem by Clement Marot. It is charming and captivating, and its flow is completely controlled by the flow of the words. Not all Parisian chansons were so simple and lyrical—other composers wrote narrative chansons that were humorous and ribald. Between them, however, Sermisy and Janequin wrote more than four hundred chansons of various sorts, some lyrical, some narrative; some chordal and others polyphonic. Sermisy

12.22 Claudin de Sermisy, *Tant que vivray*.

excelled in composing delicate love songs, while Janequin's works typically express the vivacious and irreverent side of the French character. Today, Janequin is best remembered for his long descriptive chansons—for example, *Le chant des oiseaux* (*The Song of the Birds*) — in which he explored a particular theme—in this instance bird songs, but also battles, hunts, street cries, and ladies' gossip—that allowed him to make a virtuoso display of onomatopoeia (words that sound like their reference). *The Song of the Birds* uses a series of slow-moving chords to frame a rich jumble of elaborate animal noises which make up the central point of this amusing piece.

A CRITICAL REVIEW

Our examination of the art of northern Europe has been straightforward. Some comparisons will help us build our confidence in perceiving and responding to works of art.

Using the elements of line, form, and color, compare one painting by Grünewald with one painting by Altdorfer. Now do the same exercise with Bosch and Bruegel.

In what ways did Albrecht Dürer bring the Renaissance to visual art in northern Europe?

Describe the music of the French composers Claudin de Sermisy and Clement Janequin.

SYNTHESIS
The Great Age of the Tudors

In 1485 the Wars of the Roses came to an end, and Henry VII, the first Tudor, became king. His son, Henry VIII, succeeded, at the height of the humanist Renaissance and the Lutheran Reformation, in asserting the national, independent character of the English throne. Whether through desire for a son and heir or from pure ambition, Henry VIII came in conflict with Rome over the pope's refusal to grant him a divorce, eventually rejecting Rome and proclaiming himself head of the Church of England. The turmoil with Rome took a heavy toll: in 1533 Henry was excommunicated, and two years later Henry's close advisor and a staunch Roman Catholic, Sir Thomas More, was executed for treason. Between 1536 and 1539 the Act of Dissolution dissolved all monasteries and created a nobility based on the wealth of those who were loyal to the state. After Henry's death in 1547, a period of instability followed, with Edward VI (r. 1547–53) supporting the Reformation, and Mary Tudor (r. 1553–8) instituting a "Spanish-style" Catholic reaction. Elizabeth I, who became queen in 1558, ended the uncertainty. She consolidated the Acts of Supremacy and Uniformity by which her father and brother had broken from Rome,

and she stood firm against both foreign "Papists" and rebellious Puritans at home. The 1534 Act of Supremacy had made the king head of the Church of England, and the 1559 Act of Uniformity made Elizabeth I head of the episcopal hierarchy of the new Church of England. She instituted a national religion, later called "Anglicanism," that, in effect, represented a compromise between Protestant dogmatism and episcopal discipline and hierarchy. For this reason, Anglicanism may accurately be seen as not a Protestant faith. The Anglican Church is based on two documents, the Thirty-nine Articles and the *Book of Common Prayer*. Elizabeth "allowed" her rival to the throne, Franco-Scottish Mary Stuart, Queen of Scots, to be executed in 1587, and her rule was further strengthened by the catastrophic destruction of the Spanish Armada in 1588. The forty-five years of Elizabeth's reign consolidated an English national identity and gave birth to a magnificent cultural Renaissance, especially in literature and theatre, with lesser accomplishments in music, visual art, and architecture. It was a time of empire, with Sir Francis Drake leaving in 1577 to circumnavigate the globe.

12.23 Exterior of Wollaton Hall, Nottingham, UK, 1588.

VISUAL ART AND ARCHITECTURE

During the Tudor period the greatest and most lasting influences on English visual art and architecture were not English but Italian, Netherlandish, and German, although England would achieve greatness in other arts, as we will see. Henry VIII had been so impressed by reports about Francis I's great château of Fontainebleau that he built the palace of Nonsuch, which no longer exists. Thereafter and during the reigns of Edward VI and Mary I, French influence in architecture remained paramount. Netherlandish influence followed in the reign of Elizabeth I. The reasons for these outside influences may lie in England's strong commercial ties with both France and the Netherlands, although Italianate influences were present in the scenery for the theatrical court masques of Elizabethan times, which were designed by Inigo Jones. Certainly, England had strong links with the continent in terms of the Protestant Reformation, which saw its political counterpart in Henry VIII's divorce from Catherine of Aragon, the daughter of Ferdinand and Isabella of Spain. The Act of Supremacy installed the King of England as the head of the Church of England, and England became a place of refuge for both French and Dutch Protestants fleeing from persecution in their own countries. In addition, England had early become familiar with humanist learning through the visits of Erasmus, and through the "Oxford Reformers" and Sir Thomas More.

The preeminent English architect of the period was Robert Smythson (c. 1535–1614). One of his most famous houses is Wollaton Hall near Nottingham (Fig. **12.23**). Designed for the sheriff of Nottingham, Sir Francis Willoughby, and completed in 1588, it shows Italian influences dating to Serlio (see Chapter 11), but is a unique application of the style. The tall, forceful central hall is illuminated by clerestory windows and topped by a turreted chamber that rises above the ornamented façade like an overweight crown—compare the Lescot façade of the Louvre, Figure **11.24**. The proportions established by such a design are totally without precedent. The central hall is flanked by equally fanciful toppings on the wings, whose gables resemble the façades of Renaissance Italian churches and the bell gables of the Netherlands. One might conclude that there is as much fantasy in Smythson's designs as there is in Bosch and Bruegel, and we must remember that in England this was the time of Edmund Spenser, whose fantasy in the epic poem *The Faerie Queene* we will note later in this chapter. Like Spenser's poetry, Wollaton Hall, whose first two stories would leave it sufficient, rises up in dreamlike majesty.

A German painter whose work in London made him the favorite of Henry VIII, Hans Holbein the Younger (c. 1497–1543), came from a family of Augsburg painters all of whose reputations he eclipsed. He traveled widely in France and Italy and was strongly influenced by the work of Mantegna and Leonardo (see Chapter 11). It is possible that Holbein's letter of introduction to Henry VIII came from Erasmus, who was impressed by the young artist's promise. Erasmus did provide Holbein a letter of introduction to Sir Thomas More, who became the artist's principal patron and protector during his first visit to England, when Holbein undertook an ambitious portrait of Sir Thomas More and his family, a work that has not survived. Shortly after arriving in England for the second time in 1532, Holbein became court painter to Henry VIII, who set him up in a studio in St James's Palace. Holbein painted a series of portraits of the king, including that seen in Figure **12.24**. There is such control of technique here that Henry almost comes to life in all his obesity and obsessive temperament. Equally sensitive is the portrayal of Jane Seymour (Fig. **12.25**), and the artist's vibrancy, control, and acute observation give us the sense that we know this person, who appears almost ready to leave the canvas and join us in polite conversation. There is such delicacy in the portrayal of details that the textures seem to lift off the surface. The harmony and symmetry of the pose gives the painting a quiet and yet strong elegance that mark Holbein's style.

12.24 Hans Holbein the Younger, *Henry VIII in Wedding Dress*, 1540. Oil on panel, 35¹⁄₂ × 30 ins (89 × 75 cm). Galleria Nazionale d'Arte Antica, Rome.

12.25 (*right*) Hans Holbein the Younger, *Jane Seymour*, 1536. Oil on wood, 26³/₄ × 19 ins (66 × 48 cm). Kunsthistorisches Museum, Vienna.

12.26 (*far right*) Nicholas Hilliard, *A Youth Leaning Against a Tree with Roses*, c.1590. Parchment, 5³/₈ × 2³/₄ ins (14 × 7 cm). Victoria & Albert Museum, London.

The second half of the sixteenth century gave England its first native Renaissance master in the area of painting. Nicholas Hilliard (c. 1547–1619) is best known for his miniatures and small portraits like that of the unidentified *Youth Leaning Against a Tree with Roses* (Fig. **12.26**). This miniature, barely 5 inches by 3 inches (14 x 7 centimeters), is done in watercolor on parchment. Apart from the rather dreamy expression of its subject and the romanticized setting, the work tells us more about the costume of the period than anything else, but we can sense Hilliard's delicate touch and command of fine detail, which is often more difficult in small scale than it is in large. Hilliard also shows a clear sense of balance and color quality, as he encircles the young man with green leaves, which pull the floor of the painting up to its apex, and carries the umbers of the tree, the young man's hair, and the elongated rose stems in graceful curves to balance the elliptical outline of the painting itself.

LITERATURE AND DRAMA

In England Renaissance literature and drama flowered during the last quarter of the sixteenth century. After the seemingly interminable Wars of the Roses and the turbulence of the Reformation, under Elizabeth I England entered a period of political and social stability that engendered a mood of optimism and readiness to experiment in cultural matters.

Lyric poetry enjoyed wide popularity, and the ability to compose a sonnet or to coin an original and witty phrase was regarded as essential in any courtier, while the growing and increasingly prosperous middle class—no longer confined to the large towns, but extending throughout the shires and country towns—demanded increasingly sophisticated entertainment. At the same time a large and educated readership, women as well as men, also developed. Writers and booksellers quickly responded to this new market. An early and notable testament to this upsurge in interest came in Sir Philip Sidney's *A Defense of Poesie* (published posthumously in 1595), a brilliant and forceful polemic, which laid claim to the cultural high ground for verse. Sidney (1554–86), in many ways the model English Renaissance courtier and man of letters, had read widely and judiciously in ancient Italian and French literature. His sonnets, best represented in *Astrophel and Stella*, perfectly embodied the delicacy, elegance, wit, and expressiveness of contemporary writing.

The mantel of Elizabethan poetry falls, however, on the shoulders of Edmund Spenser (c. 1552–99). Born in London to middle-class parents, he was well educated in humanist disciplines and the classics, and he also studied English composition and drama. He received two degrees from Cambridge University, where he developed a deep love of poetry and made a wide group of friends who turned out to be both intellectually stimulating and politically useful. Although he enjoyed aristocratic patronage, poetry, although popular, was not at the time a particularly desirable career, and his first work *The Shepheardes Calendar*, dedicated to Philip Sidney, was published under a pseudonym in 1579. Meticulously symmetrical, it reveals Spenser's impulse toward experimentation in verse types. The result is a quaint and moderately charming poem, in which a group of shepherds, representing Spenser and his friends, reveal their ideas about love, poetry, and religous feeling. Writing did not give Spenser a steady income, and in 1580 he took a position in Ireland as private secretary to the new Governor, Lord Grey of Wilton. Spenser lived in Ireland for the rest of his life, regarding himself as an exile and having little sympathy with the Irish. He approved of Lord Grey's cruel policy of military plunder and portrayed him sympathetically in *The Faerie Queene* and a report on the *View of the Present State of Ireland*.

The Faerie Queene, which was circulated in manuscript form long before it was published, was widely admired. In 1589 Spenser returned to London with Sir Walter Raleigh, who had read *The Faerie Queene* and who represented for Spenser a way to patronage and position. When the first parts were published in 1590, the work was dedicated to the "most mighty and magnificent" Empress Elizabeth, "the greatest Gloriana," the heroine of the poem. The work made Spenser famous, and he gained a small pension from it. However, he failed to gain either an important position or a patron, and he returned to Ireland a disillusioned man. Over the years, he published many more poems and enjoyed great fame, but had little material benefit.

In the summer of 1598 the Irish rebelled against England. Spenser's home was burned and ransacked, and he barely escaped to England with his wife and four children. He died soon after, an emotional and physical wreck. Even in death, the ironic juxtaposition of fame and ill-fortune continued, for while poets accompanied his body to burial in Westminster Abbey, a monument ordered by Queen Elizabeth was never erected.

Although his own generation revered his great skill in fashioning a new literature from the classics, Chaucer, and the French and Italian Renaissance poets, today, Spenser remains one of the least read of the great English poets. By the sixteenth century Chaucer's language had become archaic, and Spenser, seen as Chaucer's successor, so reshaped the crafting of verse, created such a rich vividness in his scenes and imagery, and developed such variety in his sounds that he became "teacher" to the great English poets who were yet to come—for example, Milton, Pope, Keats, and Tennyson. Nevertheless, *The Faerie Queene* is so poetic in its explorations and so lacking in the narrative movement and

PROFILE

Christopher Marlowe (1564–93)

The English dramatist Christopher Marlowe was an important predecessor of Shakespeare. He was the son of a Canterbury shoemaker, and he obtained a bachelor's degree from Corpus Christi College, Cambridge, in 1584, progressing to the master's degree after some difficulty about irregular attendance and a letter from the Privy Council certifying the worthwhileness of his government employment, part of which had taken him abroad as a member of the Queen's secret service. Thereafter, he resided in London and wrote actively for the theatre. Unorthodox in religious belief and behavior, he was attacked as an atheist and also sentenced to prison for a brawl in which someone was killed. He was himself killed in a quarrel over a tavern bill on May 1, 1593, at the age of twenty-nine.

Marlowe wrote a number of plays, two of which have earned acclaim—*Tamburlaine the Great* and *Doctor Faustus*. His earliest play, *Tamburlaine the Great* (1587), established blank verse as the convention for later Elizabethan and Jacobean playwrights. This verse form consists of nonrhyming lines of iambic pentameter—that is, lines of five metrical feet in which each foot has two syllables, the second one generally bearing the rhythmic stress. The play itself is in two parts, the second part—as Marlowe notes in its prologue—having been written as a result of the popularity of the first. The play tells of Tamburlaine's quest for power and luxury and possession of beauty, as he rises from being an obscure shepherd to a powerful conqueror. By Part II, the fairly sympathetic hero of Part I becomes cruel and obsessed with power; he succumbs to a fatal illness, a victim of his own weakness. In this tale, Marlowe paints an amazingly three-dimensional picture of grandeur and impotence.

Marlowe—Doctor Faustus

Marlowe's most famous play, first published in 1604, is *The Tragical History of the Life and Death of Doctor Faustus*, or simply *Doctor Faustus*. The story tells the tale of human temptation, fall, and damnation in richly poetic language.

Marlowe's source appears to have been an English translation of the German legend of Faustus that appeared in England at that time. The plot centers on the scholar Faust, who despairs of the limitations of his own learning and of all human knowledge. He turns to magic, and makes a contract with Mephistophilis, a minor devil. They agree that Mephistophilis will assist Faust and be his slave for twenty-four years. After that, Mephistophilis will claim Faust's soul, and Faust will be damned for eternity. So for twenty-four years, Faust uses his powers to the full, from playing practical jokes to calling back Helen of Troy. On the last night, he waits in agony and terror. In the end, Mephistophilis comes and carries him off to hell.

The central message is that life on this earth determines the nature of eternal life. The play harks back to the medieval morality play in which the forces of good and evil battle for control of the human soul, but at the same time, it shows the Renaissance preoccupation with the quest for knowledge. Faust is an ardent student of the classics and science. He can never know enough, and his very nature exhibits the new need to think for himself.

The tension of the drama arises from the conflict between the Renaissance desire for personal, unlimited power and the medieval promise of damnation for those who use evil means to gain those ends. Yet the play goes far beyond moralistic tensions and becomes a universal drama about the search for identity. Here is the struggle between personal potential and personal limitation, between seeking the goals that are consonant with being what we are and seeking only those goals that grant us power over others. In Christian terms, *Faustus* is about the difference between submitting to grace through repentance and regretting one's actions but failing to repent. In humanist terms, the play is about the willing corruption and eventual self-destruction of a person. In either case, the defiance of moral values leads to catastrophe.

The complexity and depth of Faust's character make the play a tragedy rather than a melodrama. Faust is a sympathetic human being with whom we can identify. He has the classical *hamartia*, or tragic flaw, that leads to his downfall, and he is a universal symbol of humanity. In Aristotelian terms, he is a figure slightly larger than life, a true tragic hero.

Marlowe's powerful poetic language was new in drama at the time. His flexible use of blank verse and the brilliance of his imagery combine to arouse emotion and rivet the audience. The imagery of terror in the final scene is among the most powerful in all drama. In addition, Marlowe's language and imagery unify the play: the patterns in Faust's references to heaven provide a subtle implication of the force from which Faust cannot escape but that he must, at the beginning, deny.

Ben Jonson's comedy stands in contrast to Marlowe's heroic tragedy. The play *Every Man in his Humor* documents the lives of a group of Elizabethan eccentrics. Jonson's wit and pen were sharp, and his tolerance was low. His plays were often vicious caricatures of contemporary individuals.

realism of character development that we find, for example, in Chaucer and Shakespeare, that he seems arcane to a modern reader.

Of course, the greatest literary genius of all was William Shakespeare (1564–1616), most of whose work was for the theatre, but who also left a remarkable sequence of sonnets in which he pushed the resources of the English language to breathtaking extremes. In his works for the theatre, Shakespeare represents the Elizabethan love of drama, and the theatres of London were patronized by lords and commoners alike. They

sought and found, usually in the same play, action, spectacle, comedy, character, and intellectual stimulation deeply reflective of the human condition. Thus it was with Shakespeare, the pre-eminent Elizabethan playwright. His appreciation of the Italian Renaissance—which he shared with his audience—can be seen in the settings of many of his plays. With true Renaissance breadth, Shakespeare went back into history, both British and classical, and far beyond, to the fantasy world of *The Tempest*. Like most playwrights of his age, Shakespeare wrote for a specific professional company, of which he became a partial owner. The need for new plays to keep the company alive from season to season provided much of the impetus for his prolific output.

Although we know only little of his life, the principal facts are well established. He was baptized in the parish church of Stratford-upon-Avon on April 26, 1564, and probably attended the local grammar school. We next learn of him in his marriage to Ann Hathaway in 1582, when a special action was necessary to allow the marriage without delay. The reason is clear—five months later, Ann gave birth to their first daughter, Susanna. The next public mention comes in 1592, when his reputation as a playwright was sufficient to warrant a malicious comment from another playwright, Robert Greene. From then on, there are many records of his activities as dramatist, actor, and businessman. In addition to his steady output of plays, he also published a narrative poem entitled *Venus and Adonis*, which was popular enough to have nine printings in the next few years. His standing as a lyric poet was established with the publication of 154 Sonnets in 1609.

In 1594 he was a founder of a theatrical company called the Lord Chamberlain's Company, in which he functioned as shareholder, actor, and playwright. In 1599, the company built its own theatre, the Globe, which came directly under the patronage of James I when he assumed the throne in 1603. Shakespeare died in 1616 shortly after executing a detailed will. Although more is known about Shakespeare than the few facts

mentioned here, playwrights were not held in high esteem in England in the sixteenth century, and there was virtually no reason to write about them. We do, in fact, know more about Shakespeare than we do most of his contemporaries.

Shakespeare's plays fall into three distinct genres: comedies, tragedies, and histories. The third category represents a particularly Elizabethan type. England's prosperity and rising greatness, accentuated by the defeat of the Spanish Armada, led to a tremendous popular interest in English history, and Shakespeare's history plays are large-scale dramatizations and glorifications of events that took place between 1200 and 1550. An occasional tragedy—*Julius Caesar*, for example—was based on history, and he often set his comedies in Renaissance Italy—for example, *The Taming of the Shrew*—but the true "histories" have a particular flavor and type and are identified by titles referring to English kings—for example, *Richard II*, *Henry V*, and so on. King Lear was a mythical English king, but the play of that title is a tragedy rather than a "history."

There is a robust, peculiarly Elizabethan quality in Shakespeare's plays. The ideas expressed in them have a universal appeal because of his understanding of human motivation and character, and his ability to probe deeply into emotion. The plays reflect life and love, action and nationalism, and they present those qualities in a magnificent poetry that explores and expands the English language in unrivaled fashion. Shakespeare's use of

12.27 The second Globe Theatre, as reconstructed, c. 1614.

tone, color, and complex or new word meanings gives his plays a musical as well as dramatic quality, which appeals to every generation.

Shakespeare was not the only significant playwright of the English Renaissance stage, however, and the plays of Christopher Marlowe (1564–93) and Ben Jonson (1573–1637) still captivate theatre audiences. Marlowe's love of sound permeates his works, and if his character development is occasionally weak, the heroic grandeur of his action has the universal qualities of Aeschylus and Sophocles.

THE ELIZABETHAN PLAYHOUSE The structure of Elizabethan theatre buildings is familiar, even though documentation is fairly sketchy. In general, we assume that the audience surrounded the stage on three sides, an inheritance from earlier times when stages were erected in the enclosed courtyards of inns. By 1576 buildings housing the professional theatre existed in London. They were round or octagonal in shape ("This wooden O," according to Shakespeare in *Henry V*). A cross-section of society attended them, from commoners in the "pit," or standing area around the stage, to nobility in the galleries, a seating area under a roof. Situated against one wall of the circular building, the stage may or may not have been protected by a canopy, but the great spectacle of Elizabethan drama was, by and large, an outdoor event. Theatres were constructed of wood; fire was a constant threat and a frequent reality. Johannes de Witt, from whose accounts of a trip to London in 1596 we derive nearly all our knowledge of the physical theatre of the era, claimed that the Swan Theatre could seat 3,000 spectators (Fig.**12.27**).

MUSIC

In sixteenth-century England, nothing compared to London, especially in music. The capital city afforded the opportunity for all kinds of musical composition and performance, it was the center of music printing, and it was the home of foreign and domestic musicians and instrument makers. In addition, London was the location of the court of the monarch whose patronage was of the upmost importance, and the sovereign supported the best musicians both secular and sacred.

In the field of sacred music, the dominant force was the Chapel Royal, although during the early and mid-sixteenth century, the liturgical tradition in the Chapel was unstable. As we have noted, the Church of England's formal separation from the Roman Catholic communion in 1534 under Henry VIII had political rather than doctrinal causes, and there was, therefore, no immediate change in liturgy or music. In 1544 Archbishop Thomas Cranmer published an English version of the litany in which the traditional chants were adapted to the vernacular, and a

second version of the service, published in the same year, had settings of the chants for five voices. Between the reigns of Henry VIII and Elizabeth I—that is, during the brief but tempestuous reigns of Edward VI and Mary Tudor—great doctrinal swings took place. In 1549, shortly after Edward VI became king, the Act of Uniformity decreed that the liturgy as prescribed in the *English Book of Common Prayer* should be used in all services. A year late John Merbecke issued his *Booke of Common Praier*, which included traditional chants and new monophonic music for the service. These compositions contained melodies that nicely matched the English words.

The reign of Mary Tudor saw the re-establishment of Roman Catholicism, but the accession of Elizabeth I in 1558, and the return of the Puritan faction, brought the restoration of English rites, and the Church of England acquired its present form. In Elizabeth's time, a period when church music was bitterly attacked by the English followers of John Calvin, the Chapel Royal remained the most important bastion of elaborate ritual. However, the Chapel Royal reflected the monarch's will, and there was little the reformers could do, as the monarch was head of the English Church. During Elizabeth I's reign, therefore, the Chapel Royal stabilized as an institution, and what is known as the Elizabethan "golden age of church music" began. Elizabeth was clearly more drawn to the elaborate ritual of Catholicism than to the austerity of the Puritans, recognizing perhaps that ceremony and trappings could glorify not only God but also the supreme Head of the Church of England as well. There were, in addition, political reasons for maintaining some vestiges of Catholicism rather than adopting wholeheartedly the simplicity of the Calvinists, for the powerful Catholic monarchies of Europe were reassured by the appearance, at least, that England had not been totally subverted by the Reformers.

Elizabeth I specifically allowed Latin to continue to be used in those collegiate chapels and churches where the language was familiar to the congregations. However, the results of her influence were in the creation of an entirely new body of English church music. During the first years of her reign, an attempt was made to build a more impressive repertory than had existed previously, and the burden of that task fell on the shoulders of the composer William Byrd (1543–1623). Byrd displayed a multifaceted musical personality, and his range, versatility, and superb quality set him apart from his contemporaries. He excelled in virtually every form—Latin Masses, motets, English anthems and services, songs and madrigals, and music for stringed and keyboard instruments. He was a pivotal figure in English music—at the same time the last great composer in the rich tradition of Catholic polyphony and the first of the Elizabethan golden age. He is the originator of the English verse anthem.

Byrd spent most of his professional life as organist

for the Chapel Royal, and served the court for nearly fifty years. Interestingly, he remained a Catholic all his life, surviving in a Protestant country that was, at times, vigorously hostile to his religion. Nonetheless, he felt secure enough to compose and publish music for the Catholic liturgy even as he maintained an important position in the Anglican church and provided music for its services. His settings were often grave, penitential, and supplicatory. Earlier English composers—such as Byrd's predecessor as organist at the Chapel Royal, Thomas Tallis—used imitative techniques and laid out their points in perfectly symmetrical patterns. Byrd adopted more flexible procedures and introduced successive voices irregularly, to give his counterpoint greater interest and complexity. Many of his motets are unusually long, and this allowed him to expand his themes and show them off in various combinations. His later motets incorporated a wide range of textures and styles, with a greater use of chromaticism and antiphonal effects, and livelier, more varied rhythms.

Some of Byrd's finest music includes complete services for the Anglican church, including settings of the morning and evening canticles and the communion service. A complete service consists of the music for the unvarying portions of morning and evening prayer,

which correspond roughly to the Roman Catholic matins and vespers, and the music for holy communion, which corresponds to the Roman Mass. An Anglican service is either a "Great Service" or a "Short Service," depending on the type of music employed. A Great Service uses contrapuntal and melismatic (more than one note per syllable of text) music; a Short Service uses chordal and syllabic music. Byrd's services employed the note-against-note counterpoint that Archbishop Thomas Cranmer had recommended to Henry VIII as the only appropriate style for church music. They also used florid counterpoint and explored fully the possible combinations of its two five-voiced choirs. The rich density and imitative texture of his Great Service make it one of the greatest in the Anglican tradition.

Byrd's instrumental music set new standards for the time. He wrote fantasies, dances, and sets of variations, and he also wrote for solo keyboard and instrumental ensembles. Although he did not write every kind of music popular in England at the time—for example, he left no lute music, no airs, and no music for the favorite English combination of lute, pandora, cittern, two viols, and flute (called the "broken consort")—his extraordinary accomplishments make him the stellar example of music during the Elizabethan Golden Age.

CHAPTER THIRTEEN

THE BAROQUE AGE

AT A GLANCE

Scientific Revolution and Systematic Rationalism
Francis Bacon
Galileo Galilei
Johannes Kepler
René Descartes
Isaac Newton
  TECHNOLOGY: Standardized Measurement

Social Theory
Thomas Hobbes
John Locke

The Counter-Reformation
The Council of Trent
The Wars of Religion

Absolutism and the Rise of the Bourgeoisie

The Visual Arts and Architecture
Baroque Style
Counter-Reformation Baroque
Aristocratic Baroque
  OUR DYNAMIC WORLD: Muslim versus Hindu Architecture
Bourgeois Baroque
  MASTERWORK: Rembrandt—The Night Watch

Literature
Poetry and Satire
The Rise of the Novel

Music
The Counter-Reformation
Baroque Style
Secular Music
  PROFILE: Johann Sebastian Bach
  MASTERWORK: Bach—Fugue in G Minor

French Neoclassical Theatre

Synthesis: English Baroque Seventeenth-century London
  MASTERWORK: Wren—St Paul's Cathedral
  PROFILE: Sir Christopher Wren

13.1 Gian Lorenzo Bernini, *Baldacchino* in St Peter's, Rome, 1624–33. Gilded bronze, c. 100 ft (30 m) high.

the color spectrum. However, his characteristic use of strongly highlighted forms—the highlight is pure white, as opposed to a higher value of the base hue—sharpens the contrasts, and this, too, intensifies the emotional tone of the work. The obvious brushwork in many places encourages the viewer to look beneath the surface reality of the painting into a special truth within.

SCULPTURE

The splendor of the baroque was particularly apparent in sculpture. Forms and space were charged with an energy that carried beyond the confines of the work. As in painting, sculpture directed the viewer's vision inward and

13.9 Gian Lorenzo Bernini, *David*, 1623. Marble, 5 ft 7 ins (1.70 m) high. Galleria Borghese, Rome.

invited participation rather than neutral observation. Feeling was the focus. Baroque sculpture tended to treat space pictorially, almost like a painting, to describe action scenes rather than single sculptural forms. To see this, we can focus on the work of Gian Lorenzo Bernini (1598–1680).

Bernini's *David* (Fig. **13.9**) exudes a sense of power and action as he curls to unleash the stone from his sling to hit Goliath, who is outside the statue's space. Our eyes sweep upward along a diagonally curved line and are propelled outward in the direction of *David*'s concentrated expression. Repetition of the curving lines carries movement throughout the work. The viewer participates emotionally, feels the drama, and responds to the sensuous contours of the fully articulated muscles. Bernini's *David* seems to flex and contract in the moment of action, rather than expressing the pent-up energy of Michelangelo's giant-slayer.

Apollo and Daphne (Fig. **13.10**) is almost whimsical by contrast. It does, however, exhibit similar curvilinearity, moving diagonally upward. The detailed hair and leaves—Daphne is being metamorphosed into a bay tree—are elegantly ornamental. Every part of this complex sculpture is clearly articulated, but each part is subordinate to the theme of the work. Although it is a statue

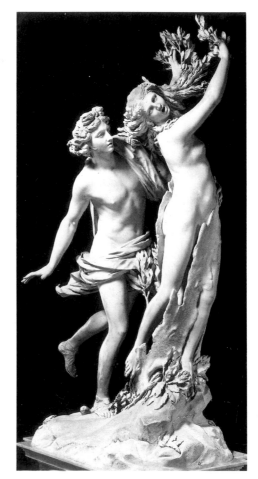

13.10 Gian Lorenzo Bernini, *Apollo and Daphne*, 1622–5. Marble, 8 ft (2.44 m) high. Galleria Borghese, Rome.

13.11 Gian Lorenzo Bernini, *The Ecstasy of St Theresa*, 1645–52. Marble, c. 11 ft 6 ins (3.5 m) high. Cornaro Chapel, Santa Maria della Vittoria, Rome.

an imaginary wind. Deep recesses and contours establish strong highlights and shadows, which further heighten the drama. The "picture" forces the viewer's involvement in an overwhelming emotional and religious experience.

ARCHITECTURE

The baroque style in architecture emphasized the same contrasts between light and shade and the same action, emotion, opulence, and ornamentation as the other visual arts of the period. Because of its scale, however, the effect was one of dramatic spectacle. There were many excellent baroque architects, among them Giacomo della Porta (1540–1602) (Figs. **13.12** and **13.13**). His Church of Il Gesù is the mother church of the Jesuit order, which was founded in 1534, and it had a profound influence on later church architecture, especially in Latin America. This church truly represents the spirit of the Counter-Reformation. Il Gesù is a compact basilica. By eliminating side aisles, the design literally forces the congregation into a large, hall-like space directly in view of the altar. Della Porta's façade (see Fig. **13.12**) boldly repeats its row of double pilasters on a smaller scale at the second level. Scroll-shaped buttresses create the transition from the wider first level to the crowning pediment of the second. The design reflects the influences of Alberti, Palladio, and Michelangelo, but in its skillful synthesis of these influences it is unique.

and therefore stationary, *Apollo and Daphne* exudes so much motion that its momentum seems to carry it beyond the confines of its actual shape. If Apollo were not frozen in mid-stride, completing his step would carry him elsewhere. Daphne's hair flies as her body, suddenly pinned to the ground, twists around. There is much more going on here than in earlier sculptures, where forms barely emerge from their marble blocks.

The Ecstasy of St Theresa (Fig. **13.11**) is a fully developed "painting" in sculptural form. It represents an experience described by St Theresa, one of the saints of the Counter-Reformation, of an angel piercing her heart with a golden flaming arrow: "The pain was so great that I screamed aloud; but at the same time I felt such infinite sweetness that I wished the pain to last forever." Accentuated by golden rays, the figure embodies St Theresa's ecstasy. Typical of baroque sculptural design, the lines of the draperies swirl diagonally, creating circular movement. Each element slips into the next in an unbroken chain, and every aspect of the work suggests motion. Figures float upward and draperies billow from

13.12 Giacomo della Porta, west front of Il Gesù, Rome, 1568–84.

up and into the background, an overwhelming stretch of deep space, depicted with intricate and graphic clarity as far as the eye can see. Poussin uses no atmospheric perspective here. The objects farthest away are as clearly depicted as those in the foreground. The various planes of the composition lead the viewer methodically from side to side, working toward the background one plane at a time. The composition is rich in human, natural, and architectural details that please the eye.

Although the *Landscape with the Burial of Phocion* is more subdued than Rubens' work, in every way the details in this painting are no less complex. The scheme is one of systematically interrelated pieces, in typically rational baroque fashion. Also typical of the baroque is the play of strong highlight against strong shadow. Although the picture does not show a real place, Poussin has depicted the architecture very precisely. He studied Vitruvius, the Roman architectural historian, and Vitruvius' accounts are the source of this detail.

13.17 Antoine Coysevox, *The Great Condé*, 1688. Bronze, 23 ins (58.4 cm) high. Louvre, Paris.

13.16 Pierre Puget, *Milo of Crotona*, 1671–83. Marble, 8 ft 10½ ins (2.71 m) high. Louvre, Paris.

SCULPTURE

Pierre Puget's (1620–94) *Milo of Crotona* (Fig. **13.16**) seems possessed by its own physical strength. The statue depicts Milo, the Olympic wrestling champion, who challenged the god Apollo. His punishment for daring to challenge the gods was death. The powerful hero, with his hand caught in a split tree-stump, is held helpless as he is mauled by a lion. Neither classical idealism nor reason has any part in this portrayal—it is pure physical pain and torment. The figure is caught in the violent agonies of pain and imminent death. The skin is about to tear under the pressure of the lion's claws—in an instant it will split open. The sweeping and intersecting arcs of the composition create intense energy of a kind that recalls the Laocoön group.

Portrait busts of the period, such as those by the French sculptor Antoine Coysevox (1640–1720), also attempt an emotional portrayal of their subjects. *The Great Condé* (Fig. **13.17**) uses dynamic line and strong and emphatic features to express the energy of the sitter.

ARCHITECTURE

Probably no monarch better personified the baroque era than Louis XIV, and probably no work of art better represents the magnificence and grandeur of the baroque style than the grand design of the Palace of Versailles, along with its sculpture and grounds. The great Versailles complex grew from the modest hunting lodge of Louis XIII into the grand palace of the Sun King over a number of years, involving several architects.

The Versailles château was rebuilt in 1631 by Philibert Le Roy. The façade was decorated by Louis Le Vau (1612–70) with bricks and stone, sculpture, wrought iron, and gilt lead. In 1668 Louis XIV ordered Le Vau to enlarge the building by enclosing it in a stone envelope containing the king's and queen's apartments (Fig. **13.18**). The city side of the château thus retains the spirit of Louis XIII, while the park side reflects classical influence (Fig. **13.19**). François d'Orbay and, later, Jules Hardouin-Mansart (1646–1708) expanded the château into a palace whose west façade extends over 2,000 feet (610 meters). The palace became Louis XIV's permanent residence in 1682. French royalty was at the height of its power, and Versailles was the symbol of the monarchy and of the divine right of kings.

As much care, elegance, and precision were employed on the interior as on the exterior. With the aim of supporting French craftsmen and merchants, Louis XIV had his court live in unparalleled luxury. He also decided to put permanent furnishings in his château, something that was unheard of. The result was a fantastically rich and beautiful set of furnishings. Royal workshops produced mirrors (Fig. **13.20**), tapestries, and brocades of the highest quality, and these goods became highly sought after all over Europe. Le Brun (1619–90) coordinated all the deco-

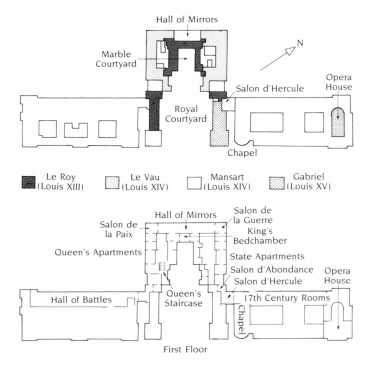

13.18 Plans of the Palace of Versailles, 1669–85.

13.19 Louis Le Vau and Jules Hardouin-Mansart, garden façade. Palace of Versailles, 1669–85.

OUR DYNAMIC WORLD

Muslim versus Hindu Architecture

The Islamic Mughal emperors of India were patrons of architecture, and the most famous of all Indian architectural accomplishments also qualifies as an example of Islamic work—the Taj Mahal at Agra (Fig. **13.24**). However, the Taj Mahal blends Islamic and indigenous Indian styles. The tomb, built by Shah Jahan as a mausoleum for his favorite wife, Mumtaz Mahal (1593–1631), was entirely without precedent in Islam, and it is possible that the building also was intended as an allegory of the day of Resurrection, for the building is a symbolic replica of the throne of God. Four intersecting waterways in the garden by which one approaches the Taj symbolized the four flowing Rivers of Paradise as described in the Koran. The scale of the building is immense, yet the details are exquisitely refined, and the proportions are well balanced and symmetrical. The effect of this huge, white octagonal structure with its impressive dome and flanking minarets is nothing short of breathtaking.

In contrast, the Hindu architectural tradition was almost defiantly anti-Islamic, with its abundance of figurative sculpture celebrating a plurality of deities. Good examples of this countervailing trend can be seen in the south of India, especially in the city of Vijayanagar, which covers 10 square miles (26 square kilometers). Here, huge and exquisite temples came alive with brilliantly colored sculpture depicting the Hindu pantheon (Fig. **13.25**). Upward-striving terraces with ornate detail reach toward a vaulted pinnacle. In Vijayanagar the concept of the temple went beyond a single shrine and encompassed an entire complex of buildings within concentric enclosures. These were entered through tall gate towers called gopuras, which were packed with friezes of the Hindu gods, and which increased in size from the inner to the outer walls.

13.24 Ustad Ahmad Lahori (architect), the Taj Mahal, Agra, India, 1632–48.

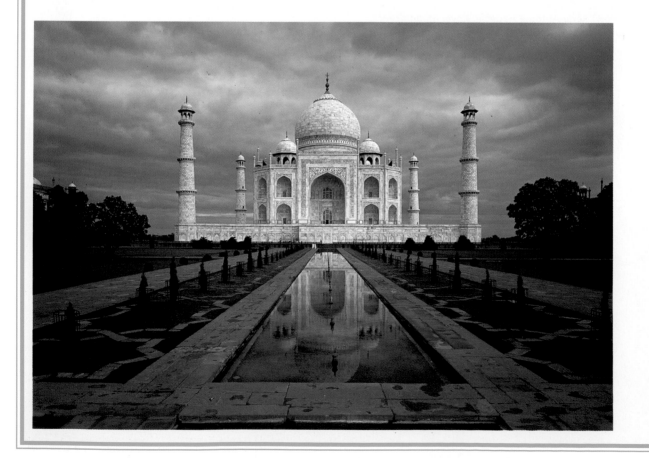

ration and furnishing of the royal residences, and supervised everything for the state apartments, such as the statues, the painted ceilings, and the silver pieces of furniture.

The apartments of the palace boast a splendor and wealth previously unseen. Each room was dedicated to one of the planetary gods. The Salon d'Abondance (Fig. **13.21**, p. 424) was not considered a part of the state apartments until the north wing was built. The ceiling here shows an allegorical figure of Magnificence, whose scepter and cornucopia are symbols of the royal prerogatives of power and provision. Around Magnificence are Immortality and the Fine Arts, symbolized by a winged figure.

The Queen's staircase (Fig. **13.22**) leads to a suite created by Le Vau for Queen Marie-Thérèse. It comprises four large rooms whose windows open to the plantings on the Parterre du Midi (Fig. **13.23**). The grounds here and elsewhere are adorned with fountains and statues. The magnificent Fountain of Apollo by Tuby (Fig. **13.26**), which sits astride the east-west axis of the grounds, was originally covered with gold. The sculpture was executed from a drawing by Le Brun and inspired by a painting by Albani. It continues the allegorical glorification of *Le Roi Soleil*, representing the break of day, as the sun-god rises in his chariot from the waters. Apollo was the perfect symbol for the Sun King, who reigned, it was thought, at God's behest and in his stead, in glorious baroque splendor, surrounded by art that was rational yet emotional,

13.25 *Gopura* (gateway tower) of the Pampapati temple, Vijayanagar, India, sixteenth century; renovated in the seventeenth century.

13.26 The Fountain of Apollo, Palace of Versailles

13.27 Balthasar Neumann, Kaisersaal, Residenz, Würzburg, Germany, 1719–44.

opulent in tone, and complex in design.

Baroque style in architecture developed later in Germany than in the rest of Europe. When it came, it took on a lighter tone than its more ponderous early cousins. We can see this trend in the works of the architect Balthasar Neumann (1687–1753) (Fig. **13.27**).

BOURGEOIS BAROQUE

Art in the bourgeois baroque style reflected the visions and objectives of the new and wealthy middle class. The wealth and opulent lifestyle of the bourgeoisie sometimes exceeded that of the aristocracy. As a result, a power struggle was at hand.

REMBRANDT

Born in Leiden, Rembrandt van Rijn (1606–69) trained under local artists and then moved to Amsterdam. His early and rapid success gained him many commissions

and students—more, in fact, then he could handle. In contrast to the work of Rubens, Rembrandt's is by, for, and about the middle class. Indeed, Rembrandt became what could be called the first "capitalist" artist. The quality of art could be gauged, he believed, not only on its own merits but also by its value on the open market. He is reported to have spent huge sums of money buying his own works in order to increase their value.

Rembrandt's genius lay in delivering the depths of human emotion and psychology in the most dramatic terms. Unlike Rubens, for example, Rembrandt uses suggestion rather than great detail. After all, the human spirit is intangible—it can never be portrayed, only alluded to. Thus in Rembrandt's work we find atmosphere, shadow, and implication creating emotion.

Rembrandt's DEPOSITION scene, *The Descent from the Cross* (Fig. **13.29**, p. 430), is at the opposite end of the emotional scale from Rubens' ascension scene, but it too has a certain sense of richness. Rembrandt uses only reds, golds, and red-browns: except for the robe of the figure pressing into Christ's body, the painting is nearly monochromatic. Contrasts are provided and forms are revealed through changes in value. The composition is open—that is, lines escape the frame at the left arm of the cross and

MASTERWORK

Rembrandt—The Night Watch

The huge canvas now in the Rijkmuseum in Amsterdam is only a portion of the original group portrait *The Night Watch* (Fig. **13.28**), which was cut down in the eighteenth century to fit into a space in Amsterdam Town Hall. So it happens that it no longer shows the bridge over which the members of the watch were about to cross.

Group portraits, especially of military units, were popular at the time. Usually the company posed in a social setting, such as a gathering around a banquet table, but Rembrandt chose to break with the norm and portrayed the company, led by Captain Cocq, as if it were out on duty. The result was a scene of great vigor and dramatic intensity, true to the baroque spirit.

As a dramatic scene, the painting is a virtuoso performance of baroque lighting and movement. There is nothing regular or mechanical about it. The result, however, angered the members of Captain Cocq's company. They had paid equally, and they expected to be treated equally in the portrait, but they are not. Some of the figures in this life-size group fade into the shadows. Others are hidden by the gestures of those placed in front of them.

Cleaning revealed the vivid color of the original. The painting is now a good deal brighter than when it was named, last century. Yet its dramatic highlights and shadows reflect no natural light source whatsoever, and no analysis of the light can solve the problem of how the figures in the painting are supposed to be illuminated. It has been suggested that perhaps the painting depicts a "Day Watch," with the intense light at the center of the work being morning sunlight. An examination of the highlights and shadows in the painting, however, shows that Rembrandt has used light for dramatic purposes only. While the figures are rendered realistically, no such claim can be made for the light sources.

Rembrandt's genius lay in depicting human emotions and characters. He suggests detail without including it, and we find him taking this approach in *The Night Watch*. Here he concentrates on atmosphere and implication. As in most baroque art, the viewer is invited to share in an emotional experience, to enter in, rather than to observe.

13.28 Rembrandt van Rijn, *The Night Watch* (*The Company of Captain Frans Banning Cocq*), 1642. Oil on canvas, 12 ft 2 ins × 14 ft 7 ins (3.7 × 4.45 m). Rijksmuseum, Amsterdam.

13.29 After Rembrandt van Rijn, *The Descent from the Cross*, c. 1655. Oil on canvas. 4 ft 8¼ ins × 3 ft 7¾ ins (1.43 × 1.11 m). National Gallery of Art, Washington D.C. (Widener Collection).

in the half-forms at the lower right border. The horizontal line of the darkened sky is subtly carried off the canvas, middle right. Again, a strong central triangle holds the composition together. From a dark, shadowed base, which runs the full width of the lower border, it is delineated by the highlighted figure on the lower right and the ladder at the lower left. Christ's upstretched arm completes the apex of the triangle as it meets an implied extension of the ladder behind the cross. The drapery leads the eye downward in a gentle sweeping curve.

VAN RUISDAEL

Rembrandt's emotional subject matter was probably hard for most collectors to cope with. More to the taste of the new, general marketplace were the subjects of the emerg-

ing landscape painters. *The Cemetery* (Fig. **13.30**), a painting by Jacob van Ruisdael (1628–82), appeals to the emotions with its rich detail and atmosphere, light and shade, and grandiose scale.

The painting is huge, nearly 5 feet (1.5 meters) high and more than 6 feet (1.8 meters) wide. The graveyard itself, along with the medieval ruins, casts a melancholy spell over the work. The absence of human life in the painting suggests its insignificance in the universe. The ruins suggest that even the traces of human presence shall also pass away. Highlight and shadow lead the eye around the composition, but not in any consecutive way. The eye's path is broken, or at least disturbed, by changes of direction, for example, in the tree trunk across the stream and in the stark tree limbs. Nature broods over both the scene and the wider universe outside the frame.

13.30 Jacob van Ruisdael, *The Cemetery*, c. 1655. Oil on canvas, 4 ft 8 ins × 6 ft 2¼ ins (1.42 × 1.89 m). Detroit Institute of Arts (Gift of Julius H. Haass, in memory of his brother Dr Ernest W. Haass).

A CRITICAL REVIEW

In this section, amid our discussion of baroque style in visual art and architecture, we saw a feature on Hindu and Muslim art in India. By this point in our study, we recognize that art of different styles is identifiable. We may not be able to pinpoint everything about a given style, but we know immediately that baroque art, Islamic art, and Far Eastern art look different from each other. The fact that we can recognize the difference means that we can recognize style. If we have studied the material closely and have learned the terminology discussed in the Introduction, we can, with confidence even, tell how and why the styles are different and do so using accurate vocabulary. That is a significant accomplishment.

Describe in aesthetic terms the differences between Hindu and Muslim art from India.

Baroque art is emotion-centered, unlike classical art, and it ought to make us feel something. Pick a work from this section and describe how it makes you feel. Then analyze *why* you think it does so.

opera house is a unique architectural entity). And in particular, in true baroque spirit, opera is primarily an overwhelming emotional experience.

Opera grew out of late fifteenth-century madrigals. Many of these madrigals, some called "madrigal comedies" and some called *intermedi*, were written to be performed between the acts of theatre productions. They were fairly dramatic, and included pastoral scenes, narrative reflections, and amorous adventures. They gave rise to a new style of solo singing, as opposed to ensemble singing. In 1600, an Italian singer–composer, Jacopo Peri (1561–1633), took a contemporary pastoral drama, *Eurydice*, by the playwright Ottavio Rinuccini, and set it to music. Peri's work is the first surviving opera. It was sparely scored, and consisted primarily of RECITATIVE, or sung monologue reflecting the pitches and rhythms of speech, over a slow-moving bass. Peri's opera, however, was weak, both musically and theatrically.

It was Claudio Monteverdi who took a firmer hand to the new art form. In *Orfeo* (1607), he expanded the same mythological subject matter, the story of Orpheus and Eurydice, into a full, five-act structure—five acts were considered classically "correct"—and gave it richer, more substantial music. The emotional effect was consequently much stronger. The mood swung widely through contrasting passages of louds and softs. (In baroque music, quick shifts in volume, speed, and expression are the musical equivalents of the strong contrasts in light and shade in baroque painting and sculpture.) Monteverdi added solos, duets, ensemble singing and dances. *Orfeo*'s melodic lines were highly embellished and ornamental. The orchestra

consisted of approximately forty instruments, including brass, woodwind, strings, and CONTINUO. The grandiose scenic designs of the great Bibiena family, one of which appears in Figure **13.31**, suggest the spectacular staging of this and other baroque operas. Monteverdi's innovation was the dramatic prototype of what we know today, and he is rightly called the "father of opera."

By the second half of the seventeenth century, opera had become an important art form, especially in Italy, but also in France, England, and Germany. A French national opera was established under the patronage of Louis XIV. French opera included colorful and rich ballet and cultivated strong literary qualities using the dramatic talents of playwrights such as Corneille and Racine. In England the court masques of the late sixteenth century led to fledgling opera during the suspension of the monarchy, when Cromwell's zealots shut down the theatres. Indeed, English opera probably owed more to a desire to circumvent the prohibition of stage plays than anything else. In Germany, a strong Italian influence spurred on opera in the courts. This German tradition led to one of the most astonishing eras in opera, during the mid-nineteenth century.

CANTATA

Another important new musical form to emerge in the late seventeenth century was the Italian CANTATA, a composition for chorus and/or solo voice(s) accompanied by an instrumental ensemble. It developed from monody, or solo singing with a predominant vocal line, centering on

13.31 Giuseppe Galli de Bibiena, design for an opera, 1719. Contemporary engraving. Metropolitan Museum of Art, New York (The Elisha Whittelsey Collection, The Elisha Whittelsey Fund, 1951).

PROFILE

Johann Sebastian Bach (1685–1750)

Although currently considered one of the giants of music, Johann Sebastian Bach was considered old-fashioned during his lifetime, and his works lay virtually dormant after his death. Not until the nineteenth century did he gain recognition as one of the greatest composers of the Western world. He was born in Thuringia, in what is now Germany, and when he was ten years old both his parents died. His oldest brother, Johann Christoph, took responsibility for raising and teaching him, and Johann Sebastian became a choirboy at the Michaelskirche in Luneburg when he was fifteen. He studied the organ and was appointed organist at Neukirche in Arnstadt, where he remained for four years. Then he took a similar post at Muhlhausen at about the same time as he married his cousin, Maria Barbara Bach. One year later, he took the position of court organist at Weimar, remaining there until 1717, when Prince Leopold of Kothen hired him as his musical director. While he was serving as musical director to Prince Leopold, Bach completed the Brandenberg Concertos in 1721.

In 1720 Bach's wife died, and one year later he married Anna Magdalena Wilcken. In 1723 he moved to Leipzig as the city's musical director at the school attached to St Thomas' Church, and among his responsibilities to the city, were to supply performers for four churches. In 1747 he played for Frederick II the Great of Prussia at Potsdam, but shortly thereafter his eyesight began to fail, and he went blind just before his death in 1750.

Bach's output as a composer was prodigious but also required as part of his responsibilities, especially at Leipzig. Over his career, he wrote more than two hundred cantatas, the *Mass in B Minor*, and three settings of the Passion story, works that illustrate Bach's deep religious faith. His sacred music allowed him to explore and communicate the profound mysteries of the Christian faith and to glorify God. His cantatas—that is, short oratorios that employ recitatives, arias, and choral passages—typify the baroque exploration of wide-ranging emotional development. They range from ecstatic expressions of joy to profound meditations on death. *The Passions*, of which the *St Matthew Passion* is typical, tell the story of the trial and crucifixion of Jesus. Written in German rather than the traditional Latin, the Passions express Bach's devotion to Lutheranism.

In addition to his sacred works, he wrote a tremendous amount of important music for harpsichord and organ, including forty-eight Preludes and Fugues, called *The Well-Tempered Clavier* and the *Golden Variations*. In the fugues, he develops a single theme, which is then imitated among the polyphonically developed voices of the composition (see the Masterwork section on the *Fugue in G Minor*, p. 436). Among his many instrumental works are twenty concertos and twelve unaccompanied sonatas for violin and cello.

a text to which the music was subservient. These works, which consisted of many short, contrasting sections, were far less spectacular than opera, and they were designed to be performed without costumes or scenery. Most cantatas were written for solo soprano voice, although many used other voices and groups of voices.

The high point of the Italian cantata came in the works of Alessandro Scarlatti (1660–1725), who composed more than six hundred of them. Typically Scarlatti's cantatas begin with a short "arioso" section, that is somewhere between recitative and ARIA (a set-piece song). A recitative follows, then a full aria, a second recitative, and a final aria in the opening key. Scarlatti's moods tended to be melancholic and tender, and his composition elegant and refined. The theme of almost all of his works is love, and particularly its betrayal.

In Germany, the cantata was a sacred work that grew out of the Lutheran chorale. Its most accomplished composers were Johann Sebastian Bach (1685–1750) and Dietrich Buxtehude (c. 1637–1707), of whom Bach is by far the greater. As a choirmaster, Bach was under a professional obligation to compose a new cantata weekly, and between 1704 and 1740, he composed more than two hundred. His cantatas were primarily contrapuntal in texture, usually written for up to four soloists and a four-part chorus.

Bach's work is one of the great responses of Protestant art to the challenge of the Counter-Reformation. His sacred music achieves extraordinary power as a humane, heartfelt expression of faith. Never theatrical, its drama derives from an inner striving, a hard-won triumph over doubt and death.

CHAPTER FOURTEEN

THE

ENLIGHTENMENT

AT A GLANCE

The Enlightenment
Technology
  TECHNOLOGY: James Watt and the Steam
    Engine
Philosophy
The Philosophes
  PROFILE: Voltaire
Economics and Politics
Aesthetics and Classicism

The Visual Arts and Architecture
Rococo Style
Humanitarianism and Hogarth

Landscape and Portraiture
Genre
Neoclassicism
  MASTERWORK: David—The Oath of the
    Horatii

Literature
Goldsmith
Johnson
The Preromantics

Music
Pre-Classical

Expressive Style
Classical Style

Theatre
Britain
America
  OUR DYNAMIC WORLD: Japanese Kabuki
    Theatre
France
Germany

**Synthesis: The Enlightened Despot—
Frederick the Great**

14.1 Jean-Honoré Fragonard, *The Swing*, c. 1768–9. Oil on canvas, 32 x 25½ ins (83 x 66 cm). Wallace Collection, London.

A CRITICAL LOOK The Enlightenment—a new descriptive label for a new century. This was the century in which most of the old order faded away to be replaced by a new sense of egalitarianism. The rising bourgeoisie wrested power from the aristocracy, concern for the welfare of all classes, especially the downtrodden, came nearer the top of the social agenda, and the idea of universal education brought ideas that were previously the prerogative of the rich to the mass of the public. Rational thought as the premier approach to human knowledge gained the upper hand. Finally, the ancient world came to life in new discoveries and new understandings. The emotionalism of the baroque submerged as a more delicate rococo style, and then a new classicism, arose.

What were the major inventions of the eighteenth century, and how did they affect life in general?

How did the philosophies of Hume and Kant differ from those of their predecessors?

What did the philosophes contribute to eighteenth-century life?

THE ENLIGHTENMENT

The eighteenth century was an age of change and revolution in some areas and prosperous stability in others. The idea of the absolute monarch was challenged, although with varying degrees of success, while the middle class rose to demand its place in society, and HUMANITARIAN-ISM—social philosophy in action—attempted to make a place for all classes in the social scheme. Knowledge, for the philosophes, was a transcendent and universal goal. The aristocracy found itself in decline, and the rococo style reflected its increasing superficiality. Then, at least for a while, the pendulum swung back from refinement and artifice to intellectual seriousness. The structural clarity of classicism returned in painting, sculpture, architecture, and, above all, in music and a remarkable century culminated in works of emotional depth and formal inventiveness. The cult of "sensibility" with which the century closed presaged the Romantic upheavals of *Sturm und Drang* that were shortly to come.

The eighteenth century has often been called the "Age of Enlightenment," but, as we noted in Chapter 13, century marks are arbitrary boundaries that tell us very little about history or art. Styles, philosophies, and politics come and go for a variety of reasons. We have already pushed half-way through the eighteenth century in some areas, without encountering any natural barriers—J.S. Bach, for example, lived and worked until 1750. The best we can say, then, is that eighteenth-century enlightenment grew out of various seventeenth-century ideas that fell on more or less fertile soil at different times in different places.

Seventeenth- and eighteenth-century thought held that people were rational beings in a universe governed by some systematic natural law. Some believed that law to be an extension of God's law. Others held that natural law stood by itself. Natural law was extended to include international law, and accords were formulated in which sovereign nations, bound by no higher authority, could work together for a common good.

Faith in science, in human rights arising from the natural law, in human reason, and in progress, were touchstones of eighteenth-century thought. The idea of progress was based on the assumption that the conditions of life could only improve with time and that each generation made life even better for those following. Some scholars—the "ancients"—held that the works of the Greeks and Romans had never been surpassed. Others—the "moderns"—held that science, art, literature, and the inventions of their own age were better since they were built upon the achievements of their predecessors.

Enlightenment, reason, and progress are secular ideas, and the age became increasingly secular. Politics and business superseded religion, wresting leadership away from the Church, of whatever denomination. Toleration increased and persecution and the imposition of corporal punishment for religious, political, or criminal offenses became less common as the era progressed, particularly in Germany and Austria.

The rapid increase in scientific discovery that followed Newton's work resulted in the development of new disciplines. Physics, astronomy, and mathematics remained primary, but fragmented inquiry was replaced by quiet categorizing. The vast body of information gathered during the late Renaissance period needed codification. The new sciences of mineralogy, botany, and zoology developed. First came classification of fossils, then classification of rocks, minerals, and plants. Carolus Linnaeus, the botanist, and Georges Buffon, the zoologist, were pioneers in their fields. Chemistry struggled under the burden of mistaken theories of combustion until the Frenchman Antoine Lavoisier correctly explained the process. In addition, he isolated hydrogen and oxygen as

	GENERAL EVENTS	LITERATURE & PHILOSOPHY	VISUAL ART & ARCHITECTURE	THEATRE & MUSIC
1700	Frederick I Louis XV War of Spanish Succession Humanitarianism		Watteau (**14.5**) de Cuvilliès (**14.10**)	Beginning of American theatre Couperin
1725	Herculaneum excavated Frederick II Maria Theresa of Austria War of Austrian Succession Crucible steel process		Hogarth (**14.11**, **14.12**) Chardin (**14.14**) Pesne (**14.30**) Krohne (**14.9**) von Knobelsdorff (**14.32**, **14.33**, (**14.35**)	Cibber Marivaux Gay
1750	Pompeii excavated *Encylopédie* published Industrial Revolution begins Lisbon earthquake Watt's steam engine George III of England	Johnson Rousseau Hume Kant Diderot Voltaire Baumgarten Goldsmith Prévost Fielding Winckelmann Herder	Boucher (**14.6**) von Menzel (**14.31**) Fragonard (**14.1**) Falconet (**14.7**)	Garrick Lessing Goldsmith Goldoni C.P.E. Bach Haydn
1775	American Revolution First iron bridge Louis XVI French Revolution	Blake Adam Smith Paine Wollstonecraft	Clodion (**14.8**) Houdon (**14.17**) Gainsborough (**14.13**) David (**14.15**, **14.18**)	Goethe Sheridan Beaumarchais Mozart
1800			Jefferson (**14.19**, **14.20**)	Beethoven

Timeline 14.1 The Enlightenment.

the two component elements of water, and he also postulated that although matter may alter its state, its mass always remains the same.

TECHNOLOGY

Science went hand in hand with technology. Telescopes and microscopes were improved. The barometer and the thermometer were invented, as were the air pump and the steam engine. By 1796, James Watt had patented a steam engine reliable enough to drive a machine. The invention of the steam engine gave rise to other machines, and paved the way for the Industrial Revolution at the end of the century.

The seventeenth and eighteenth centuries saw significant improvement in agricultural technology, as well. The technology for mechanized seed planting, developed in ancient Babylonia, had disappeared, and planting in Europe was done by hand until the eighteenth century when Jethro Tull invented the seed drill. Scientific observation also led to the implementation of the four-year system of crop rotation and the plow was greatly improved.

The use of coal fuel in place of charcoal to smelt iron revolutionized metallurgy in the early eighteenth centu-

ry. Strong coke fuel tremendously increased the capacity of blast furnaces. Coke-smelted iron initially proved to be more impure than charcoal-smelted iron, but the puddling furnace solved that problem. Around 1740 Benjamin Huntsman invented the crucible melting and casting process. Using hard coke as fuel achieved higher temperatures, and a greater blast could be gained using tall chimneys instead of the bellows. A new understanding of the properties of oxygen and chemical reagents made further advances possible. These improvements in metallurgy made possible the later use of iron and steel as structural elements, first in bridges and later in buildings. They also made possible the development of new machinery for the manufacture of yet other machinery, tools, and finely constructed hardware and instruments.

Scientific and medical inquiry in the seventeenth and eighteenth centuries created a demand for precise instruments. It is important to note here that new technology resulted from the demand created by inquiry, and not the other way around. A need for greater precision in observation and measurement led to the development of improved surveying, astronomical, and navigation instruments, and the thermometer and the barometer were refined. Advances were also made in the skills and materials used in the manufacture of instruments, resulting in

TECHNOLOGY: PUTTING DISCOVERY TO WORK

James Watt and the Steam Engine

Strictly speaking, the work of James Watt (1736–1819) on the steam engine was more a critical revision and study of an existing machine than a new composition. However, his scientific and critical innovations were so significant that science views it as a strategic invention. Watt's specific contribution lay in the concept of a separate condensing chamber for an engine invented by Thomas Newcomen and the problem of heat loss through the cooling and heating of the cylinder. The primary concept of a condensing chamber came to Watt on his regular Sunday walk. He saw that steam was an elastic body, which would rush into a vacuum, and if there were a connection between the cylinder and an exhausting vehicle, the steam would rush into it and be condensed without cooling the cylinder. He began testing his possible solution to the problem the next day with the apparatus shown in Figure **14.2**. His model proved highly efficient and demonstrated the soundness of the fundamental principles.

Watt worked rapidly from that point, refining his basic design in larger models, until he had developed a steam engine in the accurate sense of the word, and the result became a well-designed machine based on a sound scientific perception of the properties of steam. Watt's concept of the engine quickly carried him beyond the limits of current facilities for machine building, and many of the parts he required present-

14.2 James Watt's experimental condensing chamber. Water heated in a closed container (A) produced steam, which traveled through tubes (B and H) into chambers (C and K), moderated by valves (F), to create force to move pistons (D and J) and raise weight E.

ed problems that no existing iron makers could solve. Consequently, the attempt to build a working steam engine was postponed until after Watt secured a patent for it in 1769. Even with financial assistance, however, Watt was unable to pay for the construction of the engine and he was forced into bankruptcy.

greater specialization and the creation of craft shops. These included advances in making optical glass, which, in turn, led to the development of better lenses for use in telescopes and compound microscopes.

Improvements in precision tooling affected clock-making and tools such as the lathe. The introduction of cams and templates allowed even greater accuracy and intricacy in production. An instrument called the dividing engine made it possible to graduate a circle by mechanical means, and to graduate scales on surveying and navigational instruments accurately.

The field of engineering in the seventeenth and eighteenth centuries saw advances in hydraulics, road building, and bridge construction. The control of water flow in canals was aided by the development of an extremely accurate bubble-tube leveling device. The surveyor's level with a telescopic sight was another productive invention. Bridge building was improved by modifica-

tions to the construction of pier foundations, and the first iron bridge was erected at Coalbrookdale, England, in 1779.

The introduction of power machinery revolutionized the English textile industry in the late eighteenth century, but the steam engine was undoubtedly the most significant invention of the period. In replacing human, animal, wind, and water power with machine power, it changed the course of history. The first full-scale steam engine had been developed in England in 1699, and early steam engines were used to drain mine shafts. By the mid-eighteenth century, some wealthy people were using steam engines to pump domestic water supplies, but James Watt's invention of the separate condenser in 1769 brought steam engines to new levels of practicality and productivity. Further modifications primed the engine for its role as cornerstone of the Industrial Revolution. In 1800, when the patent for Watt's engine expired, new high-pressure steam engines were applied to a variety of tasks, most notably in the first successful steam locomotive in 1804. By 1820, the steam engine could generate an estimated 1,000 horsepower, and the Industrial Revolution was at hand.

PHILOSOPHY

To understand the philosophy of the eighteenth century, we must retrace our steps to the Middle Ages. In the medieval period, philosophy was closely linked to theology. As we noted in the last chapter, Descartes (1596–1650) had peeled philosophy away from theology, and allied it with the natural sciences and mathematics. Reason was supreme, and Descartes called for rejection of all that could not be proved. Descartes' philosophy is known as "Cartesianism," and it is based on the contention that human reason can solve every problem that the mind can entertain.

We have also seen how John Locke (1632–1704) challenged the Cartesian idea that knowledge stemmed from the intellect. Locke argued that knowledge derives first from the senses. He redirected philosophical energies from the vast metaphysical systems of pure rationalism to a more practical, earthbound sphere. Locke's philosophy was grounded in reason, but because he stressed sensations and experience as the primary sources of knowledge, he is known as a "sensualist" or an "empiricist."

Empiricism became the predominant philosophy of the late eighteenth century, although it was not without its critics. Locke's approach formed the basis for the later philosophical thought of Hume and Kant. David Hume (1711–76), a Scotsman, differed from Locke in his assertions that the mind is incapable of building up knowledge from sensations, and that the world we live in consists only of probabilities. Hume maintained that not only philosophy, but also natural science, existed in a cloud of doubt. Mathematics was the only true and valid science.

Hume was not the only skeptic of the age, and his philosophy might have been disregarded, were it not for the German philosopher Immanuel Kant (1724–1804). Kant's major contribution to late eighteenth-century thought was his distinction between science and philosophy and his attribution to each of separate functions and techniques. For Kant, science was concerned with the phenomenal world, or the world of appearances, which it describes by general propositions and laws. Science must not go beyond the world of appearances to concern itself with the reality beyond. That reality, the "noumenal" world, is the realm of philosophy. Kant's division of science and philosophy succeeded in giving a much-needed assurance to both philosophy and science allowing both to move forward.

THE PHILOSOPHES

The Enlightenment was concerned with more than philosophy and invention. Enlightened thought led to an active desire, called humanitarianism, to raise the downtrodden from the low social circumstances into which ignorance

14.3 Jean Huber, *The Philosophes at Supper*, c. 1750. Engraving. Bibliothèque Nationale, Paris.

PROFILE

Voltaire (1694–1778)

François-Marie Arouet (Voltaire: pronounced vole-TAIR) ranged widely through French literature during the years of the Enlightenment and leading up to the French Revolution. Born into a middle-class Parisian family, he lost his mother when he was seven and believed that his real father was not his legal one. A rebel from authority, he grew up in the company of his free-thinking godfather, the Abbé de Châteauneuf, and always maintained a clear sense of reality and a positive outlook. His schooling, at the Jesuit College of Louis-le-Grand in Paris, nurtured his love of literature, theatre, and social life, but the school's religious instruction left him skeptical. The period around 1709 saw the last years of Louis XIV accompanied by military disasters and religious persecution, events that left an indelible impression on the young Voltaire, although he continued to admire Louis XIV and to believe that kings were agents of progress.

His wit and desire to pursue a career in literature, coupled with the peculiar circumstances of the years after Louis XIV, in which the literary salon was the center of French society, soon brought Voltaire into social prominence. However, when he mocked the Regent, he found himself imprisoned for a year in the Bastille. Nonetheless, he saw himself as the Vergil of French literature and set about the serious task of writing, and he was soon back in favor. A two-year visit to England made him acquainted with the writings of Sir Isaac Newton and John Locke and gave him a greater appreciation of English literature, and he returned to France determined to use England as a model for his compatriots. Careful investments made Voltaire rich, and the independence wealth gave him allowed him to proceed on literary and social ventures of his choice. He wrote several mediocre tragedies before turning to writing history. His histories read like novels, and as he wrote, he increasingly began to insert philosophy into his texts.

However, his profound insights were not appreciated by his contemporaries, and a warrant was issued for his arrest. He retreated to the château of Mme. du Chatelet, with whom he spent the next several years studying, traveling, and writing, and during this time, Voltaire was a companion of the enlightened Prussian despot Frederick II, the Great, and frequently visited the Palace at Sans Souci (see pp. 474–7).

14.4 Jean-Antoire Houdon, *Voltaire*, 1781. Marble, 20 ins (51 cm) high. Victoria & Albert Museum, London.

However, the French court remained hostile. Voltaire committed several personal indiscretions and some of his plays failed miserably, and he was forced to lead a restless existence that eventually made him ill. In despair after the death of Mme. du Chatelet, he returned to Germany at the invitation of Frederick II. Controversy seemed to follow him, however, and by 1753 he was out of favor with Frederick and forbidden to return to Paris. He retired to Geneva, where he completed two major historical studies but also became embroiled in religious controversy with the Calvinists (see p. 381). During this time, he wrote his most famous work, *Candide* (1758). Then he purchased an estate on the French-Swiss border, which afforded him safe haven from whichever police were after him at the moment. This began the most active period of his life. Although he was constantly embroiled in minor feuds over everything from land titles to liberation for the serfs, he was world famous and the constant host for international celebrities. He used his fame to speak out on anything and everything—especially the Church—and he fought vigorously for religious toleration, material prosperity, respect for the rights of all humans, and the abolition of torture and useless punishments. He continued to write for the theatre, and it was the theatre that brought about his triumphant return to Paris in 1778. However, the excitement proved too great, and his health suffered irreparably. He died on May 30, that same year.

and tyranny had cast them. All men and women had a right, as rational creatures, to dignity and happiness. This desire to elevate the social circumstances of all people led to an examination and questioning of political, judicial, economic, and ecclesiastical institutions.

The ideas of the Enlightenment spread largely through the efforts of the philosophes (Fig. **14.3**). Although this term suggests philosophy, the philosophes were not philosophers in the usual sense of the word. Rather, they were popularizers or publicists. They were men of letters who culled thought from great books and translated it into simple terms that could be understood by a reading public. In France, the most serious of all the philosophe enterprises was the *Encyclopedia*, edited by Denis Diderot (1713–84). The seventeen-volume *Encyclopedia*, which took from 1751 to 1772 to complete, was a compendium of scientific, technical, and historical knowledge, incorporating a good deal of social criticism. Voltaire, Montesquieu, and Rousseau were among its contributors.

Immediately following the 1688 Revolution in England, John Locke wrote several treatises on government, asserting that the power of a nation came from its people as a whole. In a social contract between government and people, the people had the right to withdraw their support from the government whenever it used its power against the general will.

No philosophe undertook such a vocal or universal attack on contemporary institutions as Voltaire. Voltaire (1697–1778; his name was originally François-Marie Arouet) took Locke's ideas to France, and extolled them. It is easy to see Voltaire as an aggressive, churlish skeptic, who had nothing positive to offer as a substitute for the ills he found everywhere. In fact, his championship of deism contributed greatly to improved religious toleration. His stinging wit broadened awareness of and reaction to witch-burnings, torture, and other such abuses of human rights. Without question, his popularizing of knowledge and his broad program of social reform helped to bring about the French Revolution, which cast out the old absolutist order once and for all.

Another influential figure in the mid-eighteenth century was Jean-Jacques Rousseau (1712–72). Rousseau propounded a theory of government so purely rationalistic that it had no connection whatever with the experience of history. To Rousseau, human beings were essentially unhappy, feeble, frustrated, and trapped in a social environment of their own making. He believed people could be happy and free only in a "state of nature," or, at most, in a small and simple community. Such a philosophy stands completely in contrast to that of Diderot, who held that only accumulated knowledge would liberate humanity.

Indeed, it was an age of contrasts. Rousseau was an anarchist, and did not believe in government of any kind.

He wrote on politics, therefore, not because he was trying to improve government, but because he lived in an age of political speculation and believed he had the power to deal with every problem. His *Social Contract* (1762) was utterly rationalistic. It reasserted Locke's propositions about the social contract, sovereignty of the people, and the right of revolution. More importantly, he took Locke's concept of primitive humanity and converted such people into "noble savages" who had been subjected to progressive degradation by an advancing civilization. In an age turning to rational, intellectual classicism, Rousseau sowed the seeds of Romanticism, which were to flower in the next century. He also sounded the call for revolution: the opening sentence of the *Social Contract* reads, "Man is born free and everywhere he is in chains," a thought that predates Karl Marx by about a century.

ECONOMICS AND POLITICS

The same spirit of challenge and questioning was also applied to economics. Critics of mercantilistic government regulation and control were called "physiocrats," from the Greek *physis*, meaning "nature," because they saw nature as the single source of all wealth. Agriculture, forestry, and mining were of greater importance than manufacturing. Physiocratic theory also advocated a *laissez-faire* approach to economic endeavor. In other words, physiocrats believed that production and distribution were best handled without government interference. Government supervision should be abandoned so that nature and enterprising individuals could co-operate in the production of the greatest possible wealth. General physiocratic ideas were refined and codified in Adam Smith's *Wealth of Nations* (1776). Smith (1723–90), a Scotsman, argued that the basic factor in production was human labor (rather than nature). He believed that enlightened self-interest, without government intervention, would be sufficient to inspire individuals to produce wealth on an unheard-of scale.

On the political scene, the German states were in turmoil and flux in the eighteenth century. In 1701 Frederick I (1657–1713) became King in Prussia (the word "in" rather than "of" was used to placate Poland, which occupied West Prussia). Frederick's major political stronghold lay in a small area called Brandenburg. However, Frederick's family, the Hohenzollern, soon came to dominate the whole of Prussia. Frederick's son, King Frederick William I (r. 1713–40), perfected the structure of the army and the German civil service.

Frederick William was a notable eccentric. For example, anyone he suspected of having wealth was compelled to build a fine residence to improve the appearance of his city. He also had a craze for tall soldiers, whom he recruited from all over Europe, thereby making his palace

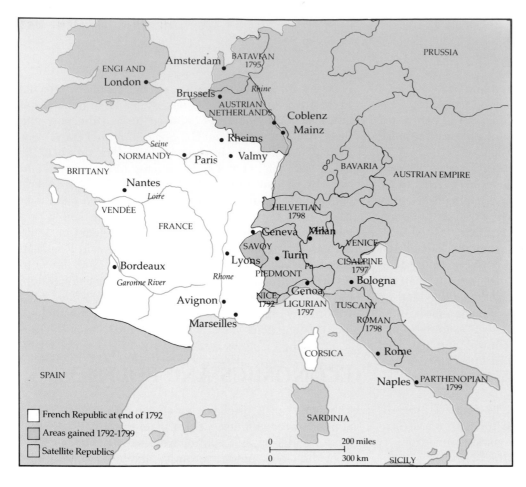

Map 14.1 Europe in the eighteenth century.

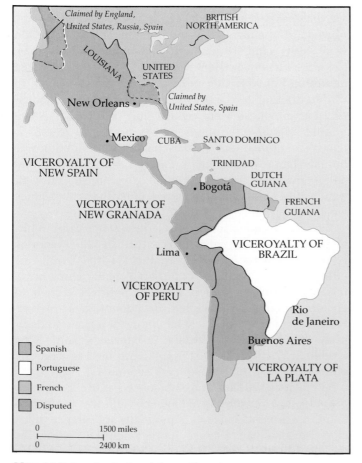

Map 14.2 America in the eighteenth century.

guard a cadre of coddled giants. Frederick William's son, who would become Frederick II, the Great, was given a rigorous training in the army and civil service.

When Frederick the Great (1712–86) assumed the throne on his father's death in 1740, he brought to it a detailed knowledge of the Prussian service, together with an intense love of arts and literature. He was a person of immense ambition, and he turned his sights very quickly on neighboring Austria. Austria's House of Hapsburg was ruled by Charles VI, who died in 1740. His daughter, the Archduchess Maria Theresa, became ruler of all the Hapsburg territories, many of which were the subject of disputed claims of possession. Scenting opportunity, Frederick the Great promptly marched into Austrian territory. A tug-of-war-and-peace between Austria and Prussia followed. Both countries emerged from these hostilities strong and socially stable, and both became centers of artistic, literary, and intellectual activity in the second half of the eighteenth century.

Frederick the Great was an "enlightened" and humanitarian ruler, a "benevolent despot." He championed thinkers throughout Europe and reformed German institutions so that they were better able to render service to all classes of society, especially the poor and oppressed (in strong contrast to Louis XV and XVI of France). When he died in 1786, he left behind a strong and renowned country.

In Austria under the Hapsburgs, too, constant warfare did not interfere with internal order and enlightened reform. Maria Theresa's husband became Emperor Francis I in 1745. He was followed, in 1765, by their son, Joseph II. Ruling jointly with his mother from 1765 to 1780 and alone until his death in 1790, Joseph II was also an enlightened monarch. He unified and centralized the Hapsburg dominions and brought Austria into line with the economic and intellectual conditions of the day.

Meanwhile, in England, King George III (1760–1820), and in France, Louis XV (1715–74) and his grandson, Louis XVI, along with his wife, Marie Antoinette (1774–89), saw revolution overtake their colonies or their country. The events and ramifications of the American Revolution are already familiar. The complexities of the French Revolution (1789), which are beyond our scope here, led from wars throughout Europe and a second revolution in 1792, through an "Emergency Republic," the "Terror," the Directory, Napoleon's *coup d'état* in 1799, to a new and politically explosive century in Europe.

AESTHETICS AND CLASSICISM

The death of Louis XIV in 1715 brought to a close a magnificent French courtly tradition that had championed baroque art (although the German baroque continued well into the eighteenth century). The French court and aristocracy moved to more modest surroundings, to intimate, elegant townhouses and salons, a milieu entirely different from the vastness and opulence of the Palace of Versailles. Charm, manners, and finesse replaced previous standards of social behavior. Enlightenment society sought refinement of detail and décor, and delicacy in everything. "Sociability" became the credo of early eighteenth-century France and the rest of Europe.

Classical influences dating from the Renaissance continued to be important, principally because a "classical education" was considered essential for all members of the upper classes. The excavation of the ruins of the Roman city of Pompeii, found virtually intact, in 1748 caused a wave of excitement. The ancient city of Herculaneum had been partly excavated in 1738. Amid this revived interest came Gottlieb Baumgarten's significant book, *Aesthetica* (1750–58). For the first time the word "aesthetics" was used to mean "the study of beauty and theory of art." Then, in 1764, came Johann Winckelmann's *History of Ancient Art*, in which the author described the essential qualities of Greek art as "a noble simplicity and tranquil loftiness … a beautiful proportion, order, and harmony."

These values brought the arts of the eighteenth century out of the baroque era. Herculaneum, Pompeii, aesthetic theory, and a return to antiquity and the simplicity of nature, closed a century marked by war and revolution, rationalism, and skepticism.

CRITICAL REVIEW below

A CRITICAL REVIEW

The term "enlightened despot" is an important one with regard to this period. As we will see in the Synthesis section at the end of the chapter, this century did away with the "absolute monarchs," although the "enlightened despots" survived. The concept describes a condition of social order that seemed to work—at least at the time. Power, although not absolute, rested in a monarch: therefore, things got done. However, the enlightened attitude of the monarch made it possible to meet the needs of even the lowest, most humble individual in society—order was kept, and the basic conditions and rights of humans were respected and maintained. Life seemed pretty good on the whole. This, at least, was true in the German states in the eighteenth century. In France, on the other hand, the roughshod ways of absolute monarchy caused a mass uprising in which the aristocracy was not only overthrown but exterminated under the guillotine. However, once the mob controlled France, conditions got even worse, and chaos reigned. Eventually, this rude sort of democracy led to the emergence, not of a king, but of a dictator: Napoleon. At the same time England had a constitutional monarchy, and the United States was on the road to establishing a republic.

Write a short essay in which you respond to the following assertion: Enlightened despotism is a better form of government than democracy.

A CRITICAL LOOK

In the next section, the arts take center stage. We will see not one but several new styles emerging from the social conditions of the eighteenth century. In effect, the pendulum will swing from emotion to intellect and back to emotion before we end the next few pages. When we finish this material, we should be able to describe the characteristics of the rococo style; identify painters associated with landscape, portraiture, and genre and describe their works; and explain the principles and characteristics of neoclassicism in visual art and architecture.

Write a page explaining why neoclassicism became popular in America.

In what sense is William Hogarth an Enlightenment painter?

Describe the literary works of Goldsmith, Johnson, and the Preromantics.

THE VISUAL ARTS AND ARCHITECTURE

ROCOCO STYLE

CRITICAL LOOK above

The change from the splendor of courtly life to the style of the small salon and the intimate townhouse was reflected in a new style of painting called "rococo." Often rococo is described as an inconsequential version of baroque, and there is some justification for such a description. Some paintings of this style display fussy detail, complex composition, and a certain superficiality. To dismiss early eighteenth-century work thus would be wrong, however.

Rococo was a product of its time. It is essentially decorative and nonfunctional, like the declining aristocracy it represented. Its intimate grace, charm, and delicate superficiality reflect the social ideals and manners of the age. Informality replaced formality in life and in painting. The heavy academic character of the baroque of Louis XIV was found lacking in feeling and sensitivity. Its scale and grandeur were simply too ponderous. Deeply dramatic action was now transmuted into lively effervescence and melodrama. Love, friendship, sentiment, pleasure, and sincerity became predominant themes. None of these characteristics conflicts significantly with the overall tone of the Enlightenment, whose major goal was refinement. The arts of the period could dignify the human spirit through social and moral consciousness as well as through the graceful sentiments of friendship and love. Delicacy and informality did not have to imply limp or empty sentimentality.

The rococo paintings of Antoine Watteau (1683–1721) are representative of many of the changing values of the aristocracy. Watteau's work is largely sentimental, but it is not particularly frivolous. *Embarkation for Cythera* (Fig. **14.5**) idealizes the social graces of the high-born classes. Cythera is a mythological land of enchantment, the island of Venus, and Watteau portrays aristocrats idling away their time in amorous pursuits as they wait to leave for that faraway place.

Soft color areas and hazy atmosphere add the qualities of fantasy to the landscape. An undulating line underscores the human figures, all posed in slightly affected attitudes. Each group of doll-like couples engages in graceful conversation and amorous games. An armless bust of Venus presides over the delicate scene. Watteau's fussy details and decorative treatment of clothing contrast with the diffused quality of the background. But underlying this fantasy is a deep, poetic melancholy.

The slightly later work of François Boucher (1703–70) continues in the rococo tradition. His work even more fully exemplifies the decorative, mundane, and somewhat erotic painting popular in the early and mid-eighteenth century. As a protégé of Madame de Pompadour, the mistress of King Louis XV, Boucher enjoyed great popularity. His work has a highly decorative surface detail and portrays pastoral and mythological settings such as *Venus Consoling Love* (Fig. **14.6**). Boucher's figures almost always appear amid exquisitely detailed drapery. His technique is nearly flawless, and, with his painterly virtuosity, he creates fussily pretty works, the subjects of which compete with their decorative backgrounds for attention. Compared with the power, sweep, and grandeur of baroque painting, Boucher's work is gentle and shallow. Here, each of the intricate and delicate details takes on a separate focus of its own and leads the eye in a disorderly fashion first in one direction and then another.

Characteristic of later Rococo style, *The Swing* (see Fig. **14.1**) by Jean-Honoré Fragonard (1732–1806) is an "intrigue" picture. A young gentleman has enticed an unsuspecting old cleric to swing the gentleman's sweetheart higher and higher so that he, strategically placed, can catch a glimpse of her exposed limbs. The young

14.5 Antoine Watteau, *Embarkation for Cythera*, 1717. Oil on canvas, 4 ft 3 ins × 6 ft 4½ ins (1.29 × 1.94 m). Louvre, Paris, France.

14.6 François Boucher, *Venus Consoling Love*, 1751. Oil on canvas, 3 ft 6⅛ ins × 2 ft 9⅜ ins (107 × 85 cm). National Gallery of Art, Washington D.C. (Chester Dale Collection).

lady, perfectly aware of his trick, gladly joins in the game, kicking off her shoe toward the statue of the god of discretion, who holds his finger to his lips in an admonishment of silence. The scene is one of frivolous naughtiness and sensuality, with lush foliage, foaming petticoats, and luxurious colors.

Sculpture struggled as an art form in the eighteenth century. The Academy of Sculpture and the French Academy in Rome encouraged the copying of antique sculpture, and resisted any changes in style. Most sculpture thus continued in a derivative baroque style.

Rococo style did find expression in the sculpture of Falconet (1716–91) and Clodion (1738–1814). Their works feature decorative cupids and nymphs, motifs that recur in painting of this style. Venus appears frequently, often in the form of a thinly disguised prominent lady of the day. Madame de Pompadour, who epitomized love,

HUMANITARIANISM AND HOGARTH

The aristocratic frivolity of rococo style was heavily counterbalanced by the biting satire and social comment of enlightened humanitarians such as William Hogarth (1697–1764). In England during the 1730s, Hogarth portrayed dramatic scenes on moral subjects. His *Rake's Progress* and *Harlot's Progress* series are attempts to correct raging social ills and to instill solid middle-class values. Hogarth attacked the foppery of the aristocracy, drunkenness, and social cruelty. In *The Harlot's Progress* series (Fig. **14.11**), the prostitute is a victim of circumstances. She arrives in London, her employer seduces her, and she ends up in Bridewell Prison. Hogarth blames her final fate more on human cruelty than on her sins. The same may be said of *The Rake's Progress*, which in a series of six tableaux, portrays the downfall of a foolish young man from comfortable circumstances. This series moves through several views of the young man as he sinks lower and lower into corruption (Fig. **14.12**) until he ends up in the Bedlam insane asylum.

Hogarth's criticism of social conditions is clear in his paintings, intended as an incitement to action, a purpose characteristic of eighteenth-century humanitarians. The fact that his paintings were made into engravings and widely sold as prints to the public illustrates just how popular were attacks on the social institutions of the day.

LANDSCAPE AND PORTRAITURE

The popularity of portraiture and landscape also increased in the eighteenth century. One of the most influential English painters of the time was Thomas Gainsborough (1727–88). His landscapes bridge the gap between the baroque and Romantic styles, and his portraits exhibit sensitive elegance. Gainsborough's full-length portraits of lords and ladies have a unique freshness and lyric grace. Occasionally art critics object to the lack of structure in his attenuated, almost weightless figures; however, such objections fade away when confronted by the beauty of Gainsborough's color and the delicacy of his touch. His landscapes reveal a freshness typically associated with the English approach to painting.

In *The Market Cart* (Fig. **14.13**) we find a delicate use of WASH reminiscent of Watteau. Here the painter explores tonalities and shapes that express a deep and almost mystical response to nature. Although the subject is pastoral, the composition has an unusual energy that derives from its diagonal composition. The tree forms on the right border are twisted and gnarled: the foremost tree leads the viewer's eye up and to the left, to be caught by the downward circling line of the trees and clouds in the background and returned on the diagonal. The human figures in the picture are not of particular interest—although they are warmly rendered, they are not individuals, and their forms remain indistinct. We see them, rather, as subordinate to the forces of nature which ebb and flow around and through them.

GENRE

A fresh bourgeois flavor could be found in the mundane subjects of France's Jean-Baptiste Siméon Chardin (1699–1779), whose paintings show an interest in the servants and life "below stairs" in well-to-do households. He was the finest STILL-LIFE and genre painter of his time. and can be seen to continue the tradition of the Dutch masters of the previous century. His early works are almost exclu-

14.13 Thomas Gainsborough, *The Market Cart*, 1786–7. Oil on canvas, 6 ft ½ ins × 5 ft ¼ ins (1.84 × 1.53 m). Tate Gallery, London.

14.14 Jean-Baptiste Siméon Chardin, *Menu de Gras*, 1731. Oil on canvas, 13 × 16⅛ ins (33 × 41 cm). Louvre, Paris.

sively still-lifes, and *Menu de Gras* (Fig. **14.14**) illustrates how everyday items could be raised to a level of unsuspected beauty.

The artist invests each item—cooking pot, ladle, pitcher, bottles, cork, a piece of meat, and other small things—with intense significance, as richness of texture and color combined with careful composition and the use of chiaroscuro make these humble items somehow noble. The eye moves slowly from point to point, carefully directed by shapes and angles, color and highlight. The work itself controls the speed at which we view it. Each new focus demands that we pause and savor its richness. Chardin urges us to look beneath our surface impressions of these objects into their deeper reality.

NEOCLASSICISM

The discovery of the ruins of Pompeii, Winckelmann's interpretation of Greek classicism, Rousseau's "noble savage," and Baumgarten's aesthetics sent the interests of late eighteenth-century artists and thinkers back into antiquity, and in particular, into nature.

A principal proponent of neoclassicism in painting was Jacques-Louis David (1748–1825). His works illustrate the newly perceived grandeur of antiquity, and this is reflected in his subject matter, composition, and historical accuracy. Propagandist in tone—he sought to inspire French patriotism and democracy—his paintings have a strong, simple compositional unity. In both *The Death of Socrates* (Fig. **14.15**) and *The Oath of the Horatii* (see Fig. **14.18**), David exploits his political ideas using Greek and Roman themes. In both cases, the subjects suggest a devotion to ideals so strong that one should be prepared to die in their defense. David's values are made dramatically clear by his sparse, simple composition.

The neoclassicism of David and others was, of course, not a simple matter of copying ancient works. Classical detail and principles were used selectively and frequently adapted to suit the artist's own purposes.

During the years just prior to the French Revolution, Jean-Antoine Houdon (1741–1828) worked in a more serious vein. His portrait busts of children, such as those of Alexandre and Louise Brongniart (Fig. **14.16** and **14.17**),

14.15 Jacques-Louis David, *The Death of Socrates*, 1787. Oil on canvas, 4 ft 3 ins × 6 ft 5¼ ins (1.29 × 1.96 m). Metropolitan Museum of Art, New York (Wolfe Fund, 1931. Catherine Lorillard Wolfe Collection).

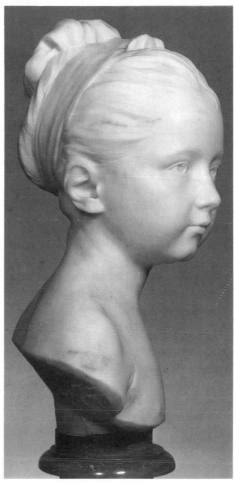

14.16 (*far left*) Jean-Antoine Houdon, *Alexandre Brongniart*, 1777. Marble, 15³/₈ ins (39.2 cm) high. National Gallery of Art, Washington D.C. (Widener Collection).

14.17 (*near left*) Jean-Antoine Houdon, *Louise Brongniart*, 1777. Marble, 14¹/₈ ins (37.7 cm) high. National Gallery of Art, Washington D.C. (Widener Collection).

show acute psychological observation as well as accurate technical execution. Houdon's works distill the personality of his subjects, and his busts of American revolutionary figures, such as Washington, Jefferson, John Paul Jones, and Benjamin Franklin, are revealing character portraits. Houdon's work seems to belong to the emerging eighteenth-century neoclassical style. The realism and truth that Houdon puts into his individual characters are much more akin to the ideals of neoclassicism than to those of the rococo.

Sculpture, like society in the eighteenth century, was in transition. Academically rooted in the baroque, yet attempting to reflect the age of the rococo and the aesthetic and antiquarian interests of the last third of the century, sculpture made little progress. That would come in the nineteenth century, with another stylistic shift.

In the mid-eighteenth century the aims of architecture altered to embrace the complex philosophical concerns of the Enlightenment. The result was a series of styles and sub-styles broadly referred to as "neoclassical." Excavations at Herculaneum and Pompeii, philosophical concepts of progress, the aesthetics of Baumgarten, and the writings of Winckelmann all expressed and created a new view of antiquity. Neoclassicism was thus a new way

of examining the past: rather than seeing the past as a single, continuous cultural flow broken by a medieval collapse of classical values, theoreticians of the eighteenth century saw history as a series of separate compartments—Antiquity, the Middle Ages, the Renaissance, and so on.

Three important approaches emerged as a result of this new idea. The archeological school saw the present as continually enriched by persistent inquiry into the past. In other words, history was the story of progress. The second approach was eclectic. It saw the artist as someone who could choose among styles, or, more importantly, combine elements of various styles. A third, modernist, approach viewed the present as unique and, therefore, capable of expression in its own terms. Each of these three concepts profoundly influenced eighteenth-century architecture and bore importantly on the other arts. From this time forward, the basic premises of art were fundamentally changed.

Neoclassicism in architecture alludes to all three concepts, and encompasses a variety of treatments and terminologies. The identifiable forms of Greece and Rome are basic to it, of course. It also took considerable impetus from the *Essai sur l'architecture* (1753) by the Abbé

MASTERWORK

David—The Oath of the Horatii

David's famous painting, *The Oath of the Horatii*, concerns the conflict between love and patriotism. In legend, the leaders of the Roman and Alban armies, on the verge of battle, decide to resolve their conflicts by means of an organized combat between three representatives from each side. The three Horatius brothers represented Rome; the Curatius sons represented the Albans. A sister of the Horatii was the fiancée of one of the Curatius brothers. David's painting depicts the Horatii as they swear on their swords to win or die for Rome, disregarding the anguish of their sister.

The work captures a directness and an intensity of expression that were to play an important role in Romanticism. But the starkness of outline, the strong geometric composition (which juxtaposes straight line in the men and curved line in the women), and the smooth color areas and gradations hold it to the more formal, classical tradition. The style of *The Oath of the Horatii* is academic neoclassicism. The scene takes place in a shallow picture box, defined by a severely simple architectural framework. The costumes are historically correct. The musculature, even the arms and legs of the women, has a surface devoid of warmth or softness, like the drapery.

It is ironic that David's work was admired and purchased by King Louis XVI, against whom David's revolutionary cries were directed and whom David, as a member of the French Revolutionary Convention, would sentence to death. Neoclassicism increased in popularity and continued through the Napoleonic era and into the nineteenth century.

14.18 Jacques-Louis David, *The Oath of the Horatii*, 1784–5. Oil on canvas, c. 14 × 11 ft (4.27 × 3.35 m). Louvre, Paris.

14.19 Thomas Jefferson, Rotunda of the University of Virginia, 1819–28.

14.20 Thomas Jefferson, Monticello, Charlottesville, Virginia, 1770–84; rebuilt 1796–1800.

Laugier. Laugier's strictly rationalistic work expressed neoclassicism in a nutshell. Discarding all architectural language developed since the Renaissance, he urged the architect to seek truth in the architectural principles of the ancient world and to use those principles to design modern buildings. Laugier's neoclassicism descended directly from the Greeks, with only passing reference to the Romans.

In Italy, the architect Giambattista Piranesi (1720–78) was incensed by Laugier's arguments, which placed Greece above Rome. He retaliated with an overwhelmingly detailed work, *Della Magnificenza ed Architettura dei Romani*, which professed to prove the superiority of Rome over Greece. This quarrel aside, both Piranesi and Laugier were instigators of the neoclassical tradition, and in general, this revival of classicism in architecture, with its high moral seriousness, was seen in many quarters as a revolt against the frivolity of the rococo.

In America, neoclassicism had special meaning, as the colonies struggled to rid themselves of the monarchial rule of George III of England. For the revolutionary colonists, classicism meant Greece, and Greece meant democracy. The designs of colonial architect Thomas Jefferson (Fig. **14.19** and **14.20**) reflect the ideas of this period. Jefferson was highly influenced by Palladio, whose popularity had soared during the significant period of English villa architecture, between 1710 and 1750. In a uniquely eighteenth-century way, Jefferson looked at architecture objectively, within the framework of contemporary thought. Strongly influenced by Lockean ideas of natural law, Jefferson believed that the architecture of antiquity embodied indisputable natural principles, and he made Palladian reconstructions of the Roman temple the foundation for his theory of architecture. His country house, Monticello, consists of a central structure with attached Doric porticos, or porches, and short, low wings

14.21 Miles Brewton House, Charleston, South Carolina (architect unknown), c. 1769.

attached to the center by continuing Doric entablatures. The simplicity and refinement of Jefferson's statement here goes beyond mere reconstruction of classical prototypes, and appeals directly to the viewer's intellect and sensibilities.

Throughout the United States, and particularly in the South, the classical revival found frequent expression. In Charleston, South Carolina, the Miles Brewton House provides us with one of the finest examples of American Georgian architecture (Fig. **14.21**). The large pedimented portico, supported by Ionic columns, indicates the boldness of American neoclassicism.

LITERATURE

Among the numerous eighteenth-century literary figures stands one who used his talents in an interdisciplinary way. William Blake (1757–1827) published his poems by personally engraving them into copper plates along with his own illustrations. He then illuminated the pages with watercolors. He defied reason and detested the rationalism of the period, championing the emotions in an age of intellect and science.

Thomas Paine (1737–1809), on the other hand, turned his energies to writing pamphlets in support of the libertarian ideals of the times. An Englishman, he worked for the American movement toward independence, and later wrote *The Rights of Man* (1792) in support of the French Revolution. He was banished from Britain, imprisoned in France, and died in poverty in the United States. 1792 also saw the publication of *A Vindication of the Rights of Woman* by Paine's fellow British writer Mary Wollstonecraft (1759–97). This well-argued treatise can be seen to mark the beginning of the feminist movement.

GOLDSMITH

Contemporary literature reflects the eighteenth-century focus on the commonplace that we saw in the genre paintings of the day. Common ordinary occurrences are frequently used as symbols of a higher reality. The work of Oliver Goldsmith (1730–74), the prominent British eighteenth-century poet and playwright, illustrates this quite clearly. Goldsmith grew up in the village of Lissoy, where his father was vicar, and *The Deserted Village*, written in 1770, describes the sights and personalities of Lissoy:

> Sweet Auburn! Loveliest village of the plain
> Where health and plenty cheered the laboring swain;
> Where smiling spring its earliest visit paid.
> And parting summer's lingering blooms delayed.
> Dear lovely bowers of innocence and ease,
> Seats of my youth, where every sport could please;
> How often have I loitered o'er thy green,
> Where humble happiness endeared each scene!

Goldsmith's portrait of the old village parson includes a lovely simile.

> To them his heart, his love, his griefs were given,
> But all his serious thoughts had rest in heaven.
> As some tall cliff that lifts its awful form,
> Swells from the vale, and midway leaves the storm,
> External sunshine settles on its head.

Finally, there is great tenderness in the way he describes his dream of ending his life amid the scenes in which it had begun.

> In all my wanderings round this world of care,
> In all my griefs—and God has given my share—
> I still had hopes, my latest hours to crown,
> Amid these humble bowers to lay me down,
> To husband out life's taper at the close,
> And keep the flame from wasting by repose....
> And as an hare whom hounds and horns pursue,
> Pants to the place from which at first she flew,
> I still had hopes my long vexations past,
> Here to return—and die at home at last.

JOHNSON

The mid-eighteenth century is often called the "Age of Johnson." Samuel Johnson (1709–84) began his literary career as a sort of odd-job journalist, writing for a newspaper. His principal achievements were as a lexicographer and essayist: the 208 *Rambler* essays cover a huge variety of topics, including "Folly of Anger: Misery of a Peevish Old Age" and "Advantages of Mediocrity: an Eastern Fable." These essays promoted the glory of God and the writer's salvation.

In 1758, Johnson began the *Idler Essays*, a weekly contribution to a newspaper called the *Universal Chronicle*. In these essays we find the moralistic, reforming tone still present, but with an increasingly comic element.

THE PREROMANTICS

The decline of drama and the rise of the novel in the eighteenth century marked a significant shift in literature. Henry Fielding's life (1707–54) mirrored this transition as he moved from a distinguished career in the theatre—he had written about twenty-five plays, mostly satirical and topical comedies—to become a pre-eminent novelist. His first full novel, *Joseph Andrews* (1742), portrays one of the first memorable characters in English fiction—an idealistic and inconsistent hero who constantly falls into ridiculous adventures. Fielding called his novel a "comic prose epic," and it is remarkable for its structure as well as its humor and its satire. His most famous novel remains *Tom Jones* (1749), a splendid romp which ranks among the greatest works in English literature.

One of the most influential of the Preromantic writers in France was Jean-Jacques Rousseau. He placed a new emphasis on emotion rather than reason, on sympathy rather than rational understanding. Others included the novelists Horace Walpole (1717–97) and Mrs Radcliffe (1764–1823), who catered to the public taste for Gothic tales of dark castles and shining heroism in medieval settings. The German Johann Gottfried von Herder (1744–1803) also contributed to the Preromantic movement. Herder's essays, *German Way and German Art* (1773), have been called the "manifesto of German *Sturm und Drang*" (storm and stress). In his greatest work, *Ideas on the Philosophy of the History of Mankind* (1784–91), he analyzed nationalism and prescribed a way of reviving "a national feeling through school, books, and newspapers using the national language."

The major thrust of Romanticism outlasted the eighteenth century and found full expression only in the nineteenth. By then, the various offshoots of Romanticism had permeated every aspect of society, as we shall see in the next chapter.

CRITICAL REVIEW below

A CRITICAL REVIEW

We have come far enough in our journey to recognize a trend. The arts seem to swing back and forth between two poles. At one pole, form and content lean toward intellectual stimulation, at the other pole, they lean toward the emotional. This alternation is sometimes known as "form versus feeling." The naturally opposing forces of intellect and emotion continue to tug at the underlying meanings of the works. Another way to describe this alternating tendency is to use a stylistic label: classicism versus anti-classicism. If you apply those characteristics to the broad periods of artistic activity that we have been pursuing in this text, we see that we have established a rhythmic swing: Classicism to anti-classicism to classicism to anti-classicism, and so on. Applying that alternating pattern to what we have studied in Chapters 3 to 14, place the various styles on a continuum, with classicism (form) on one end and anti-classicism (feeling) on the other.

Describe rococo painting, using as examples the works of Watteau and Boucher. How does rococo differ from baroque?

Explain how genre painting differs from neoclassicism. Cite specific works to support your contentions.

Which visual art styles most closely resemble the writings of Goldsmith?

A CRITICAL LOOK

In the next section, music and theatre reveal many of the same trends we saw in painting, sculpture, architecture, and literature. The pendulum swings from emotion to intellect. In this section, we will do some musical analysis, and by now our skills are fairly well tuned. We may stumble over some of the terminology, but our ability to hear subtleties in musical phrasing, structure, and tonality are better than we think. You should now be able, for example, to describe styles and identify their principal composers.

Describe the features of the classical style and the specific characteristics of its key composers.

Describe the general theatre conditions in Britain, the United States, France, and Germany during the eighteenth century.

MUSIC

PRE-CLASSICAL

CRITICAL
LOOK
p.465

As French court society and its baroque arts slipped from favor, the ornamentation, delicacy, prettiness, and pleasant artificiality of the rococo style came to music as well as to painting and sculpture. Musicians improvised "decorations" in their performances, and the practice was so common that many composers purposely left their melodic lines bare in order to allow performers the opportunity for playful trills and other ornaments. The purpose of music was to entertain and to charm.

François Couperin (1668–1733) exemplified the musical spirit of his time, but he also retained sufficient of his baroque roots to avoid excessive sentimentality or completely artificial decoration. Nevertheless, his works are appropriate to salon performance, and do not limit any one piece or movement to one emotion. He shows a pleasant blending of logic and rationality with emotion and delicacy, in true rococo fashion.

Couperin was part of a uniquely French school of keyboard music, which specialized in long dance suites, so-called "genre pieces," contrapuntal works with highly ornamented introductions, and overtures similar to those found in French opera. Many of the pieces are miniatures, and the grand sweep of the baroque era is replaced by an abundance of short melodic phrases with much repetition and profuse ornamentation. But Couperin's passacaglias and chaconnes—for example, the *Passacaille ou Chaconne* from the First Suite for Viols, 1728—still use the same indefinitely repeated four- or eight-measure harmonic patterns found in music of the seventeenth century. His trio sonatas, too, look back to the baroque era, and are among the last of this musical form to be composed. The classical period was to bring in new instrumental groupings for chamber music.

EXPRESSIVE STYLE

A second style of music, the Expressive style, paralleled the rococo style and formed a transitional stage between baroque and classical. This Expressive style (more literally, "sensitive" style), or *empfindsamer Stil*, came from Germany. It permitted a freer expression of emotions than the baroque, largely by allowing a variety of moods to occur within a single movement. Polyphonic complexities were reduced, and different themes, with harmonic and rhythmic contrasts, were introduced. Expressive style was thus simple and highly original. Composers had the freedom to use rhythmic contrasts, original melodies, and new nuances and shading of loud and soft. Yet the goal was a carefully proportioned, logical, unified whole, whose parts were clear and carefully articulated.

The principal exponent of the *empfindsamer Stil* was Carl Philipp Emanuel Bach (1714–88), one of J.S. Bach's sons. His position between the baroque and classical styles has led some scholars to call him the "founder" of the classical style. For many years he was court harpsichordist to Frederick the Great, and it is his keyboard works that are generally considered his most important compositions. He understood music to be an art of the emotions, and believed it very important that the player be involved personally in each performance.

CLASSICAL STYLE

In 1785 Michel Paul de Chabanon wrote: "Today there is but one music in all of Europe." What he meant was that music was being composed to appeal not only to the aristocracy but to the middle classes as well. Egalitarian tendencies and the popular ideals of the philosophes had also influenced artists, who now sought larger audiences. Pleasure had become a legitimate artistic purpose. Eighteenth-century rationalism saw excessive ornamentation and excessive complexity (both baroque characteristics) as not appealing to a wide audience on its own terms. Those sentiments, which coincided with the discoveries of Pompeii and the ideas of Winckelmann and Baumgarten, prompted a move toward order, simplicity, and careful attention to form. We call this style in music classical (the term was not applied until the nineteenth century), rather than neoclassical or classical revival, because although the other arts returned, more or less, to Greek and Roman prototypes, music had no known classical antecedents to revive. Music thus turned to classical ideals, though not to classical models.

One very basic characteristic of classical style was a clearly articulated structure. Each piece was organized into short statements, called "phrases," which recurred regularly and clearly. The most frequently cited example occurs in Wolfgang Amadeus Mozart's (1756–91) Symphony No. 40 in G minor, whose opening movement is based on a three-note rhythmic pattern, or motif, organized into two contrasting phrases. These phrases are then grouped into themes, which comprise sections in the movement. In contrast, for example, with the opening movement of Vivaldi's "Spring" (remember its ABACADAEA structure), the Symphony No. 40 uses only an AABA structure. Although it is part of a much longer composition than Vivaldi's, it is much simpler and more clearly expressed.

A second change was the general avoidance of polyphony. Classical music depended upon a single, unobscured melodic line that could be shaped into expressive contours and brought to a definite conclusion.

A third change from the baroque lay in rhythmic patterns. The flow of the baroque's numerous ornamented parts fostered essentially unchanging rhythmic patterns. Classical phrase structure and melodic linearity allowed far more opportunity for rhythmic variety and contrast.

Finally, classical style changed harmonic relationships, including more frequent use of key changes.

The most important forms in this period were the symphony and the sonata. Sonatas were composed for virtually every instrument, but the piano and violin predominate. The classical sonata is a work of three or four movements, each of which has a specific structure. The most important structural feature of the sonata is the typical configuration of the first movement. This structure is so important and specific that it is called "sonata form," or "sonata-*allegro* form." It is used not only in the first movement of sonatas, but also in the first movement of symphonies and chamber music. Using the traditional structural alphabet, sonata form simply goes AABA. The A section begins with a thematic statement in the home or tonic key, followed by transitional materials, called a bridge. A contrasting theme is then presented in a different key—usually the key of the dominant or the relative minor. The A section, called the "exposition," closes with a strong cadence. Usually the entire exposition section is repeated (AA). In the next section (B), called the "development," the thematic material of the exposition undergoes numerous alterations. The composer restates thematic material using different rhythms, harmonies, melodies, dynamics, and keys. Usually tension and excitement build up in this section.

Finally, tension is resolved in the recapitulation section (A). Although called a "recapitulation," this is not a strict repeat of the exposition. In particular, both the main themes are now presented in the home key. There might also, for example, be an extended coda. Not all classical sonatas, symphonies, or chamber music fit the textbook mold, but these characteristics provide a fairly accurate guide to the classical sonata form.

The symphony, which uses sonata form in its opening movement, also plays an important part in the classical music tradition. By the last quarter of the eighteenth century, the symphony, like other forms of instrumental ensemble music, had largely eliminated use of *basso continuo*, and, thereby, the harpsichord. Primary focus, then, fell on the violin section, and classical symphonies reflect that new focus. By the turn of the nineteenth century, other sections, such as the woodwind, were given more important, independent material.

The timbre of an orchestra was fairly close to what we know today. But the size, and therefore the overall volume of sound, was not. The largest orchestra of the mid-eighteenth century, at Mannheim, consisted of forty-five players, mostly strings, with six woodwind, five brass and two timpani. Haydn's orchestra between 1760 and 1785 rarely exceeded twenty-five players, and the Vienna orchestras of the 1790s averaged thirty-five. This stands in contrast to those of the nineteenth century, which had twice this many players.

HAYDN

The Austrian-born Franz Joseph Haydn (1732–1809) pioneered the development of the symphony from a short, simple work into a longer, more sophisticated one. Haydn's symphonies are diverse and numerous—some sources indicate that he wrote more than 104. Some of these are light and simple, others are serious and sophisticated.

Many of Haydn's early symphonies use the preclassical, fast-slow-fast three-movement form. These usually consist of an opening allegro, followed by an *andante* in a related key, and close with a rapid dance-like movement in triple meter. Other early works use four movements, the first of which is in a slow tempo. In contrast, the Symphony No. 3 in G major (c. 1762) has a typical four-movement structure beginning with a fast tempo: I *allegro*, II *andante moderato*, III minuet and trio, and IV *allegro*. This symphony emphasizes polyphony more than homophony, in contrast to the general classical trend, and the opening *allegro* does not use sonata form. The third movement, the minuet and trio, is a new feature, found in nearly every classical symphony. It always has a distinctive form: the minuet is played first, then the trio, and then the minuet is played again (ABA). Both minuet and trio are themselves two-part structures. Haydn's minuets contain very charming music, often emphasizing instrumental color in the trio.

Among his late works is his most famous symphony, No. 94 in G major (1792), commonly known as the "Surprise" Symphony. Its second movement contains a simple, charming theme and the dramatic musical surprise that gives the work its popular name. The movement is in the form of a theme and variations (AA'A''A'''A'''')—the apostrophes represent a VARIATION of the original material. The tempo is *andante*, and the orchestra begins with a soft statement of the theme. After presenting the theme a second time, even more quietly, Haydn inserts a tremendous *fortissimo* (very loud) chord. This is the surprise that makes those who are unfamiliar with the work jump out of their skin. With the exception of the "surprise," this movement is typical in its use of a melody based on the two main harmonies of Western music, the TONIC or home chord, and the dominant chord. It is also typical to use variation form for a slow movement. At each repetition of the theme, one or more elements—such as rhythm, texture, or instrumentation—is changed. In this instance, it is quite easy to hear that the second variation is in a minor key, unlike the rest of the movement, and the fourth variation plays around with various rhythmic features, such as triple rhythms and

14.22 Haydn, Symphony No. 94 in G major, first theme of first movement.

loud chords on weak beats.

In the opening movement of this four-movement work, Haydn uses sonata form. This is preceded by a pastoral introduction, marked *adagio cantabile*, that is, in a slow, singing style, in triple meter. The introductory material alternates between the strings and the woodwind.

The tempo switches to *vivace assai*, that is, very fast, and the strings quietly introduce the first theme in G major (Fig. **14.22**).

The last note of the theme is marked *f*, or *forte* (loud). At this point, the full orchestra joins the violins in a lively section. Just before a pause, the orchestra plays a short prefatory phrase which will recur throughout the movement (Fig. **14.23**):

14.23 Haydn, Symphony No. 94 in G major, prefatory phrase, first movement.

The first theme then reappears, with a slightly altered rhythmic pattern. This marks a bridge, or transition passage, to a new key, the dominant, D major. A quick series of scales in the violins and flutes leads to the introduction of the second theme, a lyrical theme with trills and a falling motif. The exposition section closes with a short scale figure and repeated notes, and then the entire exposition is repeated.

The development section opens with a variation of the first theme and then goes through a series of key and dynamic changes.

The recapitulation starts—as recapitulations always do—with a return to the first theme in the original key. A passage based on motifs from the first theme, a repeat and brief development of the first theme, a pause, and finally, another repeat of the first theme follow. Then the second theme appears again, now in the home key, and the movement closes with a short scale passage and a strong cadence.

MOZART

Wolfgang Amadeus Mozart (1756–91), also an Austrian, had performed at the court of Empress Maria Theresa at the age of six. As was the case throughout the classical period, aristocratic patronage was essential for musicians to earn a living, although the middle classes provided a progressively larger portion of commissions, pupil fees, and concert attendance. Mozart's short career (he died at the age of thirty-five) was dogged by financial insecurity.

His early symphonies were simple and relatively short, like those of Haydn, while his later works were longer and more complex. His last three symphonies are generally regarded as among his greatest masterpieces, and the aforementioned Symphony No. 40 in G minor is often referred to as the typical classical symphony. This work, along with Nos. 39 and 41, have clear order and restraint, yet they exhibit a tremendous emotional urgency, which many scholars cite as the beginning of the Romantic style.

The first of the four movements of Symphony No. 40, written in sonata form, begins *allegro molto*. The violins state the first theme above a soft chordal accompaniment, which establishes the tonic key of G minor (Fig. **14.24**). Three short motifs are repeated throughout the piece.

14.24 Mozart, Symphony No. 40 in G minor, first theme of first movement.

The restlessness of the rhythm is accentuated by the liveliness of the lower strings. The second theme in the woodwinds and strings provides a relaxing contrast. It is in a contrasting key, the relative major, B flat, and it flows smoothly, each phrase beginning with a gliding movement down a chromatic scale. A codetta echoes the basic motif on various instruments and finishes with a cadence in B flat major. In most performances the entire exposition section is repeated, giving the movement a classical AABA form.

The development section concentrates on the basic three-note motif and explores the possibilities of the opening theme. This section is somewhat brief, but full of drama.

The recapitulation restates the first theme in the home key, and then the second theme, also in G minor rather than in the original major. This gives the ending a more mournful character than the equivalent section in the exposition. A coda in the original key ends the movement.

The second movement, *andante*, in E flat major, also uses sonata form. The first theme of the movement is passed successively among the violas, second violins, and first violins. The horns provide a rich background.

Unlike the first movement, there is no strong contrast between the first and second themes. They are presented in E flat major and B flat major—the standard contrast of keys in a movement that starts in a major key. The development changes key further, moving into the minor, then returns to the home key with a dialogue among the woodwinds. This movement features many graceful embellishments, which were popular with the Austrian court.

The third movement, *allegretto*, returns to G minor and the emotional tension of the first movement. The meter is triple—it is a minuet and trio, which is typical for the third movement. This is a lively piece with symmetrically arranged phrases and strong cross-rhythms. The trio changes key to G major and has a more relaxed mood.

The finale, *allegro assai*, uses a compact sonata form. The violins state the subject in G minor and create a "rocket theme," that is, an upward thrusting arpeggio (Fig. **14.25**).

14.25 Mozart, Symphony No. 40 in G minor, first theme of fourth movement.

The violins play the second, contrasting theme in the related key of B flat major, and the woodwinds pick it up and embellish it. The development in this movement is very dramatic. The rocket motif bounces from instrument to instrument, creating a highly complex texture, which is increased by rapid modulation through several remote keys. The recapitulation returns, of course, to the home key of G minor, with subtle restatement and variation.

Mozart is also well known for his operas, and he was especially skilled in comic opera. *The Marriage of Figaro* (1786), for example, is fast and humorous, with slapstick action in the manner of farce, but it also has great melodic beauty.

The plot of *The Marriage of Figaro* is taken from Beaumarchais' play of the same name. It centers on the impending marriage of Count Almaviva's valet Figaro to the Countess's maid Susanna. The plot is complex and full of comic deceptions, mistaken identities, physical action, revenge, and actions at cross-purposes.

The duet "Cinque ... dieci," which opens Act I (Fig. **14.26**), gives us a good example of Mozart's style. We hear Figaro, a baritone, singing a series of deliberate motifs as he measures the bedroom which he will share with Susanna after the wedding. He calls out the measurements, "cinque" (five), "dieci" (ten), and so on:

14.26 Mozart, *The Marriage of Figaro*, first theme of "Cinque ... dieci" duet.

Figaro's passage comprises the first theme of the duet, which is *allegro*. The free form of the duet allows for the contrast between the two themes, the second of which is sung by Susanna, a soprano, who enters while Figaro is singing. She is preoccupied with trying on a new hat, and the composer lets the two singers work their themes together before Figaro responds to his fiancée. Then he joins in dialogue with her. The music begins in G major, modulates to D major, and returns to G, a typical key scheme.

BEETHOVEN

Ludwig van Beethoven (1770–1827) is often considered apart from the classical period and treated as a singular transitional figure between classicism and Romanticism. Beethoven wanted to expand the classical symphonic form to accommodate greater emotional character. The typical classical symphony has movements with contrasting and unrelated themes. Beethoven moved toward a single thematic development throughout, thereby achieving a unity of emotion in the whole work.

Beethoven's works differ significantly from those of Haydn and Mozart. They are more dramatic, and they use changing dynamics for starker emotional effects. Silence is used to pursue both dramatic and structural ends. Beethoven's works are also longer. He lengthened the development section of sonata form and did the same to his codas, many of which take on characteristics of a second development section.

He also changed traditional numbers of and relationships among movements, especially in the unusual Symphony No. 6, which has no break between the fourth and fifth movements. In the Symphony No. 5, no break occurs between the third and fourth movements. In some of his four-movement works, he changed the traditional third movement minuet and trio to a scherzo and trio of significantly livelier character. Beethoven's symphonies draw heavily on imagery, for example heroism in Symphony No. 3 and pastoral settings in Symphony No. 6. The famous Symphony No. 5 in C minor, for example, begins with a motif that Beethoven described as "fate knocking at the door." The first movement (*allegro con brio*) develops according to typical sonata form, the second and contrasting movement (*andante con moto*) is in theme-and-variation form, and the third movement (*allegro*) is a scherzo and trio in triple meter. Movement number four returns to *allegro* and to sonata form.

Beethoven's nine symphonies became progressively

TECHNOLOGY: PUTTING DISCOVERY TO WORK

Exact Tolerance

All areas of industry saw the invention and design of new machines and machine tools throughout the century. One of these was the milling machine (Fig. **15.2**), whose rotary cutting edges made possible the manufacture of parts of exact tolerance that could be interchanged in a single product. This idea of interchangeable parts is called the "American System," and is generally attributed to Eli Whitney. The armaments industry also began to use a new grinding machine that enabled machinists to shape metal parts as opposed to merely polishing or sharpening them. Further experiments refined the accuracy of grinding wheels and improved their abrasive surfaces. A new turret lathe made it possible to use several tools on a workpiece. Advances of this sort made possible a "second generation" of machine tools in the industrialized West.

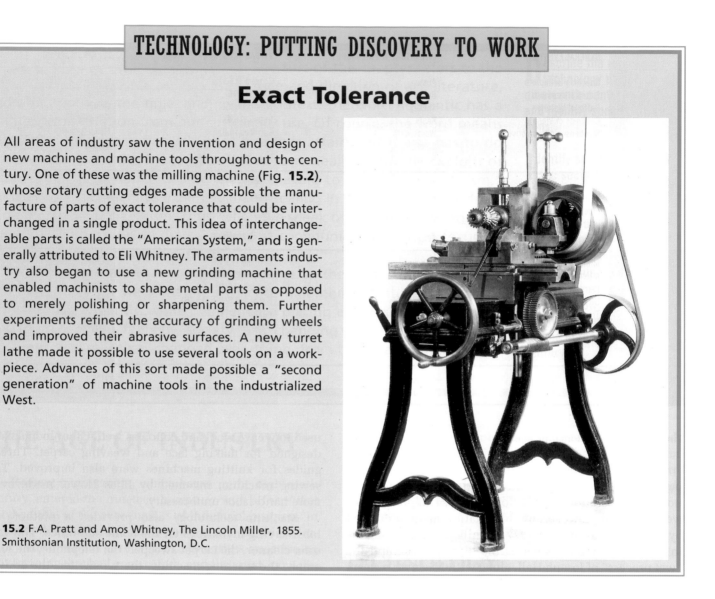

15.2 F.A. Pratt and Amos Whitney, The Lincoln Miller, 1855. Smithsonian Institution, Washington, D.C.

ishable goods could be refrigerated, and frozen goods could even be shipped across the American continent.

At the mid-point of the century, the process of pasteurization was discovered, eliminating several milk-borne diseases. Largely as a result of the experiments of Nicholas Appert, early in the nineteenth century, the use of heat in preserving food gave rise to the canning industry, and by the late 1840s, hermetic sealing was widespread.

Another major aspect of the technological revolution was the harnessing of electricity. By the nineteenth century, the wet battery provided a source for the continuous flow of current. Electrical energy was gradually applied to heating, lighting, and mechanical energy. Experiments produced a practical filament for an incandescent light bulb. The electric-powered streetcar rendered horsecars obsolete by 1888. By 1895 Niagara Falls had been harnessed for hydroelectric power. Elsewhere, long transmission lines and transformers carried electrical power throughout the Western world.

We have touched on four major areas of technological development—advances in the production of metals; the development of machine-tool industries; the introduction of precision instruments leading to standardization; and the development of efficient energy systems. There were, of course, many others, both before and during the nineteenth century. All had wide-ranging effects, and, by the turn of the twentieth century, the Western world had been fully mechanized.

SOCIAL CHANGES

Watt's steam engine of 1769 gave rise to further invention in the textile industry and elsewhere. In 1807 Robert Fulton built the first practical steamboat, and in 1825 an Englishman, George Stephenson, built a steam locomotive, which led to the first English railroad. The explosion of steamboat and railroad building that followed meant that, by the mid-nineteenth century, the world's entire

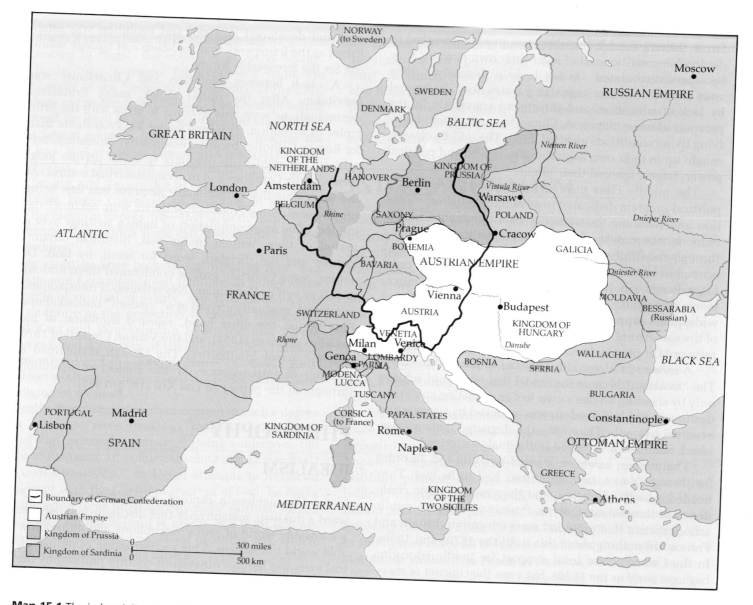

Map 15.1 The industrialized world in the nineteenth century.

transportation system had undergone a complete revolution.

Soon steam engines ran sawmills, printing presses, pumping stations, and hundreds of other kinds of machinery, and further inventions and discoveries followed on the heels of steam power. Electricity, too, was in fairly wide use before the century was over, at least in the urban centers. The discovery of electricity made the telegraph possible in 1832. Telegraph lines spanned continents and, in 1866, joined them via the first transatlantic cable. The telephone was invented in 1876, and by 1895, radio-telegraphy was ready for twentieth-century development.

The Industrial Revolution began in England and, at the conclusion of the Napoleonic wars in 1815, spread to France and the rest of Europe. It gained momentum as it spread, and irrevocably altered the fabric of civilization.

By 1871, the year of the first unification of Germany, major industrial centers had been established all over Europe.

Coal and iron production gave Britain, Germany, France, and Belgium the lead in European industry. But vast resources of coal, iron, and other raw materials, more than all Europe had, soon propelled the United States into a position of economic dominance. Throughout the Western world, centers of heavy industry grew up near the sources of raw materials and transportation routes. Colonial expansion provided world markets for new goods. Wealth increased enormously, and although the effects of investment were felt at every level of society, the principal effect of industrialization was to centralize economic control in the hands of a relatively small class of capitalists. Populations grew as the mortality rate went down. A new class of machine workers, "blue-collar workers," or labor, emerged.

Drawn from pre-industrial home industries and

MASTERWORK

Géricault—The Raft of the "Medusa"

The Raft of the "Medusa" (Fig. **15.10**) by Théodore Géricault illustrates both an emerging rebellion against classicism in painting and a growing criticism of social institutions in general. The painting tells a story of governmental incompetence that resulted in tragedy. In 1816, the French government allowed an unseaworthy ship, the *Medusa*, to leave port, and it was wrecked. Aboard a makeshift raft, the survivors endured tremendous suffering, and were eventually driven to cannibalism. In preparing for the work, Géricault interviewed the survivors, read newspaper accounts, and went so far as to paint corpses and the heads of guillotined criminals.

Géricault's painting captures the ordeal in Romantic style, tempered by classical and even High Renaissance influences. Géricault was a pupil of David, and, like David, he achieved firmly modeled flesh,

realistic figures, and a precise play of light and shade. (His treatment of the physical form reminds us of Michelangelo.) In contrast to David's ordered, two-dimensional paintings, however, Géricault used complex and fragmented compositional structures. For example, he chose to base the design on two triangles rather than a strong central triangle. In *The Raft of the "Medusa"* the left triangle's apex is the makeshift mast, which points back toward despair and death. The other triangle moves up to the right to the figure waving the fabric, pointing toward hope and life as a rescue ship appears in the distance.

Géricault captures the precise moment at which the rescue ship is sighted. The play of light and shade heightens the dramatic effect, and the composition builds upward from the bodies of the dead and dying in the foreground to the dynamic group whose final energies are summoned to support the figure waving to the ship. Thus, the painting is charged with unbridled emotional responses to the horror of the experience and the heroism of the survivors.

15.10 Théodore Géricault, *The Raft of the "Medusa"*, 1819. Oil on canvas, 16 ft × 23 ft 6 ins (4.91 × 7.16 m). Louvre, Paris.

15.11 Joseph Mallord William Turner, *The Slave Ship* (*Slavers Throwing Overboard the Dead and Dying, Typhoon Coming On*), 1839. Oil on canvas, 35³/₄ × 48¹/₄ ins (90.8 × 122.6 cm). Museum of Fine Arts, Boston (Henry Lillie Pierce Fund).

These figures are not realistically depicted people. Instead, Goya makes a powerful social and emotional statement. Napoleon's soldiers are not even human types. Their faces are hidden, and their rigid, repeated forms become a line of subhuman automatons. The murky quality of the background strengthens the value contrasts in the painting and this charges the emotional drama of the scene. Color areas have hard edges, and a stark line of light running diagonally from the oversized lantern to the lower border irrevocably separates executioners and victims. Goya has no sympathy for French soldiers as human beings here. His subjectivity fills the painting, which is as emotional as the irrational behavior he wished to condemn.

The Englishman J.M.W. Turner (1775–1851) indulged in a subjectivity even beyond that of his Romantic contemporaries, and his work foreshadows the dissolving image of twentieth-century painting. The Romantic painter John Constable described Turner's works as "airy visions painted with tinted steam." *The Slave Ship* (Fig. **15.11**) visualizes a passage in James Thomson's poem *The*

Seasons which describes how sharks follow a slave ship in a storm, "lured by the scent of steaming crowds of rank disease, and death." The poem was based on an actual event, where the captain of a slave ship dumped his human cargo into the sea when disease broke out below decks.

Turner's work demonstrates the elements of Romantic painting. His disjointed diagonals contribute to an overall fragmentation of the composition. His space is deeply three-dimensional. The turbulence of the event pictured is reflected in the loose painting technique. The sea and sky appear transparent, and the brushstrokes are energetic and spontaneous. Expression dominates form and content, and a sense of doom prevails.

Eugène Delacroix (1798–1863) employed color, light, and shade to capture the climactic moments of high emo-

15.12 Eugène Delacroix, *The 28th July: Liberty Leading the People*, 1830. Oil on canvas, 8 ft 6 ins × 10 ft 7 ins (2.59 × 3.25 m). Louvre, Paris.

tion. Delacroix has been described as "the foremost neo-baroque Romantic painter," and the intricacy and contrasts in his paintings support this label. In *The 28th July: Liberty Leading the People* (Fig. **15.12**), Delacroix shows the allegorical figure of Liberty bearing aloft the tricolor flag of France and leading the charge of a freedom-loving common people. Lights and darks provide strong and dramatic contrasts. The red, white, and blue of the French flag symbolize patriotism, purity, and freedom, and as Delacroix picks up these colors throughout the work, they also serve to balance and unify the scene.

The approach of Jean-Baptiste-Camille Corot (1796–1875) is often described as "Romantic naturalism." Corot was among the first to execute finished paintings out-of-doors rather than in the studio. He wanted to recreate the full luminosity of nature and to capture the natural effect of visual perception, that is, how the eye focuses on detail

and how peripheral vision actually works. In *Volterra* (Fig. **15.13**), he strives to this true-to-life visual effect by reducing the graphic clarity of all details except those of the central objects which he presents very clearly, just as our eyes perceive clearly only those objects on which we are focusing at the moment, while everything else in our field of vision is relatively out of focus. Corot's works are spontaneous and subjective, but he retains a formal order to balance that spontaneity.

Rosa Bonheur (1822–99), certainly the most popular woman painter of her time, has been labeled both a "realist" and a "Romantic" in style. Her subjects were mostly animals and their raw energy. "Wading in pools of blood," as she put it, she studied animal anatomy even in slaughter houses, and was particularly interested in animal psychology. *Plowing in the Nivernais* (Fig. **15.14**) captures the tremendous power of the oxen on which European agriculture had depended before the Industrial Revolution. The beasts appear almost monumental, and each detail is precisely executed. The painting clearly reveals Bonheur's reverence for the dignity of labor and her vision of human beings in harmony with nature.

15.13 Jean-Baptiste-Camille Corot, *Volterra*, 1843. Oil on canvas, 18½ × 32¼ ins (47 × 82 cm). Louvre, Paris.

15.14 John Nash, Royal Pavilion, Brighton, England, remodeled 1815–23.

PROFILE

Rosa Bonheur (1822–99)

One of the most significant and prominent women artists of the time, Rosa Bonheur (pronounced bo-NUHR) focused her artistic attention almost solely on animals. Born in Bordeaux, France, she was the eldest of four children of an amateur painter. After early instruction from her father, she studied with Leon Cogniet at the École des Beaux-Arts in Paris, and rather early on began to specialize in animal subjects, studying them wherever she could. Her early paintings won awards in Paris, and in 1848, she won a first-class medal for *Plowing in the Nivernais* (see Fig. **15.15**). By 1853 her work had reached full maturity, and she received high acclaim in Europe and the United States. Her paintings were much admired and became widely known through engraved copies. She was also well known as a sculptor, and her animal subjects led to

her success among contemporary French sculptors.

Rosa Bonheur had an independent spirit and fought to gain acceptance on a level equal to that of male artists of the time. Her ability and popularity earned her the title of Chevalier of the Legion of Honor in 1865, and she was the first woman to receive the Grand Cross of the Legion. Befriended by Queen Victoria of Britain, who became her patron, Bonheur became a favorite among the British aristocracy, although her last years were spent in France, and she died near Fontainebleau in 1899.

15.15 Rosa Bonheur, *Plowing in the Nivernais*, 1849. Oil on canvas, 5 ft 9 ins × 8 ft 8 ins (1.75 × 2.64 m). Musée Nationale du Château de Fontainebleau, France.

Romantic architecture also borrowed styles from other eras and produced a vast array of buildings that revived Gothic motifs and reflected fantasy. This style has come to be known as "picturesque." Eastern influence and whimsy abounded in John Nash's Royal Pavilion in Brighton, in the south of England (Fig. **15.14**), with its onion-shaped domes, minarets, and horseshoe arches.

"Picturesque" also describes the most famous example of Romantic architecture, the Houses of Parliament (Fig. **15.16**), a building that demonstrates one significant architectural concept that can be described as "modern." The exterior walls function simply as a screen, and have nothing to say about structure, interior design, or function. The inside has absolutely no spatial relationship to the

15.16 Sir Charles Barry and Augustus Welby Northmore Pugin, Houses of Parliament, London, 1839–52.

15.17 Sir Joseph Paxton, Crystal Palace, London, 1851.

outside. The strong contrast of forms and asymmetrical balance also suggest the modern.

If the nineteenth century was an age of industry, it was also an age of experimentation and new materials. In architecture, steel and glass came to the fore. At first, an architect needed much courage actually to display the support materials as part of the design itself. The Crystal Palace in London (Fig. **15.17**) exemplified the nineteenth-century fascination with new materials and concepts. Built for the Great Exhibition of 1851, this mammoth structure was completed in the space of nine months. Space was defined by a three-dimensional grid of iron stanchions and girders, designed specifically for mass production and rapid assembly. (In this case, disassembly was also possible—the entire structure was disassembled and rebuilt in 1852–4 at Sydenham.) Like the Houses of Parliament, the Crystal Palace demonstrated the divergence of the function of a building (as reflected in the arrangement of its interior spaces), its surface decoration, and its structure. A new style of building had arrived.

CRIT
REVI
belov

A CRITICAL REVIEW

We are at the point in history where we can spend some time in the United States. As some of the illustrations in the previous section revealed, the styles of Romanticism and classical revival shaped buildings that we can see in our home towns, and history now becomes part of our present in a way that is perhaps more obvious than has previously been the case. Even if we have never lived in a classical revival or Romantic-style house, you are almost certain to know someone who did.

Romantic style in painting shows us a definitive step away from the careful organization of classicism. However, sometimes the departures are tentative or only partial. For example, Ingres' painting *La Grande Odalisque* can be interpreted as classical and/or Romantic.

Find an example of Romantic and of classical revival architecture in your city. Write a description of it, and explain how its features conform to the general characteristics noted in the text.

Compare Géricault's The Raft of the "Medusa" and Turner's The Slave Ship, describing how each artist expresses the characteristics of Romanticism.

A CRITICAL LOOK

In the next sections, we examine literature and music. These two disciplines, perhaps more than the others, enjoyed the full flower of Romanticism because there is nothing physical in these disciplines to constrain the subjective imagination of the artist. The emotions can be turned loose to revel in sound and in the sound-power of words. In the music section, we are going to immerse ourselves in a number of sub-categories, because Romantic music took many forms, and we need to sample them in order to get the full flavor of the style and the period.

Explain the term Lieder and describe the works of Franz Schubert.

Describe the piano works of Frédéric Chopin.

Explain the term program music and describe the works of Hector Berlioz.

LITERATURE

CRITICAL
LOOK
above

The main phase of Romantic literature probably began around 1790. In the United States the Romantic spirit found among its champions Edgar Allen Poe (1809–49) and Walt Whitman (1819–92). Poe's Romantic poetry is very distinguished, but he is most remembered for his horror stories based on the Gothic novel. Whitman's writings encompass a wide range of subjects—he intended to celebrate everything. Nothing was beneath the quest for his senses. Out of the Civil War came an unexpected author, whose contributions were oratorical, but which, because of their importance, have become part of the important canon of literature; these are the speeches of Abraham Lincoln.

Romantic writers tended to form groups or partnerships. The close relationship between Goethe and Schiller was one example. In Britain, Wordsworth and Coleridge were also close colleagues, and Byron, Shelley, and Keats knew and criticized each other's work.

WORDSWORTH

William Wordsworth (1770–1850) saw transcendental and often indefinable significance in commonplace and everyday things. His worship of nature and the harmony he felt existed between people and nature led him to create a new and individual world of Romantic beauty.

In 1795 he met Samuel Taylor Coleridge (1772–1834), another British poet, and in working with Coleridge, Wordsworth found that his life and writing suddenly opened up. Out of this relationship came the Lyrical Ballads, which Wordsworth published anonymously along with four poems by Coleridge. Among these ballads, Tintern Abbey describes Wordsworth's love of nature most explicitly. That love is first presented as the animal passion of a wild young boy, then as a restorative and moral influence, and finally as a mystical communion with an eternal truth.

JANE AUSTEN

Jane Austen (1775–1817) lived and worked in the high years of the major English Romantics, but she shunned the Romantic cult of personality and remained largely indifferent to Romantic literature. She looked back to neoclassicism and the comedy of manners as her sources, and her work portrays middle-class people living in provincial towns and going about the daily routine of family life—a life of good breeding, wit, and a reasonable hope that difficulties can be resolved in a satisfactory manner. She occasionally portrayed disappointments in love and threatened or actual seduction, but, somehow, these seem less important than the ongoing and routine conversations and rituals of daily life. Merely because she portrayed a quiet form of life does not mean, however, that her characters lack depth or interest. She explored human experience deeply and with humor. She proved that one does not require spectacular events in order to provide engaging art.

Her early years produced a variety of works that parody the sentimental and romantic clichés of popular fiction. In her second period of writing, from 1810 on, she crowned her career with works like *Emma* (1815), *Persuasion* (1818), and *Mansfield Park* (1813). *Emma* shows Austen's ability to remain detached from her heroine, Emma Woodhouse, who represents self-deception, as she misreads evidence, misleads others, and discovers her own feelings only by accident. In her other works, Austen portrayed many gentle and self-effacing characters in the mode of her earlier masterpiece *Pride and Prejudice* (1813). Here, there is little of the satire of other works of the same period, but an ironic and sympathetic view of human nature and its propensity for comic incongruity.

The central comedy of *Pride and Prejudice* lies in fully developed character that reveals a sense of human realities and values. For example, in the character of Mr Bennet, Austen made a symbolic comment on intelligence that exists without will or drive. In her two opposing protagonists, Darcy and Elizabeth, who reflect the title of the book, Austen revealed character overlaid with class superciliousness and character abounding in independence and sharpness of mind that acts with prejudgment, wrong-headedness, and self-satisfaction. In all situations, Jane Austen remained detached, witty, and good-humored. Her disturbances are minor intrusions in an unshakable moral universe in which one can point out an entire range of human frailties and yet not despair.

OTHER NINETEENTH-CENTURY ROMANTICS

The life and works of Wordworth's friend Coleridge more closely resembled the temperament of German Romanticism. He is best remembered for his long poem, *The Rime of the Ancient Mariner*, which exemplifies the mystery and wonder of the Romantic spirit. Walter Scott (1771–1832) was also influenced by German Romanticism. His romances have an easy, fluent style, color, and a lack of depth. Like many nineteenth-century artists, Scott delighted in the romance of history, and he was fond of evoking the charms of the Middle Ages and of the Renaissance.

George Gordon, Lord Byron (1788–1824), was the Romantic poet *par excellence* with his colorful and dramatic private life, his support of the nationalist aspirations of the Greeks, and his energetic verse. *Don Juan*, a richly ironic ramble through human frailties, is probably his best poem. Percy Bysshe Shelley (1792–1822) wrote in a more meditative and more lyrical vein, and the passions of Romanticism are never far below the surface. The greatest of English Romantics, however, was John Keats (1795–1821). The best of his poems, such as *Ode on a Grecian Urn* and *Ode to a Nightingale*, explore the tensions between classical restraint and the Romantic determination to feel life at its most intense and to push pleasure to ecstasy.

Emily Brontë (1818–48) wrote the stormily romantic *Wuthering Heights*, while her sister Charlotte (1816–55) produced the more sophisticated *Jane Eyre*. New possibilities for the novel were opened up by the French writer Honoré de Balzac (1799–1850), whose great cycle of novels, part of his projected and only partially completed *Comédie Humaine*, sought to survey contemporary society from the palace to the gutter. The heroes and heroines of Balzac's works are figures whose experiences reveal how society really works. Charles Dickens (1812–70) had a similar aim in his novels. The best of them, such as *Bleak House*, deliver up a cross-section of the teeming society of Victorian England. Dickens's plots are dazzlingly ingenious and entertaining in their own right. But this complexity also captures the interdependence of rich and poor, and the endless ramifications of every individual act. The naturalism of writers like Gustave Flaubert (1821–80) and Émile Zola (1840–1902), which developed out of this tradition, closely parallels realism in painting.

An interest in the morbid, the pathological, and the bizarre also developed, and the "decadent" poems of Charles Baudelaire (1821–67), especially in his *Les Fleurs du Mal* (*Flowers of Evil*), typify this trend. The paths of poetry and the novel now diverged, poetry moving into symbolism, while the novel, in the hands of writers like Henry James (1843–1916), became more psychological as it explored the interior life and the nature of consciousness.

MUSIC

Richard Strauss claimed that by purely musical means he could convey to an audience the amount of water in a drinking glass! In an era of Romantic subjectivity, music provided the medium in which many found an unrivaled opportunity to express emotion. In trying to express human emotion, Romantic music made stylistic changes to classical music, and although Romanticism amounted to rebellion in many of the arts, in music it involved a more gradual and natural extension of classical principles. The classical–Romantic antithesis—form versus feeling, or intellectual versus emotional conflict—does not apply neatly to music of the eighteenth and nineteenth centuries.

As in painting, spontaneity replaced control, but the primary emphasis of music in this era was on beautiful, lyrical, and expressive melody. Phrases became longer, more irregular, and more complex than they had been in classical music. Much Romantic rhythm was traditional, but experiments produced new meters and patterns. Emotional conflict was often suggested by juxtaposing different meters, and rhythmic irregularity became increasingly common as the century progressed.

Harmony and tone color changed significantly. Harmony was seen as a means of expression, and any previous "laws" regarding key relationships could be broken to achieve striking emotional effects. Form was clearly subordinate to feeling. Harmonies became increasingly complex, and traditional distinctions between major and minor keys were blurred in chromatic harmonies, complicated chords, and modulations to distant keys. In fact, some composers used key changes so frequently that their compositions are virtually nothing but whirls of continuous modulation.

As composers sought to disrupt the listener's expectations, more and more dissonance occurred, until it became a principal focus. Dissonance was explored for its own sake, as a strong stimulant of emotional response rather than merely as a decorative way to get to the traditional tonic chord. By the end of the Romantic period, the exhaustion of chromatic usage and dissonance had led to a search for a completely different type of tonal system.

Exploring musical color to elicit feeling was as important to the Romantic musician as it was to the painter. Interest in tonal color, or timbre, led to great diversity in vocal and instrumental performance, and the music of this period abounds with solo works and exhibits a tremendous increase in the size and diversity of the orchestra. To make our way through this complex era, however, we must first look at certain basic musical forms and explore them.

LIEDER

In many ways, the "art song," or *Lied*, characterized Romantic music. A composition for solo voice with piano accompaniment and poetic text allowed for a variety of lyrical and dramatic expressions and linked music directly with literature.

The burst of German lyric poetry in this period encouraged the growth of *Lieder*. Literary nuances affected music, and music added deeper emotional implications to the poem. This partnership had various results: some *Lieder* were complex, others were simple; some were structured, others were freely composed. The pieces themselves depended on a close relationship between the piano and the voice. In many ways, the piano was an inseparable part of the experience, and certainly it served as more than accompaniment, for the piano explored mood and established rhythmic and thematic material, and sometimes had solo passages of its own. The interdependency of the song and its accompaniment is basic to the art song.

The earliest, and perhaps the most important, composer of *Lieder* was Franz Schubert (1797–1828). Schubert's troubled life epitomized the Romantic view of the artist's desperate and isolated condition. Known only among a close circle of friends and musicians, Schubert composed almost one thousand works, from symphonies to sonatas and operas, to Masses, choral compositions, and *Lieder*. None of his work was publicly performed, however, until the year of his death. He took his *Lieder* texts from a wide variety of poems, and in each case the melodic contours, harmonies, rhythms, and structures of the music were determined by the poem.

Schubert wrote two song cycles based on poems by Wilhelm Müller, *Die schöne Mülerin* (1820) includes twenty songs and begins with "Das Wandern"

("Wandering"), sung by a young miller:

Wandering is the miller's delight, wandering!
He must be a very poor miller
Who never felt like wandering, wandering.

From the water we learned this, from the water!
It does not rest by day or night,
But is always wandering, the water.

We see it also in the mill-wheels, the mill-wheels!
They never want to be still,
They nor I never tire of the turning, the mill-wheels.

The stones even, as heavy as they are, the stones!
They join the cheerful round dances
And want to go even faster, the stones.

Wandering, wandering, my delight, wandering!
O master and mistress
Let me go my way in peace and wander.

The tempo is a leisurely walking pace, and the major key indicates the happy mood. As in all *Lieder*, the piano is a partner, and it sets the scene, evoking rippling water with flowing 16th-notes. The vocal melody, characterized by skips in the scale, is completely different from the piano writing. After the piano introduction, the first theme is stated and immediately repeated. A second and third phrase follow, and the piano completes each stanza with a restatement of the opening measures.

PIANO WORKS

The development of the art song depended in no small way on nineteenth-century improvements in piano design. The instrument for which Schubert wrote had a much warmer, richer tone than earlier pianos, and improvements in pedal technique made sustained tones possible and gave the instrument greater lyrical potential.

Such flexibility made the piano an excellent instrument for accompaniment, and, more importantly, made it an almost ideal solo instrument. As a result, new works were composed solely for the piano, ranging from short, intimate pieces, similar to *Lieder*, to larger works designed to exhibit great virtuosity in performance. Franz Schubert wrote such pieces, as did Franz Liszt (1811–86). The technical demands of Liszt's compositions, and the rather florid way he performed them, gave rise to a theatricality, the primary purpose of which was to impress audiences with flashy presentation. This fitted well with the Romantic concept of the artist as hero.

The compositions of Frédéric Chopin (1810–49) were somewhat more restrained. Chopin wrote almost exclusively for the piano. Each of his ÉTUDES, or studies, explored a single technical problem, usually set around a single motif. More than simple exercises, these works

explored the possibilities of the instrument and became short tone poems in their own right. A second group of compositions included short intimate works such as preludes, nocturnes, and impromptus, and dances such as waltzes, polonaises, and mazurkas. (Chopin was a Pole living in France, and Polish folk music had a particularly strong influence on him.) A final class of larger works included scherzos, ballades, and fantasies. Chopin's compositions are highly individual, many without precedent. His style stands outside classicism, almost totally without standard form. His melodies are lyrical, and his moods vary from melancholy to exaltation.

Chopin's nocturnes, or night pieces, are among his most celebrated works. His Nocturne in E flat major (1833) illustrates the structure and style of this sort of mood piece well. It has a number of sections, with a main theme alternating with a second until both give way to a third. The piece has a complex AA'BA''B'A'''CC' structure. The nocturne is in *andante* tempo, a moderate, walking speed, and begins with the most important theme (Fig. **15.18**).

15.18 Frédéric Chopin, Nocturne in E flat major, first theme.

The melody is very graceful and lyrical over its supporting chords. The contours of the melody alternately use pitches that are close together and widely spaced. The theme is stated, then immediately repeated with ornamentation. The second theme begins in the dominant key of B flat major and returns to E flat for a more elaborate repeat of the first theme. The second theme is restated, and followed by an even more elaborate restatement of the first theme, leading to a dramatic climax in the home key. A third theme is presented and then repeated more elaborately in the tonic key. The work ends with a short cadenza, which builds through a crescendo and finishes pianissimo, very softly.

PROGRAM MUSIC

One of the new ways in which Romantic composers structured their longer works was to build them around a non-musical story, a picture, or some other idea. Music of this sort is called "descriptive." When the idea is quite specific and closely followed throughout the piece, the music is called "programmatic" or "program music."

These techniques were not entirely new—we have already noted the descriptive elements in Beethoven's

"Pastoral" Symphony—but the Romantics found them particularly attractive and employed them with great gusto. A nonmusical idea allowed composers to rid themselves of formal structure altogether. Of course, actual practice varied tremendously—some used programmatic material as their only structural device, while others subordinated a program idea to formal structure. Nevertheless, the Romantic period has become known as the "age of program music." Among the best known composers of program music were Hector Berlioz (1803–69) and Richard Strauss (1864–1949).

Berlioz's *Symphonie Fantastique* (1830) employed a single motif, called an IDÉE FIXE, to tie the five movements of the work together. The story on which the musical piece is based involves a hero who has poisoned himself because of unrequited love. However, the drug only sends him into semi-consciousness, in which he has visions. Throughout these visions the recurrent musical theme (the *idée fixe*) symbolizes his beloved. Movement 1 consists of "Reveries" and "Passions." Movement 2 represents "A Ball." "In the Country" is movement 3, in which he imagines a pastoral scene. In movement 4, "March to the Scaffold," he dreams he has killed his beloved and is about to be executed. The *idée fixe* returns at the end of the movement and is abruptly shattered by the fall of the axe. The final movement describes a "Dream of a Witches' Sabbath" in grotesque and orgiastic musical imagery.

Not all program music depends for its interest upon an understanding of its text. Many people believe, however, that the tone poems, or symphonic poems, of Richard Strauss require an understanding of the story. His *Don Juan*, *Till Eulenspiegel*, and *Don Quixote* draw such detailed material from specific legends that program explanations and comments are integral to the works and help to give them coherence. In *Till Eulenspiegels lustige Streiche* (*Till Eulenspiegel's Merry Pranks*), Strauss tells the legendary German story of Till Eulenspiegel and his practical jokes. Till is traced through three escapades, all musically identifiable. He is then confronted by his critics and finally executed. Throughout, the musical references are quite specific.

SYMPHONIES

As some Romantic composers were pursuing these relatively innovative directions, others continued to write traditional symphonies and concertos. While employing the lyrical melodic tendencies of the period, these symphonic works retain classical form and content. That is, they are built upon musical rather than literary ideals—motifs, phrases, and themes—and they maintain their unity through musical structure rather than nonmusical ideas or texts. Such works are known as "abstract," or "absolute," music.

15.19 Johannes Brahms, Symphony No. 3 in F major, opening motif of first movement.

The melodies, rhythms, and timbres of these works reflect typically Romantic characteristics, and they display an increasingly dense texture and greatly expanded dynamic range. Although their form remains traditional, their effect is emotional—the listener is bathed in sensual experience. Contrasts in dynamics and timbre are stressed, and, as in painting, form is subordinated to expression. Certain composers achieved a synthesis of classical tradition and Romantic spirit, however, in particular the German Johannes Brahms (1833–97).

An outstanding example of the Romantic symphony is Brahms's Symphony No. 3 in F major (1883). Composed in four movements, the work calls for pairs of flutes, oboes, clarinets, a bassoon, a contrabassoon, four horns, two trumpets, three trombones, two timpani, and strings—not an adventurous grouping of instruments for the period. Composed in sonata form, the first movement is *allegro con brio* (fast with spirit), and begins in F major. However, with an ambiguity characteristic of Romantic music, the composer begins by having the winds play a progression built around a minor rather than a major third (Fig. **15.19**). This motif consists of an opening, sustained, six-beat tone on F, followed by a sustained, six-beat tone on A flat (an interval of a minor third—breaking out of the home key in the second measure of the piece). The winds then jump to F, an octave above the opening note. This enigmatic motif returns throughout the movement. Following this three-note statement, Brahms firmly establishes the F major key in the first phrase of the opening theme, played by the violins. The marking here indicates that it is to be played passionately (Fig. **15.20**).

15.20 Brahms, Symphony No. 3 in F major, first theme of first movement.

The music modulates through some very remote keys such as D major and A major, and the meter shifts from duple to triple. Both the modulations and the meter change take this movement well outside the parameters of classical music. Then the tone color changes to focus on clarinets supported by pizzicato (plucked) lower strings. A second important theme is introduced quietly, softening to *pianissimo* (Fig. **15.21**).

The exposition section closes with a return to the opening motif and meter, employing rising scales and

15.21 Brahms, Symphony No. 3 in F major, second theme of first movement.

arpeggios. Then, following classical tradition, the exposition is repeated.

The development section uses both the principal themes, with changes in tonal colors, dynamics, and modulation.

The recapitulation opens with a forceful restatement of the opening motif, followed by a restatement and further development of materials from the exposition. Then comes a lengthy coda, again announced by the opening motif, and based on the first theme. A final, quiet, restatement of the opening motif and first phrase of the theme brings the first movement to an end.

NATIONALISM

The Romantic period gave birth to new nationalistic trends in music. The roots of such movements went deep into the past, but composers also wrote with the political circumstances of the century in mind. Folk tunes appear in these works as themes, as do local rhythms and harmonies. This exaltation of national identity was consistent with Romantic requirements, and it occurs in the music of nineteenth-century Russia, Bohemia, Spain, Britain, Scandinavia, Germany, and Austria.

Of all the nationalistic composers of the Romantic period, the Russian Peter Ilyich Tchaikovsky (1840–93) has enjoyed the greatest popularity. His Violin Concerto in D major (1878) remains one of the best known nineteenth-century violin concertos.

Two of the three themes in the third movement, *allegro vivacissimo* (fast and extremely lively), are based on Russian folk music. The focus is of course on the solo violin, which is backed by a large orchestra of strings, winds, and timpani. In form, this finale is a rondo that can be summarized as ABCA'B'C'A''. The dramatic quality of the movement is heightened by an increasingly fast tempo. The movement begins in A major, the dominant of the home key of D major, with a unison motif played by the entire orchestra. The solo passages begin in earnest with a lively Russian folk melody in D major, with the violin gently accompanied by the strings and woodwind. The first theme is then repeated.

The second theme, another Russian folk melody, is played by the solo violin in the key of A major, then adapted by the horns, strings, and soloist. A third theme—not a folk tune—introduces a lyrical melody, and is followed by a restatement of the first, second, and third themes, in new keys. A third restatement of the opening

theme focuses on the virtuosity of the soloist. A loud cadence from the orchestra closes the movement.

CHORAL MUSIC

Vocal music ranged from solo to massive ensemble works. The emotional requirements of Romanticism were well served by the diverse timbres and lyricism of the human voice. Almost every major composer of the era wrote some form of vocal music. Franz Schubert is remembered for his Masses, the most notable of which is the Mass in A flat major. Felix Mendelssohn's *Elijah* stands beside Handel's *Messiah* and Haydn's *Creation* as a masterpiece of oratorio. Hector Berlioz marshaled full Romantic power for his *Requiem*, which called for 210 voices, a large orchestra, and four brass bands.

One of the most enduringly popular choral works of the Romantic period is Brahms's *Ein Deutsches Requiem* (*A German Requiem*). Based on selected texts from the Bible, in contrast with the Latin liturgy of traditional requiems, Brahms's work is not so much a Mass for the dead as a consolation for the living. It is principally a choral work—the solos are minimal: two for baritone and one for soprano—but both vocal and instrumental writing are very expressive. Soaring melodic lines and rich harmonies weave thick textures. After the chorus sings "All mortal flesh is as the grass," the orchestra suggests fields of grass moving in the wind. One lyrical movement, "How lovely is thy dwelling place," remains one of the most moving choral pieces ever written. Brahms's *Requiem* begins and ends with moving passages aimed directly at the living "Blest are they that mourn." Hope and consolation underlie the entire work.

An important factor in Brahms's music is its lyricism and its vocal beauty. Brahms explored the voice as a human voice, and not as another instrument or some other mechanism unaffected by any restrictions, as other composers have done. His parts are written and his words chosen so that no voice is ever required to sing outside its natural range or technical capacity.

OPERA

The spirit and style of Romanticism are summed up in that perfect synthesis of all the arts, opera. "I have written the opera with clenched fists, like my spirit! Do not look for melody; do not look for culture: in *Marat* there is only blood!" So said Pietro Mascagni in 1921 of his new opera *Il Piccolo Marat*. But this was a final outburst at the end of an era. The preceding century and two decades produced a large proportion of the operatic repertoire that we have today. Three countries, France (especially Paris), Italy, and Germany, dominated the development of opera.

Paris occupied an important position in Romantic opera during the first half of the nineteenth century. The spectacular quality of opera and the size of its auditoriums had made it an effective vehicle for propaganda during the Revolution, and as an art form, opera enjoyed great popular appeal among the rising and influential middle classes.

A new type of opera, called "grand opera," emerged early in the nineteenth century, principally through the efforts of Louis Veron, a businessman, the playwright Eugène Scribe, and Giacomo Meyerbeer, a composer. These three broke away from classical themes and subject matter and staged spectacular productions with crowd scenes, ballets, choruses, and fantastic scenery, written around medieval and contemporary themes. Meyerbeer (1791–1864), a German, studied Italian opera in Venice and produced French opera in Paris. *Robert the Devil* and *The Huguenots* typify Meyerbeer's extravagant style; they achieved great popular success, although the composer Schumann called *The Huguenots* "a conglomeration of monstrosities." Berlioz's *The Trojans*, written in the late 1850s, was more classically based and more musically controlled. At the same time, Jacques Offenbach (1819–80) brought to the stage a lighter style, in which spoken

PROFILE

Johannes Brahms (1833–97)

Although he was born into an impoverished family, Johannes Brahms (pronounced brahmz) appears to have had a relatively happy childhood. His father was an itinerant musician, who eked out a meager living playing the horn and double bass in taverns and night clubs. The family lived in the slums of Hamburg, Germany, but despite their economic hardships, they retained close and loving family relationships. Early in life, Johannes showed evidence of considerable musical talent, and the eminent piano teacher Eduard Marxsen agreed to teach him without pay.

By the time he was twenty, Brahms had gained acclaim as a pianist and accepted an invitation to participate in a concert tour with the Hungarian violinist Eduard Remenyi. The event was invaluable to the young Brahms, because it introduced him to Franz Liszt and Robert Schumann, and through Schumann's efforts Brahms was able to publish several of his compositions, which opened the door to the wider artistic world and launched his prolific career. Brahms gained experience as musical director at the little court of Detmold and as founder and director of a women's chorus in Hamburg, for which he wrote several choral works. His musical creativity showed a deep love of folk music and a sensitivity of expression. He mastered German *Lieder* (see page 500) and remained devoted to the Romantic style throughout his career, notwithstanding his fondness for clarity of structure and form based in the classical style of the previous century.

Although Brahms wanted to stay in Hamburg, he was passed over for a position, and, feeling betrayed and neglected by his native town's rejection, he moved to Vienna. That city's rich musical ambiance enriched his talent and experience, and he gained tremendous success, serving as director of the Vienna Singakademie and as conductor of the Society of Friends of Music. In 1875, he resigned his positions and spent the rest of his days in creative endeavors. For the next twenty-two years he sacrificed his personal life in pursuit of his career, and the results gained him—in his own lifetime—recognition as one of the world's greatest artists.

His work spanned several idioms, from solo piano compositions and chamber music to full orchestral works. He was never interested in music for the stage nor in program music, but he reveled in symphonic compositions ruled by purely musical ideas (absolute music). See page 502 for a discussion of Brahms' Symphony No. 3 in F major.

15.22 Johannes Brahms in 1894.

dialogue was mixed with the music. This type of opera, called *opéra comique*, is serious in intent despite what the French word comique might suggest. It is a satirical and light form of opera, using vaudeville humor to satirize other operas, popular events, and so forth. In between the styles of Meyerbeer and Offenbach there was a third form of Romantic opera, lyric opera. Ambroise Thomas (1811–96) and Charles Gounod (1818–93) turned to Romantic drama and fantasy for their plots. Thomas's *Mignon* contains highly lyrical passages, and Gounod's *Faust*, based on Goethe's play, stresses melodic beauty.

Early Romantic opera in Italy featured the BEL CANTO style, which emphasizes beauty of sound, and the works of Gioacchino Rossini (1792–1868) epitomize this feature. Rossini's *The Barber of Seville* takes melodic singing to new heights with light, ornamented, and highly appealing work, particularly for his soprano voices.

Great artists often stand apart from or astride general stylistic trends while they explore their own themes. Such is the case with the Italian composer Giuseppe Verdi (1813–1901). With Verdi, opera is truly a human drama, expressed through simple, beautiful melody.

Verdi's long career had different phases. In the early phase, with works such as *La traviata* (*The Courtesan*) (1853), he focused on logic and structure, using recurring themes to provide unity. The story of *La traviata* was based on Alexandre Dumas *fils'* novel *La Dame aux camélias* (*The Lady of the Camellias*). Violetta, a courtesan, falls in love with Alfredo, a young man of respectable family. Violetta and Alfredo live together for a time, but at his father's urging, she nobly leaves him to save the good name of his family. Her health, already frail, breaks under the strain, and Alfredo returns to her just as she dies of tuberculosis. Violetta, a soprano, sings the aria "Ah, fors' e lui" ("Ah, perhaps it is he") when she first realizes she is in love with Alfredo. This is the first part of two important sections, each of which comprises a recitative and an aria. In the first recitative of the second section, Violetta's thoughts about the possibilities of finding true love carry her into the first aria. Two musical themes are explored, one minor and disjunct, as she thinks about the mystery of love, the other, which repeats the melody used by Alfredo in the previous scene to express his love for her, major and lyrical, as she herself is overcome by love. In the second recitative, she decides to enjoy life as she now finds it. She then sings the second aria, "Sempre libera" ("Always free"), in which she looks forward to continuing her life as a courtesan.

In the second phase of Verdi's career, he wrote works such as *Aïda* (1871), grand operas of spectacular proportions built upon tightly woven dramatic structures. Finally, in a third phase, he produced operas based on Shakespearean plays. *Otello* (1887) contrasts tragedy and *opera buffa*—comic opera, not *opéra comique*—and explores subtle balances among voices and orchestra, together with strong melodic development.

Richard Wagner (1813–83) was one of the masters of Romantic opera. At the heart of Wagner's artistry lay a philosophy that has affected the stage from the mid-nineteenth century to the present day. His ideas were laid out principally in two books, *Art and Revolution* (1849) and *Opera and Drama* (1851). Wagner's philosophy centered on the *Gesamtkunstwerk*, a comprehensive work of art in which music, poetry, and scenery are all subservient to the central generating idea. For Wagner, the total unity of all elements was supremely important. In line with German Romantic philosophy, which gives music supremacy over the other arts, music has the predominant role in Wagner's operas. Dramatic meaning unfolds through the LEITMOTIF, for which Wagner is famous, although he did not invent it. A *Leitmotif* is a musical theme that is tied to an idea, a person, or an object. Whenever that idea, person, or object appears on stage or comes to mind in the action, that theme is heard. Juxtaposing *Leitmotifs* gives the audience an idea of relationships between their subjects. *Leitmotifs* also give the composer building blocks to use for development, recapitulation, and unification.

Each of Wagner's magnificent operas deserves detailed attention. Anything we might say here by way of description or analysis would be insignificant compared to the dramatic power these works exhibit in full production. Even recordings cannot approach the tremendous effect of these works on stage in an opera house.

CRITICAL REVIEW p. 506

THEATRE

CRITICAL LOOK p. 506

"The play-going world of the West End is at this moment occupied in rubbing its eyes, that it may recover completely from the dazzle of Thursday last, when, amid the acclamations of Queen Victoria's subjects, King Richard the Second was enthroned at the Princess's Theatre." Thus began the reviewer's comments in the *Spectator*, March 14, 1857. The dazzle of scenery, revivals, and a pot-pourri of uncertain accomplishments helped a stumbling theatre to keep up with the other arts that flourished through the early years of the nineteenth century.

ROMANTICISM

Romanticism as a philosophy of art was its own worst enemy in the theatre. Artists sought new forms to express great truths, and they strove to free themselves from neoclassical rules and restraints. They did, however, admire Shakespeare as an example of new ideals and as a symbol of freedom from structural confinement. Intuition reigned, and the artistic genius was set apart from everyday people and above normal constraints. As a result,

A CRITICAL REVIEW

Many people think that the Romantic Age has never ended. To test that assertion, pick one of your favorite songs (rock or otherwise) and analyze its use of structure, melody, harmony, and text. Then present a case for its inclusion as a piece of classical music, Romantic music, or something in between. Without a doubt unbridled emotionalism, lack of idealization, and fragmentation of form can be found in today's art and popular culture, and in a moment, we will see even more evidence of how the Romantic style influences the film and television we see today. However, that is yet to come. Looking back at the material we have just studied, we need to do two things. One is to be sure that we have mastered it, and the other is to determine its relevance for today.

Identify the major writers cited in your text, and explain how their work exemplifies the characteristics of Romantic literature.

Explain how Romantic music differs from classical music.

Identify the major composers of Romantic opera and describe their works. What similarities and differences can you find between them and modern musicals?

A CRITICAL LOOK

In the next section we see more things that look familiar. In the theatre of the Romantic period lie the foundations for just about everything we see on the screen and on television.

What are the basic characteristics of Romantic theatre, including melodrama?

Romantic writers had no use for any guide but their own imagination.

Unfortunately, the theatre operates within some rather specific limits. Many nineteenth-century playwrights penned scripts that were unstageable and/or unplayable, and great writers could not or would not abide by constraints of the stage, while the hacks, yielding to popular taste, could not resist overindulgence in phony emotionalism, melodrama, and stage gimmickry. As a result, the best Romantic theatre performances came from the pen of William Shakespeare, whose work was revived in a great rush of nineteenth-century antiquarianism.

Poor as it may have been in original drama, however, the Romantic period did succeed in loosening the arbitrary rules of neoclassical convention. Thus, it paved the way for a new theatrical era in the later years of the century.

The audiences of the nineteenth century played a significant part in determining what took the stage. Royal patronage was gone, and box office receipts were needed to pay the bills. A rising middle class had swelled the eighteenth-century audience and changed its character. Then, in the nineteenth century, the lower classes began attending the theatre. The Industrial Revolution had created larger urban populations and expanded public education to a degree. As feelings of egalitarianism spread

throughout Europe and America, theatre audiences grew, and theatre building flourished. To appeal to this diverse audience, theatre managers had to put on plays for the popular as well as the sophisticated taste if they wanted to make money, so to offer something for everyone, an evening's theatre program might contain several types of fare and last over five hours. The consequence was predictable. Fewer and fewer sophisticated patrons chose to attend, and the quality of the productions declined.

By 1850 theatres began to specialize, and sophisticated play-goers came back to certain theatres, although the multi-part production remained typical until nearly the turn of the twentieth century. Audience demand was high, and theatre continued to expand.

The early nineteenth-century theatre had some very particular characteristics. First of all, there was the repertory company, with a set group of actors, including stars, which stayed in one place and staged several productions during a given season. (That is quite unlike contemporary professional theatre, in which each play is produced and cast independently and runs for as long as it shows a profit.) Gradually, better known actors capitalized on their reputations and began to go on tour, starring in local productions and featuring their most famous roles. A craze for visiting stars developed, and the most famous actors began to make world tours. This increase in touring stars led to an increase in touring companies, and, in

15.23 Charles Kean's production of Shakespeare's *Richard II*, London, 1857. Between Acts III and IV, the Entry of Bolingbroke into London. Contemporary watercolor by Thomas Grieve. Victoria & Albert Museum, London.

the United States especially, these companies, with their star attractions and complete sets of costumes and scenery, became a regular feature of the landscape. By 1886 America could boast 282 touring companies. At the same time, local resident companies became less popular, except in Germany, where a series of local, state-run theatres was established.

Although theatre design was by now very diverse, some general similarities existed. Principally, the changes in nineteenth-century stages and staging were prompted by increased interest in historical accuracy and popular demand for depiction rather than convention. Before the eighteenth century, history had been considered irrelevant to art. Knowledge of antiquity that began with archeological excavations in Pompeii, however, aroused curiosity, and the Romantic dream of escape to the long ago and far away suggested that the stage picture of exotic places should be somehow believable. At first, such detail was used inconsistently, but, by 1823, some productions claimed that they were entirely historical in every respect. Attempts at historical accuracy had begun as early as 1801, and in France, Victor Hugo and Alexandre Dumas *père* insisted on historically accurate settings and costumes during the early years of the century. However, it was Charles Kean (1811–68) who brought

the spectacle of antiquarianism in the London theatre to fruition in the 1850s (Fig. **15.23**).

The onset of accuracy as a standard for production led to three-dimensionality in settings and away from drop and wing scenery to the box set. The stage floor was leveled—since the Renaissance it had been raked—and new methods of shifting and rigging were devised to meet specific staging problems. Over a period of years, all elements of the production became integrated, much in the spirit of Wagner's totally unified artwork, the GESAMTKUNSTWERK. The distraction of numerous scene changes was eliminated by closing the curtain.

MELODRAMA

On the popular side in the nineteenth century theatre production developed a Romantically exaggerated form called "melodrama." Typically this kind of theatre is characterized by sensationalism and sentimentality. Characters are stereotyped, and everything and everyone tends to be all good or all evil. Plots are sentimental and the action is exaggerated. Regardless of circumstances, good must be rewarded and evil punished. There was often also some form of comic relief, usually through a minor character. The action of melodrama progresses at the whim of the villain, and the hero is forced to endure episode after episode of trial and suffering. Suspense is imperative, and a reversal at the end is obligatory.

The term "melodrama" implies music and drama, and, in the nineteenth century, these plays were accompanied by a musical score tailored to the emotional or dynamic character of the scene. In practice, this was very similar to the way music is used in films and television programs today, with the added attractions of incidental songs and dances that were used as curtain raisers and *entr'acte* entertainment.

Melodrama was popular throughout Europe and the United States. *Uncle Tom's Cabin*, based on the novel by Harriet Beecher Stowe (1852), took the stage by storm. The stage version was opposed by Stowe, but copyright laws did not exist to protect her. The play does retain her complex themes of slavery, religion, and love. The action involves a number of episodes, some of which are rather loosely connected. Characteristic of melodrama, *Uncle Tom's Cabin* places considerable emphasis on spectacle, the most popular of which at the time was Eliza's crossing of the ice with mules, horses, and bloodhounds in pursuit.

SYNTHESIS
The Victorians—The Nineteenth Century in Britain

The Romantic Age, also known as the Age of Industry, is also known as the Victorian Age, referring to Britain's Queen Victoria, who reigned through most of the period. Thus, because of the importance of Britain in the Industrial Revolution, the Romantic style in the arts, and the morals and mores that have become associated with the nineteenth century and Victorian England, we return to England once more for our Synthesis. In it we see the tremendous diversity that romanticism made possible by freeing artists to follow the subjective impulses of their emotions.

We have called the nineteenth century not only the Age of Industry, but also the Age of Romanticism. And

15.24 Sir Edwin Landseer, *Dignity and Impudence*, 1839. Oil on canvas, 35 × 27½ ins (89 × 70 cm). Tate Gallery, London.

15.25 Richard Dadd, *The Fairy Feller's Master Stroke*, 1855–64. Oil on canvas, 21¼ × 15¼ ins (54 × 38.5 cm). Tate Gallery, London.

indeed we find both industrialization and the philosophical and artistic aims of Romanticism at the heart of the age.

The indomitable spirit of England's great queen, Victoria, was yet another influence that reached far beyond her homeland to the continent of Europe and to North America. Victoria's presence was felt not only through her great patronage, as was the case with earlier European monarchs, but also in the force of her personality, her values, and her general social influence.

British confidence soared to great heights in the middle decades of the nineteenth century, That was when

15.26 Thomas Creswick, *Landscape*, c. 1851. Oil on canvas, 27 × 35 ins (68.5 × 89 cm). Royal Academy of Arts, London.

the British began to use the term "Victorian" to describe the era in which they were living, demonstrating their consciousness that their values dominated a distinct period. New technologies and new economics combined with social stability and traditional values. Parliament and the monarchy symbolized continuity, stability, and tradition in changing times. The new Parliament buildings reflected the antiquity of the institution of Parliament in their mock-medieval architecture. The revolutionary nature of the era was hidden behind a cloak of custom and tradition. When Victoria ascended to the throne in 1837, the British monarchy could trace its ancestry back further than any other European political institution apart from the papacy. Victoria and Albert raised the monarchy to new heights of public esteem.

The character and essence of Victorianism can be clearly seen in the single discipline of painting, which reveals a remarkable complexity and scope. "There were contradictions, movements and countermovements; endless and labyrinthine courses were explored, false

gods pursued.... If the period produced few artists of world stature, this was balanced by the cumulative effect of the rich diversity of high talent, occasionally bordering on greatness.[2] The Victorian age was compulsively multidisciplinary. G.K. Chesterton described it as "a world in which painters were trying to be novelists, and novelists trying to be historians, and musicians doing the work of school-masters, and sculptors doing the work of curates." Although official patronage had more or less disappeared, state support of artists did exist, and there was some increase in private patronage. Support groups for artists were first set up during this period, among them, Morris and Company (1861), the Art Workers Guild (1884), and the New English Art Club (1885). The Royal Academy, which had been founded in 1769, also supported artistic endeavors. On the one hand, it provided a focus for artistic activity, but on the other, it was seen as an established institution against which rebellious artists could react. The age produced historical painters, landscape painters, marine painters, sporting painters, animal painters, genre painters, fairy painters, nude and still-life painters, neoclassical painters, portrait painters, and the Pre-Raphaelites.

The Victorian love of animals is legendary, and own-

15.27 Daniel MacLise, *The Marriage of Eva and Strongbow*, first exhibited 1854. Oil on canvas, 10 ft 2 ins × 16 ft 7 ins (3.09 × 5.05 m). National Gallery of Ireland, Dublin.

ing bizarre, wild, and exotic pets became the rage, a development perfectly consistent with the Romantic tendency and outlook. In the jubilee year of 1887, thousands of prisoners all over the British Empire were released. The only criminals not released were those convicted of cruelty to animals, which Queen Victoria regarded as "one of the worst traits of human nature." In *Dignity and Impudence*, Edwin Landseer (1802–73) (Fig. **15.24**) anthropomorphizes two dogs.

Highly controversial, the Pre-Raphaelites appear to have exercised significant influence on later movements away from naturalism. They formed themselves into a group in 1848. The Pre-Raphaelites had a significant influence on art and design because of their ability to envision and paint with detailed skill and their use of a wide range of symbolism. They returned to the direct symbolism, frank naturalism, and poetic sentiment previously found in medieval art, prior to the Renaissance painter Raphael—hence the name. To such medieval qualities they added a modern analysis and profound and intellectual study of art and nature. They loved detail, and their works abound with painstaking atten-

tion to it.

Escape to legend and literature, along with a strong interest in the occult and spiritualism, led to an English fascination with fairy tales. As Charles Dickens wrote in *Household Words* (vol. 8), "In a utilitarian age, of all other times, it is a matter of grave importance that fairy tales should be respected." Fairy tales were subject matter understood and shared by artist and viewer alike. The art that emerged represents a unique, Victorian contribution to art.

The fascinating painting *The Fairy Feller's Master Stroke* (Fig. **15.25**) took the artist, who was suffering from schizophrenia, nine years to complete. Richard Dadd (1817–87) had been among the founders of a group of painters called "the Clique," and his early works had been undistinguished attempts at landscape, marine, and animal painting. After returning from an extensive trip to the Middle East and Italy, and after being rejected in the competition for the decoration of the Houses of Parliament, he stabbed his father to death. Fleeing to France, he planned to assassinate the Emperor of Austria. Captured after stabbing a passenger at Fontainebleau, he spent his remaining years institutionalized in Bedlam, or the Hospital of St Mary of Bethlehem. He was provided with painting materials, and his subsequent works have an insistent supernatural quality, as we can see in Figure **15.25**. The flat coloring and obsessive detail have been explained as a reflection of certain symptoms of schizophrenia. The main event in the painting is placed in the center, and the myriad details that surround it seem to be nothing more than highly imaginative decoration.

Victorian landscape painters produced a prodigious quantity of "pretty, undisturbed scenes" which were designed for a growing picture-buying public. The themes were mostly superficial, emotional, and repetitive, and yet for the most part the genre is highly pleasing. The genius of John Constable (1776–1837) was the guiding light as well as the shadow over other Victorian landscape artists. Constable's "chiaroscuro of nature" lent itself to easy adaptation, and his naturalistic style permeated the genre. *Landscape* (Fig. **15.26**) by Thomas Creswick (1811–69) has much in common with the work of Corot (see Fig. **15.13**), displaying a careful treatment of rocks, trees, and foliage.

Interest in history, both as a backdrop for Utopian escape and for antiquarianism, colored the arts as well as philosophy. Images of heroism and sublimity caught the imagination of the Romantic painters. Scale as well as attitude found its way onto the canvas. *The Marriage of Eva and Strongbow* (Fig. **15.27**) by Daniel MacLise (1806–70), which covers a canvas 10 feet 2 inches by 16 feet 7 inches (3.09 x 5.05 meters), depicts the twelfth-century marriage of Richard Strongbow, Second Earl of Pembroke and Strigul, to Eva, eldest daughter of Dermot. Complex and busy, the work elicits an emotional response and captures a climactic moment. Strong contrasts in tones compete with many different focal areas for the viewer's attention. The central situation is played out while everything around it is in confusion. The coloring is harsh, and the facial expressions not very real.

Victorian painting, with all its diversity, complexity, contradictions, and often mediocre quality, very effectively represents the remarkable lot of Romantics, realists, and jacks-of-all-trades who rode the crest of the first wave that swept us into our modern world.

CHAPTER SIXTEEN

THE BEGINNINGS OF MODERNISM

A T   A   G L A N C E

The World in Turmoil
European Migration
Business and Industry
Workers and Socialism
The German Reich
A Scientific Explosion
  TECHNOLOGY: Coca-Cola

Philosophy and Psychology
Friedrich Nietzsche
Sigmund Freud
Carl Jung

The Visual Arts and Architecture
Realism

MASTERWORK: Renoir—Le Moulin de la
  Galette
Impressionism
Post-impressionism
Experimentation and Art Nouveau
  PROFILE: Louis Sullivan
Cubism
  MASTERWORK: Picasso—Les Demoiselles
  d'Avignon
Mechanism and Futurism
Expressionism
Fauvism

Literature
Realism
  OUR DYNAMIC WORLD: Native American
  Women in Literature

Symbolism

Music
Impressionism
Naturalism in Opera
Nontraditional Transitions
PROFILE: Igor Stravinsky
Jazz

Theatre
Realism and Naturalism
Symbolism

Film: Art and Mechanization

Synthesis: America's Gilded Age

16.1 Claude Monet, *Rouen Cathedral, the Portal, Morning Sun, Harmony in Blue*, 1893. Oil on canvas, 35$\frac{1}{2}$ × 24$\frac{1}{2}$ ins (91 × 63 cm). Musée d'Orsay, Paris.

| | | |

A CRITICAL LOOK In this chapter we will span the time from approximately 1870 to 1920. Like all our divisions in this book, these are arbitrary dates, dependent on the subjects we are discussing. For example, in political affairs, we will stop before the outbreak of World War I (1914), and in painting, we will begin in the 1850s with styles that began in opposition to Romanticism. On occasion, we will see an illustration dating later than 1914, because it illustrates the work of an artist whose style is the product of the earlier time. It is important that we do not get lost in chronology. The study in this book is not about dates—even though they are important sometimes—but about ideas, culture, and art styles.

In the first sections of this chapter, we examine the World in Turmoil and Philosophy and Psychology, in particular the ideas of Friedrich Nietzsche, Sigmund Freud, and Carl Jung. We will see that during the years between approximately 1870 and 1914 there was tremendous upheaval in politics, business and industry, labor, and science. These years also saw important developments in psychology that remain at the center of things today. Our few pages on each topic offer us only a fleeting glimpse, as from a moving train, but they give us an idea of how tumultuous the period was.

Explain the impact on the world that resulted from the European migration in the late nineteenth century.

Describe the changes in industry that occurred during this time period.

Identify some of the important discoveries and inventions that came to pass.

Describe the impact of socialism on world labor conditions.

Identify the important scientists and developments in physics, chemistry, and biology that occurred during the late nineteenth and early twentieth centuries.

THE WORLD IN TURMOIL

EUROPEAN MIGRATION

During the eighteenth and nineteenth centuries seventy million people emigrated from Europe to other continents, mostly to North America, but others went to Siberia, Latin America, and Australia. By 1900 the total European population outside of Europe numbered approximately 560 million and represented more than one-third of the world's entire population. Not all European countries participated in this migration equally—for example, France which early adopted birth control practices, barely reproduced at replacement level, but the declining death rate resulting from better medicine and a number of other factors, allowed France's population to grow. Nevertheless, it contributed little to the great movement of European migration.

The populations of most other European countries, on the other hand, exploded and led to migration on a massive scale. Among the first to contribute to the emigration were the British and the Irish. In the mid-nineteenth century, Ireland was contributing nearly half of the immigrants to the United States, and in four successive waves

(1850, 1870, 1885, and 1910) thirteen million English and Scots left their native lands. Two-thirds of them came to the United States, half that many to Canada, and the remainder to Australia and South Africa. In the same period six million Germans left home (most of them for the United States), and two million Scandinavians did the same. Sixteen million Italians left Italy—nearly 750,000 people in 1913 alone—half went to North and South America and the other half to other parts of Europe. Central and Eastern Europeans contributed nine million people to the waves of emigration. By the end of the nineteenth century, Europeans had, literally, populated the globe.

BUSINESS AND INDUSTRY

During the nineteenth century industrial civilization changed from a system of production based on iron and coal to one based on the technology of electricity, the internal combustion engine, and the chemistry of synthetic materials. The turning point came in the 1890s, when technological development accelerated exponentially. An overview of industrial and technological development isolates three principal periods. The first began in the late eighteenth century in Britain and had moved, by the first half of the nineteenth century, to France, Belgium, Switzerland, and the United States. However,

	GENERAL EVENTS	LITERATURE & PHILOSOPHY	VISUAL ART & ARCHITECTURE	THEATRE & CINEMA	MUSIC
1870	Emigration from Europe Unification of Germany	Zola Marx Dostoevski	Courbet (**16.6**) Millet (**16.7**) Rodin (**16.14**) Manet (**16.8**) Monet (**16.1**, **16.11**) Renoir (**16.10**)	Ibsen	Bizet
1875	Flotation separation of ore Brooklyn Bridge Hydroelectric power Pasteurization Radio-telegraphy Discovery of radium Renault makes cars	La Flesche	Seurat (**16.15**) Tanner (**16.9**) Morisot (**16.12**) Cassatt (**16.13**) Gauguin (**16.17**) Van Gogh (**0.6**)	Chekhov Shaw	Debussy Ravel Mascagni Puccini Leoncavallo Wagner Strauss
1900	Rise of nationalism in Europe	Nietzsche Freud Jung Proust	Cézanne (**16.16**) Burnham and Root (**16.18**) Gaudi (**16.21**) Sullivan (**16.19**) Wright (**16.20**) Picasso (**16.22**) Braque Matisse (**16.25**) Duchamp (**16.23**) Beckmann (**16.24**)	Maeterlinck Stanislavsky Armat Lumière brothers Méliès Porter Pathé Sennet Griffith Chaplin	Stravinsky Schoenberg Jazz

Timeline 16.1 The beginnings of modernism.

with the exception of the United States, the industrial explosion slowed in these countries after the 1860s—between 1875 to 1913, on the other hand, the United States' share of world industrial output had climbed from 23 percent to 36 percent. The second period of industrial development, which occurred between 1840 and 1873, witnessed the first real world boom in railway construction and the widespread industrialization of the remainder of Europe, particularly Germany, where a much greater economic transformation took Germany to a position as the world's second largest industrial producer by the end of the century. The last wave of industrial expansion came at the very end of the nineteenth century and encompassed Russia, the Scandinavian countries, Italy, parts of Eastern Europe and Japan. By 1913, Europe and North America represented 82 percent of the world's industrial production—down by 4 percent from 1870.

The growth and spread of industry and technology created fundamental changes in the organization of the system of production. Until the 1870s the capitalist system underpinned economic activity in Europe. The social dynamic centered on the family, and its system of organization rested on the authority of one man, the omniscient entrepreneur. It was the age, as we will see in the Synthesis section at the end of this chapter, when great personal fortunes were amassed by individual businessmen. Gradually, however, especially in the United States

and Germany, business and industry placed at their center the concept of continuous production and mass distribution. The change, which might be defined as a shift from the "visible" hand of an integrated company to the "invisible" hand of the market, coincided with a growing concentration of businesses that tended to bring together in one unit the activities of production, marketing, and research. Thus, the world began to see huge corporations with multi-functional hierarchical structures. Some companies retained a family structure, but others moved toward a managerial model, with decision-making placed in the hands of salaried executives, and at the same time, the concept of marketing networks created more and more mergers and larger and larger corporations. In addition, the marketplace experienced a dynamic increase in new business centered on new products that emerged from new technologies—for example, automobiles, bicycles, the cinema, and, later, airplanes.

WORKERS AND SOCIALISM

Among the major results of industrialization were the growth of the working class, the development of its organizational forms, and its links to other elements in society who were, to varying degrees, unwilling to integrate with bourgeois society (Figs **16.2** and **16.3**). The organization of the working class came in three spurts. The first, from 1864–93, witnessed powerful popular movements and brutally repressed mass strikes. During this period, the International Working Men's Association (1864) and the socialist International (1889–93) were formed. The second spurt, which occurred between 1893 and 1905, saw the rise of trade unions and the emergence of nation-states of political parties. The last spurt, from 1905 until World War I, included a general expansion of the labor and socialist movements.

The International Working Men's Association was founded in London in 1864, and it drew much support across Europe. It was intended to be a worldwide work-ers' party through which workers could derive a sense of solidarity in their struggle to improve their conditions. The movement split in 1869, with the followers of Karl Marx going in one direction, and the others, known as "anti-authoritarian faction," going in another. Within twenty years the movement had splintered into national groups, for the simple reason that the different forms of action and militancy could not develop according to a

16.2 Käthe Kollwitz, *The Weaver's Cycle: March of the Weavers*, 1897. Etching, 8³/₈ × 11⁵/₈ ins (21.3 × 29.5 cm). University of Michigan Museum of Art.

16.3 Ford Madox Brown, *Work*, 1852-65. Oil on canvas, 4 ft 6¹/₂ ins x 6 ft 5¹/₈ ins (1.38 x 1.96 m). Manchester City Art Gallery, U.K.

single model. The movement polarized around two centers: unions and political parties.

The socialist creed continued to be spread through the organization of the Second International in 1889–91, a loose federation of organizations. According to its agenda, in order to be called a socialist, an individual had to work for the collective ownership of the means of production and to recognize the need for political and parliamentary action. Strikes became the main weapon of the union movement in Europe, but by the beginning of the twentieth century, the labor movement in Europe proved relatively impotent in the face of rising nationalism and imperialism.

THE GERMAN REICH

As we have seen in preceding chapters, unlike much of the rest of Europe, Germany remained a series of independent states under individual rule. However, on January 18, 1871, twenty-five German states, including three city states, joined together to create a unified German Reich (state) with William I, King of Prussia, as Kaiser. It was an authoritarian state, whose government was not responsible to the parliament. The previous state of Prussia dominated the remaining members of the Reich, and that gave the new state a particular civilization and type of government—that is, a conservative business class and the domination of the civil service by a powerful professional military. Bismarck, the prime minister of the Reich was a Prussian, and he began a *Kulturkampf* (campaign for secularization), which attacked Catholics, expelled the Jesuits, and placed controls on the Roman clergy. However, because such a campaign also alarmed the Protestants, it did not succeed. After two attempts were made to assassinate the Kaiser, Bismarck dissolved the Reichstag (parliament) and instituted anti-socialist laws. Despite the crash of the Viennese stock market, German industrial expansion continued, and heavy industry became more highly concentrated. The country became more and more urban, and the population grew quickly. Agriculture was modernized, and Germany,

Map 16.1 Political frontiers and national communities in Europe 1848.

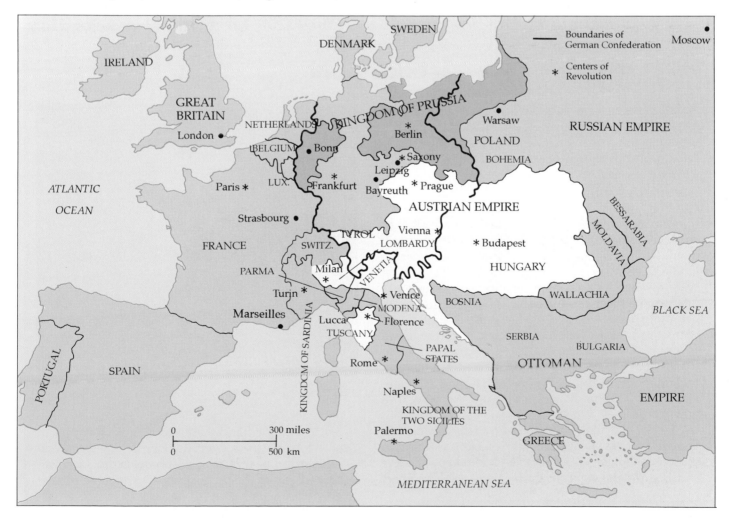

practicing a form of state capitalism, became the second most powerful nation on earth. The German aristocracy joined forces with the richest industrialists to form a strong hedge against socialism and trade unionism.

Bismarck's foreign policy sought to consolidate Germany's position in Europe by forging a set of contradictory treaties. In 1879 Germany entered an alliance with Austria-Hungary, in 1881 he engineered the Three Emperor's League, and in 1882 he produced the Triple Alliance among Germany, Austria-Hungary, and Italy. German nationalism strengthened when Kaiser William II took the throne in 1888 and began his search for Germany's "place in the sun." However, during this time, socialist influence increased and, in 1912, the Social Democratic Party (SPD) became the largest group in the Reichstag. Among its major objectives, which it tried to accomplish by demonstrations and strikes, was universal suffrage in those areas of Germany where three classes—aristocracy, bourgeoisie, and workers—still existed. This demand proved an important point in the SPD's acceptance of Germany's entry into World War I under a government of national unity on August 4, 1914.

A SCIENTIFIC EXPLOSION

PHYSICS

So much happened in science in the last quarter of the nineteenth century and the first decade of the twentieth century that a mere scratching of the surface is all that a book that is primarily about art and culture can manage.

In 1900 no law had been discovered to account for the phenomenon of heat and light radiation by a solid, white-hot body. In that year, Max Planck (1858–1947) guessed that radiation did not occur in a continuous fashion but in small discrete units, separate quantities or quanta. This theory, which enabled scientists to explain heat radiation, turned physics upside down. Building on this theory, Albert Einstein (1879–1955) explained in 1905 the photoelectric effect, by showing that light, which comprises both waves and particles, moves by quanta—that is, tiny packets of light, which were later called photons. Nils Bohr (1885–1962) used this quantum theory to build a model of an atom, in 1911, describing the movement of

---

TECHNOLOGY: PUTTING DISCOVERY TO WORK

Coca-Cola

Sugar, caffeine, and vegetable extracts are some of the ingredients of the world's most popular soft drink, although the exact proportions of these ingredients remain one of the corporate world's most jealously guarded secrets. Dr John S. Pemberton (Fig. **16.4**) never patented his original formula, which he concocted in 1886 in Atlanta, Georgia.

Pemberton, a pharmacist, developed a variety of chemical compounds for treating various human ailments—for example, Globe of Flower Cough Syrup, Indian Queen Hair Dye, and Triplex Liver Pills—and he spent much of his time in his chemical laboratory looking for new flavors to make his pharmaceutical products more tasty. Around 1880 he began to experiment with a "soft" drink that could be sold at the food soda fountain of drug stores. In 1886 he discovered a syrup that, when mixed with carbonated water, made a thirst-quenching drink. He added caffeine and vegetable extracts, for flavor, and mixed the brew in a brass kettle.

The first person to test the new drink was William Venable, the resident "soda jerk" of Jacob's Drugstore in Atlanta. Apparently, Venable liked what he drank and bought the mix on a trial basis. His customers

16.4 Dr John S. Pemberton of the Coca-Cola corporation.

loved it, and wanted to ask for it by name. One of Pemberton's partners, Frank Robinson, suggested Coca-Cola, and the next day, an elaborate script logo was produced. It and the product remain the same today.

electrons within an atom. This model enabled him to achieve remarkable results in the fields of the spectroscopy of gaseous matter and of X-ray physics.

In September 1895 Wilhelm Conrad Röntgen (1845–1923) discovered X-rays—he called the rays "X" because their nature was then unknown. It was not defined until 1912, when Max von Laue (1879–1960) managed to diffract the rays through a lattice of crystal. X-rays are electromagnetic waves with very short wavelengths that pass through material that is normally opaque to light, and their discovery gained Röntgen a Nobel Prize for Physics in 1901. In 1911 Heike Kamerlingh Onnes of the Netherlands discovered superconductivity—that is, the property of certain metals or alloys, at very low temperatures, to lose their resistance to electricity. It took until 1986 for research in superconductivity to lead to the development now being seen in contemporary physical processes.

BIOLOGY

In 1865 the Moravian-born botanist Gregor Johann Mendel (1822–84) demonstrated that hereditary characteristics are transmitted via distinct elements, which are today called genes. Mendel's findings, the discovery of chromosomes in 1888 and of mutations in 1901, founded the science of genetics. The gene itself emerged in 1909, when the Danish botanist Wilhelm Johannsen (1857–1927) coined the name "genes" for the hereditary units that produce the physical characteristics of an organism.

In microbiology, the second half of the century produced the work of Frenchman Louis Pasteur (1822–95), who explained the fermentation process as the result of the action of microscopic living organisms. Pasteur extended his research to include bacteria, thus beginning the field of bacteriology, and he promulgated the idea that living beings contain in themselves the means of fighting disease. Thus, the immune system became a serious subject for scientific study. Birth itself emerged from scientific experimentation in the early twentieth century, when in vitro cultivation—that is, a method in which a living organism is sustained outside of its natural environment—was invented in 1907.

PHILOSOPHY AND PSYCHOLOGY

FRIEDRICH NIETZSCHE

The German philosopher and poet Friedrich Wilhelm Nietzsche (1844–1900) was raised after his father's death by his religious female relatives, and, according to some,

this accounted for the attacks on religion and women that he made in his writings. His brilliance brought him the appointment as Professor of Greek at the University of Basel in 1869, but ten years later he resigned the post because of poor health and, for the next ten years, led a mostly solitary life. In January 1889 he suffered a complete mental collapse from which he never recovered, although he lived for another eleven years.

Soon after going to Basel, he published an intuitive philosophical investigation of the spiritual background of Greek tragedy entitled *The Birth of Tragedy from the Spirit of Music* (1872). Three years later he wrote *Untimely Opinions* in which he attacked the smug conceit of Bismarck's Germany. Perhaps his best known work is *Thus Spake Zarathustra* (1883–92), a series of rhapsodical sermons by an imaginary prophet and written in poetic prose modeled after the Bible.

Nietzsche was a fascinating figure. He attacked all the accepted ideas of his time—for example, Christianity, conventional morality, sympathy for the weak and helpless, and rationalism—but at the same time he reportedly warned a friend that it was not desirable for his readers to agree with him. Many of his ideas are clearly fascistic, and the followers of Adolf Hitler claimed him as their inspiration and prophet. Perhaps there is an irony in the fact that Nietzsche himself opposed nationalism, armies, the German Empire, politics, and racism, especially anti-Semitism. Understanding and interpreting Nietzsche was made exceedingly difficult by the fact that he often wrote in hyperbole—that is, by overstating his case in order to get a reaction—and whatever he wrote, he wrote with verve and caustic wit. He accepted the idea of human helplessness in a mechanical world operating under inexorable law, but he rejected Schopenhauer's pessimism. Instead, he preached courage in the face of the unknown and found this to be humanity's highest attribute. After a long selective process, Nietzsche was certain that courage would produce a race of supermen and women.

SIGMUND FREUD

One of the towering figures of modern times, the Austrian Sigmund Freud (1856–1939) was the first to develop what he called "psychoanalysis"—that is, the probing of the human "unconscious"—in the study of human behavior by exploring the world of dreams (Fig. **16.5**). Psychoanalysis is a method of understanding psychological and psychopathological phenomena, and at the same time a method of treating mental illness. Freud developed his theories around 1885 in Vienna, and although he did not invent the idea of the psychic unconscious, he undertook a systematic exploration of it. At first his ideas were met with considerable skepticism because of their novel propositions regarding sexuality. However, psychoanaly-

16.5 Max Halberstadt, photograph of Sigmund Freud, c. 1926. Courtesy of W. Ernest Freud, by arrangement with Mark Patterson and Associates and the Freud Museum, London.

sis gradually gained an important place in medicine and psychology.

Freud's principal work was *The Interpretation of Dreams* (1900), in which he showed that the discoveries of psychoanalysis about dreaming and using symbols can be applied to literature as well as to psychology and psychiatry. His ideas significantly influenced twentieth-century literature, and some of the misinterpretations of his ideas led to the exploration of the creative imagination.

Freud's impact on literature falls into three areas. The first, called literary surrealism, is based on the idea of breaking human psychological defenses and giving uncensored expression to the irrational symbolic modes of the unconscious. The second area concerns an aspect of what, in the Introduction to this text, we called "contextual criticism." Here, biographers and critics "psychoanalyze" writers, and other artists, in order to explain literary works in terms of the writer's "conditioning." The final area consists of writers, particularly novelists and dramatists, conceiving and presenting their characters in psychoanalytical terms. This is especially true of the

A CRITICAL REVIEW

The strife between labor and management that led to the socialist labor movements during the late nineteenth century was much worse than the conditions we see today—even when violent strikes occur. Any discussion of the role and value of labor unions evokes strongly held opinions on all sides of the issue, but whatever current conditions may be, the condition of laborers in the industrialized world of the late nineteenth century was little better than the role of serfs in the Middle Ages. Some might argue that it was worse, because under feudalism, the lord of the manor was at least expected to provide for all conditions of life for those who labored on his manor. All too often, industry in the late nineteenth century built riches for its owners on the pure exploitation of labor, and, as we have seen, the conditions of ownership and management were changing from the single, family entrepreneur to an impersonal corporation run by directors and managers. In the United States, a massive influx of migrants from Europe provided industry with a plentiful source of cheap labor.

Describe the ways in which labor–management structures and relationships have changed from the late nineteenth century. In what ways have they remained the same?

In a short essay speculate on the manifestations of the European migration on issues of immigration that are current in the United States today.

The unification of the German states was an important and far-reaching aspect of nationalization during this time.

Describe the issues affecting Germany from 1870 to 1914.

The late nineteenth century produced a crop of intellectual giants—Freud in psychology, Einstein in physics and Nietzsche in philosophy—whose influence still resounds a century later.

Discuss how the science, psychology, and philosophy of the time still affect the way we live and see life.

"stream-of-consciousness" school, in which the character's inner monologue imposes on the reader the job of finding the person in the midst of the material comprising his personal experience.

CARL JUNG

The idea that artistic creativity is basic to humanity has been expressed in various ways in the 20th century. To take one example, in the field of theatre, the designer Robert Edmund Jones makes the connection between imagination and dreams in his book *The Dramatic Imagination*. His concepts were closely related to the concept of intuition propounded by Carl Gustav Jung (1875–1961). Jones sees the theatre as a place that deals with magic, not logic. The supernormal is normal, the imagination is the source of creativity, "a special faculty…by means of which we can form mental images of things not present in our senses." He cautions, however, that "many people confuse imagination with ingenuity, with inventiveness. But imagination is not this thing at all. It is the power of seeing with the eye of the mind."

Jung, on the other hand, developed a working concept of intuition as "a function separate from thinking, feeling,

and sensation which was characterized by the ability to see connections between things and find the potential inherent in a situation…[it was] an active, creative process."[1] In *The Spirit in Man, Art and Literature* Jung describes intuition as "the source of [the artist's] creativeness." Jung believed not only in individual unconsciouses but in a universal unconscious—that is, in a collective unconscious shared by all human beings—in which lay a reservoir of primordial images—Jung called them "archetypal images," or ARCHETYPES—upon which any person could draw. Artists were influenced more than ordinary people by the contents of this unconscious, however, "The creative urge lives and grows in [the artist] like a tree in the earth from which it draws nourishment. We would do well, therefore, to think of the creative process as a living thing implanted in the human psyche."

What an artist creates, then, is the unconscious expression of archetypal images. And the drive to create originates in the unconscious and brings out the expression of psychic material in images and patterns that are similar throughout history and from place to place (see C.G. Jung, *Man and His Symbols*).

Whether or not we subscribe to Jung's concept of creativity, our intuitive function does suggest that the urge to create art is timeless and universal.

CRITICAL REVIEW p. 520

A CRITICAL LOOK

The world of the late nineteenth and early twentieth centuries exploded with new technologies, ideas, social patterns, and self-realization, and it is not surprising that we find a similar thrust in the arts. In earlier chapters, we could trace long periods of time and witness one, two, or perhaps three art styles emerging. Modernity changes all that. Now that artists are free from patronage and live and work on their own, their vision takes them in diverse directions. Consequently, in the short period of time we are examining in this chapter, we will study no fewer than ten new styles, each of which has its own characteristics and representative artists. Keeping them all straight will be a challenge.

Describe the characteristics of realism, impressionism, and post-impressionism and identify their key artists and works.

Describe the experiments in architecture that led us to modern approaches.

Describe the style called art nouveau and identify its representative artists and works.

THE VISUAL ARTS AND ARCHITECTURE

REALISM

A new painting style called "realism" arose in the mid-nineteenth century. The word describes various kinds of painting. "Social realism," for example, describes a number of painting styles that picture the contemporary

scene, usually from a socialist viewpoint, and always with a strong thematic emphasis on the ways in which society oppresses the individual. Others extend the "realist" label to include Manet, while still others apply the term only to Courbet. Whatever the case, the definition of "reality" in the nineteenth century took on new significance because the camera now intruded on what previously had been exclusively the painter's realm.

The style that is referred to as "realism" ran through the 1840s, 1850s, and 1860s, and its central figure was Gustave Courbet (1819–77). Courbet was influenced by the innovations of Corot in terms of the play of light on

ICAL LOOK bove

surfaces. But, unlike Corot, his aim was to make an objective and unprejudiced record of the customs, ideas, and appearances of contemporary French society, and his work depicts everyday life. *The Stone Breakers* (Fig. **16.6**) was the first painting to display his philosophy to the full. Courbet painted two men as he had seen them working beside a road. The work is lifesize, and, while the treatment seems objective, it makes a sharp comment on the tedium and laborious nature of the task. A social realist, Courbet was more intent on social message than on meditative reaction. Therefore, his work is less dramatic and nostalgic than that of others.

Jean-François Millet (1814–75) was one of a group of painters called the Barbizon School, which focused upon a realistic-Romantic vision of landscape, and typically used peasants as its subject matter. The Barbizon School did not espouse socialism, but it did exalt the honest, simple life and work on the land, as contrasted with the urban bourgeois life. In Millet's *Woman Baking Bread* (Fig. **16.7**) these themes are apparent, and the peasant emerges as an heroic figure. This quality is enhanced by the vantage point the painter has chosen. Seen from slightly below, the peasant woman has an added height and dominance which emphasizes her grandeur.

Edouard Manet (1832–83) followed in the realist tradition, although he is often regarded as an impression-ist—an association he denied. Manet strove to paint "only what the eye can see." Yet his works go beyond a mere reflection of reality to a larger artistic reality, one which suggests that a painting has an internal logic different from the logic of familiar reality. Manet liberated the painter's art from competition with the camera. *Déjeuner sur l'herbe* (Fig. **16.8**), in which Manet sought to "speak in a new voice," shocked the public when it was first shown at the Salon des Refusés in 1863. The setting is pastoral, like one we might find in Watteau, for example, but the people are real and identifiable: Manet's model, his brother, and the sculptor Leenhof. The apparent immorality of a naked frolic in a Paris park outraged the public and the critics. Had his figures been nymphs and satyrs or idealized men and women in classical dress, all would have been well. But the intrusion of reality into the sacred mythical setting, not to mention the nudity of a real woman while her male companions have their clothes on, proved more than the public could handle.

The first important black painter, the American Henry O. Tanner (1859–1937), although somewhat later, painted in a similar style (Fig. **16.9**). He studied with the

16.6 Gustave Courbet, *The Stone Breakers*, 1849. Oil on canvas, 5 ft 3 ins x 8 ft 6 ins (1.6 x 2.59 m). Formerly Gemäldegalerie, Dresden, Germany (destroyed 1945).

16.7 Jean-François Millet, *Woman Baking Bread*, 1853–4. Oil on canvas, 21³/₄ x 18 ins (55 x 46 cm). Collection, State Museum Kröller-Müller, Otterlo, The Netherlands.

16.9 Henry O. Tanner, *The Banjo Lesson*, c. 1893. Oil on canvas, 48 x 35 ins (122 x 89 cm). Hampton Institute, Hampton, Virginia.

16.8 Edouard Manet, *Déjeuner sur l'herbe* (*The Picnic*), 1863. Oil on canvas, 7 ft x 8 ft 10 ins (2.13 x 2.69 m). Louvre, Paris.

MASTERWORK

Renoir—Le Moulin de la Galette

The impressionist Pierre-Auguste Renoir (1841–1919) specialized in painting the human figure and sought out what was beautiful in the body. His paintings sparkle with the joy of life. In *Le Moulin da la Galette* (Fig. **16.10**) he depicts the bright gaiety of a Sunday afternoon crowd in a popular Parisian dance venue. The artist celebrates the liveliness and charm of these everyday folk as they talk, crowd the tables, flirt, and dance. Warmth infuses the setting. Sunlight and shade dapple the scene and create a sensation of floating in light.

There is a casualness here, a sense of life captured in a fleeting and spontaneous moment, and of a much wider scene extending beyond the canvas. This is no formally composed scene like that in David's *Oath of the Horatii* (Fig. **14.18**). Rather, we are invited to become a part of the action. People are going about their everyday lives with no sense of the painter's presence. As opposed to the realism of the classicist who seeks the universal and the typical, the realism of the impressionist seeks "the incidental, the momentary, and the passing."

Le Moulin de la Galette captures the enjoyment of a moment outdoors. The colors shimmer, and although Renoir skillfully plays off highlights against dark tones, the uniform hue of the lowest values is not black but blue. In short, the beauty of this work exemplifies Renoir's statement, "The earth as the paradise of the gods, that is what I want to paint."

16.10 Pierre-Auguste Renoir, *Le Moulin de la Galette*, 1876. Oil on canvas, 4 ft 3½ ins x 5 ft 9 ins (1.31 x 1.75 m). Louvre, Paris.

American realist painter Thomas Eakins (1844–1916), who encouraged both blacks and women at a time when professional careers were essentially closed to them. *The Banjo Lesson* presents its images in a strictly realistic manner, without sentimentality. The painting's focus is achieved through the contrast of clarity in the central objects and less detail in the surrounding areas. In many respects this technique follows Corot. Tanner skillfully captures an atmosphere of concentration and shows us a warm relationship between teacher and pupil.

IMPRESSIONISM

The realists' search for spontaneity, harmonious colors, subjects from everyday life, and faithfulness to observed lighting and atmospheric effects led to the development of a style used by a small group of painters in the 1860s, and described by a hostile critic in 1874 as "impressionism." The "impressionists" created a new way of seeing reality and sought to capture "the psychological perception of reality in color and motion."[2] Their style emerged in competition with the newly invented technology of the camera, and these painters tried to outdo photography by portraying those essentials of perception that the camera cannot capture.

The style lasted only fifteen years in its purest form, but it profoundly influenced all painting that followed. Working out-of-doors, the impressionists concentrated on the effects of natural light on objects and atmosphere. They discovered that color, for example, is not inherent in an object but in our perceptions of that object, as mod-

16.11 Claude Monet, *On the Seine at Bennecourt*, 1868. Oil on canvas, 31⁷/₈ x 39¹/₂ ins (78.5 x 100.5 cm). Courtesy the Art Institute of Chicago (Potter Palmer Collection).

ified by the quality of existing light. Their experiments resulted in a profoundly different vision of the world around them and way of rendering that vision. This "revolution of the color patch," as it has been called, taught that the painted canvas was, first of all, "a material covered with pigments—that we must look at it, not through it." As we look at an impressionist painting, we see that the canvas is filled with small "color patches," and that our impression of the reality there comes through the total effect of those "flickering" patches. The result is a lively, vibrant image.

Impressionism was as collective a style as any we have seen thus far. In an individualistic age, this style reflected the common concerns of a relatively small group of artists who met frequently and held joint exhibitions. The subjects painted are impressions of landscapes, rivers, streets, cafés, theatres, and so on.

However, it is generally considered that Claude Monet and Pierre-Auguste Renoir brought impressionism to its birth. They spent the summer of 1866 at Bougival on the River Seine, working closely together, and from that collaboration came the beginnings of the style. In his paintings, Claude Monet (1840–1926) tried to find an art of modern life by recording everyday themes with on-the-spot, objective observations. He sought to achieve two aims: representation of contemporary subject matter and optical truth—that is, the way colors and textures really appear to the eye. Monet's paintings reflect an innocent joy in the world around him and an intensely positive view of life. He had no specific aesthetic theory—in fact, he detested theorizing—but he did seek to bring realism to its peak. His work encompasses scientific observation, the study of optics, and other aspects of human perception. Monet translated objects into color stimuli. He told a young American artist in 1889 that he should disregard the actual trees, houses, fields; rather, he should see only "a square of blue...an oblong of pink...a streak of yellow" by using exact colors and shapes, until a naive impression of the scene before him was created.

On the Seine at Bennecourt (Fig. **16.11**) by Monet illustrates these concerns. It conveys a pleasant picture of the times, an optimistic view rather than the often pessimistic outlook of the Romantics. It also suggests a fragmentary and fleeting sensory image. This was a new tone for a new era. We sense the quickly applied pigment. Brushstroke suggests form, and although the scene is a landscape panorama, the vision leaves us with no deep space. The background colors are as vibrant as the foreground. There is no linear perspective, and the overall effect brings the entire painting into the foreplane. The

scene is bright, alive, and pleasant. We are comfortable in its presence.

The best-known central figures in the development of impressionism were Monet, Renoir, and Degas. But also included in this original group of impressionists was Berthe Morisot (1841–95). Her works have a gentle introspectiveness, often focusing on family members, and her view of contemporary life is edged with pathos and sentimentality. In *In the Dining Room* (Fig. **16.12**), she gives a penetrating glimpse into psychological reality. The servant girl has a distinct personality, and she stares back at the viewer almost impudently. The painting captures a moment of disorder—the cabinet door stands ajar with what appears to be a used table cloth flung over it. The little dog playfully demands attention. Morisot's brushstrokes are delicate, loose, and casual.

In 1877, another woman joined the impressionists. Mary Cassatt (1845–1926) came to Paris from Philadelphia, a minor center for artists at the time.

16.13 Mary Cassatt, *The Bath*, 1891. Oil on canvas, 39½ x 26 ins (100 x 66 cm). Art Institute of Chicago.

16.12 Berthe Morisot, *In the Dining Room*, 1886. Oil on canvas, 24⅛ x 19¾ ins (61 x 50 cm). National Gallery of Art, Washington, D.C.

16.14 Auguste Rodin, *The Burghers of Calais*, 1866. Bronze, 6 ft 10½ ins (2.1 m) high. Hirshhorn Museum and Sculpture Garden, Smithsonian Institution, Washington, D.C.

Thanks to her financial independence, she overrode her family's objections to a career deemed unsuitable for a woman, especially a woman of wealth. In fact, it was her wealth and connections with wealthy collectors in the United States that helped the impressionists gain exposure and acceptance in this country. In *The Bath* (Fig. **16.13**), she depicts her favorite subjects—women and children. In this painting, Cassatt's brushwork is far less obvious than that in other impressionist works, and this helps conventional viewers to understand the work and relate closely to the scene. Painted in clear, bright colors, Cassatt's subjects do not make eye contact with the viewer. Their forms are purposeful, and they awaken our interest, rather than our emotions.

The surface and textural concerns of the impressionist can be seen in the work of the century's most remarkable sculptor, Auguste Rodin (1840–1917). Although his style is not easy to classify, we find plenty of idealism and social comment—for example, in his powerful work *The Burghers of Calais* (Fig. **16.14**), a piece celebrating the noble, if humiliating, surrender of the city. Rodin's textures are impressionistic: his surfaces appear to shimmer as light plays on their irregularities, but they are more than reflective surfaces. They give his works dynamic and dramatic qualities. Although Rodin worked fairly realistically, he nevertheless created a subjective reality beyond the surface, and the subjectivity of his viewpoint is even more clear and dramatic in his pessimistic later sculptures.

POST-IMPRESSIONISM

In the last two decades of the nineteenth century, impressionism evolved gently into a collection of rather disparate styles called simply "post-impressionism." In subject matter, post-impressionist paintings were similar to impressionist paintings—landscapes, familiar portraits, groups, and café and nightclub scenes—but the post-impressionists gave their subject matter a complex and profoundly personal significance.

Georges Seurat (1859–91), often described as a neo-impressionist"—he called his approach and technique "divisionism"—departed radically from existing painting technique with his experiments in optics and color theory. His patient and systematic application of specks of paint is called POINTILLISM, because paint is applied with the point of the brush, one small dot at a time. *A Sunday Afternoon on the Island of La Grande Jatte* (Fig. **16.15**) illustrates both his theory of color perception and his concern for the accurate depiction of light and colorations of objects. The composition of this work shows attention to perspective, and yet it willfully avoids three-dimensionality. Japanese influence is apparent here, as it was in much post-impressionist work. Color areas are fairly uniform, figures are flattened, and outlining is continuous. Throughout the work we find conscious systematizing. The painting is broken into proportions of three-eighths and halves, which Seurat believed represented true har-

16.15 Georges Seurat, *A Sunday Afternoon on the Island of La Grande Jatte*, 1884–6. Oil on canvas, 6 ft 9¹/₂ ins x 10 ft ³/₈ ins (2.06 x 3.06 m). Courtesy of the Art Institute of Chicago (Helen Birch Bartlett Memorial Collection).

16.16 Paul Cézanne, *Mont Sainte-Victoire seen from Les Lauves*, 1902–4. Oil on canvas, 27¹/₂ x 35¹/₄ ins (69.8 x 89.5 cm). Philadelphia Museum of Art (George W. Elkins Collection).

16.17 Paul Gauguin, *The Vision after the Sermon*, 1888. Oil on canvas, 28³/₄ x 36¹/₄ ins (73 x 92 cm). National Gallery of Scotland, Edinburgh.

mony. He also selected his colors by formula. For Seurat, the painter's representation of physical reality was simply a search for a superior harmony, for an abstract perfection.

The post-impressionists called for a return to form and structure in painting, characteristics they believed were lacking in the works of the impressionists. Taking the evanescent light qualities of the impressionists, Gauguin, Seurat, Van Gogh, and Cézanne brought formal patterning to their canvases. They used clean color areas, and applied color in a systematic, almost scientific manner. The post-impressionists sought to return painting to traditional goals while retaining the clean palette of the impressionists.

Paul Cézanne (1839–1906), considered by many to be the father of modern art, illustrates concern for formal design, and his *Mont Sainte-Victoire seen from Les Lauves* (Fig. **16.16**) shows a nearly geometric configuration and balance. Foreground and background are tied together in a systematic manner so that both join in the foreground to create two-dimensional patterns. Shapes are simplified, and outlining is used throughout. Cézanne believed that all forms in nature are based on geometric shapes—the cone, the sphere, and the cylinder.

Employing these forms, he sought to reveal the enduring reality that lay beneath surface appearance.

Paul Gauguin (1848–1903) brought a highly imaginative approach to post-impressionist goals. An artist without training, and a nomad who believed that European society and all its works were sick, Gauguin devoted his life to art and to wandering, spending many years in rural Brittany and the end of his life in Tahiti and the Marquesas Islands. His work shows his insistence on form and his resistance to naturalistic effects. Gauguin was influenced by non-Western art, including archaic and "primitive" styles. *The Vision after the Sermon* (Fig. **16.17**) has Gauguin's typically flat, outlined figures, simple forms, and the symbolism for which he and his followers, sometimes called "Nabis," from the Hebrew word for prophet, were known. In the background of this painting, the biblical figure of Jacob wrestles with the Angel while, in the foreground, a priest, nuns, and women in

Breton costume pray. The intense reds are typical of Gauguin's symbolic and unnatural use of color, used here to portray the powerful sensations of a Breton folk festival.

Vincent van Gogh (1853–90) took yet another approach to post-impressionism. His intense emotionalism in pursuing form was unique. Van Gogh's turbulent life included numerous short-lived careers, impossible love affairs, a tempestuous friendship with Gauguin, and, finally, serious mental illness. Biography here is essential because Van Gogh gives us one of the most personal and subjective artistic viewpoints in the history of Western art. Frenetic energy explodes from his brushwork in paintings such as *The Starry Night* (see Fig. **0.6**). Flattened forms and outlining reflect Japanese influence. Tremendous power surges through the painting, especially in focal areas, and we can sense the dynamic, personal feeling and mental turmoil barely contained by the painting's surface.

EXPERIMENTATION AND ART NOUVEAU

A new age of experimentation also took nineteenth-century architects in a different direction—upward. Late in the period, the skyscraper was designed in response to the need to create additional commercial space on the limited land space in burgeoning urban areas. Burnham and Root's Monadnock Building in Chicago (Fig. **16.18**) was an early example. Although this prototypical "skyscraper" is all masonry—that is, it is built completely of brick and requires increasingly thick supportive walls toward its base—it was part of the trend in architecture to combine design, materials, and new concepts of space.

When all these elements were finally combined, the skyscraper emerged, almost exclusively in America. Architects erected buildings of unprecedented height without increasing the thickness of lower walls by using structural frameworks—first of iron, later of steel—and by treating walls as independent partitions. Each story was supported on horizontal girders. The concept of the skyscraper could not be realized comfortably, however, until the invention of a safe and reliable elevator.

One of the most influential figures in the development of the skyscraper and philosophies of modern architecture was Louis Sullivan, the first truly modern architect. Working in the last decade of the nineteenth century in Chicago, then the most rapidly developing metropolis in the world, Sullivan designed buildings of great dignity, simplicity, and strength. Most important, however, he created a rubric for modern architecture with his theory that form flowed from function. As Sullivan said to an observer of the Carson, Pirie, and Scott building (Fig. **16.19**): "It is evident that we are looking at a department

16.18 Daniel Hudson Burnham and John Wellborn Root, the Monadnock Building, Chicago, 1889–91.

store. Its purpose is clearly set forth in its general aspect, and the form follows the function in a simple, straightforward way."

In the final years of the nineteenth century, a new style of architectural decoration evolved called ART NOUVEAU. It is not primarily an architectural mode but, like rococo, which it resembles, it provides a decorative surface—one that is closely associated with graphic art—that imparts a unique character to any building.

Frank Lloyd Wright (1867–1959) was one of the most influential and innovative architects of the twentieth century. He wished to initiate new traditions. One such new tradition was the prairie style, which Wright developed around 1900. In creating these designs, Wright drew on the flat landscape of the Midwest as well as the simple horizontal and vertical accents of the Japanese style. Wright followed Louis Sullivan in his pursuit of form that expressed function, and he took painstaking care to devise practical arrangements for his interiors and to make the exteriors of his buildings reflect their interior

Louis Sullivan (1856–1924)

Born in Boston, Louis Sullivan became one of the leaders in modern architectural design in the United States. He studied briefly at the Massachusetts Institute of Technology and worked for W. le Baron Jenney, an architectural pioneer in the use of the steel skeleton type of building construction, before finishing his education at the École des Beaux-Arts in Paris.

When he was twenty-five years old, Sullivan entered into a partnership with the engineer Dankmar Adler (1844–1900) in Chicago, and the next fourteen years, in partnership with Adler, were the most productive period of Sullivan's career. Between 1886 and 1890 he redesigned the interior of the huge masonry Auditorium building in Chicago, and over the next four years, Sullivan designed two buildings—the Wainwright Building in St Louis and the Guaranty Building in Buffalo—in which he initiated a new set of aesthetics for tall, steel-frame office buildings.

Sullivan rejected historic styles and proposed organically designed buildings that were as expressive of their nature and function as living things are of theirs, and his philosophy was summarized in the phrase "form follows function." His pioneering work made him the father of the modern skyscraper, and, although his designs thrust upward in vertical composition, he embellished them with lively, plantlike ornament very much like art nouveau.

By 1893, however, his star had begun to fade. His colorful Transportation Building at the Columbian Exposition of that year brought little praise, and at the same time, the country experienced a depression, and Sullivan ended his partnership with Adler. Uncompromising in attitude, Sullivan received very few commissions after the dissolution of the partnership. Nonetheless, he built the Carson, Pirie and Scott Department Store in Chicago (1899–1904), replete with strong verticals and horizontals contrasting with lush cast iron foliage, and he also designed a few Midwestern banks. He died in poverty in Chicago on April 24, 1924, but his influence spread into the twentieth century, principally through the success of his young pupil, Frank Lloyd Wright.

16.19 Louis Henry Sullivan, Carson, Pirie, and Scott Department Store, Chicago, 1899–1904.

spaces. He also tried to relate the exterior of the building to its context—that is, its site or natural environment.

Wright also designed some of the furniture for his houses. In doing so, comfort, function, and integration with the total design were his chief criteria. Textures and colors in the environment were duplicated in the materials, including large expanses of wood, both in the house and for its furniture. He made a point of giving furniture several functions. Tables, for example, might also serve as cabinets. All spaces and objects were precisely designed to present a complete environment. Wright was convinced that houses profoundly influence the people who live in them, and he saw the architect as a "molder of humanity." Wright's works range from the simple to the complex, from the serene (Fig. **16.20**) to the dramatic, and from interpenetration to enclosure of space. He was always experimental, and his designs explore the various interrelationships between space and geometric design.

Art nouveau is connected in some ways with the doctrines of nineteenth-century artistic symbolism, and its identifying characteristic is the lively, serpentine curve,

16.20 Frank Lloyd Wright, Robie House, Chicago, 1907–9.

16.21 Antoni Gaudí, Casa Batlló. Barcelona, Spain, 1904–6.

known as the "whiplash." The style also reflects a fascination with plant and animal life and organic growth. The influence of Japanese art, which had been widely plundered late in the nineteenth century, is evident in the undulating curves. Art nouveau incorporates organic and often symbolic motifs, usually languid-looking flowers and animals, and treats them in a flat, linear, and relief-like manner. The twentieth century had arrived.

One of the greatest exponents of Art Nouveau, which continued into the early years of the twentieth century, was Antoni Gaudí (1852–1926). Gaudí designed a number of important buildings in Spain, including townhouses. At Casa Batlló (Fig. **16.21**) in Barcelona he refaced an older building with colored tiles, adding a steep but undulating roof that flows from orange to blue-green. The bay windows, rippling stone entrance, and sinister balconies are his too.

At the same time, widespread experimentation with new forms and materials continued. Many attempts have been made to categorize general tendencies and to label specific ones. But attempts at far-ranging categorizing have not met with universal acceptance. Terms such as "rational," "functional," and "international" have been suggested, but perhaps only the vague term "modern" covers most cases. Rather than pursue such categories, we shall, instead, focus as much as possible on individual work. It is individualism, after all, that has been the hallmark of the arts in our century.

CUBISM

CRITICAL LOOK above

Between 1901 and 1912, an entirely new approach to pictorial space emerged, an approach called CUBISM. Cubist space violates all usual concepts of two- and three-dimensional perspective. Until this time, the space within a composition had been thought of as an entity separate from the main subject of the work—that is, if the subject were removed, the space would remain, unaffected.

Pablo Picasso (1881–1973) and Georges Braque (1882–1963) changed that relationship. In their view the artist should paint "not objects, but the space they engender." The area around an object became an extension of the object itself, and if the object were removed, the space around it would collapse. Cubist space is typically quite shallow and gives the impression of reaching forward out of the frontal plane toward the viewer.

Essentially, the style developed as the result of independent experiments by Braque and Picasso with various ways of describing form. Newly evolving notions of the time–space continuum were being proposed by Albert Einstein at this time. We do not know whether the Theory of Relativity influenced Picasso and Braque, but it was being talked about at the time, and it certainly helped to make their works more acceptable. The results of both painters' experiments brought them to remarkably similar artistic conclusions.

Picasso has influenced the arts of the twentieth century more than any other painter. Born in Spain, in 1900 he moved to France, where he lived for most of his life. In Paris he was influenced by Toulouse-Lautrec and the late works of Cézanne, particularly in organization, analysis of forms, and use of different points of view. Very early on Picasso began to identify deeply with society's misfits and cast-offs. In the period from 1901 until around 1904 or 1905, known as Picasso's Blue Period, these oppressed subjects appear in paintings, in which blue tones predominate. In his Rose Period, from 1904 to 1906, he became more concerned with make-believe, which he expressed as portraits of circus performers, than with the tragedy of poverty. Cubism was born in 1907, with the creative revelation of *Les Demoiselles d'Avignon* (see Fig. **16.22**). Its simplified forms and restricted color were adopted by many cubists, as they reduced their palettes in order to concentrate on spatial exploration.

Like Picasso, Braque took a new approach to spatial construction and reduced objects to geometric shapes. It was from Braque's geometric forms that the term "cubist" first came. Unfortunately, the label has led many observers to look for solid cubic shapes rather than for a new kind of space "which was only visible when solid forms became transparent and lost their rigid cubical contours."[3]

MASTERWORK

Picasso—Les Demoiselles D'Avignon

This landmark painting deliberately breaks with the traditions of Western illusionistic art. Picasso's discovery of primitive African art and sculpture led him to borrow its flat forms and its exaggeration of certain features. Three of the heads in this painting are adaptations of African masks. Picasso used primitive art as a "battering ram against the classical conception of beauty."[4] The painter denies both classical proportions and the organic integrity and continuity of the human body. One critic wrote that the canvas "resembles a field of broken glass."

Les Demoiselles d'Avignon (Fig. **16.22**) is aggressive and harsh. Forms are simplified and angular, and colors are restricted to blues, pinks, and terracottas.

Subjects are broken into angular wedges, which convey a sense of three-dimensionality. We are unsure whether the forms protrude out or recess in. In rejecting a single viewpoint, Picasso presents "reality" not as a mirror image of what we see in the world, but as images that have been reinterpreted within the terms of new principles. Understanding thus depends on knowing rather than seeing.

The canvas is large—it measures 8 feet by 7 feet 8 inches (2.44 x 2.34 meters)—and its effect is one of great violence. The work began as a temptation scene in a brothel, but the narrative element has been dislodged by Picasso's concentration on aggression and savage eroticism.

16.22 Pablo Picasso, *Les Demoiselles d'Avignon*, 1907. Oil on canvas, 8 ft x 7 ft 8 ins (2.44 x 2.34 m). The Museum of Modern Art, New York (Acquired through the Lillie P. Bliss Bequest).

MECHANISM AND FUTURISM

Themes dealing with mechanism proved to be popular in the early twentieth century, as life became more and more dominated by machines. A brief movement in Italy, mechanism, sought to express the spirit of the age by capturing speed and power through representation of vehicles and machines in motion. Mechanistic themes can be seen clearly in the works of Marcel Duchamp (1887–1968), who is often associated with the dada movement and whose famous *Nude Descending a Staircase, No. 2* (Fig. **16.23**) is sometimes called "protodadaist." To Duchamp, apparently, men and women were machines that ran on passion as fuel. Like those of the dadaists,

16.23 Marcel Duchamp, *Nude Descending a Staircase, No. 2*, 1912. Oil on canvas, 58 x 35 ins (147 x 89 cm). Philadelphia Museum of Art (Louise and Walter Arensberg Collection).

many of Duchamp's works also exploit chance and accident.

Sculptors now turned to further explorations of three-dimensional space and what they could do with it. Technological developments and new materials also encouraged the search for new forms to characterize the age. This search resulted in a style called "futurism," which was really more of an ideology than a style. Futurism encompassed more than just the arts, and it sought to destroy the past—especially the Italian past—in order to institute a totally new society, a new art, and new poetry. Its basis lay in "new dynamic sensations." In other words, the objects of modern life, such as "screaming automobiles" that run like machine guns, have a new beauty—speed—that is more beautiful than even the most dynamic objects of previous generations. Futurists found in the noise, speed, and mechanical energy of the modern city a unique exhilaration that made everything of the past drab and unnecessary. The movement was particularly strong in Italy and among Italian sculptors. In searching for new dynamic qualities, the Italian futurists in the visual arts found that many new machines had sculptural form. Their own sculptures followed mechanistic lines and included representations of motion.

Umberto Boccioni's *Unique Forms of Continuity in Space* (see Fig. **17.1**) takes the mythological subject of Mercury, messenger of the gods (compare Bologna's *Mercury*, Fig. **11.22**), and turns him into a futuristic machine. The overall form is recognizable and the outlines of the myth move the viewer's thoughts in a particular direction. Nonetheless, this is primarily an exercise in composition. The intense sense of energy and movement is created by the variety of surfaces and curves that flow into one another in a seemingly random, yet highly controlled pattern. The overall impression is of the motion of the figure rather than of the figure itself.

EXPRESSIONISM

"Expressionism" traditionally refers to a movement in Germany between 1905 and 1930. Broadly speaking, however, it includes a variety of approaches, mostly in Europe, that aimed at eliciting in the viewer the same feelings the artist felt in creating the work—a sort of joint artist/viewer response to elements in the work of art. Any element—line, form, color—might be emphasized to elicit this response. The subject matter itself did not matter. What mattered was that the artist consciously tried to stimulate in the viewer a specific response similar to his or her own. The term EXPRESSIONISM as a description of this approach to visual art and architecture first appeared in 1911. It emerged following six years of work by an organized group of German artists who called themselves *Die Brücke* ("The Bridge"). Trying to define their purpos-

16.24 Max Beckmann, *Christ and the Woman Taken in Adultery*, 1917. Oil on canvas, 4 ft 10¼ ins x 4 ft 1⅛ ins (1.49 x 1.27 m). Saint Louis Art Museum (Bequest of Curt Valentin).

es, the painter Ernst Ludwig Kirchner (1880–1938) wrote: "He who renders his inner convictions as he knows he must, and does so with spontaneity and sincerity, is one of us." The intent was to protest against academic naturalism. They used simple media such as woodcuts and

created often brutal, but nonetheless powerful effects that expressed inner emotions.

The early expressionists maintained representationalism to a degree, but later expressionist artists, for example those of the Blue Rider group between 1912 and 1916, created some of the first completely abstract or nonobjective works of art. Color and form emerged as stimuli extrinsic to subject matter, and without any natural spatial relationships of recognizable objects, paintings took a new direction in internal organization.

In Max Beckmann's *Christ and the Woman Taken in Adultery* (Fig. **16.24**), the artist's revulsion against physical cruelty and suffering is transmitted through distorted figures crushed into shallow space. Linear distortion, changes of scale and perspective, and a nearly Gothic spirituality communicate Beckmann's reactions to the horrors of World War I. In this approach, the meaning of the painting—that is, the painter's meaning—is carried by very specific visual means of communication.

FAUVISM

Closely associated with the expressionist movement was the style of the fauves (the French word for "wild beasts"). The label was applied in 1905 by a critic in response to a sculpture which seemed to him "a Donatello in a cage of wild beasts." Violent distortion and outrageous coloring mark the work of the fauves, whose two-dimensional surfaces and flat color areas were new to European painting.

The best-known artist of this short-lived movement was Henri Matisse (1869–1954). Matisse tried to paint pictures that would "unravel the tensions of modern exis-

16.25 Henri Matisse, *Blue Nude* (*Souvenir de Biskra*), 1907. Oil on canvas, 3 ft ¼ in x 4 ft 7¼ ins (92.1 x 140.4 cm). Baltimore Museum of Art (The Cone Collection, formed by Dr Claribel Cone and Miss Etta Cone of Baltimore, Maryland).

tence." In his old age, he made a series of very joyful designs for the Chapel of the Rosary at Venice, not as exercises in religious art but as expressions of joy and the nearly religious feeling he had for life.

The *Blue Nude* (Fig. **16.25**) illustrates the wild coloring and distortions in the paintings of Matisse and the other fauves. The painting takes its name from the energetically applied blues, which occur throughout the figure as dark accents. For Matisse, color and line were indivisible devices, and the bold strokes of color in his work both reveal forms and stimulate a purely aesthetic response. Matisse literally "drew with color." His purpose was not, of course, to draw a nude as he saw it in life. Rather, he tried to express his feelings about the nude as an object of aesthetic interest. Thus Matisse, along with the other fauve painters, represents one brand of expressionism. There were others, including the Bridge and Blue Rider groups, and artists such as Kandinsky, Rouault, and Kokoschka.

CRITICAL REVIEW below

LITERATURE

REALISM

CRITICAL LOOK below

We have seen how realism took hold as a style in painting, and we shall see it again later in the chapter. Realism as a literary style held that the purpose of art is to depict life with absolute honesty—that is, to show things "as they really are." In pursuit of that goal, realists look for specific, verifiable details rather than for sweeping generalities, and they value impersonal, photographic accuracy more than the individual interpretation of experience. The triumph of realism, which began in the eighteenth century, came to full flower in the nineteenth and early twentieth centuries, and it was influenced by the growth of science and by a revolt against the sweeping emotionalism of Romanticism. Because realists sought to avoid idealism and Romantic "prettifying," they tended to

A CRITICAL REVIEW

In earlier chapters we discussed whether art is a reflection of its time or whether it derives purely from the artistic drives of the artist. We also considered if art should serve a purpose or not. The intense subjectification of art brought on by Romanticism turned artists more and more into themselves, with the result that art in the subjective mode is personal in that, as Zola put it, it "filters reality through a personality." That raises the question of whether art has become a vision of human reality communicated to others or merely a self-centered caprice. Of course, we are generalizing here, but the issues are as real as the current debate over artistic freedom of speech, artistic responsibility, and federal subsidy of the arts.

Using the styles of the previous section and Goethe's criteria for judgment (see the Introduction) as your guides, pick one of the works just studied and write a critical judgment of its success in communicating. Include an assessment of your own biases and/or perceptual weaknesses, and support your assessment with sound reasoning.

A CRITICAL LOOK

The arts have always shown some interconnectedness, and it should not be surprising to us when we find similar trends in separate art forms. As we have seen before, however, not all art forms lend themselves to the expressions of others—for example, the uninhibited emotional expression of Romanticism in music and literature was less possible in sculpture and theatre. In the sections that follow, we will not find the intensely individualized expressions of the fauves and cubists in literature and music, although theatre, having visual components, will be a more conducive medium for stylistic expression. Finally, we come to an entirely new artistic medium, a product of modern technology—film.

Explain the literary styles of realism and symbolism.

Characterize impressionism in music and naturalism in opera.

Identify and describe the work of representative composers in the previous areas as well as of nontraditional composers and works of the period.

stress the commonplace and, often, sordid and brutal aspects of life. There were a number of great realist writers, but we will focus on only one: Feodor Dostoevski.

Russian novelist Feodor Dostoevski (1821–81) was born and raised in Moscow. Both his parents died while he was in his teens—his father was murdered by his own serfs—and although he was interested in literature early on, he did not begin writing until he had finished military school and a two-year stint in the army. In 1846 he published a short story, "Poor Folk," which made him an instant success. He then became associated with a group of political revolutionaries and utopian reformers, and when the group was arrested, Dostoevski was sentenced to death, being pardoned by the Czar at the last moment. Apparently, the Czar had planned to pardon the prisoners all along, but he let the matter proceed, right up to the point where they stood before the firing squad, more as a whimsical joke than anything else. Dostoevski was sent to Siberia for five years and then forced back into the army. In 1859 he was finally pardoned, but these experiences, plus the fact that he suffered from epilepsy, left him bitter. He believed that his imprisonment gave him an opportunity to expiate his sins, and his beliefs that humans required penitence and that salvation comes through suffering reached the point of obsession and recur constantly in his novels.

We know Dostoevski best for two works from among his many: *The Brothers Karamazov* and *Crime and Punishment*. *Crime and Punishment* (1866) is a psychological novel that explores multiple personality—that is, the hidden and confused motivations of human behavior—and its constant theme is moral redemption through suffering. Perhaps the most outstanding characteristic of the novel is its capacity to force the reader to think seriously about the many problems it presents. Dostoevski accomplishes this by refusing to allow us to confuse oversimplification with deep thought. For example, in tackling the issue of distinguishing between morality and respectability, Dostoevski gives us one truly good character, the prostitute Sonia, who at the same time is the most openly disreputable, and contrasts her with a truly evil character, Raskolnikov's sister, who is the most respectable of the characters. Thus, he forces us to see that morality consists of what a person is, while respectability is the front that we put up in public, and that there need not be any connection between the two. He also shows that morality and respectability are not opposites, because, that, too, would be an oversimplification. The work forces us, through the objectively detailed manner of the realist, to think seriously about money, social position, sanity and insanity, and, above all, about crime and punishment. Dostoevski presents these issues with such compelling insight that we cannot escape them or explain them away with superficial responses.

OUR DYNAMIC WORLD

Native American Women in Literature

Literacy among Native Americans began to take hold in the late eighteenth century as the result of missionary activity, particularly that of the Methodists and Presbyterians, and a century later increased interest in America's heritage gave rise to the publication of tribal histories written by Native Americans.

Fiction writing among Native Americans appeared as early as 1823, but between 1870 and 1920 Native American culture underwent tremendous change: tribal autonomy decreased, and all tribes within the territory of the United States were confined to reservations. By the end of 1870, the federal government had become actively involved in Native American education, and a subsequent increase in literacy produced what may be called a tribal intellectual elite. As a result, numerous authors emerged, many of them women, one of whom was Susette La Flesche. Her story, "Nedawi," was first published in 1881 in a popular magazine for children, and it probably represents the first short story written by a Native American that is not a reworking of a legend. The author's gender testifies to the prominence of women in Native American—as well as in American—literature, and the story, subtitled "An Indian Story from Real Life," is representative of much Native American fiction prior to 1920. Describing a past way of life, in nostalgic terms, "Nedawi" emphasizes ethnocentric detail, has a strong moralistic tone, and appeals to young readers.

SYMBOLISM

Another literary movement of the late nineteenth century was symbolism, a conscious and deliberate attempt to use symbols because, as its proponents believed, the transient objective world is not true reality but a reflection of the invisible absolute. Symbolists rebelled against the techniques of the realists, which were designed to capture the transient world, believing instead that the inner eternal reality could only be suggested. They achieved intensity and complexity by using condensed syntax and minor images centered around one main METAPHOR, so that one sense impression was translated into another and both became symbols of the original impression. Although their writing was often as arcane as that assertion, that was acceptable to them, because they wished their writing to be "an enigma for the vulgar." They rejected sociological and ethical themes, and held that art pursues sensations of beauty that are quite separate from moral or social responsibility. The symbolists subscribed to the theory of "art for art's sake"—any theme or perception was appropriate as long as it captured the writer's subtle intuitions and contributed to an overall design. They were contemptuous of their environment and middle-class morality, often flaunting their perversions and despair, but they freed literature from its conventional subject matter and emphasized technique. Of those who used symbolist techniques, Marcel Proust stands out.

French novelist Marcel Proust (1871–1922) was a legend in French literary circles. Reclusive, frail, and asthmatic, he was allergic to noise, to light, and to dust, and he kept his room soundproofed, overheated, and in semi-darkness. He spent long periods in bed, during which he wrote the long novels on which he thrived. He was, in fact, a bold literary experimenter, who was able to put in writing remarkable sensory and imaginative experience. His magnum opus was *Remembrance of Things Past*, published in 16 volumes between 1913 and 1927, in which Proust sought to write the past—time lost and apparently irrecoverable—into permanence. He is preoccupied with time, which becomes an ever-present fact as the memory of the narrator shuttles back and forth without regard for chronology. Proust explores the distinctions between mechanical and psychological time by drawing up his own past experiences, and as he juxtaposes past against present, he shows us the fraudulent values of high society and strips away its glitter. Proust uses the techniques of the symbolists to achieve his ends—that is, metaphor, symbol, and image—as he tries to recreate the atmosphere of the mind, and thus we find his main themes—love, art, human ways of seeing and feeling life, homosexuality, rituals of the aristocracy, and architecture. In a sense, all of civilization trudges across his pages.

MUSIC

IMPRESSIONISM

The anti-Romantic spirit also produced a style of music analogous to that of the impressionist painters. A free use of chromatic tones marked later nineteenth-century style, even among the Romantics. However a parting of the ways occurred, the effects of which still permeate contemporary music. Some composers made free use of chromatic harmony and key shifts but stayed within the parameters of traditional major/minor tonality. Others rejected traditional tonality completely, and a new ATONAL harmonic expression came into being. This rejection of traditional tonality led to impressionism in music, a movement international in scope, but limited in quantity and quality. There was some influence from the impressionist painters, but the impressionist composers turned mostly to the symbolist poets for inspiration.

Impressionist music was international, but its substance can best be found in the work of its primary champion, the Frenchman Claude Debussy (1862–1918), although he did not like to be called an "impressionist"—the label, after all, had been coined by a critic of the painters and was meant to be derogatory. Debussy maintained that he was "an old Romantic who has thrown the worries of success out the window," and he sought no association with the painters. There are, however, similarities. His use of tone color has been described as "wedges of color," much like those the painters provided with individual brushstrokes. Oriental influence is also apparent, especially in Debussy's use of the Asian six-tone scale. He wished above all to return French music to fundamental sources in nature and move it away from the heaviness of the German tradition. He delighted in natural scenes, as did the impressionist painters, and he sought to capture the effects of shimmering light in music.

Unlike his predecessors, Debussy reduced melodic development to limited short motifs, and in perhaps his greatest break with tradition he moved away from traditional progressions of chordal harmonies. For Debussy, and impressionists in general, a chord was considered strictly on the merits of its expressive capabilities, apart from any idea of tonal progression within a key. As a result, gliding chords, that is, the repetition of a chord up and down the scale, became a hallmark of musical impressionism. DISSONANCE and irregular rhythm and meter further distinguish Debussy's works. Here, again, form and content are subordinate to expressive intent. His works suggest rather than state, leaving the listener only with an impression, perhaps even an ambiguous one.

Freedom, flexibility, and nontraditional timbres mark Debussy's compositions, the most famous of which is

Prélude à l'après-midi d'un faune, based on a poem by Mallarmé. The piece uses a large orchestra, with emphasis on the woodwinds, most notably in the haunting theme running throughout. Two harps also play a prominent part in the texture, and antique cymbals are used to add an exotic touch near the end. Although freely ranging in an irregular $\frac{9}{8}$ meter and having virtually no tonal centers, the *Prélude* does have the traditional ABA structure.

NATURALISM IN OPERA

Romanticism in all the arts saw many counter-reactions, and late nineteenth-century opera was no exception. In France, an anti-Romantic movement called "naturalism" developed. It opposed stylization, although it maintained exotic settings, and included brute force and immorality in its subject matter. The best operatic example of naturalism is Georges Bizet's *Carmen* (1875). Unlike earlier Romantic operas, the text for *Carmen* is in prose rather than poetry. Set in Spain, its scenes are realistic, and its music is colorful and concise. The libretto comes from a literary classic, a story by Prosper Mérimée, whose heroine, Carmen, is a seductive employee in a cigarette factory in nineteenth-century Seville (Fig. **16.26**). She flirts with Don José, a soldier, and so enraptures him that he deserts from the army to follow her to her haunt, a disreputable tavern, and then to a mountain pass where gypsy smugglers have their hideout. Carmen soon tires of

Don José, however, and becomes interested in the toreador Escamillo. On the day of a bullfight in Seville, Carmen arrives with Escamillo, who is welcomed as a hero. After Escamillo enters the bullring, Don José is seen, dishevelled and distraught. He pleads with Carmen to return to him, and when she refuses, he stabs her with a dagger. Emerging from his bullfight, Escamillo finds Don José weeping over Carmen's dead body.

Carmen began as *opéra-comique*. When Bizet first wrote his score, he used spoken dialogue, and this is the way *Carmen* was heard at the Opéra-Comique in Paris on March 3, 1875, and, incidentally, the way it is still played in that house. Elsewhere, however, dialogue was replaced by recitatives prepared not by the composer himself but by Ernest Guiraud (1837–92). As we now hear it, *Carmen* differs in a further way from the way it was introduced— today a number of ballet sequences, using background music from other Bizet compositions, are interpolated. As an opéra-comique in 1875, *Carmen* had no ballets.

Carmen herself is a fascinating character. Bizet uses her as a symbol of "Woman," and every passage he gave her to sing is a new mask, mirroring the man she is addressing. Bizet's sympathetic portrayal shows uncanny realism in her change of tone as she addresses the passers-by, José, Zuniga, the smugglers, and Escamillo. To each of the men she is a different women, changing the sound of her voice, the character of her melody, her mood, her tempo.

There was much in Carmen to disturb audiences in

16.26 Georges Bizet, *Carmen*, 1875. José Carreras as Don José and Agnes Baltsa as Carmen in this 1986–7 New York production.

16.27 Giacomo Puccini, *Manon Lescaut*, 1893. Opera Company of Philadelphia.

1875. The vivid portrayal of a character as immoral as Carmen was shocking, never before had an opera presented girls onstage smoking cigarettes, and some listeners objected to the music, thinking it was too Wagnerian, because Bizet assigned such importance to the orchestra and occasionally used a leading-motive (*leitmotif*) technique. Nevertheless, Carmen was by no means the total failure that some of Bizet's early biographers suggested. Some critics hailed it, a publisher paid a handsome price for the publication rights, and the opera company kept it in its repertory the following season.

Bizet's naturalism was similar to that of Italian *verismo* opera, which emerged at the turn of the twentieth century. The spirit of *verismo*—that is, of verisimilitude or true-to-life settings and events—is the same hot-blooded vitality that was implicit in Mascagni's statement quoted in Chapter 15 (page 503). The works of Mascagni, Puccini (Fig. **16.27**), Leoncavallo, and others exemplify this *verismo* tradition in musical drama, which concentrates on the violent passions and common experiences of everyday people. Adultery, revenge, and murder are frequent themes. Mascagni's *Cavalleria Rusticana*, Leoncavallo's *I Pagliacci*, and to some extent Puccini's *Tosca* are the best known examples of this melodramatic form.

NONTRADITIONAL TRANSITIONS

If twentieth-century painting and sculpture took a path that diverged radically from their nineteenth-century heritage, so did twentieth-century music. Its new directions parted with past traditions in three essential ways.

The first was rhythmic complexity. Since the Middle Ages, tradition had emphasized the grouping of beats together in rhythmic patterns, called "meter." The characteristic accents of double and triple meters helped to unify and clarify compositions, as well as to give them certain flavors. For example triple meter, with its one-two-three, one-two-three accent patterns, created lilting dance rhythms, of which the waltz was characteristic. The alternating accents of double meter, one-two, one-two, or one-two-three-four, suggested the regularity of a march. But modern composers did away with these patterns and the regularity of accents, choosing instead to employ complex, changing rhythms in which it is often virtually impossible to determine meter, or even the actual beat.

The second change consisted of a focus on dissonant harmonies. Before the late nineteenth century, CONSONANCE was the norm, and all harmonic progressions returned to it. Dissonance was used to disturb the norm, to enable the music to return to consonance. All art, of course, requires a disturbance of some status quo to create interest. A play, for example, must become complicated in order to move forward, then something more must happen to resolve the problem. Dissonances in music fulfilled much the same role, but they were expected to be brief and passing, then return to consonance. In the late nineteenth century there was significant tampering with that principle, however. By the twentieth century, composers were using more and more dissonance, and not necessarily resolving it.

The third important change involved a rejection of traditional TONALITY, or sense of key, altogether. Traditional thinking held that one note, the *doh*, or tonic, of a scale, was the most important. All music was composed in a specific key. Modulations into distant or related keys occurred, but the tonic of the basic key was the touchstone to which everything related. Many composers now chose to pursue two other paths. One was to get rid of any tonal center. Thus, no one tone was more important than the other. All twelve semitones of the chromatic scale in effect became equal. The systems that resulted from this new tonality were called TWELVE-TONE composition, and SERIAL MUSIC. The second, less radical, approach denied traditional major/minor tonality, but maintained some sense of a tonal center.

The works of the French impressionist Debussy are generally seen as carrying the transition from the nineteenth to the twentieth century, but several other traditions were also current. One, of German-Italian influence, built upon the works of Richard Wagner and was called the "cosmopolitan" style. The principal composer in this group was César Franck (1822–90). The works of Camille Saint-Saëns (1835–1921) represent the more classically

oriented style that continued into the twentieth century.

The French composer Maurice Ravel (1875–1937) began as an impressionist, but his style became more and more classical as years went by. Even in his earlier works, however, Ravel did not adopt Debussy's complex sonorities and ambiguous tonal centers. Ravel's *Boléro* (1928) exhibits strong primitive influences and the relentless rhythm of certain Spanish dance music. More typical works of Ravel—for example, his Piano Concerto in G— use Mozart and traditional classicism as their models. Thus, some composers stayed completely within established neo-classical conventions of Western music well into the twentieth century.

STRAVINSKY

Another nontraditionalist, Igor Stravinsky (1882–1971), came to prominence with *The Firebird* (1910). *The Rite of Spring* (1912–13) created an even greater impact. Both works were ballets. *The Firebird* was a commission for the Russian impresario Serge Diaghilev, and it was premièred successfully at the Paris Opéra. Another commission, *The Rite of Spring*, created a riot because of its revolutionary orchestrations and driving, primitive rhythms.

Why was *The Rite of Spring* such a disaster? The third of his ballet commissions for Diaghilev, it is subtitled *Pictures of Pagan Russia*, and it depicts the cruel rites of spring that culminate in the sacrifice of a virgin, who dances herself to death accompanied by frenetic music. It is those compelling rhythms that give the work its

PROFILE

Igor Stravinsky (1882–1971)

The son of an opera singer, Igor Stravinsky (Strah-VIN-skee) responded early in life to his musical surroundings. He started to compose before he had received any formal training, but when he began studying music in his early twenties, he did so with a master, the renowned Russian composer Nikolai Rimsky-Korsakov (1844–1908). Stravinsky was born near St Petersburg, Russia, and developed an early affinity for Russian folk music. Before he was thirty, he had written *The Firebird* (1910) for Diaghilev. Two more ballets followed in quick succession—*Petrushka* in 1911 and *The Rite of Spring* in 1913. His use of dissonance, complexity, and changing rhythms in the latter separated Stravinsky from all previous traditions and placed

him in the vanguard of modern music.

He left Russia before World War I and lived in France, where he wrote a variety of compositions, including *The Soldier's Tale* (1918). An interest in religion is evident in the 1930 *A Symphony of Psalms*.

In 1939 Stravinsky left France and moved to the United States, where he became a citizen in 1945. This change in citizenship appears to have marked a change in his interest in Russian folklore, as well. When he was in his seventies, he began to experiment with the twelve-tone method of composition. By the time of his death in 1971, Stravinsky's influence on contemporary music had reached legendary status in Europe, England, and the United States.

impressive character. Rapid, irregular mixtures of very short note values create an almost intolerable tension, or at least a tension that was intolerable to the public of that day. The melodic material is quite unconventional—short driving motifs that stop short of thematic fulfillment. Such melodies as there are are short and fragmentary.

After World War I, Stravinsky embraced neo-classicism in a series of works with classical and baroque references. He was flexible enough to create serial compositions too toward the end of his life.

SCHOENBERG

The movement that drew the most attention in the first half of the twentieth century grew out of German romanticism, but it took a radical turn into atonality. At the root of the movement was Arnold Schoenberg (1874–1951). Between 1905 and 1912 Schoenberg moved away from the gigantic post-Romantic works he had been composing and began to adopt a more contained style, writing works for smaller ensembles, and treating instruments in a more individual manner. His orchestral works of this period display swiftly alternating timbres, in contrast with the massive orchestral texture of earlier works. They also employ increased complexity in their rhythms, harmonies, and fragmented melodies.

Although the word "atonality," meaning without tonality, is used to describe Schoenberg's works, he preferred the term "pantonality"—that is, inclusive of all tonalities. In his compositions Schoenberg used any combination of tones without having to resolve chord progressions, a concept he called "the emancipation of dissonance." In 1912 Schoenberg created one of his most famous works, *Pierrot Lunaire* (*Moonstruck Pierrot*), a cycle of twenty-one songs based on French surrealist poems translated into German. The cycle uses a female solo voice accompanied by various instruments, and important in this work is the stylized use of the speaking voice, *Sprechgesang*.

By 1923 Schoenberg was composing in twelve-tone technique. This involves "tone rows." A tone row presents the twelve semitones of a chromatic scale only once, in an order chosen by the composer. This series of notes can be used in various ways—as melodies and harmonies, upside down, backward, upside down and backward—that is, in whatever order or form the composer chooses. The structure of this technique is fairly mathematical and formal, but a good composer can maintain a balance between emotion and mechanics. The important thing to understand about these works is that they are specifically and logically organized so as to be completely atonal. When the listener knows the concepts behind them, Schoenberg's dramatic and experimental compositions can be heard as artistic entities just as much as more traditional music can.

JAZZ

Undoubtedly the most significant African-American contribution to American music, and, in turn, a uniquely American contribution to the world of music, jazz began near the turn of the century, and from there went through many changes and forms. Jazz includes many sophisticated and complicated styles, but all of them feature improvised variations on a theme.

The earliest form, blues, went back to the rhythmic music of the slaves, and consisted of a repeated line, with a second, concluding line (AAB). This was music of oppression, and early singers, such as Bessie Smith (1894–1937), evoked an emotional quality which the instruments tried to imitate.

At approximately the same time came ragtime, a piano style with a strict, two-part form. Syncopation played an important role in this style, whose most famous exponent was Scott Joplin (1868–1917). New Orleans, the cradle of jazz, also produced traditional jazz, which featured improvisational development from a basic, memorized chordal sequence. All this was followed in the thirties and forties by swing, bebop, and cool jazz.

THEATRE

REALISM AND NATURALISM

In line with trends in philosophy and the other arts, a conscious movement toward realism in the theatre emerged around the middle of the nineteenth century, and by 1860 dramatic literature was striving for the truthful portrayal of the real world. Objectivity was stressed, and knowledge of the real world was seen as possible only through direct observation. (Corot's approach to painting was based on a similar viewpoint, as was the realism of writers like Dostoevski.) Thus, everyday life, with which the playwright was directly familiar, became the subject matter of drama. Interest shifted from the past to human motives and experience, or, more likely, idealized versions of these. Exposure to such topics on the stage was not particularly pleasant, and many play-goers objected that the theatre was turning into a "sewer or a tavern." Playwrights countered the criticisms by saying that the way to avoid such ugly depictions on the stage was to change society.

The acknowledged master of realist drama was Norway's Henrik Ibsen (1828–1906). Ibsen took the format of Eugene Scribe's well-made play, eliminated many of its devices, and built powerful, realistic problem-dramas around carefully selected detail and plausible character-to-action motivations. His plays usually bring to conclusion events that began well in the past, and his exposition is usually meticulous. Ibsen's concern for realistic detail carries to the scenery and costumes, and his plays contain detailed descriptions of settings and properties, all of which are essential to the action. The content of many of Ibsen's plays was controversial, and most deal with questions about moral and social issues that are still valid. In his late plays, however, Ibsen abandoned realism in favor of symbolist experiment.

Realism spread widely, finding expression in the work of Anton Chekhov (1860–1904), although, like Ibsen, Chekhov incorporates symbolism into his works. Chekhov is regarded by many as the founder of modern realism. He drew his themes and subject matter from Russian daily life, and they are realistic portrayals of frustration and the depressing nature of existence. His structures flow in the same apparently aimless manner as the lives of his characters. While short on theatricality and compact structure, his plays are skillfully constructed to give the appearance of reality.

In Britain, the Irish writer George Bernard Shaw (1856–1950) embodied the spirit of nineteenth-century realism, although his career overlapped the nineteenth and twentieth centuries. This witty, brilliant artist was above all a humanitarian, and although many Victorians considered him a heretic and a subversive (because of his devotion to Fabian socialism), his faith lay in humanity and its infinite potential.

Shaw's plays deal with the unexpected, and they often appear contradictory and inconsistent in characterization and structure. His favorite device was to build up a pompous notion and then destroy it. For example, in *Man and Superman*, when a respectable Victorian family learns that their daughter is pregnant, they react with predictable indignation. A character who appears to speak for the playwright comes to the girl's defense, attacking the family's hypocrisy and defending the girl. She, however, explodes in anger, not against her family, but against her defender. She had been secretly married all the time, and, as the most respectable of the lot, she condemns her defender's (and possibly the audience's) free thinking.

Shaw opposed the doctrine of "art for art's sake," and he insisted that art should have a purpose. He believed that plays were better vehicles for social messages than speeches or pamphlets, and he is most often successful in getting his messages across through drama, despite his somewhat weak characterizations. Although each play usually has a character who acts as the playwright's mouthpiece, Shaw does more than sermonize. His characters probe the depths of the human condition, often discovering themselves through some lifelike crisis.

Naturalism, a style closely related to realism, also flourished in the same period. Émile Zola (1840–1902) was a leading proponent, although he was more a theoretician and novelist than a playwright. Both realism and naturalism insisted on a truthful depiction of life, but naturalism went on to insist on the basic principle that behavior is determined by heredity and environment. Absolute objectivity, not personal opinion, was the naturalistic goal.

SYMBOLISM

To amplify our earlier discussion, late in the nineteenth century, and very briefly, there was an anti-realistic literary movement called "symbolism," also known as "neo-Romanticism," "idealism," or "impressionism." Symbolism was briefly popular in France, and it has recurred occasionally in the twentieth century. The idea behind symbolism is that truth can be grasped only by intuition, not through the senses or rational thought. Thus, ultimate truths can be suggested only through symbols, which evoke in the audience various states of mind that correspond vaguely with the playwright's feelings.

One of the principal dramatic symbolists, Maurice Maeterlinck (1862–1949), believed that every play contains a "second level" of dialogue that speaks to the soul. Through verbal beauty, contemplation, and a passionate portrayal of nature, great drama conveys the poet's idea of the unknown. Therefore, plays that present human actions can only, through symbols, suggest higher truths gained through intuition. The symbolists did not deal at all with social problems. Rather, they turned to the past and tried to suggest universal truths independent of time and place, as Maeterlinck did, for example, in *Pelléas and Mélisande* (1892).

FILM: ART AND MECHANIZATION

On 23 April, 1896, at Koster and Bial's Music Hall in New York, the Leigh Sisters performed their umbrella dance. Then the audience was astonished to see waves breaking upon the shore. Thus was launched a new process for screen projection of movies—the Vitascope. Invented by Thomas Armat (although Thomas Edison has received much of the credit), the Vitascope was the latest in centuries of experiments on how to make pictures move. Relying on the persistence of vision and basic photographic techniques, the Vitascope captured real objects in motion and presented those images on a screen.

Technological experiments in rapid-frame photography were common in the last half of the nineteenth century, but it remained for Thomas Armat and others to perfect a stop-motion device essential to screen projection. Two Frenchmen, the Lumière brothers, are usually credited with the first public projection of movies on a large screen in 1895. By 1897, the Lumières had successfully exhibited their *cinématographie* all over Europe, and their catalogue listed 358 films. They opened in America three months after the première of the Vitascope. Later that year, the American Biograph made its début using larger film and projecting twice as many pictures per minute, creating the largest, brightest, and steadiest picture of all.

At that point, movies did nothing more than record everyday life. George Méliès (1861–1938) in France and Edwin S. Porter (1870–1941) in the United States would demonstrate the narrative and manipulative potential of the cinema. Between 1896 and 1914, Méliès turned out more than a thousand films. Edwin S. Porter, who was in charge of the Edison Company Studios, studied the narrative attempts of Méliès. Then, acting as his own scriptwriter, cameraman, and director, he spliced together old and freshly shot film into *The Life of an American Firefighter*. In 1903 Porter made *The Great Train Robbery*, the most popular film of the decade. It ran a total of twelve minutes. The popular audience was entranced, and flocked to electric theatres to see movies that could excite and thrill them with stories of romance and adventure. The movies were a window to a wider world for the poor of America.

By 1910 the young film industry counted a handful of recognized stars who had made more than four hundred films for the screen's first mogul, Charles Pathé. Short films remained the staple of the industry, but there was a growing taste for more spectacular fare, especially in Europe. The Italian film *Quo Vadis* was produced in 1912, complete with lavish sets, chariot races, Christians, lions, and a cast of hundreds. A full two hours long, it was a huge success.

Lawsuits over patents and monopolies marked the first decade of the century. In order to escape the constant badgering of Thomas Edison's lawyers, independent filmmakers headed west to a sleepy California town called Hollywood, where, among other things, the weather, the natural light, and the exotic, varied landscape were much more conducive to cinematography. By 1915 over half of all American movies were being made in Hollywood.

That year also witnessed the release of D.W. Griffith's *The Birth of a Nation* (Fig. **16.28**), which ran for three hours. Popular and controversial, the film was destined to become a landmark in cinema history. It unfolds the story of two families during the Civil War and the Reconstruction period. Now condemned for its depiction of leering, bestial blacks rioting and raping white women, and for the rescue of whites by the Ku Klux Klan, the film is nonetheless a work of great artistry. Griffith defined and refined nearly every technique in film-making: the fade-

16.28 D.W. Griffith, *The Birth of a Nation*, 1915.

in, fade-out, long shot, full shot, close-up, moving camera, flash-back, CROSSCUTTING, and juxtaposition. In addition, Griffith virtually invented film editing and preshooting rehearsals.

As if *The Birth of a Nation* were not colossal enough, Griffith followed it in 1916 with *Intolerance*, a $2 million epic of ancient Babylon, biblical Judea, sixteenth-century France, and contemporary America. As the film progressed, brilliant crosscutting increased at a frantic pace to heighten suspense and tension. However, audiences found the film confusing. It failed miserably at the box office, and the failure ruined Griffith financially.

The same era produced the Mack Sennet comedies, which featured the hilarious antics and wild chase scenes of the Keystone Kops. Sennet was one of Griffith's partners in the Triangle Film Company. A third partner was Thomas Ince, who brought to the screen the prototypical cowboy hero, William S. Hart, in such works as *Wagon Tracks*.

Nothing better represents the second decade of the twentieth century, however, than the work of the genius, Charlie Chaplin, the "little fellow." Chaplin's characters represent all of humanity, and he communicates through the silent film as eloquently and deeply as anyone ever has. In an era marked by disillusionment, Chaplin represented resilience, optimism, and an indomitable spirit. By the end of World War I Chaplin shared the limelight with that most dashing of American heroes, Douglas Fairbanks.

A CRITICAL REVIEW

One of the ways in which we can identify how the arts interrelate is to take examples from more than one general grouping and compare them. For example, we have become accustomed in this text to referring to painting, sculpture, and architecture not only by their individual names, but also by the term "visual arts." This general term has the effect of separating these disciplines, which more or less stand still from another group of arts called the "performing arts," which include music and theatre and which represent arts in which the basic visions of composer or playwright are interpreted or performed by other artists, who lend some of their own vision to the artwork. Thus, we can find a useful means of comparison if we take an example of visual art and compare it with an example of performing art.

Choose two examples of visual art and compare them with two examples from the same style chosen from the performing arts.

Identify and describe the major realist and naturalist playwrights.

Describe the development of film as an art form and identify its early practitioners.

SYNTHESIS

America's Gilded Age

The short feature, Our Dynamic World, in which we briefly looked at the role of Native American women in literature, reflects what was happening in other realms. Despite the conditions we loosely refer to as "democracy" in the United States and Europe, society, even without a powerful aristocracy, tended to be two-tiered. In Native American culture those who maintained tribal customs and racial purity were distinct from those who had been educated in the Western ways or who were "half-breeds" (we will see more of this in the next chapter). In the rest of society, especially in the United States, a new class of super-rich separated themselves from the remainder of society. The worlds represented by these differences were as apart as earth and moon, and those worlds did not include the African-American, who, although "free" because of the Civil War, lived in a state of cultural limbo.

To synthesize what was happening in society, we turn to the world of the wealthy and the homes they built. These homes bring together in a physical location, the general conditions of society in America at the time. As you read about these homes and the individuals who built them, compare them with current housing directions in the United States. In the period after World War II the typical suburban house had about 1,200 square feet (110 square meters) of space and contained as many as four bedrooms. Today a typical suburban home has 3,000 square feet (280 square metres) of space and the same number of bedrooms.

After the Civil War (1861–5) America boomed economically as it had never done before. The United States expanded westward and reached out across the oceans to secure its share of the world's trade and empire. However, viewed from the vantage point of history, the period was not an honorable one—political corruption reigned among ineffectual presidents, state political machines, big-city bosses, and legislators whose votes were for sale to the highest bidder.

Reconstruction in the South soon saw the return of the white aristocracy, and blacks, free but without land, were forced to become sharecroppers for landowners who demanded higher and higher portions of the crops they grew. Blacks remained second-class citizens who were discriminated against and denied the right to vote. While farmers' organizations agitated for reform, and labor unions struggled to gain a foothold, the overall economic picture was, nevertheless, rosy. The nation grew rapidly, the population doubling every twenty-five years, and its resources seemed endless. Europe provided the United States with an almost inexhaustible supply of capital and people, and the nation benefited from rapid technological advances. There was a spirit in the land that anyone could go from rags to riches if one steadfastly applied entrepreneurial energy.

Railroads stretched across the continent—the United States had more miles of railroad than all of Europe—and between 1877 and 1892 the output of American factories tripled. By the end of the century the United States led the world in both agriculture and industry. Big business developed with huge corporations emerging and hiring. The boom produced America's legendary financial and corporate giants—for example, J. Pierpont Morgan, Andrew Carnegie, John D. Rockefeller, Cornelius Vanderbilt, and Henry Flagler. To the reformers of the time, these were the "robber barons" of the United States, men who seemed able, through all kinds of conditions, to manipulate and, through ruthlessness, to build their personal empires to phenomenal heights. They were symbols of monopoly and exemplars of what Americans considered to be the "American Dream"— that is, success. It was the gilded age of America—before income and inheritance taxes despoiled personal fortunes—and the homes of these members of America's aristocracy, which was of money, not birth, symbolize and synthesize the opulent, overindulgent ostentation of the time.

THE BREAKERS

During this golden period, the burning ambition of those who had access to power and money was to be accepted in high society, and they would go to almost any lengths to achieve this aim. The acknowledged leaders of New York society were Mr and Mrs Cornelius Vanderbilt. Cornelius Vanderbilt (1843–99) was President of the New York Central Railroad, and, in 1893, one year after his brother, William, had built an unrivaled statement about his own power—a mansion called Marble House—Cornelius engaged Richard Morris Hunt to build The Breakers. His vision was a sixteenth-century Italian palace, and money was no object. The

16.29 Richard Morris Hunt,
The Breakers, Newport,
Rhode Island, 1893–5

16.30 Carrère and Hastings
Whitehall, Palm Beach,
Florida, 1900–01.

house had to be fireproof, finished quickly, and be the finest house in all of Newport. Workers from all over the world worked day and night for two years to create an exquisite seventy-room, $7 million palace (Fig. **16.29**). Unique among American homes, it was equipped with electricity and with gas, in case the new power source should fail, and the structure integrated steel framing, which represented a major departure in construction techniques. It was a house perfectly suited to the grand style of entertaining that the Vanderbilts enjoyed.

The interior boasted an enclosed courtyard with a ceiling painted to resemble the sky, complete with wind-swept clouds. The dining room, which covered 2,400 square feet (222 square meters), sat thirty-four, and was adorned with two Baccarat crystal chandeliers. The house is an example of social ritual, with particular spaces divided to provide specific activities representing the structured daily and nightly life of the social elite. The exterior landscape was also designed for social ritu-al, with acres of formal gardens, for which the sod was imported from Britain.

WHITEHALL

Henry Flagler was a visionary who had made his millions in partnership with John D. Rockefeller in the Standard Oil Company. He went to Florida in 1877, at a time when the state was little more than a wilderness, and saw its potential. Beginning with the Ponce de Leon Hotel in St Augustine, Flagler spent the next twenty-five years building hotels throughout Florida, transforming the state from swampland to playground. Called the Taj Mahal of North America, Flagler's home, Whitehall (Fig. **16.30**), became the envy of America's social elite. It con-tained seventy-three rooms on 6 acres (2.4 hectares) overlooking Lake Worth in Palm Beach. It was a castle worthy of a king, and seventy-one-year-old Flagler and his thirty-five-year-old, third wife ruled Palm Beach soci-ety.

Construction began in 1900 and took a mere eigh-teen months to complete. As many as a thousand work-men created elaborate marble designs with wooden accents. Each of the rooms reflects a different European style, and the house features treasures from around the world. Despite the $4 million spent on building and the further $1.5 million for interior furnishings, Whitehall was used for only two months of the year, January and February. It was an entertainment pavilion designed to impress, and, unlike The Breakers, it was not a home.

16.31 Hunt and Olmstead, Biltmore House, North Carolina, 1895.

BILTMORE HOUSE

Without doubt, the grandest house from this period is George Vanderbilt's ultimate dreamhouse, Biltmore House (Fig. **16.31**). The grandson of Commodore Vanderbilt, George had traveled the world and seemed to disdain the kind of ostentation that typified his family's palaces in Newport. Nonetheless, in the mountains of North Carolina, on 125,000 acres (50,590 hectares), George built a 225-room palace that is still America's largest private home. During his travels George had come to admire the country estates of the European nobility, and Biltmore House was built to realize a dream. It was to be a self-sustaining working estate, on which all the necessary provisions for the house—everything from beef to agricultural crops and forestry—could be produced to support the house and its guests. The entire project was the responsibility of two friends of the Vanderbilt family, architect Richard Morris Hunt, who had designed The Breakers, and landscape architect Frederick Law Olmstead, who designed New York's Central Park (a smaller project than Biltmore House). At the time Biltmore House was built, both architects were very old, and neither lived to see the completion of the project.

The work took five years to complete, and thousands of people were employed. The house, which was completed in 1895, occupied 4 acres (1.6 hectares) of floor space and had sixty-five fireplaces. The gallery, 90 feet (27 meters) long, contains three huge sixteenth-century tapestries representing the victory of virtue over vice. Rich furnishings and magnificent art grace every room. Over ten thousand books occupy the shelves of the library. The medieval banquet hall covers more than 3,000 square feet (910 meters), with a 70-foot arched ceiling, and a triple fireplace at one end. It had an indoor pool, a gym, and a bowling alley. Although all but 8,000 acres (3,240 hectares) have been sold to become the Pisgah National Forest, Biltmore House remains a private estate today.

CHAPTER SEVENTEEN

MODERNISM

AT A GLANCE

The Modern World in Conflict
The Economy Before World War I
Toward World War I
The Great War
Revolution and Civil War in Russia
The Aftermath

Between the Wars
The Great Depression
Hitler's Conquests

World War II
Europe and Africa
The Pacific

Science and War
TECHNOLOGY: Computers

Philosophy
Pragmatism
Existentialism

Literature
The Novel
PROFILE: Langston Hughes
Poetry
OUR DYNAMIC WORLD: Native American
Fiction

The Visual Arts and Architecture
Abstraction
Dada
Surrealism
American Painting
PROFILE: Georgia O'Keeffe
African and Primitive Influences
MASTERWORK: Moore—Recumbent Figure

Architectural Modernism
MASTERWORK: Wright—Kaufmann House

Music
Modern Traditionalism
Departures

Theatre
Expressionism
Epic Theatre
Absurdism

Film
European Film
The Glorious Twenties
The Thirties

Synthesis: The Bauhaus—Integration of the Arts

17.1 Umberto Boccioni, *Unique Forms of Continuity in Space*, 1913. Bronze (cast 1931), 3 ft 7⁷⁄₈ ins (1.1 m) high. Museum of Modern Art, New York (Acquired through the Lillie P. Bliss Bequest).

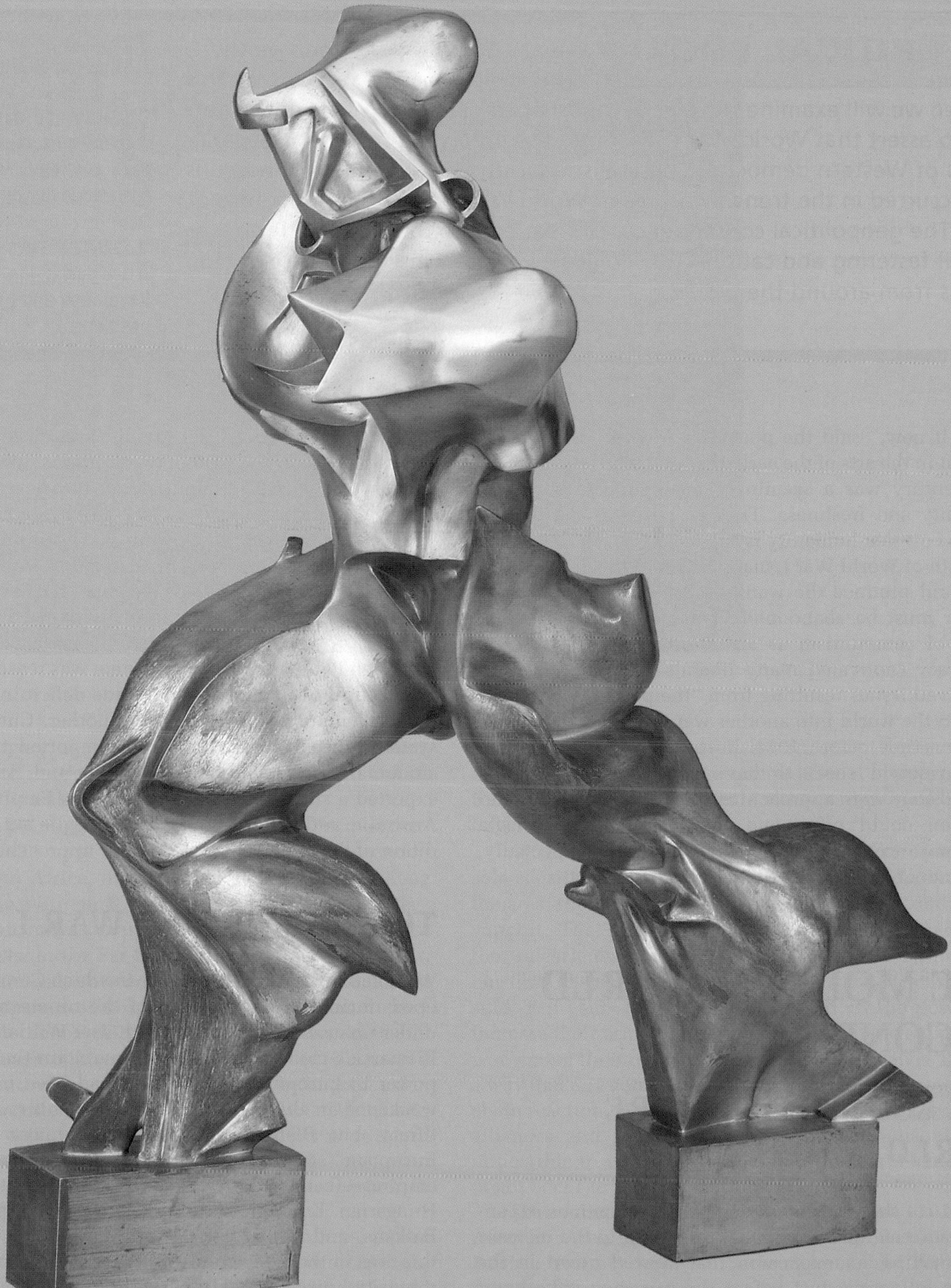

THE GREAT WAR

Between 1914 and 1918 the military commands of both sides changed strategies repeatedly. On one hand, they would pursue a "strong point" strategy, in which they attacked the enemy in order to break its resistance, then they would switch to a "weak point" strategy, which aimed to disorganize the enemy and reduce the number of its allies.

In 1914 the Germans attacked the strong point in the west. This maneuver, the Schlieffen plan, aimed to encircle and destroy the British and French armies with an attack from the west. The attack failed, with the decisive battle coming at the River Marne. At the same time, the Russians attacked the Germans and were defeated by Hindenburg at Tannenberg. In the end, despite each side's strong thrust at the enemy's perceived strongest points, nothing was accomplished, although the cost in terms of lives and expenditure was enormous. No decisive victory was possible, and the effect was a general paralysis on all fronts, which consisted of an elaborate series of trenches. A year later, Allied offensives in Champagne and Artois, and German and Austrian attacks in Poland—again after tremendous expenditure of men and materials—reached the same impasse.

Given the lack of military success, the antagonists turned to targeting perceived weaknesses in the enemy's coalition. This strategy produced a series of mindless massacres—for example, a massed Allied attack on the Turks at the Dardanelles, and the German and Austrian attempts to punish Italy, which switched sides in 1916 by joining the Allies—which accomplished nothing strategically but took material away from other locations where a decisive victory might have been secured. Thus, the enemies returned to the earlier strategy, but further battles at Verdun and the Somme in the west and Isonzo and Asiago in the east proved indecisive. The same occurred

Map 17.1 World War I and its aftermath in Europe.

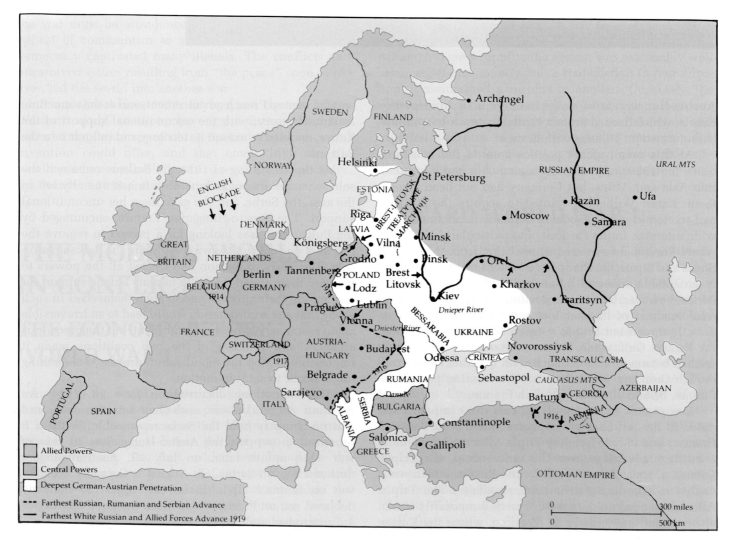

	GENERAL EVENTS	LITERATURE & PHILOSOPHY	VISUAL ART & ARCHITECTURE	THEATRE & CINEMA	MUSIC
1900	Triple Entente Balkan wars Women's suffrage (USA)	Dewey Yeats Frost Hughes e.e. cummings Lawrence Joyce	Boccioni (**17.1**) Gilbert (**17.24**)	Strindberg Toller	
1914	World War I Russian Revolution Treaty of Versailles	Gide Mann Kafka	de Chirico (**17.11**) Lipchitz (**17.21**) Malevich (**17.9**) Ernst (**17.10**) Davis (**17.14**)	Wiene (**17.26**) Lang Eisenstein Rice	
1920	Einstein German rearmament Japanese Invasion of Manchuria Great Depression		O'Keeffe (**17.13**) Mondrian (**17.8**) Wood (**17.15**) Brancusi (**17.19, 17.21**) Gropius (**17.27**) Rivera (**17.18**) Dali (**17.12**) Douglas (**17.16, 17.17**) Le Corbusier (**17.23**)	O'Neill Brecht Pirandello DeMille Vidor Disney Ford	Schuman Prokofiev Bartók Hindemith Berg
1939	World War II Pearl Harbor	Woolf Eliot Faulkner Hemingway Pound Dos Passos Steinbeck Camus Auden Sartre	Wright (**17.25**) Moore (**17.22**)		Ives Copland

Timeline 17.1 Modernism.

in 1917, and even the Russian Revolution in that year left things virtually unchanged.

However, the situation began to change in 1917. What had been a European conflict took on global dimensions when Britain mounted offensives in Egypt, Iraq, and elsewhere in the Arab world. Then Japan and China entered the conflict. Finally, Germany's submarine attacks, which came as a result of its policy of unrestricted naval warfare, brought the United States into the war on April 6, 1917.

Both sides used strategies designed to disrupt the other side's efforts. This, as we noted, comprised the "weak point" strategy. The main thrust of the Triple Alliance Powers (Germany, *et al.*) consisted of trying to provoke non-Russian nationalities into rebelling against the Tsarist empire. This consisted of publishing a Bulletin of the Nationalities of Russia, forming a Finnish legion, and proclaiming the independence of Poland. As part of the same strategy, they lent support to the Irish nationalists, which resulted in the Easter Rising against Britain in 1916, and in Belgium Germany tried to disrupt

the Allies by trying to reawaken the ideal of Flemish nationhood. The Triple Alliance also tried to inflame Islamic sentiments into jihads (holy wars) in their enemies' empires. The Allies pursued the same strategy by promising independence (on victory) to every oppressed minority in central Europe—for example, the Croats, Slovenes, Czechs, and Slovaks—which weakened enemy morale somewhat, but proved not to be much of a factor, although it was more effective against the Ottoman Empire. In Armenia nearby Russian advances led to a massacre that killed over a million people in 1915, and Arab uprisings led by the Englishman T.E. Lawrence, Lawrence of Arabia, eventually led to the reconstitution of Syria—a nation that had been lost for several centuries.

The general strategy was complemented by the Allies' attempts to destroy the Triple Alliance's seaborne trade and so to destroy the foundations of their economies, a strategy that provoked the Central Powers into unlimited submarine warfare, which had the unfortunate effect of provoking the United States into entering the war on the side of the Allies. In the end, the effects of the weak point strategy were difficult to evaluate, although it does appear to have caused the United States to enter the war. The deterioration of the Russian economy and the resultant shortages played a major role in the Russian Revolution in 1917. However, eventually, the war was won by military rather than economic means. In 1917 things began to go badly for Germany and her partners on the western front, and by 1918 the Germans realized that they could no longer hope to turn things in their own favor. The first armistices were signed at the end of October and in November 1918.

REVOLUTION AND CIVIL WAR IN RUSSIA

A combination of military defeats, shortages, and hatred of the aristocracy made an explosive combination for Russia, and in an uprising that lasted for five days in Petrograd, the revolution triumphed and Tsar Nicholas II abdicated. Power was shared by a government made up of former members of the Russian Duma (parliament) and a Soviet of Workers and Soldiers' Deputies (Fig. **17.3**). Under the leadership of Alexander Kerensky, this alliance between the bourgeois and proletarian revolutions proved inca-

pable of either winning or ending the war and unable to put into effect the necessary reforms to transform the social order. Opposition arose from, on the one side, the factory and soldiers' committees that were headed by the Bolsheviks or anarchists and, on the other, the military high command and the industrial bourgeoisie. They were opposed to the reforms desired by the socialists. In the end, the Soviets and workers' and soldiers' committees— led by the Bolsheviks under Lenin—easily overthrew the provisional government in the October uprising.

In 1918 the Bolsheviks negotiated the Treaty of Brest-Litovsk, which separated the Baltic states, Poland, and part of the Ukraine from the former empire. However, civil war broke out between the Bolsheviks and other socialists and the democrats and a volunteer army under former military commanders (called the White Army). The Allies supported the Whites: British and Canadian troops landed at Archangel, later, American troops landed at Vladivostock, and French troops landed at Odessa. The intervention of foreign forces only discredited the Whites at home, however, and led to their ultimate defeat.

The revolution, which had both political and social consequences, gave a temporary incentive for states of the old empire to seek independence, something that the Bolsheviks hinted at in a declaration of the people's right to self-determination. Once the revolution had succeed-

17.3 Alexandr Nikolayevich Samochvalov, *V.I. Lenin Entering the Second All Russian Congress,* 1940. Oil on canvas, 11 ft 7³/₈ ins × 9 ft 3³/₈ ins (3.54 × 2.83 m). Russian State Museum, St Petersburg.

ed, however, Lenin and Stalin put the clamps on the nationalist movements, and at the end of the world war and the revolution, only the Baltic States, Poland, and Finland had preserved their independence.

THE AFTERMATH

After months of negotiations, a series of agreements called the Treaty of Versailles formally ended the war. Almost immediately, these agreements were contested, and after twenty years the treaty was totally repudiated. It failed for four reasons. The first reason was called the "principle of nationalities." For centuries, the three great empires—that is, the Austro-Hungarian, Russian, and Ottoman—had within them groups of oppressed minorities under a dominant community that gave them only minimal rights. These groups had tried to gain independence throughout the nineteenth century, and during the war, as part of its weak point strategy, the Allies tried to exploit this ideal. However, within the empires, the minorities were intermingled, and it proved impossible to draw up political borders that were also ethnic ones. In one case, the problem was resolved by a massive repatriation: 400,000 Turks moved from Macedonia to Turkey, and 1,300,000 Greeks moved from Asia Minor to Greece. That did little to dampen Greek and Turkish ill-feeling, and elsewhere ethnic populations simply stayed put. Large German populations became included in Czechoslovakia, and others found themselves in Poland. This "principle of nationalities" later gave Hitler one of his most effective propaganda themes.

The second reason the treaty failed had to do with the problem of non-European territories. German colonies and non-Turkish territories of the Ottoman Empire were divided up between the victors, and from that time onward, the Middle East became a thorn in the side of both France and Britain.

The third reason had to do with Germany itself. Judged responsible for the war, she was disarmed and condemned to pay reparations. A set of fifty-year payment plans was established, and then revised and abandoned. Even though the Allies had not come close to invading Germany, the Treaty of Versailles regarded Germany as the guilty party. That label and the crippling reparations were seen by all Germans as unfair, and the rejection of the Versailles *diktat* would be the Nazi's first priority.

Finally, there was no way that the territorial divisions stipulated in the treaty and the payment of reparations could be enforced. The United States refused to ratify the treaty, and the new League of Nations, the forerunner of the United Nations, which was designed to act as a type of world parliament, had no means of external action. As early as 1920 the Turks rebelled against the terms of the treaty and forced a revision, called the Treaty of Lausanne. Between 1935 and World War II Hitler did everything he could simply to abolish the treaty unilaterally. He reintroduced military service, remilitarized the left bank of the Rhine River, annexed the German border region of Bohemia, and made a claim on the Polish corridor. The spirit of the Versailles Treaty was simply anathema to the Nazis.

CRITICAL REVIEW below

A CRITICAL REVIEW

An all-too-prevalent view of any generation is the tendency to see itself as the first and only generation to have suffered a collapse of expectations, deprivation, uncertainty, cynicism, and fear. In reality, of course, every generation has had such feelings, with the only difference being the level of expectations that defines deprivation in terms of perceived needs. That is why it is occasionally difficult for one generation to take particularly seriously the sense of deprivation felt by another, whose deprivation may be in a different area than their own. In most respects, the collapse of dreams results from two tendencies that were recognized thousands of years ago as the primary obstacles to healthy living—self-pity and fear. Aristotle speaks of this when he describes the outcomes of Greek tragedy as ridding the soul of pity and fear. The collapse of dreams was an understandable outcome of World War I and its devastation.

What political or spiritual conditions exist today that can be traced to the aftermath of World War I? You are being asked here to speculate, but be sure to support your answer with specific examples.

A CRITICAL LOOK

Another set of dreams collapsed with the stock market in 1929, just when life in most countries seemed to have recovered from the trauma of World War I. However, one section of Europe that never did recover from World War I was Germany, and, as we shall see, the failure of the Treaty of Versailles laid the groundwork for a resurgent Germany, bent on revenge. The rise of Nazi Germany brings with it some of the most terrible memories of history in terms of humankind's treatment of its fellow humans. Although it did not cause the concentrated loss of life seen in World War I, World War II reached further and involved more nations than did its predecessor. We will trace it around the globe, from Europe to the Pacific. Finally, we will study the beginnings of the computer, the harbinger of our own time.

Describe the conditions of the Great Depression.

Describe the process by which Hitler initiated World War II.

Identify and describe the tactics used by Germany during the war.

Explain Japan's objectives in the war.

BETWEEN THE WARS

THE GREAT DEPRESSION

The crisis that began in the United States not only reflected the deep strains and stresses in world capitalism, but was also a continuation of problems occurring in Europe since the second half of the previous century. Low consumer spending, currency crises, and credit and international trade problems combined in a sequence of events that gathered pace from the end of the Great War. Inflation, which had been spectacular in Germany, ruined people almost everywhere. International currencies were extremely fragile, and the power of the banks increased. Then, a wave of speculation on Wall Street caused the stock market to crash on October 24, 1929 (Fig. **17.4**), and stocks and shares plummeted until 1932.

The crisis spread throughout the world, and bankruptcies mushroomed in any country whose credit system had ties to the United States. The crisis in business

17.4 Wall Street, during the collapse of share prices on the New York Stock Exchange, October 25, 1929 (Black Friday).

and banking caused an industrial crisis, which, in turn, affected agriculture. Agricultural prices fell by 50 percent in the United States. In 1932 alone forty million people were out of work and on the dole, and the lack of any social security systems in many countries increased the scale of human tragedy.

Social and political unrest increased. Around the world there were protest marches and uprisings by people who could not understand a system by which, for example, corn was burned to maintain prices while children starved. Confidence in the "free enterprise" system was deeply shaken, and a call to get the economy moving at any cost reverberated around the world. New political forces came to power, and government intervention was demanded by businessmen, farmers, and workers.

Spurred on by violence in the streets, different countries adopted different solutions, depending on the depth of the crisis and the influence and make-up of the various factions in society. The United States witnessed the New Deal; Germany saw Nazism; France and Spain experienced the Popular Front. Many countries returned to protectionism, and currencies were devalued. Nothing seemed to work. Wealthier nations then turned to public works, as in the United States, increases in wages, as in France, or closer links with colonies, as in Britain, while countries such as Italy, Germany, and Japan chose the path of rearmament and preparation for war, which seemed to some countries the only logical way out of the crisis.

17.5 Nazi Party Labor convention at Nuremberg, September 7–13, 1937

HITLER'S CONQUESTS

On January 30, 1933, Adolf Hitler became Chancellor of Germany. It took less than a year for him to have his party declared the only legal one and to bring all sectors of public life into line through an orchestrated campaign of intimidation and violence (Fig. **17.5**). Once assured of compliance at home, Hitler had the means to effect the final blows against the hated Treaty of Versailles. He reintroduced compulsory military service and rearmed the Rhineland. Making such a show of strength enabled Hitler to assess the lack of resolve on the part of France and Britain and to achieve a *rapprochement* with the states of central and southeastern Europe. He also aided Franco's forces in the Spanish Civil War and formalized an Axis with Benito Mussolini ("Il Duce") and Italy.

Although it was supposedly disarmed, Germany was actually militarily superior to the rest of Europe, and Hitler was, therefore, able to effect a solution to what he saw as the "problem of Greater Germany." The first step was to annex lands inhabited by Germans, and in the spring of 1938 the Wehrmacht, Germany's war machine, moved into Austria, earning only a mild rebuke from Paris and London. In the classic act of "appeasement,"

British prime minister Neville Chamberlain negotiated the Munich Agreement, which effectively dismantled Czechoslovakia and added the Sudetenland to Hitler's growing list of annexations to the Reich. In March 1939 Bohemia-Moravia disappeared from the map of Europe, and Germany grew accordingly. Hitler had completed the second stage of his campaign for *Lebensraum* (living room) in the east.

When Hitler turned toward Poland, however, neither Paris and London could retreat for fear of losing further face with the threatened smaller countries of Europe. Britain joined France in guarantees to Poland, and the Soviets were also included. Poland balked at the prospect of Soviet forces within its borders, and the talks ground on. Meanwhile, talks began in Moscow that led to a secret Nazi-Soviet non-aggression pact, which effectively divided Poland between Germany and the Soviet Union. Hitler offered an agreement to Britain in which they would divide the world between them, but the British refused. On September 1, 1939, Hitler invaded Poland, and Europe was again at war. Three years later, Japan attacked Pearl Harbor, and World War II reached around the globe.

WORLD WAR II

EUROPE AND AFRICA

After success in Poland, Germany launched a *Blitzkrieg* (lightning war) in the spring of 1940, in which it seized the Danish straits, the Norwegian coast, the Netherlands, Belgium, and France in a period of six weeks. After heavily bombing Britain, Hitler turned his focus to the Mediterranean and the Balkans. In a fateful move, Operation Barbarossa, the German invasion of the Soviet Union, began on June 22, 1941. Despite the tremendous amount of territory involved and the severity of the Russian winter, German forces contined to advance until November 1942, when they had reached the Caucasus Mountains and the River Volga.

Depending on a number of factors—for example the Nazi's racial doctrines that led to the Holocaust—con-quered areas suffered under varying degrees of oppression and economic exploitation. Millions of individuals died in the Reich's concentration camps, but Hitler's "New Order" actually succeeded in breeding internal resistance movements, which proved vital in the eventual liberation of Europe.

At the end of 1942 fortunes began to change. British and Americans forces landed in North Africa, and British Field Marshal Montgomery won an important victory at El Alamein. At the same time, Hitler's General Paulus was forced to surrender at Stalingrad. The war on several fronts gave the Allies superiority, and Hitler's decision to break his treaty with Stalin and invade Russia ultimately proved catastrophic. Using North Africa as a base, the Allies invaded Italy and brought about the fall of Hitler's henchman, the Italian dictator Benito Mussolini. The Red Army began counterattacking, and the draining of German forces to the eastern front left Hitler vulnerable to a European invasion that commenced on D-Day, June 6,

Map 17.2 World War II in Europe.

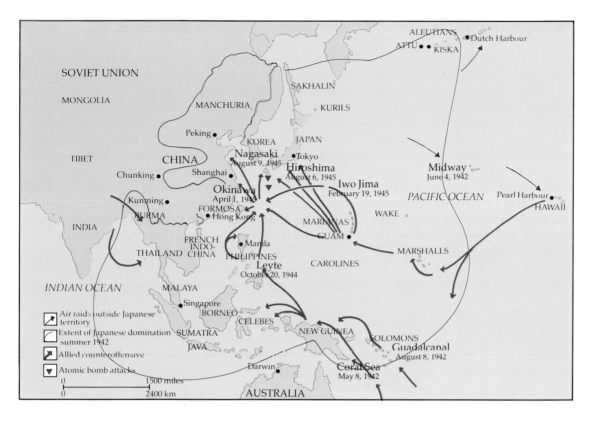

Map 17.3 World War II in the Pacific.

1944. By the fall of that year, Germany's Fortress Europe was crumbling, and many of its allies had been forced to sign armistices.

Hitler's scientists had made enormous strides in the area of rocketry, and the unmanned rocket-bombs, the V1 and V2, had rained terror on Britain from Belgium. However, even these and German counteroffensives in the Ardennes and Budapest, could not halt the Allied advance, and Germany collapsed from both east and west as the Allies and Soviets headed through Germany toward Berlin. On April 30, 1945, Hitler committed suicide in his Berlin bunker. The task of negotiating with the Allies fell to Admiral Doenitz, and unconditional surrender occurred on May 8, 1945.

THE PACIFIC

The Japanese attack on Pearl Harbor on December 7, 1941, illustrates the eagerness with which the Japanese approached war with the United States, which had opposed the Japanese invasion of China. In addition, the Japanese were determined to seize the resources of Indochina and the Dutch East Indies after their rulers had fallen to Germany in 1940. In moves as swift and decisive as the German *Blitzkrieg*, the Japanese swept through the eastern Pacific and threatened India and Australia. Perhaps expecting the United States to seek a peaceful solution, the Japanese got, instead, an all-out response that included the bombing of Tokyo as early as 1942.

Decisive United States' victories at Midway and the Coral Sea weakened the Japanese forces to the point that the overextended communications and forces of the Empire of the Sun were unable to prevent the three-year pincer movement. The American forces strategically leap-frogged Japanese concentrations and worked their way toward the Philippines. Japanese resistance was stubborn and fanatic, however, *Kamikaze* pilots committed suicide by crashing their planes into American ships, and ground forces fought to the death rather than be dishonored by surrender. At the beginning of 1945, American forces had inched their way to Iwo Jima and Okinawa, where they won strategic victories and gained bases from which bombers could reach Japan for saturation bombing and ships could intercept supplies heading to Japan.

Nonetheless, Japan refused to surrender, and it still held Indochina, the Dutch East Indies, and the coast of China. The American high command did not expect to be able to launch an invasion of Japan until 1946, and believed that such an invasion would cost the lives of a million American men. Resolution came when President Truman decided to drop two atomic bombs: one on Hiroshima on August 6, 1945, and one on Nagasaki on August 9, 1945. In the meantime, Russia entered the war in Asia and invaded the Japanese-held areas of Manchuria and Korea. Emperor Hirohito intervened personally and forced his ministers and military leaders to accept surrender. The surrender document was signed on the deck of the battleship *Missouri* in the Bay of Tokyo on September 2, 1945. World War II had ended.

SCIENCE AND WAR

The possibilities of a nuclear bomb and its world-changing consequences came as a result of a number of factors and individuals. In the 1930s the situation across the world was, as we have already discussed, in flux, and in different parts of Europe and in America, physicists worked separately, but aware of each other's progress, to find ways to split the atom and so create large quantities of energy. Later, during World War II, in Germany and the United States these scientists worked feverishly against each other to create an atomic bomb.

The British scientist Sir James Chadwick discovered the neutron in 1932. He was able to split this electrically charged neutral particle in the atom by bombarding it with alpha rays from radium. The Italian-born Enrico Fermi continued the work on nuclear fission, and was able to split uranium. In 1938 Fermi won the Nobel Prize, and was sent to Sweden by Mussolini. However, Fermi defected to the United States, where he continued his work to create an atomic pile that could sustain a chain reaction and create a constant flow of energy.

In 1939 three physicists, including Albert Einstein, wrote to President Roosevelt to warn of Germany's progress toward developing a nuclear reactor. As a result, the United States government supported Fermi's research, and in 1942, the first nuclear reaction occurred. It lasted twenty-eight minutes. From that point, a team of scientists, including Fermi, worked at Los Alamos, New Mexico, and by August 1945, Fermi's nuclear reactor had become the world's most destructive bomb. After the war, Fermi's discovery was harnessed to create energy, nuclear devices for medicine, and other peaceful applications.

CRITICAL REVIEW p. 565

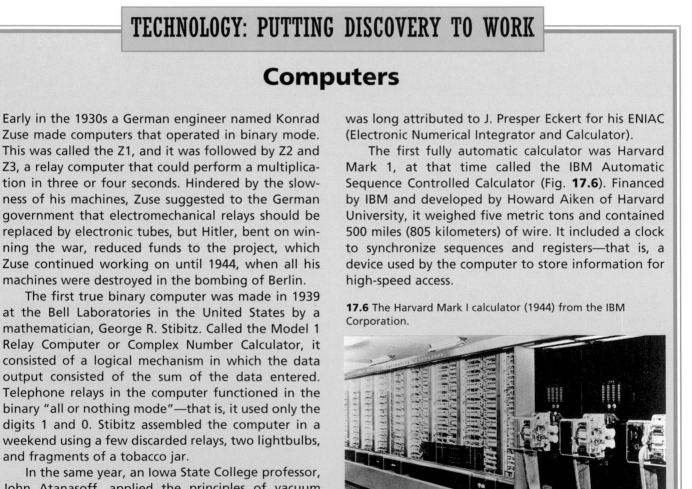

TECHNOLOGY: PUTTING DISCOVERY TO WORK

Computers

Early in the 1930s a German engineer named Konrad Zuse made computers that operated in binary mode. This was called the Z1, and it was followed by Z2 and Z3, a relay computer that could perform a multiplication in three or four seconds. Hindered by the slowness of his machines, Zuse suggested to the German government that electromechanical relays should be replaced by electronic tubes, but Hitler, bent on winning the war, reduced funds to the project, which Zuse continued working on until 1944, when all his machines were destroyed in the bombing of Berlin.

The first true binary computer was made in 1939 at the Bell Laboratories in the United States by a mathematician, George R. Stibitz. Called the Model 1 Relay Computer or Complex Number Calculator, it consisted of a logical mechanism in which the data output consisted of the sum of the data entered. Telephone relays in the computer functioned in the binary "all or nothing mode"—that is, it used only the digits 1 and 0. Stibitz assembled the computer in a weekend using a few discarded relays, two lightbulbs, and fragments of a tobacco jar.

In the same year, an Iowa State College professor, John Atanasoff, applied the principles of vacuum tubes to digital calculation. The result, designed to solve the complex equations used in physics, became known as the ABC (Atanasoff Berry Computer). However, neither Atanasoff nor Iowa State registered a patent; thus, the invention of the tube computer was long attributed to J. Presper Eckert for his ENIAC (Electronic Numerical Integrator and Calculator).

The first fully automatic calculator was Harvard Mark 1, at that time called the IBM Automatic Sequence Controlled Calculator (Fig. **17.6**). Financed by IBM and developed by Howard Aiken of Harvard University, it weighed five metric tons and contained 500 miles (805 kilometers) of wire. It included a clock to synchronize sequences and registers—that is, a device used by the computer to store information for high-speed access.

17.6 The Harvard Mark I calculator (1944) from the IBM Corporation.

A CRITICAL REVIEW

What is the relationship between money and crime? In the Great Depression, when so many people had so little of material value, people could leave their doors unlocked. What is poverty? Is it lack of material things, is it a condition of the human spirit, or is it a combination of both?

Talk to people who lived through the Great Depression and World War II, and listen to their descriptions of life at that time. Try to avoid comparisons with your own time, and instead try to see life as they saw it from the only vantage point possible for them: what was facing them at that time.

Construct an "oral history" of the time from the end of World War I to the end of World War II by writing down the recollections of at least two people who lived through the time. Then chronicle your own reactions to their stories.

A CRITICAL LOOK

In the next sections we examine the topics of Philosophy and Literature. We will study two schools of philosophy, pragmatism and existentialism, and meet a number of writers and poets.

Explain approaches to the novel and poetry taken in the period 1914–44 and identify important writers and their works.

PHILOSOPHY

PRAGMATISM

Philosophy had lost credit in the nineteenth century. Unlike their former colleagues in the sciences, philosophers came to be regarded as useless appendages to social progress. More and more people began to believe that sensory and intellectual powers were insufficient to solve the problems posed by philosophy.

Early in the twentieth century a reorientation occurred. A new philosophy, pragmatism, emerged in America, championed by John Dewey (1859–1952). Pragmatism abandoned the search for final answers to great problems, such as the existence of immortality, and instead contented itself with more modest goals in the realm of social experience. Using the scientific method, pragmatism pursued such issues as what moral and aesthetic values might be in a democratic, industralized society, and how one might achieve the highest personal fulfillment through education. Its value as a philosophy or as an adjunct of sociology remains to be seen.

Dewey's concept of "art as experience"—he used this title for his analysis of aesthetics—is enlightening, challenging, and sometimes frustrating. "Experience" is fundamental to Dewey's philosophy in all areas, but it appears most significant in his philosophy of aesthetics. Human experience, as interpreted by his aesthetics, presents a significant challenge to philosophy. According to Dewey, the philosopher needs to go to aesthetic experience in order to understand experience in general. Dewey is building on Hegel's concept of truth as a whole here,

and he shares Schelling's belief that aesthetic intuition is "the organ of philosophy," and so aesthetics is "the crown of philosophy."

EXISTENTIALISM

Existentialism is a philosophical doctrine that holds as its fundamental tenet an insistence on the actual existence of an individual as the basic and important fact, rather than a reliance on theories and abstractions. The idea itself is relatively ancient, but it was brought into a modern statement by Sören Kiergegaard (1813–55). Philosophers like Karl Jaspers and Martin Heidegger worked with the idea, and it can be seen in the writings of Dostoevski, for example (see Chapter 16), and Kafka (see p. 566). It became associated with a literary school in the 1940s with the writings of Jean-Paul Sartre among others (see p. 583).

The central doctrine of existentialism is that humans are what they make of themselves. They are not predestined by God, society, or biology, but have free will and the responsibility that goes with it. If people refuse to choose or allow outside forces to determine them, they are contemptible. Existentialists stress the basic elements in humankind, including the irrationality of the unconscious and subconscious act, and consider life to be dynamic and in a constant state of flux. Human life is not an abstraction but a series of consecutive movements. Existentialists insist on the concrete rather than the abstract, on existence itself rather than the idea of existence. Christian existentialism holds that the positive act of the will is a matter of religious choice and must ultimately lead to God.

LITERATURE

THE NOVEL

Between 1914 and 1939 the novel came to the fore as a literary medium. The economic, moral, and intellectual chaos of the interwar period required complex literary forms to express it. The novel—"fiction in prose of a certain extent," as the French critic Abel Chevally and, later, the British writer E.M. Forster called it—proved adaptable enough to handle a multitude of ideas and experiences, and thus became a catch-all form, which replaced tighter mediums of expression such as the drama, the essay, and the epic poem. Improving standards of education created a new reading public that was receptive to fiction "of a certain extent." In an age of revolt against old certainties, the novel seemed immune to rules and restrictions.

As a result, subject matter was enriched, and so was technique. Novelists now challenged the traditional forms of the novel as well as traditional concepts of time and space. Edouard, a character in *Counterfeiters* (1925) by André Gide (1869–1951) says: "My novel hasn't got a subject…'slice of life,' the naturalistic school used to say. The great defect of that school is that it always cuts its slice in the same direction; in time, lengthwise. Why not in breadth? Or in depth? As for me, I should not like to cut it at all. Police notwithstanding, I should like to put everything in my novel."

The interwar period produced an Irish novelist of extraordinary quality, James Joyce (1882–1941). Like Gide's Edouard, Joyce in *Ulysses* did "put everything in [his] novel." In this case, however, the police *were* a factor to be reckoned with. The serial publication of *Ulysses* in the United States was stopped by the American courts, although the finished work appeared in Paris in 1922. It was banned by the British authorities until 1941. Using STREAM OF CONSCIOUSNESS methods new to fiction, Joyce spins out actions and thoughts in great detail. The whole novel is the account of a single day in the life of Leopold Bloom. While the overall form is epic, virtually all other conventions of the novel are broken down, parodied, and recombined. Joyce also explored the unconscious mind in greater depth in *Finnegans Wake* (1939), a work of dazzling originality and great difficulty, in which the English language is replaced by a kind of polyglot punning.

The novels of D.H. Lawrence (1885–1930), such as *Sons and Lovers* and *Women in Love*, were more traditional in technique. His rejection of contemporary mass culture and the materialistic society that produced it, together with his messianic faith in "natural" (which included "sexual") things, links him strongly with the Romantics of the nineteenth century. The novels and short stories of Virginia Woolf (1882–1941) painstakingly explore the inner landscape of feeling and emotion, particularly that of women.

Woolf, who committed suicide after the first bombings of England during World War II, was one of the most gifted and innovative of the stream of consciousness writers. Her explorations are intensely subjective, and she worked toward high condensation and glimpses of moments of experience rather than attempting the illusion of a total picture. She advocated the freedom for the novelist to capture the "shower of atoms" and the discontinuity of experience, and she pictured men and women as enclosed in their "envelope" of consciousness from birth to death. In *A Room of One's Own* (1929) she spoke out for women's liberation.

The German writer Thomas Mann (1874–1955) created a richly symbolic picture of the fatal contradictions that beset European intellectuals between the wars in his masterpiece, *The Magic Mountain* (1924). The Austrian novelist Franz Kafka (1883–1924) lived and wrote in Prague of the Austro-Hungarian Empire. Although he finished law school, he did not practice, but took a minor clerical position in the department of workmen's compensation, which made him tremendously aware of the bureaucracy and red tape in which life can become entangled. He never developed the ability to assert himself, writing but never publishing, and he could not bring himself to marry even though he was engaged several times. His early death resulted from tuberculosis, and he directed his executor to destroy all his manuscripts. Instead, his executor published them. Kafka never finished any of his novels, but even in their incomplete state, they captured the fancy of Europeans caught in a world of rising dictatorships. *The Trial* (1925) and *The Castle* (1926) portray an incomprehensible world and authority—for example, when the hero finds himself unexpectedly arrested. Unlike the stream of consciousness writers, Kafka explored the intangible inner world as if it were an outward reality. It is never clear whether what takes place in the story is actual reality or merely part of the character's fantasy. He portrays guilt-obsessed people who trip themselves up and are never aware of their identity or relation to authority.

What all these writers had in common was a certain dissatisfaction with their times and a sense of alienation from them. In America, the response was different. Powerful, vital novels of social realism began to appear. William Cuthbert Faulkner (1897–1962) wrote both novels and short stories, and in 1929, he published his most admired work, *The Sound and the Fury*, in which he made use of the stream of consciousness technique. His methods of narration included moving from the present to the past and presenting two or more seemingly unrelated stories juxtaposed against each other. He wrote more than twenty novels based on characters in the imaginary Southern Yoknapatawpha County.

PROFILE

Langston Hughes (1902–67)

Langston Hughes is often referred to as the "poet laureate of Harlem." An African-American poet, he portrayed the life of the ordinary black individual in the United States, and his poetry is particularly meaningful to young people. He speaks of the basic qualities of life—love, hate, aspirations, and despair—yet he writes with a faith in humanity in general. He interprets all life as it is experienced in the real world as well as in idealism. At the same time, some of his work contains militant ideas that carry broad socio-political implications. He struggled within himself between what he wanted to write and what his audience expected him to write.

He was born in Joplin, Missouri, and soon after his birth his parents separated, his father, embittered by racial discrimination, moving to Mexico where he practiced law and pursued other business ventures. Langston was raised by his mother and grandmother. After his grandmother's death, he and his mother moved frequently, finally living in

17.7 Langston Hughes (1902–67).

Cleveland, where he finished high school. An unhappy year with his father in Mexico followed, as did a year at Columbia University. Then he traveled in West Africa and Europe, finished a degree at Lincoln University in 1929, and settled in Harlem, which he called the "great dark city."

Hughes received considerable attention as a poet as early as 1921 with his poem "The Negro Speaks of Rivers." His poetry and his involvement in social causes often intertwined, but although he is sometimes identified with the political left, his works often defy political interpretation. He experimented with numerous literary forms, and his collected works include thirty-two books, including poetry, short stories, an autobiography, drama, and history. His fictional character, Jesse B. Simple, revealing the uncensored thoughts of a native young urban youth, became a legend among African-Americans. In his novel *Not Without Laughter* Hughes created a brilliant portrayal of an African-American's passage into manhood.

Ernest Hemingway (1898–1961) erased the dividing line between journalism and literature. His style is characterized by the terse representation of simple acts, sparse dialogue, and understatement of emotion. His themes emphasize the sensual side of life, with overassertive males and two-dimensional women who exist for the pleasure of men.

POETRY

Bold new directions were also taken in poetry. Among the numerous important poets of the early twentieth century we must certainly mention the Irish William Butler Yeats (1865–1939) and the American Robert Frost (1874–1963), both of whom brought their own individual touch to an age of ever-expanding and experimental styles. The most

famous work of T.S. Eliot (1888–1965), *The Waste Land* (1922), marked the full emergence of modernism in poetry. Here Eliot cast aside traditional meters and rhymes in favor of free verse. This new kind of writing needs to be read with great care if it is to make any sense at all. The *Cantos* of Ezra Pound (1885–1972) and the works of e. e. cummings took this approach even further. Not all poets, however, responded to the complexity of their times by pursuing this strenuous route. W.H. Auden (1907–73), for example, reflected the mood of the 1930s in rhymed, epigrammatic satirical poetry that harked back to the eighteenth century.

The African-American poet Langston Hughes (1902–67), caught with sharp immediacy and intensity the humor, pathos, irony, and humiliation of being black in America. As early as 1921, Hughes received considerable attention with his poem "The Negro Speaks of Rivers."

CRITICAL REVIEW
p. 568

Native American Fiction

As we discussed in Chapter 16, the period from 1870 to 1920 produced a profound change in Native American culture and circumstances. Confinement to reservations and an increase in formal education changed both the Indian way of life and its tradition of oral transmission of culture. The perception of Indian and white cultures as being incompatible was a frequent issue for both cultures, and these conflicts were a common preoccupation and central theme for Indian writers, many of whom were "half-breeds" and the products of the white man's education. "Half-breeds" were popular subjects in the nineteenth and early twentieth centuries, and writers who focused on transculturation give us a profound insight into the Native American mind.

Gertrude Bonnin, a South Dakota Yankton Sioux, who had a full-blooded mother and an Anglo-American father, wrote under the penname of Red Bird (Zitkala-Sa). The mixed-blood protagonist of "The Soft-Hearted Sioux," a short story published in 1901, reflects the conflicts of the Native American caught between cultures. Unable to function in either world, he is given no alternative but to face a violent death. Here is a short excerpt.

On the day after my father's death, having led my mother to the camp of the medicine-man, I gave myself up to those who were searching for the murderer of the paleface.

They bound me hand and foot. Here in this cell I was placed four days ago.

The shrieking winter winds have followed me higher. Rattling the bars, they howl unceasingly: "Your soft heart! your soft heart will see me die before you bring me food!" Hark! something is clanking the chain on the door. It is being opened. From the dark night without a black figure crosses the threshold.... It is the guard. He tells me that tomorrow I must die. In his stern face I laugh aloud. I do not fear death.

Yet I wonder who shall come to welcome me in the realm of strange sight. Will the loving Jesus grant me pardon and give my soul a soothing sleep? or will my warrior father greet me and receive me as his son? Will my spirit fly upward to a happy heaven? or shall I sink into the bottomless pit, an outcast from a God of infinite love?

Soon, soon I shall know, for now I see the east is growing red. My heart is strong. My face is calm. My eyes are dry and eager for new scenes. My hands hang quietly at my side. Serene and brave, my soul awaits the men to perch me on the gallows for another flight. I go.[1]

A CRITICAL REVIEW

John Dewey's concept of art as experience speaks to something we may find familiar from emerging attitudes in medicine: a holistic view of humankind. According to Dewey, approaching life through aesthetic experience helped make a person "whole." Being developed as whole human beings is a right that we should expect to be fulfilled, even when it does not seem to have immediate practical payoffs.

What are the differences between John Dewey's philosophy and that of the existentialists?

Compare the viewpoint of Langston Hughes with that of Gertrude Bonnin.

A CRITICAL LOOK

We turn again to the visual arts and architecture. Whatever we may have thought about the art of the 1913 Armory Show, one thing was still clear: the subject matter for the most part was recognizable. All that is about to change. We are about to see some art that moves completely away from the observable world. We will examine three new styles—abstraction, dada, and surrealism—the last of which returns the objective image—however distorted. Then we will take a look at some American painters in order to bring our discussion a little closer to home. Finally, we will see the beginnings of "modern" architecture as a style.

Identify six major American painters of the period and describe their work.

Identify specific artists who reflect primitive and African influences and describe their work.

Identify at least three "modern" architects and describe their work.

THE VISUAL ARTS AND ARCHITECTURE

ABSTRACTION

We have used the phrase "dissolving image" to describe tendencies in nineteenth-century visual art to move away from recognizable, or objective, reality. This is what most people think of when they describe "modern" art as ABSTRACT art. A more precise term, however, is NONREPRE-SENTATIONAL art. All art is abstract, of course—that is, it is not the real thing itself, but a representation of something made from a distance, literally, "standing apart from it." Thus, paintings, sculptures, plays, and symphonies are abstractions, regardless of how realistic they are.

Abstract or nonrepresentational art, however, contains minimal reference to natural objects—that is, objects in the world we perceive through our senses. In many ways, abstract art stands in contrast to impressionism and expressionism in that the observer can read little or nothing in the painting of the artist's feelings for anything outside the painting. Abstract art seeks to explore the expressive qualities of formal design elements and materials in their own right. These elements are assumed to stand apart from subject matter. The aesthetic theory underlying abstract art maintains that beauty can exist in form

17.9 Kasimir Malevich, *Suprematist Composition: White on White*, c. 1918. Oil on canvas, 31¼ ins × 31¼ in (79.4 × 79.4 cm). Museum of Modern Art, New York.

alone and that no other quality is needed. Many painters explored these approaches, and several subgroups, such as *de Stijl*, the suprematists, the constructivists, and the Bauhaus painters, have pursued its goals. The works of Piet Mondrian and Kasimir Malevich illustrate many of the principles at issue in abstract painting.

Mondrian (1872–1944) believed that straight lines and right angles represented the fundamental principles of life. A vertical line signified activity, vitality, and life, while a horizontal line signified rest, tranquility, and death. The crossing of the two in a right angle expressed the highest possible tension between these forces, positive and negative. Mondrian's exploration of this theory in *Composition in White, Black, and Red* (Fig. **17.8**) is typical of all his linear compositions. The planes of the painting are close to the surface of the canvas, creating, in essence, the shallowest space possible. The palette is restricted to three hues. Even the edges of the canvas take on expressive possibilities as they provide additional points of interaction between lines. Mondrian believed that he could create "the equivalence of reality" and make the "absolute appear in the relativity of time and space" by keeping visual elements in a state of constant tension.

Another movement within the nonrepresentational tradition was suprematism. The works of the suprematist painters puzzle many people. A work such as *Suprematist Composition: White on White* (Fig. **17.9**) by Kasimir Malevich (1878–1935) seems simple but confusing, even by abstract standards. For Malevich, such works

17.8 Piet Mondrian, *Composition in White, Black, and Red*, 1936. Oil on canvas, 3 ft 4¼ ins × 3 ft 5 ins (1.02 × 1.04 m). Museum of Modern Art, New York (Gift of the Advisory Committee).

go beyond reducing painting to its basic common denominator of oil on canvas. Rather, he sought basic pictorial elements that could "communicate the most profound expressive reality."

DADA

The horrors of World War I caused tremendous disillusionment. One expression of this was the birth of a movement called "dada." (Considerable debate exists about when and how the word "dada"—it is French for "hobbyhorse"—came to be chosen. The dadaists themselves accepted it as two nonsense syllables, like one of a baby's first words.) During the years 1915 and 1916, many artists gathered in neutral capitals in Europe to express their disgust at the direction Western societies were taking. Dada was thus a political protest, and in many places the dadaists produced more left-wing propaganda than art.

By 1916, a few works of art began to appear, many of them FOUND OBJECTS and experiments in which chance played an important role. For example, Jean Arp (1888–1966) produced collages that he made by dropping haphazardly cut pieces of paper onto a surface and pasting them down the way they fell. Max Ernst (1891–1976) juxtaposed strange, unrelated items to produce unexplainable phenomena. This use of conventional items placed in circumstances that alter their traditional meanings is characteristic of dadaist art. Irrationality, meaninglessness, and harsh, mechanical images are typical effects, as shown in *Woman, Old Man, and Flower* (Fig. **17.10**). This is a nonsensical world in which pseudo-human forms with their bizarre features and proportions suggest a malevolent unreality.

17.10 Max Ernst, *Woman, Old Man, and Flower*, 1923–4. Oil on canvas, 3 ft 2 ins x 4 ft 3¼ ins (96.5 x 130.2 cm). Museum of Modern Art, New York.

SURREALISM

As the work of Sigmund Freud became popular, artists became fascinated by the subconscious mind. By 1924 a surrealist manifesto stated some specific connections between the subconscious mind and painting. Surrealist works were thought to be created by "pure psychic automatism." Its advocates saw surrealism as a way to discover the basic realities of psychic life by automatic associations. Supposedly, a dream could be transferred directly from the unconscious mind of the painter to canvas without control or conscious interruption.

The metaphysical fantasies of Giorgio de Chirico (1888–1978) have surrealist qualities. In works such as *The Nostalgia of the Infinite* (Fig. **17.11**), strange objects are irrationally juxtaposed: they come together as in a dream. These bizarre works reflect a world that human beings do not control. In them, "there is only what I see with my eyes open, and even better, closed."

Surrealism is probably more accurately represented by the paintings of Salvador Dali, however. Dali (1904–89) called his works, such as *The Persistence of Memory* (Fig. **17.12**), "hand-colored photographs of the subconscious," and the almost photographic detail of his work, coupled with the nightmarish relationships of the objects he pictures, has a forceful impact. The whole idea of time is destroyed in these "soft watches" (as they were called by those who first saw this work) hanging limply and crawling with ants. And yet the images are strangely fascinating, perhaps in the way we are fascinated by the world of our dreams. While the anti-art dadaism of Max Ernst may seem repulsive, the irrationality of de Chirico and Dali can be entrancing. The starkness and graphic clarity of Figures **17.11** and **17.12** speak of the unpolluted light of another planet, yet nonetheless it reveals a world we seem to know.

AMERICAN PAINTING

Until the early twentieth century painting in the United States had done little more than adapt European trends to the American experience. Strong and vigorous American painting emerged in the early twentieth century, however, and it encompasses so many people and styles that we will have to be content with only a few representative examples.

An early group called "the Eight" appeared in 1908 as painters of the American "scene." They were Robert Henri, George Luks, John Sloan, William Glackens, Everett Shinn, Ernest Lawson, Maurice Prendergast, and Arthur B. Davies. These painters shared a warm and somewhat sentimental view of American city life, and they presented it both with and without social criticism. Although uniquely American in tone, the works of the

17.11 Giorgio de Chirico, *The Nostalgia of the Infinite*, c. 1913–14, dated 1911 on painting. Oil on canvas, 4 ft 5¼ ins × 2 ft 1½ ins (135.2 x 64.8 cm). Museum of Modern Art, New York.

Eight often revealed European influences, for example, of impressionism.

The modern movement in America owed much to the tremendous impact of the International Exhibition of Modern Art (called the Armory Show) in 1913. There, rather shocking European modernist works, such as

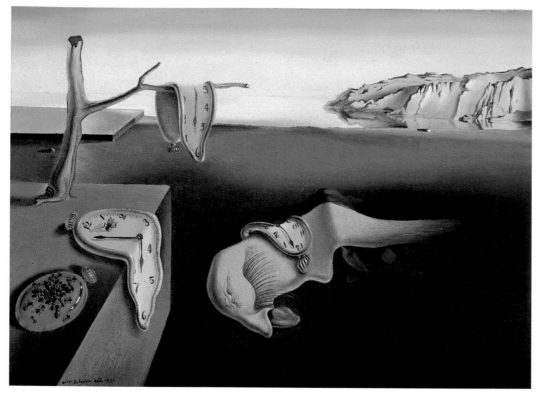

17.12 Salvador Dali, *The Persistence of Memory*, 1931. Oil on canvas, 9 ½ x 13 ins (24 x 33 cm). Museum of Modern Art, New York.

Duchamp's *Nude Descending a Staircase, No. 2* (see Fig. **16.23**) and the cubist work of Braque and Picasso, were first revealed to the American public.

Georgia O'Keeffe (1887–1986), an American, proved to be one of the most original artists of the century. Her imagery draws on a wide variety of objects that she abstracts in a uniquely personal way. She takes, for example, an animal skull and transforms it into a form of absolute simplicity and beauty. In *Dark Abstraction* (Fig. **17.13**) an organic form becomes an exquisite landscape which, despite the modest size of the painting, appears monumental. Her lines flow gracefully upward and outward with a skillful blending of colors and rhythmic grace. The painting expresses a mystical reverence for nature, whatever we take its subject matter to be. O'Keeffe creates a sense of reality that takes us beyond our usual perceptions into something much deeper.

Precisionists, such as Stuart Davis (1894–1964), took real objects and arranged them into abstract groupings, as in *Lucky Strike* (Fig. **17.14**). These paintings often use the strong, vibrant colors of commerical art (and are much like those of pop art in the 1960s). At every turn, this subject matter surprises us. At first we wonder at the frame within the frame. The gray textured border provides a strong color contrast to the interior form, which, were it not for the curved form at the top, would look very much like a window. The curve is repeated in reverse near the bottom of the picture, and the slight slant of these two opposing lines is encountered by the reverse slant of the white and black arcs. The strength of this work lies in the

17.13 Georgia O'Keeffe, *Dark Abstraction*, 1924. Oil on canvas, 24⅞ x 20⅞ ins (63 x 53 cm). St Louis Art Museum (Gift of Charles E. and Mary Merrill).

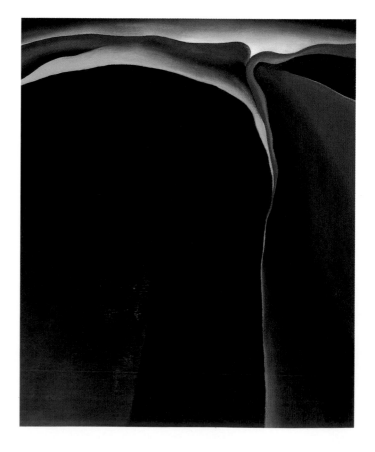

PROFILE

Georgia O'Keeffe (1887–1986)

American painter Georgia O'Keeffe was born near Sun Prairie, Wisconsin. She grew up on the family farm in Wisconsin before deciding that she wanted to be an artist. She spent 1904–5 at the Art Institute of Chicago and 1907–8 at the Art Students League of New York, then supported herself by doing commercial art and teaching at various schools and colleges in Texas and the South. Her break came in 1916 when her drawings were discovered and exhibited by the famous American photographer Alfred Stieglitz, who praised and promoted her work vigorously. They maintained a lifelong relationship, marrying in 1924, and O'Keeffe became the subject of hundreds of Stieglitz's photographs. After meeting Stieglitz, O'Keeffe spent most of her time in New York, with occasional periods in New Mexico, but she moved permanently to New Mexico after her husband's death in 1946.

Her early pictures lacked originality, but by the 1920s she developed a uniquely individualistic style. Many of her subjects included enlarged views of skulls and other animal bones, flowers, plants, shells, rocks, mountains, and other natural forms. Her images have a mysterious quality about them, with clear color washes and a suggestive, psychological symbolism, that often suggests eroticism. Her rhythms undulate gracefully. The works bridge the gap between abstraction and biomorphic form (see Figure **17.13**).

Perhaps her best known work was created in the 1920s, 1930s, and 1940s, but she remained active as a painter almost until her death in 1986. Her later works exalt the New Mexico landscape for which she had so much love.

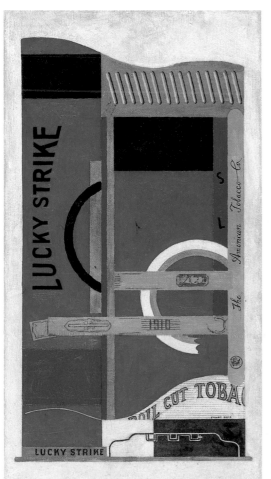

17.14 Stuart Davis, *Lucky Strike*, 1921. Oil on canvas, 33¼ x 18 ins (84.5 x 45.7 cm). Museum of Modern Art, New York (Gift of the American Tobacco Company, Inc.).

17.15 Grant Wood, *American Gothic*, 1930. Oil on beaver board, 29⅞ x 24⅞ ins (79 x 63.2 cm). Friends of American Art Collection, courtesy of Art Institute of Chicago.

juxtaposition of complementary colors, rectilinear and curvilinear forms, and opposing values, that is, lights and darks.

The realist tradition continued in the works of Grant Wood (1892–1942). The painting *American Gothic* (Fig. **17.15**) is a wonderful celebration of the simple, hard-working people of America's heartland. There is a lyric spirituality behind the façade of this down-home illustration. The elongated forms are pulled up together into a pointed arch which encapsulates the Gothic window of the farmhouse and escapes the frame of the painting through the lightning rod (just as the Gothic spire released the spirituality of the earth into heaven at its tip). Rural American reverence for home and labor is celebrated here with gentle humor.

THE HARLEM RENAISSANCE

From 1919 to 1925, Harlem, a neighborhood in upper Manhattan, became the international capital of black culture. "Harlem was in vogue," wrote the black poet Langston Hughes. Black painters, sculptors, musicians, poets, and novelists joined in a remarkable artistic outpouring. Some critics at the time attacked this work as isolationist and conventional, and the quality of the Harlem Renaissance still stirs debate.

The movement took up several themes: glorification of the black American's African heritage, the tradition of black folklore, and the daily life of black people. In exploring these subjects, Harlem Renaissance artists broke with previous black artistic traditions. But they celebrated black history and culture and defined a visual vocabulary for black Americans.

Black intellectuals such as W.E.B. Du Bois (1868–1963), Alain Locke (1886–1954), and Charles Spurgeon spearheaded the movement. Among the notable

17.16 Aaron Douglas, *Aalta*, 1936. Oil on canvas, 18 x 23 ins (45.7 x 58.4 cm). Afro-American Collection of Art, The Carl Van Vechten Gallery of Fine Arts, Fisk University, Nashville, Tennessee.

17.17 Aaron Douglas, *Aspects of the Negro Life* (detail), 1934. Oil on canvas, entire work 5 ft x 11 ft 7 ins (1.52 x 3.53 m). Schomburg Center for Research in Black Culture, New York Public Library, Astor, Lenox and Tilden Foundations.

17.18 Diego Rivera, *Enslavement of the Indians*, 1930–1. Fresco. Palace of Cortez, Cuernavaca, Mexico.

artists were social documentarian and photographer James van der Zee (1886–1983), painter William Henry Johnson (1901–70), painter Palmer Hayden (1890–1973), painter Aaron Douglas (1899–1979), and sculptor Meta Vaux Warrick Fuller (1877–1968).

Aaron Douglas was arguably the foremost painter of the Harlem Renaissance. In his highly stylized work, he explores a palette of muted tones. Douglas was particularly well known for his illustrations and cover designs for many books by black writers. His portrait of *Aalta* (Fig. **17.16**) is warm and relaxed, and its color and line express dignity, elegance, and stability. *Aspects of the Negro Life* (Fig. **17.17**), at the New York Public Library's Cullen branch, documents the emergence of a black American identity in four panels. The first portrays the African background in images of music, dance, and sculpture. The next two panels bring to life slavery and emancipation in the American South and the flight of blacks to the cities of the North. The fourth panel returns to the theme of music. The master of many styles, Douglas was extremely effective in his realistic work.

CENTRAL AMERICAN PAINTING

Diego Rivera (1886–1957) revived the fresco mural as an art form in Mexico in the 1920s. Working with the support of a new revolutionary government, he produced large-scale public murals that picture contemporary subjects in a style that blends European and native traditions. The fresco painting *Enslavement of the Indians* (Fig. **17.18**) creates a dramatic comment on that chapter in Mexican history. The composition is not unlike that of Goya's *The Third of May 1808* (Fig. **15.9**). A strong diagonal sweeps across the work, separating the oppressed from the oppressor, and provides a dynamic movement that is stabilized by the classically derived arcade framing the top of the composition.

AFRICAN AND PRIMITIVE INFLUENCES

The direct influence of African art can be seen in the sculptures of Constantin Brancusi (1876–1957) (Figs **17.19** and **17.20**). Yet beyond this, the smooth, precise surfaces of much of his work seem to have an abstract, machined quality. Brancusi's search for essential form led to very economical presentations, often ovoid and simple, yet ani-

17.19 Constantin Brancusi, *Mlle Pogany*, 1931. Marble on limestone base, 19 ins (48 cm) high. Philadelphia Museum of Art (Louise and Walter Arensberg Collection).

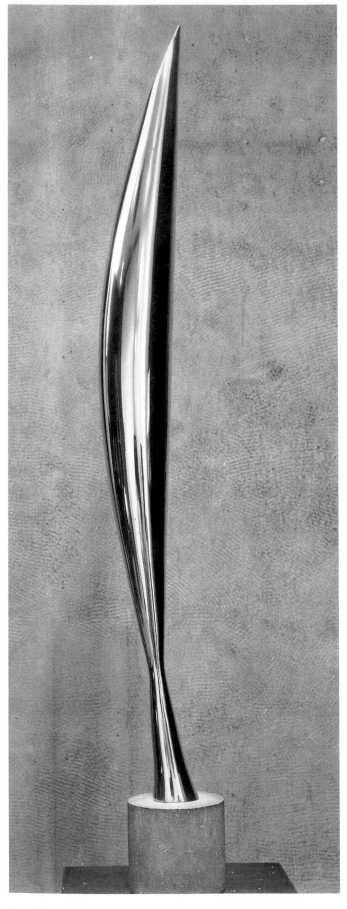

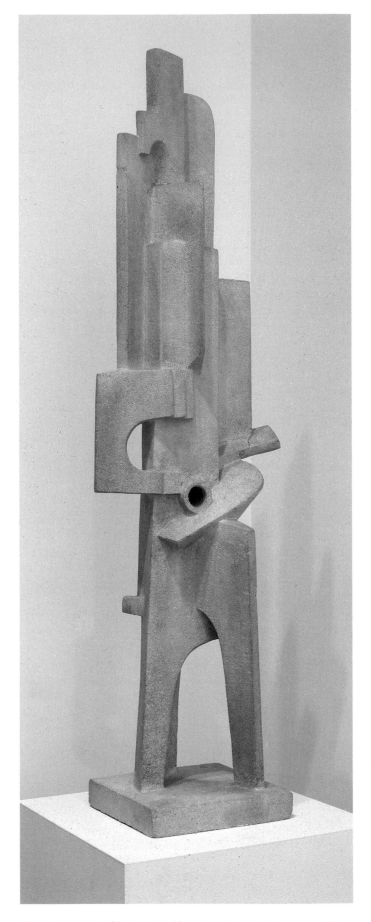

17.20 Constantin Brancusi, *Bird in Space*, c. 1928. Bronze (unique cast), 4 ft 6 ins (1.37 m) high. Museum of Modern Art, New York.

17.21 Jacques Lipchitz, *Man with a Guitar*, 1915. Limestone, 38¼ ins (97.2 cm) high. Museum of Modern Art, New York (Mrs Simon Guggenheim Fund).

MASTERWORK

Moore—Recumbent Figure

The British sculptor Henry Moore (1898–1986) explored many ways of depicting the human figure. These various treatments are unified by a deep feeling for the dignity of the human form, however. In *Recumbent Figure* (Fig. **17.22**), the humanity of the piece emerges perhaps more strongly than it would in a purely naturalistic expression.

Moore's work reflects the "primevalism" inherent in some sculpture even today, and his early work was influenced by the monoliths of Stonehenge. However, *Recumbent Figure* also displays a certain classicism.

The sense of the resting form recalls that of Dionysus in the sculptures from the pediment of the Parthenon. In a very modern way, the stone is not disguised, but rather profoundly exploited. Perhaps the most "famous" features of Moore's sculptures are the "holes," or "negative spaces," that he inserts. The negative space provides a counterpoint to the interlocking shapes of the solids in his work.

17.22 Henry Moore, *Recumbent Figure*, 1938. Green Hornton stone, 4 ft 7 ins (1.4 m) long. Tate Gallery, London.

17.23 Le Corbusier, Villa Savoye, Poissy, France, 1928–30.

mate. Certainly, great psychological complexity exists in *Bird in Space*. Its highly polished surface and upward striving line has a modern sleekness, and yet somehow its primitive essence remains, reminding us of the work of African or aboriginal tribes. Brancusi's *Mlle Pogany* (see Fig. **17.20**), despite the superbly polished surface and accomplished curves which lead the eye inward, has an enigmatic character that is reminiscent of an African mask.

In 1925, Jacques Lipchitz (1891–1973) created a series of "transparents" made from cardboard cut and bent to approximate the cubism of Picasso's paintings. He thus opened up the interiors of these works, to achieve a radical new understanding of space: interior spaces need not be voids, but, rather, could become integral parts of the sculptural work itself. Thus, he arrived at the concept of negative space, which played an important role in sculpture, especially in the work of Henry Moore.

Lipchitz's *Man with a Guitar* (Fig. **17.21**) predates his discovery of negative space, but clearly it reflects his interest in form, space, cubism, and archaic and primitive art. Here, these influences appear in the way forms are combined to create a multifaceted shape that has the appearance of being viewed from several directions at once. At the same time, the work has an archaic, geometric solidity. The primitive influence is apparent in its proportions—an elongated torso and head and shortened legs. The interaction of angles and curves draws the viewer in to examine the work from many different observation points.

ARCHITECTURAL MODERNISM

After World War I many new concepts occurred in architecture, and in the United States, the pre-eminence of Frank Lloyd Wright, whose Prairie Style we studied in the last chapter, remained. His insistence on the integration of the context of the building and the creation of indoor space that was an extension of outdoor space led him to

17.24 Cass Gilbert, The Woolworth Building, New York, 1913.

MASTERWORK

Wright—Kaufmann House

Frank Lloyd Wright is one of the greatest American artists in any medium. His primary message is the relationship of architecture to its setting, a lesson that some modern architects seem to have forgotten. Wright's buildings seem to grow out of, and never violate, their environment.

One of his most inventive designs is the Kaufmann House, Falling Water, at Bear Run, Pennsylvania (Fig. **17.25**). Cantilevered over a waterfall, its dramatic imagery is exciting. The inspiration for this house was probably the French Renaissance château of Chenonceaux, built on a bridge across the River Cher. However, "Falling Water" is no house built on a bridge. It seems to erupt out of its natural rock site,

and its beige concrete terraces blend harmoniously with the colors of the surrounding stone. Wright has successfully blended two seemingly dissimilar styles: the house is a part of its context, yet it has the rectilinear lines of the International Style, to which Wright was usually opposed. He has taken those spare, sterile boxes and made them harmonize with their natural surroundings.

Wright's great asset, and at the same time his greatest liability, was his myopic insistence on his own vision. He could work only with clients who would bend to his wishes. So, unlike many architects, whose designs are tempered by the vision of the client, what Wright built was Wright's, and Wright's only.

17.25 Frank Lloyd Wright, Kaufmann House, Falling Water, Bear Run, Pennsylvania, 1936–7.

even more dramatic projects. The horizontality of the Prairie Style remains, but we see it in a completely different mode in the exciting Kaufmann House (see Fig. **17.25**).

Other new concepts in design appeared in the works of Le Corbusier (1887–1965) during the 1920s and 1930s. Le Corbusier was concerned with integrating structure and function, and he was especially interested in poured concrete. He demonstrated his belief that a house was "a machine to be lived in" in several residences of that period. By "machine," Le Corbusier did not mean something depersonalized. Rather, he meant that a house should be efficiently constructed from standard, mass-produced parts, and logically designed for use, on the model of an efficient machine.

Le Corbusier had espoused a domino system of design for houses, using a series of slabs supported on slender columns. The resulting building was boxlike, with a flat roof, which could be used as a terrace. The Villa Savoye (Fig. **17.23**) combines these concepts in a building whose supporting structures free the interior from the necessity of weight-supporting walls. In many ways, the design of the Villa Savoye reveals a classical Greek inspiration, from its columns and human scale to its precisely articulated parts and coherent, unified whole. The design is crisp, clean, and functional.

Many traditional approaches to architecture continued through the period. Cass Gilbert's Woolworth Building (Fig. **17.24**) is one such example. It has not only stimulated considerable discussion, including the appelation "Woolworth Gothic," but it has also inspired a wave of Gothic skyscrapers, including Howells and Hood's Tribune Tower in Chicago (1923–25).

CRITICAL
REVIEW
below

A CRITICAL REVIEW

Some of the disillusionment brought on by the modern world, its wars, dehumanization, and broken promises, can be seen in the art of this period. Certainly the anti-art art called dada brings home that idea. However, the direction that seems most often to offer itself is the direction of a turn further inward. In Chapters 15 and 16 we talked about subjectivity as an increasing force in art, but what we are now seeing seems to be something more personal and unreflective of an external world shared by the artist and the viewer—we are seeing the results of artists dabbling with the unconscious and subconscious mind.

We are used to communicating through ordered syntax, and we are used to discussing recognizable images that reveal the surfaces and essences of the world we recognize. Some of the artists we have just considered do not care about our perceptions of the recognizable world, but are more concerned with evocative images that stir something more primal in us.

When art gets so personal—or impersonal—it moves to a different plane from the one we might be used to. That plane may or may not be a deeper one. Sometimes it offers nothing but self-centered drivel, sometimes it can be more profound than more "beautiful" or representational art, and sometimes it is hard to know which is which because the language of images to which we are accustomed no longer is used. All of which leads us back to the fundamental question: what is art supposed to do? As frustrating as it may be, there are no simple answers to that question.

Discuss the question, "What is art supposed to do?" with your peers and professor. Do you share any common perceptions?

<table>
<tr><td>

A CRITICAL LOOK

</td><td>

At the beginning of the book we discussed how important process

</td></tr>
</table>

sometimes is—more important than coming up with "right" answers to all the questions—and this is one of those occasions. One of the curiosities of studying the arts is the fact that often the art of our own time is the most difficult for us to come to grips with. It may be that we do not like the message we are getting about ourselves, or it may be that contemporary artists are so self-indulgent that they have forgotten what art is supposed to be about. Or it may be that we just need a little more time and space to let things settle. In the next section we find music that departs from the established conventions of the past three hundred years. We close this chapter with theatre and film, two art forms highly accessible to us.

Identify composers who followed traditional and nontraditional paths and explain the characteristics of music that account for such conclusions.

Describe the theatrical movements labeled expressionism, epic theatre, and absurdism.

Identify and describe the major conditions and personages in film during the 1920s and 1930s.

MUSIC

MODERN TRADITIONALISM

Traditional tendencies continued through the 1930s and 1940s in various quarters, for example, in the music of the American William Schuman (1910–92). Schuman's symphonies have bright timbres and energetic rhythms, and focus on eighteenth- and nineteenth-century American folklore. The inspiration of the eighteenth-century American composer William Billings (1746–1800) figures prominently in Schuman's *William Billings Overture* (1943) and the *New England Triptych* (1956), which is based on three pieces by Billings. *American Festival Overture* (1939) is perhaps his most famous work. Traditional tonality also appears in the works of the Russian composer Sergei Prokofiev (1891–1953). With all its traditional tonality, however, Prokofiev's *Steel Step* reflected the encroachment of mechanization of the 1920s. The machine as a symbol for energy and motion found its way into music, and in *Steel Step* Prokofiev intentionally dehumanized the subject of his music in order to reflect contemporary life.

DEPARTURES

HINDEMITH

Paul Hindemith (1895–1963) departed from traditional tonality in his compositions. He presented his systematized approach to problems of musical organization and their theoretical solutions in *The Craft of Musical Composition*. Hindemith's work was extremely chromatic and almost atonal. Although his system of tonality

used centers, it did not include the concepts of major and minor keys. He hoped that his new system would become a universal music language, but it did not.

Hindemith was, however, extremely influential in twentieth-century composition, both as a composer and a teacher. His works are broad and varied, encompassing nearly every musical genre, including ten operas, art songs, cantatas, chamber music, requiems, and symphonies. *Kleine Kammermusik für fünf Bläser* is a delightful composition for five woodwinds in five contrasting movements. Its overall form is very clear, as are its themes. Its dissonant harmonies and untraditional tonalities typify Hindemith's works. Yet Hindemith criticized "esoteric isolationism in music," and he tried to write works that the general public could understand and that the amateur musician could play.

BARTÓK

The Hungarian composer Béla Bartók (1881–1945) took another nontraditional approach to tonality. He was interested in folk music, and a number of his compositions show nationalistic elements. Eastern European folk music does not use Western major/minor tonalities, and thus Bartók's interest in it and in nontraditional tonality in general went hand in hand. Bartók invented his own type of harmonic structure, which could accommodate folk melodies.

As nontraditional as some of Bartók's work is, however, he also employs traditional devices and forms. His style is precise and well structured, and he occasionally uses sonata form. He often develops his works from one or two very short motifs, and his larger works are unified by repeating thematic material. Bartók's textures are largely contrapuntal, with strong melodies but little conventional harmony, and dissonances occur frequently.

Bartók's employment of traditional devices was always bent to his own desires and nearly always lay outside the traditional tonal system. He contributed significantly to string quartet literature, and his six quartets each set out a particular problem which is then solved, using simple motifs combined with complex tonality. One characteristic of his melodic development was octave displacement, in which successive notes of a melody occur in different octaves. This device apparently came from the folk music in which he was so interested. When peasants found the notes of a melody too high or low, they simply jumped up or down an octave so as to sing them comfortably.

Rhythm is a notable feature of Bartók's music. His works tend to have a lot of rhythmic energy; he employs devices such as repeated chords and irregular meters to generate dynamic rhythms. He also uses polyrhythms, that is, various juxtaposed rhythms at a time, to create a nonmelodic counterpoint of unique quality.

BERG

Alban Berg (1885–1935) was a close friend and disciple of Schoenberg, and his compositions are based on the serial technique. However, Berg's lyricism means that, despite their atonality, his works are not as disconnected as much serial music. Many of the characteristics of his work can be found in his *Lyric Suite* (1927), a string quartet in six movements. This work is based on several different tone rows.

The opening movement of the *Lyric Suite* starts with a brief chordal introduction, followed by the first tone-row (the main theme, played by the first violin). The second theme, derived from the tone-row, is more peaceful. Both themes are then freely recapitulated, and the movement closes with a brief coda. The rhythm is varied, changing constantly between quadruple and duple meter. Much of the meaning of the piece to the listener depends upon an accurate dynamic rendering by each of the four string players; Berg indicates the volume and articulation he requires in great detail. The remaining five movements use contrasting tempos, heightening the dramatic impact of the whole work.

The story on which this piece is based, that is, its "program," alludes to an extramarital affair. This information, however, remained a secret for nearly fifty years. It was published for the first time only after the death of Berg's widow.

IVES AND COPLAND

The Americans Charles Ives and Aaron Copland both had experimental and highly personal styles.

Charles Ives (1874–1954) was so experimental that many of his compositions were considered unplayable, and did not receive public performances until after World War I. Content to remain anonymous and disinclined to formulate a "system," as Schoenberg did, Ives went unrecognized for many years. His melodies spring from folk and popular songs, hymns, and other, often familiar, material, which he treated in unfamiliar, complex ways. His rhythms are very irregular and are often written with only an occasional bar line to indicate an accent. His counterpoint is so dissonant that frequently it is impossible to distinguish one melodic line from another. Some of the tone clusters in his piano music are unplayable without using a block of wood to depress all the keys at once. Ives' experiments, such as *The Unanswered Question* (1908), employ ensembles placed in various locations to create STEREOPHONIC effects. Ives' work reflects his idea that all music relates to life's experiences and ideas, some of which are consonant and some dissonant.

Aaron Copland (1900–91) integrated American idioms—jazz, dissonance, Mexican folk songs, and Shaker hymns—into his compositions. The last of these figure prominently in Copland's most significant work, *Appalachian Spring* (1944). First written as a ballet, it was later reworked as a suite (set of movements) for symphony orchestra. Copland employed a variety of styles, some harmonically complex, some simple. He often used all the tones of the DIATONIC scale simultaneously, as he does in the opening chord of *Appalachian Spring*. His style is nonetheless traditionally tonal, and his unique use of rhythms and chords has been highly influential in twentieth-century American music.

THEATRE

EXPRESSIONISM

In Chapter 16 we studied expressionism as a style in the visual arts. As seems always the case, visual art styles filter slowly into the theatre. Expressionism brought more disillusion than realism to the theatre. But the theatre is both visual and oral. The painters' revolt against naturalism came to the theatre in scenic design, and it was settings that followed expressionist fashion. For playwrights, expressionism was merely an extension of realism or naturalism, and it allowed them to express their reactions to the universe more fully. August Strindberg (1849–1912), for example, turned inward to the subconscious in expressionistic plays such as the *Ghost Sonata*. In so doing, he created a "presentational" rather than "representational" style.

The plays of Ernst Toller (1893–1939) typify German expressionistic disillusionment after World War I. Toller's personal struggles, his communist idealism, and his opposition to violence are reflected in the heroine of

Man and the Masses (1923). Sonia, a product of the upper class, leads a strike for peace. Her desire to avoid violence and bloodshed is opposed by the mob spirit (the "Nameless One"), who seeks just those results, and to destroy the peace the strike intends to achieve. For leading the disastrous strike, Sonia is imprisoned and sentenced to death.

Expressionism also found its way to America. Elmer Rice's *Adding Machine* (1923) introduces the viewer to Mr Zero, a cog in the great industrial machinery of twentieth-century life, who stumbles through a pointless existence. Finding himself replaced by an adding machine, he goes berserk, kills his employer, and is executed. Adrift later in the hereafter, he is too narrow-minded to understand the happiness offered to him there. He becomes an adding machine operator in heaven.

EPIC THEATRE

The theatre of social action found a successful exponent in Bertolt Brecht (1898–1956) and his epic theatre. Although most of Brecht's plays were written before the war, they were not produced until after it. With his Berliner Ensemble, Brecht brought his theories and productions to a wide audience. Drawing heavily on the expressionists, Brecht developed complex theories about theatre and its relationship to life, and he continued to mold and develop these theories until his death.

Brecht was in revolt against dramatic theatre. Essentially, he tried to move the audience out of the role of passive spectator and into a more dynamic relationship with the play. To this end, Brecht postulated three circumstances—historification, alienation, and epic.

Historification removed events from the lifelike present to the past in order to make the actions presented seem strange. According to Brecht, the playwright should make the audience feel that if they had lived under the conditions presented in the play, they would have taken some positive action. Understanding this, the audience should see that things have changed since then and thus they too can make changes in the present.

Brecht believed the audience should not confuse the theatre with reality. The audience should always watch the play critically as a comment on life. In order for the spectators to judge the action in the play and apply it to life outside, however, they must be separated—or alienated—from the play's events, even though they might be emotionally involved in them. Historification was one kind of alienation. Other devices could also be used to make things strange, such as calling attention to the make-believe nature of a production or inserting songs, film sequences, and so on. Brecht did not subscribe to the idea of a unified production. Rather, he saw each element as independent, and thus each was a device that could be employed to produce further alienation.

Finally, Brecht called his theatre "epic" because he believed that his plays resembled epic poems more than they did traditional drama. His plays present a story from the point of view of a storyteller, and they frequently involve narration and changes of time and place that might be accomplished with nothing more than an explanatory sentence.

ABSURDISM

Many artists of this period had lost faith in religion, realism, science, and humanity itself. In their search for meaning, they found only chaos, complexity, grotesque laughter, and perhaps insanity. The plays of Luigi Pirandello (1867–1936) obsessively ask the question "What is real?" with brilliant variations. *Right You Are If You Think You Are* (1917) presents a wife, living with her husband in a top-floor apartment, who is not permitted to see her mother. She converses with her daily, the mother in the street and the daughter at a garret window. Soon a neighbor demands an explanation from the husband. He answers, but so does the mother, who has an equally plausible but different answer. Finally, someone approaches the wife, who is the only one who can clear up the mystery. Her response, as the curtain falls, is loud laughter! Pirandello's dismay at an incomprehensible world was expressed in mocking laughter directed at those who thought they knew the answers.

Pirandello's work was one factor in the emergence of a movement called "absurdism." A philosophy that posited the essential meaninglessness—or unknowable meaning—of existence, and thus questioned the meaning of any action, was also emerging. This philosophy, "existentialism," also contributed to absurdist style, especially in the literary arts. From such antecedents came numerous dramas, the best known of which were written by the French existentialist philosopher, writer, and playwright Jean-Paul Sartre (1905–80). Sartre held that there were no absolute or universal moral values and that humankind was part of a world without purpose. Therefore, men and women were responsible only to themselves. His plays attempted to draw logical conclusions from "a consistent atheism." Plays such as *No Exit* (1944) translate Sartre's existential views into dramatic form.

Albert Camus (1913–60) was the first writer to apply the term "absurd" to the human condition. This he took to be a state somewhere between humanity's aspirations and the meaninglessness of the universe which is the condition of life. Determining which way to take a chaotic universe is the theme of Camus' plays, such as *Cross-Purposes* (1944). Absurdism continued as a theatrical genre after World War II, and will be discussed further in the next chapter.

FILM

EUROPEAN FILM

Film-making revived and spread rapidly throughout Europe after World War I. The German director Fritz Lang's futuristic *Metropolis* (1926) tells the story of life in the twenty-first century. Critics called the plot ludicrous, but marveled at the photographic effects. In France, film found its first real aesthetic theorist in Louis Delluc, and came to be regarded as a serious art form.

German expressionism made its mark in film as well as in the visual and other performing arts. In 1919, its most masterful example, Robert Wiene's *Cabinet of Dr Caligari* (Fig. **17.26**), astounded the film-going public. Macabre sets, surrealistic lighting effects, and distorted properties, all combined to portray a menacing postwar German world.

In Russia Sergei Eisenstein wrote and directed the great film *Battleship Potemkin* (1925). This cruel story of the crew of the ship *Potemkin* contains one of the most legendary scenes in all cinema. A crowd of citizens is trapped on the great steps of Odessa between the Czar's troops and mounted Cossacks. The editing of the massacre scenes that follow is truly riveting. The sequence showing the carnage is a montage of short, vivid shots—a

face, a flopping arm, a slipping body, a pair of broken eye glasses—deftly combined into a powerful whole.

THE GLORIOUS TWENTIES

The 1920s were the heyday of Hollywood. Its films were silent, but its extravagance, its star system, and its legions of starlets dazzled the world. It was the beginning of the big studio era—MGM, Paramount, Universal, Fox, and Warner Brothers all began now. Fantastic movie houses that rivaled baroque palaces in their opulence were built all over the United States. The scandals, the intrigues, the often "immoral" glamor were the stuff of legends. Out of this rather premature decadence came Cecil B. DeMille and *The Ten Commandments* (1923).

Twenty thousand movie theatres existed around the country, and to keep apace of demand, movie studios turned out one film after another—mostly on a formula basis. The decade, nevertheless, produced some great artistry, for example Erich von Stroheim's *Greed* (1924). Although cut from nine hours to two by MGM, the film was a brilliant treatment of a slight story about a boorish dentist, practicing without a license, who murders his greedy wife.

This was the era of Fairbanks and Pickford and an immigrant Italian tango dancer, whom the studio named

17.26 Robert Wiene, *The Cabinet of Dr Caligari*, 1919.

Rudolph Valentino, who thrilled women in movies such as the *Sheik*. After Valentino's death, John Gilbert and his co-star (and, for a time, fiancée) Greta Garbo became matinee idols. On the lighter side were Harold Lloyd, Buster Keaton, and Laurel and Hardy.

Although the sound-track had been invented many years earlier, and short talking films had been released, the *Jazz Singer* in 1927 heralded the age of talkies with Al Jolson's famous line "You ain't heard nothin' yet!" The film industry was not particularly enthusiastic about introducing talking films, however. The public was quite satisfied with silent movies. Profits were enormous, and the new invention required a vast capital investment to equip movie theatres with sound projection equipment.

But the die was cast. For some it meant continued stardom, while for others, whose voices did not match their faces, it meant obscurity. Early successes in using sound came from directors King Vidor in *Hallelujah* and Rouben Mamoulian in *Applause* (1929). Lewis Milestone's *All Quiet on the Western Front* used sound to unify visual compositions in a truly unforgettable anti-war statement.

THE THIRTIES

The early thirties produced films about crime and violence. Films such as *Little Caesar* (1930), with Edward G. Robinson, kept Hollywood's coffers full during the Depression. But the gangster genre fell out of favor amid public cries that such glorified violence was harming American youth. The sexually explicit dialogue of Mae West added a titillating dimension to the cinema. But the Production Code—that is, censorship—was strengthened, and West was toned down.

From the mid-1930s on, new types of film emerged, including the musicals of Fred Astaire and Ginger Rogers who danced through a sleek world of black and white. The glitter of these musicals was intended to bolster sagging attendances and divert a Depression-weary populace. There were Jeanette MacDonald and Nelson Eddy, Maurice Chevalier, Shirley Temple, and a new star, Judy Garland, in the *Wizard of Oz* (1939). Wholesomeness came in as happiness poured out.

The most popular star of the thirties, however, was created by Walt Disney. Mickey Mouse led a parade of animated characters in films, the popularity of which continues today. The Western continued, and in 1939, John Ford's classic, *Stagecoach*, made John Wayne the prototypical cowboy hero. This superbly edited film exemplified the technique of CUTTING WITHIN THE FRAME, which became a Ford trademark. (It also prevented others from re-editing and tampering with the product.) The 1930s also featured the slapstick of the Marx Brothers and the alcoholic ill-humor of W.C. Fields.

Chaplin continued to produce comedy into the thirties. *City Lights* (1931) was a silent relic in an age of sound, but its consummate artistry made it a classic. The story depicts Chaplin's love for a blind girl, who erroneously believes he is rich. He robs a bank and pays for an operation that restores her sight. He is apprehended and sent to prison. Years later she happens to cross a tramp being chased by a group of boys. Amused and yet saddened, she offers the tramp a coin and a flower. At the touch of his hand, she recognizes him, but she is stunned that her imagined rich and handsome lover is really nothing more than a comical tramp. The film ends with the knowledge that their relationship is doomed. Among the great comic sequences in this film is a scene in which Chaplin swallows a whistle at a society party, then, in a fit of hiccups, disrupts a musical performance and calls a pack of dogs and several taxicabs.

The epic of the decade was David O. Selznick's *Gone with the Wind*, a three-and-three-quarter-hour extravaganza with an improbable plot and stereotypical characters. Nonetheless, the performances of Clark Gable, Vivien Leigh, Leslie Howard, and Olivia de Havilland, along with its magnificent cinematography, have made this film eternally popular.

The rise of Nazism in Germany had virtually eliminated the vigorous German film industry by the late thirties. Fritz Lang, however, had already produced his psychological thriller *M.*, which employed subtle and deft manipulation of sound, including a Grieg *Leitmotif*. Peter Lorre's peformance as a child-murderer was significant. From Europe during the 1930s also came the master of suspense and shot manipulation, Alfred Hitchcock.

Throughout this era, Hollywood film unabashedly pursued entertainment as its primary goal. It did so with artistry and virtuosity, and it clearly succeeded in shaping images on a celluloid strip into aesthetically coherent works of art.

SYNTHESIS
The Bauhaus—Integration of the Arts

The Bauhaus is our Synthesis for this chapter because it represents a conscious attempt to integrate the arts into a unified statement. For the most part, the story of the Bauhaus and its goals will be told in the philosophy of its founder and primary visionary, Walter Gropius. Although it was secular in spirit, the Bauhaus represents a vision of artistic accomplishments, such as were seen in the great churches and palaces of the past—a true integration of vision wrapped in a common purpose. That vision may, in fact, be returning in the performance art of the last few years.

In the early twentieth century, pluralism prevents us from finding a movement or direction that truly synthesizes the arts. However, a movement did occur whose philosophies attempted to integrate or synthesize the arts in order to bring them to focus on architecture and the visual environment. That approach came from Germany in the mid-1920s. Led by Walter Gropius and Adolph Meyer, the Bauhaus School of Art, Applied Arts, and Architecture approached aesthetics from the point of view of engineering. Experimentation and design were based on technological and economic factors rather than on formal considerations. The Bauhaus philosophy sought to establish links between the organic and technical worlds and thereby to reduce contrasts between the two. Spatial imagination, rather than building and construction, became the Bauhaus objective. The design principles of Gropius and Meyer produced building exteriors that were completely free of ornamentation. Several juxtaposed, functional materials form the external surface, underscoring the fact that exterior walls are no longer structural, merely a climate barrier. Bauhaus buildings evolved from a careful consideration of what people needed their buildings to do, while, at the same time, the architects were searching for dynamic balance and geometric purity (Fig. **17.27**).

In 1919 Walter Gropius (1883–1969) wrote what has been called the "Bauhaus Manifesto." The major thrust of his ideas was that "all the arts culminate in architecture." He was inspired by a vision of buildings as a new type of organic structure created by integrating all the arts and expressing the contemporary situation. What Gropius sought to do in his new vision was to bring back into the architectural environment the work of painters and sculptors—who, by the twentieth century, had been virtually excluded from the building crafts. Gropius wanted to create a new unity between art and technology, not by returning to the styles of the past, but, in fact, by abandoning contemporary artistic vocabulary—which he viewed as "sterile" and meaningless—and evolving a new architectonic outlook.

As he viewed the past, Gropius realized that ornamentation of buildings was considered to be the major function of the visual arts, and thus these arts had played a vital part in the creation of great architecture. However, in the twentieth century, visual art stood apart from architecture, as self-sufficient. Gropius believed that architects, painters, and sculptors needed to work together, exchanging ideas, to rediscover the many aspects of great building.

So, guided by this idea of a fundamental unity underlying all branches of design, Gropius founded the original Bauhaus during World War I. At the invitation of the Grand Duke of Sachsen-Weimar-Eisenach, Gropius took over the Weimar School of Arts and Crafts and the Weimar Academy of Fine Art. His primary plan was to shape instruction throughout the school so that students could be trained "to grasp life as a whole, a single cosmic entity" rather than to be trained in specialized classes. He tried to combine imaginative design and technical proficiency by producing a new type of artist-collaborator, who could be molded so as to achieve equal proficiency in design and technology. He made his students complete apprenticeships with the local building trades and insisted on manual instruction in order to provide the student with good all-round hand and eye training.

The Bauhaus workshops were laboratories for solving real problems. They sought to work out practical new designs for everyday goods and to improve models for mass production. All of this required a very special staff who had wide, general cultural backgrounds and skills in both practical application of design and in design theory. They needed to be able to build by hand and to translate designs into prototypes for mass production—two radically different skills. The Bauhaus philosophy maintained that the difference between industry and handicraft was due less to the nature of the tools involved than to the assignment of labor. That is, in handicraft, one person controls the entire process and product, while in industry the labor is subdivided among

17.27 Walter Gropius, Professor Gropius's own house at Dessau, Germany, 1925.

several individuals. For Gropius and the Bauhaus, these two approaches—handicraft and industry—were opposite poles that were gradually approaching each other. According to Bauhaus thinking, in the future, handicraft would become chiefly preparation for evolving experimental new types and forms for mass production.

Gropius believed that talented craftspersons, who could turn out individual designs and market them, would always exist. However, the Bauhaus concentrated on a different direction, that would prevent human "enslavement by the machine by giving its products a content of reality and significance, and so saving the home from mechanistic anarchy." This idea was also applicable to architecture.[2]

During the years of its existence, the Bauhaus embraced a wide range of visual arts: architecture, planning, painting, sculpture, industrial design, and theatre stage design and technology. The Bauhaus sought a new and meaningful working relationship among all the

processes of artistic creation, culminating in a new "cultural equilibrium," as Gropius described it, in the visual environment. Teachers and students worked together in a community effort, trying to become vital participants in the modern world. One of the fundamental precepts of the Bauhaus was that the teacher's own approach should never be imposed on the student. In fact, any attempt by the student to imitate the teacher was ruthlessly suppressed: stimulation from the teacher was solely to help students to find their bearings.

The Bauhaus was a synthesis of the arts, attempting the lofty goal of totally redesigning the visual environment by merging visual art and architecture. Although highly influential in its time, it soon became an isolated style of its own. Many famous artists participated in the Bauhaus School, but perhaps the intrinsic pluralism of the twentieth century and the constant striving for something "new" doomed the Bauhaus to a brief life. It was a synthesis—perhaps the only synthesis of its time—and a forerunner of the interdisciplinary art of the current age; however, the age itself made that synthesis impossible to sustain.

CHAPTER EIGHTEEN

AN AGE OF PLURALISM

AT A GLANCE

A Pluralistic World Order
Decolonization
The Cold War
A Unified Europe
  TECHNOLOGY: Robots
Science and Liberty
Toward Another Millennium

The Visual Arts and Architecture
Abstract Expressionism
Pop Art
Op Art
Hard Edge
Photorealism and conceptualism
Neo-expressionism
Primary Structures
Abstraction
Found Sculpture and Junk Culture

Minimalism
Light Art
Ephemeral and Environmental Art
  PROFILE: Robert Smithson
Installations
Postmodernism
Neo-abstraction
Video Art
Architectural Modernism
Architectural Postmodernism

Pluralism in Literature

Music
Serialism
Aleatory Music
Improvisation
Electronic Music

Pluralism
  PROFILE: Krzysztof Penderecki
Pop Music

Theatre
Realism
Absurdism
Pluralism
Spectacularism

Film
Neorealism
The Demise of the Studio
Pluralism

Synthesis: Native American and African-American Arts

18.1 Louise Nevelson, *Black Wall*, 1959. Wood, 9 ft 4 ins × 7 ft 1¼ ins × 2 ft 1½ ins (264 × 217 × 65 cm). Tate Gallery, London.

A CRITICAL LOOK

We have come to the last chapter in our journey through time. In the physical world things have changed dramatically since the time of our Paleolithic ancestors, and the pace of change seems to be accelerating. However, in terms of the fundamentals of who we are as human beings, the changes may be purely superficial. The accumulation of articles and the appearance of change in the world around us may camouflage more important issues that have to do with the creative impulse and those qualities of what it means to be human.

In the first sections of this chapter, we travel through the political and physical context from which, in which, and about which the arts speak. These are events within the lifetime of the "babyboomers," who were born as the dust settled after World War II.

Explain how the concept of a Third World and movements such as Islamic Fundamentalism have affected late twentieth-century life.

Explain the development and importance of robots, including Asimov's three rules for robotics.

A PLURALISTIC WORLD ORDER

Our vision of ourselves and where we are going is probably as unclear to us as it was to our Paleolithic ancestors. As we are threatened with being drowned out by the clamor of our machines, overwhelmed by social prob- lems, poisoned by our own waste, and swamped by the inane, we struggle to understand what it means to be human, turning to the arts of the past for inspiration, if not for answers. In the same spirit we must also examine the art that is being created in our own time. As we strive to cope with our own finiteness from day to day, it is there that we may find the clues to who and what we are, and who we might become.

Increasingly, we recognize that even as our human-

	GENERAL EVENTS	LITERATURE & PHILOSOPHY	VISUAL ART	THEATRE & CINEMA	MUSIC
1945	Hiroshima Korean War Start of Vietnam War Cold War		Le Corbusier (**18.33**) van der Rohe (**18.31**) Wright (**18.32**) Noguchi ((**18.18**) Johnson (**18.31**) Pollock (**18.3**) de Kooning (**18.4**) Rothko (**18.5**) Giacometti (**18.21**) Nevelson (**18.1, 18.17**) Nervi (**18.34**) Fuller (**18.35**)	Beckett Miller Ionesco Williams Genet Welles Rossellini Ford Hitchcock Fellini Kurosawa	Babbitt Parker Gillespie Stockhausen Boulez Cage
1960	Decolonization Cuban missile crisis	Wiesel Narayan Heller Kawabata Solzhenitsyn Yevtushenko Walker	Hepworth (**18.19**) Calder (**18.20**) Kosuth (**18.13**) Oldenburg (**18.8**) Segal (**18.10**) Warhol (**18.9**) Lichtenstein (**18.7**) Vasarély (**18.11**) Smithson (**18.24**)	Bergman	Foss Penderecki Carter Berio Reich Davis Haley Presley Beatles
1975 1990	Disintegration of communism Fall of Berlin Wall Gulf War	Abu-Khalid Khamis	Piano and Rogers (**18.38**) Shapiro (**18.27**) Bofill (**18.36**) Moore (**18.39**) Graves (**18.37**) Frankenthaler (**18.6**)	Spielberg	

Timeline 18.1 The late twentieth century.

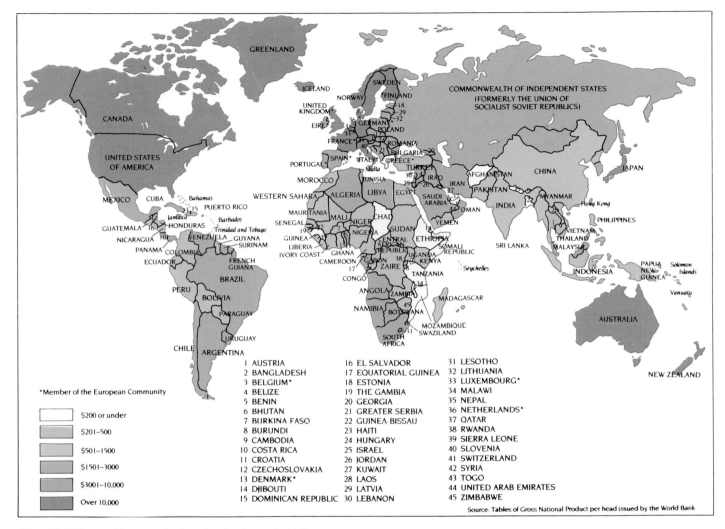

Map 18.1 The world economic situation in the early 1990s.

ness unites us, there are manifold expressions of individuality in that togetherness. To paraphrase St Paul, the body that represents humanity is not all ears or eyes or feet. It takes diverse members, each with different purposes, to make a complete body. Thus, in the late twentieth century, the evidence, indeed, the celebration, of pluralism—of difference—has become an important theme.

DECOLONIZATION

Before the end of World War II, a large portion of the globe, especially in what we call the Third World, existed under the colonial rule of outside nations. After World War II that order changed. During the late 1940s, decolonization was spurred by nationalist wars of independence, although the Dutch and the British, for example, had actually planned for the independence of their colonies in Egypt, India, and Malaysia. In the 1950s, as the Cold War polarized the entire world, violent popular revolutions challenged the remnants of colonialism in North Africa and Southeast Asia. By the 1960s several African countries had undergone sweeping changes and had achieved independence with the more-or-less freely given consent of their previous overlords.

The effects of decolonization have been widespread and, to a large extent, problematical. Violent conflicts among tribal powers, oppressive military dictatorships, suppression of human rights, the use of unusually cruel weapons of war, and famine, for example, have replaced the injustices of colonial rule. Even today, with Eastern Europe having thrown off communism, the absence of any strong central authority has resulted in an explosion of ethnic violence that had lain dormant under the Soviets. Everywhere, those who have struggled for "freedom" have begun to learn that "independence" is not an automatic state of grace. Freedom has been confused with economic comfort, and when unrealistic expectations are

592 AN AGE OF PLURALISM

not immediately fulfilled, disillusionment brings about more violent uprisings to no clear purpose.

In 1952, Alfred Sauvy, using an analogy referring to the Third Estate at the time of the French Revolution, called the emerging states that belonged to neither the Western or Eastern bloc, the "Third World." A Third World Movement emerged from the Bandung Conference of 1955, with the goal of bringing together subjugated peoples and dominated states in a common defense of their political interests and national security. Today the countries of the Third World do not constitute a unified bloc—the extreme diversity of their social formations, cultures, and histories make this impossible—but they have their own specific problems and strengths, and they represent pluralistic economic strategies and conditions that have yielded plural experiences and results. On one hand are the petroleum-exporting countries, and on the other, those whose economies remain vulnerable to fluctuations in oil prices. Some are newly emerging industrial countries; others are still devastated by war and famine. In addition, the countries of the Third World are divided into regional organizations—for example, the Organization of African Unity—and religious and linguistic ones—for example, the Arab League or the Islamic Conference.

THE COLD WAR

After World War II the United States and the Soviet Union dominated the world. The two former allies quickly grew apart as each sought to protect its sphere of influence from the other, and a period of tense conflict, sometimes called "peaceful coexistence," lasted for the next forty-five years.

The period of greatest conflict, the Cold War years of 1946–62, witnessed strain between the two great powers over the division of Germany, the Marshall Plan for the rebuilding of Europe, and the Berlin crisis, and the antagonism took an extended military form in Korea (1950–3). Toward the end of the 1950s, with the United States and the Soviet Union experiencing the beginnings of détente, the scene of international conflict shifted to Southeast Asia. The changing power relations between the USA, the USSR, and China destabilized the region after the French were thrown out of the area at the end of the Indochina War. The conflict was centered on Vietnam. Plans for the unification of the country, provided for in the 1954 Geneva Accords, collapsed, and war resumed in the south of the country. From 1955 a government led by Ngo Dinh Diem tried, with US backing, to annihilate the communist opposition. In 1958 the communists set up the NLF (National Liberation Front), and its guerilla army made significant inroads in South Vietnam. Pressure from the United States led to Diem's overthrow in 1963 because he

was unable to overcome the NLF and he sought neutralism in the conflict. The United States wanted to create in South Vietnam a military state like that in South Korea, which would be capable of resisting the communist insurgency. A strong anti-war movement in the United States and a strong offensive attack by the NLF, called the Tet Offensive, eventually spelled the end of American policy in South Vietnam.

In 1962, the Cuban missile crisis brought a direct threat of Soviet hegemony to the United States. The resulting brinkmanship taught both the Soviet Union and the United States that they could at least contain their mutual hostility, and the subsequent nuclear "balance of power" kept conflict decentralized and led to "peaceful coexistence."

For over two decades since the late 1960s, another movement has rapidly grown in importance, and that is the rise of Arab nationalism in the Middle East. Defeat in the 1967 Arab-Israeli war and the death of Egypt's President Nasser in 1970, left the door open for the return of religious leaders on the political scene. Fundamentalist protest grew strong on the disillusionment with progress and on the failure of various attempts at social and economic development, and, eventually, became a destabilizing factor.

A UNIFIED EUROPE

As the Soviet Union under Mikhail Gorbachev and world communism in general have disintegrated in the early 1990s, the large conflicts now seem to turn upon economics. Japan has more or less succeeded in dominating the world marketplace, a victory of sorts that it could not accomplish militarily in World War II. In fact, it could be argued that, having been forbidden by the peace treaty of 1945 to maintain military forces, Japan has been able to focus its economy more effectively than have the United States and the Soviet Union, both of which have expended enormous resources in competing militarily with each other.

Since the defeat of Germany in 1945, the nations of Western Europe have moved slowly but systematically toward an economically unified European community. In 1992 that movement was called into question by the European Community, because many of the partners disagreed about goals and operating details. Where it goes from there, of course, remains to be seen. Germany is struggling as it strives to overcome the economic drag of its reunification. Providing aid to the former Soviet Union presents additional challenges for the European Community as well as for the individual states there.

The problems of China and Africa and the ongoing conflicts in the Middle East also have profound effects on the West. The joint European and American action

TECHNOLOGY: PUTTING DISCOVERY TO WORK

Robots

Robots—at least as an idea—occur in ancient mythology, and as long ago as 1738 a Parisian inventor made an artificial duck that quacked, ate grain, swam, and flapped its wings. The word Robot was coined in 1923 in Karel Čapek's play *R.U.R.* (Rossum's Universal Robots), and it is the Czech word for worker. In the 1940s Isaac Asimov, a science fiction writer, described the first benevolent robots, whose purpose was to serve humans.

The first actual robots derived from the work of Joseph Engelberger, a physicist devoted to Isaac Asimov, and the inventor George C. Devol. Engelberger had studied the development of digital controls, which had been used in World War II to aim and fire guns from ships, and which automatically adapted to changes in the position of the ship and the motion of the water. Devol had developed a Programmed Article Transfer device that Engelberger knew could become a robot. The two joined forces to create Unimates, robots that would replace humans in jobs that were tedious, limiting, and dangerous. After being turned down by everyone they approached, they eventually found a manufacturer willing to invest $25,000 in the experiment.

At first, the business was not successful, mainly because of the short-term view of economics taken by management (not the fear of losing jobs by labor). Today, Engelberger works to create and sell robots

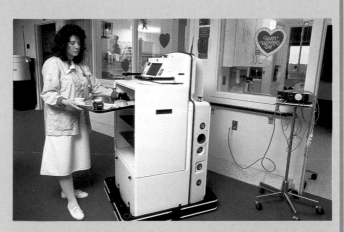

18.2 "Helpmate" robot being used to carry patients' meals at a hospital.

designed for a service economy—for example, robots that can clean floors and toilets. One popular robot, called "Helpmate," is an all-purpose hospital aide that delivers meals, mail, and medicine, runs errands, gives directions, and speaks English (Fig. **18.2**). Engelberger's robots always conform to Asimov's three laws of robotics: (1) a robot must not harm a human being, nor through inaction allow one to come to harm; (2) a robot must always obey human beings, unless that is in conflict with the first law; (3) a robot must protect itself from harm, unless that is in conflict with the first or second laws.[1]

against Saddam Hussein in the Gulf War (1991), under the auspices of the United Nations, places the European Community on the front line of any attempts at peace—or war—in the Middle East.

SCIENCE AND LIBERTY

As science and technology race on, questions of ethics and governmental control stubbornly resist clear solution. These vital concerns set the stage for military ventures, civil technology, and fundamental issues of individual liberty and social order. The development of nuclear weapons maintained by major and minor powers—of which Israel, Iran, Pakistan, and North Korea are only a few—rocket technology and "Star Wars" defenses, and "simpler" systems of warfare, such as the effective pairing of "scud" and "patriot" missiles in the Gulf War,

are but three threats to contemporary cultures that drain resources which might otherwise go to more civilized pursuits.

The American government's ignorance of the after effects of the bombing of Hiroshima and Nagasaki during World War II, and the intense nuclear testing that went on long after that, led to incalculable human and environmental damage. In essence, the globe became a modern laboratory, and its living inhabitants guinea pigs.

Who controls whom, how, and for what, remain critical issues as human knowledge and understanding of its applications expand. Who should control decisions about prolonging life through mechanical means? Who should control the dissemination of birth control devices and drugs such as the "abortion pill"? Is there a right to die and who has it? Is there a right to live, and who has that? These are a few of the difficult issues facing a pluralistic society with a rigid tradition of individual freedoms.

TOWARD ANOTHER MILLENNIUM

The second half of the twentieth century is now drawing to a close. Societies exist in a global environment in which actions of even the smallest nation can have ramifications around the world that are often well beyond the importance of the original cause. The 1991 Iraqi invasion of Kuwait and the subsequent, if brief, war, which people around the world watched as it happened on television, demonstrate how tentative, tender, and unstable our "world order" really is.

The uncritical optimism spawned by the victory of democracy over totalitarianism in World War II has faded, to be replaced by a more realistic, if less positive, appreciation of social inequities within democracy itself. The inevitable conflict that arises when a state pursues individual liberties as well as social rights, and the question of where one ends and the other begins, are among the most vexing problems of our era. The questions of individual responsibility versus individual rights, and of accommodating minority differences while maintaining cultural integrity, trouble us at every turn.

Multinational corporations function as supranational governments, and the creation of life in a test-tube is a scientific reality. Mechanization has assumed universal proportions, and computer-generated conclusions threaten to replace human reason as the source of problem solving.

Technocrats are poised to rule a world of individuals whose education, if any, has consisted solely of job training. Philosophy in many quarters is considered unproductive speculation, and usefulness alone has become the touchstone of value. In short, many of our contemporaries seem to have progressed to the point that they, in Oscar Wilde's cynical words, "know the price of everything and the value of nothing."

Very few expect an end of the world and a judgment day with the second coming of Christ in the year 2000 as Christians, at least, believed would happen in the year 1000. Our problem is that, of many terrible possibilities, we don't know what to expect.

CRITICAL REVIEW below

THE VISUAL ARTS AND ARCHITECTURE

ABSTRACT EXPRESSIONISM

The first fifteen years following the end of World War II were dominated by a style called "abstract expressionism." The style originated in New York, and it spread rapidly throughout the world on the wings of modern mass communications. Two characteristics identify abstract expressionism. One is nontraditional brushwork, and the other is nonrepresentational subject matter. This

CRITICAL LOOK p. 595

A CRITICAL REVIEW

At least one contemporary historian and scholar has suggested that we have come to the end of history. He maintains that the last great idea was democratic capitalism and that nothing new has happened since. That challenging theory invites us to consider whether anything really "new" has happened to humanity at any time in history. Questions about ourselves, our relationships to other people, and to an ultimate creator or force beyond us are fundamental to our humanity, and they seem just as mysterious to us today as they were at the dawn of history when we know, through artifacts, that humans already contemplated them. The breakdown of the social order, as devastating to us as it may be, probably is not much different from similar breakdowns that have occurred many times before. Reshuffling the political maps seems to change history, but the concept of a "country" is as ephemeral as some of the art we will see in the next sections.

These are speculative questions. There is no "right" or "wrong" answer but do give them deep thought. Here again, the process is more important than the final product.

What do you think? Is the current drift of the physical world anything new, or does it portend anything any more catastrophic than at any other time in history? Are the terms "Third World" and "communism" representative of significant changes, or are they purely superficial?

What is history all about? Do the changes in the physical world really matter, or is life about more basic conditions like human relationships and spiritual wholeness?

A CRITICAL LOOK

Things move rapidly in the modern world, and in keeping with the title of this chapter and the individualism of the century, we should not be surprised to learn that in the next section, in which we study painting, we will discover no fewer than six new styles. As we work through these, we concentrate on three concepts—abstract art, nonobjective art, and conceptualism—focusing on the differences among them, the artists' varying purposes, and the way they use or do not use works of art.

Explain the differences implied by the three terms just mentioned.

Identify and describe the characteristics and approaches of op, pop, and hard edge, citing artists and works representing each style.

complete freedom to reflect inner life led to the creation of works with high emotional intensity. Absolute individuality of expression and the freedom to be irrational underlie this style. This may have had some connection with the confidence inspired by postwar optimism and the triumph of individual freedom: as the implications of the nuclear age sank in, abstract expressionism all but ceased to exist.

The most acclaimed painter to create his own particular version of this style was Jackson Pollock (1912-56). A rebellious spirit, Pollock came upon his characteristic approach to painting only ten years before his death.

Although he insisted that he had absolute control, his compositions consist of what appear to be simple dripping and spilling of paint onto huge canvases, which he placed on the floor in order to work on them. His work (Fig. 18.3), often called "action painting," conveys a sense of tremendous energy. The viewer seems to feel the painter's motions as he applied the paint.

Willem de Kooning (b. 1904) took a different approach to abstract expressionism. Sophisticated texture

18.3 Jackson Pollock, *Number 1*, 1948. Oil on canvas, 5 ft 8 ins x 8 ft 8 ins (1.73 x 2.64 m). Museum of Modern Art, New York.

(Fig. **18.8**) presents an enigma to the viewer. What are we to make of it? Is it a celebration of the mundane? Or is a serious comment on our age implicit in these objects? Certainly Oldenburg calls our attention to the qualities of design in ordinary objects by taking them out of their normal contexts and changing their scale.

The influence of the pop movement can also be seen in the plaster figures of George Segal (b. 1924). Working from plaster molds taken from living figures, Segal builds scenes from everyday life with unpainted plaster images (Fig. **18.10**).

In the 1960s Andy Warhol (1928–87) focused on pop-

18.8 Claes Oldenberg, *Two Cheeseburgers, with Everything* (*Dual Hamburgers*), 1962. Burlap soaked in plaster, painted with enamel, 7 ins (17.8 cm) high. Museum of Modern Art, New York (Philip Johnson Fund).

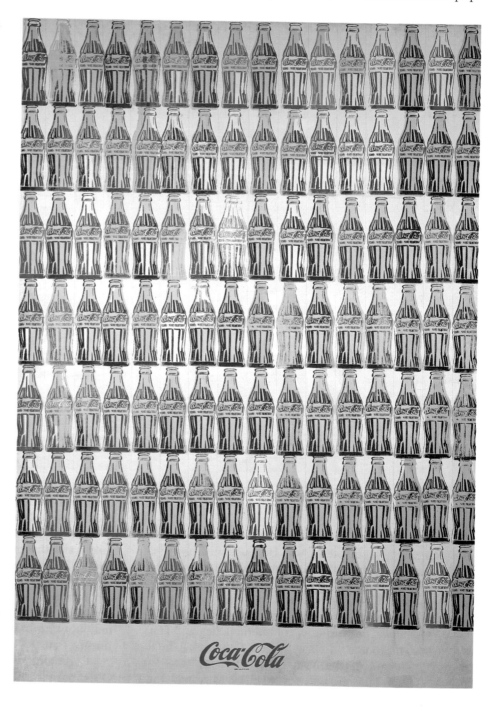

18.9 Andy Warhol, *Green Coca-Cola Bottles*, 1962. Oil on canvas, 6 ft 10 ins x 4 ft 9 ins (1.97 x 1.37 m). Whitney Museum of American Art, New York (Purchase, with funds from the Friends of the Whitney Museum of American Art).

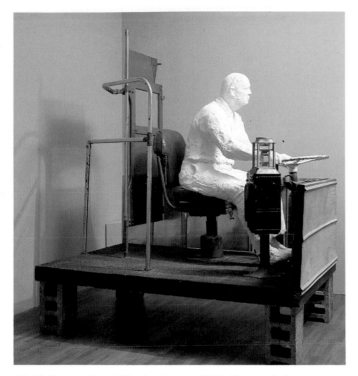

18.10 George Segal, *The Bus Driver*, 1962. Figure of plaster over cheesecloth; bus parts including coin box, steering wheel, driver's seat, railing, dashboard, etc. 6 ft 3 ins (1.91 m) high overall. Museum of Modern Art, New York (Philip Johnson Fund).

18.11 Victor Vasarély, *Arcturus II*, 1966. Oil on canvas, 5 ft 3 ins x 5 ft 3 ins (1.51 x 1.51 m). Hirshhorn Museum and Sculpture Garden, Smithsonian Institution, Washington, D.C.

ular culture and contemporary consumerism in his ultra-representational art. The very graphic *Green Coca-Cola Bottles* (Fig. **18.9**) is a good example of his style. The starkness and repetitiousness of the composition are broken up by subtle variations. The apparently random breaks in color, line, and texture create moving focal areas, none of which is more important than another, yet each significant enough to keep the viewer's eye moving continuously through and around the painting. In these subtle variations, the artist takes an almost cubistlike approach to the manipulation of space and image.

OP ART

Op art plays on the possibilities offered by optics and perception. Emerging from work done in the 1950s, op art was an intellectually oriented and systematic style, very scientific in its applications. Based on perceptual tricks, the misleading images in these paintings capture our curiosity and pull us into a conscious exploration of what the optical illusion does and why it does it.

Victor Vasarély (b. 1908) bends line and form to create a deceptive sense of three-dimensionality. Complex sets of stimuli proceed from horizontal, vertical, and diagonal arrangements. Using nothing but abstract form, Vasarély creates the illusion of real space.

The psychological effects of his images depend on extremely subtle repetition of shape and gradation of color. In *Arcturus II* (Fig. **18.11**), the symmetrical imagery seems to come into and out of focus because of the apparent brightness of the individual colors. Shape and color combine to create the optical experience, and what at first glance seems simple and straightforward, becomes complicated and deceptive. The more we look, the more we are convinced that we are "seeing things."

HARD EDGE

Hard edge, or hard-edged abstraction, also came to its height during the 1950s and 1960s, in the work of Ellsworth Kelly and Frank Stella (b. 1936), among others. Its flat color areas have hard edges which carefully separate one area from another. Essentially, hard edge is an exploration of design for its own sake. Stella often abandoned the rectangular format of most canvases in favor of irregular shapes in order to be sure that his paintings bore no resemblance to windows. The odd shape of the canvas thus became part of the design itself, as opposed to being a frame or a formal border within which the design was executed.

Some of Stella's paintings have iridescent metal powder mixed into the paint, and the metallic shine further enhances the precision of the composition. *Tahkt-I-Sulayman I* (Fig. **18.12**) stretches just over 20 feet (6

18.12 Frank Stella, *Tahkt-I-Sulayman I*, 1967. Polymer and fluorescent paint on canvas, 10 ft ¼ in x 20 ft 2¼ ins (3.04 x 6.15 m). Pasadena Art Museum, California (Gift of Mr and Mrs Robert A. Rowan).

meters) across, with interspersed surging circles and half-circles of yellows, reds, and blues. The intensity of the surface, with its jarring fluorescence, counters the grace of its form, while the simplicity of the painted shapes is enriched by the variety of the repetitions.

PHOTOREALISM AND CONCEPTUALISM

Photorealism is related to pop art in that it, too, relies on pre-existing images. As can be guessed from the name of the movement, it is a form of art that involves working directly from photographs, rather than from the original subjects. It came to the fore during the 1970s, in the work of people such as Richard Estes (b. 1932) and Chuck Close (b. 1940). Photorealism acknowledges the role that the camera plays in shaping our understanding of reality, and suggests obliquely that contemporary life is often centered more around manufactured than natural objects.

Conceptual art challenges the relationship between art and life in a different way, and, in fact, challenges the definition of art itself. Essentially anti-art, as was dada, conceptual art attempts to divorce the imagination from aesthetics. Ideas are more important than visual appearances. It insists that only the imagination and not the artwork is art. Therefore, artworks can be done away with. The creative process needs only to be documented by

some incidental means—a verbal description, or a simple object like a chair. But, of course, despite its claims, conceptual art depends on something physical to bridge the gap between the artist's imagination and the viewer's.

One and Three Chairs (Fig. **18.13**) by Joseph Kosuth (b. 1945) depicts three different realities. The first is that of the actual chair that sits between the photograph and the printed definition. The second reality is the life-size photographic image of the same chair represented in the first reality. The third reality is the verbal description of the same chair. Using the third reality, we form in our mind an idea of the chair, and that might be termed a "conceptual reality." So the conceptual artwork, that is, the combination of actuality, photo image, and verbal description, presents a relationship "between an object and communicative methods of signifying that object."[2]

NEO-EXPRESSIONISM

A recent controversial and momentarily successful movement has been called "neo-expressionism." One of its most promising adherents, the Italian Francesco Clemente (b. 1952), records images "that the rest of us repress." In *Untitled from White Shroud* (Fig. **18.14**), he forces the viewer to confront what may well be repulsive images. The painting has nightmarish qualities, and yet the fluid, watercolor medium gives it a softening, translucent quality. The contrasts of the cool blues in the background and the bright red and yellow of the fishes capture our interest. Thus, the composition successfully balances form and color.

Like the expressionists, neo-expressionists also seek to evoke a particular emotional response in the viewer.

18.13 Joseph Kosuth, *One and Three Chairs*, 1965. Wooden folding chair, 32³/₈ ins (76.8 cm) high; photograph of chair, 36 x 24 ins (86.4 x 57.6 cm); photographic enlargement of dictionary definition of chair, 24 x 25 ins (57.6 x 60 cm). Collection, Museum of Modern Art, New York (Larry Aldrich Foundation Fund).

18.14 Francesco Clemente, *Untitled from White Shroud*, 1983. Watercolor. Kunsthalle, Basel, Switzerland.

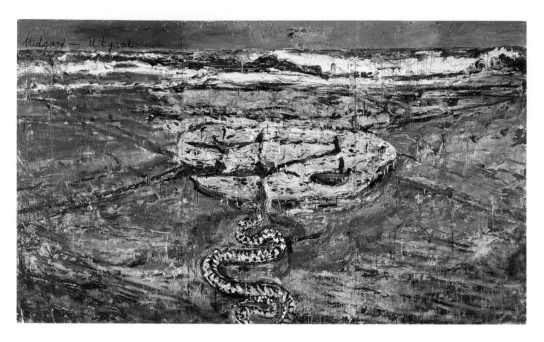

18.15 Anselm Kiefer, *Midgard*, 1980–5. Oil and emulsion on canvas, 11 ft 10 ins x 19 ft 9 3/4 ins (3.6 x 6.04 m). Carnegie Museum of Art, Pittsburgh.

German artist Anselm Kiefer (b. 1945) invests his work with strong emotive and empathetic content. In *Midgard* (Fig. **18.15**), he draws upon Nordic mythology to portray a desolate landscape of despair. "Midgard" means "middle garden," the term given by the Norse gods to the earth. In Nordic myth, the earth is destroyed by the Midgard serpent and other demons after three years of winter. Standing before this enormous painting, we find its scale and emotional power profoundly affecting. It takes up our whole field of vision and seems to surround us.

CRITICAL
REVIEW
below

PRIMARY STRUCTURES

CRITICAL
LOOK
p. 603

The "primary structures" movement pursues two major goals: extreme simplicity of shapes and a kinship with architecture. A space–time relationship distinguishes primary structures from other sculpture. Viewers are invited to share an experience in three-dimensional space in which they can walk around and/or through the works. Form and content are reduced to their most "minimal" qualities.

Cubi XIX (Fig. **18.16**) by David Smith (1906–65) rises to nearly 10 feet (3 meters), and its seemingly precarious balance and its curious single cylinder convey a sense of urgency. Yet the work is in perfect balance. The texture of the luminescent stainless steel has a powerfully tactile effect, yet it also creates a shimmering, almost impressionistic play of light. The forms are simple rectangles, squares, and a cylinder, and scale gives them a vital importance.

Louise Nevelson (1900–88) overcame the notion that sculpture was a man's profession because it involved heavy manual labor and became perhaps the first major

A CRITICAL REVIEW

Some of the fundamental issues we have just covered include differences among abstract, nonobjective, and conceptual art. Each of these approaches places the artwork in a different position between the artist and the respondent. In abstract works visual effects are derived from objects in the "real world" but have been simplified or rearranged to satisfy the artists' purposes. The content in nonobjective art is wholly subjective or invented, and the ability to respond to art *form* is an absolute must, whereas in conceptual art the idea behind the work is foremost and the product is somehow negligible.

Is an actual work of art necessary for aesthetic communication between artist and respondent? Use specific examples from the text to support your conclusions.

Using "communication" as your yardstick, compare Jackson Pollock's Number 1 with Roy Lichtenstein's Whaam!

A CRITICAL LOOK

In the world of sculpture and architecture during the last fifty years, the titles of styles and movements carry intriguing implications. In the next sections we will examine "primary structures," "found" and "junk culture," video art, modernism, and postmodernism, to name a few. We move beyond keeping straight the titles, works, and artists to deeper questions about what it is that these artists are trying to do with their art and to us, the viewers.

Like some abstract expressionist painting, much contemporary sculpture rejects traditional materials in favor of new ones. In particular, it favors materials that do not require molds or models. Inventive shapes have severed sculpture, as far as is possible, from the natural world. Even so, abstract sculpture often has titles that link nonobjective expression to objective associations.

Analyze Louise Nevelson's Black Wall and America—Dawn as examples of the primary structures movement.

Identify the characteristics and describe the differences among the styles of abstraction, found and junk culture, and minimalism.

Explain the differences between architectural modernism and postmodernism and identify architects and works representative of each style.

woman sculptor of the twentieth century. In the 1950s Nevelson began using found pieces of wood as her medium. At first miniature cityscapes, her work grew larger and larger. Painted a monochromatic flat black, *Black Wall* (see Fig. 18.1) is a relief-like wall unit, whose pieces suggest the world of dreams. Their meaning remains a puzzle, although they make an intense appeal to the imagination.

Her *America—Dawn* (Fig. 18.17) is similarly ambivalent. The decoration on her ivory-colored wooden blocks seems to have a primitive, mythic quality, but on the other hand one also senses the busy organization and sheer modernity of a circuit board or a complex machine. A Stonehenge or a city of skyscrapers?

ABSTRACTION

Less concerned with expressive content than other sculptors, Isamu Noguchi (1904–88) began experimenting with abstract sculptural design in the 1930s. His creations have gone beyond sculpture to provide highly dynamic and suggestive set designs for the choreography of Martha Graham, with whom he was associated for a number of years. Noguchi's *Kouros* figures (Fig. 18.18) do seem to be abstractly related to archaic Greek sculpture, and they too exhibit exquisitely finished surfaces and masterly technique.

Another kind of abstraction of the human form appears in *Sphere with Internal Form* (Fig. 18.19). Here

18.16 David Smith, *Cubi XIX*, 1964. Stainless steel, 9 ft 5 ins (2.87 m) high. Tate Gallery, London.

18.17 Louise Nevelson, *America—Dawn*, 1962. Painted wood, 18 x 14 x 10 ft (5.49 x 4.27 x 3.05 m). Art Institute of Chicago (Grant J. Pick Purchase Fund, 1967, 387).

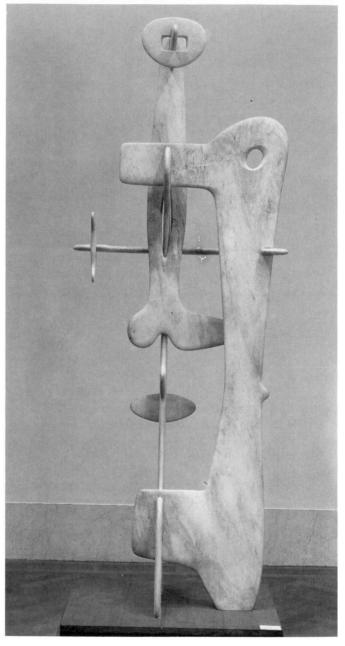

18.18 Isamu Noguchi, *Kouros* (in nine parts), 1944–5. Pink Georgia marble, slate base, c. 9 ft 9 ins (2.97 m) high. Metropolitan Museum of Art, New York (Fletcher Fund, 1953).

18.19 Dame Barbara Hepworth, *Sphere with Internal Form*, 1963. Bronze, 3 ft 4 ins (1.02 m) high. Collection, State Museum Kröller-Müller, Otterlo, The Netherlands.

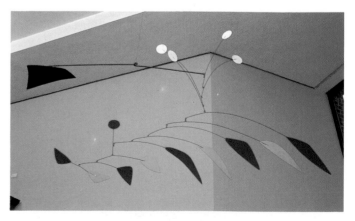

18.20 Alexander Calder, *Spring Blossoms*, 1965. Painted metal and heavy wire, 4 ft 4 ins (1.32 m) high. Museum of Art, Pennsylvania State University.

Barbara Hepworth (1903–75) incorporates two sculptural devices—a small form resting inside a large, enclosing form, and the piercing of the form. Piercing gives the piece a sense of activity, as it admits light into the work and provides tonal contrasts.

The MOBILES of Alexander Calder (1898–1976) (Fig. **18.20**) finally put abstract sculpture into motion. Deceptively simple, these colorful shapes turn with the slightest air currents or by motors. Calder's pieces show us that sculpture can be created by the movement of forms in undefined space.

The figures of Alberto Giacometti (1901–66) mark a return to objectivity. Giacometti was a surrealist sculptor

18.21 Alberto Giacometti, *Man Pointing*, 1947. Bronze, 6 ft 8½ ins (1.79 m) high. Museum of Modern Art, New York (Gift of Mrs John D. Rockefeller III).

in the 1930s, but he continued to explore the likeness of the human figure and the depiction of surface, as Figure **18.21** shows. Here form is reduced to its essence. The tortured fragmentation of the figure makes an emotional statement about what it feels like to be human in the contemporary world.

FOUND SCULPTURE AND JUNK CULTURE

Yet another approach to have emerged since World War II is found sculpture—that is, objects taken from life and presented as art for their inherent aesthetic value and meaning. Perhaps developed out of cubist collages, the movement called "junk culture" also took natural objects and assembled them to create single artworks. Interpretations of this kind of assemblage art vary widely, but they usually imply that the artist is making some value judgment on a culture to which built-in obsolescence and throwaway materials are fundamental.

MINIMALISM

In the late 1950s and 1960s a style called "minimalism" in painting and sculpture sought to reduce the complexity of both design and content as far as possible. Instead, minimalist artists concentrated on nonsensual, impersonal, geometric shapes and forms. No communication was to pass between artist and respondent, no message was to be conveyed. Rather, the minimalists, such as Toby Smith, wanted to present neutral objects free of their own interpretations and leave response and "meaning" entirely up to the viewer.

LIGHT ART

Since the 1960s the use of light as an element in sculpture has gained in popularity. Its adherents see light as an independent aesthetic medium, and they use it in a variety of innovative ways.

Typical of artists working with light, (Varda) Chryssa (b. 1933) creates technically precise blinking neon sculptures using very simple shapes. Neon, so indicative of the commercialism and mechanization of modern life, serves as a symbolic comment on the modern era. Chryssa's innovative constructions, such as *Fragments for the Gates to Times Square* (Fig. **18.22**), explore the experience of contemporary technology. His works also explore environmental space in a highly theatrical fashion, in this case surrounding the viewer with a garish ambience like that of Times Square or the Las Vegas Strip.

18.22 Chryssa, *Fragments for the Gates to Times Square*, 1966. Neon and plexiglas, 6 ft 9 ins x 2 ft 10½ ins x 2 ft 3½ ins (206 x 88 x 70 cm). Whitney Museum of American Art, New York (Gift of Howard and Jean Lipman).

18.23 Jean Dubuffet, *Jardin d'Émail*, 1973–4. Concrete, epoxy paint, and polyurethane, 66 ft 8 ins x 100 ft (20 x 30 m). State Museum Kröller-Müller, Otterlo, The Netherlands.

18.24 Robert Smithson, *Spiral Jetty*, 1969–70. Black rock, salt crystals, earth, and red water (algae), 160 ft (48.7 m) diameter; coil 1500 ft (457 m) long and 15 ft (4.6 m) wide. Great Salt Lake, Utah.

EPHEMERAL AND ENVIRONMENTAL ART

Ephemeral art has many possible justifications. The conceptualists, for example, insist that "art is an activity of change, of disorientation and shift, of violent discontinuity and mutability."

Environmental art sets out to create an inclusive experience. In the *Jardin d'Émail* by Jean Dubuffet (b. 1901) (Fig. **18.23**), an area made of concrete is painted with white paint and black lines. Surrounded by high walls, the whole construction is capricious in form. Inside the sculptural environment we find a tree and two bushes of polyurethane. Here Dubuffet has tried to push the boundaries of art to their known limits, perhaps. He has consistently opted for chaos, for *art brut*—the art of children, psychotics, and amateurs. The *Jardin d'Émail* is one of several projects in which he has explored this chaotic, disorienting, and inexplicable three-dimensional form.

The dynamic and dramatic landscape of *Spiral Jetty* (Fig. **18.24**) by Robert Smithson (1928–73), in the Great Salt Lake of Utah, is another example of environmental art. A number of concepts and ideas are represented here. The spiral shape represents the early Mormon belief that the Great Salt Lake was connected to the Pacific Ocean by an underground canal, which from time to time caused great whirlpools on the lake's surface. In addition, the jetty is intended to change the quality and color of the water around it, thereby creating a color-shift, as well as making a linear statement. Finally, the design is meant to be ephemeral as well as environmental. Smithson knew that eventually the forces of wind and water would transform, if not obliterate, the project. And, in fact, high water has submerged the jetty in recent years.

Designed to be transitory, ephemeral art makes its statement, then ceases to exist. Undoubtedly the largest works of sculpture ever designed were based on that concept. *The Umbrellas, Japan–USA, 1984–91* (Fig. **18.25 A** and **B**, p. 609) by Christo (Christo Jachareff, b. 1935) was an event and a process, as well as a sculptural work. In a sense, Christo's works are conceptual in that they call attention to the experience of art, rather than any actual permanent form. At the end of a short viewing period, *The Umbrellas* were removed and ceased to be.

Robert Smithson (1928–73)

Visual artist Robert Smithson grew up in Passaic, New Jersey, and when he was young he built a small museum in the basement of his home for his collection of minerals and shells. He particularly liked rocks and fossils, and the earth and its contents dominated his interest and, later, manifested itself in his art. During his senior year in high school, he commuted to New York City on Saturdays to attend classes at the Art Students League. These Saturday sessions comprised his only formal art education. He spent six months in the army, hitchhiked around the country, and then moved to New York City. Working in the minimalist tradition, he enjoyed early success, but not much satisfaction, so he turned away from minimalism, withdrew from the New York scene, and began studying crystalline structures and organic processes. As a result, he realized that he was interested not merely in the finished product of art but also in the on-going process of a work of art.

Smithson became attracted to Frederick Law Olmstead, a turn-of-the-century landscape architect and designer of New York's Central Park. Particularly important was Smithson's realization that Central Park was not a "thing to look at" but a process to enter into and experience. Also, it was accessible to everyone. As a result, Smithson developed an interest in working directly with nature. He studied ecosystems, archeology, geology, evolution, and organic processes and incorporated them into his work (see Fig. **18.24**). He created earthworks and thought of them as meditations on the role that art could play in our ability to understand ourselves and our environment. His work sought to show us that there was a price to pay for everything: something was gained and something was lost. An optimist, he saw decay and ugliness as essentially positive elements that merely awaited an artist's transforming vision.

More importantly, he visualized a new role for the viewer—that is, a direct experience of the earth and a contemplation of the contemporary landscape. Smithson's intense dislike of the gallery experience of art led to his involvement in "land art." He believed that most contemporary art was myopically self-centered and overly specialized, and that it lacked the intellect and ability to engage viewers in a dialogue about the contemporary world. He wanted a new, more public art that would raise issues and give new realizations about ugliness and beauty, progress and destruction. As a result, Robert Smithson's art became public and accessible to anyone. Likewise, it could never be "owned"—only understood.

He referred to his early pieces as "non-sites." Usually each one consisted of a topographical map mounted on the wall, with a rock-filled metal bin directly below it. He gathered materials from the spot indicated on the map and brought them to the gallery to reveal the relationship between the map—or "concept"— and the reality of the natural objects. His later work is based on geologic time and randomness. Order and disorder, disintegration, and reconstruction reflected the workings of the universe and life itself.

Although he was killed in a plane crash in 1973, his work and ideas continue to exert a strong influence on the way artists shape and viewers respond to art and nature.

INSTALLATIONS

"Environments" which have been expanded into room-size settings are now called "installations." The installations of Judy Pfaff (b. 1946) employ a variety of materials, including those of painting, in order to shape and charge architectural space. The art historian H.W. Janson likens her work to "exotic indoor landscapes," and finds her spontaneous energy similar to that of Jackson Pollock's action painting (see Fig. **18.3**). Nature seems to have inspired her installation *Dragons* (Fig. **18.26**). Swirling tendrils hang like brightly colored jungle foliage. Fiery reds predominate, although Pfaff uses the entire color spectrum. All this stands out against the white walls of the room. The sweeping diagonals seem carefully juxtaposed against linear verticals while, at the same time, a jumble of stringlike things in the far corner emanates confusion. The strong colors and proliferation of lines suggest that paint has been flung into space and, magically, suspended there.

POSTMODERNISM

The period from the late 1960s through the 1980s witnessed a variety of mostly individualistic reactions to the

18.25 A and **B** Christo, *The Umbrellas, Japan–USA, 1984–91*. (A) Valley north of Los Angeles, CA, 1,760 yellow umbrellas; (B) Valley in prefecture of Ibaraki, Japan, 1,340 blue umbrellas. Combined length: 30 miles (48 km) © Christo 1991.

18.26 Judy Pfaff, *Dragons*, mixed media. Installation view at 1981 biennial, Whitney Museum of American Art, New York.

styles of the past—including the recent past of the twentieth century. Like the collective styles of the end of the nineteenth century, which were called post-impressionist, these "new" styles, which seem to have no common thread, have been lumped together as postmodernist styles. They are highly individualistic, although some artists prefer to return art to the anonymity of pre-Renaissance times. One recognizable aspect of the postmodernist styles appears to be a desire to return recognizable content or meaning to works of art, and the artists following these paths were reacting to what they felt was a clutter and lack of content in previous styles. To recount our earlier attribution from Ezra Pound, these artists sought to "make it new" and took great pains to be "different." The question of difference, however, became complicated by the fact that many, like the postmodernist architects, took great delight in eclectically borrowing from the past. They mixed old styles to create something "new."

One artist who can represent this melange of styles is the sculptor Joel Shapiro. He was born, raised, and educated in New York, and his art gradually evolved into the production of miniature clay, glass, copper and lead works shaped objectively. One particular aspect of his

18.27 Joel Shapiro, *Untitled*, 1980–1. Bronze, 4 ft 4⁷/₈ ins x 5 ft 4 ins x 3 ft 9¹/₂ ins (1.34 x 1.62 x 1.15 m). Collection of the Whitney Museum of American Art, New York.

18.28 Lynda Benglis, *Passat*, 1990. Aluminum, 78 x 52 x 27 ins (198 x 132 x 68.5 cm). Paula Cooper Gallery, New York (Photograph by Douglas Parker) © Lynda Benglis/DACS, London/VAGA, New York, 1994.

works illustrates the art of the 1980s—that is, the use of a variety of media and techniques, some of which are new and require new techniques. The mixture of media in previously untried ways provides new avenues of experimentation and mastery as well as providing works of art that have a different appearance from those of the past. Shapiro's works graduated from clusters of small geometric pieces—spread out on the floors of galleries in which the actual space in which they were assembled became an important element—to large-scale stick figures exhibiting precarious balance such as *Untitled* (Fig. **18.27**).[3] It is cast in metal but retains the texture and apparent construction methods of the wood from which it was originally constructed.

NEO-ABSTRACTION

By the mid-1980s other young artists sought to make their mark by reacting against the postmodernist trends. Their work returned to abstract and near-abstract works, including hard edge. These neo-abstractionists, like the postmodernists, make up a loose confederation of mostly individualistic approaches. Like the postmodernists, the neo-abstractionists borrow freely from others by modifying or changing the scale, media, or color of older works to give them a new framework and, hence, new meaning. Occasionally, the new meanings include sarcasm and satire and often comment on the decadence of American society in the 1980s. An example is the work of Lynda Benglis, a painter who turned to sculpture. Her work also

represents process art—that is, taking molten materials, letting them flow freely on the floor, and then adding color and/or shape to them. *Passat* (Fig. **18.28**) illustrates her recent work, in which she shapes knots, bows, and pleats insectlike sculptures in shiny metal.

VIDEO ART

What next? Is television our next art medium? *Video Composition X* by Nam June Paik (b. 1932) turned a large room into a garden of shrubbery, ferns, and small trees. As one looked up from the greenery, thirty television sets were all running the same program in unison. Bill Viola's *He Weeps for You* featured a drop of water forming at the end of a thin copper pipe and then falling on a drumhead. The image was blown up on a large television screen, and the sound of the falling drop was amplified into a thunderous boom. MIT's *Centerbeam* was a 220-foot (67-meter) long contraption using holograms, video, colored steam, and laser beams.

In fact, a wide-ranging genre of sculpture called "video art" has emerged from the rebellions of the 1960s as a reaction against conventional broadcast television. Since then, inexpensive portable recording and playback video equipment has made it possible for this art form to flourish. Video art has moved from a nearly photojournalistic form to one in which outlandish experiments exploit new dimensions in hardware and imagery.

Nam June Paik is perhaps the most prominent of the video artists. His work pioneered the use of television went before. The continuing careers of architects who had achieved significant accomplishment before the war soon bridged the gap, however. The focus of new building shifted from Europe to the United States, Japan, and even South America. The overall approach still remained modern, or international, in flavor.

A resurgence of skyscraper building occurred in the 1950s. Lever House (1951–2) in New York City (Fig. **18.30**) illustrates the glass-and-steel box approach that began then and continues today. A very important consideration in this design is the open space surrounding the tower. Created by setting the tower back from the perimeter of the site, the open space around the building creates its own envelope of environment, or its context. Reactions against, and alternatives to, the all-over glazing of the Lever Building have occurred throughout the last forty years—aluminum surfaces pierced by small windows, for example. An intensification of the glazed exterior has also taken place, where metalized rather than normal glass forms the surface. Such an approach has

18.29 Nam June Paik, *TV Bra for Living Sculpture*, 1969. Performance by Charlotte Moorman with television sets and cello. Courtesy Holly Solomon Gallery, New York.

18.30 Gordon Bunshaft (Skidmore, Owings, and Merrill), Lever House, New York, 1950–2.

imagery in performance and other multimedia art. It takes television well beyond its primary function of reproducing imagery. Indeed, Nam June Paik's video art creates its own imagery. In *TV Bra for Living Sculpture* (Fig. **18.29**), he creates interactive images of a performance of classical music and miniature televisions with their own images. The combined video and live situations function as a third, overriding experience. The effect is bizarre, startling, fascinating, and, unlike the moment captured in the illustration, constantly changing.

ARCHITECTURAL MODERNISM

In a sense, the task of evaluating contemporary architecture is the most difficult of all the arts. In our day the human element in artistic creation has been blurred by the contributions of architectural firms rather than individual architects. In addition, the contemporary observer sees a sameness in the glass and steel boxes of the International Style that dominate our cities and easily misses some truly unique approach to design that is visible in some housing project in an obscure location.

The ten-year break in architectural construction during World War II separated what came after from what

been particularly popular in the Sun Belt, because metalized glass reflects the sun's rays and their heat. Whatever materials are used on the façade, however, the functional, plain rectangle of the International Style has continued as a standard architectural form.

The rectangle, which has so uniformly and in many cases thoughtlessly become the mark of contemporary architecture, leads us to the architect who, before World War II, was among its advocates. Ludwig Mies van der Rohe (1886–1969) insisted that form should not be an end in itself but that the architect should discover and state the function of the building. Mies pursued those goals, taking mass-produced materials—bricks, glass, and manufactured metals—at their face value and expressing their shapes honestly. This was the basis for the rectangularization that is the common ground of twentieth-century architecture. His search for proportional perfection can be traced, perhaps, back to the German Pavilion of the Barcelona Exposition in 1929, and it was consummated in large-scale projects such as New York's Seagram Building (Fig. **18.31**).

The simple straight line and functional structure that were basic to Mies' vision were easily imitated and readily reproduced. This multiplication of steel and glass boxes, however, has not overshadowed exploration of other forms. Contemporary design has ultimately answered in various ways the question put by Louis I. Kahn, "What form does the space want to become?"

In the case of Frank Lloyd Wright's Guggenheim Museum (Fig. **18.32**), space has become a relaxing spiral that reflects the leisurely progress one should make through an art museum. Eero Saarinen's Trans-World Airline Terminal emulates the shape of flight in its curved lines and spaces, carefully designed to accommodate large masses of people and channel them to and from waiting aircraft. (Shapes like this can be executed only using modern construction techniques and materials such as reinforced concrete.) Le Corbusier's dynamic church, Notre Dame du Haut (Fig. **18.33**), which is more like a piece of sculpture than a building, also suggests flight. The function of this pilgrimage church cannot easily be surmised from its form. Rather, the juxtaposed rectilinear windows and curvilinear walls and the overwhelming roof nestled lightly on thin pillars above the walls appear a "pure creation of the spirit."

Two other noteworthy architects have their own signatures, the arch of Pier Luigi Nervi (1891–1979), and the dome of Richard Buckminster Fuller (1895–1983). The unencumbered free space of their work contrasts sharply with the self-contained boxes of the International Style. Nervi's Small Sports Palace (Fig. **18.34**) and Fuller's

18.31 Mies van der Rohe and Philip Johnson, Seagram Building, New York, 1958.

18.32 Frank Lloyd Wright, Solomon R. Guggenheim
Museum, New York, 1942–59.

18.33 Le Corbusier, Notre Dame du Haut, Ronchamp,
France, 1950–4, from the southeast.

18.34 Pier Luigi Nervi, Small Sports Palace, Rome, 1957.

18.35 Richard Buckminster Fuller, Climatron, St Louis, 1959.

18.36 Ricardo Bofill, Palace of Abraxas, Marne-la-Vallée, near Paris, 1978–83.

Climatron (Fig. **18.35**) illustrate the practical need for free space. They also illustrate the trend toward spansion architecture, which stretches engineering to the limits of its materials. (In the case of the Kansas City Hyatt Regency Hotel a spansion design went beyond practicality, with tragic results.)

ARCHITECTURAL POSTMODERNISM

Beyond these trends, contemporary architecture has been pluralistic. Postmodern, or "revisionist," architecture takes past styles and does something new with them. The Spanish architect Ricardo Bofill (b. 1939) and the Italian Aldo Rossi (b. 1931) both derive much of their architectural language from the past. As Bofill remarked, his architecture takes "without copying, different themes from the past, but in an eclectic manner, seizing certain moments in history and juxtaposing them, thereby prefiguring a new epoch." We see this eclectic juxtaposition in

his public housing development called, with typical grandiosity, the Palace of Abraxas (Fig. **18.36**). Here columnar verticality is suggested by glass bays and by the cornice/capitals over them which give the appearance of a dynamic classicism. In Japan, postmodern architects such as Arata Isozaki (b. 1931) portray in their buildings the restrained elegance and style of traditional Japanese art. In the United States, Michael Graves (b. 1934) has reacted to the repetitive glass, concrete, and steel boxes of the International Style by creating a metaphorical allusion to the keystone of the Roman arch (Fig. **18.37**). The bright red pilasters suggest fluted columns, and fiberglass garlands recall both art deco and rococo.

Postmodern architecture focuses on meaning and symbolism, and it embraces the past. The postmodernist seeks to create buildings "in the fuller context of society and the environment." Function no longer dictates form, and ornamentation is acceptable. The goals of postmodern architecture are social identity, cultural continuity, and sense of place.

Another clear repudiation of the glass-and-steel box

18.37 (*left*) Michael Graves, Portland Public Office Building, Portland, Oregon, 1979–82.

18.38 Renzo Piano and Richard Rogers, Pompidou Center, Paris, 1971–8.

18.39 Charles Moore, Piazza d'Italia, New Orleans, 1978–9.

of the International Style and other popular forms in mainstream architecture can be seen in the design for the Pompidou Center in Paris (Fig. **18.38**). Here the building is turned inside out, with its network of ducts, pipes, and elevators color-coded and externalized, and its internal structure hidden. The interior spaces have no fixed walls, but temporary dividers can be arranged in any configuration that is wanted. The bright primary colors on the exterior combine with the serpentine, plexiglass-covered escalators to give a whimsical, lively appearance to a functional building. The Pompidou Center has become a tourist attraction rivaling the Eiffel Tower, and, while controversial, it has gained wide popular acceptance.

The highly colorful Piazza d'Italia (Fig. **18.39**), designed for the Italian-American community in New Orleans, comes alive at night with neon lighting that complements its columns, its temple front, and its fountain that spills out onto a map of Italy. The architect, Charles Moore (b. 1925), was inspired by his conception of the "American dream," which he found embodied in Disneyland, and he applied that idea to this project.

CRITICAL REVIEW below

A CRITICAL REVIEW

In the world of sculpture—whose parameters seem stretched by the examples we have seen in this section—questions of permanent versus ephemeral art arise frequently. In the material we have just studied, a continuum has been exposed. At one end is sculpture that has constant and permanent form, while at the other end is sculpture that is put up for a short period and is then removed. Somewhere in the middle is sculpture that is permanent but is intended to change at the whims of nature.

We have moved out of the modern era into a postmodern era—we may, indeed, already be out of that and into something else.

Explain the characteristics of light art, ephemeral and environmental art, and video art, and identify the artists and works that represent each.

Choose one work of each style and write a comparative analysis based on use of line, form, texture, proportion, and scale.

A CRITICAL LOOK	In the next two sections, which cover literature and music, we will

meet a number of contemporary writers and composers who, true to the pluralistic nature of the age, take a variety of approaches to their art. These artists come from around the world and represent a variety of traditions. In this regard, we are stepping outside of our avowed purpose—that is, pursuit of the Western tradition—without putting in feature boxes the non-Western materials. During the last fifty years the world has become so interwoven in many of its traditions, and the Western tradition has become so pervasive, that separating traditions becomes more and more difficult—perhaps, indeed, futile. In any case, this material is true to the title of this chapter: it represents the pluralistic nature of the world we now live in.

Describe the works of writers like Joseph Heller, R.K. Narayan, Alice Walker, Yasunari Kawabata, and Alexander Solzhenitsyn.

Explain the musical terms serialism, aleatory, improvisation, electronic music, and pop music.

Identify major musical composers linked to these styles and others, and describe their works.

PLURALISM IN LITERATURE

ITICAL LOOK above

In the field of literature, "schools, movements, and ideologies have not only proliferated but fragmented in the last decades, with a restlessness born of a nagging dissatisfaction with the reigning modes," particularly in America. Pluralism abounds. In fiction we find naturalism and realism, novels of manners, Southern fiction, Jewish fiction, black fiction, Western fiction, the beats, and metafiction. In poetry we find formalist/academic poets, black mountainists, San Francisco/beats, confessionalists, the New York poets, deep imagists, black poets and the independents. This wide-ranging nature of literature of the late twentieth century makes it impossible for us to do more than glance at a few luminaries. The age has been beset, at least briefly, by an approach to literary criticism called "deconstruction," which attempted to remove meaning from the work. Nonetheless, amid the clamor of the times, we can find a cross-section of genres and styles, written by authors from every continent.

Following the horrors of World War II, various media have been used to try to document the inhumanity of Nazism, from documentary film and harrowing nonfiction to the short stories and novels of writers such as Elie Wiesel (b. 1928). Wiesel is a European Jew who survived incarceration in a concentration camp, and in his very moving autobiographical novel *Night* (1960) one gets a strong impression of the conflict between faith and human evil.

The American novelist Joseph Heller (b. 1923) also writes about the dreadful impact of modern warfare, but in a completely different style. Heller attacks it with black humor, satire, and a surrealistic streak that juxtaposes sit-

uations in bizarre ways. His most famous work is *Catch-22*, which pokes fun at bureaucracy as well as war.

India's foremost contemporary novelist, R.K. Narayan (b. 1906), writes in English for an international audience, and centers his fiction around middle-class life in southern India, painting a sympathetic but gently humorous portrait of social change, the struggle for identity, and the conflicts between generations.

Wit and irony are tools used by black American author Alice Walker (b. 1944) in her novels, poetry, and critical writings. The battles she fights are for rights for blacks and women. However, she is prone to satirize political activists just as much as their opponents. Her life and writings reflect the tensions and ideals of a "womanist," a word she coined for a black feminist. Her work focuses on what she calls the "twin afflictions" of the civil rights and black power movements and the women's movement. However, she pursues a larger purpose in chronicling the fortunes of black Americans during the twentieth century—for example, *The Color Purple*, which spans the period 1920–42.

Walker came from a family of Georgia sharecroppers and was one of eight children. Because a childhood accident left her blind in one eye, she was able to attend Spelman College, a prestigious black women's college in Atlanta, on a state rehabilitation scholarship, and she continued her education at Sarah Lawrence, New York, graduating in 1965. Her identity as a black and a woman were challenged by an unwanted pregnancy, an abortion, and a trip to Africa. She wrote of these in her first published work of poetry, *Once* (1968). She returned to the South and married a Jewish civil rights leader, from whom she was divorced in 1976.

In addition to her novels, her short stories indicate a preoccupation with the "oppressions, the insanities, the loyalties, and the triumphs of black women," in which she documents a variety of black women. Some of her works are highly controversial and deal with topics like abortion, sadomasochism, and interracial rape—for example, "Advancing Luna."

Yasunari Kawabata, a Japanese novelist (1899–1972) won the 1968 Nobel Prize for literature for a series of poetic novels in which he explored the nature of love and the alienation of the individual. His best known novel is *Snow Country* (*Yukiguni,* 1947), which describes the passions of a country geisha and the alienated state of one of her lovers. *The Master of Go* (1972) portrays a six-month championship match of the ancient Japanese game of Go, in which a brash young challenger defeats an elderly, tradition-bound master, thereby illustrating the tragic difference in sensibility between the young and the old. Kawabata was deeply influenced by the symbolists (see page 545) and traveled and lectured widely in the West. He committed suicide in 1972.

Alexander I. Solzhenitsyn (b. 1918) is a Russian novelist and playwright. His fame gained impetus from his anti-Stalinist writings, particularly *One Day in the Life of Ivan Denisovich* (1962), and his other works, published in the United States, were not published in the Soviet Union under the communist regime. *August 1914*, in which he vociferously explores Russian participation in World War I, has tremendous sweep, power, and compassion. Solzhenitsyn was imprisoned after war service for an alleged slur on Stalin, and his subsequent work focused on the Soviet prison system, on which he writes with extremely human sensitivity and insight. He was expelled from the Soviet Writers' Union in 1969 because of his "radical" views. He defined these views in his undelivered acceptance speech for the 1970 Nobel Prize for literature: the indivisibility of truth and the "perception of world literature as the one great heart which beats for the concerns and misfortunes of our world."

Another Russian, the poet Vevgeny Alexandrovich Yevtushenko (b. 1933), has become the spokesman for the younger generation of Russian poets, and his autobiographical work "Zima Junction" (1953), made him instantly famous and popular. He writes with a lyric tone of such quality that many of his poems have been set to music. His autobiography deals with the social and personal themes surrounding the important year 1953, when Stalin died, and he looks back on the past as it affects his present sensibilities on his return to his childhood home in Siberia (Zima). Yevtushenko's insights reveal a passionate love of his country and hopes for its future, his honesty, his sense of moral justice, and his refusal to be silenced by political dogma.

From the Middle East, the age of pluralism has produced women writers of great vision and courage. Fawziyya Abu-Khalid (b. 1955) came from a Westernized upper-middle-class family in Saudi Arabia. Her earliest poems, written when she was a young girl, were published in the local newspaper and were included in her first volume of poetry, published in Lebanon. Included in that volume was a poem with the provocative title "Until When Will They Go on Raping You on Your Wedding Night?" It was banned in Saudi Arabia.

One of the few popular poets to emerge from the United Arab Emirates is Zabyah Khamis (b. c. 1958). In 1987 she was arrested briefly by the security police apparently because of several articles, including one on the status of women, and poems she had written that were critical of the UAE authorities. No charges were ever filed, but her arrest came amid a general clampdown of freedom of expression in several Gulf countries at the time. Among her recent collections are *Qasa'id Hubb* (*Love Odes*), which are written in traditional rhymes and meters.

MUSIC

After World War II music developed along several distinctly different lines, and the different schools became further polarized. Two general directions have been taken, one toward control and formality, and the other toward less control to the point of randomness and total improvisation. The serialism of Milton Babbitt (b. 1916) in America and Pierre Boulez (b. 1925) in France are clear examples of a move toward tighter control and predetermination of events. The improvisational works of Earle Brown (b. 1926) and the various approaches taken by John Cage (b. 1912) exemplify a move away from composer control, leaving decisions to performers or to chance. At the same time, a number of composers have continued in more traditional styles, which stemmed from the musical principles of Hindemith, the neoclassicism of Stravinsky and Prokofiev, and the nationalistic styles of Bartók and Copland.

SERIALISM

Postwar serialism reflects a desire to exert more control and to apply a predetermined hierarchy of values to all elements of a composition. Before the war, composers using the twelve-tone technique created a set, or row, of twelve pitches arranged in a specific order. Although the order could be manipulated in a number of ways, certain relationships between the pitches of the tone-row were constant and provided the underlying structure and much of the flavor of this style. To some extent, structural decisions were made before the actual writing of the composition itself. The composer was then subject to fairly strict limitations on the selection of pitches as the work progressed, since all pitch order was pre-established.

Proponents of the technique argued that composers

have always worked within limitations of some kind and that the discipline required to do so is an essential part of the creative problem-solving process. Opponents argued that writing music this way was more a mathematical manipulation that appealed to the intellect and less the function of a composer's ear.

Three Compositions for piano by Milton Babbitt, written in 1947–8, is one of the earliest examples of serial technique applied to elements other than pitch. In this work, rhythm and dynamics are also predetermined by serial principles.

ALEATORY MUSIC

While some composers were developing techniques and even systems of highly controlled composition in the late 1940s, others went in the opposite direction. John Cage has been a major force in the application of ALEATORY, or chance, procedures to composition with works such as *Imaginary Landscape No. 4* for twelve radios and *The Music of Changes* (1951). Cage relied on the *I Ching*, or *Book of Changes*, for a random determination of many aspects of his works. (The *I Ching*, which dates from the earliest period of Chinese literature, contains a numerical series of combinations based on the throwing of yarrow sticks—not unlike the throwing of dice or coins.) The ultimate example of chance music is a piece that could be considered non musical—Cage's *4' 33"* (1952)—in which the performer makes no sound whatever. The sounds of the hall, audience, traffic outside—that is, whatever occurs—forms the content of the composition.

Cage toured Europe in 1954 and 1958 and is thought to have influenced composers such as Boulez and Karlheinz Stockhausen to incorporate aspects of chance and indeterminacy into their music. Boulez's Third Piano Sonata and Stockhausen's *Klavierstück*, both dating from 1957, for example, give options to the performer concerning the overall form of the work or the order of specific musical fragments. But they are, for the most part, conventionally notated, and thus controlled.

IMPROVISATION

An open, improvisatory tradition was carried on by composers like Lukas Foss, who wrote a suite for soprano and orchestra that includes jazz improvisation. He founded the Improvisation Chamber Ensemble, and a number of other improvisation groups sprang up in the United States during the 1960s. During this period, there was also intense exploration of new sound possibilities using both conventional and electronic instruments.

ELECTRONIC MUSIC

The development of the SYNTHESIZER and the establishment of the Columbia-Princeton Electronics Music Center provided an opportunity for composers such as Milton Babbitt to pursue the application and further development of primarily serial techniques. Many aleatory composers found electronic sound a congenial way to achieve their musical goals of indeterminacy, as John Cage did in *Imaginary Landscape No. 5*. Mainstream and jazz composers did not pay serious attention to the electronic medium until the 1960s, however.

PLURALISM

In the 1960s and early 1970s the "ultrarational" and "antirational" schools of music went to further extremes. The desire constantly to create something new also intensified, at times superseding most other considerations. Karlheinz Stockhausen (b. 1928), for example, became more interested in the total manipulation of sound and the acoustic space in which the performance was to take place. His work *Gruppen* (1957), for three orchestras, is an early example. As he became more and more interested in timbre modulation, his composition—for example, *Microphonie I* (1964)—used more and more sound sources, both electronic and acoustic.

Elliott Carter (b. 1908) developed a highly organized approach toward rhythm often called "metric modulation" in which the mathematical principles of meter, standard rhythmic notation, and other elements are carried to complex ends. Carter's use of pitch is highly chromatic and exact, and his music requires virtuoso playing both from the individual and the ensemble.

Virtuoso playing produced an important composer–performer relationship in the 1960s, and many composers, such as Luciano Berio (b. 1925), wrote specifically for individual performers, such as trombonist Stewart Dempster. In the same vein, percussionist Max Neuhaus was associated with Stockhausen, and pianist David Tudor with John Cage.

Experimentation with MICROTONES has been of interest to composers and music theorists throughout history, and many non-Western cultures employ them routinely. Microtones can be defined as intervals smaller than a half step. The usual Western system divides the octave into twelve equal half steps. But why might the octave not be divided into twenty-four, fifty-three, ninety-five, or any number of parts? The possibilities are limited only by our ability to hear such intervals and a performer's ability to produce them. Alois Haba experimented in the early part of the century with quarter tones (twenty-four per octave) and sixth tones (thirty-six per octave) and Charles Ives did much the same thing. A number of instruments were designed to produce microtones, and experimentation and composition have been carried out widely.

Composers also questioned the limitations of the traditional concert hall. Early work by Cage and others led to theatre pieces, multimedia or mixed media pieces, so-called danger music, biomusic, soundscapes, happenings, and total environments which might include stimulation of all the senses in some way. Thus the distinctions between the composer and the playwright, the film-maker, the visual artist, and so on, were often obscured.

Since the early 1960s, electronic instruments that can be used in live performance have had a powerful influence on music composition. Live performances were mixed with prerecorded tape in the 1950s, and by the 1960s, it became common to alter the sound of live performers by electronic means. Computer technology has been added to the composition and performance of music, and the options available through computer application are now virtually endless.

Theatre music, sometimes called "experimental music," may be relatively subtle, with performers playing or singing notated music and moving to various points on the stage, as in Berio's *Circles* (1960). Or it may be more extreme, as in the works of La Monte Young, where the performer is instructed to "draw a straight line and follow it," or to exchange places with the audience. In Nam June Paik's *Homage to John Cage*, the composer ran down into the audience, cut off Cage's tie, dumped liquid over his head, and ran out of the theatre. Later he phoned with the message that the composition had ended. Needless to say, such compositions contain a considerable degree of indeterminacy.

Some works were never intended to be performed, but only conceptualized, such as Nam June Paik's *Danger Music for Dick Higgins*, which instructs the performer to "creep into the vagina of a living whale" or Robert Moran's *Composition for Piano with Pianist*, which instructs the pianist to climb into the grand piano.

There was also a return to minimal materials. Stockhausen's *Stimmung* (*Tuning*), dating from 1968, has six vocalists singing only six notes. Minimal music can be defined as music which uses very little musical material, but often for an extended length of time. *One Sound* for string quartet by Harold Budd and the electronic piece *Come Out* (1966) by Steve Reich are clear examples.

Many so-called "mainstream" composers continued writing throughout the 1960s and early 1970s. The source of much of this music is a combination of nineteenth-century Romantic tradition, the folk styles of Bartók and Copland, harmonies of Hindemith, the tonal systems of Debussy and Ravel, and the neoclassicism of Prokofiev and Stravinsky. By this period, a noticeable element of controlled indeterminacy has crept into the music, however. The late 1960s and 1970s brought a greater acceptance of varying aesthetic viewpoints and musical styles as avant-garde techniques joined the mainstream.

A similar freedom from melodic, rhythmic, and formal restraints appeared in jazz, and free jazz became the style of the 1960s. Saxophonist Ornette Coleman was one of its earliest proponents. Others, such as John Coltrane, developed a rhythmically and melodically free style based on more modal materials, while Cecil Taylor developed more chromatic music. In the mid to late sixties, Miles Davis arrived at a sophisticated blend of control and freedom in his *Bitches Brew* album of 1967. A number of musicians who originally worked with Miles Davis became leading artists in the 1970s, developing a style called "jazz-rock" or "fusion."

PENDERECKI

The Polish composer Krzysztof Penderecki (b. 1933) is widely known for instrumental and choral works, including a major composition, the *Requiem Mass* (1985). Most notably, Penderecki has experimented with techniques to produce new sounds from conventional stringed instruments.

His *Polymorphia* (1961) uses twenty-four violins, eight violas, eight cellos, and eight double basses. He has invented a whole new series of musical markings that are listed at the beginning of the score. In performance, his timings are measured by a stop watch and there is no clear meter. *Polymorphia* uses a free form, achieving its structure from textures, harmonies, and string techniques. The piece is dissonant and atonal.

It begins with a low, sustained chord. The mass of sound grows purposefully, with the entry of the upper strings, and then the middle register. Then comes a section of glissandos (slides), which can be played at any speed between two given pitches, or with what amounts to improvisation. A climax occurs, after which the sound tapers off. Then a number of pizzicato (plucked) effects are explored. Fingertips are used to tap the instruments, and the strings are hit with the palms of the hands, leading up to a second climax. After another section, in which bowed, sustained, and sliding sounds are explored, a third climax is reached. After an almost total dearth of melody and defined pitch, the work ends with a somewhat surprising C major chord.

The postwar period has been one of rapid change in its constant quest for something new—new sounds, new applications of new technology, new notation, new formal parameters, new ways of presenting music, or combining music with visual and other stimuli. This insatiable appetite for change has led to extremism among both conservative and avant-garde composers. It peaked during the 1970s, however, and, in the 1980s, it gave way to a re-evaluation and an increased tolerance of all styles as valid.

The influence of music composition for films and

PROFILE

Krzysztof Penderecki (b. 1933)

Born in Debica, Poland, composer Krzysztof Penderecki (pronounced KRIS-tov pen-der-ET-skee) won world-wide acclaim for his novel and masterful treatment of musical orchestration. In 1958 he graduated from the Superior School of Music in Krakow, Poland, and returned to the school as a professor, when his principal area of study was music composition. In the year after his graduation, he drew wide attention at the third Warsaw Festival of Contemporary Music through the performance of his piece *Strophes* for soprano, speaker, and ten instruments. One year later, two new works were premièred at the Donaueschingen Festival. One of these, *Threnody for the Victims of Hiroshima* for fifty-two strings, revealed a wonderfully skilled treatment of instrumentation using quarter-tone clusters—that is, close groupings of notes a quarter step apart. The piece also utilized glissandi (sliding pitches), faint, eerie tones produced by partial string vibrations called whistling harmonics, and other unusual effects. Since that time, his prolific works have continued to explore the wide range of musical—especially string—possibilities (see page 620 for an analysis of *Polymorphia*). Simple, linear treatments emerge from some of his compositions, and he regularly combines traditional and experimental elements. Works like the *Passion According to St Luke* resemble large baroque Passions like those of J.S. Bach. He uses a chantlike freedom of meter and the twelve-tone row—that is, ordering of the twelve notes of the chromatic scale. At the same time, he introduces aleatory (chance) elements, percussive vocal treatments, and nontraditional musical notation. He is recognized widely as a leader of the European avant-garde in music.

---

television made the era an interesting one. It brought together various styles for dramatic purposes, and used new sounds and technologies in order to appeal to a wide audience. This may well be one of the most productive new directions for music in the 1990s.

POP MUSIC

Perhaps the most pervasive cultural phenomenon of the years since World War II has been that of popular music, which forms the core of popular culture. Whether or not popular culture represents what some might see as "proper" subject matter for a text that traces the history of essentially "high" art in the Western tradition is a debate that we will leave for you and your instructors to decide. Even those who would agree that popular music represents an important genre and warrants inclusion here, may disagree about what constitutes popular music. Certainly, rock 'n' roll merits inclusion, but if we include rock 'n' roll, what of its roots in, and the continuity of, country and folk music and rhythm and blues?

Country, folk, and rhythm and blues, which are considered by many to be "the" distinctive American music, form the springboard from which came rock. Country music has become a national phenomenon, breaking out of its regional boundaries in the music of Elvis, the Byrds, the Eagles, and Linda Ronstadt among many. Even the Beatles used it for comic effect in "Act Naturally." It leapt to the charts in the early 1980s after the success of the movie *Urban Cowboy*. Nonetheless, it remains the most conservative of the popular music genres. Although basic ensembles have been electrified, they remain essentially string bands, with pickers, pluckers, and strummers. Its roots are constantly returned to by contemporary artists of each decade—for example, Waylon Jenings, Willie Nelson, Ricky Scraggs, Randy Travis, and Wynona Judd— and its abiding popularity may lie in its appeals to "traditional values."

The themes of country music emerge from its lyrics and fall into eight general categories: (1) satisfying and fulfilling love relationships, almost always depicted within the framework of marriage; (2) unsatisfactory love relationships—the most prominent theme—usually involving a marriage gone sour; (3) home and family; (4) country—that is, a state of mind and a way of life; (5) work; (6) individual worth; (7) rugged individualism; and (8) patriotism.[4]

Rhythm and blues also has a secure place in the history of rock 'n' roll. From it came the basic musical ensemble of rock, and also the beat, structure, and form of many of the songs, plus the harmonic progressions, vocal styles, and melodic and riff formulas used by rock musicians. Rhythm and blues (R & B) represents another chapter in the long history of the contribution made by American blacks to the musical tradition. In the 1960s it was called soul, which exemplifies the deep vitality, energy, and feeling that underlies this form of popular music. In addition, R&B typifies the creative impulse that lies at the heart of making music.

The remaining roots of rock 'n' roll lie in the soil of folk music, which grew from the popular music of Woody Guthrie and the Weavers in the 1940s and 1950s, and it drew the college audiences of the 1960s to music in the pioneering work of Bob Dylan and the Byrds. Folk music provided the social matrix of the political unrest of the 1960s, and it lay at the heart of the civil rights marches of the 1950s and 1960s. Today, folk music seems to have come full circle in the works of John Mellancamp, U-2, Sting, and Bruce Springsteen, who often performs "This Land is Your Land"—it all goes back to Woody Guthrie.

Guthrie has become a folk hero in many senses, and his popularity lies in the universal appeal of his humanity, love of people, and respect for the dignity of every person. He had an optimistic, "can-do" attitude toward individual ability to control one's own destiny, and he maintained that optimism until his death from Huntington's Chorea (a progressive disease of the central nervous system) in 1967.

Rock 'n' roll itself may be seen as representing the central theme of American popular music, a theme that is too vast for us to do more in this space than spotlight a few artists and trends. It all began in the 1950s with one song—Bill Haley's "Rock around the Clock." Its success and longevity were remarkable, if for no other reason than in 1957, one of the strongest years in early rock, teenagers represented only 12 percent of the total audience for popular music. In less than ten years, rock had become pervasive. However, like their forebears (and successors), the youth of the 1950s were trying to carve a niche in a world that seemed destined to come to an end in an apocalyptic nuclear holocaust. It was the age of rebels. Marlon Brando is asked in *The Wild One*, "What are you rebelling against?" He responds, "Whataya got?" Rock 'n' roll represented the music of a new order, and this carried into the social turmoil of the 1960s, with its antiwar protests and civil rights struggles in the music of Chuck Berry, Pete Townshend, and Bob Dylan, for example. Of course,

the king of rock 'n' roll was Elvis Presley, and his passion symbolized the new order. Essentially, rock 'n' roll represented a rhythmic revolution. It had a strong, rhythmic beat "that you could dance to," but there was more—themes ran from rebellion to teenage love, death, and a fascination with UFOs.

In the 1960s, the Beatles represented a changing attitude toward love, and their music ran from the innocence of "I Want to Hold Your Hand," to the emerging sexual revolution of "Norwegian Wood" and beyond to a more profound understanding in "Hey Jude." Then the Beatles told youth to "Let It Be," and the "Me Generation" was born.

In the 1970s, the Beatles broke up, and Blind Faith, and Crosby, Sills and Nash were on a course of self-destruction. Jimi Hendrix and Janis Joplin died of drug overdoses, and The Rolling Stones had the Hell's Angels as their "bodyguards." At the end of the decade, Bob Seger lamented that "The old music ain't got the same soul, Not like that old time rock 'n' roll." But the old time rock 'n' roll had fragmented. The Beatles introduced a sophisticated pop style, the Rolling Stones, the Animals, and others brought a hard rhythm and blues orientation. By the end of the decade, one could find acid rock, folk rock, country rock, art rock, punk rock, and many more.

The Me Generation, which produced James Taylor, Elton John, and Carole King, expanded popular music's language from rock to classical and jazz. But rock remained the mainstay, and that carried into the 1980s with Michael Jackson, Madonna, Prince, Bruce Springsteen, John Mellancamp, and the advent of MTV. The climate has changed, and pop and rock continue to produce a range of positions that youth culture can occupy. In fact, they have produced a cultural power and created a "youth culture." However, pop and rock music have gone beyond youth culture to permeate nearly all levels and ages of our society, perhaps because the generation that started it all still clings to rock 'n' roll as tenaciously as rock 'n' roll—through its seemingly unending permutations—clings tenaciously to each age.

CRITICAL REVIEW below

A CRITICAL REVIEW

The previous sections on literature and music have provided us with information about artists and approaches. Although we may or may not go beyond that material in class, with examples of music or readings from the literature, any critical insights we make about the literature and music of the last fifty years may be void of its actual artifacts. We can, however, comment on the relationship of pop music to its "high art" cousins, a debate we probably already have had with parents, teachers, and friends.

Debate with your classmates both sides of the question of the significance of pop music in speaking to life's fundamental questions: does it provide important answers or only emotional outbursts and escapism?

A CRITICAL LOOK

In the next sections we see how theatre and film have moved through the last fifty turbulent years. We will see novel approaches that upset previous understandings about the foundations of the art. We will note important people who have shaped and pushed their art in both traditional and avant-garde directions.

Describe the difference between theatrical realism and absurdism and identify the playwrights associated with each.

Identify and explain the major developments and practitioners in the cinema during the last fifty years.

THEATRE

REALISM

Realism flourished throughout the postwar era, most notably in the works of Tennessee Williams (1912–83) and Arthur Miller (b. 1915). Realism now included a great deal more than its nineteenth-century definition had allowed. It included more theatrical staging devices such as fragmented settings, and also many more nonrealistic literary and presentational techniques such as symbolism. As far as the theatre was concerned, stage realism and the realism of everyday life had parted company.

Tennessee Williams skillfully blended the qualities of realism with whatever scenic, structural, or symbolic devices were necessary to achieve the effects he wanted. His plays, such as *The Glass Menagerie* and *A Streetcar Named Desire*, deal sensitively with the psychological problems of common people. One of his great interests and strengths is character development, and this often carries his plays forward as he explores the tortured lives and the illusions of his larger-than-life characters.

Arthur Miller probed both the social and the psychological forces that destroy contemporary people in plays such as *Death of a Salesman*.

ABSURDISM

Following on from the work of Pirandello, Camus, and Sartre came a series of absurdists, who differed quite radically from them. While early absurdists strove to bring order out of absurdity, the plays of Samuel Beckett, Eugene Ionesco, and Jean Genet all tend to point only to the absurdity of existence and to reflect the chaos in the universe. Their plays are chaotic and ambiguous, and their absurd and ambiguous nature makes direct analysis purely a matter of interpretation. *Waiting for Godot* (1958), the most popular work of Samuel Beckett (b.

1906), has been interpreted in so many ways to suggest so many different meanings that it has become an eclectic experience in itself. Beckett, like minimalist sculptors, left it to the audience to draw whatever conclusions they wished about the work confronting them. The plays of Ionesco (b. 1912) are even more baffling, using nonsense syllables and clichés for dialogue, endless and meaningless repetition, and plots that have no development. He called *The Bald Soprano* (1950) an "antiplay." The absurdist movement has influenced other playwrights and production approaches, from Harold Pinter to Edward Albee.

PLURALISM

The great social turmoil of the late 1960s and early 1970s made its impression on the arts. It was a revolutionary period, and the theatre was deeply affected. Happenings, group gropes, and participatory performances were a new kind of theatre, performed not in traditional theatre buildings, but in streets, garages, on vacant lots and so on. Convention was ignored and traditional theatre split at the sides. Life began to imitate art, and scenes of ritualized madness seemed more like a synthesis of Brecht, Artaud, Genet, and Ionesco than real life.

Since the 1960s, theatre has remained vital because of its diversity. It still requires that the playwright bring to the theatre new works for production—in whatever style. The commercial limitations of theatre production cause great difficulty in this regard. Significant efforts, such as those of the Actors' Theatre of Louisville, are greatly responsible not only for helping new playwrights, but also for bringing new works to production, and for keeping theatre vital in areas of the United States not next door to New York City and Broadway.

The significance of these efforts can be seen in two productions: *The Gin Game* and *Agnes of God*. D.L. Coburn's *The Gin Game* emerged from the Actors' Theatre's First Festival of New Plays in 1976–7. Its story evolves around an elderly man and woman who meet in

18.40 D.L. Coburn, *The Gin Game*, The Actors' Theatre of Louisville, 1978. Georgia Healslip (left), Will Hussung (right).

18.41 John Pielmeier, *Agnes of God*, 1980. The Actors' Theatre of Louisville. Mia Dillon (left), Adale O'Brien (right).

a retirement home. The vehicle for their reviews, debates, and intimacy is an on-going card game (Fig. **18.40**). *The Gin Game* won a Pulitzer Prize in 1978 and enjoyed a successful Broadway run. John Pielmeier's *Agnes of God* (Fig. **18.41**) was produced as part of the Fourth Festival of New American Plays, 1979–80. It deals with a psychiatrist who becomes obsessed with an unusually mystical nun who has been charged with murdering her child at birth. These and other Actors' Theatre of Louisville plays, such as Beth Henley's *Crimes of the Heart* (1978–9), continued to make a significant contribution to the contemporary theatre, often finding their way to the commercial forum of Broadway and the film.

SPECTACULARISM

The 1980s saw a decline in commercial Broadway productions but a rise in regional theatre productions and stunning advances in the field of design. Training has increased technical skills and artistry (Fig. **18.42**).

No longer is the design merely the environment of the play. Now it is frequently the essence of the play, establishing its mood, rhythm, and content (Fig. **18.43**). In musicals like *Starlight Express* and *Phantom of the Opera*, the design may *be* the production. Today's designers move easily among theatre, opera, ballet, and television, and readily adapt to the locations and stage require-

ments (Fig. **18.44**). Current productions are graced by lavish settings which challenge audiences with the designer's ingenuity. Technological advances and flexibility are the keys to the preeminence of modern set design.

FILM

NEOREALISM

World War II and its aftermath brought radical change to the form and content of the cinema. A film came out in 1940 that stunned even Hollywood. Darryl Zanuck produced and John Ford directed John Steinbeck's *Grapes of Wrath*, an artistic visualization of Steinbeck's portrayal of the Depression. Here was social criticism with superb cinematography and compelling performances. Social commentary appeared again in 1941 with *How Green Was My Valley*, which dealt with exploited coal miners in Wales, and *Citizen Kane*, a grim view of wealth and power in the United States. This film, thought by some to be the best movie ever produced, blazed a new trail in its cinematic techniques. Orson Welles, its director and star, and Greg Toland, its cinematographer, brilliantly combined deep-focus photography, unique lighting effects, rapid cutting, and moving camera sequences.

As Italy recovered from World War II, a new concept

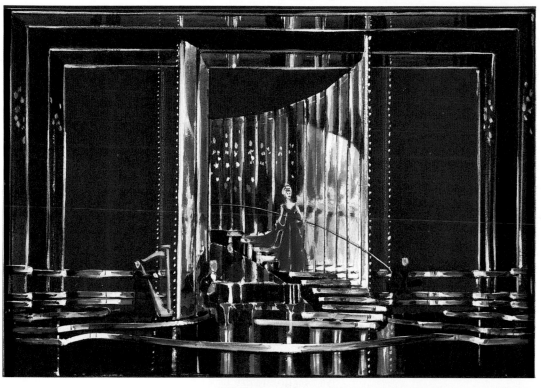

18.42 Hal Tiné, scene design for *Jerry's Girls*, National Tour, USA.

18.43 Tom Benson, scene design for *Cabaret*, Mainstage, University of Arizona, Tucson.

18.44 Peter Wexler, scene design for *The Happy Time*, Broadway Theatre, New York City.

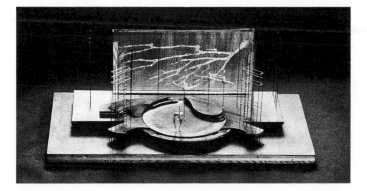

of film set the stage for many years to come. In 1945, Roberto Rossellini's *Rome, Open City* showed the misery of Rome during the German occupation. It was shot on the streets of Rome using hidden cameras and mostly non professional actors and actresses. Technically, the quality of the work was somewhat deficient, but its objective viewpoint and documentary style changed the course of cinema and inaugurated an important style called neorealism.

THE DEMISE OF THE STUDIO

The 1940s and 1950s saw a revival of musical comedies, more John Wayne, and an unforgettable genre of forgetable Saturday matinée series from *Captain Video* to *Buck Rogers*. Elvis Presley arrived on the screen in 1956, as Judy Garland left it. Elizabeth Taylor in *National Velvet* and Audrey Hepburn in *Roman Holiday* became stars. The most unforgettable actress of the period, however, was Marilyn Monroe. *The Misfits* (1962) brought her and Clark Gable together for their last film appearances.

The foreign film tradition was still dominated by neo-realism, Federico Fellini directed *La Strada* (1954) and *La Dolce Vita* (1960). The stunning artistry of Akiro Kurosawa's *Rashomon* (1951) and *Seven Samurai* (1954) penetrated the human condition to great depths or slid over its surface, and tied together East and West. Heavy Scandinavian symbolism marked the films of Sweden's Ingmar Bergman. In *The Seventh Seal*, *Wild Strawberries*, and the *Virgin Spring*, among other films, Bergman delved into human character, suffering, and motivation.

The sixties was the era of international films and of the independent producer. Studios no longer undertook programs of film production, nor did they keep stables of contract players. Now each film was an independent project whose artistic control was in the hands of the director. A new breed of film-maker came to prominence.

PLURALISM

Film has taken curious directions in the seventies and eighties. Devotees came to regard film as an art form significant enough to be studied in depth. More and more films were made for very specific and sophisticated audiences, and even movies made for commercial success have elements in them aimed at those in the know. Steven Spielberg's *Star Wars*, for example, consists of a carefully developed series of quotations from old movies and satires of them. Not recognizing these allusions does not hamper one's enjoyment of the film, but knowing about them enhances one's pleasure.

In the nineties, we do not know whether cable television and pay TV, in which first-run films are released not to movie theatres but to television outlets, will mean the end of the theatre film. Television will certainly have a significant effect on the aesthetics of film-making. Films shot for theatre screens are basically long-shot oriented, because the size of the screen enhances broad visual effects. Television, on the other hand, is a close-up medium. Its small viewing area cannot show wide-angle panoramas. Details are simply too small. Television must rely mostly on the close-up and the medium shot. Television movies must hook an audience in the first few minutes to prevent viewers from changing channels. A theatre movie can develop more slowly. Film aesthetics are already somewhat compromised. Directors with one eye on the theatre box office and the other on a lucrative pre-release to television try to meet the aesthetic requirements of both media. Only the mass marketplace will decide what the art of the cinema will be in the future, because whether it is taken to be art, entertainment, or both, cinema depends upon commercial success for its existence.

A CRITICAL REVIEW

Since World War II theatre and film have witnessed a number of changes. Some of these can be summarized and evaluated in terms of their lasting effect on the art form—for example, although absurdism was popular during the 1950s and 1960s, it has, to all intents and purposes, faded into an historical footnote. Like dada, its anti-art sentiment faded quickly. Other movements are less easy to assess. The current explosion of multimedia "performance art" pieces seems strong, but our tendency to view the art of our own times without any kind of summary judgment may not let us get the most out of it. We do not know how lasting it will be, and we will not live long enough to know whether today's art, as radical as it sometimes seems, will have a similar impact on generations two thousand years from now, as Aeschylus and Sophocles had on ours.

Pick any of the art forms discussed in these sections and write a descriptive narrative of its characteristics. Give your opinion of how well the form speaks to you. Give sound reasons for your conclusions, including an assessment of your own predilections about what art or art works should be.

SYNTHESIS
Native American and African-American Arts

The title of this chapter is An Age of Pluralism. We have already seen the wide diversity of artistic styles that the half-century since World War II has produced: some of these stretch the traditional definitions and purposes of art almost to breaking point. However, pluralism in our society, as we are well aware, includes stretching the bounds of the way Americans think of their very society itself. Whatever importance the traditional Western canon of art and literature may have, ethnicity, positively or problematically, has taken on new emphasis. In some portions of the United States, traditional "minorities" are now the majority. Culture, of whatever tradition, is part of being, and it seems fitting that, in an age of pluralism, the arts of Native Americans and African-Americans should close our text as a synthesis of what is happening in the United States at the end of the twentieth century.

Our Synthesis begins with Native American poetry, then moves to Native American ceramics, painting, and music. Following that, we study African-American popular music, specifically jazz. We close with the very strong movements in African-American theatre and literature. By separating these two ethnic traditions from the remainder of our text, which centers on the Western tradition, we do not marginalize them—rather, we point to the fact that they are significant cultural entities in and of themselves and merit considerable attention.

Pluralism in the United States has taken many foci, as we have just seen. However, in terms of cultural reality, pluralism means ethnic diversity as well. That diversity includes the contemporary artistic endeavors of both Native and African-Americans. Thus, we close our text with a brief examination of those accomplishments in contemporary American society.

NATIVE AMERICAN POETRY

In the last twenty years Native Americans have struggled to avoid succumbing to a sense of despair about their culture's demise as it is assimilated into the general American "melting pot." Writers in particular have made the assault on such feelings a major focus of their works. In 1969 Scott Momaday's novel *House Made of Dawn* won a Pulitzer Prize and made a new generation of Native American writers aware of a powerful message:

people caught between cultures can, despite a variety of problems, find ways to survive.

Paula Gunn Allen, a representative of many Native American writers, believes that Momaday's book created a new future for her: it "brought my land back to me." She believes that she and many Native Americans suffer from "land sickness"—that is, a deep sense of exile caused by the loss of their land and birthright. In the passages of *House Made of Dawn* she found that she shared a familiarity with the places Momaday described: "I knew every inch of what he was saying." It gave her the strength and inspiration—the will—to continue. In her poem "Recuerdo" she creates images of movement, loss, and of searching. She looks for a sense of "being securely planted."

NATIVE AMERICAN CERAMICS AND PAINTING

Pottery was the greatest of the prehistoric arts, and it continues today—even though it is now almost completely an aesthetic activity. Early pottery vessels, however, were designed for everyday use, and technique gave way to practical concerns—the time taken for exquisite finishing techniques was sacrificed in favor of getting the object into use. Today, clay bowls such as those made by Lucy Lewis reflect the time-honored traditions of southwest art, but they have risen in quality of finish and design to the status of high art, and thus the culture has been sustained. Other artistic forms found among these peoples include silversmithing—the popular silver and turquoise jewelry is still made—and sand painting, which incorporates important religious meanings, so that many rituals cannot be performed without it.

In addition to the traditional materials of Native American art—that is, indigenous, easily accessible materials—contemporary Native American artists also work in the media of traditional artists—for example, watercolor. In Figure **18.45**, one of the foremost Navajo painters, Harrison Begay, documents typical Native American life, in this case, women picking corn. One aspect of Native American watercolor of the middle of the century that seems fairly typical is Begay's use of space—the painting stays on the surface plane and only the important subjects are depicted, with no background being shown. We are concerned only with the women and the corn, and

18.45 Harrison Begay, *Women Picking Corn*, mid-twentieth century. Watercolor, 15 x 11½ ins (38.1 x 29.2 cm). National Museum of the American Indian, Smithsonian Institution.

no spatial environment is added. The subjects are rendered in two dimensions, and the only hint of space beyond the frontal plane—that is, three-dimensional space or perspective—is the diminutive size of the woman on the left. The horizon line, or viewer's eye level, is at the bottom of the painting.

NATIVE AMERICAN MUSIC

Native American music continues to be an important aspect of cultural reality. For example, the music of the Inuit people has developed into a highly complex art form, exhibiting complex rhythms that use contrasting accents and meters. The tonal range of melodies tends to be limited, so that changes of pitch occupy only brief distances, thus creating a gentle, undulating quality. The style of Inuit music is often declamatory—that is, it is similar to the operatic technique of recitative in Western music.

Northwest coast Native American music has a number of unique qualities. The first of these is the concept of ownership of a song—that is, only the owner of a

song can perform it. It is, however, possible to buy a song, to inherit it, or even to obtain it by murdering the owner, provided, of course, that the murderer could justify the claim. In addition, songs are owned by secret societies within the tribes. In musical terms, northwest Native American music requires part singing, and in a similar style to some African music, music of these tribes makes use of parallel harmonies and drone notes. The rhythms of this music tend toward strongly percussive and intricate patterns.

The songs of the southwest Native Americans, especially the Pueblos, reveal complex tonal arrangements. Songs are based on six- or seven-note scales and appear to keep within a rather low register—that is, the pitches stay among the low notes of the range. This is in contrast to the music of the Plains Indians, who tend to use high pitches for their music. Nearly every social occasion, holy day, and ceremony has its own special music.

AFRICAN-AMERICAN POPULAR MUSIC—JAZZ

Styles stemming from traditional jazz proliferated after World War II, when there was a gradual move away from the big bands to smaller groups and a desire for much more improvisation within the context of the compositions. The term "be-bop" was coined as a result of the characteristic long-short triplet rhythm that ended many phrases, and the prime developers of this style were alto saxophonist Charlie "Bird" Parker (Fig. **18.46**) and trumpeter Dizzie Gillespie. The Cool Jazz style developed in the early 1950s with artists like Miles Davis, and although the technical virtuosity of be-bop continued, a certain lyric quality, particularly in the slow ballads, was emphasized and, more importantly, the actual tone quality, particularly of the wind instruments, was a major distinction.

Were our space unlimited, we could look further into this African-American form and include such gifted performers as Thelonius Monk, John Coltrane, and Cecil Taylor. John Coltrane, for example, whose personality and charisma projected to black Americans in his albums *A Love Supreme*, *Ascension Meditations*, and those that followed, has had a tremendous influence on black society in the United States. These works acted as a spiritual reservoir for black people and have cast a hugely influential shadow over jazz ever since.

AFRICAN-AMERICAN THEATRE

MAINSTREAM The realistic tradition in modern theatre gave rise to a number of black, as well as white, playwrights. Garland Anderson wrote *Appearances*, the first black play to open on Broadway, in 1925. Other playwrights included Langston Hughes (1902–67), Paul Green

(1894–1981), and, most notably, Lorraine Hansberry (1930–65), whose masterful play *A Raisin in the Sun* dealt with crisis and redemption in the life of a black family on the south side of Chicago.

THE BLACK LIBERATION MOVEMENT The theatrical black liberation began in the 1960s, and continues to the present. One manifestation of the civil rights movement of the 1950s and 1960s was led by angry, militant blacks who espoused black consciousness. Many converted to the Black Muslim version of Islam, and many longed for a completely separate black nation. Radical groups talked about destroying Western society, and a number of American blacks turned toward Africa and sought a new identity in the Third World. In the 1980s, there was a change in self-description from "black" to "African-American."

Many of these ideas were expressed in the dramatic works of playwrights such as LeRoi Jones, who became Imamu Ameer Baraka (b. 1934). His theatrical visions in *Dutchman* and *A Black Mass* dramatize the dangers of blacks allowing whites into their private lives and call for racial separation. Charles Gordonne's *No Place to Be Somebody* renews Baraka's cause, and espouses violence as legitimate action in the penetrating story of a fair-skinned black searching for his own racial identity.

Many new black theatre companies also emerged in the sixties. The Negro Ensemble Company, for example, founded by Douglas Turner Ward, is one enduring example. From that company came the moving production of *Home* (1979) by Samm-Art Williams (b. 1946).

[*Home*] traces the life of a Southern black, Cephus, from his farmboy youth, through escape to the big city, draft evasion and jail, joblessness and welfare, disease and despair, to his return to the honest labor and creative values on the farm. What makes *Home* more than a typical change-of-fortune melodrama are the poetic language and the conventions of its production format. Cephus is played by a single actor, but all the other roles—old, young, male, female, black, white—are played by two women who take on whatever role they wish by a simple costume addition.... Sometimes they are characters in Cephus's odyssey, other times they act as a chorus, helping the audience to collapse time and space and see the whole of Cephus's life from the larger viewpoint of American black history and culture.... The fact that the place itself never changes, though Cephus is constantly on the move, and the fact that the actors

18.46 Saxophonist Charlie Parker in performance with Tommy Potter. Parker died prematurely in 1955, aged 35, but by that time he was already a legendary figure.

never change, though they play multitudes of different roles, suggest that "home" is right there all the time, ready to be grasped once the inner yearning is acknowledged, ready to be offered once others are willing to help, to extend themselves, to choose roles of grace instead of confrontation.[5]

The son of a white father and a black mother, August Wilson (b. 1945) writes with an ear tuned to the rhythms and patterns of the blues and the speech of the black neighborhoods. Founder of the Playwrights Center in Minneapolis, his plays range from *Jitney* (1982) to a planned series of ten plays beginning with *Ma Rainey's Black Bottom* (1984). Wilson believes that the American black has the most dramatic story of all humankind to tell. His concern lies with the stripping away of important African traditions and religious rituals from blacks by whites. In plays such as *The Piano Lesson* (1987), he portrays the complexity of African-American attitudes toward themselves and their past. The conflicts between black and white cultures and attitudes form the central core of Wilson's work and can be seen in plays such as *Fences*.

Fences treats the lives of black tenement-dwellers in Pittsburgh in the 1950s. Troy Maxson, a garbage collector, takes great pride in his ability to hold his family together and to take care of them. As the play opens, Troy discusses his challenge to the union concerning blacks' access to doing the same "easy" work as whites. He is frustrated and believes that he has been deprived of the opportunities to get what he deserves—and this becomes a central motif. He describes his wrestling match with death in 1941 when he had pneumonia, and he also tells of his days in the Negro baseball leagues because he was not allowed to play in the majors—because of his race.

AFRICAN-AMERICAN WRITERS

Earlier in the chapter, we met Alice Walker, an African-American novelist, poet, and short-story writer (see page 647). Another contemporary African-American writer is Gayl Jones (b. 1949), who grew up in the streets and segregated schools of Lexington, Kentucky. A graduate in English from Connecticut College and with two graduate degrees in writing from Brown University, she taught creative writing and African-American literature at the University of Michigan from 1975 until 1983, when she left the United States. Her writings reflect black vernacular culture and treat the terror of constant sexual warfare, the obsessive extremes of sexuality and violence, and the joining of pleasure and pain. In her work, madness is not an ailment of an individual but of society. Her first novel, *Corregidora* (1975), tells the story of Ursa Corregidora, a descendant of the incest of the Portuguese slave owner of her maternal ancestors. Her husband's violence makes her incapable of having children, and she comes to the realization that "the ritual hatred for men found in the folklore of black women overlooks the perverse longing of all human beings for their own oppression."[6] Her second novel, *Eva's Man* (1976), was no less controversial. It tells the story of a horrendous sex crime committed by a woman who has been tormented by a lifetime of masculine sexual animosity. She recounts her story from a mental asylum and reveals the origins of her madness in everyday sexual violence.

GLOSSARY

a cappella. Choral music without instrumental accompaniment.

abacus. The uppermost member of the capital of an architectural column; the slab on which the architrave rests.

absolute music. Music that is free from any reference to nonmusical ideas, such as a text or program.

abstract, abstraction. Nonrepresentational; the essence of a thing rather than its actual appearance.

absurdism. A style dealing with life's apparent meaninglessness and the difficulty or impossibility of human communication.

academy. From the grove (the Academeia) where Plato taught; the term has come to mean the cultural and artistic establishment which exercises responsibility for teaching and the maintenance of standards.

accent. In music, a stress on a note. In the visual arts, any device used to highlight or draw attention to a particular area, such as an accent color. See also *focal point*.

acoustics. The scientific study of sound and hearing.

action theatre. A contemporary phenomenon in which plays, happenings, and other types of performance are strongly committed to broad moral and social issues with the overt purpose of effecting a change for the better in society.

aerial perspective. The indication of distance in painting through use of light and color.

aesthetics. A branch of philosophy dealing with the nature of beauty and art and their relation to human experience.

affective. Relating to feelings or emotions, as opposed to facts. See *cognitive*.

aleatory. Chance or accidental. A term used for twentieth-century music in which the composer deliberately incorporates elements of chance.

allegory. Expression by means of symbols to make a more effective generalization or moral commentary about human experience than could be achieved by direct or literal means.

altarpiece. A painted or sculpted panel placed above or behind an altar to inspire religious devotion.

ambulatory. A covered passage for walking, found around the apse or choir of a church.

amphitheatre. A building, typically Roman, that is oval or circular in form and encloses a central performance area.

amphora. A two-handled vessel for storing provisions, with an opening large enough to admit a ladle, and usually fitted with a cover.

animism. The belief that objects as well as living organisms are endowed with soul.

antiphonal. A responsive style of singing or playing, in which two groups alternate.

anthropomorphic. With human characteristics attributed to nonhuman beings, or things.

apse. A large niche or niche-like space projecting from and expanding the interior space of an architectural form such as a basilica.

arcade. A series of arches side by side.

arch. In architecture, a structural system in which space is spanned by a curved member supported by two legs.

archetype. An original model or type after which other similar things are patterned.

architrave. In post-and-lintel architecture, the lintel or lowest part of the entablature, resting directly on the capitals of the columns.

aria. An elaborate solo song found primarily in operas, oratorios, and cantatas.

art song. A solo musical composition for voice, usually with piano accompaniment.

articulation. The connection of the parts of an artwork. In music or speech, the production of distinct sounds.

artifact. An object produced or shaped by human workmanship.

Art Nouveau. A style of decoration and architecture first current in the 1890s, characterized by curvilinear floral forms.

atonality. The avoidance of tonal centers or keys in musical compositions.

atrium. An open courtyard within or related to a building.

avant-garde. A term used to designate innovators, the "advanced guard," whose experiments in art challenge established values.

balance. In composition, the equilibrium of opposing or interacting forces.

ballad. In folk music, a narrative song usually set to relatively simple music.

ballade. A verse form usually consisting of three stanzas of eight or ten lines each, with the same concluding line in each stanza, and a brief final stanza, ending with the same last line as that of the preceding stanzas. In musical composition, either a medieval French song, or a lyrical piano piece from the nineteenth century.

baroque. A seventeenth- and eighteenth-century style of art, architecture, and music that is highly ornamental.

barrel vault, tunnel vault. A series of arches placed back to back to enclose space.

basilica. In Roman times a term referring to building function, usually a law court; later used by Christians to refer to church buildings and a specific form.

bel canto. An Italian baroque style of operatic singing characterized by rich tonal lyricism and brilliant display of vocal technique.

binary form. A musical form consisting of two sections.

biomorphic. Representing life forms as opposed to geometric forms.

bridge. A musical passage of subordinate importance played as a link between two principal themes.

broken consort. A group containing string and woodwind instruments. A *whole* consort was made up of all woodwind or all strings.

buttress. A support, usually an exterior projection of masonry or wood, for a wall, arch, or vault.

cadence. In music, the specific harmonic arrangement that indicates the closing of a phrase.

cameo. A gem, hardstone, or shell with two layers of color, the upper of which can be carved in relief while the lower is used as a ground. Also a brief but dramatic appearance of a prominent actor or actress in a single scene in film, television, and stage.

canon. A body of principles, rules, standards or norms; a criterion for establishing measure, scale, and proportion. In music, a composition for two or more voices or instruments, where one enters after another in direct imitation of the first.

cantata. A type of composition developed in the baroque period, for chorus and/or solo voice(s) accompanied by an instrumental ensemble.

cantilever. Part of a beam or structure that projects beyond its support. A beam that is fixed at only one end.

capital. The transition between the top of a column and the lintel.

carbon-dating. A scientific method of determining the origin or date of ancient objects.

caryatid. A sculpted female figure standing in the place of a column.

cast. See *sculpture*.

catharsis. The cleansing or purification of the emotions through the experience of art, the result of which is spiritual release and renewal.

cella. The principal enclosed room of a temple; the entire body of a temple as opposed to its external parts.

chamber music. Vocal or instrumental music suitable for performance in small rooms.

chiaroscuro. Light and shade. In painting, the balance of light and shade across the whole picture. See also *modeling*. In theatre, the use of light to enhance plasticity of human and scenic form.

chorale. A Protestant hymn, for voices or organ.

chord. Three or more musical tones played at the same time.

choreography. The composition of a dance work; the arrangement of patterns of movement in dance.

citadel. A fortress or a fortified place.

city-state. A sovereign state consisting of an independent city and its surrounding territory.

classical. Adhering to traditional standards. May refer to Greek and Roman art in which simplicity, clarity of structure, and appeal to the intellect are fundamental.

clerestory. A row of windows in the upper part of a wall.

cloister. A covered walk with an open colonnade on one side, running along the inside walls of buildings that face a quadrangle. A place devoted to religious seclusion.

coffer. A recessed panel in a ceiling.

cognitive. Facts and objectivity as opposed to emotions and subjectivity. See *affective*.

collage. An artwork constructed by pasting together various materials, such as newsprint, to create textures, or by combining two- and three-dimensional media.

colonnade. A row of columns usually spanned or connected by lintels.

colonnette. A tall, narrow, engaged column; colonnettes are grouped together to form piers which support structural arches in buildings such as Gothic cathedrals.

coloristic. Reflecting the skillful use of color and painterly skills.

column. A cylindrical post or support which often has three distinct parts: base, shaft, and capital.

commedia dell'arte. A type of comedy developed in Italy in the sixteenth century, characterized by improvisation from a plot outline and by the use of stock characters.

composition. The arrangement of line, form, mass, color, and so forth, in a work of art.

compression, compressive strength. In architecture, stress that results from two forces moving toward each other.

concerto. A composition for one or more solo instruments, accompanied by an orchestra, typically in three movements.

concerto grosso. A baroque composition for a small group of solo instruments and a small orchestra.

conjunct melody. In music, melody comprising neighboring notes in the scale. The opposite of *disjunct melody*.

consonance. The feeling of a comfortable relationship between elements of a composition. Consonance may be both physical and cultural in its ramifications. The opposite of *dissonance*.

constructivism. A movement in art using such materials as iron, glass, and plaster to bridge the gulf between life and art.

continuo, basso continuo. In baroque music, a bass line played on a low melodic instrument, such as a cello, while a keyboard instrument (or other chord-playing instrument) also plays the bass line and adds harmonies.

contrapposto, counterpoise. In sculpture, the arrangement of body parts so that the weight-bearing leg is apart from the free leg, thereby shifting the hip/shoulder axis.

Corinthian. A specific order of Greek columns employing an elaborate leaf motif in the capital.

cornice. A crowning, projecting, architectural feature.

counterpoint. In music, two or more independent melodies played in opposition to each other at the same time.

crosscutting. In film, alternation between two independent actions that are related thematically or by plot to give the impression of simultaneous occurrence.

crossing. The area in a church where the transept crosses the nave.

cross-section. A view of an object shown by cutting through it.

cruciform. Arranged or shaped like a cross.

crypt. A vaulted chamber, wholly or partly underground, that usually contains a chapel. Found in a church under the choir.

cubism. A revolutionary art form from the early decades of the twentieth century involving the use of geometric shapes to represent objects and figures.

curvilinear. Formed or characterized by curved line.

cutting within the frame. Changing the viewpoint of the camera within a shot by moving from a long or medium shot to a close-up, without cutting the film.

dénouement. The section of a play's structure in which events are brought to a conclusion.

deposition. A painting or sculpture depicting the removal of the body of Christ from the cross.

design. A comprehensive scheme, plan or conception.

diatonic. Referring to the seven tones of a standard major or minor musical scale.

diptych. A painting on two hinged panels.

disjunct melody. In music, melody characterized by skips or jumps. The opposite of *conjunct melody*.

dissonance. The occurrence of inharmonious elements in music or the other arts. The opposite of *consonance*.

Doric. A Greek order of column having no base and only a simple slab as a capital.

drames bourgeois. Pseudo-serious plays utilizing middle-class themes and settings, with an emphasis on pathos and morality.

dynamics. The various levels of loudness and softness of sounds.

echinus. In the Doric order, the round, cushion-like element between the top of the shaft and the abacus.

eclecticism. A combination of several differing styles in a single composition.

empathy. Emotional and/or physical involvement in events to which one is a witness but not a participant.

empirical. Based on experiments, observation, and practical experience, without regard to theory.

engaged column. A column, often decorative, which is part of and projects from a wall surface.

entablature. The upper portion of a classical architectural order above the column capital.

entasis. The slight convex curving on classical columns to correct the optical illusion of concavity which would result if the sides were left straight.

ephemeral. Transitory, not lasting.

epic. A long narrative poem in heightened style about the deeds and adventures of a hero.

étude. Literally, a study, a lesson. An instrumental composition, intended for the practice or display of some technique.

exposition. The introductory material or opening section of a play or a musical composition.

expressionism. A style of painting that seeks to express the artist's emotions rather than accurately represent line or form.

façade. The front of a building, or the sides, if they are emphasized architecturally.

fan vaulting. An intricate style of traceried vaulting, common in the late English Gothic style, in which ribs arch out like a fan from a single point such as a capital.

farce. A theatrical genre characterized by broad, slapstick humor and implausible plots.

ferro-concrete. Concrete reinforced with rods or webs of steel.

fluting. Vertical ridges in a column.

flying buttress. A semi-detached buttress.

focal point, focal area. A major or minor area of visual attraction in pictures, sculpture, dance, plays, films, landscape design, or buildings.

foreground. The area of a picture, usually at the bottom, that appears to be closest to the viewer.

form. The shape, structure, configuration, or essence of something.

found object. An object taken from life that is presented as an artwork.

four-part harmony. A standard musical texture, where four tones fill out each chord.

fresco. A method of painting in which pigment is mixed with wet plaster and applied as part of the wall surface.

frieze. The central portion of the entablature: any horizontal decorative or sculptural band.

fugue. Originated in the baroque period from a Latin word meaning "flight." A musical composition in a fixed form in which a theme is developed by counterpoint.

full-round. See *sculpture*.

genre. A category of artistic composition characterized by a particular style, form, or content.

geometric. Based on man-made patterns such as triangles, rectangles, circles, ellipses, and so on. The opposite of *biomorphic*.

Gesamtkunstwerk. A complete, totally integrated artwork; associated with the music dramas of Richard Wagner in nineteenth-century Germany.

gesso. A mixture of plaster of Paris and glue, used as a base for low relief or as a surface for painting.

Greek cross. A cross in which all arms are the same length.

Gregorian chant. A medieval form of monophonic church music, also called plainchant or chant, sung unaccompanied, and named for Pope Gregory I.

groin vault. The ceiling formation created by the intersection of two tunnel or barrel vaults.

half cadence. A type of harmonic ending to a musical phrase which does not have a feeling of finality because it does not end on the home or tonic chord.

hamartia. The "tragic flaw" in the character of the protagonist of a classical tragedy.

harmony. The relationship of like elements such as musical notes, colors, and patterns of repetition. See *consonance* and *dissonance*.

Hellenistic. Relating to the time from the reign of Alexander the Great to the first century B.C.

heroic. Larger than lifesize.

hierarchy. Any system of persons or things that has higher and lower ranks.

hieratic. A style of depicting sacred persons or offices, particularly in Egyptian and Byzantine art.

hieroglyph, hieroglyphic. A picture or symbol of an object standing for a word, idea, or sound; developed by the ancient Egyptians into a system of writing.

homophony. A musical texture characterized by chordal texture supporting one melody. See *monophony* and *polyphony*.

horizon line. A real or implied line across the picture plane which, like the horizon in nature, tends to fix the viewer's vantage point.

hubris. Pride; typically the "tragic flaw" found in the protagonist of a classical tragedy. See *hamartia*.

hue. The spectrum notation of color; a specific, pure color with a measurable wavelength. There are primary hues, secondary hues, and tertiary hues.

humanitarianism. The ideas and philosophies associated with people who are concerned about human need and the alleviation of human suffering.

hymnody. The singing, composing, or study of hymns; the hymns of a particular period or church.

hypostyle. A building with a roof or ceiling supported by rows of columns, as in ancient Egyptian architecture.

Icon. A Greek word meaning "image." Used to identify paintings which represent the image of a holy person.

Iconography. The meanings of images and symbols.

idealization. The portrayal of an object or human body in its ideal form rather than as a true-to-life portrayal.

Idée fixe. A recurring melodic motif representing a nonmusical idea; used by, among others, the composer Berlioz.

illumination. The practice of decorating the pages of books—especially medieval manuscripts—with colorful pictures or motifs.

improvisation. Music or other art produced on the spur of the moment, spontaneously.

intensity. The degree or purity of a hue. In music, theatre, and dance, that quality of dynamics denoting the amount of force used to create a sound or movement.

interval. The difference in pitch between two tones.

intrinsic. Belonging to a thing by its nature.

Ionic. A Greek order of column that has a scroll-like capital with a circular base.

jamb. The upright piece forming the side of a doorway or window frame.

key. A system of tones in music based on and named after a given tone—the tonic.

kouros. An archaic Greek statue of a standing, nude youth.

krater. A bowl for mixing wine and water, the usual Greek beverage.

kylix. A vase turned on a potter's wheel; used as a drinking cup.

lancet window. A tall, narrow window whose top forms a lancet or narrow arch shaped like a spear.

lantern. A relatively small structure on the top of a dome, roof, or tower, frequently open to admit light into the area beneath.

Latin cross. A cross in which the vertical arm is longer than the horizontal arm, through whose midpoint it passes.

Leitmotif. A "leading motif" used in music to identify an individual, ideal, object, and so on; associated with Wagner.

lekythos. An oil flask with a long, narrow neck adapted for pouring oil slowly; used in funeral rites.

Lied. German secular art song. Normally applied to a nineteenth-century solo song with piano accompaniment; also a term for a three-part Early Renaissance song.

linear perspective. The creation of the illusion of distance in a two-dimensional artwork through the convention of line and foreshortening. That is, the illusion that parallel lines come together in the distance.

lintel. The horizontal member of a post-and-lintel structure in architecture, or a stone bridging an opening.

loggia. A gallery open on one or more sides, sometimes with arches or with columns.

lost-wax, cire-perdue. A method of casting sculpture in which the basic mold is created by using a wax model, which is then melted to leave the desired spaces in the mold.

low relief. See *sculpture*.

lyric. A category of poetry differentiated from dramatic or narrative. In music, the use of sensual sound patterns.

madrigal. An unaccompanied musical composition for two to five independent voices using a poetic text.

masonry. In architecture, stone or brickwork.

mass. Actual or implied physical bulk, weight, and density. Also, the most important rite of the Catholic liturgy, similar to the Protestant communion service.

medium. The process employed by the artist. Also the binding agent used to hold pigments together.

melismatic. Music where a single syllable of text is sung on many notes.

melodrama. A theatrical genre characterized by stereotyped characters, implausible plots, and an emphasis on spectacle.

melody. In music, a succession of single tones; a tune.

metaphor. A figure of speech in which one object is used to represent another in order to imply characteristics.

microtone. A musical interval smaller than a half-step.

mime. A form of ancient Greek and Roman drama in which realistic characters and situations were farcically portrayed and mimicked on stage.

miniature. An artwork, usually a painting, done in very small scale.

mobile. A constructed structure whose components have been connected by joints to move by force of wind or motor.

mode. A particular form, style, or manner. In music, a scale; often used with reference to non-Western music.

modeling. The shaping of three-dimensional forms. Also the suggestion of three-dimensionality in two-dimensional forms.

modulation. The changing from one key to another in a musical composition.

monody. A style of musical composition in which one melodic line predominates; a poetic form expressing personal lament.

monolith. A large block of stone used in architecture or sculpture.

monophony. In music, a texture employing a single melody line without harmonic support.

montage. The process of making a single composition by combining parts of others. A rapid sequence of film shots bringing together associated ideas or images.

monotheism. The belief that there is only one God.

monumental. Works actually or appearing larger than lifesize.

mosaic. A decorative work for walls, vaults, floors, or ceilings, composed of pieces of colored material set in plaster or cement.

motet. A polyphonic musical composition based on a sacred text and usually sung without accompaniment.

motif, motive. In music, a short, recurrent melodic or rythmic pattern. In the other arts, a recurrent element.

mullions. The vertical elements dividing windows into separate sections.

mural. A painting on a wall, usually large.

musique concrète. A 20th-century musical approach in which conventional sounds are altered electronically and recorded on tape to produce new sounds.

narthex. A portico or lobby of an early Christian church, separated from the nave by a screen or railing.

naturalistic. Carefully imitating the appearance of nature.

nave. The great central space in a church, usually running from west to east, where the congregation sits.

neo-Attic. Literally, "new Greek." A reintroduction of the classical Greek and Hellenistic elements of architecture and visual art.

neoclassicism. Various artistic styles that borrow the devices or objectives of classical art.

niche. A recess in a wall in which sculpture can be displayed.

nimbus. The circle of radiant light around the head or figures of God, Christ, the Virgin Mary, and the saints.

nonobjective. Without reference to reality; may be differentiated from "abstract."

nonrepresentational. Without reference to reality; including abstract and nonobjective.

obelisk. A tall, tapering, four-sided stone shaft with a pyramidal top.

octave. In music, the distance between a specific pitch vibration and its double; for example, concert A equals 440 vibrations per second, the A one octave above that pitch equals 880, and the A one octave below equals 220.

oculus. A circular opening in the top of a dome.

oligarchy. Government by a small, select group.

opus. A single work of art.

oratorio. A large choral work for soloists, chorus, and orchestra, developed in the baroque period.

orchestra. A large instrumental musical ensemble; the first-floor seating area of a theatre; the circular playing area of the ancient Greek theatre.

organum. Singing together. Earliest form of polyphony in Western music, with the voices moving in parallel lines.

ornament. Anything used as a decoration or embellishment.

palette. In the visual arts, the composite use of color, including range and tonality.

palmette. A decoration taking the form or abstracting the form of a palm branch.

pantomime. A genre of Roman drama in which an actor played various parts, without words, with a musical background.

pantheon. A Greek word meaning all the gods.

pathos. The "suffering" aspect of drama usually associated with the evocation of pity.

pediment. The typically triangular roof piece characteristic of classical architecture.

pendentive. A triangular part of the vaulting which allows the stress of the round base of a dome to be transferred to a rectangular wall base.

perspective. The representation of distance and three-dimensionality on a two-dimensional surface. See also *linear perspective* and *aerial perspective*.

picaresque. An artwork referring to the environment of rogues and adventurers.

piers. Upright architectural supports—usually rectangular.

pietà. A painting or sculpture of the dead Christ supported by Mary.

pigment. Any substance used as a coloring agent.

plainsong, plainchant. Medieval liturgical music sung without accompaniment and without strict meter.

plan. An architectural drawing that reveals in two dimensions the arrangement and distribution of interior spaces and walls, as well as door and window openings, of a building as seen from above.

plaque. A decorative or informative design placed on a wall.

plasticity. The capability of being molded or altered. In film, the capacity to be cut and shaped. In painting and theatre, the accentuation of dimensionality of form through chiaroscuro.

pointillism. A style of painting in which the paint is applied to the surface by dabbing the brush so as to create small dots of color.

polyphony. Literally, "many sounds." See *counterpoint*.

polyrhythm. The use of contrasting rhythms at the same time in music.

post-and-lintel. An architectural structure in which horizontal pieces (lintels) are held up by vertical columns (posts).

program music. Music that refers to nonmusical ideas through a descriptive title or text. The opposite of *absolute music*.

proportion. The relation, or ratio, of one part to another and of each part to the whole with regard to size, height, width, length, or depth.

proscenium. A Greek word meaning "before the skene." The plaster arch or "picture frame" stage of traditional theatres.

prototype. The model on which something is based.

psalmody. A collection of psalms.

putti. Nude male children—usually winged—especially shown in Renaissance and later art.

pylon. A gateway or a monumental structure flanking an entranceway.

quatrefoil. A carved ornament with four leaflets or lobes arranged around a common center.

rake. To place at an angle. A raked stage is one in which the floor slopes slightly upward from one point, usually downstage, to another, usually upstage.

realism. A style of painting, sculpture, and theatre based on the theory that the method of presentation should be true to life.

recitative. Sung monologue or dialogue, in opera, cantata, and oratorio.

reinforced concrete. See *ferro-concrete*.

relief. See *sculpture*.

representational. Art showing objects that are recognizable from real life.

requiem. A mass for the dead.

rhythm. The relationship, either of time or space, between recurring elements of a composition.

rib. A slender architectural support projecting from the surface in a vault system.

ribbed vault. A vault to which slender, projecting supports have been added. A structure in which arches are connected by diagonal as well as horizontal members. See *vault*.

rite. A customary form for conducting religious or other solemn ceremonies.

ritornello form. A baroque musical form in which a recurrent orchestral theme alternates with solo passages.

rondeau. A medieval French secular song based on a poetic form.

rondo form. A predominantly classical form of musical composition based around recurrence of the main theme, alternating with contrasting themes.

sarcophagus. A stone coffin.

saturation. In color, the purity of a hue in terms of whiteness; the whiter the hue, the less saturated it is.

scale. In music, a graduated series of ascending or descending musical tones. In architecture, the mass of the building in relation to the human body.

scenography. The art and study of scenery design for the theatre and film.

schema. A summarized or diagrammatic representation.

sculpture. A three-dimensional art object. Among the types are 1. *cast*: created from molten material utilizing a mold. 2. *relief*: attached to a larger background. 3. *full-round*: free-standing.

semidome. A roof covering a semicircular space; half a dome.

serial music. A twentieth-century musical style utilizing the tone row; can also employ serialization of rhythms, timbres, and dynamics.

sfumato. A smoky or hazy quality in a painting, with particular reference to Leonardo da Vinci's work.

shaft. The main trunk of a column.

shape. A two-dimensional area or plane with distinguishable boundaries.

silhouette. A form as defined by its outline.

skene. The stage building of the ancient Greek theatre.

skyphos. A two-handled ancient Greek drinking pot with an open top, tapering bowl, and flat, circular base.

sonata. Instrumental composition of the seventeenth through twentieth centuries, consisting of a group of movements played in succession.

statuary. Free-standing, three-dimensional sculpture.

stereophonic. Sound reproduction in which two channels are used to simulate a natural distribution of sources.

still life. In the visual arts, an arrangement of inanimate objects used as a subject of a work of art.

strainer arch. An arch in an internal space that prevents the walls from being pushed inward.

stream of consciousness. A style of writing in which the author reveals character and event by expressing a continuous flow of a character's thoughts.

strophic form. Form of vocal music in which all stanzas of the text are sung to the same music.

stucco. A plaster or cement finish for interior and exterior walls.

style. The characteristics of a work of art that identify it with an artist, a group of artists, an era, or a nation.

stylized. A type of depiction in which verisimilitude has been altered for artistic effect.

stylobate. The foundation immediately below a row of columns.

suite. A grouping of musical movements, usually unrelated except by key.

summa. An encyclopedic summation of a field of learning, particularly in theology or philosophy.

symbol. A form, image, or subject standing for something else.

symmetry. The balancing of elements in design by placing physically equal objects on either side of a center line.

symphony. A lengthy orchestral composition, usually in four movements.

syncopation. In a musical composition, the displacement of accent from the normally accented beat to the offbeat.

synthesis. The combination of independent factors or entities into a compound that becomes a new, more complex whole.

synthesizer. An electronic instrument that produces and combines musical sounds.

temperament. In music, a system of tuning. Equal temperament—the division of the octave into twelve equal intervals—is the most common way of tuning keyboard instruments.

tempo. The rate of speed at which a musical composition is performed. In theatre, film, or dance, the rate of speed of the overall performance.

tensile strength. The ability of a material to resist bending and twisting.

text painting. See *word painting*.

theatricality. Exaggeration and artificiality; the opposite of *verisimilitude*.

theme. The subject of an artwork, whether melodic or philosophical.

timbre. The characteristic of a sound that results from the particular source of the sound. The difference between the sound of a violin and the sound of the human voice, caused by different patterns of sound waves, is a difference in timbre, also called color.

toccata. A baroque keyboard composition intended to display technique.

tonality. In music, the specific key in which a composition is written. In the visual arts, the characteristics of value.

tondo. A circular painting.

tonic. In music, the root tone (*doh*) of a key.

tragedy. A serious drama or other literary work in which conflict between a protagonist and a superior force (often fate) concludes in disaster for the protagonist.

tragicomedy. A drama combining the qualities of tragedy and comedy.

transept. The crossing arm of a cruciform church, at right angles to the nave.

travertine. A creamy-colored type of calcium carbonate used as a facing in building construction.

triforium. The section of the nave wall above the arcade and below the clerestory windows.

triptych. An altarpiece or devotional picture composed of a central panel and two wings.

trompe l'oeil. "Trick of the eye" or "fool the eye." A two-dimensional artwork so executed as to make the viewer believe that three-dimensional subject matter is being perceived.

trope. A medieval dramatic elaboration of the Roman Catholic mass or other offices.

tundra. A treeless area between the ice cap and the tree line of arctic regions, with a permanently frozen subsoil and supporting low-growing vegetation such as lichens, mosses, and stunted shrubs.

tunnel vault. See *barrel vault*.

twelve-tone technique. A twentieth-century atonal form of musical composition associated with Schoenberg.

tympanum. The space above the door beam and within the arch of a medieval doorway.

value, value scale. In the visual arts, the range of tonalities from white to black.

vanishing point. In linear perspective, the point on the horizon toward which parallel lines appear to converge and at which they seem to vanish.

variation. Repetition of a theme with small or large changes.

vault. An arched roof or ceiling usually made of stone, brick, or concrete.

verisimilitude. The appearance of reality or the nearness to truth in works of art; the opposite of *theatricality*.

virtuoso. Referring to the display of impressive technique or skill by an artist or performer.

volute. A spiral architectural element found notably on Ionic and other capitals, but also used decoratively on building façades and interiors.

wash. A thin layer of translucent color or ink used in watercolor painting and brush drawing.

woodcut. A block of wood with an engraved design; a print made from such a piece of wood.

word painting. The use of language by a poet or playwright to suggest images and emotions; in music, the use of expressive melody to suggest a specific text.

NOTES

See Further Reading for full bibliographical details of all cited works

Chapter 1
1. Murray, *Egyptian Sculpture*, p. 23

Chapter 3
1. Hofstadter and Kuhns, *Philosophies of Art and Beauty*, p. 4
2. *Ibid.*
3. Fuller, *A History of Philosophy*, p. 172
4. Snell, *Discovery of the Mind: The Greek Origins of European Thought*, p. 247
5. *Ibid.*
6. Robertson, *A Shorter History of Greek Art*, p. 123
7. Hamilton, trans. in *Three Greek Plays*
8. Arrowsmith, trans. in *The Complete Greek Tragedies*, vol. vi (New York, Random House, 1958)
9. *Ibid.*
10. *Ibid.*
11. Hamilton, *op. cit.*
12. Arrowsmith, *op. cit.*

Chapter 4
1. Fuller, *op. cit.*, p. 266
2. "Rings around the Pantheon," *Discover*, March, 1985, p. 12
3. Vergil, *The Aeneid*, trans. Theodore C. Williams, New York: Houghton Mifflin Co., 1938, p. 1
4. Garraty and Gay, *A History of the World*, p. 209
5. Andreae, *The Art of Rome*, p. 109

Chapter 5
1. McGiffert, *A History of Christian Thought*, p. 7
2. Fuller, *op. cit.*, p. 353
3. *Ibid.*
4. Hofstadter and Kuhns, *op. cit.*, p. 172
5. Barclay, *The Gospel of Luke*, pp. 15-16

Chapter 6
1. Garraty and Gay, *op. cit.*, p. 431
2. Roberts, *History of the World*, p. 321
3. Mango, *Byzantium*, p. 235
4. Nicoll, *The Development of Theatre*, p. 48

Chapter 8
1. Fuller, *op. cit.*, p. 377

Chapter 10
1. Hartt, *Italian Renaissance Art*, p. 187

Chapter 11
1. Hartt, *op. cit.*, p. 592
2. Campos (ed.), *Art Treasures of the Vatican*, p. 7

Chapter 14
1. Helm, *Music at the Court of Frederick the Great*, p. 94

Chapter 15
1. Hofstadter and Kuhns, *op. cit.*, p 381
2. Maas, *Victorian Painters*, p. 10

Chapter 16
1. McDermot, "Creative Evolution," *Theatre Journal*, 1984, pp. 217-18
2. Gardner, *Art Through the Ages*, p. 760

3. Hamilton, *Nineteenth and Twentieth Century Art: Painting, Sculpture, Architecture, p. 211*
4. *Janson,* A Basic History of Art, p. 682

Chapter 17
1. Zitkala-Sa (Gertrude Bonnin), "The Soft-Hearted Sioux," (copyright 1989 The Arizona Board of Regents). Reprinted from *The Singing Spirit*, edited by Bernd C. Peyer.
2. Gropius *The New Architecture and the Bauhaus*, pp. 51-5

Chapter 18
1. Valerie-Anne Giscard d'Estaing and Mark Young (eds.), *Inventions and Discoveries 1993*, New York: Facts on File Inc., 1993, p. 220
2. Wilkins and Schultz, *Art Past Art Present*, p. 506
3. Otto G. Ocvirk *et al.*, *Art Fundamentals* (7th ed.), p. 309
4. John Buckley, "Country Music and American Values," in Scheurer (ed.), *American Popular Music: Readings from the Popular Press, vol. ii: The Age of Rock*, pp. 25-7
5. Kernodle and Pixley, *Invitation to the Theatre*, pp. 287-8
6. Arkin and Shollar (eds.), *Longman Anthology of World Literature by Women*, p. 1039

FURTHER READING

Achtemeier, Paul (ed.), *Harper's Bible Dictionary*. San Francisco: Harper & Row, 1985

Anderson, Bernhard, *Understanding the Old Testament*, Englewood Cliffs, NJ: Prentice Hall, 1975

Andreae, Bernard, *The Art of Rome*, New York: Harry N. Abrams, Inc., 1977

Armstrong, Karen, *Muhammad: A Western Attempt to Understand Islam*, San Francisco: HarperCollins, 1992

Arkin, Marian, and Shollar, Barbara (eds.), *Longman Anthology of World Literature by Women*, New York: Longman, 1989

Arnason, H.H., *History of Modern Art*, Englewood Cliffs, NJ: Prentice Hall, Inc., 1977

Arnott, Peter D., *An Introduction to the Greek Theatre*, Bloomington, IN: Indiana University Press, 1963

Artz, Frederick, *From the Renaissance to Romanticism*, Chicago: University of Chicago Press, 1962

Aston, M., *The Fifteenth Century: The Prospect of Europe*, New York: Harcourt, Brace, & World, 1968

Balsdon, J.P.V.D., *Rome: The Story of an Empire*, New York: McGraw Hill, 1970

Bainton, Roland, *Here I Stand: A Life of Martin Luther*, New York: New American Library, 1950

Barclay, William, *The Gospel of Luke*, Philadelphia: Westminster Press, 1975

Barraclough, G., *The Medieval Papacy*, New York: Harcourt, Brace, & World, 1968

Barrett, W., *Time of Need: Forms of Imagination in the Twentieth Century*, New York: Harper & Row, 1972

Bataille, Georges, *Lascaux*, Switzerland: Skira, n.d.

Bazin, Germain, *The Baroque*, Greenwich, CN: New York Graphic Society, 1968

Beckwith, J., *Early Medieval Art*, New York: Praeger, 1973

Bentley, Eric (ed.), *The Classic Theatre*, (4 vols), Garden City, NY: Doubleday Anchor Books, 1959

Bevan, G.M., *Early Christians of Rome*, London: Society for Promoting Christian Knowledge, 1927

Beye, C.R., *Ancient Greek Literature and Society*, Ithaca: Cornell University Press, 1987

Bieber, M., *The Sculpture of the Hellenistic Age*, New York: Columbia University Press, 1955

Bishop, M., *Petrarch and His World*, Bloomington, Indiana University Press, 1963

Boardman, J., *The Greeks Overseas*, Baltimore: Penguin, 1973

Boardman, J., Jasper, G., and Murray, O. (eds.), *The Oxford History of the Classical World*, Oxford: Oxford University Press, 1986

Boardman, J., *et al.*, *Greek Art and Architecture*, New York: Abrams, 1967

Bohn, T.W., Stomgren, R.L., and Johnson, D.H., *Light and Shadows, A History of Motion Pictures*, (2nd ed.), Sherman Oaks, CA: Alfred Publishing Co., 1978

Bony, Jean, *French Gothic Architecture of the Twelfth and Thirteenth Centuries*, Berkeley: University of California Press, 1983

Booth, Michael, *Victorian Spectacular Theatre 1850-1910*, Boston: Routledge & Kegan Paul, 1981

Borroff, Edith, *Music in Europe and the United States: A History*, Englewood Cliffs, NJ: Prentice Hall, Inc., 1971

Bovini, G., *Ravenna Mosaics*, Greenwich, CT: New York Graphic Society Publishers, Ltd., 1956

Boyd, M., *Bach*, London: Dent, 1983

Brandon, S.G.F., *Religion in Ancient History*, New York: Charles Scribner's Sons, 1969

Brendel, O.J., *Etruscan Art*, Baltimore: Penguin, 1978

Brindle, Reginald Smith, *The New Music: The Avant-Garde Since 1945*, London: Oxford University Press, 1975

Brion, Marcel, *Dürer, His Life and Work*, New York: Tudor Publishing, 1960

Brockett, Oscar G., *History of the Theatre*, Boston: Allyn and Bacon, Inc., 1968

Brondsted, Johannes, *The Vikings* (trans. Kalle Skov), New York: Penguin Books, 1960

Brown, Howard M., *Music in the Renaissance*, Englewood Cliffs, NJ: Prentice Hall, 1976

Brown, P., *Augustine of Hippo*, London: Faber, 1967

Brucker, Gene, *Renaissance Florence*, New York: Wiley, 1969

Bruzelius, Carline A., *The 13th-Century Church at St-Denis*, New Haven, CT: Yale University Press, 1985

Burcket, W., *Ancient Mystery Cults*, Cambridge: Harvard University Press, 1987

Burckhardt, Jakob, *The Civilization of the Renaissance in Italy*, New York: Harper Torchbooks, 1958

Burn, A.R., *The Pelican History of Greece*, New York: Penguin, 1966

Campos, D. Redig de (ed.), *Art Treasures of the Vatican*, Englewood Cliffs, NJ: Prentice Hall, Inc., 1974

Carsten, F.L., *The Rise of Fascism* (2nd ed.), London: Batsford, 1980

Carter, Tim, *Music in the Late Renaissance and Early Baroque*, Portland, OR: Amadeus Press

Chadwick, H., *The Early Church*, New York: Penguin, 1967

Cheney, Sheldon, *The Theatre: Three Thousand Years of Drama, Acting, and Stagecraft* (rev. ed.), New York: Longmans, Green, 1952

Clough, Shepard B. *et al.*, *A History of the Western World*, Boston: D.C. Heath & Co., 1964

Cochrane, Eric, *The Late Italian Renaissance, 1525-1630*, New York: Harper Torchbooks, 1970

Conisbee, P., *Painting in Eighteenth-century France*, Ithaca: Cornell University Press, 1981

Cope, David H., *New Directions in Music*, Dubuque, IA: William C. Brown & Co., 1981

Corrigan, Robert, "The Search for New Endings: The Theatre in Search of a Fix, Part III," *Theatre Journal*, vol. 36, No. 2, May 1984, pp. 153-63

Coryell, Julie, and Friedman, Laura, *Jazz-Rock Fusion*, New York: Delacorte Press, 1978

Crawford, M., *The Roman Republic*, Cambridge MA: Harvard University Press, 1982

Crocker, Richard, *A History of Musical Style*, New York: McGraw-Hill, 1966

Cronin, Vincent, *The Florentine Renaissance*, New York: E.P. Dutton & Co., 1967

Crosby, Sumner McKnight, *The Royal Abbey of Saint-Denis*, New Haven: Yale University Press, 1987

Dallmayr, Fred R., *Critical Encounters: Between Philosophy and Politics*, Notre Dame, IN: University of Notre Dame Press, 1987

Daly, Lowrie, *The Medieval University: 1200-1400*, New York: Sheed & Ward, 1961

Diderot, Denis, *Encyclopedia: Selections* (ed. and trans. S.J. Gendzier), New York: Harper & Row, 1967

Diehl, Charles, *Byzantium*, New Brunswick, NJ: Rutgers University Press, 1957

Drinkwater, John, *The Outline of Literature*, London: Transatlantic Arts, 1967

Dunlop, D.M., *Arab Civilization to A.D. 1500*, London: Longman, 1971

Engel, Carl, *The Music of the Most Ancient Nations*, Freeport, NY: Books for Libraries Press, 1970

Epstein, Isidore, *Judaism*, Middlesex, U.K.: Penguin Books, 1968

Ernst David, *The Evolution of Electronic Music*, New York: Schirmer Books, 1977

Esposito, John, *Islam: The Straight Path*, New York: Oxford University Press, 1991

Esser, Kajetan, *Origins of the Franciscan*

Order (trans. Aedan Daly and Irina Lynch), Chicago: Franciscan Herald Press, 1970.

Fenlon, Iain (ed.), *The Renaissance*, Englewood Cliffs, NJ: Prentice Hall, 1989.

Finley, M.I., *Early Greece: The Bronze and Archaic Age*, New York: Norton, 1981

Fleming, William, *Arts and Ideas*, New York: Holt, Rinehart, & Winston, 1980

Fletcher, Jefferson, B., *Literature of the Italian Renaissance*, New York: The Macmillan Co., 1934

Frankfort, Henri, *Kingship and the Gods*, Chicago: University of Chicago Press, 1948

Freedley, George, and Reeves, John, *A History of the Theatre* (3rd ed.), New York: Crown Publishers, 1968

Frend, W.H.C., *The Rise of Christianity*, Philadelphia: Fortress, 1983

Friedrich, C.J., *The Age of the Baroque: 1610-1660*, New York: Harper Torchbooks, 1961

Fuller, B.A.G., *A History of Philosophy*, New York: Henry Holt and Company, 1945

Gardner, Helen, *Art Through the Ages* (8th ed.), New York: Harcourt Brace Jovanovich, 1986

Garraty, John, and Gay, Peter, *A History of the World* (2 vols), New York: Harper & Row, 1972

Gassner, John (ed.), *A Treasury of the Theatre*, New York: Holt, Rinehart, & Winston, 1967

Gilbert, Creighton, *History of Renaissance Art Throughout Europe: Painting, Sculpture, Architecture*, New York: Harry N. Abrams, Inc., 1973.

Giscard d'Estaing, Valerie Anne, and Young, Mark (eds.), *Inventions and Discoveries 1993*, New York: Facts on File, Inc., 1993

Glasstone, Victor, *Victorian and Edwardian Theatres*, Cambridge, MA: Harvard University Press, 1975

Goethe, Johann Wolfgang von, *Faust: Part I* (trans. Philip Wayne), Baltimore: Penguin Books, 1962

Goldwater, R., *Symbolism*, New York: Harper & Row, 1979

Gottfried, Robert S., *The Black Death: Natural and Human Disaster in Medieval Europe*, New York: Free Press, 1983

Grabar, Andre, *The Art of the Byzantine Empire*, New York: Crown Publishers, Inc., 1966

Grant, M., *Roman Literature*, New York: Penguin, 1964

Grant, M., *From Alexander to Cleopatra: The Hellenistic World*, London: Weidenfeld & Nicolson, 1982

Graves, R., *The Greek Myths*, Garden City, NY: Doubleday, 1981

Graziosi, Paolo, *Palaeolithic Art*, New York: McGraw-Hill, 1960

Griffiths, Paul, *A Concise History of Avant-Garde Music*, New York: Oxford University Press, 1978

Grimm, Harold, *The Reformation Era*, New York: Macmillan Co., 1954

Groenewegen-Frankfort and Ashmole, Bernard, *Art of the Ancient World*, Englewood Cliffs, NJ and New York: Prentice Hall, Inc. and Harry N. Abrams, Inc., n.d.

Gropius, Walter (ed.), *The Theatre of the Bauhaus*, Middletown, CN: Wesleyan University Press, 1961

Gropius, Walter, *The New Architecture and the Bauhaus*, Cambridge, MA: M.I.T. Press, 1965

Grout, Donald Jay, *A History of Western Music* (rev. ed.), New York: W.W. Norton & Co., Inc., 1973

Hale, J.R., *Florence and the Medicis*, London: Thames & Hudson, 1977

Hall, A. Rupert, *The Revolution in Science 1500-1750*, London: Longman, 1983

Hamilton, Edith, *Three Greek Plays*, New York: W.W. Norton & Co., Inc., 1965

Hamilton, George Heard, *Nineteenth and Twentieth Century Art: Painting, Sculpture, Architecture*, New York: Harry N. Abrams, Inc., 1970

Hampson, N., *A Cultural History of the Enlightenment*, New York: Pantheon, 1968

Hartt, Frederick, *Art* (2 vols). Englewood Cliffs, NJ and New York: Prentice Hall, Inc. and Harry N. Abrams, Inc., 1979

Hartt, Frederick, *Italian Renaissance Art* (3rd ed.), Englewood Cliffs, NJ and New York: Prentice Hall, Inc. and Harry N. Abrams, Inc., 1987

Hawkes, Jacquetta, and Wooley, Sir Leonard, *History of Mankind: Prehistory and the Beginnings of Civilization*, New York: Harper & Row, 1963

Hay, Denys, and Law, John, *Italy in the Age of the Renaissance, 1380-1530*, London: Longman, 1989

Hayman, Ronald, *Kafka: A Biography*, New York: Oxford University Press, 1981

Hayes, C.J.H., *A Generation of Materialism*, New York: Harper & Row, 1963

Held, Julius, and Posner, D., *Seventeenth and Eighteenth Century Art*, New York: Harry N. Abrams, Inc., n.d.

Helm, Ernest, *Music at the Court of Frederick the Great*, Norman, OK: University of Oklahoma Press, 1960

Henderson, W.O., *The Industrialization of Europe, 1780-1914*, London: Thames & Hudson, 1969

Henig, Martin (ed.), *A Handbook of Roman Art*, Ithaca, NY: Cornell University Press, 1983

Hewett, Bernard, *Theatre USA*, New York: McGraw-Hill Book Company, 1959

Hitchcock, Henry-Russell, *Architecture: Nineteenth and Twentieth Centuries*, Baltimore: Penguin, 1971

Hofstadter, Albert, and Kuhns, Richard, *Philosophies of Art and Beauty*, Chicago: University of Chicago Press, 1976

Hofstatter, H.H., *Art of the Late Middle Ages* (trans. R.E. Wolf), New York: Abrams, 1968

Honour, Hugh, and Fleming, John. *The Visual Arts: A History* (3rd ed.), Englewood Cliffs, NJ: Prentice Hall, Inc., 1992

Hoppin, Richard, *Medieval Music*, New York: W.W. Norton & Co., Inc., 1978

Hornstein, Lillian, Percy, G.D., and Brown, Sterling, *A World Literature* (2nd ed.), New York: Mentor, 1973

Hubatsch, Walther, *Frederick the Great of Prussia*, London: Thames & Hudson, 1975

Hubert, J., Porcher, J., and Volbach, W.F., *The Carolingian Renaissance*, New York: George Braziller, 1970.

Jackson, W.T.H., *Medieval Literature: A History and a Guide*, New York: Collier Books, 1966

Jacobs, Lewis, *An Introduction to the Art of the Movies*, New York: Noonday Press, 1967

Janson, H.W., *A Basic History of Art* (2nd ed.), Englewood Cliffs, NJ and New York: Prentice Hall, Inc. and Harry N. Abrams, Inc., 1981

Johnston, Leonard, *A History of Israel*, New York: Sheed & Ward, 1963

Jung, Carl G., *Man and His Symbols*, New York: Doubleday & Co., Inc., 1964

Kane, George, *Chaucer*, New York: Oxford University Press, 1984

Karsavina, Tamara, *Theatre Street*, New York: E.P. Dutton, 1961

Katz, Bernard, *The Social Implications of Early Negro Music in the United States*, New York: Arno Press and *The New York Times*, 1969

Keck, George R., and Martin, Sherrill V., *Feel the Spirit*, New York: Greenwood Press, 1988

Kernodle, George and Portia, and Pixley, Edward, *Invitation to the Theatre* (3rd ed.), San Diego: Harcourt Brace Jovanovich, 1985

Keutner, Hubert, *Sculpture: Renaissance to Rococo*, Greenwich, CT: New York Graphic Society, 1969

King, Margaret, *Women of the Renaissance*, Chicago: University of Chicago Press, 1991

Kirby, E.E., *A Short History of Keyboard Music*, New York: Macmillan Co., 1966

Kjellberg, Ernst, and Saflund, Gosta, *Greek and Roman Art*, New York: Thomas Y.

Crowell Co., 1968

Knight, Arthur, *The Liveliest Art: A Panoramic History of the Movies* (rev. ed.), New York: Macmillan, Inc., 1978

Knowles, David, *Christian Monasticism*, New York: McGraw-Hill, 1969

Kratzenstein, Marilou, *Survey of Organ Literature and Editions*, Ames IA: Iowa State University Press, 1980

Krehbiel, Henry Edward, *Afro-American Folksongs*, New York: G. Schirmer, n.d. (c. 1914)

Kristeller, P.O., *Renaissance Thought: The Classic, Scholastic, and Humanist Strains*, New York: Harper Torchbooks, 1955

Lange, Kurt, and Hirmer, Max, *Egypt*, London: Phaidon, 1968

Leish, Kenneth, W., *Cinema*, New York: Newsweek Books, 1974

Levey, Michael, *High Renaissace*, New York: Penguin, 1975

Liddell Hart, B.H., *History of the Second World War*, New York: Putman, 1971

Lippard, Lucy R., *Pop Art*, New York: Oxford University Press, 1966

Lloyd, Seton, *The Archaeology of Mesopotamia*, London: Thames & Hudson, 1978

Lockyear, Roger, *Hapsburg and Bourbon Europe*, London: Longman, 1974

Lommel, Andrea, *Prehistoric and Primitive Man*, New York: McGraw-Hill, 1966

Lull, James (ed.), *Popular Music and Communication*, Newbury Park, CA: Sage Publications, 1987

Maas, Jeremy, *Victorian Painters*, New York: G.P. Putnam's Sons, 1969

McDermott, Dana Sue, "Creativity in the Theatre: Robert Edmond Jones and C.G. Jung," *Theatre Journal*, May 1984, pp. 212-30

MacDonald, William, *Early Christian and Byzantine Architecture*, New York: George Braziller, 1967

McGiffert, Arthur, *A History of Christian Thought*, New York: Charles Scribner's Sons, 1961

Machiavelli, Niccolò, *The Prince* (trans. George Bull), Baltimore: Penguin Books, 1963

Machlis, Joseph, *The Enjoyment of Music* (3rd ed.), New York: W.W. Norton & Co., 1955

McLeish, Kenneth, *The Theatre of Aristophanes*, New York: Taplinger Publishing Co., 1980

McNeill, William H., *The Shape of European History*, New York: Oxford University Press, 1974

Mango, Cyril, *Byzantium*, New York: Charles Scribner's Sons, 1980

Marshack, Alexander, *The Roots of Civilization*, New York: McGraw-Hill, 1972

Milburn, Robert, *Early Christian Art and Architecture*, Berkeley: University of California Press, 1988.

Montet, Pierre, *Lives of the Pharaohs*, Cleveland: World Publishing Co., 1968

Moortgat, Anton, *The Art of Ancient Mesopotamia*, London: Phaidon, 1969

Morford, M.P.O., and Lenardon, P.J., *Classical Mythology*, New York: Longman, 1977

Murray, Margaret, *Egyptian Sculpture*, New York: Charles Scribner's Sons, 1930

Muthesius, Stefan, *The High Victorian Movement in Architecture 1850-1870*, London: Routledge & Kegan Paul, 1972

Myers, Bernard S., *Art and Civilization*, New York: McGraw-Hill Book Co., Inc., 1957

Nicoll, Allardyce, *The Development of the Theatre* (5th ed.), London: Harrap & Co. Ltd., 1966

Nyman, Michael, *Experimental Music: Cage and Beyond*, New York: Schirmer Books, 1974

Ocvirk, Otto G., et. al., *Art Fundamentals* (7th ed.), Madison, WI: Brown Benchmark, 1994

Ogg, D., *Europe in the Seventeenth Century* (rev. ed.), New York: Collier Books, 1968

Oman, Sir Charles, *The Sixteenth Century*, Westport, CN: Greenwood Press, 1975

Oppenheim, A. Leo, *Ancient Mesopotamia*, Chicago: University of Chicago Press, 1964

Ostransky, Leroy, *Understanding Jazz*, Englewood Cliffs, NJ: Prentice Hall, Inc., 1977

Pfeiffer, John E., *The Creative Explosion*, New York: Harper & Row, 1982

Pignatti, Terisio, *The Age of Rococo*, London: Paul Hamlyn, 1969

Plumb, J.H., *The Italian Renaissance*, New York: Harper Torchbooks, 1961

Powell, T.G.E., *Prehistoric Art*, New York: Frederick Praeger Publishers, 1966

Raphael, Max, *Prehistoric Cave Paintings*, Washington, D.C.: Pantheon, 1946

Read, Benedict, *Victorian Sculpture*, New Haven: Yale University Press, 1982

Read, Herbert E., *Art and Society* (2nd ed.), New York: Pantheon Books, Inc., 1950

Redhead, Steve, *The end-of-the-century party*, Manchester, UK: Manchester University Press, 1990

Rice, David Talbot, *The Art of Byzantium*, New York: Harry N. Abrams, Inc., n.d.

Richter, Gisela, *Greek Art*, Greenwich, CN: Phaidon, 1960

Roberts, J.M., *History of the World*, New York: Alfred A. Knopf, Inc., 1976

Robertson, Martin, *A Shorter History of Greek Art*, Cambridge, U.K.: Cambridge University Press, 1981

Robinson, David, *The History of World Cinema*, New York: Stein & Day Publishers, 1973

Rorig, F., *The Medieval Town* (trans. D.J.A. Matthew), Berkeley: University of California Press, 1969

Roters, Eberhard, *Painters of the Bauhaus*, New York: Frederick Praeger Publishers, 1965

Rotha, Paul *The Film Till Now*, London: Spring Books, 1967

Rowell, George, *The Victorian Theatre* (2nd ed.), Cambridge, U.K.: Cambridge University Press, 1978

Sachs, Curt, *The Rise of Music in the Ancient World*, New York: W.W. Norton & Co., 1943

Sadie, Stanley (ed.), *The New Grove Dictionary of Music and Musicians*, Washington, D.C.: Grove's Dictionaries; London: Macmillan, 1980

Salzman, Eric, *Twentieth Century Music: An Introduction*, Englewood Cliffs, NJ: Prentice Hall, Inc., 1967

Sandars, N.K., *Prehistoric Art in Europe*, Baltimore: Penguin Books, 1968

Scheurer, Timothy E., *American Popular Music: Reading from the Popular Press, Vol. II: The Age of Rock*, Bowling Green, OH: Bowling Green State University Popular Press, 1989

Schevill, Ferdinand, *A History of Europe*, New York: Harcourt Brace & Co., Inc., 1938

Schonberger, Arno, and Soehner, Halldor, *The Rococo Age*, New York: McGraw-Hill, 1960

Sherrard, Philip, *Byzantium*, New York: Time Inc., 1966

Shirer, William L., *The Rise and Fall of the Third Reich*, New York: Simon & Schuster, 1960

Singleton, Charles, *The Divine Comedy of Dante Alighieri* (6 vols), Princeton: Princeton University Press, 1972

Sitwell, Sacheverell, *Great Houses of Europe*, London: Spring Books, 1970

Smart, Alastair, *The Renaissance and Mannerism in Northern Europe and Spain*, London: Harcourt, Brace Jovanovich, Inc., 1972

Smith, Hermann, *The World's Earliest Music*, London: W. Reeves, n.d.

Smith, W. Stevenson, *The Art and Architecture of Ancient Egypt*, Baltimore: Penguin Books, 1958

Snell, Bruno, *Discovery of the Mind: The Greek Origins of European Thought*, New York: Harper, 1960

Snyder, J., *Northern Renaissance Art*, Englewood Cliffs, NJ: Prentice Hall, 1985

Southern, Richard, *The Seven Ages of the Theatre*, New York: Hill and Wang, 1961

Sperry, Roger, *Science and Moral Priority: Merging Mind, Brain, and Human*

Values, New York: Columbia University Press, 1983

Spitz, Lewis (ed.), *The Protestant Reformation*, Englewood Cliffs, NJ: Prentice Hall, Inc., 1966

Sporre, Dennis J., *Perceiving the Arts*, Englewood Cliffs, NJ: Prentice Hall, Inc., 1981

Sporre, Dennis J., *The Arts*, Englewood Cliffs, NJ: Prentice Hall, Inc., 1985

Staley, Edgcombe, *Famous Women of Florence*, London: Archibald Constable & Co., 1909

Stamp, Kenneth M., and Wright, Esmond (eds.), *Illustrated World History*, New York: McGraw-Hill Book Co., 1964

Stinger, Charles, *The Renaissance in Rome*, Bloomington: Indiana University Press, 1985

Strayer, Joseph, and Munro, Dana, *The Middle Ages*, Pacific Palisades: Goodyear Publishing Co., 1970

Thompson, S. Harrison, *Europe in Renaissance and Reformation*, New York: Harcourt, Brace & World, 1963

Tierney, Brian, and Painter, Sidney, *Western Europe in the Middle Ages*, New York: Alfred A. Knopf, 1974

Tirro, Frank, *Jazz: A History*, New York: W.W. Norton & Co., Inc., 1977

Ucko, Peter J., and Rosenfeld, Andree, *Paleolithic Cave Art*, London: World University Library, 1967

Ulrich, Homer, *Music: A Design for Listening* (3rd ed.), New York: Harcourt, Brace & World, Inc., 1970

Van Der Kemp, Gerald, *Versailles*, New York: The Vendrome Press, 1977

Vidal-Naquet, Pierre (ed.), *The Harper Atlas of World History*, New York: Harper & Row, 1986

Ward-Perkins, J.B., *Roman Imperial Architecture* (2nd ed.), New York: Penguin, 1981

Waterhouse, E., *Painting in Britain 1530-1790* (4th ed.), New York: Penguin, 1978

Watt, W.M., *Muhammad: Statesman and Prophet*, New York: Oxford University Press, 1974

Wheeler, Robert Eric Mortimer, *Roman Art and Architecture*, New York: Frederick Praeger Publishers, 1964

White, John, *Art and Architecture in Italy 1250-1400*, Baltimore: Pelican, 1966

Wilkins, David G., and Schultz, Bernard, *Art Past Art Present*, Englewood Cliffs, NJ and New York: Prentice Hall Inc. and Harry N. Abrams, Inc., 1990

Willey, B., *The Seventeenth-century Background*, New York: Columbia University Press, 1967

Wolf, J.B., *Louis XIV*, New York: Norton, 1968

Zarnecki, George, *Art of the Medieval World*, Englewood Cliffs, NJ: Prentice Hall, Inc., 1975

INDEX

Bold references are to picture and map captions.

A

Aachen 224
  Palatine Chapel 244-5, **7.27**, **7.28**
Aalto (Douglas) 575, **17.16**
Abd-al-Malik, Calif 210
Abelard, Peter 256, 275
Abraham 154, 155, 157
Absalom and Achitophel (Dryden) 432
absolutism 414
Abstract art 569-70, 603, 605, 610
Abstract Expressionism 594-6
absurdism 583, 623
Abu Bakr, Caliph 208
Abu-Khalid, Fawziyya 618
Acharnians, The (Aristophanes) 107
Adding Machine (Rice) 583
Adler, Dankmar 532
Advancement of Learning (Bacon) 407
"*Advancing Luna*" (Walker) 618
Aeneid (Vergil) 148, 149, 259
Aeschylus 83, 104-6, 108, 120, 192
Aesthetica (Baumgarten) 453
Africa 170
  Igbo-Ukwu 234
  Nok style 108
African-American culture 548
  Harlem Renaissance 574-5
  literature 630
  music 544, 628
  theatre 628-30
Agamemnon (Aeschylus) 105
Agnes of God (Pielmeier) 623-4, **18.40**
agricultural technology 447, 481
Aïda (Verdi) 505
Aiken, Howard 564
Akbar 345
Akhenaton 50, 52, 53, **1.24**
Alaric I 174
Alba Madonna (Raphael) 357-8, **11.17**
Albee, Edward 623
Alberti, Leon Battista 316-17, 322-3, **10.2**, **10.6**
Albertus Magnus 257
Aldus Manutius 377
aleatory music 619
Alexander the Great 86, 111, 159, 345, **3.28**
Alexandre Brongniart (Houdon) 460-1, **14.16**
Alexandria 111, 113, 169, 192
All Quiet on the Western Front (Milestone) 585
Allen, Paula Gunn 627
Alloway, Laurence 597
Altdorfer, Albrecht 389, 390, **12.14**
Amenophis II, Pharaoh 155
America
  architecture 463-4, 487, 489, 531-2, 548-51, 578-80
  film 546-7
  literature 566-7, 568, 574-5
  music 581, 582
  painting 522, 525, 534, 571-5, 594-6, 599-600
  theatre 470
America-Dawn (Nevelson) 603, **18.17**
American Festival Overture (Schuman) 581
American Gothic (Wood) 574, **17.15**
"American System" 482
Amiens Cathedral 264, **8.17**
Analects (Confucius) 89
Anaximander 84
Anderson, Garland 628

Angelico, Fra 236-8, **10.21**
Animals, the 622
Anthemius of Tralles 213, **6.30**
Anthony, St 201
Antioch 169, 192
Apollo Belvedere 342
Apollo and Daphne (Bernini) 418-19, **13.10**
Apollodorus of Damascus **4.16**, **4.17**
Apology (Plato) 86
Appalachian Spring (Copland) 582
Appeal to the German Nation, An (Luther) 379
Appearances (Anderson) 628
Appert, Nicholas 482
Applause (Mamoulian) 585
Apuleius 149
Arabian Nights, The 209
Architectura, De (Vitruvius) 129, 310
architecture 21-2
  20th-c. 578-80, 586-7, 611-16
  Art Nouveau 531, 532-3
  Assyrian 42
  Baroque 419, 422-5, 427-8, 440-2
  Byzantine 203-5, 213 17
  Carolingian 244
  Decorated style 302
  early Christian 179-81
  Egyptian 43, 45-6, 48, 50-3
  Expressionism 536
  Federal style 487, 489
  Gothic 260-6, 275-7, 288-90, 302-5
  Greek 58, 99-103, 117-18
  Greek Orders 72-3, 102-3, **2.20**, **3.21**
  Hellenistic 117-18, 130
  High Renaissance 361-3
  Indian 426
  International style 611, 612
  Islamic 209-12, 426
  Jewish 162-3
  Modernism 578-80, 611-14
  neo-classical 461, 464, 487
  Perpendicular style 305
  postmodernism 614-16
  Renaissance 316-19, 361-3
  revisionist 614
  rococo 457, 477
  Roman 130, 143-7, 179-80
  Romanesque 231-5
  Romantic 496
  skyscrapers 22, 531, 532, 611-12
  structure 21-2
Arcturus II (Vasarély) 599, **18.11**
Arena Chapel, Padua 295-6, **9.17**
Ariosto, Ludovico 366-7
Aristophanes 15, 105, 107, 108, 112, 192, 437
Aristotle 82, 86, 107, 109, 131, 148, 171, 192, 193, 256-7, 309, 406
Ark of the Covenant 158, 163
Armat, Thomas 545
Arnolfini Marriage, The (van Eyck) 297, **9.20**
Arnolfo di Cambio 336
Arp, Jean 570
ars antiqua 271
ars nova 299, 301
Art Nouveau 531, 532-3
Art and Revolution (Wagner) 505
art theories 13-17, 85-6, 565
  Aristotle 86
  Augustine 171
  Baumgarten 453
  criticism 26-7
  evaluation 24-7
  Goethe 27
  Hegel 484-5
  Plato 171
  Plotinus 136
  Winckelmann 453
Art Workers Guild 509
Artaud, Antonin 623

Ashton, Anthony 470
Asimov, Isaac 593
Aspects of the Negro Life (Douglas) 575, **17.17**
Assumption of the Virgin, The (Titian) 358, **11.19**
Assyrian Empire 42, 158, **1.10**, **1.11**
Astaire, Fred 585
astronomy 383-4, 407
Atanasoff, John 564
Athanasius of Alexandria 201
Athenodorus 117, **3.31**
Athens 82-3, 104, 108, 111, 192
  Parthenon 94, 96, 100-1, 103, **3.1**, **3.11**, **3.12**, **3.18-20**
  Propylaea 103, **3.22**
  Temple of Athena Nike 103, **3.23**
  Temple of Olympian Zeus 117, 130, **3.34**, **4.7**
Attila the Hun 188
Auden, W.H. 567
August 1914 (Solzhenitsyn) 618
Augustine, St 222, 230
Augustine of Hippo, St 170-1, 376, 378
Augustus, Emperor 124, 132-3, 136, 137, 139, 148, 149, 150-1, **4.1**, **4.15**, **4.27**, **4.28**
Augustus, Philip, King of France 250
Austen, Jane 499
Austria 452-3, 467-9
Autun Cathedral 236, **7.19**

B

Babbitt, Milton 618, 619
Babylonian Empire 40-1, 158, **1.3**
Bacchae, The (Euripides) 107
Bach, Carl Philipp Emanuel 466, 476
Bach, Johann Sebastian 435-6, 446, 476, **13.32**
Bacon, Francis 406-7
Bald Soprano, The (Ionesco) 623
Baldacchino (Bernini) **13.1**
Baltimore Cathedral (Latrobe) 487, 489, **15.6**
Balzac, Honoré de 499
Banjo Lesson, The (Tanner) 522, **16.9**
Baraka, Imamu Ameer 629
Barbarians 173-4
Barbarossa, Frederick 192
Barber of Seville, The (Beaumarchais) 472
Barber of Seville, The (Rossini) 505
Barberini Ivory 198, **6.11**
Barbizon School 522
Baroque style 414-30
  architecture 419, 422-5, 427-8, 440-2
  music 433-7, 442-3
  painting 415-18, 420-2, 428-31
  sculpture 418-19, 422
  theatre 443
Barry, Sir Charles 496, **15.16**
Bartók, Béla 581-2, 618, 620
Basilica of the Assumption, Baltimore (Latrobe) 487, 489, **15.6**
Bath, The (Cassatt) 527, 528, **16.13**
Battle of Alexander and Darius on the Issus (Altdorfer) 389, 390, **12.14**
Battle of San Romano (Uccello) 328, 338, **10.22**
Battleship Potemkin (Eisenstein) 584
Baudelaire, Charles 500
Bauhaus 569, 586-7
Baumgarten, Gottlieb 453, 460, 461, 466
Beatles, the 621, 622
Beaumarchais, Pierre de 469, 472
bebop 544
Beckett, Samuel **0.15**, 25, 623
Beckmann, Max 537, **16.24**

Beethoven, Ludwig van 469-70, **14.27**
Begay, Harrison 627-8, **18.45**
Beggars Opera, The (Gay) 470
Belamy Mansion, Wilmington (Bunnell) 489, **15.7**
Benedict, St 238
Benglis, Lynda 610, **18.28**
Benson, Tom **18.43**
Beowulf 238
Berg, Alban 582
Bergman, Ingmar 626
Berio, Luciano 619, 620
Berlioz, Hector 502, 503, 504
Bernard of Clairvaux, St 252, 254
Bernini, Gian Lorenzo 418-19, **11.33**, **13.1**, **13.9-11**
Bernward of Hildesheim 232
Berry, Chuck 622
Bessel brothers 481
Bible, The 159-60, 165-7, 181, 439
Billings, William 581
Biltmore House, North Carolina (Hunt and Olmstead) 551, **16.31**
biology 484, 519
Bird in Space (Brancusi) 578, **17.20**
Birds, The (Aristophanes) 15
Birth of a Nation (Griffith) 546-7, **16.28**
Birth of Tragedy from the Spirit of Music (Nietzsche) 519
Birth of Venus (Botticelli) 329, **10.27**
Bismarck 517-18, 554
Bizet, Georges 541-2, **16.26**
Black Death, The 283
Black Mass, A (Baraka) 629
Black Wall (Nevelson) 603, **18.1**
Blake, William 464
Bleak House (Dickens) 500
Blind Faith 622
Blissett, Francis **14.29**
Blue Nude (Souvenir de Biskra) (Matisse) 537, **16.25**
Blue Rider group 537, 538
Boccaccio, Giovanni 287-8
Boccioni, Umberto 536, **17.1**
Bofill, Ricardo 614-15, **18.36**
Bohr, Nils 518
Boléro (Ravel) 543
Bologna, Giovanni da 361, 536, **11.22**
Bonheur, Rosa 494, 496, **15.15**
Bonnin, Gertrude 568
Book of Hours of Jeanne d'Evreux 296, **9.19**
Book of Pastoral Care (Pope Gregory I) 222
Bosch, Hieronymus 389-90, **12.15**
Botticelli, Sandro 329, 332, **10.23**, **10.27**
Boucher, François 454, **14.6**
Boulez, Pierre 618, 619
Bourgeois Gentilhomme, Le (Molière) 436
Brahms, Johannes 502, 503, 504, **15.19-22**
Bramante, Donato 361, 368, **11.23**, **11.35**
Brancusi, Constantin 575, 578, **17.19**, **17.20**
Brando, Marlon 622
Braque, George 534, 572
Breakers, The (Hunt) 548-50, **16.29**
Brecht, Bertolt 583, 623
Britain *see* England
Brontë, Charlotte 499
Brontë, Emily 499
Bronzino 360, 417, **11.21**
Brothers Karamazov, The (Dostoevski) 539
Brown, Earle 618
Brown, Ford Madox **16.3**
Brücke, Die 536, 538
Bruegel, Pieter, the Elder 390-2,

12.16-18
Brunelleschi, Filippo 288, 317-19, **10.7-10**, **10.14**
Bryennius, Nicephorus 192
Buck Rogers 626
Budd, Harold 620
Buddha 89, **3.5**
Buddha (Frankenthaler) 596, **18.6**
Buddhism 89, 111, 272
Buffon, Georges 446
Bunnell, Rufus H. 489, **15.7**
Bunshaft, Gordon 611, **18.30**
Burckhardt, Jacob 308
Burghers of Calais, The (Rodin) 528, **16.14**
Burgundian school 334
Burnham, Daniel Hudson 531, **16.18**
Bus Driver, The (Segal) 598, **18.10**
Buxtehude, Dietrich 435
Byrd, William 402-3
Byrds, the 621, 622
Byron, George Gordon, Lord 499
Byzantine Empire 188-92, **6.1**
architecture 203-5, 213-17
hieratic style 196-7
Isaurian Emperors 190
literature 192, 200-1
manuscript illumination 197-8
mosaics 195-7, 215
music 201, 203
philosophy 192-3
pictorial style 193-5
sculpture 198-9
theatre 201

C

Cabaret **18.43**
Cabinet of Dr Caligari (Wiene) 584, **17.26**
Cage, John 618, 619, 620
Calder, Alexander 605, **18.20**
Calling of St Matthew, The (Caravaggio) 416-17, **13.6**
Calvin, John 374, 381-2, 402, **12.6**
Camus, Albert 583, 623
Candide (Voltaire) 450
Canova, Antonio 487, **15.5**
Canterbury Tales, The (Chaucer) 287
Cantos (Pound) 567
Capek, Karel 593
capitalism 313, 382, 480
Captain Video 626
Caravaggio 416-17, **13.6**, **13.7**
Carmen (Bizet) 541, **16.26**
Carnegie, Andrew 548
Carolingian Renaissance 220, 224-6, 240-5
Carrère **16.30**
Carter, Elliott 619
Cartesianism 449
Casa Batlló, Barcelona (Gaudí) 533, **16.21**
Cassatt, Mary 527-8, **16.13**
Castiglione, Baldassare 366, **11.29**
Castle, The (Kafka) 566
Catch 22 (Heller) 617
Cavalleria Rusticana (Mascagni) 542
Cemetery, The (Ruisdael) 430, **13.30**
Centerbeam (MIT) 610
ceramics
Chinese 116, 140, 393
Greek 66-8, 92-3
Japanese 165
Native American 627-8
Nok style 108
Cervantes, Miguel 432
Cesare e Cleopatra (Graun) 475
Cézanne, Paul 530, 534, **16.16**
Chabanon, Michel Paul de 466
Chadwick, Sir James 564
Chambord, Château of 393, **12.20**
Champeaux, William of 256
Chant des oiseaux, Le (Janequin)

395
Chaplin, Charlie 547, 585
Chardin, Jean-Baptiste Siméon 459 60, **14.14**
Charioteer (Delphi) 94, **3.8**
Charlemagne 224-6, 237, 239, 240 5, **7.4**
Charles V, Emperor 349
Chartres Cathedral 262-4, **8.11-14**, **8.18-20**
Chéteauneuf, Abbé de 450
Chaucer, Geoffrey 287, 399, **9.6**
Chekhov, Anton 545
Chesterton, G.K. 509
Chevalier, Maurice 585
Chevally, Abel 566
Chicago
Carson, Pirie and Scott Department Store (Sullivan) 531, 532, **16.19**
Monadnock Building (Burnham and Root) 531, **16.18**
Robie House (Wright) 532, **16.20**
Tribune Tower (Howell and Hood) 580
China
architecture 331
Han Dynasty 140-1
influence 209
literature 44
metalwork 44
Ming Dynasty 330-1, 393
painting 17, 140-1
Qin Dynasty terracotta warriors 116
Shang Dynasty 44
theatre 202
chivalry 250-1
Chopin, Frédéric 501, **15.18**
Chrétien de Troyes 258
Christ *see* Jesus Christ
Christ and the Woman Taken in Adultery (Beckmann) 537, **16.24**
Christianity 114, 154, 164-83
Apostolic mission 167-8
Church reform 241, 251-2
Church schism 188, 285-6
early Christian art 175-83
early Roman church 221-2
Gospels 165-7, 181
iconoclastic controversy 190
Jesus Christ 164, 165-7
mystery plays 271, 273-4, **8.27**
mysticism 192, 252
Papacy *see* Papacy, the
theology and philosophy 170-1
Westernization 184-5
Christo (Christo Jachareff) 14, 607, **18.25**
Chronicles (Froissart) 288
Chrysippus 131
Chryssa, (Varda) 605, **18.22**
Chu Ta **0.5**, 17
Cicero 132, 149
Cid, Le (Corneille) 437-8, 472
Cimabue 292-3, **8.5**, **9.14**
cinema *see* film
Circles (Berio) 620
cities, development 52-3, 61-2, 248 9
Citizen Kane (Welles) 624
City of God (St Augustine) 170, 171
City Lights (Chaplin) 585
Classical Greek style 92-110
Classical music 466-70
classical revivals 225, 241, 244-5, 309-10, 453, 460, 487
Clemente, Francesco 600, **18.14**
Climaton, St Louis (Fuller) 612, 614, **18.35**
Clodion (Claude Michel) 455-7, **14.8**
Close, Chuck 600
Clouet, Jean 393-4, **12.21**
Cluny Abbey 233-4, **7.15-17**
Coburn, D.L. 623-4, **18.40**
Coca-Cola 518

Cold War 592
Coleman, Ornette 620
Coleridge, Samuel Taylor 498, 499
Color Purple, The (Walker) 617
Coltrane, John 620, 628
Come Out (Reich) 620
Comédie Humaine (Balzac) 499
Commedia dell'Arte 364-5
Commentary on the True and False Religion (Zwingli) 380
Comnena, Anna 192
Composition X (Paik) 610
Composition (Miro) **0.7**, 17
Composition for Piano with Pianist (Moran) 620
Composition in White, Black and Red (Mondrian) 569, **17.18**
computer 564
Comte, Auguste 485
Conceptual art 600
Concerning Architecture (Alberti) 316-17
Concerning Human Understanding, An Essay (Locke) 410
Concerning Remarkable Mechanical Devises (Anthemius) 213
Confessions (St Augustine) 170
Confucius 89, 202
Conquistadors, the Age of the 344
Constable, John 493, 511
Constantine I, Emperor (the Great) 169, 171, 173, 174, 188, 220, **5.17**
Constantine V, Emperor 190
Constantinople 173, 190, 195, 220
Council of 169
St Sophia 213, 215-17, **6.30**, **6.33** 6
constructivism 569
cool jazz 544
Copernicus, Nicholas 383-4, 406
Copland, Aaron 582, 618, 620
Corelli, Arcangelo 437
Corneille, Pierre 437-8
Corot, Jean-Baptiste-Camille 494, 511, 521-2, 544, **15.13**
Corpus Juris Civilis (Justinian) 189
Corregidora (Jones) 630
Cortona, Domenico da 393
Cossutius 118
Counter-Reformation 349-50, 410 13
Counterfeiters (Gide) 566
country music 621
Couperin, François 466
Courbet, Gustave 521-2, **16.6**
Courtier, The (Castiglione) 366
Coysevox, Antoine 422, **13.17**
Craft of Musical Composition, The (Hindemith) 581
Cranach, Lucas, the Elder **12.3**
Creation (Haydn) 503
Creswick, Thomas 511, **15.26**
Crime and Punishment (Dostoevski) 539
Crimes of the Heart (Henley) 624
Cromwell, Oliver 382, 441
Crosby, Sills and Nash 622
Cross-Purposes (Camus) 583
Crusades, the 192, 252-4, **8.1-3**
Cubi XIX (Smith) 602, **18.16**
Cubism 534-5, 578
cummings, e.e 567
Cuvilliès, Jean Françoise de 457, **14.10**
Cynicism 113
Cyrus the Great 63, 158

D

Dada movement 570
Dadd, Richard 510-11, **15.25**
Dagulf Psalter 244, **7.25**
Dali, Salvador 571, **17.12**
Damascus, Great Mosque 212, **6.25**, **6.26**
Dame aux camélias, La (Dumas) 505

dance 542, 543
Danger Music for Dick Higgins (Paik) 620
Dante Alighieri 255, 258-9, 310
Dark Abstraction (O'Keeffe) 572, 573, **17.13**
Dark Ages 220
Darwin, Charles 484
David, Jaques-Louis 460, 462, 487, 492, **14.15**, **14.18**
David (Bernini) 418, **13.9**
David (Donatello) 321, **10.11**
David (Michelangelo) 19, 353, 355, 356, **11.16**
Davies, Arthur B. 571
Davis, Miles 620, 628
Davis, Stuart 572, 574, **17.14**
de Chirico, Giorgio 571, **17.11**
de Kooning, Willem 595-6, **18.4**
de Stijl 569
Death of a Salesman (Miller) 623
Death of Socrates, The (David) 460, **14.15**
Death of the Virgin, The (Caravaggio) 416-17, **13.7**
Debussy, Claude 540-1, 543, 620
Decameron (Boccaccio) 287, 288
decolonization 591-2
Decorated style 302
Defense of Poesie, A (Sidney) 398
Defoe, Daniel 433
Degas, Edgar 527
Déjeuner sur l'herbe (Manet) 522, **16.8**
Delacroix, Eugène 493-4, **15.12**
Deliverance of St Peter, The (Raphael) 358, **11.18**
Della Magnificenza ed Architettura dei Romani (Piranesi) 463
Della Porta, Giacomo 368, **11.31**
DeMille, Cecil B. 584
Democritus 65
Demoiselles d'Avignon, Les (Picasso) 534, 535, **16.22**
Dempster, Stewart 619
des Prés, Josquin 334, 363
Descartes, René 407-8, 449, **13.2**
Descent from the Cross (after Rembrandt) 428, 430, **13.29**
Descent from the Cross (van der Weyden) 385, **9.21**
Deserted Village, The (Goldsmith) 464
Deutsches Requiem, Ein (Brahms) 503
Devol, George C. 593
Dewey, John 565, 568
Diaghilev, Serge 543
Dickens, Charles 500, 510
Diderot, Denis 451
Dignity and Impudence (Landseer) 510, **15.24**
Diocletian, Emperor 171, 173, **5.16**
Diogenes 113
Diogenes of Babylon 131
Dipylon Vase, The 67
Discobolus (Myron) 95, **3.10**
Discourse on Method (Descartes) 408
Disney, Walt 585
Divine Comedy (Dante) 255, 258-9, **8.6**
Doctor Faustus (Marlow) 399, 400
Dolce Vita, La (Fellini) 626
Don Juan (Byron) 499
Don Juan (Strauss) 502
Don Quixote (Cervantes) 432
Don Quixote (Strauss) 502
Donatello 320-1, 338, **10.11-13**, **10.31**
Donne, John 432
d'Orbay, François 423
Dostoevski, Feodor 539, 544, 565
Douce Apocalypse 270, **8.22**
Douglas, Aaron 575, **17.16**, **17.17**
Douris 93, **3.7**
Dragons (Pfaff) 608, **18.26**

Dramatic Imagination, The (Jones) 521
Dryden, John 432
Du Bois, W.E.B. 574
Dubuffet, Jean 607, **18.23**
Duccio 293, **9.15**
Duchamp, Marcel 536, 572, **16.23**
Dufay, Guillaume 334
Dulle Griet (Mad Meg) (Bruegel) 392, **12.18**
Dumas, Alexandre 505
Dumas, Alexandre (père) 507
Dunciad, The (Pope) 432
Dunstable, John 334
Duran, Diego **11.2**
Dürer, Albrecht 385-7, **10.2**, **12.8-11**
Dutch painting 428-31
Dutchman (Baraka) 629
Dying Gaul, The 115-16, **3.33**
Dylan, Bob 622

E

Eagles, the 621
Eakins, Thomas 525
Eckert, J.Presper 564
Ecloga 190
Eclogues (Vergil) 148
Ecstasy of St Theresa, The (Bernini) 419, **13.11**
Eddy, Nelson 585
Edison, Thomas 545, 546
Egyptian civilization
    hieroglyph writing 48, 50
    Middle Kingdom 45, 50
    music 51
    New Kingdom 50
    Old Kingdom 45, 49
    painting 45, 48, 49, 50
    pharaohs 43-5, 49, 50
    philosophy and religion 43-4, 52-3
    pyramids and tombs 43, 45-6, 48, 50-1
    sculpture 46, 49, 53
Eight, the 571
Einstein, Albert 13, 518, 534, 564
Eisenstein, Sergei 584
El Greco 417-18, **13.8**
Eleanor of Aquitaine 250
Elgin Marbles 96
Elijah (Mendelssohn) 503
Eliot, T.S. 567
Elizabeth I 396, 399
Ely Cathedral 304, **9.27**
Embarkation for Cythera (Watteau) 454, **14.5**
Emma (Austen) 499
Empedocles of Acragas 65
Encyclopedia (Diderot) 451
Enemy of the People, An (Ibsen) 15
Engelbart, Joseph 593
England 230, 250, 255, 281-3, 285
    architecture 265, 302-5, 440-2, 457, 496-7
    Baroque style 439-43
    literature 238, 287, 302, 398-42, 407, 432-3, 464-5, 493, 499, 566
    music 334, 402-3, 433, 442-3
    Norman period 234-5
    painting 230, 270, 302, 397-8, 458-9
    philosophy 410, 485
    science 406-7, 408-9
    theatre 273-4, 302, 443, 470, 545
    Tudor age 396-403
    Victorian Age 508-11
Enlightenment, The 444-77
Ennead (Plotinus) 136
Enslavement of the Indians (Rivera) 575, **17.18**
environmental art 607-8
ephemeral art 607-8
Epictetus 136
Epicureanism 113, 114, 136
Epicurus 114
Erasmus, Desiderius 376, 377, 397,

12.2
Ernst, Max 570, **17.10**
Essai sur l'architecture (Abbé Laugier) 461, 463
Essay Concerning Human Understanding (Locke) 410
Estes, Richard 600
Etruscan civilization 124, **4.2**
Euclid 92
Euripides 104-5, 106-7, 120-1, 437
Eurydice (Rinuccini) 434
Eva's Man (Jones) 630
Every Man in his Humor (Jonson) 400
Everyman (morality play) 301
Excavation (de Kooning) 596, **18.4**
Exeter Cathedral 302, **9.25**
existentialism 565
exploration 343-4
Expressionism 536-7, 582-3
Eyck, Jan van 297, 298, **9.20**
Ezra 158

F

Faerie Queene, The (Spenser) 397, 399
Fairbanks, Douglas 547
Fairy Feller's Master Stroke, The (Dadd) 510-11, **15.25**
Falconet, Étienne-Maurice 455-6, **14.7**
Faulkner, William Cuthbert 566
Faust (Goethe) 472
Faust (Gounod) 505
Fauvism 537-8
Federal style architecture 487, 489, **15.8**
Fellini, Federico 626
Fences (Wilson) 630
Fermi, Enrico 564
Fichte, Johann 484, 485
Ficino, Marsilio 310, 312, 333
Fielding, Henry 465
Fields, W.C. 585
film 23-4, 545-7, 584-5
    demise of studio 625-6
    neorealism 624-5
    pluralism 626
    television movies 626
Finnegans Wake (Joyce) 566
Firebird, The (Stravinsky) 543
Five Classics, The 89
Flagler, Henry 550
Flanders
    music 334
    painting 296-8, 389-92
    sculpture 291
    theatre 273-4
Flaubert, Gustave 500
Flemish art *see* Flanders
Fleures du Mal, Les (Baudelaire) 500
Florence 193, 317-19, 321-9, 336-9, **10.29**
    Baptistery 323, **10.16**, **10.17**
    Cathedral 288-9, 317-18, **9.8**, **10.7**, **10.8**
    Foundling Hospital 318, **10.9**
    Pazzi Chapel 319, **10.10**
    Santa Maria Novella **10.20**
folk music 621-2
Fontana, Dominico 368
Ford, John 585, 624
Forster, E.M. 566
Foss, Lukas 619
4' 33" (Cage) 619
Four Books on Architecture (Palladio) 363
Four Horsemen of the Apocalypse, The (Dürer) 385-6, **12.9**
Fragments for the Gates to Times Square (Chryssa) 605, **18.22**
Fragonard, Jean-Honoré 454-5, **14.1**
France 224, 250, 251, 252, 255-6, 281-3

architecture 231-4, 260-4, 266, 275-7, 368, 422-5, 427, 580
    the Enlightenment 453-6
    film 546
    Gargas cave 32
    Lascaux cave 34
    literature 193, 245, 288, 499-500, 566
    music 238, 271, 299, 301, 395, 433, 466, 540-1, 543
    opera 503-5, 541-2
    painting 32, 34, 241, 296, 454-5, 459-60, 496, 521-2, 524, 525-7, 528-31, 534-6, 537-8
    philosophy 384, 450, 485
    Revolution 453, 462
    School of Fontainebleau 392-4
    sculpture 236-7, 267-8, 304, 455-7, 460-1, 487, 528
    theatre 239, 273-4, 335, 437-8, 472
Francis I, King of France 363, 392-3, **12.21**
Francis of Assisi, St 257, **8.5**
Franck, César 543
Frankenthaler, Helen 596, **18.6**
Frederick II, Emperor (the Great) 450, 452, 466, 474-7, **14.30**
Frederick II Hohenstaufen, Emperor 192
Freud, Sigmund 519-20, 571, **16.5**
Friedrich, Caspar David **15.1**
Frogs, The (Aristophanes) 105
Froissart, Jean 288
Frost, Robert 567
Fuller, Meta Vaux Warrick 575
Fuller, Richard Buckminster 612, 614, **18.35**
Fulton, Robert 482
Futurism 536, **17.1**

G

Gable, Clark 585, 626
Gainsborough, Thomas 458, **14.13**
Galileo Galilei 407
Garbo, Greta 585
Garden of Earthly Delights, The (Bosch) 389-90, **12.15**
Gargas cave 32
Garland, Judy 585, 626
Gates of Paradise, The (Ghiberti) 323, **10.16**, **10.17**
Gaudí, Antoni 533, **16.21**
Gauguin, Paul 530, **16.17**
Gay, John 470
Gelasius, Pope 222
Genet, Jean 623
Georgics (Vergil) 148
Géricault, Théodore 491, 492, **15.10**
German Way and German Art (Herder) 465
Germany 224, 229, 252, 451-2
    architecture 288, 428, 457, 474-7
    Bauhaus 586-7
    Expressionism 536-7
    film 585
    German Reich 517
    literature 465, 500-1, 566
    music 237, 238, 394-5, 435, 466, 469-70, 500
    opera 503-5
    painting 384-0, 536-7
    philosophy 484-5
    sculpture 232-3, 290-1
    theatre 273, 472, 582-3
Ghiberti, Lorenzo 321-3, **10.15**, **10.16**, **10.17**
Ghost Sonata (Strindberg) 582
Giacometti, Alberto 605, **18.21**
Gide, André 566
Gilbert, Cass 585, **17.24**
Gilbert, John 585
Gilgamesh Epic 36-7, 40
Gillespie, Dizzie 628
Gin Game, The (Coburn) 623-4, **18.40**

Giorgio, Francesco di **10.5**
Giotto 293-6, 336, **9.16**, **9.17**
Girl Before a Mirror (Picasso) **0.10**, 19
Glackens, William 571
Glass Menagerie, The (Williams) 623
Gloucester Cathedral 305, **9.30**, **9.31**
Godfrey, Thomas 471
Goethe, Johann Wolfgang von 27, 472, 486, 498, 505
Goetz von Berlichingen (Goethe) 472
Golden Ass (Apuleius) 149
Golden Haggadah **5.3**
Goldsmith, Oliver 464
Gombert, Nicholas 363
Gone with the Wind (Selznick) 585
Gorbachev, Mikhail 592
Gordonne, Charles 629
Gospel Book of Godescale 241, **7.21**
Gospel Book of Saint Médard of Soissons 241, **7.22**
Gothic style 260-6, 275-7, 288-90, 302-5
Goths 220
Gounod, Charles 505
Goya, Francisco de 491, 493, 575, **15.9**
Grande Odalisque, La (Ingres) 487, **15.4**
Grapes of Wrath (Steinbeck) 624
Grateful Dead 14
Graun, Karl Heinrich 474, 475
Graves, Michael 615, **18.37**
Great Condé, The 422, **13.17**
Great Depression, The 560-1, **17.4**
Great Train Robbery, The (Porter) 546
Greed (Stroheim) 584
Greek civilization 192
    archaic period 56-77
    architecture 58, 99-103, 117-18
    city-states 61-2
    Classical period 92-110
    Hellenistic period 111-19
    literature 86-8, 90-1, 103-7, 112-13, 200
    music 73-4, 109-10
    painting 57, 58
    philosophy 64-5, 84-6, 113-14
    science 208
    sculpture 68-72, 115-17
    sport 62
    theatre 15, 22, 83, 103-9, 112-13, 120-1
    vase painting 66-8, 92-3
Green, Paul 628-9
Green Coca-Cola Bottles (Warhol) 599, **18.8**, **18.9**
Greene, Robert 401
Gregorian chant 237
Gregory I, Pope 222, 223, 237, **7.3**
Griffith, D.W. 546-7, **16.28**
Gringoire, Pierre 335
Gropius, Walter 586-7, **17.27**
Grünewald, Matthias 387-8, **12.12**, **12.13**
Gruppen (Stockhausen) 619
Guiraud, Ernest 541
Gulliver's Travels (Swift) 432
Gupta **3.5**
Guthrie, Woody 622

H

Haba, Alois 619
Hagesandrus 117, **3.31**
hagiography 201
Halberstadt, Max **16.5**
Haley, Bill 622
Hall, Joseph 481
Hallelujah (Vidor) 585
Hals, Frans **13.2**
Hammurabi 40
Handel, George Frederick 439, 442-3, 503

Hansberry, Lorraine 629
happenings 623
Happy Time, The **18.44**
Harbaville Triptych 197, 199, **6.12**
Hard-edged abstraction 599-600
Hardouin-Mansart, Jules 423, **13.19**, **13.20**
Harlem Renaissance 574-5
Harlot's Progress, The (Hogarth) 458, **14.11**
Hastings **16.30**
Havilland, Olivia de 585
Hayden, Palmer 575
Haydn, Franz Joseph 467-8, 503, **14.22**, **14.23**
He Weeps for You (Viola) 610
Hecuba (Euripides) 120-1
Hegel, Georg Wilhelm Friedrich 484-5, 565
Heidegger, Martin 565
Hellenistic period 111-19, 127, 130, 194
Heller, Joseph 617
Hell's Angels 622
Hemingway, Ernest 567
Hendrix, Jimi 622
Henley, Beth 624
Henri IV Receiving the Portrait of Maria de Medici (Rubens) 420, **13.14**
Henri, Robert 571
Henry V (Shakespeare) 401
Henry VIII, King of England 396, 397, **12.24**
Hepburn, Audrey 626
Hepworth, Barbara 605, **18.19**
Heraclitus 84, 189
Herbert, George 432
Herculaneum 137-9, 453, 461
Herder, Johann Gottfried von 465
Hero 113, **3.29**
Herodotus 91
Hesiod 60, 63, 75, 192, 200
High Renaissance 342-71
  architecture 361-3
  painting 351-5, 357-60
Hildesheim Cathedral 232-3, **7.11**
Hilliard, Nicholas 398, **12.26**
Hindemith, Paul 581, 618, 620
Hippocrates 92
historiography 200
History of Ancient Art (Winckelmann) 453
History of the Persian Wars (Herodotus) 91
Hitchcock, Alfred **0.14**, 23, 585
Hitler, Adolf 519, 559, 561, 564
Hobbes, Thomas 410
Hogarth, William 458, **14.11**, **14.12**
Holbein, Hans the Younger 397, **12.24**, **12.25**
Holy Roman Empire 349, **11.1**
Holy Trinity, The (Masaccio) 324-6, **10.20**
Homage to John Cage (Paik) 620
Home (Williams) 629-30
Homer 58, 60, 63, 76-7, 192, 200
Hominis dignitate oratio, De (Mirandola) 312
Hood, Raymond 580
Horace 133, 149
Horatian Ode (Marvell) 432
Houasse, René-Antoine **13.21**
Houdon, Jean-Antoine 460-1, **14.4**, **14.16**, **14.17**
House of Fame, The (Chaucer) 287
House Made of Dawn (Momaday) 627
Household Words (Dickens) 510
How Green Was My Valley 624
Howard, Leslie 585
Howe, Elias 481
Howells, John Mead 580
Hrosvitha 239
Huber, Jean **14.3**
Hudon, Jean-Antoine **14.4**
Hughes, Langston 567, 574, 628,

17.7
Hugo, Victor 507
Huguenots, The (Meyerbeer) 504
humanism 84, 193, 310
Hume, David 449
Hundred Years' War, The 280, 281-3
Huns 174, 188, 220
Hunt, Richard Morris 548-50, 551, **16.29**
Hunter, Richard 470
Huntsman, Benjamin 447
Huss, John 285, 374

I
Ibsen, Henrik 15, 544
Ice Age 12, 30-2
iconoclasm 190
idealism 484, 545
Ideas on the Philosophy of the History of Mankind (Herder) 465
Idler Essays (Johnson) 465
Igbo-Ukwu 234
Il Piccolo Marat (Mascagni) 503
Iliad (Homer) 58, 63-4, 76-7
illuminated manuscripts 230-1, 241, 268, 270, 296, **5.3**, **7.1**, **7.8**
  Byzantine 197-8, **6.7**, **6.8**
  Carolingian 241-3, **7.21**, **7.22**, **7.24-6**
  Islamic 208-9, **6.21**, **6.22**
Imaginary Landscape No. 4 (Cage) 619
Imaginary Landscape No. 5 (Cage) 619
Impressionism
  music 540-1
  painting 524, 525-8, **16.10-13**
  theatre 545
In the Dining Room (Morisot) 527, **16.13**
In Praise of Folly (Erasmus) 377
Ince, Thomas 547
India 111, 345, **11.3**
Industrial Revolution 447-9, 480-4
industrialization 514-15, 517
Ingres, Jean-Auguste-Dominique 487, **15.4**
Inquisition, Holy Office of 284
installation art 608
Institutes of the Christian Religion (Calvin) 374, 381
intellectualism 84
International Gothic 291
International style 611, 612
internationalism 485-6
Interpretation of Dreams, The (Freud) 520
Intolerance (Griffith) 547
Ionesco, Eugene 623
Ireland 230, 399
Isaac, Heinrich 394
Isaiah 158
Isaiah Davenport House, Georgia 489, **15.8**
Isenheim altarpiece (Grünewald) 387-8, **12.12-13**
Isidorus of Miletus 215
Islam 154, 205-12, 238, 252-4, 256
  architecture 209-12, 426
  literature 209
  Muhammad 205-7, 208, 209, **6.22**
  painting 208-9
  The Koran 205, 208, 209
  theology and philosophy 205-8
Isozaki, Arata 615
Israel, Judaism *see* Judaism
Israel and Egypt (Handel) 442
Italian Wars 346-7
Italy 192, 255, 346-7, 349
  architecture 288-90, 316-19, 361-3, 612
  Etruscans 124
  film 546
  literature 258-9, 286-8, 366-7
  music 333, 363-4, 433

opera 503-5, 542
painting 292-6, 324-32, 416-17, 600
Romans *see* Roman civilization
sculpture 291-2, 320-3, 356, 361
theatre 273, 335, 364-5
Ives, Charles 582, 619
ivory 197, 198, 199
Izumo, Takeda 471

J
Jackson, Michael 622
Jacquard loom 481
James, Henry 500
Jane Eyre (Brontë) 499
Janequin, Clement 395
Janson, H.W. 99, 100, 608
Japan 563
  architecture 272
  painting 272
  sculpture 165, 272
  theatre 300, 471
Jardin d'Émail (Dubuffet) 607, **18.23**
Jaspers, Karl 565
jazz 544, 582, 619, 620, 627, 628
Jefferson, Joseph **14.29**
Jefferson, Thomas 363, 461, 463-4, **14.19**, **14.20**
Jenings, Waylon 621
Jerome, St 238
Jerry's Girls **18.42**
Jerusalem 158, 169
  Dome of the Rock 209-10, **6.23**, **6.24**
  Holy Sepulchre 210
  Temple of Solomon 158, 159-63, **5.7-11**
Jesus Christ 164, 165-7. *See also* Christianity
Jitney (Wilson) 630
Joan of Arc 282, 283, **9.3**
John II, Emperor 201
John, Elton 622
John of Damascus 192
Johnson, Philip **18.31**
Johnson, Samuel 464-5
Johnson, William Henry 575
Jolson, Al 585
Jones, Gayl 630
Jones, Inigo 397, 443, **13.39**
Jones, LeRoi *see* Baraka, Imamu Ameer
Jones, Robert Edmund 521
Jonson, Ben 400, 402
Joplin, Janis 622
Joplin, Scott 544
Joseph Andrews (Fielding) 465
Joshua 157
Joyce, James 566
Judaism 154-64, 171, 206
  arts 161, 164
  history 155-9, **5.1**
  Patriarchs 155-6
  Ten Commandments 157
  the Torah 160
Judd, Wynona 621
Julius Caesar (Shakespeare) 401
Jung, Carl Gustav 521
junk culture 605
Justinian, Emperor 188-9, 192, 194, 201, 203-4, 213, 215-17, 222, **6.6**
Juvenal 149

K
Kabuki theatre 471, **14.28**
Kafka, Franz 565, 566
Kahn, Louis I. 612
Kandinski, Wassily 538
Kant, Immanuel 449, 484, 485
Kaufmann House (Wright) 579, **17.25**
Kawabata, Yasunari 618
Kayonaga, Torri **14.28**
Kean, Charles 507, **15.23**

Keaton, Buster 585
Kelly, Ellsworth 599
Kepler, Johannes 312, 407
Khamis, Zabyah 618
Kiefer, Anselm 602, **18.15**
Kiergegaard, Sören 565
King, Carole 622
Kirchner, Ernst Ludwig 537
Klavierstück (Stockhausen) 619
Kliene Kammermusik für fünf Bläser (Hindemith) 581
Klinger, Friedrich von 472
Knobelsdorff, Georg Wenzelaus von 474, 477, **14.32-5**
Knossos 57-8, **2.2**
Know Thyself (Abelard) 256
Knox, John 382
Kokoschka, Oskar 538
Kollwitz, Käthe **16.2**
Koran, The 205, 208, 209
kore 71-2, **2.16**
Kosuth, Joseph 600, **18.13**
kouros 69-71, **21.14**, **21.15**
Kouros (Noguchi) 603, **18.18**
Kresilas **3.3**
Kritios Boy 72, **2.18**
Krohne, G.H. **14.9**
Kurosawa, Akiro 626

L
La Flesche, Susette 539
Lahori, Ustad Ahmad 426, **13.24**
Lamentation, The (Giotto) 295-6, **9.17**
Landscape with the Burial of Phocion (Poussin) 421-2, **13.15**
Landscape with the Fall of Icarus (Bruegel) 390, 392, **12.16**
Landseer, Edwin 510, **15.24**
Lang, Fritz 584, 585
Laocoön (Hagesandrus, Polydorus, Athenodorus) 95, 117, 342, **3.31**
Lascaux cave 34, **1.5**
Last Supper, The (Leonardo) 325, 351-2, **10.19**
Latrobe, Benjamin H. 487, 489, **15.6**
Laue, Max von 519
Laugier, Abbé 461, 463
Laurana, Luciano **10.5**
Laurel and Hardy 585
Lavoisier, Antoine 446
law
  code of Hammurabi 40-1
  early Christian 170
  Ecloga 190
  Justinian 189, 192
  Roman 135-6
Lawrence, D.H. 566
Lawrence, T.E. 557
Lawson, Ernest 571
Le Brun, Charles 423, 427, **13.20**
Le Corbusier 580, 612, **17.23**, **18.33**
Le Roy, Philibert 423
Le Vau, Louis 423, 427, **13.19**
Leiden des Jungen Werthers, Die (Goethe) 472
Leigh, Vivien 585
Leo I, Pope 169
Leo III, Pope 224, 240
Leo X, Pope 342, 349, 377, 379
Leo XIII, Pope 484
Leo III, Emperor 190
Leonardo da Vinci 325, 342, 348, 351-2, 353, 392, **10.4**, **10.19**, **11.5**, **11.6**, **11.8-10**
Leoncavallo, Ruggiero 542
Leontius of Byzantium 192
Lescot, Pierre 363, **11.24**
Lessing, Gotthold Ephraim 472
Leucippus 65
Leviathan (Hobbes) 410
Lewis, Lucy 627
Lichtenstein, Roy 597, **18.7**
lieder 394, 500-1, 504
Life of an American Firefighter, The (Porter) 546

light art 605
Lincoln, Abraham 498
Lincoln Cathdral 304, **9.29**
Lindisfarne Gospels 230, **7.8**
Linnaeus, Carolus 446
Lipchitz, Jacques 578, **17.21**
Lippi, Fra Filippo 326
Liszt, Franz 501, 504
literature
  17th-c. 432
  19th-c. 538-40
  20th-c. 520, 566-8
  African-American 630
  Ancient Egypt 50
  Byzantine 192, 200-1
  Chinese 44
  Elizabethan 398-402
  genres 23
  Greek 86-8, 90-1, 103-7, 112-13, 200
  hagiography 201
  Hellenistic 112-13
  historiography 200
  Islamic 209
  Jewish 161
  Middle Ages 245, 258-9, 286-8
  Native American 539, 548, 568, 627
  the novel 566-7
  Realism 538-9
  Roman 148, 149, 181
  Romantic movement 498-500
  Sumerian 36, 38, 40
  Symbolism 540, 545
Little Caesar 585
Livy 149
Lloyd, Harold 585
Locke, Alain 574
Locke, John 410, 441, 449, 450, 451
Lombard, Peter 193, 257
London
  Crystal Palace 498, **15.17**
  Hampton Court Palace 441-2, **13.33**
  Houses of Parliament 496, **15.16**
  St Paul's Cathedral 439, 440-1, 442, **13.34-6**
  Westminster Abbey **9.28**
Lorenzetti, Pietro 296, **9.18**
Lorre, Peter 585
Lorsch Gospels 244, **7.26**
Lotus (Chu Ta) **0.5**, 17
Louis IX, King of France 250, 268
Louis XIV, King of France (the Sun King) 414, 422-3, 427, 438, 450
Louis XVI, King of France 453, 462
Louise Brongniart (Houdon) 460-1, **14.17**
Low Countries *see* Flanders
Loyola, Ignatius 412
Lu Chi 330, **10.24**
Lucan 149
Lucky Strike (Davis) 572, 574, **17.14**
Luks, George 571
Lumière brothers 545-6
Luther, Martin 376, 377-80, 394, **12.1, 12.3, 12.4**
Lyell, Sir Charles 484
Lyric Suite (Berg) 582
Lysippus 99, **3.17**
Lysistrata (Aristophanes) 15

M

Ma Rainey's Black Bottom (Wilson) 630
MacDonald, Jeanette 585
Machaut, Guillaume de 299, 300
Machiavelli, Niccolò 311, 335, 342, **10.3**
MacLise, Daniel 511, **15.27**
Madame de Pompadour (Falconet) 455-6, **14.7**
Maderno, Carlo 368, **11.37**
Madonna 622
Madonna with the Long Neck (Parmigianino) **11.1**

Madonna of the Rocks, The (Leonardo) 351, **11.8**
Maeterlinck, Maurice 545
Magic Mountain, The (Mann) 566
Maître Pierre Pathélin 335
Makron 67, **2.11**
Malevich, Kasimir 569-70, **17.9**
Mallory, Thomas 258
Mamoulian, Rouben 585
Man with a Guitar (Lipchitz) 578, **17.21**
Man and His Symbols (Jung) 521
Man and the Masses (Toller) 583
Man Pointing (Giacometti) 605, **18.21**
Man and Superman (Shaw) 545
Mandragola (Machiavelli) 335
Manet, Edouard 522, **16.8**
Mann, Thomas 566
Mannerism 359-60, 361, 363, 374
Manon Lescaut (Puccini) 542, **16.27**
Mansfield Park (Austen) 499
Mantegna, Andrea 333, **10.1, 10.28**
Manuel I, Emperor 201
manuscript illumination *see* illuminated manuscripts
Marcus Aurelius 135, 136
Market Cart, The (Gainsborough) 458-9, **14.13**
Marlowe, Christopher 399, 400, 402
Marot, Clement 395
Marriage of Eva and Strongbow (MacLise) 511, **15.27**
Marriage of Figaro (Beaumarchais) 472
Marriage of Figaro (Mozart) 469, **14.26**
Martel, Charles 208, 224
Martial 149
Marvell, Andrew 432
Marx, Karl 451, 484, 516
Marx Brothers 585
Marxsen, Eduard 504
Masaccio (Tommaso di Giovanni) 324-6, **10.18, 10.20**
Mascagni, Pietro 503, 542
masque 443
Master of Go, The (Kawabata) 618
match, invention 182
materialism 485
Matisse, Henri 537-8, **16.25**
Maximum the Confessor 192
Mecca 205, 206, 207, 210
Medici, Cosimo de 310, 337-8, **10.30**
Medici, Lorenzo de 312, 333, 339, 349, **10.32**
Medici, Piero de 338-9, 346
Medina 207
Méliès, George 546
Mellancamp, John 622
melodrama 507
Menander 112, 131, 437
Mendel, Gregor Johann 484, 519
Mendelssohn, Felix 503
Menu de Gras (Chardin) 459-60, **14.14**
Menzel, Adolf von **14.31**
Mercury (da Bologna) 361, 536, **11.22**
Mérimée, Prosper 541
Mesopotamian civilization 36-42
Messiah (Handel) 442-3, 503, **13.37-8**
Metropolis (Lang) 584
Mexico 69, 344, 349, 575
Meyer, Adolph 586
Meyerbeer, Giacomo 504
Michelangelo Buonarroti 14, 342, 353-7, 368, **0.1, 5.25, 11.11-16, 11.30-3, 11.36**
Microphonie I (Stockhausen) 619
Middle Ages 220
  early 218-45, **7.1**
  High 246-77, **8.1**
  Late 278-305, **9.1**
Midgard (Kiefer) 602, **18.15**

Mies van der Rohe, Ludwig 612, **18.31**
Mignon (Thomas) 505
Milan Cathedral 289, **9.9**
Miles Brewton House, Charleston 464, **14.21**
Milestone, Lewis 585
Miller, Arthur 623
Millet, Jean-François 522, **16.7**
Milo of Crotona (Puget) 422, **13.16**
Milton, John 432
Minghuang, Emperor 202
minimalism 605
Minoan civilization 57-8
Mirandola, Pico della 312
Miro, Joan **0.7**, 17
Misfits, The 626
Mithraism 136, 137, **4.11**
Mlle Pogany (Brancusi) 575, **17.19**
mobile 605
Modernism 552-87
Modest Proposal, A (Swift) 432
Molière 26, 438
Moll Flanders (Defoe) 433
Momaday, Scott 627
Mona Lisa (Leonardo) 354, **11.10**
monasticism 190, 192, 222-4, 238, 252, 257
Mondrian, Piet 569, **17.8**
Monet, Claude 527, **16.11**
Monk, Thelonius 628
Monroe, Marilyn 626
Mont Sainte-Victoire (Cézanne) 530, **16.16**
Montaigne, Michel de 384
Monteverdi, Claudio 433, 434
Monticello (Jefferson) 463, **14.20**
Moore, Charles 616, **18.39**
Moore, Henry 577, 578, **17.22**
Moran, Robert 620
More, Sir Thomas 396, 397
Morgan, J. Pierpont 548
Morisot, Berthe 527, **16.12**
Morley, Thomas 433
Morris and Company 509
Morte d'Arthur (Mallory) 258
mosaic 195-7, 212, 215, **6.3-6, 6.24, 6.29**
Moses 155-6
Moses (Michelangelo) **0.1**
Moulin de la Galette, Le (Renoir) 524, **16.10**
Mouton, Abbot Gabriel 409
Mozart, Wolfgang Amadeus 14, 15, 466, 468-9, **14.24-6**
Mughal art 345, 11.3
Muhammad 205-7, 208, 209, **6.22**. See also Islam
Müller, Wilhelm 500
music
  20th-c. 542-4, 581-2
  African-American 544, 628
  aleatory 619
  Ancient Egypt 51
  Ancient Greece 51, 73-4, 109-10
  ars antiqua 271
  ars nova 299, 301
  Baroque 433-7, 442-3
  bebop 544
  Byzantine 201, 203
  cantata 434-5
  Classical style 466-70
  cool jazz 544
  country 621
  dissonance 542-3
  early Christian 181-3
  electronic 619, 620
  elements of 22
  Elizabethan 402-3
  Expressive style 466
  folk 621-2
  fusion 620
  German reformation 394-5
  Gregorian chant 237
  hymns 182-3, 201, 203
  Impressionism 540-1
  improvisation 619

jazz 544, 582, 619, 620, 627, 628
jazz-rock 620
Jewish 164
lieder 394, 500-1, 504
microtonality 619-20
Middle Ages 237-8, 271
Native American 628
opera *see* opera
plainchant 237
pluralism 619-20
progam music 501-2
ragtime 544
Renaissance 333-4, 363-4
rhythm and blues (R & B) 621-2
rock 'n' roll 621-2
Roman 148, 181-2
Romantic 468, 469, 500-5
sacred 201, 237
serialism 543, 618-19
sonata form 467
Sumerian 40
swing 544
symphonic form 467-9, 502-3
Syrian 201, 203
theatre (experimental) 620
vocal 74, 394, 395, 500, 503, 504
Music of Changes, The (Cage) 619
Musica Nova (Willaert) 363
musical instruments 40, 51, 74, 92, 238, 403, 433, 436
Muslim culture *see* Islam
Mycenaean civilization 58-9, **2.4**
Myron 94, 95, **3.10**

N

Nabis, The 530
Napoleon Bonaparte 453, 485, 487, 491, **15.3**
Napoleon III 485
Narayan, R.K. 617
Nash, John 496, **15.14**
Nasmyth, James 481
National Velvet 626
nationalism 503
Native American culture 44, 69, 548
  ceramics and painting 627-8
  literature 539, 548, 568, 627
  music 628
naturalism 541-2, 544-5
"Nedawi" (La Flesche) 539
Nefertari, Tomb of 48-9, **1.17, 1.18**
Negro Speaks of Rivers, The (Hughes) 567
Nehemiah 158
Nelson, Willie 621
neo-abstraction 610
neo-classicism 437, 453, 460, 487-9. *See also* classical revivals
neo-classicism, French 437-8
neo-expressionism 600, 602
neo-Platonism 136, 137, 170-1, 192, 193, 310, 312, 353
neo-realism 624-5
neo-Romanticism 545
Nervi, Pier Luigi 612, 614, **18.34**
Netherlands *see* Dutch painting; Flanders
Neuhaus, Max 619
Neumann, Balthasar 428, **13.27**
Nevelson, Louise 602-3, 18.1, 18.17
New England Triptych (Schuman) 581
New English Art Club 509
New York
  Guggenheim Museum 612, **18.32**
  Lever House 611-12, **18.30**
  Seagram Building 612, **18.31**
  Woolworth Building 580, **17.24**
Newcomen, Thomas 448
Newton, Sir Isaac 13, 408-9, 446, 450, **13.4**
Nicea, Council of 169
Niebelungenlied 238
Nietzsche, Friedrich Wilhelm 519
Nigeria 234

Night Watch, The (Rembrandt) 429, **13.28**
Night (Wiesel) 617
Nijinsky, Vaslav 25
Nike of Samothrace 115, 116, **3.30**
Ninety-five Theses (Luther) 379, **12.4**
No Exit (Sartre) 583
No Place to Be Somebody (Gordonne) 629
Noguchi, Isamu 603, **18.18**
Noh theatre 300
Nok style 108
Nonrepresentational art *see* Abstract art
Norman style 234-5
Nostalgia of the Infinite, The (de Chirico) 571, **17.11**
Not Without Laughter (Hughes) 567
Notker Balbulus 237
Notre Dame du Haut, Ronchamp (Le Corbusier) 612, **18.33**
nuclear weapons 563, 564
Nude Descending a Staircase, No.2 (Duchamp) 536, 572, **16.23**

O

Oath of the Horatii (David) 460, 462, 524, **14.18**
Ode on a Grecian Urn (Keats) 499
Ode to Joy (Schiller) 470
Ode to a Nightingale (Keats) 499
Odo of Metz 244
Odyssey (Homer) 58
Oedipus the King (Sophocles) 106
Offenbach, Jacques 504-5
O'Keeffe, Georgia 572, 573, **17.13**
Oldenburg, Claes 597-8, **18.8**
Olmstead, Frederick Law 551, 608, **16.31**
Olympic games 62, 94
On the Fabric of the Human Body (Vesalius) 383
On the Gods (Protagoras) 84-5
On the Motion of Mars (Kepler) 407
On the Revolutions of the Celestial Orbs (Copernicus) 383-4
On the Seine at Bennecourt (Monet) 527, **16.11**
Once (Walker) 617
One Day in the Life of Ivan Denisovich (Solzhenitsyn) 618
One Sound (Budd) 620
One and Three Chairs (Kosuth) 600, **18.13**
Onnes, Heike Kamerlingh 519
Op art 599
opera 433-4, 469, 470, 474-5, 503-4, **13.31**
    19th-c. 541-2
    naturalism 541-2
Opera and Drama (Wagner) 505
Oresteia (Aeschylus) 105
Orfeo (monteverdi) 434
Organon (Aristotle) 256
Origin of Species, The (Darwin) 484
Orlando Furioso (Ariosto) 367
Orta Oinu (Turkish theatre) 201
Orthodox Church 188-90
Oscott Psalter 270, **8.23**
Ostrogoths 188, 213
Otello (Verdi) 505
Ottoman Empire 346, 349
Ottonian period 220, 229, 232-3

P

Pacific War 563, **17.3**
Pagliacci, I (Leoncavallo) 542
Paik, Nam June 610-11, 620, **18.29**
Paine, Thomas 464
painting 17, 18
    20th-c. 569-74, 575
    Abstract art 569-70, 610
    Abstract Expressionism 594-6
    Ancient Egypt 45, 48, 49, 50

Barbizon School 522
Baroque 415-18, 420-2, 428-31
Blue Rider group 537, 538
Byzantine 197
Carolingian 241
Chinese 17, 140-1
Cubism 534-5, 578
Dada 570
de Stijl 569
Die Brücke 536, 538
early Christian 177-8, 194, 229-30
Expressionism 536-7
Fauvism 537-8
genre 459-60
Gothic 269-70, 292-8
Hard-edged abstraction 599-600
illuminated manuscripts *see* illuminated manuscripts
Impressionism 524, 525-8
Islamic 208-9
Jewish 161
Mannerism 359-60
miniature 398
minimalism 605
Mughal 345
Nabis 530
Native American 627-8
neo-expressionism 600, 602
Nonrepresentational 569-70
Op art 599
Photorealism 600
Post-Impressionism 528-31
Realism 521-3, 525, 574
reformation 384-94
Renaissance 324-32, 351-5, 357-60
rococo 454-5
Roman 127-9, 137, 139
Romanticism 489, 491-6
Stone Age cave 32, 34
suprematists 569
Surrealism 571
Victorian 508-11
Palace of Abraxas, Marne-la-Vallée (Bofill) 615, **18.36**
Palazzo Rucellai, (Alberti) 317, **10.6**
Palestrina, Giovanni Pierluigi da 433
Palladio, Andrea 363, 364, 443, **11.25**, **11.27**
Panaetius 131
Panini, Giovanni Paolo **4.22**
Papacy, the 169, 189, 221-3, 252, 314, 347, 349, 368-71
Paradise Lost (Milton) 432
Paris
    Abbey Church of Saint-Denis 260-2, 275-7, **8.7**, **8.8**, **8.28-30**
    Louvre 363, **11.24**
    Notre-Dame 262, **8.9**, **8.10**
    Pompidou Center 616, **18.38**
Parker, Charlie "Bird" 628, **18.46**
Parliament of Fowls (Chaucer) 287
Parmigianino **11.1**
Passat (Benglis) 610, **18.28**
Passion According to St Luke, The (Penderecki) 621
Pasteur, Louis 519
Pathé, Charles 546
Paul, St 184-5, **5.31**
Pauline Borghese as Venus Victrix (Canova) 487, 15.5
Paxton, Sir Joseph 498, 15.17
Pelagius 171
Pelléas and Mélisande (Maeterlinck) 545
Penderecki, Krzysztof 620-1
Pergamon, Altar of Zeus 118, **3.35**
Peri, Jacopo 434
Pericles 82, 83, 100, **3.3**
Perpendicular style 305
Persistence of Memory, The (Dali) 571, **17.12**
Persuasion (Austen) 499
Peruzzi, Baldassare **11.26**
Pesne, Antoine **14.30**
Petrach 286-7, 310, 363
Petronius 149

Pfaff, Judy 608, **18.26**
Phaedo (Plato) 85, 86-8, 90-1
Phantom of the Opera 624
Phèdre (Racine) 438
Phidias 83, 98, **3.14**
Philip II, King of Spain 349-50
Philosophy of the History of Mankind, The (Herder) 465
philosophy and religion 377, 383, 407, 484-5, 598
    18th-c. 449-51
    Ancient Egypt 43-4, 52-3
    Buddhism *see* Buddhism
    Byzantine period 192-3
    Cartesianism 449
    Christianity *see* Christianity
    Confucianism 89
    Cynicism 113
    Epicureanism 113, 114, 136
    existentialism 565
    Greek 63-5, 84-6, 113-14
    Hellenistic 113-14
    humanism 84, 193, 310
    idealism 484, 545
    Islam *see* Islam
    Judaism *see* Judaism
    Middle Ages 255-8
    neo-Platonism 136, 137, 170-1, 192, 193, 310, 312, 353
    Nietzsche 519
    Pauline 184-5
    Platonism 85, 86-8, 89, 90-1, 110, 171, 192, 256, 312
    pragmatism 565
    Renaissance 310, 312
    Roman 129, 131-2, 136-7
    Shinto 165
    Skepticism 113
    Sophists 84-5
    Stoicism 113-14, 131-2, 136, 137, 149, 170, 384
    Sumerian 36-7
    Taoism 89, 202
phisiology 383
Photius 192
Photorealism 600
physics 518-19
Piano, Renzo 616, 18.38
Piano Lesson, The (Wilson) 630
Piazza d'Italia, New Orleans (Moore) 616, **18.39**
Picasso, Pablo **0.10**, 13, 19, 534, 535, 572, 578, **16.22**
Piccolo Marat, Il 503
Pielmeier, John 624, **18.41**
Pierrot Luniare (Schoenberg) 544
Pietà (Michelangelo) 353, 355, 357, **11.15**
Pinter, Harold 623
Pirandello, Luigi 583, 623
Piranesi, Giambattista 463
Pisano, Giovanni 291-2, **8.1**, **9.13**
Pisano, Nicola 291-2
Pius IX, Pope 484
Plack, Max 518
plague 283
plainchant 237
Plato 62, 85, 86-8, 89, 90-1, 110, 171, 192, 256, 312
Plautus 131
Pliny the Younger 201
Plotinus 136, 170
Plowing in the Nivernais (Bonheur) 494, 496, 15.15
pluralism 590-4, 619-20, 623-4, 626, 627
Poe, Edgar Allen 498
Poetics (Aristotle) 86, 107, 109
Pollock, Jackson 595, 608, **18.3**
Polyclitus 94, **3.9**
Polyclitus the Younger 109, **3.27**
Polydorus 117, **3.31**
Polymedes of Argos 95, **2.14**
Polymorphia (Penderecki) 620, 621
Pompeii 453, 460, 461, 466, 507
Pope, Alexander 432
Porta, Giacomo della 361, 419,

11.31, 13.12, 13.13
Porter, Edwin S. 546
Portland Public Office Building, Portland (Graves) 615, **18.37**
Posidonius 131
positivism 485
Post-Impressionism 528-31, **16.15-17**
postmodernism 608-10, 614-16
Potter, Tommy **18.46**
Pound, Ezra 554, 567
Poussin, Nicolas 421-2, **13.15**
pragmatism 565
Pratt, F.A. 482, **15.2**
Praxiteles 98-9, **3.15**, **3.16**
Pre-Raphaelites 510
Precisionists 572
Prélude à l'après-midi d'un faune (Debussy) 541
Prendergast, Maurice 571
Preromantic movement 465
Presley, Elvis 621, 622, 626
Pride and Prejudice (Austen) 499
Primary structures movement 602-3
Primavera, La (Botticelli) 329, **10.23**
Prince 622
Prince, The (Machiavelli) 311
Prince of Parthia, The (Godfrey) 471
Principia (Newton) 408-9
Principles of Geology (Lyell) 484
printing 284, 363, 377, 379, **12.4**
Procopius of Caesarea 201
Prodromos, Theodore 201
Prokofiev, Sergei 581, 618
Prometheus Bound (Aeschylus) 120
Protagoras 84-5
Proust, Marcel 540
Psalter of St Louis 268, **8.21**
Psellus, Michael 192
Puccini, Giacomo 542, **16.27**
Pucelle, Jean 296, **9.19**
Puget, Pierre 422, **13.16**
Pugin, A.W.N. 496, **15.16**
pyramids *see* Egyptian civilization
Pyrrho of Elis 113
Pythagoras 64, 110

Q

Qasa'id Hubb (*Love Odes*) (Khamis) 618
Quo Vadis 546

R

Rabelais 308
Racine, Jean 438
Radcliffe, Mrs 465
Raft of the "Medusa" (Géricault) 491, **15.10**
ragtime 544
railroads 482, 548
Raisin in the Sun, A 629
Rake's Progress, The (Hogarth) 458, **14.12**
Rambler essays (Johnson) 464
Rape of the Lock, The (Pope) 432
Raphael 342, 357-8, 368, 371, **11.17**, **11.18**, **11.29**, **11.38**
Rashomon (Kurosawa) 626
Ravel, Maurice 543, 620
Ravenna 213-15, 244
    Apollinare in Classe **5.1**
    San Vitale 213-15, 216, **6.6**, **6.27-9**, **6.32**
Realism
    literature 538-9
    painting 521-3, 525, 574
    theatre 544-5, 623
"Recuerdo" (Allen) 627
Recumbent Figure (Moore) 577, **17.22**
Reformation 349, 372-403
Reich, Steve 620
Rembrandt van Rijn 13, 428-30, **13.28, 13.29**

Remembrance of Things Past
  (Proust) 540
Remenyi, Eduard 504
Renaissance
  architecture 316-19, 361-3
  Early 306-39
  High 340-71
  literature 366-7
  music 333, 363-4
  painting 324-32, 351-5, 357-60
  philosophy 310, 312
  sculpture 320-3
  technology 313-14, 315
  theatre 335, 364-5
Rene Descates (Hals) **13.2**
Renoir, Pierre-Auguste 524, 527,
  16.10
Republic (Plato) 86, 110
revisionist architecture 614
rhythm and blues (R & B) 621-2
Riace Warriors 96, 98, **3.14**
Rice, Elmer 583
Richard II (Shakespeare) 507, **15.23**
*Right You Are If You Think You
  Are* (Pirandello) 583
Rights of Man, The (Paine) 464
Rime of the Ancient Mariner, The
  (Coleridge) 499
Rimski-Korsakov, Nikolai 543
Rinuccini, Ottavio 434
Rite of Spring, The (Stravinsky) 25,
  543-4
Rivera, Diego 575, **17.18**
Robert the Devil (Meyerbeer) 504
Robinson, Edward G. 585
Robinson Crusoe (Defoe) 433
robot 593
rock 'n' roll 621-2
Rockefeller, John D. 548
rococo style 454-7
  architecture 457, 477
  music 466
  painting 454-5
  sculpture 455-6
Rodelinda (Graun) 475
Rodin, Auguste 528, **16.14**
Rogers, Ginger 585
Rogers, Richard 616, **18.38**
Rolling Stones, the 622
Roman civilization
  architecture 130, 143-7, 179-80
  Christianity 171, 173-83, 221-2
  Empire 124, 132-49, 171, 173-4,
    220, **4.2, 4.3, 4.9, 5.5**
  law 135-6
  literature 148, 149, 181
  music 15, 148, 181-2
  painting 127-9, 137, 139
  philosophy and religion 129, 131-
    2, 136-7
  Republic 124-31, **4.1**
  sculpture 129-30, 139, 141-3, 150-
    1, 174-5
  theatre 15, 129, 130-1
Roman Holiday 626
Romance of Amir Hamza, The **11.3**
Romanesque style 220, 231-7
  architecture 231-5
  Norman Romanesque 234-5
  sculpture 235-7
Romantic movement 446, 480-511
  literature 498-500
  music 468, 469, 500-5
  opera 503-4
  painting 489, 491-4
  philosophy 484-5
  theatre 505-7
Romanus IV, Emperor 199
Rome 134, 173, 192, 220, 221-2,
  4.9, 4.10
  Ara Pacis 151, **4.31**
  Arch of Titus 147, **4.24**
  Basilica of Constantine 179, **5.26,
    5.27**
  Baths of Diocletian **5.25**
  catacombs 177-8, **5.15, 5.22**
  Colosseum 143, 147, **4.19, 4.23**

Forum of Augustus 151, **4.29,
  4.30**
foundation 124
Gesó, Il 419, **13.12, 13.13**
Old St Peter's Basilica 180, 181,
  5.28
Pantheon 144-5, 216, 288, **4.20-2**
St Peter's 361, 368-71, **11.30-3,
  11.35-7, 13.1**
San Paolo Fuori le Mura 181, **5.29**
Sistine Chapel 353, 354-5, **11.12-
  14, 11.34**
Small Sports Palace (Nervi) 612,
  614, **4.2, 18.34**
Tempietto, San Pietro in Montorio
  361, **11.23**
Temple of Fortuna Virilis 130, **4.8**
Trajan's Column 141-3, **4.16-18**
Vatican 368-71, **11.32, 11.38**
Rome, Open City (Rossellini) 625
Ronstadt, Linda 621
Röntgen, Wilhelm Conrad 519
Room of One's Own, A (Woolf) 566
Root, John Wellborn 531, **16.18**
Rosselli, Francesco **10.29**
Rossellini, Roberto 625
Rossi, Aldo 614
Rossini, Gioacchino 505
Rothko, Mark 596, **18.5**
Rouault, Georges 538
Rousseau, Jean-Jaques 451, 460, 465
Royal Academy 509
Royal Pavilion, Brighton (Nash)
  496, **15.14**
Rubens, Peter Paul 417, 420-1,
  13.14
Ruffe, L. **17.2**
Ruisdael, Jacob van 421, 430, **13.30**
Running Fence (Christo) **0.3**, 14
Russia
  literature 539
  music 543, 581
  Revolution and Civil War 558-9
  theatre 545

S

Saarinen, Eero 612
Sacrifice of Isaac (Brunelleschi)
  321, **10.14**
Sacrifice of Isaac (Ghiberti) 321,
  10.15
St Albans Cathedral 234-5, **7.18**
St George (Donatello) 320, **10.13**
St James Led to Execution
  (Mantegna) 333, **10.28**
St Jerome (El Greco) 417, **13.8**
St Mark Freeing a Christian Slave
  (Tintoretto) 359, **11.20**
St Matthew Passion (Bach) 435
St Michael Quelling the Dragon
  (Dürer) 386-7, **12.10**
Saint-Saëns, Camille 543
Salisbury Cathedral 265, 285, **8.15,
  8.16, 9.1**
Samochvalov, Alexandr
  Nikolayevich **17.3**
Samuel 158
Sans Souci Palace, Potsdam
  (Knobelsdorff) 450, 477, **14.31-5**
Sappho 74-5
Sargon II 42
Sartre, Jean-Paul 565, 583, 623
Satyr and Bacchante (Clodion) 455-
  7, **14.8**
Saul 158
Sauvy, Alfred 592
Savonarola 312, 347
Scarlatti, Alessandro 435
Schelling, Friedrich 484, 485, 565
Schiller, Johann Christoph
  Friedrich von 470, 498
Schloss Nymphenburg, Munich
  457, **14.10**
Schoenberg, Arnold 544, 582
Schöne Mülerin, Die (Müller) 500-1
Schopenhauer, Artur 485, 519

Schubert, Franz 500-1, 503
Schuman, William 581
Schumann, Robert 504
science *see* technology and science
Scopas **3.13**
Scott, Walter 499
Scotus Erigena 193
Scribe, Eugène 504, 544
Scraggs, Ricky 621
sculpture 19
  19th-c. 528
  20th-c. 597-8, 602-5
  Abstraction 603, 605
  African 234, 575
  Ancient Egypt 46, 49, 53
  Archaic Greek 69-71
  Baroque 418-19, 422
  Byzantine 198-9
  Carolingian 244
  carved ivory 197, 198, 199
  Classical Greek 94-9
  early Christian 231
  environmental 607-8
  ephemeral 607-8
  found sculpture 605
  Futurism 536
  Gothic 267-8
  Hellenistic 115-17
  installations 608
  Japanese Shinto 165
  late Gothic 290-2, 304
  Mannerist 361
  minimalism 605
  mobiles 605
  neo-classical 460-1, 487
  Ottonian 232-3
  postmodernism 608-10
  Primary structures movement
    602-3
  Renaissance 320-3
  rococo 455-6
  Roman 129-30, 139, 141-3, 150-1,
    174-5
  Romanesque 235-7
  Stone Age 12, 33-4
  Sumerian 39, 40
  video 610
Seasons, The (Thomson) 493
Seasons, The (Vivaldi) 437, 466
Second Shepherd's Play 302
Segal, George 598, **18.10**
Seger, Bob 622
Selznick, David O. 585
Seneca 136
Sennet, Mack 547
serfdom 226, 228-9
serialism 543, 618-19
Serlio, Sebastiano 364, 397, 443,
  11.28
Sermisy, Claudin de 395, **12.22**
Sermon on the Mass (Luther) 379
Seurat, Georges 528, **16.15**
Seven Samurai (Kurosawa) 626
Seventh Seal, The (Bergman) 626
Shakespeare, William 400-2, 472,
  506, **15.23**
Shapiro, Joel 609-10, **18.27**
Shaw, George Bernard 545
Shelley, Percy Bysshe 499
Shepheardes Calendar, The
  (Spenser) 398
Shinn, Everett 571
Shinto 165
Sidney, Sir Philip 398
Skepticism 113
skyscrapers 22, 531, 532, 611-12
Slave Ship (Turner) 493, **15.11**
Sloan, John 571
Sluter, Claus 291, **9.12**
Smith, Adam 451
Smith, Bessie 585
Smith, David 602, **18.16**
Smithson, Robert 607, 608, **18.24**
Smythson, Robert 397
Snell, Bruno 95
Snow Country (Yukiguni)
  (Kawabata) 618

social classes 226, 249-50
Social Contract (Rousseau) 451
social theory 409-10
socialism 484, 515-17
sociology 485
Socrates 62, 83, 85, 89, 91, 256, 384
"Soft-Hearted Sioux, The" (Bonnin)
  568
Solomon 159
Solzhenitsyn, Alexander I. 618
Song of Roland (Turold) 245
Sons and Lovers (Lawrence) 566
Sophists 84-5
Sophocles 83, 104, 106, 108, 437
Sound and the Fury, The (Faulkner)
  566
Spain 224, 255, 256, 349-50
  architecture 21, 533
  literature 432
  painting 417-18
  theatre 273
spectacularism 624
Spencer, Herbert 485
Spenser, Edmund 397, 398-9
Sphere with Internal Form
  (Hepworth) 603, 605, **18.19**
Spielberg, Steven 626
Spiral Jetty (Smithson) 607, 608,
  18.24
*Spirit in Man, Art and Literature,
  The* (Jung) 521
Spring Blossoms (Calder) 605, **18.20**
Springsteen, Bruce 622
Spurgeon, Charles 574
Stagecoach (Ford) 585
stained glass 263-4
Star Wars (Spielberg) 626
Starlight Express 624
Starry Night, The (van Gogh) 17, **0.6**
steam turbine 113, **3.29**
Steel Step (Prokofiev) 581
Steinbeck, John 624
Stella, Frank 599-600, **18.12**
Stephenson, George 482
Stibitz, George R. 564
Stieglitz, Alfred 573
Stimmung (Stockhausen) 620
Sting 622
Stocker, Gaspar 363
Stockhausen, Karlheinz 619, 620
Stoicism 113-14, 131-2, 136, 137,
  149, 170, 384
Stone Age 30-5
  painting 32, 34
  sculpture 12, 33-4
Stone Breakers, The (Courbet) 522,
  16.6
Stowe, Harriet Beecher 507
Strada, La (Fellini) 626
Stradivari, Antonio 437
Strato 113
Strauss, Richard 500, 502
Stravinsky, Igor 25, 543-4, 618, 620
Streetcar Named Desire, A
  (Williams) 623
Strindberg, August 582
Stroheim, Erich von 584
Strophes (Penderecki) 621
Sturm und Drang (Klinger) 472
Suger, Abbot 260, 275-7
Suleiman I, Emperor (the
  Magnificent) 346, **11.4**
Sullivan, Louis 531, 532, **16.19**
Sumerian civilization
  literature 36, 38, 40
  music 40
  religion 36-7
  sculpture 39, 40
Summa contra Gentiles (Aquinas)
  257
Summa Theologiae (Aquinas) 257
*Sunday Afternoon on the Island of
  La Grande Jatte* (Seurat) 528,
  16.15
*Suprematist Composition: White on
  White* (Malevich) 569-70, **17.9**
suprematists 569

Surprise Symphony (Haydn) 467, **14.22**, **14.23**
Surrealism 571
Swift, Jonathan 432
Swing, The (Fragonard) 454-5, **14.1**
swing music 544
Switzerland 374, 380, 381
Syllabus of Errors (Pope Pius IX) 484
Symbolism 540, 545
Symphonie Fantastique (Berlioz) 502
Symposium (Plato) 312
synthsizer 619

T

Tahkt-I-Sulayman I (Stella) 599-60, **18.12**
Taj Mahal, Agra 426, **13.24**
Tallis, Thomas 403
Tamburlaine the Great (Marlowe) 399
Taming of the Shrew, The (Shakespeare) 401
Tanner, Henry O. 522, 525, **16.9**
T'ao Ku 182
Taoism 89, 202
Tartuffe (Molière) 26, 438
Taylor, Cecil 620, 628
Taylor, Elizabeth 626
Taylor, James 622
Tchaikovsky, Peter Ilyich 503
Teatro Olimpico, Vicenza (Palladio) 364, **11.27**
technology and science 86, 208, 249, 382-4, 406-7, 514-15, 593
  18th-c. 447-9
  19th-c. 447
  agriculture 249, 447, 481
  astronomy 383-4, 407
  biology 484, 519
  bridge building 146, 448, 481
  building techniques 531
  Chinese 116
  computers 564
  energy systems 249, 447, 482-3
  Leonardo 348
  machine tools 448, 482
  matches 182
  measurement 38, 127, 285, 409
  metal production 234, 284, 447, 481, 482
  Middle Ages 249, 284, 285
  naval artillery 383
  olive press 63
  phisiology 383
  physics 518-19
  Renaissance 313-14, 315
  robots 593
  Roman 145, 146
  ship design 227
  spanning space 145, 216
  steam turbine 113, **3.29**
  Sumerian 38
  textiles 284, 448, 480-1
  tools 32
  the wheel 38
Tempest, The (Shakespeare) 400
Temple, Shirley 585
Ten Commandments, The 157
Ten Commandments, The (DeMille) 584
Terence 131
Tertullian 170
textiles 198, 284, 448, 480-1, **6.9**
  Jacquard loom 481
Thales of Miletus 65, 84
theatre 14, 15, 16, 25-6, 476, 505
  19th-c. 544-5
  20th-c. 582-3
    absurdism 583, 623
    African-American 628-30
    Baroque 443
    black liberation movement 629-30
    Byzantine 201
    Chinese 202

Commedia dell'Arte 364-5
  elements of 22-3
  Elizabethan 400-2, **12.27**
  epic 583
  Expressionism 582-3
  French neo-classical 437-8
  Greek 15, 22, 83, 103-9, 112-13, 120-1
  Hellenistic 112-13
  idealism 545
  Impressionism 545
  Kabuki 471, **14.28**
  masque 443
  melodrama 507
  Middle Ages 237, 238-9, 271, 273-4, 301, **8.26**, **8.27**
  morality plays 301
  mystery plays 271, 273-4, **8.27**
  naturalism 545
  neo-Romanticism 545
  Noh 300
  opera *see* opera
  passion plays 302
  pluralism 623-4
  Realism 544-5, 623
  Renaissance 335, 364-5
  Roman 129, 130-1, 239
  Romantic movement 505-7
  set design 364
  spectacularism 624
  Symbolism 545
Thebes, rock tombs 50-1
Themistocles 81
Theocritus 112-13
Theodora, Empress 201, 215, **6.1**
Theodosius I, Emperor (the Great) 169, 188, 198
Theogony (Hesiod) 63, 75
Theophanes Continuatus 200
Theophilus, Emperor 190
Thespis 107-8
Third of May 1808, The (Goya) 491, 575, **15.9**
Thomas, Ambroise 505
Thomson, James 493
Thothmes III, Pharaoh 155
Threnody for the Victims of Hiroshima (Penderecki) 621
Thucydides 82, 92, 201
Thus Spake Zarathustra (Nietzsche) 519
Till Eulenspiegel (Strauss) 502
Tiné, Hal **18.42**
Tintoretto (Jacopo Robusti) 342, 358-9, **11.20**
Titian (Tiziano Vecellio) 342, 358, **11.19**
Toland, Greg 624
Toller, Ernst 582-3
Tom Jones (Fielding) 465
Torah, The 159, 160
Torroja, Eduardo 21
Toulouse-Lautrec, Henri 534
Townshend, Pete 622
Traviata, La (Verdi) 505
Travis, Randy 621
Treatises of Government (Locke) 410, 441
Trent, Council of 410-13, **13.5**
Trial, The (Kafka) 566
Tribute Money, The (Masaccio) 324-5, **10.18**
Triumph of Death, The (Bruegel) 392, **12.17**
Troilus and Criseyde (Chaucer) 287
Trojans, The (Berlioz) 504
Tuby, J.-B. 427, **13.26**
Tudor, David 619
Tull, Jethro 447
Turkey 201, 252, 346
Turner, J.M.W. 493, **15.11**
Tutankhamun 50
TV Bra for Living Sculpture (Paik) 611, **18.29**
28th July: Liberty Leading the People (Delacroix) 493-4, **15.12**
Two Cheeseburgers, with Everything

(Oldenberg) 598, **18.8**

U

U-2 622
Uccello, Paolo 328, 338, **10.22**
Ulysses (Joyce) 566
Umbrellas, Japan-USA, 1984-91, The (Christo) 607, **18.25**
Unanswered Question, The (Ives) 582
Uncle Tom's Cabin (Stowe) 507
Unique Forms of Continuity in Space (Boccioni) 536, 17.1
United Kingdon *see* England
United States *see* America
universities 255-6
University of Virginia, Rotunda (Jefferson) 463, **14.19**
"Until When Will They Go on Raping You on Your Wedding Night?" (Abu-Khalid) 618
Untimely Options (Nietzsche) 519
Untitled from White Shroud (Clemente) 600, **18.14**

V

Valentino, Rudolph 585
van Gogh, Vincent **0.6**, 17, 531
Vandals 174, 220
Vanderbilt, Cornelius 548, 550
Vanderbilt, George 551
Vasarély, Victor 599, **18.11**
Venice 192, 289, 358-9, 363, **11.25**
  Doge's Palace 289-90, 9.10
Venus and Adonis (Shakespeare) 401
Venus Consoling Love (Boucher) 454, **14.6**
Verdi, Giuseppe 505
Vergil 147, 148, 149, 259
Veron, Louis 504
Versailles, Palace of 422-5, 427, **13.18-23**, **13.26**
Vesalius, Andreas 383, 406
Victoria, Queen 508-9
video art 610-11
Vidor, King 585
Vijayanagar 426, **13.25**
Vikings 227
Villa Rotonda, Vicenza (Palladio) 363, **11.25**
Villa Savoye, Poissy (Le Corbusier) 580, **17.23**
Vindication of the Rights of Woman (Wollstonecraft) 464
Viola, Bill 610
Virgil *see* Vergil
Virgin and Child with St Anne (Leonardo) 352, 354, **11.9**
Virgin Spring (Bergman) 626
Visigoths 174, 188, 220
Vision after the Sermon, The (Gauguin) 530, **16.17**
Vita Nuova, La (Dante) 258
Vitruvius 100, 129, 310, 317, 422
Vitry, Philippe de 299
Vivaldi, Antonio 436-7, 466
Voltaire (François-Marie Arouet) 450, 451, 474, **14.4**
Volterra (Corot) 494, **15.13**
Vroom, Hendrik Cornelisz **11.7**

W

Wagner, Richard 505, 543
Waiting for Godot (Beckett) **0.15**, 25-6, 623
Walker, Alice 617-18, 630
Walpole, Horace 465
Walpole, Sir Robert 470
Walter, Johann 394
Wan Li **12.19**
Wanderer above the Mists, The (Friedrich) **15.1**
Ward, Douglas Turner 629

Warhol, Andy 13, 598-9, **18.9**
Wars of Religion 413
Waste Land, The (Eliot) 567
Watt, James 447, 448, 482, **14.2**
Watteau, Antoine 454, **14.5**
Wavrin, Jean de **9.2**
Wayne, John 585, 625-6
Wealth of Nations (Smith) 451
Weavers, the 622
Weaver's Cycle, The (Kollwitz) **16.2**
Well-Tempered Clavier, The (Bach) 435, 436
Welles, Orson 624
Wells Cathedral 302, **9.26**
West, Mae 585
Wexler, Peter **18.44**
Weyden, Rogier van der 298, 385, **9.21**
Whaam! (Lichtenstein) 597, **18.7**
wheel, the 38
Whitehall, Palm Beach (Carrère and Hastings) 550, **16.30**
Whitman, Walt 498
Whitney, Amos 482, **15.2**
Whitney, Eli 480, 482
Wiene, Robert 584, **17.26**
Wiesel, Elie 617
Wild One, The 622
Wild Strawberries (Bergman) 626
Wilde, Oscar 594
Willaert, Adrian 363
William of Aquitaine 251
William Billings Overture (Schuman) 581
Williams, Samm-Art 629-30
Williams, Tennessee 623
Wilson, August 630
Winckelmann, Johann 453, 460, 466, 485
Wizard of Oz, The 585
Wolgemut, Michael 385
Wollaton Hall **12.23**
Wollstonecraft, Mary 464
Woman, Old Man, and Flower (Ernst) 570, **17.10**
Woman Baking Bread (Millet) 522, **16.7**
women, status of 140, 185, 190, 202, 226, 228, 250-1, 464
Women in Love (Lawrence) 566
Women Picking Corn (Begay) 627-8, **18.45**
Wood, Grant 574, **17.15**
Woolf, Virginia 566
Wordsworth, William 498, 499
Work (Brown) **16.3**
Works and Days (Hesiod) 75
World War I 554-8, **17.1**
World War II 561-3, **17.2**, **17.3**
Wren, Sir Christopher 440, 441-2, 457, **13.33-6**
Wright, Frank Lloyd 531-2, 578-80, 612, **16.20**, **17.25**, **18.32**
writing 38
  cuneiform 38, 41, **1.6**
  hieroglyphs 48, 50
Wuthering Heights (Brontë) 499
Wycliffe, John 285

Y

Yeats, William Butler 567
Yevtushenko, Vevgeny Alexandrovich 618
Young, La Monte 620

Z

Zanuck, Darryl 624
Zee, James van der 575
Zeno of Citium 113, 131
"Zima Junction" (Yevtushenko) 618
Zola, Émile 491, 500, 538, 545
Zuse, Konrad 564
Zwingli, Ulrich 380, **12.5**